2000
Funk & Wagnalls
New Encyclopedia
YEARBOOK

■■■ A REVIEW OF THE EVENTS OF 1999 ■■■

FUNK & WAGNALLS
Publishers Since 1876

An Imprint of World Almanac Education Group

Published 2000 by World Almanac Education Group, Inc.

Funk & Wagnalls and F&W are registered trademarks of World Almanac
Education Group, Inc.

This annual is also published under the title *The 2000 World Book Year Book*
© 2000 World Book, Inc.

Library of Congress Catalog Card Number: 62-4818
ISBN: 0-8343-0115-6

Printed in the United States of America.

Staff

Contributors

Contributors not listed on these pages are members of the editorial staff.

- ALEXIOU, ARTHUR G., B.S.E.E., M.S.E.E.; Senior assistant secretary, UNESCO/IOC. [Ocean]

- ANDREAS, JAMES R., SR., B.A., M.A., Ph.D.; Professor of English, Clemson University and director of the Clemson Shakespeare Festival. [Literature, World Special Report: In Love with Shakespeare]

- ANDREWS, PETER J., B.A., M.S.; Free-lance writer. [Chemistry]

- APSELOFF, MARILYN FAIN, B.A., M.A.; Professor of English, Kent State University, Ohio. [Literature for children]

- ASKER, JAMES R., B.A.; Washington bureau chief, *Aviation Week & Space Technology* magazine. [Space exploration]

- BARBER, PEGGY, B.A., M.L.S.; Associate executive director for communications, American Library Association. [Library]

- BARNHART, BILL, B.A., M.S.T., M.B.A.; Financial markets columnist, *Chicago Tribune*. [Stocks and bonds]

- BARRETT, NORMAN., M.A.; Free-lance writer. [Soccer]

- BAYNHAM, SIMON, B.A., M.A., Ph.D.; Consultant, Research Institute for the Study of Conflict and Terrorism, London. [Africa and African country articles]

- BOULDREY, BRIAN, B.A., M.F.A.; Free-lance editor. [Hinduism; Literature, World; Nobel Prizes; Poetry; Pulitzer Prizes; San Francisco]

- BOYD, JOHN D., B.S.; Economics reporter, *Bridge News*. [Economics; International trade; Manufacturing]

- BRADSHER, HENRY S., A.B., B.J.; Foreign affairs analyst. [Asia and Asian country articles]

- BRETT, CARLTON E., B.A., M.S., Ph.D.; Professor of geology, University of Cincinnati. [Paleontology]

- BRODY, HERB, B.S.; Senior editor, *Technology Review* magazine. [Internet]

- BUERKLE, TOM, B.A.; Correspondent, *International Herald Tribune*. [Europe and Western European nation articles]

- CAMPBELL, GEOFFREY A., B.J.; Free-lance writer. [Congress of the United States; Courts; Human rights; Supreme Court of the United States; United States, Government of the; United States, President of the]

- CAMPBELL, LINDA P., B.A., M.S.L.; Senior reporter, legal affairs, *Fort Worth Star-Telegram*. [Congress of the United States; Courts; Human rights; Supreme Court of the United States; United States, Government of the; United States, President of the]

- CARDINALE, DIANE P., B.A.; Assistant communications director, Toy Manufacturers of America. [Toys and games]

- CASEY, MIKE, B.S., M.A.; Assistant editor, *Kansas City Star*. [Automobile]

- CORNELL, VINCENT J., B.A., M.A., Ph.D.; Associate professor of religion, Duke University. [Islam]

- DeFRANK, THOMAS M., B.A., M.A.; Washington bureau chief, *New York Daily News*. [Armed forces]

- DILLON, DAVID, B.A., M.A., Ph.D.; Architecture and design editor, *The Dallas Morning News*. [Architecture]

- DUCKHAM, DAVID, Free-lance writer and marketing consultant and former professional rugby player. [Rugby football]

- EATON, WILLIAM J., B.S., M.S.; Curator, Hubert H. Humphrey Fellowship Program, University of Maryland. [Cabinet, U.S.; Democratic Party; Elections; Immigration; Republican Party; Social security; Taxation; Welfare]

- ELLIS, GAVIN, Editor, *The New Zealand Herald*. [New Zealand]

- FARR, DAVID M. L., D.Phil.; Professor emeritus of history, Carleton University. [Canada; Canadian provinces; Canadian territories; Canada, Prime Minister of]

- FISHER, ROBERT W., B.A., M.A.; Free-lance writer. [Labor and employment]

- FITZGERALD, MARK, B.A.; Midwest editor, *Editor & Publisher* magazine. [Newspaper]

- FOX, THOMAS C., B.A., M.A.; Publisher, *The National Catholic Reporter*. [Roman Catholic Church]

- FRICKER, KAREN, B.A., M.A.; Free-lance theater critic. [Theater]

- FRIEDMAN, EMILY, B.A.; Health-policy and ethics analyst. [Health-care issues]

- GADOMSKI, FRED, B.S., M.S.; Meteorologist, Pennsylvania State University. [Weather]

- GATTY, ROBERT C., Vice President of Communications and Marketing, Food Distributors International. [Food]

- GOLDEN, JONATHAN J., B.A., M.J.; Ph.D. student, Brandeis University. [Judaism]

- GOLDNER, NANCY, B.A.; Free-lance dance critic. [Dance]

- GRIFFITHS, PAUL J., B.A., M.Phil., Ph.D.; Professor of the philosophy of religions, University of Chicago. [Buddhism]

- HARAKAS, STANLEY SAMUEL, B.A., B. Th., Th.D.; Archbishop Iakovos Professor (Emeritus) of Orthodox Theology, Holy Cross Greek Orthodox School of Theology. [Eastern Orthodox Churches]

- HAVERSTOCK, NATHAN A., A.B.; Affiliate scholar, Oberlin College. [Latin America and Latin American country articles]

- HELMS, CHRISTINE, B.A., Ph.D.; Writer and Middle East analyst. [Middle East Special Report: A Century of Struggle; Middle East and Middle Eastern country articles; North African country articles]

- HENDERSON, HAROLD, B.A.; Staff writer, Chicago *Reader*. [Chicago]

- HOFFMAN, ANDREW J., B.S., M.S., Ph.D.; Assistant professor of organizational behavior, Boston University. [Environmental pollution]

- JOHANSON, DONALD C., B.S., M.A., Ph.D.; Director and professor, Institute of Human Origins. [Anthropology]

- JONES, TIM, B.S.; Media writer, *Chicago Tribune*. [Telecommunications]

- KENNEDY, BRIAN, M.A.; Copy editor; *Outback* magazine. [Australia; Australia, Prime Minister of; Australian rules football]

- **KILGORE, MARGARET,** B.A., M.B.A.; Editor, Phillips-Van Buren, Incorporated. **[Los Angeles]**

- **KING, MIKE,** Reporter, *The* (Montreal) *Gazette.* **[Montreal]**

- **KLINTBERG, PATRICIA PEAK.,** B.A.; Washington editor, *Farm Journal.* **[Agriculture]**

- **KNIGHT, ROBERT,** B.A., M.M.; Freelance writer. **[People in the news]**

- **KRONHOLZ, JUNE,** B.S.J.; Staff reporter, *The Wall Street Journal.* **[Education]**

- **LAWRENCE, ALBERT,** B.A., M.A., M.Ed.; President, OutExcel! **[Chess]**

- **LEWIS, DAVID C.,** M.D.; Director, Brown University Center for Alcohol and Addiction Studies. **[Drug abuse]**

- **LIEBENSON, DONALD,** B.A.; Freelance writer. **[Baseball Special Report: Where Have You Gone, Joe DiMaggio?]**

- **LYE, KEITH,** B.A., F.R.G.S.; Freelance writer and editor **[Cricket]**

- **MARCH, ROBERT H.,** A.B., M.S., Ph.D.; Professor of physics and liberal studies, University of Wisconsin at Madison. **[Physics]**

- **MARSCHALL, LAURENCE A.,** B.S., Ph.D.; Professor of physics, Gettysburg College. **[Astronomy]**

- **MARTY, MARTIN E.,** Ph.D.; Fairfax M. Cone Distinguished Service Professor Emeritus, University of Chicago. **[Protestantism]**

- **MAUGH, THOMAS H., II,** Ph.D.; Science writer, *Los Angeles Times.* **[Biology]**

- **MAY, SALLY RUTH,** B.A, M.A.; Freelance art writer. **[Art]**

- **McLEESE, DON,** B.A., M.A.; Associate editor, *Midwest Living* magazine. **[Popular music]**

- **McWILLIAM, ROHAN,** B.A., M.A.; D. Phil; Senior lecturer in history, Anglia Polytechnic University, U.K. **[Ireland; Northern Ireland; United Kingdom; United Kingdom, Prime Minister of]**

- **MESSENGER, ROBERT,** B.A.; Editor, *New Criterion.* **[City; Crime; Literature, American; Washington, D.C.]**

- **MINER, TODD J.,** B.S., M.S.; Meteorologist, Pennsylvania State University. **[Weather]**

- **MORITZ, OWEN,** B.A.; Urban-affairs editor, *New York Daily News.* **[New York City]**

- **MORRIS, BERNADINE,** B.A., M.A.; Free-lance fashion writer. **[Fashion]**

- **MULLINS, HENRY T.,** B.S., M.S., Ph.D.; Professor of Earth science, Syracuse University. **[Geology]**

- **NESBITT, ELEANOR M.,** M.A., M.Phil., Ph.D.; Lecturer in religion and education, Institute of Education, University of Warwick. **[Sikhism]**

- **NGUYEN, J. TUYET,** M.A.; United Nations correspondent, Deutsche Presse-Agentur. **[Population; United Nations]**

- **OGAN, EUGENE,** B.A., M.A., Ph.D.; Professor emeritus of anthropology, University of Minnesota. **[Pacific Islands]**

- **PAETH, GREGORY,** B.A.; Television and radio writer, *The Cincinnati Post.* **[Radio]**

- **PANEK, RICHARD,** B.S.J., M.F.A.; Astronomy columnist for *Natural History* magazine and author. **[Astronomy Special Report: Astronomy Through a Millennium]**

- **REID, RON,** B.A.; Sportswriter, *The Philadelphia Inquirer.* **[Sports articles]**

- **ROSE, MARK J.,** B.A., M.A., Ph.D.; Managing editor, *Archaeology* magazine. **[Archaeology]**

- **RUBENSTEIN, RICHARD E.,** B.A., M.A., J.D.; Professor of conflict resolution and public affairs, George Mason University. **[Terrorism]**

- **SARNA, JONATHAN D.,** Ph.D.; Joseph H. & Belle R. Braun Professor of American Jewish History, Brandeis University. **[Judaism]**

- **SAVAGE, IAN,** B.A., M.A., Ph.D.; Assistant professor of economics and transportation, Northwestern University. **[Aviation; Transportation]**

- **SEGAL, TROY,** B.A.; Free-lance writer. **[Television]**

- **SHAPIRO, HOWARD,** B.S.; Travel editor, *The Philadelphia Inquirer.* **[Philadelphia]**

- **SOLNICK, STEVEN L.,** B.A., M.A., Ph.D.; Assistant professor of political science, Columbia University. **[Baltic states and other former Soviet republic articles]**

- **STEIN, DAVID LEWIS,** B.A., M.S.; Urban affairs columnist, *The Toronto Star.* **[Toronto]**

- **STOCKER, CAROL M.,** B.A.; Reporter, *The Boston Globe.* **[Gardening]**

- **STUART, ELAINE,** B.A.; Managing editor, Council of State Governments. **[State government]**

- **TANNER, JAMES C.,** B.S.J.; Former news editor—energy, *The Wall Street Journal.* **[Energy supply]**

- **TATUM, HENRY K.,** B.A.; Associate editor, *The Dallas Morning News.* **[Dallas]**

- **THOMAS, PAULETTE,** B.A.; Staff writer, *The Wall Street Journal.* **[Bank]**

- **TONRY, MICHAEL,** A.B., LL.B.; Sonosky professor of law and public policy, University of Minnesota Law School. **[Prison]**

- **von RHEIN, JOHN,** B.A.,; Classical-music critic, *Chicago Tribune.* **[Classical music]**

- **WALTER, EUGENE J., Jr.,** B.A.; Free-lance writer. **[Conservation; Zoos]**

- **WATSON, BURKE,** B.A.; Assistant suburban editor, *Houston Chronicle.* **[Houston]**

- **WOLCHIK, SHARON L.,** B.A., M.A., Ph.D.; Professor of political science and international affairs, George Washington University. **[Yugoslavia Special Report: Yugoslavia: A Decade of Ruin; Eastern European country articles]**

- **WOODS, MICHAEL,** B.S.; Science editor, *The Toledo* (Ohio) *Blade* and *Pittsburgh Post-Gazette.* **[AIDS; Computer; Drugs; Electronics; Magazine; Medicine; Mental health; Public health and safety]**

- **WRIGHT, ANDREW G.,** B.A., Senior editor, *Engineering News-Record.* **[Building and construction]**

- **WUNTCH, PHILIP,** B.A.; Film critic, *The Dallas Morning News.* **[Motion pictures]**

Contents

Major News Stories 8

The editors' pick of the most memorable, exciting, or important news stories of 1999.

The Year in Brief 11

A month-by-month review of the major news stories of 1999.

▲ Page 257

▼ Page 270

Update 36 to 448

The major world events of 1999 are reported in more than 250 alphabetically arranged Update articles—from "Afghanistan" and "Africa" to "Zimbabwe" and "Zoos." Included are Special Reports that provide an in-depth focus on especially noteworthy developments.

ASTRONOMY: Astronomy Through a Millennium **68**
by Richard Panek
Through the science of astronomy, human knowledge of the universe has expanded enormously since the year 1000.

BASEBALL: Where Have You Gone, Joe DiMaggio? **98**
by Donald Liebenson
Yankee star Joe DiMaggio, who died in March 1999, set baseball records that have stood for nearly 60 years and made headlines on and off the baseball field.

EMPIRES: Great Empires of the Millennium **180**
by David Dreier
The last thousand years have been dominated by nations seeking great empires, but a new, international era may be dawning.

HUMAN RIGHTS: A Century of Civil Rights **226**
by Jay Lenn
Since 1900, legislation and court cases have expanded the civil rights of women, African Americans, and other once-oppressed groups.

LITERATURE, WORLD: In Love with Shakespeare **270**
by James R. Andreas, Sr.
William Shakespeare after 400 years remains a reigning king of popular culture.

MIDDLE EAST: A Century of Struggle **296**
by Christine Helms
From the fall of Ottoman and colonial rule to the rise of Islamic fundamentalism, the Mideast has undergone great change since 1900.

YUGOSLAVIA: A Decade of Ruin **434**
by Sharon L. Wolchik
The war in Kosovo in 1999 was the latest of a series of conflicts that have devastated Yugoslavia in the 1990's.

TIME CAPSULES

The 2000 edition contains a special feature called Time Capsule, which serves as a souvenir of the 20th Century. To create each Time Capsule, the editors selected excerpts from articles dating back to 1922. These articles chronicle some of the most interesting and important developments and events of the past century.

▲ Page 409

▼ Page 334

▲ Page 249

Index
449

A cumulative index covering the contents of the 1999 and 2000 editions of **The Yearbook.**

The Year's Major News Stories

From a North Atlantic Treaty Organization bombing campaign to end violence against the ethnic Albanian majority in the Serbian province of Kosovo to worldwide preparations for a new millennium, 1999 was a year of memorable news events. On these three pages are stories that the editors picked as some of the most important of the year, along with details on where to find information about them in this volume. *The Editors*

Parisians celebrate the new century and millennium on January 1 with a spectacular fireworks display staged at the Eiffel Tower.

Millennium celebrations

School violence

Public concern over school violence rose in the wake of tragic shootings at Columbine High School in Littleton, Colorado. Two teen-age boys entered the school on April 20 armed with automatic weapons and went on a shooting rampage. They killed 12 fellow students and a teacher and wounded more than 20 other people before killing themselves. See **Crime,** page 153.

War in Yugoslavia

Ethnic Albanians (left) flee the Serbian province of Kosovo in March after being driven from their homes by Serb forces. This "ethnic cleansing" led to a NATO bombing campaign (above) against Yugoslavia. See **Armed forces,** page 379; **Yugoslavia,** page 433; **Yugoslavia** Special Report: **Yugoslavia: A Decade of Ruin,** page 434.

Clinton acquitted

On February 12, the U.S. Senate acquitted President Bill Clinton of impeachment charges passed two months earlier by the House of Representatives. See **Congress of the United States,** page 142; **United States, President of the,** page 421.

Earthquakes

The town of Golcuk, Turkey, lies in ruins in August after a severe earthquake shakes northwestern Turkey, killing more than 17,000 people. A second quake strikes the same area in November, and Greece is rocked by another earthquake in September. See **Greece,** page 56; **Turkey,** page 405.

Mideast peace process

In September, Israel's newly elected prime minister, Ehud Barak, and Palestinian leader Yasir Arafat renewed the Mideast peace process by signing an agreement setting a schedule for final peace negotiations. Barak, the most decorated soldier in Israeli history, was elected prime minister in May. See **Israel,** page 248; **Middle East,** page 293.

The Bundestag, the lower house of Germany's parliament, convenes in the newly renovated Reichstag in Berlin in April after the capital is moved back to that city. See **Germany,** page 214.

German government returns to Berlin

Panama Canal Turnover

On December 31, the United States handed over control of the Panama Canal to the government of Panama and evacuated the the military installations of the Canal Zone after 96 years. See **Panama,** page 331.

Independence for East Timor

A young man in Dili, the capital of East Timor, holds a sword to his throat in August in a ritual defiance of troops trying to intimidate supporters of East Timor's independence from Indonesia. On August 30, the people of East Timor voted overwhelmingly for independence. See **Asia,** page 62; **Indonesia,** page 240.

January February March April May June July August September

1999 YEAR IN BRIEF

A month-by-month listing of the most significant world events that occurred during 1999.

October November December

Chicagoans dig out from 18.6 inches (47.2 centimeters) of snow—the largest snowfall in the city's recorded history—the day after the January 2 storm.

1 **Eleven of the 15 member nations of the European Union (EU)** launch the euro, Western Europe's first single currency in more than 1,500 years. While euro notes and coins will not go into general circulation until 2002, trading in the new currency begins in European banks and stock exchanges when markets open on Monday, Jan. 4, 1999. Three EU members— Sweden, Denmark, and Great Britain— chose not to participate. Greece was disqualified from participation for economic reasons.

2 **A storm over the United States** drops massive amounts of rain and snow over much of the South and Midwest. Chicago, Detroit, and Milwaukee are hard hit by snow. Highways and airports throughout the northern Midwest are closed on one of the busiest travel days of the year. Along the storm's southern edge, freezing rain downs power lines in Arkansas, North Carolina, and South Carolina. Florida is hit by tornadoes and torrential rains.

6 **National Basketball Association (NBA) officials** settle a 191-day lockout of players by team owners just one day before owners were to vote on whether to cancel the rest of the season. While both sides made concessions, the players failed to stop the NBA from capping player salaries and the players' share of league revenues.

7 **William H. Rehnquist,** chief justice of the United States Supreme Court, opens the first presidential impeachment trial in more than 130 years by swearing in as jurors the 100 members of the U.S. Senate. The senators are to decide if President Bill Clinton should be removed from office for his alleged perjury and obstruction of justice in a civil suit that centered around Clinton's extramarital relationships.

13 **The government of Brazil** devalues the country's currency, the real, by more than 8 percent. The move triggers sell-offs of stocks on European and U.S. markets. In November 1998, Brazil received $41.5 billion in loans arranged by the International Monetary Fund (IMF), a United Nations-affiliated organization that provides short-term credit to member nations. The IMF rescue plan, which required Brazil to carry out a variety of economic reforms, was designed to help Brazil avoid the possibility of a currency devaluation.

14 **The Canadian government** sends more than 400 soldiers into Toronto to help the city cope with the latest storm, which is expected to add 10 inches (25 centimeters) of snow to the 30 inches (75 centimeters) that has fallen since January 3.

16 **International observers** monitoring the cease-fire in Kosovo accuse Serbian security forces of massacring at least 45 ethnic Albanians. Many of the victims' bodies—which were discovered in a ravine—were mutilated, observers say.

reau estimates, as many as 4 million people from this segment of the population were missed in the 1990 count. The use of statistical sampling was endorsed by Democrats and opposed by Republicans. Seats in the U.S. House of Representatives are apportioned according to census figures.

26 **King Hussein of Jordan** returns to the United States for medical treatment only hours after naming his eldest son, Prince Abdullah, heir to the throne. Abdullah replaces the king's brother, Hassan, as crown prince. Hassan ruled as regent in Jordan for six months in 1998 while Hussein was undergoing an earlier round of cancer treatments at the Mayo Clinic in Rochester, Minnesota.

27 **Sierra Leone's government** reports that hospital officials in Freetown, the capital, estimate that at least 3,000 people have died in fighting that began in early January. The restoration of the democratically elected government of President Ahmed Tejan Kabbah in 1998 failed to end fierce resistance from rebels allied with the remnants of the military regime that held power from May 1997 until March 1998.

21 **As many as 36 tornadoes** cut through Arkansas, touching down in Little Rock before moving into western Tennessee. Eight people die in the storms. Tornadoes left nine people dead in Tennessee on January 17.

24 **Juan Antonio Samaranch** of Spain, leader of the International Olympic Committee (IOC), announces that the IOC executive board, meeting in Lusanne, Switzerland, has asked six IOC members to resign. Observers describe the call for resignations as an attempt to control a widening scandal involving allegations that cities hoping to host Olympic Games in 2000 and 2002 bought the support of IOC board members with various valuable gifts.

25 **The U.S. Supreme Court** rules that the 2000 census must be conducted by head count, rather than through a combination of actual count and statistical sampling. The Census Bureau had proposed using statistical sampling to count residents in urban neighborhoods largely populated by ethnic minorities and the poor. According to Bu-

29 **The United States and its European allies** warn Yugoslav President Slobodan Milosevic to negotiate a peace settlement for Kosovo or face a series of air attacks. Meeting in London, Secretary of State Madeleine Albright and representatives of Britain, France, Germany, Russia, and Italy issue an ultimatum summoning representatives from the governments of Yugoslavia and Serbia and representatives of the Kosovar Albanians to a summit in Rambouillet, France, no later than February 6.

31 **The Denver Broncos** beat the Atlanta Falcons 34-19 to win football's Super Bowl.

Researchers report that the AIDS virus probably originated in chimpanzees and was transmitted to humans during hunting in Africa sometime in the past 50 years. Since the virus does not appear to cause disease in chimpanzees, the finding may open an avenue toward treatment.

1 **An explosion of unknown origin** rocks the Ford Motor Company's River Rouge complex in Dearborn, Michigan, killing 1 employee and injuring at least 30 others.

2 **Navies and merchant fleets** worldwide abandon use of the Morse code and the SOS distress call, adopted three months after the Titanic sank in 1912. The International Maritime Organization replaced SOS with the Global Maritime Distress and Safety System, a satellite network that pinpoints the locations of ships from their signals.

3 **The Colorado Division of Wildlife** releases a 3-year-old female lynx, weighing 18 pounds (85 kilograms), into the Weminuche Wilderness area of the San Juan Mountains. The animal is the first of 50 lynxes the state agency plans to release in 1999. In the last 100 years, lynxes, which were once common in the area, have been sighted in Colorado only 22 times. The last lynx was sighted in 1973.

4 **Deutsche Bank A.G.,** Germany's largest financial institution, releases documents that reveal that the bank helped finance the construction of the Auschwitz concentration camp, where approximately 1.25 million Jews, Gypsies, and homosexuals were murdered by German Nazis between 1941 and 1945. Deutsche Bank continues to face class action suits involving survivors' claims that the institution seized property and other wealth from German Jews during World War II (1939–1945).

6 **French President Jacques Chirac** opens a Kosovo peace conference in Paris by advising a 13-member delegation of the Serbian-dominated government and 16 ethnic Albanian negotiators from Kosovo to put aside their differences for the sake of peace. At least 2,000 people have died in Kosovo, a province of Serbia, since February 1998, when Yugoslavian President Slobodan Milosevic began to crack down on the independence movement among the province's ethnic Albanians.

7 **King Hussein of Jordan,** who was widely admired for his role as a peace-maker in the Middle East, dies at age 63. He had ruled since 1952. Abdullah, Hussein's oldest son, becomes Jordan's new king.

12 **The United States Senate** acquits President Bill Clinton on both charges for which the House of Representatives impeached him in December 1998. Senators reject the charge of perjury 55 to 45, with 10 Republicans breaking ranks to vote against conviction. The vote on whether the president willfully obstructed justice by attempting to conceal his relationship with a former White House intern ties 50 to 50. No Democrats break with the president in either vote. The U.S. Constitution specifies that a two-thirds majority of the Senate—67 members—must vote to remove the president from office. The voting culminates a five-week trial, which was only the second presidential impeachment in the 210-year history of the republic.

14 **American Indians** are more than twice as likely as other ethnic groups in the United States to be victims of violent crime, according to the first comprehensive study of Indians and crime conducted by the U.S. Justice Department. Justice officials report that unlike whites and blacks, Indians are more likely to be the victims of violent crimes committed by members of a race other than their own.

15 **The influenza** that killed between 20 million and 50 million people worldwide in 1918 was caused by an ordinary virus similar to today's swine influenza virus, according to a report by Jeffrey K. Taubenberger in the *Proceedings of the National Academy of Sciences.* Taubenberger notes that he and his associates, working with virus samples taken from lung tissue preserved since 1918, have been unable to uncover why the flu was so deadly.

16 **Kurds,** an ethnic group from Southwest Asia, stage demonstrations in 15 countries in response to the arrest of Abdullah Ocalan, leader of an autonomy movement for 20 million Kurds in Turkey, Iran, Iraq, and Armenia. Ocalan was seized by Turkish agents on February 15 when he left the Greek embassy in Nairobi, Kenya. Kurds respond with attacks on Greek and Kenyan embassies and consulates in 28 European, Canadian, and Australian cities. In Istanbul, more than 1,000 demonstrators march through the streets, setting fire to cars. In London, Stuttgart, and Copenhagen, protesters set themselves on fire.

18 **Danish physicist Lene Vestergaard Hau** announces in the journal *Nature* that she and a research team at the Cambridge, Massachusetts-based Rowland Institute for Science have succeeded in slowing light to the lowest speed ever observed. By beaming lasers through an extremely dense cloud of sodium atoms chilled to within a fraction of a degree of absolute zero, Hau slowed light to 38 miles (61 kilometers) per hour—20 million times slower than light's highest speed of 186,282 miles (299,792 kilometers) per second. Atoms cooled to near *absolute zero* (theoretically, the lowest possible temperature) form into a state of matter in which they act as a single atom. Precise control over the speed of light has a number of potential applications, including uses in communication systems, optical computers, and high-speed switches.

22 **U.S. and British warplanes** bomb weapons depots, missile sites, and communication centers in northern Iraq. According to a Clinton administration spokesperson, the attacks are a response to Iraqi antiaircraft fire on U.S. jets and the intrusion of Iraqi MiG warplanes in no-flight zones.

24 **Senior U.S. Army officials** say that no new remains will be placed in the Tomb of the Unknowns in Arlington National Cemetery in Virginia. Scientists have concluded that genetic tests have made all remains identifiable.

27 **The United Nations Security Council,** called into emergency session, passes a resolution demanding that Ethiopia and Eritrea cease hostilities and resolve the border dispute that ignited the current war, which began in May 1998.

28 **Former general Olusegun Obasanjo** is declared president of Nigeria after receiving 62 percent of the vote. The February balloting was Nigeria's first free election after 15 years of military dictatorship.

President Bill Clinton is acquitted on February 12 on the charges of perjury and obstruction of justice for which he was impeached by the U.S. House of Representatives in December 1998.

NATO bombs explode over Pristina, the capital of Kosovo, a province of Serbia, on March 24. NATO attacked after Yugoslav President Slobodan Milosevic rebuffed a peace plan with ethnic Albanian separatists.

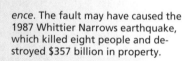

1 **Eight tourists** and four guides trekking through the Bwindi Impenetrable Forest in Uganda, are killed by rebels armed with machetes and rifles. The attackers, a roving band of approximately 150 men, are believed to be remnants of the Hutu rebel army that killed some 500,000 Tutsi in Rwanda before fleeing into the forests of Uganda and Congo (Kinshasa) in 1994. The victims were British, American, and New Zealand sightseers who hoped to glimpse rare mountain gorillas while visiting the park.

2 **California officials** announce that the Pacific Lumber Company has accepted a $480-million federal and state offer to purchase 10,000 acres (4,047 hectares) of redwoods in the Headwaters Forest, 250 miles (400 kilometers) north of San Francisco. The Headwaters Forest was the world's last privately owned grove of ancient redwoods.

3 **The United States** protests European barriers on certain brands of bananas by doubling *tariffs* (import taxes) on selected European goods. U.S. trade representatives accuse the European Union (EU)—an organization of 15 Western European nations that promotes economic cooperation among its members—of favoring bananas imported from former European colonies in Africa and the Caribbean.

4 **Scientists** announce the discovery of a major blind-thrust fault under downtown Los Angeles in the journal *Sci-*

ence. The fault may have caused the 1987 Whittier Narrows earthquake, which killed eight people and destroyed $357 billion in property.

12 **Poland, Hungary, and the Czech Republic,** former members of the Warsaw Pact military alliance, join NATO. The military alliance of 19 Western nations was formed in 1949 to discourage an attack on Western Europe by the former Soviet Union.

14 **The U.S. Justice Department** announces that the U.S. jail and prison population climbed to 1.8 million in June 1998, a record high.

15 **Amtrak's City of New Orleans train,** traveling 70 miles (113 kilometers) per hour from Chicago to New Orleans, collides with a semitrailer truck loaded with steel bars at a railroad crossing in Bourbonnais, Illinois, 55 miles (88 kilometers) south of Chicago. The derailment mangles the train's first five cars, injuring more than 100 people. A fire,

Missiles from U.S. Navy cruisers in the Adriatic and bombers flying from Great Britain, Germany, and Italy target military bases and antiaircraft sites in Serbia and Montenegro, Yugoslavia's two republics, and Kosovo, a Serbian province. The air strikes mark the first time in the 50-year history of NATO that the defense alliance has attacked a sovereign nation. The offensive is a response to Yugoslav President Slobodan Milosevic's rebuff of a peace plan. The U.S.-brokered plan was designed to restore the autonomy that Serbia stripped from Kosovo's ethnic Albanian majority in 1989.

26 **Jack Kevorkian,** a physician who claims to have assisted in the suicides of at least 130 people, is found guilty of murdering a 52-year-old man suffering from amyotrophic lateral sclerosis (Lou Gehrig's disease). Although prosecutors in Michigan charged Kevorkian with first-degree murder, the jury, after deliberating for 13 hours, reduced the charge to second-degree murder.

28 **Ethnic Albanians,** fleeing Serbian military forces, are crossing from Kosovo into Albania at a rate of 1,000 per hour. Refugees report a 10-mile- (16-kilometer-) column of between 150,000 and 200,000 persons attempting to escape Yugoslav President Slobodan Milosevic's policy of "ethnic cleansing" in Kosovo. NATO observers believe that Milosevic wants to drive ethnic Albanians from Kosovo, where Serbs constitute only 10 percent of the population.

Raul Cubas, president of Paraguay, resigns hours before the Paraguayan Senate was scheduled to remove him from office for his alleged involvement in the March 23 assassination of Vice President Luis Maria Argana.

fed by diesel fuel spilling from the twin engines, engulfs a crushed sleeper car, killing 11 passengers.

16 **The entire European Union (EU) Commission,** the executive body that runs the day-to-day affairs of the 15-nation trade group, resigns in response to an official report that accuses the commissioners of corruption.

21 **The first balloonists to circle the world,** Bertrand Piccard and Brian Jones, end their 20-day voyage by landing in the desert 300 miles (483 kilometers) south of Cairo, Egypt. The 180-foot (55-meter) silver balloon, the Breitling Orbiter 3, actually completed the first nonstop balloon trip around the world over the African country of Mauritania on March 20.

24 **NATO** launches a broad offensive against Yugoslavia in an effort to force the Serbian-controlled government in Belgrade to end its year-long assault on ethnic Albanian separatists in Kosovo.

29 **The Dow Jones industrial average** of selected stocks on the New York Stock Exchange closes above 10,000 for the first time in history.

30 **The Japanese Economic Planning Agency** announces that Japan's current unemployment rate—4.6 percent of the work force—is the highest since record keeping began in 1953.

1 **Canada** divides the eastern half of the Northwest Territories to create a new territory, Nunavut. The new territory is to be governed by native Inuit, or Eskimos, who make up 85 percent of Nunavut's 25,000 people.

Yugoslav army officials announce the capture of three U.S. soldiers inside Serbia. The men were pictured on Yugoslav television in what appeared to be a bruised condition.

3 **Six people** die and at least 100 others are injured when a tornado strikes Benton, Louisiana.

5 **Libya** turns over to the United Nations (UN) two men, described as international terrorists, who are suspected of planting a bomb aboard Pan Am Flight 103 in 1988. The destruction of the airplane, which took place over Lockerbie, Scotland, killed all 270 passengers and crew members.

6 **Archaeologists** announce the discovery of three extremely well-preserved mummies of Inca children in the Andes. Scientists believe that the boy and two girls were killed in a ritual sacrifice about 500 years ago.

9 **The president of the West African country of Niger,** Ibrahim Bare Mainassara, is assassinated, allegedly by members of his personal security guard. Mainassara's military govern-

Citizens of Littleton, Colorado, mourn the 13 victims of the Columbine High School shooting spree on April 20. The tragedy focused national attention on the issues of gun control and school safety.

ment, which took power in a *coup* (overthrow) in 1996, is locked in a political battle with civilian leaders over February 1999 election results.

10 **President Bill Clinton** announces that the number of people in the United States receiving welfare benefits dropped from 12.2 million in 1996, before the federal welfare system was overhauled, to 7.6 million in 1999.

12 **Judge Susan Webber Wright** of U.S. District Court in Little Rock, Arkansas, finds President Bill Clinton in civil contempt of court for giving false testimony about his relationship with former White House intern Monica Lewinsky in the Paula Jones sexual harassment lawsuit. The suit had been dismissed by Judge Wright on April 1, 1998, for lack of evidence.

14 **The Pakistani military** tests a medium-range missile capable of carrying a nuclear warhead. The test is conducted three days after India carries out a similar test.

15 **NATO officials** acknowledge that a U.S. pilot mistakenly dropped a bomb on a convoy of ethnic Albanian refugees in Kosovo on April 14. Serbian leaders claim that at least 70 refugees died during NATO attacks on two different civilian convoys.

Astronomers associated with the Harvard-Smithsonian Center for Astrophysics announce the discovery of three large planets orbiting Upsilon Andromedae, a star 44 light-years from Earth. A light-year is the distance light travels in one year—5.9 trillion miles (9.5 trillion kilometers). Upsilon Andromedae is the first star with multiple planets discovered in a stable solar system similar to the sun's.

18 **Wayne Gretzky**, center for the New York Rangers, ends his National Hockey League (NHL) career after 20 seasons. Gretzky holds or shares 61 NHL records.

20 **Two teen-agers** enter Columbine High School in Littleton, Colorado, and begin shooting classmates. Fifteen people, including both gunmen, die, and more than 20 others are wounded. The shooting is described as the worst incident of school violence in U.S. history.

23 **Leaders of all 19 member nations of NATO** assemble in Washington, D.C., for a three-day summit regarding the current military strikes on Yugoslavia. The summit also commemorates the 50th anniversary of the treaty organization.

The discovery of 2.5-million-year-old fossils of a skull and bones believed to have belonged to a direct human ancestor is announced in the journal *Science* by Tim White, a paleontologist at the University of California. The fossils, which White and an international team of collaborators have declared a new species, *Australopithecus garhi*, were found in the Afar Rift area of Ethiopia.

26 **The president of India,** Kircheril Raman Narayanan, dissolves the lower house of parliament and calls for a general election, India's third in three years. After Prime Minister Atal Behari Vajpayee lost a parliamentary vote of confidence on April 17, Sonia Gandhi, widow of former Prime Minister Rajiv Gandhi and unofficial head of the opposition Congress Party, failed to build a political coalition upon which to form a government.

Ankylosaur dinosaurs at least 25 million years older than any similar dinosaur type previously found in North America have been discovered near Price, Utah, according to Utah's state paleontologist James Kirkland. The fossils are dated at 98.4 million years old.

27 **U.S. government officials** report that in 1994 and 1995, a Taiwanese-born scientist, Wen Ho Lee, transferred millions of lines of top-secret computer code to a highly accessible computer network. The scientist, who was employed at the Los Alamos National Laboratory in Los Alamos, New Mexico, is suspected of transferring the files to give Chinese officials access to information about U.S. nuclear warheads. Lee and the Chinese government later deny the accusation.

1 **President Slobodan Milosevic of Yugoslavia** releases three captive U.S. soldiers through the efforts of Jesse Jackson, who led an interfaith delegation to Yugoslavia to plead for their release.

The Liberty Bell 7 Mercury space capsule, lost in the Atlantic Ocean on July 21, 1961, is discovered by an underwater salvage team approximately 300 miles (480 kilometers) off the Florida coast. The capsule sank during splashdown after astronaut Gus Grissom successfully completed a 15-minute space flight.

Charismatic, a 31-to-1 long shot, wins the 125th running of the Kentucky Derby, beating Menifee by a neck and Cat Thief by one length.

3 **Storms in Kansas and Oklahoma** spawn tornadoes that destroy at least 9,000 buildings and leave more than 40 people dead and 500 people injured. The National Weather Service reports 45 separate tornadoes. In Moore, Oklahoma, a suburb south of Oklahoma City, a 1-mile- (1.6-kilometer-) wide funnel with winds of 300 miles (483 kilometers) per hour levels 500 houses in a swath 6 blocks wide and 3 miles (4.8 kilometers) long. Weather service officials estimate the tornado exceeds the F5 level force on the Fujita Scale, the strongest classification.

8 **Thousands of Chinese college students** besiege the U.S. embassy in Beijing, protesting the May 7 NATO bombing of the Chinese embassy in Yugoslavia. NATO officials say that the bombing was accidental.

9 **A chartered bus,** carrying more than 45 senior citizens on a Mother's Day excursion to a Gulf Coast gambling casino, runs off a highway in New Orleans and crashes into an embankment, killing 22 people.

12 **Russian President Boris Yeltsin** fires a prime minister for the third time in 15 months. Yeltsin nominates interior minister Sergei Stepashin to replace Yevgeny M. Primakov. Political experts believe Yeltsin distrusted Primakov for his growing popularity and for his ties

to Communist politicians who are attempting to wrench control from him.

15 **An attempt by Russian Communists** to impeach President Boris N. Yeltsin fails in the Duma, the lower house of Russia's parliament.

17 **Israeli voters** overwhelmingly reject Prime Minister Benjamin Netanyahu in favor of Ehud Barak, a war hero and political moderate who heads the One Israel Party. Barak, who is Israel's most decorated soldier, receives approximately 56 percent of the vote, which political experts interpret as a ringing endorsement of the long-delayed Israeli-Palestinian peace process.

18 **Bruce Babbitt,** secretary of the U.S. Department of the Interior, announces plans to restore 26,000 square miles (67,340 square kilometers) of natural habitat in southern Florida's Everglades. The project, which needs Congressional funding, includes strategies to save 68 endangered and threatened species, including the manatee and American crocodile.

24 **The U.S. Supreme Court** rules that school districts and schools and universities are liable under federal law for ignoring student complaints of severe sexual harassment by other students.

25 **The universe** is about 12 billion years old, astronomers announce. The team of 27 scientists, who participated in an eight-year research project funded by NASA, used measurements taken from the Hubble Space Telescope to figure distances between Earth and 800 stars. These measurements were used to calculate the speed at which the galaxies of the universe are moving apart.

26 **Queen Elizabeth II of Great Britain** presides over the opening of the National Assembly of Wales, the first political assembly to meet in the Welsh capital of Cardiff in nearly 600 years.

India launches combat jets and helicopters to dislodge 500 to 600 Muslim guerrillas entrenched along high ridges in the Himalaya in an area of Kashmir held by India. According to India, the guerrillas are Pakistan-sponsored Islam-

A protester in Beijing, China, waves the Chinese flag above military police guarding the U.S. embassy in May. The protest was sparked by the accidental NATO bombing of the Chinese embassy in Belgrade, Yugoslavia.

ic militants who crossed a 50-year-old cease-fire line to take up strategic positions. Pakistan denies knowledge of the group. The attack is the most serious incident between the two nations since India and Pakistan earned world condemnation in 1998 by conducting underground nuclear tests along each other's borders. India and Pakistan both claim sovereignty over the territory of Jammu and Kashmir, a dispute that has triggered three wars since the two nations gained independence from Great Britain in 1947.

27 **The International Criminal Tribunal for the former Yugoslavia,** a panel of prosecutors established by the United Nations (UN), issues a 42-page arrest warrant indicting Slobodan Milosevic, president of Yugoslavia, on charges of crimes against humanity in the Yugoslav province of Kosovo. The warrant, issued in all UN member nations, charges Milosevic with ordering the forced deportation of more than 740,000 ethnic Albanians and the murder of at least 340 Kosovars since Jan. 1, 1999.

29 **Olusegun Obasanjo,** a retired army general, is sworn in as president of Nigeria. He is Nigeria's first legitimately elected head of state since a military *coup* (overthrow) toppled the government in 1983.

Polish police remove more than 300 crosses from land near Auschwitz, a Nazi death camp in Poland. The crosses began appearing in 1998 after Jewish groups demanded the removal of a large cross built at Auschwitz in 1979 to commemorate the 152 Polish Catholics who died in the camp. Jewish groups claimed the cross insults the memory of the more than 1 million Jews who died there and at other nearby camps. The cross remains standing, despite a new law banning religious symbols within 300 feet (91 meters) of former Nazi camps in Poland.

Ethnic Albanians survey the remains of their neighborhood in Jakovo, a town in the Serbian province of Kosovo, after the departure of Serb forces in June. Jakovo had reportedly been ravaged by the Serbs.

1 **American Airlines Flight 1420,** en route from Dallas to Little Rock, Arkansas, skids off a Little Rock National Airport runway while attempting to land in a severe thunderstorm. The jet, a Super MD-80, with 145 passengers and crew members aboard, spins out of control and crashes into a steel beacon tower, killing 11 people.

3 **The African National Congress (ANC)** party takes nearly two-thirds of all seats in the South African Parliament in a landslide election that guarantees that Thabo Mbeki, deputy president of South Africa, will replace Nelson Mandela as president. Mandela, who stepped down as head of the ANC in 1997, chose Mbeki to succeed him as both party head and president.

8 **Taiwan** joins Hong Kong, Malaysia, the Philippines, Singapore, South Korea, and Thailand in banning a variety of European Union (EU) farm products

in the wake of revelations that Belgian-produced chicken, eggs, butter, pork, and beef may be contaminated with dioxin, a cancer-causing chemical.

9 **NATO and Serb generals,** meeting in a tent at a helicopter base in Macedonia, sign an accord requiring all Serb forces to withdraw from the Serbian province of Kosovo over an 11-day period that begins on June 10. The Serbs agree to the introduction into Kosovo of a multinational peacekeeping force consisting of 50,000 NATO-led soldiers. The accord ends the largest allied military action in Europe since the close of World War II (1939–1945). NATO's campaign against Yugoslavia, which began on March 24, was the first military action in history waged entirely from the air and fought in the name of human rights.

10 **NATO** suspends its bombing campaign against Yugoslavia in response to Yugoslav President Slobodan Milosevic's withdrawal of Serbian troops from Kosovo. NATO dropped more than 23,000 bombs and missiles in the 78 days of the campaign, which was waged to halt Serbian aggression against ethnic Albanians in Kosovo.

11 **Russian troops** march into Kosovo, enter the provincial capital of Pristina, and take control of the airport. U.S. officials call Russia's unexpected attempt to join the NATO peacekeeping effort in post-war Kosovo "confusing."

13 **Voters in Belgium** turn the Christian Democrat and Socialist coalition government out of office after 12 years of rule. Two conservative groups, the Liberal Party and the anti-immigrant Vlaams Blok party, take the majority of parliamentary seats.

14 **The median age of U.S. citizens** is 35.2 years, the highest in the nation's history, reports the U.S. Census Bureau.

15 **South Korean warships** fire on North Korean boats in a disputed area of the Yellow Sea, hitting a torpedo boat that catches fire and sinks. All 17 members of the crew are killed. On June 7, North Korea demanded that South Korean ships leave the disputed area, which is a rich fishing ground, and South Korea launched additional warships into the Yellow Sea.

A powerful earthquake, registering 6.7, rocks central Mexico, and 25 people are killed under falling debris. While the quake's epicenter is near Huajuapan de Leon in Oaxaca, the worst damage is in the neighboring state of Puebla. Destruction is particularly severe in the city of Puebla, where a large number of churches and colonial-era buildings are damaged in the town's center.

18 **The United States and Russia** agree that 3,600 Russian troops will be integrated into the NATO peacekeeping force in Kosovo. The agreement ends three days of negotiations, held in Helsinki, Finland.

19 **Prince Edward,** third son of Queen Elizabeth of Great Britain, marries So-

phie Rhys-Jones, a commoner, at the 500-year-old St. George's Chapel at Windsor Castle, west of London. Rhys-Jones is a public relations executive.

22 **An estimated 150,000 to 200,000 people** in Zimbabwe are expected to die of AIDS in 1999, report Zimbabwe Ministry of Health officials. Officials with Zimbabwe's National AIDS Coordination Program believe that at least 25 percent of the country's 12.5 million people are infected with HIV, the virus that causes AIDS.

24 **Israeli fighter jets** bomb bridges, power stations, and guerrilla strongholds in Lebanon in retaliation for a Hezbollah rocket attack on northern Israel. Hezbollah, or Party of God, is a Lebanon-based militant Islamic group dedicated to the destruction of Israel. Six Lebanese and two Israelis are killed in the exchange, which occurs only days after Israeli Prime Minister-elect Ehud Barak and Syrian President Hafez al-Assad, who also controls much of Lebanon, announce their mutual intentions to reopen peace negotiations.

26 **The San Antonio Spurs** win the NBA championship by defeating the New York Knicks 78-77 in a game lasting into the early morning at New York City's Madison Square Garden. San Antonio's Tim Duncan, who scored 31 points in the game, is named most valuable player in the best-of-seven match series, which the Spurs win four games to one.

28 **The Yugoslav Red Cross** reports that one quarter of the Serbs living in Kosovo, more than 75,000 people, have fled the province for Serbia since the June 10 withdrawal of Serbian forces. NATO commanders in Kosovo suggest that the Serbs fear vengeance from returning Kosovar Albanians. Since June 10, more than 415,000 ethnic Albanians have returned to Kosovo, where 90 percent of the population was ethnic Albanian before the war.

29 **Abdullah Ocalan,** leader of Turkey's rebel Kurds, is found guilty of treason and sentenced to death. Thousands of Armenian and Turkish Kurds living in Europe respond with public protests.

U.S. soccer team member Brandi Chastain exults upon kicking the winning penalty shot to clinch the 1999 Women's World Cup final against China on July 10.

3 **Winds of 20 miles (32 kilometers) per hour** drive a forest fire over more than 2,000 acres (809 hectares) outside Lewiston in northern California, forcing the evacuation of at least 500 people. Outside Reno, Nevada, strong winds drive a second wildfire across 3,000 acres (1,214 hectares).

4 **Tennis players from the United States** sweep singles tennis at Wimbledon, England, for the first time in 15 years. Lindsay Davenport wins her first Wimbledon title by beating seven-time champion Steffi Graf 6-4, 7-5. Defending champion Pete Sampras takes a sixth Wimbledon title—a record in this century—by crushing Andre Agassi 6-3, 6-4, 7-5.

A police chase in southern Illinois ends when an avowed white supremacist, Benjamin Smith, dies of a self-inflicted gunshot wound. Police sought the 21-year-old man in connection with a three-day shooting spree that left two people dead and 11 injured.

5 **A 19-year-old Kurdish woman,** flashing a "V for victory" hand signal, detonates bombs strapped to her body, killing herself and wounding 17 people on the streets of Adana, Turkey. The bombing is the third major attack on Turkish civilians by Kurdish guerrillas since a Turkish court found Kurdish rebel leader Abdullah Ocalan guilty of treason on June 29 and condemned him to death.

6 **Massive flooding** in China's Yangtze River Valley forces the evacuation of more than 1.8 million people. The flood has killed about 240 people and threatens the safety of 60 million.

7 **A Florida jury** decides in the first class-action lawsuit brought by ailing smokers that tobacco companies defraud the public by producing "defective and unreasonably dangerous" products. The same companies are found guilty of conspiring to keep information from the public about the dangers of smoking and the addictive nature of cigarettes.

10 **The U.S. women's soccer team** beats the Chinese team on a penalty kick after a scoreless tie to win the 1999 World Cup championship. The match, held at the Rose Bowl in Pasadena, California, was played before 90,185 people, the largest stadium crowd to ever attend a women's sporting event.

12 **Violent protests** continue in Iran's capital, Teheran. University students began demonstrating peacefully against Iran's government on July 7, after conservatives banned the liberal Islamic newspaper *Salam* and enacted a law to curb freedom of the press. But protests turned violent after police and Islamic paramilitary groups attacked the students in their dormitories on July 8, killing at least two people.

15 **Texas Governor George W. Bush** declares that he will not accept matching federal campaign funds in his bid for the Republican presidential nomination in 2000. The refusal frees Bush from conforming to the spending limits applied to candidates who receive public campaign money. With the first presidential straw poll and primary still in the future, Bush has raised a record $37 million for his campaign.

16 **A small plane** piloted by John F. Kennedy, Jr., disappears into the Atlantic Ocean off Martha's Vineyard near Cape Cod, triggering a search for the son of the late U.S. president. Kennedy was traveling with his wife, Caroline Bessette Kennedy, and her sister, Lauren Bessette. The U.S. Coast Guard locates the three bodies within days.

23 **King Hassan II of Morocco,** who ruled for 38 years, dies at the age of 70. Hassan's eldest son and successor, Sidi Mohammed, is expected to continue in his father's role as a Mideast peace-process mediator.

24 **Ross Perot,** who twice ran unsuccessfully for the U.S. presidency, refuses to relinquish his position as head of the Reform Party, which he founded. The Reform Party's most successful candidate to date, Minnesota Governor Jesse Ventura, suggested in a speech at the party's national convention in Dearborn, Michigan, on July 23, that it was time for Perot to step aside.

25 **Lance Armstrong,** the 27-year-old leader of the U.S. Postal Service bicycle team, wins the 86th running of the Tour de France. Armstrong is only the second American to win the race.

26 **Chinese police** arrest 1,200 government employees in the latest round of an official campaign to stamp out the Falun Gong spiritual movement. More than 5,000 people have been taken into custody since the ban went into effect on July 19. Prisoners are sent to camps for instruction in Marxist ideology and Chinese Communist doctrine. Falun Gong, which adherents claim is apolitical, combines slow-motion exercise, meditation, and breathing techniques with ideas from Buddhism and Taoism. Sect leader Li Hongzhi claims there are more than 70 million Falun Gong adherents in China. By comparison, the Communist Party claims 60 million members in China.

28 **Scientists** have turned normal human cells into cancer cells, reports Massachusetts Institute of Technology Professor Robert A. Weinberg in the journal *Nature*. Researchers believe the discovery could lead to an early test for cancer as well as to new treatments and a possible cure.

30 **A heat wave,** which began in mid-July, bakes the eastern two-thirds of the United States. In the Middle Atlantic States, temperatures shoot above 100 °F (38 °C). More than 50 deaths are attributed to the heat in Chicago, where a power station fails.

3 **More than 90 people** are killed and thousands evacuated in Manila, capital of the Philippines, when torrential rains from Tropical Storm Olga trigger flash floods and the collapse of whole hillsides. In South Korea, Olga's rains swell rivers, flood more than 8,500 houses, and kill at least 50 people. Strong winds and heavy rains in North Korea leave thousands of acres of crops underwater.

5 **The U.S. Senate** votes 81 to 16 to confirm Richard C. Holbrooke as U.S. representative to the United Nations. Holbrooke formerly served as U.S. ambassador to Germany, and he was the architect of the 1995 Dayton Accord that ended the war in Bosnia-Herzegovina.

7 **Russian airmen in helicopter gunships** fight a fierce battle in the southern republic of Dagestan with hundreds of gunmen who had crossed the border into Russia from the breakaway republic of Chechnya. The Chechen gunmen appear to belong to the Wahhabi Islamic fundamentalist movement, which authorities in Moscow blame for an attack made earlier in August in the nearby Tsumadi district of the republic. Officials in Chechnya deny any connection with the gunmen.

9 **Russian President Boris Yeltsin** replaces his prime minister for the fourth time in 17 months. Dismissing Sergei Stepashin after three months in office, Yeltsin appoints Vladimir V. Putin, a former spy who headed Russia's main intelligence agency. Political experts believe that Yeltsin is attempting to set up Putin as his successor to the presidency.

10 **A gunman** sprays 20 to 30 shots from an automatic weapon into a Jewish Community Center in suburban Los Angeles, wounding five people, including three boys attending a day camp. Later in the day, the same gunman kills a Filipino American letter carrier.

11 **The last solar eclipse** of the millennium occurs. An estimated 2 billion skywatchers from Nova Scotia off the east coast of Canada to the Bay of Bengal are able to observe the phenomenon.

14 **Texas Governor George W. Bush** wins the Iowa Republican straw poll for president. The poll is a high-profile, but nonbinding, event designed to raise money for the Iowa Republican Party. Multimillionaire publisher Steve Forbes places second, and Elizabeth Dole, a cabinet officer in the administrations of Reagan and Bush, comes in third.

15 **Marxist guerrillas in Colombia** kidnap Roman Catholic Bishop Jose de Jesus Quintero Diaz. The kidnappers identify themselves as the Simon Bolivar Guerrilla Coordinators, a terrorist group made up of members of Colombia's two leading Marxist rebel armies.

17 **More than 17,000 people** are killed and thousands more injured in western Turkey in an earthquake registering 7.4 in magnitude. The quake is the most powerful ever recorded in the region. The epicenter is 50 miles (80 kilometers) east of Istanbul near the industrial city of Izmit.

The National Ice Center, a government service organization that monitors icebergs, issues a warning that a berg approximately the size of the state of Rhode Island, 24 by 48 miles (41 by 77 kilometers), threatens shipping between South America and Antarctica. The iceberg, from which smaller bergs are breaking off, is drifting southeast at approximately 8 miles (13 kilometers) per hour.

19 **An estimated 150,000 Serbs** defy riot police to gather in the streets of Belgrade, Yugoslavia, demanding the resignation of President Slobodan Milosevic. Milosevic led the country into a series of ruinous wars that have left the economy near collapse.

20 **Three Japanese banks** announce a plan to merge, creating the world's largest financial institution with assets of $1.1 trillion. Economists suggest the merger is a response by the Japanese financial community to the country's deep recession and an attempt to combat the intense global competition of U.S. and European banks.

Residents of the town of Sakarya, in western Turkey, pass by buildings toppled by a powerful earthquake that struck Turkey on August 17, killing more than 17,000 people.

23 **German's chancellery moves** from Bonn to Berlin, establishing Germany's first Berlin-based government since the collapse of Adolf Hitler's regime at the end of World War II (1939–1945).

26 **The first discovery of liquid water in an object from space** is announced by Michael E. Zolensky, a scientist at NASA's Johnson Space Center in Houston. NASA scientists found the water trapped in an extraterrestrial rock that a group of boys playing basketball saw blaze to Earth in the west Texas town of Monahans.

27 **Two Russian cosmonauts and a French astronaut,** the last scheduled crew aboard Mir, leave the Russian space station in preparation for its abandonment. After Mir's systems are switched off from Mission Control on Earth, the station is due to fall from outer space during 2000 and burn up in the atmosphere.

30 **The people of East Timor,** a former Portuguese colony occupied by Indonesia since 1976, vote on whether to become an autonomous part of Indonesia or a sovereign nation. The referendum, brokered by the United Nations (UN) and Portugal and monitored by UN officials, is carried out under the threat of violence by the Indonesian army. Indonesian President B. J. Habibie earlier announced that if the people of East Timor voted against autonomy, he would let the province pursue full independence. About 99 percent of the East Timorese vote. More than 78 percent reject the idea of autonomy and thus cast their ballots indirectly in favor of independence.

31 **Mireya Moscoso** becomes the first female president of Panama. Moscoso, the widow of former president Arnulfo Arias, is the second freely elected president since the United States deposed General Manuel Noriega in 1989.

1 **A strain of mice** that is significantly more intelligent than normal mice was created by neurobiologist Joe Z. Tsien of Princeton University, reports the journal *Nature*. Tsien, who engineered the strain by manipulating a gene involved in memory formation, believes his work may provide a foundation for fighting memory loss in the elderly.

4 **Israeli Prime Minister Ehud Barak and Palestinian leader Yasir Arafat** sign a new peace accord, called Wye Two. A revision to a 1998 agreement, the accord deals with long-standing disputes regarding Palestinian refugees and water rights. It specifies that Israel will turn over to the Palestinians partial or full control of more than 40 percent of the West Bank by Jan. 20, 2000.

5 **Islamic militants from Chechnya** cross into Dagestan and seize three villages. Hundreds of residents flee into the countryside to avoid the intense fighting between the rebels and Russian and Dagestani troops.

8 **Bill Bradley,** a one-time professional basketball star and a former U.S. senator from New Jersey, announces that he is challenging Vice President Al

Hurricane Floyd hits land at Cape Fear, North Carolina, on September 16, where the storm drops 19 inches (48 centimeters) of rain, causing widespread flooding.

Gore for the Democratic Party's presidential nomination.

11 **Serena Williams** wins the women's finals of the United States Open tennis championship by defeating Martina Hingis, 6-3, 7-6 (7-4). Hingis knocked Serena Williams's sister, Venus, from the semifinals on September 10.

Half of all the babies born in sub-Saharan Africa are infected with HIV, the virus that causes AIDS, according to UNAIDS, a United Nations agency that works to fight the spread of HIV. AIDS has cut life expectancy to an average of 25 years in 21 African countries.

12 **Indonesian President B. J. Habibie** bows to international pressure and invites a United Nations peacekeeping force to restore order in the Indonesian province of East Timor. In the last week, nearly 100,000 East Timorese fled into West Timor to escape the violence of anti-independence militias, which human rights groups claim are backed by the Indonesian military.

13 **A bomb** explodes in an eight-story Moscow apartment building, killing 78 of some 150 residents. The explosion is the fourth in Russia in two weeks. Authorities in Moscow blame the violence on Islamic Chechen rebels.

15 **A man toting a large-caliber handgun** enters the sanctuary of the Wedgwood Baptist Church in Fort Worth, Texas, and shoots into a crowd attending an evening teen prayer service. Seven worshipers are killed and seven wounded before the man turns the gun on himself.

16 **Hurricane Floyd** hits land at Cape Fear on the North Carolina coast and drops 19 inches (48 centimeters) of rain in Wilmington, North Carolina, before moving to the northeast. Losing strength over land, the hurricane is downgraded to a tropical storm but still causes massive flooding as far north as New England. More than 1 million households lose electricity. Airports are closed up and down the Eastern Seaboard, disrupting air traffic across the nation. One of the largest hurricanes to ever strike the United States, Floyd prompted the largest evacuation in U.S. history.

17 **U.S. President Bill Clinton** eases an economic embargo against North Korea in response to North Korea's promise to halt the testing of long-range missiles. The relaxing of trade restrictions allows North Korea to purchase goods from the United States and to transport cargo and passengers to and from the United States.

22 **Prime Minister Ehud Barak of Israel** pays a state visit to Chancellor Gerhard Schroeder in Germany's newly restored capital, Berlin. Barak is the first Israeli leader to make an official visit to a city many Israelis associate with Adolf Hitler and his systematic extermination of millions of Jews during World War II (1939-1945).

23 **Russian warplanes** attack the breakaway republic of Chechnya with missiles and bombs. The attack comes only days after Moscow officials announced that military strikes in Chechnya would be confined to rebel camps on the mountainous border with Dagestan.

26 **A team of 12 U.S. golfers** moves from four points behind to a 14 ½-13 ½ victory over the European team to win the Ryder Cup at The Country Club in Brookline, Massachusetts. The triumph gives the cup to a U.S. team for the first time since 1993.

30 **Officials at the National Aeronautics and Space Administration** announce that the Mars Climate Orbiter, a $125-million space probe, was lost because two engineering teams used different measurement systems. The confusion threw the orbiter off course, and ground controllers lost track of the probe as it entered the atmosphere of Mars on September 23.

Workers at a Japanese nuclear fuel plant release 35 pounds (15.9 kilograms) of uranium, seven times the specified amount, into a purification tank containing nitric acid, setting off a chain reaction. The reaction exposes 35 people in the plant to high levels of radioactivity. Nearby residents are ordered to remain indoors.

3 **More than 44 million U.S. citizens,** 16.3 percent of the population, lack health insurance, the U.S. Census Bureau reports. In 1998, the number of people in the United States without health insurance rose by 883,000.

5 **A high-speed express,** en route to London's Paddington Station, plows through a commuter train. More than 30 people are killed and 175 injured.

7 **Days of ceaseless rain** trigger flooding and mudslides in nine Mexican states, driving hundreds of thousands of people from their homes. About 350 people are confirmed dead.

India's Hindu nationalist Bharatiya Janata Party, leader of a coalition of 24 political parties, emerges victorious in parliamentary elections. The triumph guarantees that Atal Behari Vajpayee will continue as prime minister.

8 **A British court** rules that General Augusto Pinochet can be extradited to Spain to stand trail on charges that he committed torture when he was dictator of Chile. Pinochet was arrested in Great Britain in October 1998 on charges brought by a Spanish judge that between 1973, the year he grabbed power in Chile, and 1988 Pinochet carried out kidnappings and committed murders and genocide.

12 **The human population of the Earth** hits 6 billion, according to estimates made by population experts at the United Nations based upon national birth and death rates. The world's population was 2 billion in 1927, 4 billion in 1974, and 5 billion in 1987.

General Pervaiz Musharraf leads a bloodless military *coup* (overthrow) in Pakistan that topples Prime Minister Nawaz Sharif's government. Crowds of Pakistanis who blame Sharif for Pakistan's poor economy and corruption in government gather in the streets and sing "Long live the army." Sharif had removed Musharraf from his post as chief general of Pakistan's army just hours before the coup.

13 **The U.S. Senate** votes against the Comprehensive Test Ban Treaty. Experts in international relations label the vote a major defeat for President Bill Clinton, who in 1996 was the first head of state to sign the agreement at the United Nations. Most senators vote along party lines, with Republicans—who hold a majority of the seats in the Senate—voting against the treaty, and Democrats voting in favor of it. The vote marks the first time that the Senate has rejected an arms control treaty. The treaty, to go into effect, must be ratified by 44 nations posessing nuclear weapon capabilities.

14 **Tanzania's former president Julius Nyerere** dies in a London hospital at the age of 77. Nyerere helped free Tanzania from British colonial rule during the early 1960's. He served as president from 1962 until his retirement in 1985.

16 **Doctors Without Borders,** a volunteer medical group dedicated to treating people in danger from war, disease, civil strife, or natural disasters, receives the Nobel Peace Prize. Doctors Without Borders, founded by French physicians in 1971, consists of about 2,000 physicians working in about 80 countries.

19 **Republicans in the U.S. Senate** use a filibuster to block proposed legislation that would overhaul the campaign finance system. The measure would have banned "soft money"—that is, unlimited and unregulated donations to political parties, rather than to specific candidates.

20 **The People's Consultative Assembly** chooses Abdurrahman Wahid as Indonesia's first democratically elected president. Wahid, a Muslim clergyman and scholar, pledged to steer the country toward recovery from its political and financial turmoil of the late 1990's. He replaces President B. J. Habibie.

22 **Scientists** announce the discovery in Madagascar, an island country off the coast of Africa, of what may be the world's oldest dinosaur fossils. Researchers found jawbones from two kangaroo-sized dinosaurs, according to a report published in the journal *Science*. The dinosaurs, classified as prosauropods, had small heads

On October 30, the last Indonesian troops leave East Timor, marking the end of 24 years of Indonesian occupation.

and long necks and could walk on either two or four legs. Scientists believe they were *herbivores* (plant-eaters) that lived between 225 and 230 million years ago.

25 **Israel** opens certain roads to serve as a safe passage route between the West Bank and the Gaza Strip for Palestinian residents. Israel's Prime Minister Ehud Barak and Palestinian leader Yasir Arafat agreed to the route as part of the ongoing Mideast peace process.

The United Nations (UN) Security Council votes unanimously to establish a temporary government under the UN flag in East Timor. The government will serve until East Timor is able to function as a stable, self-governing nation.

26 **Teen-age birth rates** in the United States fell in 1998, officials for the National Center for Health Statistics report. Births in the 15-to-19-year-old age group fell 5 percent from 1997. The birth rate among girls aged 10 to 14 decreased by 6 percent.

27 **The New York Yankees** beat the Atlanta Braves to win their 25th World Series championship of the century.

30 **The last Indonesian soldiers** leave East Timor 24 years after Indonesia invaded the region.

31 **EgyptAir Flight 990**, traveling from New York City to Cairo, plunges into the Atlantic Ocean off the coast of Massachusetts. All 217 passengers and crew members are killed.

Seattle police use tear gas to push back protesters disrupting a World Trade Organization (WTO) conference on November 30. Most of the protesters were environmentalists or members of labor unions.

1 **A U.S. federal judge** rules that New York City Mayor Rudolph W. Giuliani violated the First Amendment of the U.S. Constitution when he cut city financing of the Brooklyn Museum of Art in October over a controversial art exhibit, "Sensations: Young British Artists from the Saatchi Collection." The exhibit included a painting of the Virgin Mary decorated with elephant dung.

4 **A judge in Laramie, Wyoming,** sentences Aaron J. McKinney to two life terms in prison for the murder in 1998 of Matthew Shepard, a University of Wyoming college student who was openly gay. A jury found McKinney guilty of second-degree murder, robbery, and kidnapping on Nov. 3, 1999.

5 **A female panda, Lun-Lun, and a male panda, Yang-Yang,** arrive at Zoo Atlanta in Atlanta, Georgia, as part in a 10-year research project designed to result in the reproduction in captivity of rare giant pandas.

Thomas Penfield Jackson, presiding judge in the U.S. government's antitrust suit against software giant Microsoft Corporation of Redmond, Washington, issues a preliminary judgment in the case. He rules that Microsoft holds a nearly complete monopoly over the manufacturing and sale of computer operating systems and notes that Microsoft is guilty of using its dominance in certain types of software to crush competition. Jackson writes in the judgment that Microsoft has harmed consumers and discouraged innovation among competitors.

6 **Australians, voting in a referendum,** reject a proposal to change their Constitution to become a republic. Queen Elizabeth II of the United Kingdom will remain Australia's official head of state.

7 **Scientists at Children's Hospital in Boston** report that they have successfully grown heart valves from the heart cells of sheep and have transplanted the valves into living sheep, where the valves performed normally. The researchers suggested that their success with sheep transplants may lead to similar transplants in human beings. Currently, patients who need new heart valves must rely on either human or animal donors or on prosthetic valves.

8 **President Bill Clinton** becomes the first U.S. president to participate in a live Internet chat by responding to questions posted online in a virtual town hall meeting. The event attracted 50,000 participants.

9 **The Professional Golfers' Association of America (PGA)** awards Tiger Woods the Vardon Trophy for setting the lowest adjusted golf score average of the year. Woods's 1999 score average—68.43—is also the lowest in history. The previous record, set by Greg Norman in 1994, was 68.81. On Nov. 7, 1999, Woods defeated Miguel Angel Jimenez on the first hole of a playoff to win the World Golf Championship in Spain.

10 **The Russian government** bans the import of all foreign goods into Chechnya in an attempt to isolate Chechen rebels. Russia also suspends all flights between southern Russia and countries in the Caucasus and the Middle East. Russian officials believe that Chechen rebels have used such flights to smuggle weapons into Chechnya, where Russia is attempting to put down a rebellion by separatist Muslim rebels.

14 **Jesse Jackson,** a prominent civil rights spokesperson, leads some 2,000 people on a march in Decatur, Illinois, to force the Decatur School Board to readmit six African American high school students. The board on September 17 expelled the students for two school years for allegedly taking part in a brawl in the stands at a football game.

16 **Investigators for the National Transportation and Safety Board** and the U.S. Federal Bureau of Investigation suggest that a copilot aboard an EgyptAir Boeing 767, which plunged into the Atlantic Ocean off the coast of Massachusetts on October 31, may have caused the crash as an act of suicide. The investigators reportedly base their conclusion on flight data and voice recordings. All 217 people aboard the flight were killed.

18 **A log pyramid at Texas A&M University** at College Station, Texas, collapses, killing 12 people and injuring 28 others. The students were building the pyramid for the school's traditional pep rally bonfire before the annual game between Texas A&M and the University of Texas.

21 **The first Chinese spacecraft designed to carry human beings** returns to China after orbiting Earth 14 times in 21 hours. The unmanned test mission moves China closer to its goal of sending people into outer space.

23 **More than 2.6 million people died** from AIDS in 1999, according to researchers at the World Health Organization and UNAIDS, a United Nations agency that works to fight the spread of HIV, the virus that causes AIDS. The agencies also report that 5.6 million people were infected with HIV in 1999.

26 **Mount Kilimanjaro,** Africa's tallest peak, is shorter than previously thought by approximately 10 feet (3 meters), a team of German and Tanzanian scientists reports. The scientists scaled Killimanjaro and interpreted data from satellites to determine that the mountain is actually 19,331 feet (5,892 meters) high.

30 **Thousands of protesters,** including environmentalists and members of labor unions, disrupt the first meeting of a four-day World Trade Organization conference in Seattle. When the protests turn violent, Seattle Mayor Paul Schell declares a state of emergency and imposes a 7 p.m. curfew. Washington State Governor Gary Locke calls out National Guard units to maintain order.

2 **Researchers in the Human Genome Project** announce in the journal *Nature* that they have determined the exact sequence of approximately 33.5 million chemical units—called bases—in the human chromosome 22.

The British Parliament hands substantial power over Northern Ireland to the Northern Ireland Assembly. A leader of the Protestant Ulster Unionist Party, David Trimble, becomes First Minister. A Roman Catholic moderate, Seamus Mallon, is made Deputy First Minister. Two representatives from Sinn Fein, the political arm of the Irish Republican Army, hold seats in the Assembly. The United Kingdom assumed control of the government of Northern Ireland in 1972 in an effort to end the centuries-old violence between Protestants and Roman Catholics.

3 **U.S. and Mexican officials** announce a joint investigation of a mass grave near Ciudad Juarez, Mexico, where six bodies have been unearthed so far. Officials believe the victims were murdered by drug traffickers.

4 **Military officials in Moscow** announce that Russian troops have surrounded Grozny, capital of the breakaway Russian republic of Chechnya.

7 **The National Aeronautics and Space Administration** announces that the Mars Polar Lander is probably lost. The spacecraft, which was due to make a soft landing about 620 miles (1,000 kilometers) from the planet's south pole on December 3, failed to make radio contact with Earth. The vehicle carried two "microprobes" to analyze the Martian soil and a microphone to detect sounds on the planet's surface.

8 **A civil trial jury in Memphis, Tennessee,** concludes that slain civil rights leader Martin Luther King, Jr., was not the victim of a lone racist gunman but of a conspiracy. The jury awards King's family a symbolic $100 in damages, the amount the family sought in the wrongful-death suit against Loyd Jowers, a former Memphis restaurateur, who had once claimed on television to have hired King's assassin.

9 **The U.S. Department of State** orders the expulsion from the United States of a Russian diplomat who was discovered monitoring a listening device hidden in a conference room at State Department headquarters in Washington, D.C. U.S. officials claimed that a foreign intelligence service had never before penetrated State Department headquarters with such a device.

11 **Pope John Paul II** presides over a ceremony marking the completion of a 20-year project to restore the Sistine Chapel in the Vatican in Rome. The chapel contains Michelangelo's murals on the ceiling vault and his "The Last Judgement" on the altar wall. Other Renaissance masters decorated the side walls.

12 **More than 20 percent of people in the United States** experience a mental disorder in any given year, according to a comprehensive report by the U.S. surgeon general. The report also discloses that approximately half of all Americans experience mental disorders at some point in their lives.

14 **Former U.S. President Jimmy Carter** joins Panamanian President Mireya Moscoso in Panama City, Panama, for the ceremonial transfer of the Panama Canal. Carter signed a treaty in 1977 that gave Panama official control over the canal on Dec. 31, 1999. The ceremony was held before the actual transfer in order to avoid conflicts with New Year's celebrations commemorating the millennium.

15 **Israeli Prime Minister Ehud Barak** and Syrian foreign minister Farouk al-Shara meet in Washington, D.C., to renew peace talks. Representatives of Israel and Syria last met to discuss peace between the two countries in 1996.

17 **The German government** and some 70 German corporations that used Nazi prisoners as slave laborers during World War II (1939-1945) agree to compensate some surviving victims of the Holocaust. The agreement ends months of negotiations between Holocaust victims, various Jewish groups, Germany, Israel, and the United States.

20 **The Supreme Court of Vermont** rules that gay and lesbian couples in Vermont are entitled, according to the state's constitution, to the same protections and benefits as heterosexual married couples. The court leaves it to the Vermont legislature to decide between granting marriage licenses to same-sex couples or setting up a broad domestic partnership system.

21 **"Mad cow disease"** in cattle and Creutzfeldt-Jakob disease, a fatal brain disorder in humans, may be the same disease, scientists report in the journal *Proceedings of the National Academy of Sciences.* The findings were based on lab experiments conducted on mice.

24 **Hijackers** seize an Indian Airlines jet after it takes off from Kathmandu, Nepal. After stops in India, Pakistan, and the United Arab Emirates, the five hijackers force the crew to land in Afghanistan. The hijackers, who are holding more than 150 passengers and crew members aboard the plane, demand that India give them $200 million and release imprisoned Kashmiri militants and a Pakistan-born Kashmiri activist.

25 **General Robert Guei,** a former army chief, takes control of the government of the Ivory Coast after ousting President Henri Konan Bedie.

31 **Boris Yeltsin** announces his immediate resignation as president of Russia and names Prime Minister Vladimir V. Putin as acting president.

Hijackers free 155 passengers and crew members from an Indian Airlines jet in Kandahar, Afghanistan, after India releases three Kashmiri militants. The hijackers, who took control of the aircraft on December 24 and killed one passenger, had originally demanded $200 million and the release of a larger number of militants.

Dec. 31-Jan. 1 A new millennium is celebrated around the world—from Sydney, Tokyo, and Beijing to Moscow, Paris, and New York City—as clocks strike midnight throughout the day.

Exploding rockets illuminate the sky above the Great Pyramids, which have survived 4,000 years, during Egypt's millennium celebration on Jan. 1, 2000.

Ocean

Geology

Architecture

Biology

South Africa

Transportation

Nobel Prizes

Economics

Canada

New York City

Chemistry

Popular music

Archaeolog

People in the news

Spac

Astronomy

Disasters

2000 UPDATE

Stocks and bonds

Conservation

Australia

Classical music

The major events of 1999 are summarized in more than 250 alphabetically arranged articles, from "Afghanistan" to "Zoos." Included are Special Reports that offer in-depth looks at subjects ranging from the development of astronomy over the past 1,000 years to the tribulations of Yugoslavia. The Special Reports can be found on the following pages under their respective Update article titles.

■ **ASTRONOMY:**
Astronomy Through a Millennium...................**68**

■ **BASEBALL:**
Where Have You Gone, Joe DiMaggio? **98**

■ **EMPIRES:**
Great Empires of the Millennium..................**180**

■ **HUMAN RIGHTS:**
A Century of Civil Rights...........................**226**

■ **LITERATURE, WORLD:**
In Love with Shakespeare **270**

■ **MIDDLE EAST:**
A Century of Struggle...............................**296**

■ **YUGOSLAVIA:**
Yugoslavia: A Decade of Ruin **434**

Afghanistan. The civil war in Afghanistan continued through 1999 despite two United Nations (UN)-sponsored peace conferences that took place in March and July. The conferences, held in Turkmenistan and Uzbekistan, brought together Afghanistan's two main factions—the Taliban, a fundamentalist Muslim group composed primarily of Pashtuns, Afghanistan's largest ethnic group; and the Northern Alliance of smaller ethnic groups from northeastern Afghanistan. The Taliban, which held about 85 percent of the country, was allied in 1999 with Pakistan and Saudi Arabia. Iran, Russia, and Uzbekistan backed the Northern Alliance, led by Ahmed Shah Massoud.

Taliban offensive. On July 28, the Taliban launched a major offensive in an attempt to destroy Northern Alliance forces. The offensive proved inconclusive when the Northern Alliance launched a hard-hitting counteroffensive a week later. Fighting surged back and forth just north of the capital, Kabul. According to refugees from combat areas, Taliban troops, accompanied by Pakistani volunteers, employed a "scorched-earth" policy throughout the countryside and committed numerous atrocities against civilians. Some 65,000 refugees fled to the Panjshir Valley, high in the Hindu Kush, a rugged mountain chain in the center of Afghanistan.

Sanctions. The United States in July 1999 banned trade with Afghanistan and froze Afghan assets in U.S. territory. In 1998, U.S. officials had demanded that the Taliban turn over Osama bin Laden, an exiled Saudi millionaire alleged to have masterminded the bombing in August 1998 of two U.S. embassies in East Africa. In August 1999, Taliban officials again refused to surrender bin Laden. A Taliban spokesman acknowledged that bin Laden was living in Afghanistan under Taliban protection. Bin Laden reportedly moved about frequently out of fear that U.S. agents would attempt to kidnap him.

The UN Security Council voted on October 15 to impose economic sanctions on Afghanistan if the Taliban did not surrender bin Laden. The sanctions went into effect on November 14. Angry mobs in a number of Afghan cities responded to the sanctions with attacks on UN offices.

Assassination attempt. A truck bomb exploded on August 24 outside the residence of the Taliban leader, Mullah Mohammad Omar, in the southern city of Qandahar. The explosion killed at least 10 people, including relatives of Omar.

Drug trade. Afghanistan became the world's largest producer of opium in 1999. The Taliban taxed and protected trade in the drug, which Western journalists alleged funded the regime.

□ Henry S. Bradsher

See also **Asia; Terrorism.**

Africa

The majority of African countries enjoyed relative peace and stability in 1999. However, violent disorder continued to afflict some areas of the continent, as civil conflict escalated in Angola, large-scale fighting continued between Ethiopia and Eritrea, and Sierra Leone remained wracked by chaos. Probably the most pressing question in Africa in 1999 was how to achieve a workable cease-fire in the Democratic Republic of Congo, also known as Congo (Kinshasa) and formerly as Zaire. The civil war there directly involved at least seven other African nations.

Niger, Guinea-Bissau, and Comoros, where military officers seized power from civilian governments, also remained unstable through much of 1999. The military staged a coup in Ivory Coast in December. The continuing flow of hundreds of thousands of economic and political refugees within and between countries and the unchecked spread of HIV, the virus that causes AIDS, created severe problems.

The restoration of democracy in Nigeria—the continent's most populous nation—and the second multiracial national elections to be held in South Africa offered hope that democracies might flourish in Africa. In addition, Mozambique, nearly destroyed by civil war in the 1980's and early 1990's, in December 1999 successfully held its second democratic national elections.

Nigeria and South Africa. On May 29, General Abdulsalam Abubakar, Nigeria's leader since June 1998, kept his pledge to end military rule and transfer power to a democratically elected leader by May 1999. Olusegun Obasanjo was elected president in February with 63 percent of the vote, and became the country's first civilian president since 1983. Earlier in February 1999, Nigerian voters had elected representatives to the National Assembly, the country's parliament.

The transition to civilian government led to Nigeria's readmission in April to the Commonwealth of Nations, an association of independent countries and other political units that have lived under British law and government. The organization had expelled Nigeria in 1995 because of widespread human rights abuses committed by its military regime.

In South Africa's second all-race elections, the African National Congress on June 2, 1999, retained its overwhelming parliamentary majority, winning almost two-thirds of the national vote. The elections, which occurred in a largely peaceful atmosphere, represented a significant step toward the consolidation of democracy in that

Refugees from Congo (Kinshasa) unload their belongings in the neighboring Central African Republic in January 1999, after fleeing advancing rebels attempting to overthrow the government of President Laurent Kabila. A cease-fire brokered by Zambia collapsed in November.

Country	Population	Government	Monetary unit*	Foreign trade (million U.S.$)	
				Exports†	Imports†
Algeria	31,158,000	President Abdelaziz Bouteflika; Prime Minister Ahmed Benbitour	dinar (66.76 = $1)	14,000	8,500
Angola	13,074,000	President Jose Eduardo dos Santos	readj. kwanza (257,128.00 = $1)	3,400	2,200
Benin	6,255,000	President Mathieu Kerekou	CFA franc (614.05 = $1)	424	665
Botswana	1,434,000	President Festus Mogae	pula (4.57 = $1)	2,250	2,430
Burkina Faso	11,708,000	Popular Front Chairman, Head of State, & Head of Government Blaise Compaore	CFA franc (614.05 = $1)	205	530
Burundi	5,835,000	President Pierre Buyoya	franc (585.77 = $1)	65	158
Cameroon	15,245,000	President Paul Biya	CFA franc (614.05 = $1)	1,859	1,358
Cape Verde	448,000	President Antonio Mascarenhas Monteiro; Prime Minister Carlos Wahnon Veiga	escudo (103.21 = $1)	43	215
Central African Republic	3,731,000	President Ange Patasse	CFA franc (614.05 = $1)	182	155
Chad	7,307,000	President Idriss Deby	CFA franc (614.05 = $1)	245	242
Comoros	552,000	Head of State Assoumani Azzali	franc (460.54 = $1)	11	70
Congo (Brazzaville)	2,970,000	President Denis Sassou-Nguesso	CFA franc (614.05 = $1)	1,700	803
Congo (Kinshasa)	51,136,000	President Laurent Kabila	Congolese franc (4.50 = $1)	1,600	819
Djibouti	588,000	President Ismail Omar Guelleh; Prime Minister Barkat Gourad Hamadou	franc (177.72 = $1)	40	201
Egypt	69,146,000	President Hosni Mubarak; Prime Minister Atef Mohammed Obeid	pound (3.41 = $1)	3,130	16,166
Equatorial Guinea	452,000	President Teodoro Obiang Nguema Mbasogo; Prime Minister Serafin Seriche Dougan	CFA franc (614.05 = $1)	197	248
Eritrea	4,025,000	President Isaias Afworki	nafka (7.60 = $1)	95	514
Ethiopia	63,785,000	President Negasso Gidada	birr (8.12 = $1)	550	1,300
Gabon	1,227,000	President El Hadj Omar Bongo; Prime Minister Jean-François Ntoutoume-Emane	CFA franc (614.05 = $1)	2,100	890
Gambia	1,291,000	Head of State Yahya Jammeh	dalasi (11.80 = $1)	27	245
Ghana	20,172,000	President Jerry John Rawlings	cedi (2,920.00 = $1)	1,635	2,307
Guinea	7,759,000	President Lansana Conte	franc (1,300.00 = $1)	695	560
Guinea-Bissau	1,192,000	President Malan Bacai Sanha	CFA franc (614.05 = $1)	27	87
Ivory Coast (Cote d'Ivoire)	16,761,000	National Committee of Public Salvation Head Robert Guei	CFA franc (614.05 = $1)	4,141	2,741
Kenya	32,577,000	President Daniel T. arap Moi	shilling (75.55 = $1)	2,007	3,194
Lesotho	2,338,000	King Letsie III; Prime Minister Pakalitha Mosisili	maloti (6.05 = $1)	200	880
Liberia	3,013,000	President Charles Taylor	dollar (1 = $1)	1,100	3,650

Country	Population	Government	Monetary unit*	Foreign trade (million U.S.$)	
				Exports[†]	Imports[†]
Libya	6,387,000	Leader Muammar Muhammad al-Qadhafi; General People's Committee Secretary (Prime Minister) Muhammad Ahmad al-Manqush	dinar (0.45 = $1)	6,800	6,900
Madagascar	15,020,000	President Didier Ratsiraka	franc (5,220.00 = $1)	169	465
Malawi	10,136,000	President Bakili Muluzi	kwacha (44.04 = $1)	481	623
Mali	12,559,000	President Alpha Oumar Konare; Prime Minister Ibrahim Boubacar Keita	CFA franc (614.05 = $1)	562	689
Mauritania	2,580,000	President Maaouya Ould Sid Ahmed Taya	ouguiya (205.02 = $1)	562	552
Mauritius	1,179,000	President Sir Cassam Uteem; Prime Minister Navinchandra Ramgoolam	rupee (25.23 = $1)	1,734	2,183
Morocco	29,637,000	King Mohamed VI; Prime Minister Abderrahmane Youssoufi	dirham (9.76 = $1)	7,219	10,262
Mozambique	18,991,000	President Joaquim Alberto Chissano; Prime Minister Pascoal Manuel Mocumbi	metical (11,495.00 = $1)	295	965
Namibia	1,752,000	President Sam Nujoma; Prime Minister Hage Geingob	rand (6.05 = $1)	1,440	1,480
Niger	10,805,000	Chairman, National Reconciliation Council Daouda Malam Wanke; Prime Minister Ibrahim Assane Mayaki	CFA franc (614.05 = $1)	269	363
Nigeria	128,786,000	President Olusegun Obasanjo	naira (95.41 = $1)	11,519	13,624
Rwanda	7,640,000	President Pasteur Bizimungu	franc (333.70 = $1)	60	285
São Tomé and Príncipe	146,000	President Miguel Trovoada	dobra (2,390.00 = $1)	5	19
Senegal	9,495,000	President Abdou Diouf; Prime Minister Mamadou Lamine Loum	CFA franc (614.05 = $1)	535	1,651
Seychelles	77,000	President France Albert Rene	rupee (5.25 = $1)	113	340
Sierra Leone	5,069,000	President Ahmad Tejan Kabbah	leone (1,930.20 = $1)	17	92
Somalia	14,470,000	No functioning government	shilling (2,620.00 = $1)	123	60
South Africa	46,215,000	President Thabo Mvuyelwa Mbeki	rand (6.05 = $1)	25,396	28,277
Sudan	32,079,000	President Umar Hasan Ahmad al-Bashir	pound (2,568.00 = $1)	596	1,915
Swaziland	980,000	King Mswati III; Prime Minister Barnabas Sibusiso Dlamini	lilangeni (6.05 = $1)	972	1,200
Tanzania	31,992,000	President Benjamin William Mkapa; Prime Minister Frederick Sumaye	shilling (797.00 = $1)	675	1,452
Togo	5,198,000	President Gnassingbe Eyadema	CFA franc (614.05 = $1)	346	503
Tunisia	9,694,000	President Zine El Abidine Ben Ali; Prime Minister Hamed Karoui	dinar (1.19 = $1)	5,750	8,338
Uganda	24,618,000	President Yoweri Kaguta Museveni; Prime Minister Apollo Nsibambi	shilling (1,459.90 = $1)	500	1,413
Zambia	10,754,000	President Frederick Chiluba	kwacha (2,475.00 = $1)	914	818
Zimbabwe	12,514,000	President Robert Mugabe	dollar (38.35 = $1)	2,397	2,817

*Exchange rates as of Oct. 8, 1999, or latest available data.   †Latest available data.

country. On June 16, Thabo Mbeki, deputy president under Nelson R. Mandela, took over as head of state. Mandela, the country's first black president, resigned, as planned, after the elections. He had served as president since the end of *apartheid* (official racial separation) in 1994.

Renewed war in Angola. The Angolan government in 1999 found itself once again locked in full-scale conflict with rebel forces led by Jonas Savimbi. In December 1998, the government had launched a major offensive against Savimbi's forces, after Savimbi refused to hand over rebel-controlled territory to the government according to a 1994 peace accord. On Feb. 26, 1999, the United Nations (UN) Security Council voted to withdraw its peacekeepers—about 1,000 mostly civilian observers—from Angola. The action came on the recommendation of UN Secretary General Kofi Annan, who said the renewed fighting had destroyed hopes of implementing the peace pact.

During 1999, Savimbi denied claims made by President Eduardo dos Santos that several African countries—including Rwanda, Uganda, and Zambia—were helping to rearm the rebels. Savimbi contended that Cuban military advisers were backing Angola's national army.

The heaviest combat in Angola in 1999 occurred in the mineral-rich northeast and in the central highlands. International aid agencies said in September that some 40,000 new civilian refugees fleeing the fighting had arrived in the city of Kuito in just 10 days. By the end of 1999, the war, which began in the 1970's and had claimed at least 1 million lives, reached a stalemate. Rebels controlled most of the countryside, and government troops held most urban areas.

The Great Lakes region. A renewal of civil war in Congo (Kinshasa) in 1998 continued to pull in the majority of nations in the Great Lakes region of central Africa in 1999. During the first half of 1999, rebels backed by Uganda and Rwanda maintained their offensive to oust Congo's President Laurent Kabila. At the same time, three southern African countries—Zimbabwe, Angola, and Namibia—deployed thousands of troops in support of Kabila.

Numerous international efforts to broker a pact led to a Zambian-sponsored truce agreement on August 31. The agreement proposed a cease-fire to be monitored by regional peacekeepers, probably led by Nigeria and South Africa. By November, however, fighting had broken out in several areas, with the rebels accusing the government of violating the truce by killing civilians in rebel-held areas and launching military offensives.

Ethiopia and Eritrea, two impoverished former allies in the Horn of Africa, launched fresh attacks against each other along their disputed 625-mile (1,000-kilometer) border in the barren and remote Yiroga Triangle in early 1999. After an uneasy lull of eight months, during which international organizations attempted to broker peace, heavy fighting on two fronts erupted in February and continued into March. Each side accused the other of reigniting the conflict.

After the Ethiopians broke through Eritrean defenses to recapture the town of Badme in late February, Eritrea announced that it would accept a peace plan drawn up by the Organization of African Unity (OAU), an association of more than 50 African nations. Although both countries accepted the OAU plan in principle in July, Ethiopia rejected the plan on September 4. The Ethiopians claimed the plan did not guarantee Eritrean withdrawal from the disputed territory. By late 1999, the conflict, which most observers regarded as a trivial dispute over patches of arid territory, had resulted in the mobilization of more than 500,000 soldiers, the death of thousands of combatants, and the displacement of hundreds of thousands of civilians.

Sierra Leone. Some 3,000 people were killed in January when rebel forces invaded Sierra Leone's capital, Freetown, in an unsuccessful effort to topple President Ahmad Tejan Kabbah's democratically elected government. A Nigerian-led military force evicted the guerrilla fighters in mid-January.

In July, the government and rebels signed a peace pact in which the government granted the rebels amnesty for their actions, which included mutilating civilians by cutting off their hands. The rebels were also offered a role in the government. The UN approved the peace treaty but refused to agree to any amnesties for "gross violations of human rights." The power-sharing agreement also aroused significant opposition in Sierra Leone.

Congo (Brazzaville). During 1999, intermittent but fierce fighting broke out in Congo (Brazzaville) between the army of President Denis Sassou-Nguesso and militia forces loyal to the former president, Pascal Lissouba. Between 150,000 and 200,000 people reportedly fled into the countryside from rebel strongholds west of Brazzaville, the capital, after government forces captured the towns.

Zambia. Fourteen bombs exploded in a 14-hour period in Lusaka, Zambia's capital, on February 28. The explosions killed one person and cut off the city's water supply. The government blamed the violence on "an external enemy." Before the bombings, Angola had accused Zambia of allowing rebels fighting the Angolan government to smuggle weapons across the countries' border. Zambia denied the charges.

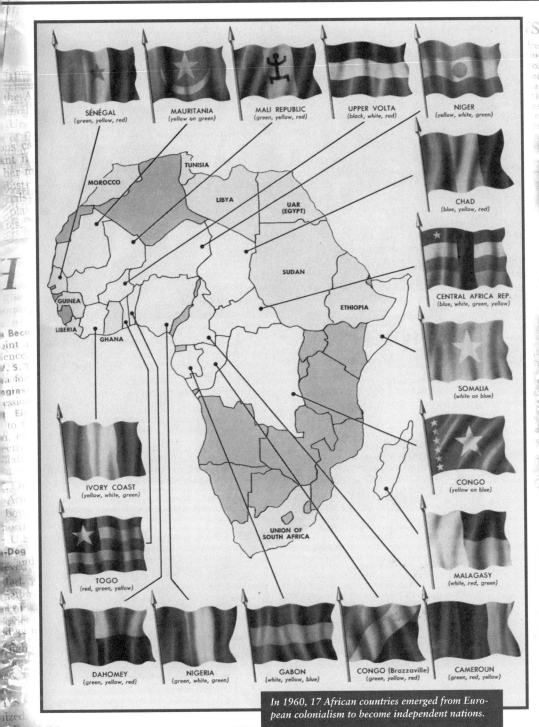

SÉNÉGAL
(green, yellow, red)

MAURITANIA
(yellow on green)

MALI REPUBLIC
(green, yellow, red)

UPPER VOLTA
(black, white, red)

NIGER
(yellow, white, green)

CHAD
(blue, yellow, red)

CENTRAL AFRICA REP.
(blue, white, green, yellow)

SOMALIA
(white on blue)

CONGO
(yellow on blue)

MALAGASY
(white, red, green)

IVORY COAST
(yellow, white, green)

TOGO
(red, green, yellow)

DAHOMEY
(green, yellow, red)

NIGERIA
(green, white, green)

GABON
(white, yellow, blue)

CONGO (Brazzaville)
(green, yellow, red)

CAMEROUN
(green, red, yellow)

MOROCCO
TUNISIA
LIBYA
UAR (EGYPT)
GUINEA
LIBERIA
GHANA
SUDAN
ETHIOPIA
UNION OF SOUTH AFRICA

In 1960, 17 African countries emerged from European colonialism to become independent nations.

Coups and elections. Niger's President Ibrahim Bare Mainassara, who had seized power in 1996 from the country's first democratically elected government, was killed by members of his presidential guard in a military *coup d'etat* (takeover) on April 9, 1999. The assassination came in the wake of political turmoil over the results of local and regional elections held in February. In April, Niger's supreme court annulled the results of some elections that the opposition coalition claimed it had won. Major Daouda Mallam Wanke, head of the presidential guard involved in the assassination, was proclaimed head of state on April 11. He promised to restore democracy by Jan. 1, 2000.

On Comoros, a three-island nation in the Indian Ocean, Colonel Assoumani Azzali seized office from a civilian government in a bloodless coup in April 1999. He said his objective was to restore order following violent protests triggered by a breakdown in talks over greater independence for the two smaller islands in the republic. The two islands had declared their independence in 1997. Azzali said he would relinquish power to a civilian government in one year and implement an April 1999 pact to establish a new government.

President Joao Bernardo Vieira of Guinea-Bissau, who had survived an army mutiny and a five-month civil war in 1998, lost power in a military coup in May 1999. The coup followed the breakdown in January of a cease-fire that had ended the civil war. Former army chief Brigadier General Ansumane Mane, whose dismissal from the army by President Vieira had triggered the conflict, led the coup.

After assuming power, Mane appointed Malan Bacai Sanha acting president and promised that presidential elections would be held in November as scheduled. On November 28, voters completed the first round of the election, with no candidate winning a majority. Independent observers declared the election honest and largely peaceful. A runoff vote was scheduled for January 2000.

In the Ivory Coast, a pay mutiny by rebellious troops on December 23 led to yet another coup, and General Robert Guei replaced President Henri Konan Bedei. On December 27, Guei announced that he would form a mixed military-civilian government early in 2000.

African development. In 1999, the UN Human Development Index reported that the world's 22 least developed countries were all in Africa. The index ranks 174 countries on the basis of deprivation, rather than income, taking into consideration such factors as low life expectancy, lack of education, and inaccessibility of clean water. Sierra Leone, with an average life expectancy of 37 years, ranked at the bottom of the list. Niger, Ethiopia, Burkina Faso, and Burundi also ranked very low.

In a report released on World Food Day, October 16, the UN warned that African countries south of the Sahara faced growing starvation. According to the report, 60 percent of the region's anticipated population of 1 billion would be chronically malnourished by 2025. Between 1960 and 1999, the number of seriously undernourished people in sub-Saharan Africa doubled, to 200 million of the region's 550 million people.

The UN said the crisis was largely the result of deteriorating soil conditions and declining farm yields. The Food and Agriculture Organization of the United Nations estimated that a program to improve African crop production would cost an average of $100 million to $500 million per country per year for 10 years.

Children at risk. In April, the United Kingdom Coalition to Stop the Use of Child Soldiers, a coalition of human rights and peace organizations, announced that more than 120,000 children under the age of 18—some as young as 7—served as soldiers in Africa during 1999. The report added that government-backed and opposition militias in many countries forced thousands of boys as well as girls to enlist in armed forces at gunpoint.

The UN Children's Fund (UNICEF) announced in July that children in sub-Saharan Africa faced higher health risks than children anywhere else in the world. UNICEF based its report on five indicators. These included child weight, mortality, educational availability, incidence of conflict, and infection rates for full-blown AIDS and HIV, the virus that causes AIDS. Angola, Sierra Leone, Somalia, and Ethiopia scored lowest on the report.

AIDS has become "the greatest obstacle to development" in Africa, health experts told an international conference on AIDS in Africa, convened in Lusaka, Zambia, in September. By 1999 the disease had killed an estimated 11.5 million Africans, accounting for more than 80 percent of AIDS deaths worldwide.

In 1999, more than 22 million people in sub-Saharan Africa—1 in every 12 people—were infected with HIV. The experts reported that AIDS was forecast to cut life expectancy in that region by 25 percent between 2005 and 2010. Experts reported that AIDS had become Africa's biggest killer. In 1999, health-care officials said that the disease killed more people in Africa than either war, famine, or such diseases as malaria and tuberculosis.

Sports. More than 6,000 athletes from 50 countries competed in the seventh All-Africa Games in Johannesburg, South Africa, in September. The games were the biggest sporting event ever held on the continent of Africa. South Africa led the competition with 69 gold medals, followed by Nigeria with 64.   ☐ Simon Baynham

See also the various African country articles.

Agriculture. Farmers in the United States in 1999 harvested abundant crops despite drought in the East and hurricane-driven floods in the Southeast. However, bumper crops worldwide and lingering financial problems in Southeast Asia and Russia continued to push world commodity prices downward. The third-largest U.S. soybean crop ever and sluggish exports drove soybean prices to their lowest level since 1972.

As prospects for a quick turnaround in the agricultural economy grew dimmer, farmers increasingly complained about the Federal Agricultural Improvement and Reform Act of 1996 (FAIR). The law gave U.S. farmers more freedom to plant crops to meet world demand in return for reduced federal income subsidies. Although FAIR provided help against bad harvests, it failed to provide a buffer against collapsing world crop prices. For the second consecutive year, the U.S. Congress in 1999 stepped in with emergency farm aid, passing an $8.7-billion assistance package that was signed into law by President Bill Clinton on October 22.

World crop production. According to a U.S. Department of Agriculture report released in December, world production of wheat and small grains declined slightly in 1999 from 1998 levels, while harvests of oilseeds, rice, and cotton rose. Global wheat production in 1999 totaled 584 million metric tons, down 2 percent from 1998. Increases in Canada, Kazakhstan, Argentina, and Australia offset lower U.S. production. Produc-

A Maryland farmer examines a field of corn stunted by the drought that affected much of Northeastern and Middle Atlantic sections of the United States in the summer of 1999. Despite the drought, the 1999 U.S. corn crop was the third-largest corn harvest on record.

tion of small grains, including corn, rye, grain sorghum, barley, oats, and millet, totaled 876 million metric tons. Russia and Kazakhstan harvested larger barley crops, and Mexico produced more grain sorghum and corn. Global rice production reached a record 396 million metric tons, largely because of increases in China and the United States.

Global oilseed production in 1999 totaled 297 million metric tons, up 3.3 million metric tons. Record rapeseed production in Canada and Europe offset smaller soybean crops in the United States, Argentina, and Bolivia. World cotton production rose 3 percent to 87 million bales, due to increases in the United States, India, Pakistan, Turkmenistan, and Uzbekistan.

U.S. crop production. In 1999, U.S. farmers harvested 9.54 billion bushels of corn—the third-largest harvest on record—though they planted less acreage of corn in 1999 than they did in 1998. Farmers also planted less soybeans. Although the soybean harvest of 2.67 billion bushels was 2 percent below 1998 levels, it was still the third-largest harvest ever. The 1999 wheat crop totaled 2.3 billion bushels, down 1 percent from 1998, while the rice crop—at 6.9 million metric tons—rose 13 percent higher. The U.S. cotton crop, at 16.9 million bales, was 21 percent above 1998's drought-damaged harvest.

Exports. Weak demand from Asia and abundant global harvests combined to push sales of U.S. farm products down to $49 billion in 1999, from $54.4 billion in 1998. That total included 5 million metric tons of wheat purchased by the U.S. government for export as food aid.

Mergers. In July 1999, the U.S. Department of Justice approved the merger of Cargill, Inc. of Minnetonka, Minnesota, the largest U.S. grain company, with the grain division of Continental Grain of New York City, the fifth-largest U.S. grain company. In May, Case Corporation of Racine, Wisconsin, merged with the Netherlands-based New Holland N.V. Both companies manufactured farm machinery. In September, Smithfield Foods, Inc. of Smithfield, Virginia, the largest U.S. hog producer, announced plans to buy Murphy Family Farms of Rose Hill, North Carolina, its closest competitor. Many farmers feared that such consolidations would increase prices and drive smaller producers from the market.

Beef ban. On July 29, the United States imposed a 100-percent tariff on $117 million worth of gourmet products, including pork, cheese, goose liver pate, and truffles, from Italy, Germany, France, and Denmark. The action came after the European Union (EU), an organization of 15 Western European countries, failed to meet a May 13 deadline to lift its ban on imports of U.S. beef that was produced using hormones.

In 1997, the World Trade Organization (WTO) in Geneva, Switzerland—the arbiter of trade disputes among member countries—had ruled against the ban. The WTO said trade could not be limited because of allegations of health risks that were not supported by scientific studies. Early in July 1999, the WTO ruled that the United States could impose tariffs on $117 million of European goods, far below the $202 million in retaliation sought by the United States and the $500 million in damages claimed by U.S. cattle producers.

On August 1, the European Commission, the EU's governing body, ruled that British beef was free from bovine spongiform encephalopathy, or "mad cow disease," which some scientists believe causes a brain disease in humans. All member countries except France lifted their bans.

Anti-GM sentiment. In 1999, U.S. farmers planted 50 percent of American soybean acreage with genetically modified (GM) soybeans. GM plants, also called transgenic crops, contain genes from other species that confer new traits on the crops, such as pest resistance and greater productivity. Approximately 30 percent of U.S. corn acreage was planted with GM seed containing a gene from the bacterium *Bacillus thuringiensis* (Bt) that makes the corn toxic to the corn borer pest.

Environmental and consumer groups stepped up their campaign against GM crops in 1999. France and the United Kingdom banned GM crops, while Japan, New Zealand, and Australia pledged to label foods that contain GM ingredients by 2001.

Anti-GM sentiment increased in the United States with the May 1999 publication of a study by scientists at Cornell University in Ithaca, New York, which found that Bt corn pollen could be hazardous to caterpillars of the monarch butterfly. Later studies, however, concluded that Bt corn pollen posed little risk to the butterfly.

In December, a group of U.S. farmers supported by a coalition of anti-GM and environmental protection organizations, including Greenpeace, sued the Monsanto Company, a large drug and agricultural company based in St. Louis, Missouri. The lawsuit, filed in a federal court in Washington, D.C., alleged that Monsanto failed to properly test the safety of its GM corn and soybean seeds. Monsanto denied the charges.

Seattle trade talks. The collapse of a WTO planning meeting for a new round of world-trade talks set back U.S. efforts to negotiate new rules governing agricultural exports. The WTO meeting was held in Seattle from November 30 to December 4. The United States had hoped that the talks would lead to new agreements to reduce high export subsidies and domestic farm support programs among many WTO members. Farmers in the United States had long wanted a reduction in foreign tariffs, which averaged 40 percent above U.S. levels in 1999.

International trade experts suggested that President Bill Clinton's efforts to link labor standards and environmental protection to future trade agreements contributed to the failure of the conference. Many developing countries balked at linking the three. They argued that low production costs provided their chief competitive edge against industrialized nations.

China. On November 15, the United States agreed in principle to sponsor China for membership in the WTO after China agreed to trade concessions with the United States. The deal called for China to reduce tariffs on U.S. farm products, create near-tariff-free quotas for imports of such products, and eliminate export subsidies.

Canada. Skirmishes between the United States and Canada over agricultural trade in 1998 bore fruit in 1999. Under the terms of an agreement signed in 1998, Canada streamlined its regulations in October 1999, for admitting live hogs from the United States. The move was expected to expand slaughter facilities for U.S. hogs. On November 3, the International Trade Commission, a U.S. government agency, announced that it would end duties on imports of live hogs from Canada on Jan. 1, 2000. □ Patricia Peak Klintberg

See also **Biology.**

AIDS. Researchers from the United States and Uganda announced in July 1999 the discovery of a simple, low-cost treatment for reducing the likelihood that a pregnant woman infected with HIV, the virus that causes AIDS, will transmit the virus to her infant during childbirth. In the study, sponsored by an agency of the National Institutes of Health (NIH) in Bethesda, Maryland, scientists found that the new therapy was more effective and about 200 times less expensive than the treatment commonly used in the United States. The NIH study provided welcome news to health care professionals in developing nations, where an estimated 1,800 HIV-infected babies are born daily.

The new treatment involves administering a single oral dose of the antiviral drug nevirapine to an HIV-infected woman during labor and another to her baby within three days of birth. Nevirapine halts the action of an enzyme essential to HIV's reproduction. The standard treatment in developed nations for blocking mother-to-infant transmission of HIV involves multiple doses of the more expensive drug AZT over a much longer period.

World's most deadly infectious disease. AIDS overtook tuberculosis (TB) as the world's most deadly infectious disease in 1998, the World Health Organization (WHO), based in Geneva, Switzerland, reported in May 1999. WHO an-

NEW DEADLY SYNDROME. Physicians were baffled and alarmed by the rapid spread in 1982 of a diverse array of medical problems called acquired immune deficiency syndrome (AIDS). These included rare infections and cancers typically found only in the elderly or in the weakened recipients of cancer chemotherapy. Epidemiologist James W. Curran, head of an AIDS task force at the Centers for Disease Control (CDC) in Atlanta, Georgia, reported in August that the incidence of AIDS rose from one case per day in the first six months of 1982 to two or three per day in the second half of the year. By October, a total of 684 cases had been reported. About 300 of them were fatal.

Most AIDS victims were previously healthy homosexual men, many of whom reported having numerous sexual partners and using illicit drugs. AIDS also has been diagnosed in several heroin addicts, among a group of Haitian immigrants, and in some hemophiliacs.

nounced that AIDS killed an estimated 2.28 million people in 1998. TB killed 1.5 million people in 1998. AIDS also moved from the seventh to the fourth leading cause of all deaths worldwide.

Vaccine. The first clinical trials in Africa of an AIDS vaccine began in February 1999 in Uganda, where about 25 percent of the population was infected with HIV. The one-year study, sponsored by the NIH, enlisted 40 healthy volunteers. Half the volunteers received a vaccine that contains three genes from HIV. The vaccine cannot cause the disease. The researchers hoped to learn how the vaccine activates the body's immune system and what kind of side effects can occur.

Origin of HIV. The HIV-1 virus that has caused most cases of AIDS worldwide developed from a closely related virus that infects a subspecies of chimpanzee living in central and western Africa where the HIV virus was first identified. That finding was reported in February by scientists at the University of Alabama at Birmingham. The virus apparently is harmless to these chimpanzees. The scientists theorized that HIV-1 first appeared in human beings who were exposed to infected blood while butchering chimpanzees for food.

□ Michael Woods

Air pollution. See Environmental pollution.
Alabama. See State government.
Alaska. See State government.

Albania. The war in the Serbian province of Kosovo dominated political life in Albania for the first half of 1999. More than 400,000 ethnic Albanian refugees from neighboring Kosovo had crossed the border into Albania by early May, having fled a campaign of "ethnic cleansing" by Serbian forces.

Kosovo crisis. Leaders from Albania's Socialist and Democratic parties adopted a common policy on the Kosovo conflict. In early 1999, Albania urged Kosovar Albanian leaders to participate in the internationally sponsored talks with Yugoslav officials in Rambouillet, France. When attempts at a diplomatic resolution failed, Albania supported the North Atlantic Treaty Organization's (NATO) campaign of air strikes against Yugoslavia, which began on March 24 and ended on June 10.

During the fighting, Albanian military units engaged in sporadic clashes with Yugoslav troops along the Albanian-Yugoslav border. Yugoslav officials accused rebel forces in Kosovo of opening a corridor across the Albanian border to smuggle fighters, weapons, and supplies into Kosovo.

The United Nations (UN) and other international organizations established refugee camps to help the Albanian government deal with the influx of refugees. They also helped defray the expense of caring for the refugees. In April, the World Bank (a United Nations agency that provides long-term loans to countries for development) promised $30 million in aid to Albania. France pledged an additional $28 million. In May, an organization of international donors pledged $200 million to Albania.

Hungry Kosovar refugees in line for food at a camp in Albania in April 1999 clamor for loaves of bread. Albania, Europe's poorest country, struggled to feed and shelter the more than 400,000 ethnic Albanians who fled there from Kosovo in 1999.

Economy. Most of the Kosovar refugees left Albania and returned home soon after the end of NATO bombing and the withdrawal of Serb troops in June. But the strain of the refugee crisis damaged Albania's already fragile economy and threatened to reverse the economic progress the country had made in 1998. However, officials of the International Monetary Fund (IMF) expressed optimism in June 1999 that Albania's *gross domestic product* (the value of all goods and services produced in a country in a given year) would grow by 8 percent in 1999. The IMF is a United Nations-affiliated organization that provides short-term credit to member nations.

Majko resigns. Prime Minister Pandeli Majko resigned on October 25, after being voted out as chairman of the Socialist Party on October 11. The Socialists chose Fatos Nano as their new chairman. Nano had resigned as Albania's prime minister in 1998, after violent protests erupted in Tirana, the capital, following the murder of a Democratic Party official. Deputy Premier Ilir Meta succeeded Majko as prime minister on Oct. 27, 1999.   □ Sharon L. Wolchik

See also **Europe; Macedonia; Yugoslavia.**

Algeria. Nearly 99 percent of Algerian voters on Sept. 16, 1999, endorsed a referendum on President Abdelaziz Bouteflika's "civil concord" plan to end Algeria's civil war. Some 85 percent of the nation's eligible voters participated in the referendum. The civil war, between Islamic militants and Algeria's military-backed government, began in 1992 after the military halted parliamentary elections that the Islamic Salvation Front (known as the FIS) was slated to win. An estimated 100,000 people were killed in the conflict between 1992 and 1999.

Bouteflika's plan granted partial amnesty to militants who renounced violence and turned themselves in to authorities. Under the plan, militants, except those who were convicted of murder, bombings, or rape, would serve reduced prison sentences. As a good-will gesture, Bouteflika pardoned and released thousands of Islamic-extremist prisoners and sympathizers who had been convicted of first offenses.

Bouteflika adopted his amnesty policy in June, after the armed wing of the FIS, the Islamic Salvation Army (AIS), formally renounced its armed struggle against the government. Most members of the AIS and some other militant groups accepted the government's amnesty offer.

Many analysts viewed the results of the referendum as an endorsement of a harsh clampdown on dissent that the government planned to institute in January 2000, when the amnesty offer was scheduled to expire. As a prelude to this clamp-down, Bouteflika announced in July 1999 that the FIS would continue to be banned from participating in future political activity. FIS leaders had urged Bouteflika to rescind the ban, which was enacted in 1992.

FIS leader assassinated. Abdelkader Hachani, a moderate leader of the FIS, was assassinated in the Algerian capital of Algiers on Nov. 22, 1999. The Algerian interior ministry announced on December 14 that authorities had arrested Fouad Boulemia, reportedly a member of the Armed Islamic Group (GIA), for the assassination. The GIA was a radical Islamic group suspected of being responsible for some of the most deadly incidents in the Algerian conflict. The slaying came after the worst week of violence in Algeria since Bouteflika's April election. The violence complicated Bouteflika's reconciliation efforts.

Election. Bouteflika won Algeria's presidential election with 74 percent of the vote on April 15, after all six of the other contestants dropped out of the race. Bouteflika's opponents charged that the election was unfair because the military backed Bouteflika.   □ Christine Helms

See also **Africa; Middle East: A Special Report.**

Angola. See Africa.

Animal. See Biology; Conservation; Zoos.

THE DISCOVERY OF A NEW FOSSIL MAN by Dr. L. S. B. Leakey in East Africa excited anthropologists throughout the world. Leakey, who named his discovery *Homo habilis*, expressed the belief that its skull resembles modern man so closely that anthropologists could well regard the fossil Neanderthal man, Java man, and Peking man as overspecialized offshoots from the generally accepted family tree of man.

Although all anthropologists were agreed on the importance of *Homo habilis*, not all accepted the position that the Neanderthals, Java men, or Peking men should be removed from the list of man's ancestors. Some argued that Neanderthals were really only a subspecies of *Homo sapiens* (modern man). Others pointed out that in the past it had been thought that a near-man, such as some *Australopithecus*, must have been ancestral to any *Homo*, and now Leakey's *Homo habilis* could be said to be the very *Australopithecus* that would take that place on man's family tree.

Anthropology. The discovery of the skeleton of a child who may have been descended from both Neanderthals—prehistoric humans who vanished from the fossil record approximately 30,000 years ago—and human beings who looked like people today, was announced in April 1999 by Joao Zilhao, director of the Portuguese Institute of Archaeology in Lisbon. The boy, who was about 4 years old when he died 24,500 years ago, was found in the Lapedo Valley, 90 miles (145 kilometers) north of Lisbon.

An analysis of the skeleton by Neanderthal expert Erik Trinkaus of Washington University in St. Louis, Missouri, revealed that it had a mixture of modern-human and Neanderthal features. The body was stocky with short legs and a broad chest—similar to that of a Neanderthal. The lower jaw had a prominent chin, absent in Neanderthals but characteristic of modern humans.

This discovery supported a school of thought among anthropologists that Neanderthals and modern humans mated with each other and that the disappearance of Neanderthals resulted from this interbreeding. Although the Portugese skeleton supported this theory, some anthropologists maintained that Neanderthals and modern humans were too different to be able to interbreed. These scientists suggested that the skeleton is merely that of a stocky modern human.

Chimpanzees, like humans, develop *culture* (the social, or nongenetic, transmission of behavior within populations), according to a June 1999 report by a team of zoologists that included noted chimp researcher Jane Goodall. The scientists observed, for example, that different groups of chimpanzees use sticks as tools in different ways.

Neanderthal cannibals? Neanderthals sometimes ate one another, according to a September report by a team of anthropologists led by Alban Defleur of the Universite de la Mediterranee in France. While investigating a cave in the Ardeche region of southeastern France, the team discovered 100,000-year-old bones of at least six Neanderthals. The bones were cut and marked with other signs suggesting butchering. The French team interpreted these signs as evidence of cannibalism. Other anthropologists countered that the cuts could have been made during ritual mutilation practices.

Mystery skull. A fossil skull of a human ancestor was discovered in March in a small New York City shop, Maxilla and Mandible, Ltd., that sells natural history items. The skull, of the species *Homo erectus,* was between 100,000 and 1 million years old and may help anthropologists learn where and how modern humans, *H. sapiens,* evolved.

The shop owner, Henry Galiano, noticed the skull when he was examining an estate collection of Indonesian rocks and curios he had recently purchased. Galiano contacted Eric Delson, a paleoanthropologist at the City University of New York, who set out to investigate the fossil's origins by contacting colleagues in Indonesia, where *H. erectus* fossils have long been unearthed. Delson determined that the skull had previously been examined by an Indonesian scientist and that it originated in the village of Poloyo in central Java.

Anthropologists found the skull interesting because, unlike other known skulls of *H. erectus,* it has a high forehead—more like *H. sapiens.* In addition, the braincase suggested similarities to modern humans in the shape of the brain.

New hominid species. A team of anthropologists led by Berhane Asfaw of Rift Valley Research Services in Ethiopia announced in April 1999 that it had discovered fossils of a new species of *hominid* (humans and their ancestors). Asfaw believed that *Australopithecus garhi,* found in 2.5-million-year-old geological strata at Bouri, Ethiopia, was probably an ancestor of modern humans and a descendent of the hominid species *A. afarensis.* The most complete *A. afarensis* specimen is the 3.2-million-year-old "Lucy" skeleton discovered in 1974. The projecting, apelike face and small brain of *A. garhi* resemble Lucy, though the teeth are much larger.

Butchered animal bones with cut marks from stone tools were also found in the sediment that yielded the fossils. The scientists said this indicated that *A. garhi* may have been a tool-making meat eater. ☐ Donald C. Johanson

See also **Archaeology.**

Archaeology.

The earliest known *phonetic* alphabet (an alphabet in which spoken sounds are represented by symbols or letters) is considerably older than archaeologists once believed, according to research reported in November 1999. Archaeologist John Darnell and colleagues at Yale University in New Haven, Connecticut, described two inscriptions in Egypt that combine Middle Kingdom (1991 to 1786 B.C.) hieroglyphic symbols with Semitic letters. Hieroglyphics are picture symbols that represent sounds and ideas. Semitic languages include Hebrew, Arabic, and a number of extinct, ancient languages. The inscriptions, which date from approximately 1900 to 1800 B.C., predate by 200 to 300 years the earliest previously known Semitic scripts.

The archaeologists discovered the inscriptions in a remote desert area through which ancient trade and military routes once passed. They speculated that the inscriptions may have been created by Semitic *mercenaries* (soldiers hired to fight for a foreign ruler) from Canaan (the approximate region of contemporary Israel).

Maya throne and tomb. Archaeologists working at Palenque, a major center of Mayan culture in the Mexican state of Chiapas, announced in April 1999 that they had uncovered both an inscribed platform—possibly a throne—and a rich burial site. The Maya were an American Indian people whose civilization reached its peak between A.D. 250 and 900. The archaeologists were led by Arnoldo Gonzalez Cruz of the National Institute of Anthropology and History in Mexico City and Alfonso Morales of the University of Texas in Austin.

The platform, which is 5 feet (1.5 meters) wide by 9 feet (2.7 meters) long, is inscribed with more than 200 hieroglyphic symbols and 12 figures, including a representation of Kinich Ahkal Mo' Nab, the ruler of Palenque from A.D. 721 to 764. In a nearby mound, the archaeologists discovered a tomb with 11 pots and many pieces of worked jade. Wall paintings in the tomb, which include a depiction of the Maya lightning god, were the first to be found intact at Palenque.

Tombs of the Eurasian steppe. Excavations near the town of Ipatovo in southern Russia in 1999 uncovered evidence of the wealth of the ancient nomads of the Eurasian *steppe* (a dry area covered by short grasses that extends from southwestern Russia to central Asia). Archaeologists Vladimira Petrenko of the Russian Academy of Sciences in Moscow and Heinrich Harke of the University of Reading in England reported in March that they had uncovered the tomb of a woman from the 300's or early 200's B.C. The woman had been buried with elaborate gold bracelets and gold necklaces.

Egyptian archaeologist Mohammed Ayadi inspects mummies with gold-covered masks discovered in Egypt's Western Desert in June 1999. The mummies, from approximately A.D. 1 to 200, were among thousands that archaeologists believe are buried in a cemetery at the Bahariya Oasis.

ARCHAEOLOGY

THE TOMB OF TUTANKHAMEN. Late in 1922 the scientific world was electrified by the discovery of the tomb of this ruler, who was one of the less known pharaohs, and of whose period really little has been learned, although earlier discoveries had located his place in history. He began to rule about 1395 B.C.; it would appear that his reign was brief—probably only six years.

The finding of the tomb of Tutankhamen is called the

Archaeologists remove a tray of relics from the tomb of King Tutankhamen, discovered in 1922.

greatest archaeological exploit of modern times. The excavation is not as large as that uncovered when the adjacent tomb of Rameses VI was found, but two chambers and rooms leading to the burial chamber which have been explored were filled with rarer and more priceless relics than ever before were seen. The richness of the objects found in the first chamber dazzled beholders, but the second held such amazing splendors that all previous discoveries in the Valley were declared insignificant in comparison. . . .

In the first chamber observers saw three magnificent state couches, all gilt, with exquisite carving and animal heads of typhon, Hathor, and lion. On these rested beds, beautifully carved, gilded, and inlaid with ivory and semiprecious stones; there were found also innumerable boxes of exquisite workmanship. One of these boxes was inlaid with ebony and ivory, with gilt inscriptions; another contained emblems of the lower world; on a third, which contained royal robes, handsomely embroidered precious stones and golden sandals, were beautifully-painted hunting scenes.

There was a stool of ebony inlaid with ivory, with the most delicately carved duck's feet; also a child's stool of fine workmanship. Beneath one of the couches was the State Throne of King Tutankhamen, probably one of the most

beautiful objects of art ever discovered. There was also a heavily gilt chair, with portraits of the King and Queen, the whole encrusted with turquoise, cornelian, lapis, and other semiprecious stones.

Two life-sized bitumenized statues of the king, with gold work, holding a golden stick and mace, faced each other, the handsome features, the feet, and the hands delicately carved, with eyes of glass and headdress richly studded with gems. . . .

The door to a third chamber cut still farther into the rock was found, and it was the opinion of the explorers that in this inner room would be found the embalmed remains of the pharaoh. The tomb was sealed without further exploration, late in March, and a strong guard against every unwarranted approach was placed at its entrance. . . .

Several shrines enclosing the burial casket were removed with the utmost care, and on Jan. 5, 1924, the granite casket of the pharaoh was revealed. Before it could be opened it was necessary to take steps to preserve the fabulously rich discoveries. . . . When the coffin is eventually opened and all possible scientific facts have been secured, it will again be reverently sealed, and the remains of King Tutankhamen will not again be disturbed.

In October, a team of French, Italian, and Kazakh archaeologists reported the discovery of 12 sacrificed horses in the burial ground of two Scythian nobles near the village of Berel in Kazakhstan, a country south of Russia. Scythians were an ancient nomadic people who lived north of the Black Sea. The burials dated from approximately 500 B.C. Archaeologists found a pair of carved wooden ibex horns covered in gold leaf near the head of one horse. A wooden carving of a *griffin* (a mythological creature that is part eagle and part lion) with leather ears was also found with the horses.

Early iron smelting. Excavations at Tell Hammeh, Jordan, reported in December 1999, revealed the earliest known evidence of iron smelting—from the 700's B.C. Archaeologists from Yarmouk University in Jordan and Leiden University in the Netherlands announced that they had discovered a layer of ash, charcoal, and *slag* (waste material left over from smelting), along with what appeared to be pieces of *tuyeres* (nozzles through which air is forced into a furnace) and the collapsed remains of five furnaces.

The furnaces were round, built of large mud bricks, and contained ash, slag, and burnt brick. Analysis of the slag indicated that it had been produced at the high temperatures needed to smelt iron.

Kennewick Man. Archaeologists with the United States National Park Service (NPS) reported in October 1999 their findings on the skeleton known as Kennewick Man. American Indians demanded that the remains, which were found in 1996 near Kennewick, Washington, be reburied. Scientists wanted the remains available for future study. A 1990 law stipulated that American Indians could claim any remains that dated from before the arrival of Europeans in 1492 and shared a "cultural affiliation" with a modern tribe.

The NPS scientists reported that the remains were those of a male, 45 to 50 years old, who resembled south Asian and *Ainu* (native inhabitants of northern Japan) people, rather than American Indians or Europeans. Initial *radiocarbon dating* (a dating method based on the amount of radioactive carbon in a specimen) of a single specimen placed the remains at 7,000 to 9,000 years old. Additional radiocarbon datings were scheduled to be completed in early 2000, at which time the fate of the skeleton would be decided.

Roman ships on land. Remains of 11 Roman ships, dating from between the 100's B.C. and A.D. 400's, were unearthed in early 1999 in what had been the harbor of ancient Pisa, Italy, but today is dry land. Scientists at the Archaeological Superintendency of Tuscany in Italy said most of the ships were coastal traders.   □ Mark Rose

See also **Anthropology; Geology; Miami.**

Architecture. Architect Michael Graves of Princeton University in New Jersey turned the $6-million restoration of the Washington Monument in Washington, D.C., into a civic celebration in 1999. Using aluminum scaffolding and blue mesh, Graves created a temporary second skin for the most famous obelisk in the United States. The scaffolding traced the monument's tapering form, while the mesh simulated the pattern of its stone work. At night, the monument took on a serene glow that made it appear both ruggedly familiar and strikingly new.

The restoration was scheduled to be completed in July 2000, though many residents of Washington hoped that Graves's elegant shell could be preserved in another location.

Radio City Music Hall, in New York City, reopened in October 1999 following an extensive renovation by Hardy Holzman Pfeiffer Associates (HHPA) of New York City. Opened in 1932 as part of Rockefeller Center, the Music Hall had hosted a wide variety of popular entertainment over the years, including rock concerts and a famous yearly Christmas show featuring the high-kicking Rockette dancers. By the 1990's, however, it had become a dark and depressing vestige of its former self.

HHPA restored the hall's original splendor, such as the grand foyer with its sweeping staircase and 40-foot- (12-meter-) high decorated ceilings. Most of the original fixtures and furnishings were restored or replicated, including a superb mural by the American painter Stuart Davis (1894-1964) in one of the lounges. The restoration reminded the public of how seamlessly integrated art and architecture used to be.

Pennsylvania Station. In May 1999, U.S. President Bill Clinton and New York Governor George Pataki unveiled a $484-million plan for a new Pennsylvania Station on the same New York City block as the one demolished in 1963. Architect David Childs of Skidmore, Owings & Merrill's New York office proposed converting the James A. Farley post office into the new station.

The plan called for the construction of an arching steel-and-glass roof over the building's main entrance, which would lead to a monumental ticket lobby reminiscent of the waiting room in the old Penn Station. Passengers would then descend through a series of concourses to the trains. Shops, theaters, and restaurants would be added later. Construction was expected to begin in the summer of 2000 and be completed by 2004. Much of the cost was to be covered by federal, state, and local grants.

Alfred Lerner Hall, the student center at Columbia University in New York City, was one of the most anticipated buildings of 1999. Designed by Bernard Tschumi, the dean of Columbia's ar-

The Reichstag, the German parliament building, reopened in April 1999 following a renovation that included the addition of a glass dome designed by the British architect Sir Norman Foster. Foster was awarded the 1999 Pritzker Prize for such projects as the critically acclaimed Reichstag renovation.

chitecture school, the building consists of a pair of brick-and-granite wings containing offices and meeting spaces flanking a soaring glass atrium filled with zigzagging ramps. The atrium was conceived as a gigantic performance space in which students on the move are the main show.

Lerner Hall opened in September to mixed reviews. Some critics praised its energy and structural inventiveness, while others called it confused and fragmented.

Santa Fe art village. The Santa Fe Art Institute and the Visual Arts Center, both on the campus of the College of Santa Fe in New Mexico, opened in May. Designed by Mexican architect Ricardo Legorreta, the two institutions create a village of boldly colored buildings—in such bright hues as fuschia, cadmium yellow, and enchilada red—grouped around outdoor gardens and courtyards. Each building is angular and asymmetrical in a modern way, yet also reminiscent of the rambling construction seen in many older buildings in New Mexico.

Massachusetts museum. The Massachusetts Museum of Contemporary Art, the largest contemporary art museum in the United States, reopened in May in renovated mill buildings dating from the 1800's. The museum is located in North Adams, a blue-collar town in the state's northwest corner, which local officials hope to trans-

form into the cultural hub of western New England.

The architecture firm of Bruner/Cott & Associates in Cambridge, Massachusetts, respected the gritty, episodic character of the original buildings, while renovating them to accommodate monumental paintings and sculptures by Robert Rauschenberg, James Rosenquist, and other contemporary masters. The museum buildings also provide space for theater, dance, and recording companies.

Awards. The 1999 Gold Medal of the Washington, D.C.-based American Institute of Architects, the largest association of U.S. architects, was awarded to Frank Gehry, designer of the Guggenheim Museum in Bilbao, Spain, the Loyola School of Law in Los Angeles, and other celebrated buildings. Gehry, who was an artist before he became an architect, is known for his collage-like designs featuring quirky, irregular shapes.

Sir Norman Foster of Great Britain won the 1999 Pritzker Prize, the most prestigious award in architecture. In such projects as the Hong Kong and Shanghai Banking Corporation tower in Hong Kong and the renovated Reichstag (German parliament building) in Berlin, Foster combined modern technology with unparalleled lyricism. ☐ David Dillon

See also **Art; Building and construction.**

Argentina. Fernando de la Rua of the center-left Alianza (Alliance) coalition was sworn in for a five-year term as president on Dec. 10, 1999. He had campaigned on a promise to end government corruption and the immunity from prosecution enjoyed by many well-connected Argentines.

Political analysts had credited de la Rua, the mayor of the capital, Buenos Aires, for balancing the city's budget while improving public services. The new president was expected to face significant challenges in fixing Argentina's stagnant economy, however, because Alianza representatives did not win a majority in the lower house of Congress, and the Senate and judiciary were controlled by his political opponents.

Menem's legacy. Outgoing President Carlos Saul Menem had proved skillful during his 10 years in office in stabilizing the troubled Argentine economy. His administration was plagued, however, with scandals that had worn away at public confidence. When Menem left office, the country was also burdened with an unemployment rate of about 14.5 percent and widespread poverty. According to a January report by Equis International, a research group based in Salt Lake City, Utah, some 7 million people, about one-fifth of Argentina's population, earned little more than $2 a day in 1998. The Equis study noted that in areas of central and northern Argenti-

na, the average annual income was only $464.

Protests. On May 8, 1999, Education Minister Susana Decibe resigned to protest a $280-million cut in education funds from the national budget. On May 12—after a week of protests by students, teachers, and university administrators—the Argentine Congress restored the funds.

On July 8, tens of thousands of truckers halted a three-day national strike after Congress voted to postpone a new vehicle tax, which was intended to make up for money restored to the education budget. The Argentine government was forced to look elsewhere for means of balancing its books as the national deficit grew to an estimated $5.1 billion by the end of 1999.

World Bank. In October, the Argentine government sold $1.5 billion in bonds to help finance its $17-billion budget for 2000. The World Bank, a United Nations agency that provides long-term loans to countries for development, offered a new program to back the bonds. The entire bond package was divided into six parts of $250 million each. The World Bank pledged to back one portion at a time and then roll the credit over to the next portion when the previous one is paid off.

Oil company purchase. In May 1999, Repsol S.A. of Madrid, Spain, a large oil and natural gas company, acquired Yacimientos Petroliferos Fiscales (YPF), an Argentine oil company that had

---

TIME CAPSULE 1952
ARGENTINA

Evita Peron

ARGENTINA in 1952 was the scene of the remarkable last days, death, and funeral of a dictator's wife. She was Eva Peron, the wife of President Juan Peron. . . .

On July 26, after a long period of suffering, the President's wife, affectionately called Evita, died at the age of 33. Her body lay in state in the Ministry of Labor until August 9. Hundreds of thousands of persons viewed it. Four were killed and 2,500 were injured in the crush. A movie crew was imported from Hollywood to photograph the funeral ceremony. After Evita's death, the Government decreed general mourning in which all Argentine men were to wear black ties "in perpetuity," or forever.

On August 9 the capital of the state of Buenos Aires, which had been known as the City of La Plata, was renamed the City of Evita Peron. Throughout the country all streets and plazas which had borne the name of Bartolome Mitre were renamed in honor of Evita Peron.

On August 22 the General Federation of Labor required that its 600,000 members give up one day's wages, estimated at $10,000,000, to be used to erect a huge bronze and marble monument to Evita Peron. On September 29 the Union-controlled newspaper La Prensa announced that the face in the moon was now that of Evita Peron.

been privatized in the early 1990's. Repsol paid $2 billion for a 15-percent stake in YPF in January 1999 and $13.4 billion for the remaining 85 percent in May. The takeover created Latin America's largest privately managed oil company and made Repsol the world's ninth-ranking company in oil and natural gas reserves.

Falkland Islands. On July 14, Argentina and the United Kingdom agreed to reinstate commercial flights between Argentina and the Falkland Islands, a British dependency off Argentina's southeastern coast. British rule was established on the islands in 1833, but Argentina had also long claimed ownership. In 1982, Argentine troops briefly occupied the islands but were forced off by the British military. The resumption of commercial flights in 1999 marked a continued normalization of relations between the two nations. In March, Great Britain's Prince Charles laid a wreath at a memorial in Buenos Aires, honoring some 650 Argentine soldiers who had died in the 1982 conflict.

Air crash. On Aug. 31, 1999, a Boeing 737 jet crashed during takeoff from a downtown airport in Buenos Aires. Sixty-four of the 100 people on board the plane died, and 10 people on the ground were killed.   □ Nathan A. Haverstock

See also **Latin America.**

Arizona. See **State government.**

Arkansas. See **State government.**

Armed forces. North Atlantic Treaty Organization (NATO) military forces launched the largest allied military attack in Europe since World War II (1939–1945) on March 24, 1999. NATO fighter planes and cruise missiles bombed targets in Yugoslavia to stop the "ethnic cleansing" of ethnic Albanians in the Yugoslav province of Kosovo.

NATO officials ordered the attack after Yugoslav President Slobodan Milosevic rejected a peace plan for Kosovo and continued a systematic campaign of repression against the province's Albanian majority. Hundreds of U.S. aircraft from bases in Germany, Great Britain, and Italy took part in the campaign. Scores of cruise missiles were fired from B-52 bombers, submarines, and surface ships as well. Two B-2 stealth bombers made their combat debut, flying missions from a base in Missouri.

After 10 weeks of bombing and intensive diplomatic negotiations, Milosevic agreed to a peace plan on June 3. The 78-day air war officially ended June 9, when NATO officials ordered a cease-fire. Serbian troops began withdrawing from Kosovo the next day, and peacekeeping troops from several NATO countries and Russia fanned out across the province.

NATO combat casualties were amazingly light. On March 31, Serbian forces captured three U.S.

soldiers patrolling the Yugoslav-Macedonian border. Milosevic ordered the release of the soldiers on May 1, following an appeal by U.S. civil rights activist Jesse Jackson.

Serbian forces shot down a U.S. Air Force F-117A Nighthawk fighter on March 27. Although the pilot was rescued, the loss of the plane was an embarrassment to Pentagon officials because its stealth technology supposedly rendered it invulnerable to enemy radar.

Pentagon officials said that while military leaders had taken precautions to reduce accidental bombings, there were several incidents where civilians were killed and nonmilitary buildings were destroyed. The most controversial such incident occurred on May 7, when a U.S. jet fighter bombed the Chinese Embassy in Belgrade, the Yugoslav capital. Chinese officials said that three Chinese nationals were killed. The incident, which was attributed to faulty intelligence data, triggered widespread demonstrations against U.S. diplomatic sites in China and caused increased tensions between the two nations.

In June, the U.S. Congress passed a $12-billion spending package financing U.S. participation in the air campaign. The spending measure also included money for weapons, training, and other items not related to the war but designed to rebuild a military force. Many critics claimed that U.S. troops were losing their fighting edge because of budget cuts and frequent peacekeeping deployments.

Bosnia-Herzegovina deployment. About 6,000 U.S. soldiers remained on NATO peacekeeping duty in Bosnia-Herzegovina, a former Yugoslav republic, in 1999. U.S. Army officials had planned to reduce the American presence by 2,000 troops but postponed those plans after the hostilities in Serbia began. A 1999 General Accounting Office study revealed that the combat capability of U.S. infantry and armored units in Bosnia had been degraded for lack of training while on peacekeeping duty.

Military experts said in 1999 that the Kosovo and Bosnian deployments were among several global peacekeeping operations that were stretching the U.S. military to its limits. U.S. Armed Services leaders ordered a review of such commitments in hopes of bringing some soldiers home and reducing a rise in resignations and early retirement from the military.

Iraq bombings. U.S. fighter jets policing "no-fly zones" in northern and southern Iraq bombed military targets throughout the country in what became an almost daily ritual in 1999. The no-fly zones were established by the United States after the Iraqi military put down uprisings in the areas following the end of the Persian Gulf War in 1991. The aerial patrols, routinely flown since the

D-DAY IN NORMANDY. About 6:30 a.m., on June 6, shortly before dawn, a vast flotilla of some 4,000 ships of all sizes and sorts began to land troops at four points along a 40-mile strip of beach between the mouth of the Seine and the Cotentin Peninsula. The marvelous American "ducks"—heavy trucks which could go 40 miles an hour on a road or plunge into the water and keep afloat in even a quite choppy sea—ferried troops ashore and went back to the ships for more loads. The weather was still quite rough, so that many soldiers were spilled into the surf. An additional difficulty came from numerous German underwater beach defenses—steel rails and timbers planted in concrete and intended to upset landing craft. But as the landing took place at low tide, these obstacles stuck up in full sight and were demolished by specially trained engineer corps. A sky umbrella of some eight thousand Allied planes covered the operation. At some points the Germans offered bitter resistance, but at others there was almost no opposition. Allied casualties on the first day were far less than had been feared. In the first 24 hours the Allies performed the almost incredible feat of putting 250,000 men ashore.

Allied troops land on the beach at Normandy, France, in June 1944.

end of the Gulf War, had escalated in December 1998 after Iraqi antiaircraft batteries began targeting U.S. planes.

U.S. and British jets flew more than 10,000 combat missions against more than 400 Iraqi military targets in 1999. U.S. and British military officials claimed that aircraft targeted only Iraqi air defense sites that were firing on their planes, though the Iraqi military claimed that many civilian sites were bombed during the raids.

About 22,000 U.S. military personnel remained on duty in the Persian Gulf region at the end of the year. Plans to reduce the size of the U.S. presence were placed on hold as a result of the increased Iraqi threat to U.S. jet fighters.

Gulf War syndrome. A panel appointed by President Bill Clinton to examine claims of illnesses suffered by U.S. soldiers who served in the Persian Gulf War announced on August 27 that it had not been able to identify the causes of the ailments. The panel recommended in an interim report that the U.S. government explore whether the genetic makeup of some soldiers made them prone to unexplained illnesses.

On November 30, however, researchers at the University of Texas Southwestern Medical Center in Dallas reported that veterans who complained of illness also had lower-than-normal levels of a chemical called N-acetyl-aspartate. The researchers said that the low chemical level indicates damage to parts of the brain that control reflexes, movement, memory, and emotion.

Since returning from the region at the end of the Persian Gulf War, more than 20,000 veterans of the war have complained of mysterious maladies, including fatigue, joint pain, and memory loss, since returning from the region. The veterans claimed that the symptoms were related to their service in the Gulf. The panel was scheduled to release its final report in 2000.

Defense budget. The Department of Defense submitted its $267.2-billion budget request for fiscal 2000 to Congress on Feb. 1, 1999. The department requested $4.3 billion for continued development of a ballistic missile defense system, the largest amount for a single weapon in history. The budget also included a $4.4-billion pay raise for U.S. soldiers, the largest since 1983, and $1.8 billion for Bosnian peacekeeping operations.

The Defense Department requested $3.6 billion for 15 C-17 jet cargo planes, $3.1 billion for six F-22 Raptor stealth fighters, $3.1 billion for 36 F/A-18 Hornet jet fighters, $2.9 billion for three Burke-class Aegis guided missile destroyers, $1.2 billion for 10 V-22 Osprey vertical take-off and landing aircraft, $658 million to upgrade M-1 battle tanks, and $537 million for 12 Trident II submarine-launched ballistic missiles.

A U.S. F-16 fighter pilot prepares for take-off from the Aviano air base in northern Italy for a NATO bombing mission over Yugoslavia in April 1999. The mission was one of thousands flown to force Serbs to end their offensive in Kosovo.

Weapons systems. Development on a variety of new weapons systems, including a new nuclear attack submarine, two air-to-ground missiles, an advanced air-to-air missile, a joint strike fighter, and the Crusader self-propelled howitzer, continued throughout 1999.

In a rare defeat for the military, a U.S. House of Representatives appropriations subcommittee on July 12 rejected a $1.8-billion budget request by the Air Force to purchase six F-22 jet fighters. The committee, however, approved a $1.2-billion request for research and development. The Defense Department wants to build 438 of the planes at an estimated cost of more than $60 billion. Critics charged that the aircraft, which had been plagued by development problems, was too expensive in an era of shrinking budgets.

Tomb of the Unknowns. The Defense Department announced in February 1999 that it would not place the remains of a Vietnam War (1957–1975) veteran in the Tomb of the Unknowns at Arlington National Cemetery in Virginia. The department concluded that new genetic tests had eliminated the chance that any remains from that war could not be identified. The remains of a Vietnam War serviceman buried at the tomb in 1984 were identified in 1998 as those of an Air Force pilot who had been shot down near An Loc in South Vietnam in 1972.

Italian ski tragedy. A military jury on March 4, acquitted a U.S. Marine Corps pilot of involuntary manslaughter in the deaths of 20 people at a ski resort near Cavalese, Italy, in 1998. Captain Richard Ashby was on a training mission when his EA-6B Prowler surveillance aircraft cut the cable of a gondola, plunging the victims to their deaths. Military prosecutors charged the pilot with flying his plane at only 370 feet (110 meters) in an area where Air Force personnel were prohibited from flying below 1,000 feet (300 meters).

In May 1999, the military jury convicted Ashby of conspiring to destroy evidence and obstruction of justice for helping to destroy a videotape of the flight. He was sentenced to six months in a military prison and dismissed from the service.

Ashby's navigator, Captain Joseph Schweitzer, pleaded guilty to an obstruction of justice charge and conspiracy charge for destroying the videotape and was dismissed from the U.S. Marine Corps. Manslaughter charges against Schweitzer were dropped after Ashby's acquittal on the same charges.

"Don't ask, don't tell." A U.S. military policy intended to make it easier for homosexuals to serve in the armed forces came under fire in December 1999. First Lady Hillary Rodham Clinton, a possible candidate for the U.S. Senate from New York, said that she disagreed with the policy and would work to overturn it if elected. Under the policy, commonly called "don't ask, don't tell," homosexual members of the military can continue to serve so long as they keep their sexual orientation private. Military superiors are also forbidden to investigate a subordinate's sexual orientation if the subordinate has kept his or her orientation private.

Clark steps down. The Department of Defense in July ordered Army General Wesley Clark to step down as NATO's military commander. The Pentagon said that Clark would leave the post in April rather than July 2000. Air Force General Joseph Ralston, vice chairman of the Joint Chiefs of Staff, was named as his successor.

Command changes. In June 1999, General Eric K. Shinseki was sworn in as Army Chief of Staff, succeeding General Dennis Reimer. A native of Hawaii, Shinseki was the first Japanese American to head the U.S. Army. General James L. Jones, Jr., was sworn in as commandant of the Marine Corps in June, succeeding General Charles C. Krulak. The U.S. Senate on July 31 confirmed F. Whitten Peters as Secretary of the Air Force. Peters had served as acting secretary since 1997.

☐ Thomas M. DeFrank

See also **Congress of the United States; United States, Government of the; Yugoslavia.**

Armenia. See Asia.

Art. The problem of art treasures looted by the Nazi government of Germany before and during World War II (1939-1945) remained a major issue in the art world in 1999. Spurred by international guidelines adopted in December 1998, the United States and European countries began the slow process of identifying Nazi-plundered art and returning it to its rightful owners. Much of the art had belonged to Jewish collectors killed during the *Holocaust*, (the systematic killing during World War II of millions of Jews and other people considered undesirable by Germany's Nazi government). Heirs of Holocaust victims have mounted numerous lawsuits to reclaim family property.

Matisse returned. The Seattle Art Museum settled the first lawsuit against a U.S. museum over looted art in June 1999 by returning *Odalisque* (1925) by French artist Henri Matisse to the heirs of Paul Rosenberg, a prominent Jewish art dealer in Paris in the 1930's. The Nazis had confiscated the painting in 1941 from the bank vault where Rosenberg had stored it before fleeing to the United States. The Seattle museum's suit against the New York City gallery that had purchased the painting in Paris in 1954 remained unsettled at the end of 1999.

Schiele dispute. A New York state appeals court ruled on March 16, that the Museum of Modern Art (MOMA) in New York City may not

---

TIME CAPSULE 1937

ART

GUERNICA, a small Basque town, seat of the oldest parliament in Europe, was bombed by the rebels in the Spanish civil war on April 27. Picasso, an ardent loyalist, took the horrible devastation of that tragic event for his theme in the great mural which was the most discussed painting of the Paris Exposition. Symbolic in form, almost frenzied in emotion, the painting, despite its avowed propagandic purpose, resolves itself, as does so much of Picasso's late work, into a subtle decorative scheme of mathematical shapes, areas, and sequences.

Pablo Picasso's Guernica

John Singer Sargent's *Madame X*, which created a tempest when first exhibited in Paris in 1884, was one of more than 100 paintings by Sargent exhibited in a 1999 retrospective of the American artist's work at the National Gallery in Washington, D.C., and the Museum of Fine Arts in Boston.

return two paintings, allegedly looted by the Nazis, to Austria until Manhattan District Attorney Robert M. Morgenthau concludes a criminal investigation into who owns the works. The Leopold Foundation of Vienna had loaned the paintings by Egon Schiele to MOMA for a 1997 exhibition. In January 1998, Morgenthau, acting on behalf of the heirs of the original owners, issued a legal order forbidding the museum from returning the works until the question of ownership was settled. The appellate court decision in 1999 overturned a lower court ruling that allowed the museum to release the paintings. The appeals court argued that a New York law protecting the free

movement of art into and out of the state does not apply to stolen art. The museum said it would appeal the decision.

Malevich accord. In June 1999, MOMA and heirs of the Russian artist Kasimir Malevich reached an agreement on 16 works that had been smuggled out of Nazi Germany by a MOMA director in 1935. The settlement allowed MOMA to keep 15 of the works in exchange for a cash payment. The museum was to return one painting, valued at about $10 million, to the artist's heirs in Russia. The 16 paintings had been made part of the museum's permanent collection in 1963 after no one had claimed them. Malevich's heirs came forward in 1993, after the breakup of the Soviet Union in 1991.

Rothschild art sale. More than 200 works of art stolen by the Nazis in 1938 from the Austrian branch of the Rothschild banking family brought $89.5 million at a London auction in July 1999. Although the works had been returned to Austria after World War II, the Austrian government had passed a law forbidding the export of the art or its sale abroad. In early 1999, the government repealed the law and returned the art to the heirs of the former owners.

The Last Supper. The public was shown Leonardo da Vinci's *The Last Supper* in Milan, Italy, on May 28, after one of the most technologically advanced art restorations ever undertaken. The 20-year, $8-million cleanup, directed by Italian restorer Pinin Brambilla Barcilon, was the seventh restoration of the approximately 500-year-old mural. The celebrated artwork depicts the moment Jesus Christ tells his apostles that one of them will betray him. Because Leonardo used an experimental painting technique, the mural began deteriorating within a few years of its completion in about 1497.

Art experts hailed the mural's remarkable clarity and rich colors after the removal of centuries of dirt, grease, and paint and other materials from previous restorations. In their attempt to recover Leonardo's original work, the restorers found such long-obscured details as facial expressions, shiny glassware, a fish platter, and an orange.

Some art experts, however, criticized the restorers' decision to remove most of the previous restoration work. The critics also deplored the use of beige watercolors to cover areas of the mural where the original pigments had been completely lost. Project officials said the restoration had saved about half of Leonardo's original work. The critics claimed that less than 20 percent remains.

Brooklyn controversy. An exhibit described as "sick stuff" and "an attack on religion" triggered a major battle over freedom of expression and public funding of the arts in New York City in autumn 1999. The exhibit, "Sensations: Young British Artists from the Saatchi Collection," opened on October 2 at the Brooklyn Museum of Art. The exhibit's most controversial work was a painting of a black Madonna decorated with elephant dung and pornographic images. Artist Chris Offili said African artists have long used elephant dung to lend spiritual significance to artifacts.

New York City Mayor Rudolph Giuliani on September 28 cut the city's $7.2-million annual allocation to the museum—a third of the museum's budget—arguing that art that is offensive to the public should not receive public funds. On November 1, a federal judge ordered the city to restore the funding, ruling that the cutoff violated the constitutional right to free speech.

Museum boom. Museums in the United States continued to experience unprecedented growth in 1999. An informal survey by *The New York Times,* published in April, identified nearly 60 U.S. museums that were enlarging their facilities. In 1997, 68 million adults visited U.S. art museums, according to the National Endowment for the Arts, a government agency.

On April 20, 1999, the Metropolitan Museum of Art (the Met) in New York City opened seven new galleries with the largest permanent exhibit of ancient Greek art in the Western Hemisphere. Six of the galleries open off a Beaux Arts barrel-vaulted corridor. The restoration included uncovering immense skylights that had been hidden because of security blackouts during World War II. On May 23, the National Gallery of Art in Washington, D.C., unveiled a 6-acre (2.4-hectare) outdoor sculpture garden.

A former electric company complex in North Adams, Massachusetts, was transformed into the $37-million Massachusetts Museum of Contemporary Art, or MASS MoCA, which opened in May. The 27-building museum includes sites for the performing arts. The new Scottsdale (Arizona) Museum of Contemporary Art, which opened in February in a former multiplex cinema, offered another inventive marriage of art and a recycled structure.

Work continued in 1999 on a new wing of the Milwaukee Art Museum and the conversion of San Francisco's Old Main Library into a new Asian Art Museum. Art museums in Portland, Oregon, and Kansas City, Kansas, also expanded their facilities in 1999.

Major exhibits. More than 1 million visitors viewed "Van Gogh's Van Goghs: Masterpieces from the Van Gogh Museum, Amsterdam" at the National Gallery in Washington, D.C., and at the Los Angeles County Museum of Art during 1999.

American museums in 1999 offered a look back to ancient Egypt with three major exhibits. "Egyptian Art in the Age of the Pyramids," which opened at the Met in September, included 250 works from more than 30 museums. "Pharaohs of the Sun: Akhenaten, Nefertiti, Tutankhamen" at Boston's Museum of Fine Arts focused on the period from 1353 to 1336 B.C., during which King Akhenaten (also spelled Akhenaton) adopted the idea of a single god. "Splendors of Ancient Egypt" at the Virginia Museum of Fine Arts in Richmond and the Phoenix Art Museum explored 3,000 years of Egyptian art.

The Whitney Museum of American Art in New York City showcased modern U.S. artists in the first part of a planned two-part exhibit. "The American Century: Art & Culture 1900-2000" presented more than 1,200 paintings, sculptures, photographs, and prints.　　□ Sally Ruth May

See also **Architecture.**

Conflicts flared across southern Asia during 1999, and armed tensions escalated in the northeast. But 1999 also saw a number of Asian nations recover peacefully from two years of severe economic troubles.

Conflict and unrest. Civil wars continued to ravage three Asian nations. In Afghanistan, foreign support and supplies fueled battles between the Taliban, Islamic fundamentalists who controlled most of the country, and ethnic minorities in the northeast. In Sri Lanka, guerrilla warfare between the army and Tamils, an ethnic minority seeking a separate state, flared in northeastern jungles, while terrorists used suicide bombers to kill opponents elsewhere in the country. A low-level guerrilla war continued to flare sporadically in the southern Philippines, where Muslim separatists and loosely allied Communists attacked the army and police.

Other fighting erupted during 1999 in Kashmir, a Himalayan region disputed by India and Pakistan, when fighters from the Pakistani side of a cease-fire line crossed into Indian-held territory. The fighters were later forced to withdraw from mountaintop posts.

In East Timor, a former Portuguese colony seized by Indonesia in 1975, violence allegedly provoked by the Indonesian Army followed in the wake of a vote on Aug. 30, 1999, for independence. An Australian-led international peacekeeping force was sent to the island in September. Indonesia gave East Timor its freedom, and the United Nations established a transitional regime there. Ethnic, religious, and separatist clashes troubled several other parts of Indonesia, causing some citizens to worry that the nation might be torn apart by regional divisions.

Tensions flared between the governments of China and Taiwan, both of which have long claimed sole legitimacy in China. Taiwan took the position that mutual discussions should be on a state-to-state basis, while China insisted on treating Taiwan's government as a provincial administration. China repeated threats to invade Taiwan if it declared independence, but Taiwan had in fact exercised independence for half a century.

Security concerns. North Korea sent ships into both South Korean and Japanese waters in 1999. In separate incidents, defense forces of the two nations fired upon the intruding North Korean ships. In early August, Japan and South Korea held their first joint naval maneuvers. North Korea, which had caused alarm in the region in 1998 by firing a missile over Japan, announced on

Sept. 12, 1999, that it would freeze its missile testing program. However, North Korea's government continued to defy international sanctions by supplying missile parts and technology to embargoed countries, such as Iran.

The United States held talks in 1999 with government officials of Japan, South Korea, and Taiwan about the possibility of setting up a joint missile defense system. The prospect of such an arrangement angered China, which suspected that a strong defense might encourage Taiwan to declare independence. Russia also objected to the idea, claiming that it would violate a 1972 U.S.-Soviet ban on missile defenses.

Economic recovery. The economies of most of the Asian nations that had been hit hard by recession beginning in mid-1997 recovered in 1999. The Asian Development Bank (ADB), an affiliate of the United Nations, reported in September 1999 that "in just a few short months, Asia has made great strides in recovering from the worst economic crisis in a generation." South Korea, Thailand, Malaysia, Singapore, and the Philippines led the way with vigorous economic growth.

The ADB report noted that the crisis had caused unemployment and falling incomes, lowered enrollment in schools, reduced food consumption, and decreased use of health services. Some 900 million Asians subsisted on incomes of less than $1 a day during the recession. The report suggested that ADB loans, which had helped in the recovery, would be refocused on reducing poverty.

Population continued to grow rapidly in much of Asia in 1999, when, according to some experts, India's population surpassed 1 billion. At the 1999 growth rate, India's population will surpass China's in 2040. Although China had 1.3 billion people in 1999, its population increased at a slower rate than India's. Economists worried that most economic growth was going toward merely maintaining low living standards because of the rapidly increasing numbers of people—rather than improving standards.

ASEAN, the Association of Southeast Asian Nations—an organization fostering cooperation among members—admitted Cambodia on April 30, 1999. With Cambodia's inclusion, ASEAN finally embraced all 10 nations in Southeast Asia. Although founded in 1967 in reaction to the regional spread of Communism, ASEAN accepted Vietnam as its first Communist member in 1995 and then Laos in 1997. Myanmar (formerly Bur-

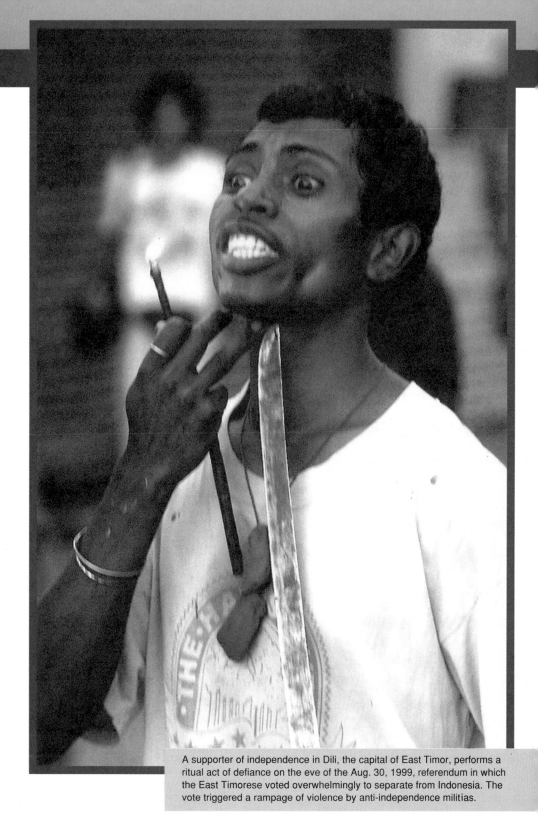

A supporter of independence in Dili, the capital of East Timor, performs a ritual act of defiance on the eve of the Aug. 30, 1999, referendum in which the East Timorese voted overwhelmingly to separate from Indonesia. The vote triggered a rampage of violence by anti-independence militias.

Country	Population	Government	Monetary unit*	Foreign trade (million U.S.$)	
				Exports†	Imports†
Afghanistan	26,674,000	No functioning government	afghani (4,750.00 = $1)	80	150
Armenia	3,813,000	President Robert Kocharian	dram (543.17 = $1)	233	892
Australia	19,222,000	Governor General William Deane; Prime Minister John Howard	dollar (1.52 = $1)	55,896	64,668
Azerbaijan	7,969,000	President Heydar A. Aliyev	manat (3,975.00 = $1)	781	794
Bangladesh	134,417,000	President Mustafizur Rahman; Prime Minister Sheikh Hasina Wajed	taka (49.45 = $1)	3,778	6,896
Bhutan	1,842,000	King Jigme Singye Wangchuck	ngultrum (43.42 = $1)	99	131
Brunei	312,000	Sultan Sir Hassanal Bolkiah	dollar (1.68 = $1)	2,273	1,915
Cambodia (Kampuchea)	11,637,000	King Norodom Sihanouk; Prime Minister Hun Sen	riel (3,820.00 = $1)	736	1,100
China	1,284,597,000	Communist Party General Secretary and President Jiang Zemin; Premier Zhu Rongji	renminbi yuan (8.28 = $1)	183,589	140,305
Georgia	5,527,000	President Eduard Shevardnadze	lari (2.21 = $1)	230	931
India	1,022,021,000	President Kircheril Raman Narayanan; Prime Minister Atal Behari Vajpayee	rupee (43.42 = $1)	32,880	42,213
Indonesia	212,731,000	President Abdurrahman Wahid	rupiah (7,817.00 = $1)	53,443	41,694
Iran	74,644,000	Supreme Leader Ayatollah Ali Hoseini-Khamenei; President Mohammed Khatami-Ardakani	rial (1,750.00 = $1)	22,391	16,274
Japan	126,472,000	Emperor Akihito; Prime Minister Keizo Obuchi	yen (107.54 = $1)	388,167	280,674
Kazakhstan	16,288,000	President Nursultan Nazarbayev	tenge (128.00 = $1)	5,339	4,242
Korea, North	21,935,000	Korean Workers' Party General Secretary Kim Chong-il	won (2.20 = $1)	743	1,830
Korea, South	47,149,000	President Kim Dae-jung; Prime Minister Kim Chong-pil	won (1,204.00 = $1)	132,313	93,282
Kyrgyzstan	4,683,000	President Askar Akayev	som (43.09 = $1)	605	677
Laos	5,602,000	President Khamtai Siphandon; Prime Minister Sisavat Keobounphan	kip (7,680.00 = $1)	359	706
Malaysia	22,299,000	Paramount Ruler (King) Sultan Salahuddin Abdul Aziz Shah; Prime Minister Mahathir bin Mohamad	ringgit (3.80 = $1)	73,304	58,326

ma) also gained admission in 1997. Cambodia's admission had been delayed after its Communist leaders slaughtered political opponents in 1997.

Observers in Asia suggested that ASEAN, a loose organization operating by consensus, was in decline in 1999 as it did little about regional economic and security problems. Criticism of ASEAN's passive role in the East Timor crisis appeared in the regional press.

Two meetings between ASEAN and the European Union (EU), a political and economic alliance of Western European nations, were canceled in early 1999 because the Europeans refused to meet with representatives of Myanmar, a dictatorship. But the two associations worked out a plan to meet in Bangkok in May.

Spratly Islands. ASEAN struggled to deal with another regional issue, control of a group of shoals and reefs in the South China Sea known as the Spratly Islands. China claimed the area and refused to negotiate with four ASEAN nations—Brunei, Malaysia, the Philippines, and Vietnam—that claimed various parts of the island group.

China allegedly continued to fortify several reefs while insisting it was only building fishing shelters. A Philippine naval vessel that was trying

Country	Population	Government	Monetary unit*	Foreign trade (million U.S.$)	
				Exports†	Imports†
Maldives	285,000	President Maumoon Abdul Gayoom	rufiyaa (11.77 = $1)	76	354
Mongolia	2,661,000	President Natsagiyn Bagabandi; Prime Minister Rinchinnyamin Amarjargal	tugrik (1,014.73 = $1)	317	472
Myanmar (Burma)	48,866,000	Prime Minister, State Peace and Development Council Chairman Than Shwe	kyat (6.03 = $1)	1,076	2,669
Nepal	24,842,000	King Birendra Bir Bikram Shah Dev; Prime Minister Krishna Prasad Bhattarai	rupee (68.48 = $1)	474	1,243
New Zealand	3,759,000	Governor General Sir Michael Hardie-Boys; Prime Minister Jennifer Shipley	dollar (1.94 = $1)	12,074	12,499
Pakistan	145,246,000	Chief Executive General Pervez Musharraf	rupee (51.83 = $1)	8,500	9,315
Papua New Guinea	4,809,000	Governor General Sir Silas Atopare; Prime Minister Sir Mekere Morauta	kina (2.89 = $1)	1,667	1,189
Philippines	74,575,000	President Joseph Estrada	peso (40.49 = $1)	25,088	38,277
Russia	145,552,000	Acting President Vladimir Putin	ruble (25.82 = $1)	71,800	58,500
Singapore	3,777,000	President Ong Teng Cheong; Prime Minister Goh Chok Tong	dollar (1.68 = $1)	109,865	101,605
Sri Lanka	19,504,000	President Chandrika Kumaratunga; Prime Minister Sirimavo Bandaranaike	rupee (71.30 = $1)	4,734	5,917
Taiwan	22,322,000	President Lee Teng-hui; Vice President Lien Chan	dollar (31.79 = $1)	122,100	114,400
Tajikistan	6,260,000	President Emomali Rahmonov; National Assembly Chairman Safarali Rajabov	ruble (1,283.75 = $1)	602	771
Thailand	61,909,000	King Phumiphon Adunyadet; Prime Minister Chuan Likphai	baht (40.29 = $1)	54,455	42,971
Turkmenistan	4,551,000	President Saparmurat Niyazov	manat (5,200.00 = $1)	1,939	777
Uzbekistan	25,383,000	President Islam Karimov	som (111.90 = $1)	3,528	3,289
Vietnam	82,648,000	Communist Party General Secretary Le Kha Phieu; President Tran Duc Luong; Prime Minister Phan Van Khai	dong (13,997.50 = $1)	7,256	11,144

*Exchange rates as of Oct. 8, 1999, or latest available data.
†Latest available data.

to chase two Chinese boats away from the Scarborough Shoal on May 23 hit and sank one Chinese boat. On July 19, a Philippine ship again sank a Chinese fishing boat. Malaysia built a structure on a shoal, approximately equidistant from its state of Sabah and the Philippines, and refused to discuss a Philippine protest. The Philippines sought U.S. help to improve its armed forces, too weak in naval and air power to protect its Spratly claims.

Piracy continued to plague the South China Sea and adjacent waters in 1999. In a February report, the Paris-based International Maritime Bureau identified the waters around Indonesia's islands as the world's "highest risk area" for piracy and warned that hijackings were becoming increasingly violent. Heavily armed pirates in fast boats ruthlessly attacked unarmed ships in the area, often killing the entire crew and stealing the ships and cargo. Governments in the region did little to halt the piracy, and some observers even accused Indonesian and Chinese coast guards and customs officials of being involved.

Boat people. In July, the EU ended a program that had helped *repatriate* (return to their home country) nearly 50,000 "boat people" who had fled Vietnam during the massive migration of the 1970's and 1980's. EU officials pronounced the program a success, but critics pointed out that returnees still faced many problems, including economic hardship. In Hong Kong, Vietnamese refugees long confined to a camp rioted in June 1999, causing at least 17 injuries. About 2,400 Vietnamese remained in Hong Kong refugee camps in 1999.

Australia was an increasingly popular destination in 1999 for Asians seeking better livelihoods. Australian officials blamed criminals in southern China for organizing and dispatching boatloads of Chinese who landed in Australia to seek jobs.

Smog caused by burning rain forests in Indonesia returned to Southeast Asia in 1999, two years after severe smoke had provoked an environmental crisis in the region. The renewed smog created new dangers to health and tourism and interfered with ship and air traffic. People in the hardest-hit nations—Malaysia, Singapore, and Brunei—blamed the Indonesian government for failing to control small farmers and big agricultural businesses that cleared land by burning. Weather forecasters noted that a 1998 drought made forests more flammable.

Weather was harsh across Asia in 1999. Unusually heavy monsoon rains in July and August caused floods that killed hundreds of people in the Philippines, Thailand, Vietnam, China, and North and South Korea. Flooding along the Yangtze River in China left as many as 5.5 million people homeless. Governments in both China and North Korea were blamed for inadequate and shoddy work on dikes and embankments built to hold back floodwaters.

Nepal held elections in May 1999 after five years of political bickering and frequently changing coalitions of political parties. Voters gave the Nepali Congress Party a working majority of 110 of 205 seats in parliament, while a Communist group took 68 seats. A 74-year-old Congress leader, Krishna Prasad Bhattarai, became prime minister on May 31. Bhattarai faced a large budget deficit, high unemployment, and a shortage of badly needed foreign investment. In remote areas of Nepal, Communist insurgents, who had caused hundreds of deaths in more than two years of clashes with authorities, fought on through 1999.

Mongolia. On July 30, the Mongolian parliament named Rinchinnyamin Amarjargal, a 38-year-old economist, the fourth prime minister in 16 months. The previous government lost a vote of confidence over the transfer of Mongolia's largest copper mine to private owners as the former Communist country struggled to stabilize its economy. □ Henry S. Bradsher

See also the various Asian country articles.

Astronomy. In 1999, astronomers discovered the first system of planets orbiting another sunlike star. Data from orbiting satellites provided close-up views of Mars and of Jupiter's moon Europa. Astronomers also discovered new moons around Uranus and watched as Pluto again became the farthest planet from the sun.

New solar system. Astronomers in April announced that they had found evidence of a solar system orbiting a star similar to the sun. Geoffrey Marcy and R. Paul Butler of San Francisco State University, together with astronomers from the Harvard-Smithsonian Center for Astrophysics and the High Altitude Observatory in Boulder, Colorado, discovered three planets that seem to be circling the star Upsilon Andromedae, located 44 light-years from Earth. A light-year is the distance light travels in one year, about 5.9 trillion miles (9.5 trillion kilometers). The astronomers believe the three planets are large gaseous bodies similar to Jupiter and Saturn, with no solid surface and unable to support life.

The astronomers discovered the solar system by measuring variations in the light from Upsilon Andromedae. The variations are caused by tiny wiggles in the star's orbit as it is pulled by the planets' gravity. Since 1995, astronomers using similar techniques had reported more than 20 nearby stars with solitary planets orbiting them. In November 1999, astronomers observed an extrasolar planet for the first time.

The surface of Mars. Two spacecraft that were to study Martian weather were lost in 1999. The Mars Climate Orbiter was lost in September because of improper instructions from Earth. The Orbiter approached too close to the Martian surface and was damaged beyond repair when one engineering team used metric units of measure-

TIME CAPSULE 1930

ASTRONOMY

PLUTO, THE NEW PLANET. A ninth world has been added to the family of the sun. Far out on the rim of the solar system, 900,000,000 miles beyond Neptune, lies Pluto, the discovery of which was the major astronomical event of 1930. . . . It is over four billion miles from us, and through large telescopes it appears only as a faint star. Many may wonder why Pluto is so called. . . . The [name] was based on the feeling that the "line of Roman gods for whom other planets are named should not be broken."

ment while another used English units. Engineers lost contact with Mars Polar Lander on December 3, as it tried to land near the south pole. The lander was to transit data about the Martian surface back to Earth.

The Mars Global Surveyor spacecraft, which arrived on Mars in 1997, took 27 million measurements of the planet's surface between its arrival and April 1999. Using these measurements, astronomers constructed the first three-dimensional map of Mars, accurate within 42 feet (13 meters). Data recorded by the Surveyor revealed a huge impact basin, named Hellas, in the southern hemisphere. The basin, created about 4 billion years ago when a large body collided with the planet, measured 6 miles (9 kilometers) deep and 1,300 miles (2,100 kilometers) across.

Data from the Surveyor also provided evidence that water once flowed across the Martian surface, producing snaking erosion beds and debris-strewn flood plains. The three-dimensional map of the planet's polar icecaps, which contain all of the known water on the planet in frozen form, suggested that the total amount of water on the caps is no more than 5 percent of the water in the Pacific Ocean on Earth.

The Surveyor also mapped surface magnetism. Instruments aboard the spacecraft revealed striped patterns—broad bands of magnetized rock. In one band, the rocks are magnetically oriented in one direction, while in a second band, they are oriented in the opposite direction. Scientists have detected similar patterns on Earth's ocean floor where new sea floor is forming as the plates of the Earth's crust drift apart. Astronomers theorized that continental drift may have occurred on Mars, as on Earth.

In December, astronomers reported that Surveyor measurements provided compelling evidence that the northern lowlands of Mars once contained a deep, wide ocean with long beaches.

Jupiter's moon Europa. The Galileo spacecraft, in orbit around Jupiter and its four large moons since 1995, continued to provide evidence in 1999 that one of the moons—Europa—has an ocean of liquid water beneath its icy surface. Photographs taken by Galileo revealed curved cracks, resembling waves in a scallop shell, that extend for hundreds of miles near Europa's south pole. Planetary scientists Gregory Hoppa and Paul Geissler, with colleagues at the University of Arizona in Tucson, used computer models to show that the source of the cracks could be the rise and fall of tides in a liquid ocean below.

In October, Robert W. Carlson of the National Aeronautic and Space Administration's Jet Propulsion Laboratory in Pasadena, California, report-

Details of the surface of Mars are revealed in the first three-dimensional map of the planet, created from data collected by the Mars Global Surveyor spacecraft and released in May 1999. One of the most prominent features on the map is the Hellas basin (the blue crater, above left), which is 1,300 miles (2,100 kilometers) across.

ed that he had used other instruments aboard Galileo to examine the chemical composition of Europa's surface. Carlson detected the presence of sulfuric acid. Although water and sulfuric acid are a corrosive mixture, there are creatures on Earth (near undersea volcanoes) that live in similar environments. Astronomers continued to consider the possibility that life may exist on Europa.

Uranus's new moons. In July, Canadian astronomers announced that they had discovered, using a telescope atop Mauna Kea in Hawaii, what appear to be three previously unknown moons orbiting Uranus. If the discovery is confirmed, the number of known moons orbiting Uranus would be 21, more than any planet in the solar system. Saturn has 18 moons.

Pluto's orbit. In February, Pluto resumed its position as the outermost planet in the solar system for the first time since 1979. Because of its eccentric orbit, Pluto spends 20 years of its 248-year journey around the sun inside Neptune's orbit. Pluto will remain the outermost planet until the year 2227.　　　　□ Laurence A. Marschall

See also **Astronomy: A Special Report; Space exploration.**

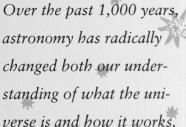

Over the past 1,000 years, astronomy has radically changed both our understanding of what the universe is and how it works.

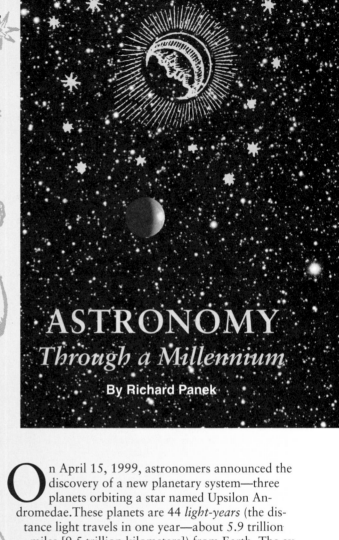

ASTRONOMY
Through a Millennium

By Richard Panek

On April 15, 1999, astronomers announced the discovery of a new planetary system—three planets orbiting a star named Upsilon Andromedae. These planets are 44 *light-years* (the distance light travels in one year—about 5.9 trillion miles [9.5 trillion kilometers]) from Earth. The existence of other worlds around another star—a subject of speculation for ages—had become a fact. The discovery underscored how radically the human view of the universe has changed over the course of the last 100 years, as well as the revolutionary changes that astronomy itself has undergone through the past millennium.

During the last 1,000 years, investigations in the field of astronomy yielded a new understanding of the universe. Assumptions about what the universe is and how it works changed at almost every level, from conceptions about the Earth and the other planets through ideas about galaxies and the farthest reaches of space, a distance that astronomers now calculate at 13 billion light-years.

This new planetary system was discovered in 1999. Three planets circle the star Upsilon Andromedae in an artist's rendering (above).

Astronomy in ancient times

In A.D. 1000, human understanding of the *cosmos* (the universe thought of as an orderly, harmonious system) was fundamentally the same as when human beings first began to study the heavens. Early skywatchers believed that Earth rested at the center of the universe; Earth was a stationary object around which the other objects in the sky revolved. These first astronomers also divided celestial objects into two categories. There were the bodies that appeared to move in relation to one another—the moon and sun and the planets Mercury, Venus, Mars, Jupiter, and Saturn. (The word planet comes from the Greek for "wanderer.") There were also celestial objects that did not move in relation to one another—the so-called fixed stars.

People in ancient times, by carefully studying the sky, realized that the motions of each of these objects followed specific patterns. The sun returned every day. The moon changed through its phases every 28 days. The planets appeared at certain places in the sky in varying lengths of time. The stars and constellations rotated through the sky every 365 days. Ancient astronomers also noticed that these patterns repeated themselves over time, making it possible to predict the positions of celestial objects. For example, these astronomers determined the place on the

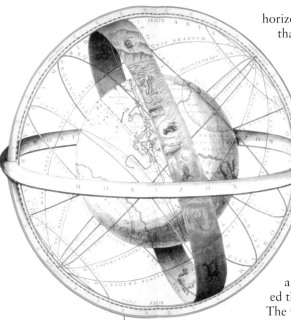

A 1660 model of the universe, engraved by Dutch mathematician and geographer Andreas Cellarius, shows the Earth as a stationary object around which the sun, planets, and stars of the universe revolve.

The author

Richard Panek is an astronomy columnist for *Natural History* and the author of *Seeing and Believing: How the Telescope Opened Our Eyes and Minds to the Heavens.*

horizon where the sun rose on the day that marked the *summer solstice* (the longest day of the year—about June 21 in the Northern Hemisphere—when the sun reaches its most northerly point above the Earth).

The ancient Greeks, to account for these elaborate patterns, hypothesized that the heavens moved along a series of circular spheres, one each for the sun, moon, and five known planets, and one for the fixed stars. These spheres were both *concentric* (having the same center), so that they nested together around the Earth, and interlocking, so that each affected the movement of its neighbor.

The Greek philosopher Aristotle (384-322 B.C.) summarized this system in his writings and added important elements. He treated the spheres not as if they were imaginary, but as if they were real objects made of a transparent substance he called "aither." He suggested that a single source, the Prime Mover, turned the starry vault, the outermost sphere, and set in motion the interlocking spheres. To account for the varying motions and rates of rotation of the planets, Aristotle proposed other, counterturning, spheres for each celestial object. In Aristotle's system, the night sky included 56 spheres.

Aristotle's model explained how the cosmos might work in principle. A practical model of this concept was not developed until approximately A.D. 150. The Egyptian astronomer Claudius Ptolemaeus—better known as Ptolemy—presented an elaborate mathematical accounting of the movements of the spheres in *The Mathematical Collection* (or, *Almagest*, from an Arabic translation). He accounted for both the motions and the periods of celestial objects. (The period of a celestial body is the length of time it takes the object to complete one revolution.) Ptolemy's computations and predictions proved to be so sound and reliable that the Ptolemaic model of the cosmos endured for well over a thousand years.

A new model of the universe

By the 1500's, however, predictions based on the Ptolemaic system began diverging from actual occurrences. Weeks separated the change of seasons on the calendar and the actual onset of seasons during the year. The projected arrival of celestial events and their actual occurrences varied by a month or more. Ptolemy's calculation for the length of a year—based on the idea that the sun and planets revolved around a stationary Earth—was min-

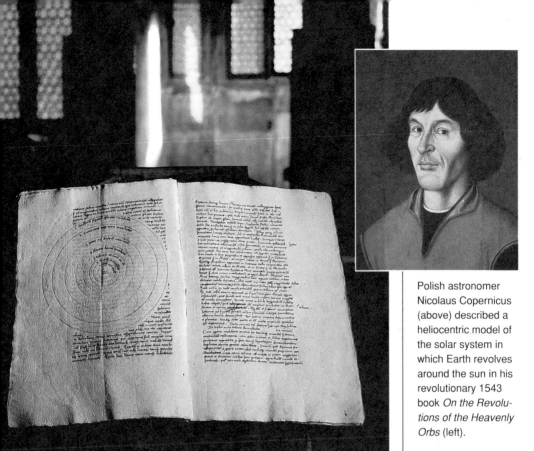

Polish astronomer Nicolaus Copernicus (above) described a heliocentric model of the solar system in which Earth revolves around the sun in his revolutionary 1543 book *On the Revolutions of the Heavenly Orbs* (left).

utes too long, and over the centuries, the minutes added up to days. The Ptolemaic model clearly needed a thorough mathematical update.

Polish astronomer Nicolaus Copernicus published a comprehensive overhaul of the Aristotelian and Ptolemaic models of the universe in 1543, the year of his death. He rejected the earlier models, not on principle, but for practical reasons. Copernicus wanted to create a new model that would keep pace with the calendar. To accomplish this, he found it necessary to hypothesize a cosmos with the sun, rather than the Earth, at the center. Copernicus's new method of accounting for the motions of the stars and planets was so accurate that astronomers incorporated many of them into Pope Gregory XIII's 1582 reform of the calendar. His idea of a *heliocentric,* or sun-centered, universe, however, was largely ignored.

Copernicus was not the first scholar to hypothesize a heliocentric cosmos. During Aristotle's lifetime, Heraclides of Pontus (an ancient country that was located in present-day Turkey) suggested that it was the Earth that rotated upon its axis every day, not the sun. One hundred years later, Aristarchus of Samos (an island in the Aegean Sea) suggested that the Earth moved around the sun, not the sun around the Earth. Copernicus's hypothesis that the cosmos is heliocentric met the same fate as earlier arguments. To anyone looking up into the heavens, the celestial bodies appeared to move around the Earth, and so the idea of an Earth-centered cosmos endured into the early 1600's.

In 1609, the Italian astronomer, physicist, and mathematician Galileo Galilei heard about a device for seeing distant objects as if they were close at hand. The so-called "perspective tube" was a novelty, little more than a toy, but Galileo understood that such an instrument might prove useful as a military or navigational aide. In August 1609, Galileo made his own "perspective tube," or telescope, and presented it to the elders of Venice as a way to gain their favor and to secure his faculty position at a local university. By the autumn of 1609, Galileo had improved the magnification of the instrument and had turned it skyward at night. There he discovered several startling phenomena.

Galileo saw that the surface of the moon was not perfectly smooth, as Aristotle had claimed. It had mountains and valleys, just like Earth. He also saw that planets were not the pinpoints of light they appeared to be. Instead, they were shaped like disks, just as the moon is. Planets that looked like the moon, which in turn looked like the Earth, suggested a logical chain of associations that raised the question: Could Earth be just another planet, one more "wanderer" in the heavens?

Galileo continued looking. Magnification of the night sky revealed many more stars than were visible with the naked eye. In January 1610, he made another discovery that astonished him. Galileo found four "stars" that appeared to accompany the planet Jupiter. After observing their motions in relation to one another for several nights in a row, he realized that they were not stars, but rather moons of Jupiter. The presence of satellites around Jupiter proved that the universe could have more than one center of rotation, meaning that the moon might indeed move around the Earth, while together the two traveled around the sun. Galileo began to publish his findings in 1610. His support of Copernicus's idea of a sun-centered solar system brought him into conflict with the Roman Catholic Church. At first, many of Galileo's fellow astronomers and mathematicians resisted the heliocentric model, but in the end, they could not deny the evidence.

Italian astronomer, physicist, and mathematician Galileo Galilei (1564-1642) provided evidence that the Earth was one of several planets revolving around the sun.

Proof of a heliocentric universe

As Galileo made observations that would change humanity's model of the cosmos, German mathematician and astronomer Johannes Kepler refined Copernicus's computations. Kepler, after years of struggle, realized that there was really no reason the orbit of a planet around the sun had to be circular—the supposedly perfect form favored by Aristotle and other ancient philosophers. Kepler hypothesized that planets follow elliptical paths. He also realized that as planets travel in these slightly elongated orbits, they slow down as they move away from the sun and speed up as they near it. Finally, Kepler arrived at a formula that showed the precise relationship between a planet's average distance from the sun and the time it takes to complete one orbit.

Kepler's findings allowed astronomers, for the first time in history, to mathematically plot the locations of objects in the night sky that actually agreed with their observations. In 1687, the English physicist and mathematician Isaac Newton applied Kepler's laws of planetary motion to the enormous amount of information that had been revealed by the telescope and derived a universal law of gravitation: Every object attracts every other object with a force that depends on the amount of matter in the bodies being attracted and the distance between the bodies.

The universal law of gravitation was both significant in itself and in what it suggested about the human capacity for knowledge about the workings of nature. In Aristotle's model of the universe, the cosmos was divided into two parts, Earth and sky. Each had its own set of physical laws, and what happened in the heavens was forever unknowable to human beings on Earth. According to Newton, no fundamental physical difference existed between Earth and sky, and an understanding of what happened in the heavens was within the grasp of human comprehension.

The use of the telescope as an investigative tool and the decisive role it played in developing Newtonian physics deeply impressed natural philosophers, as scientists were then known. Some historians of science believe the telescope, in effect, ushered in the scientific revolution. In biology, anatomy, botany, and other scientific disciplines, natural philosophers adopted a scien-

No one is certain who invented the telescope. One of the earliest models—which Galileo used in 1609—was a refracting instrument, with glass lenses that bent light to magnify the image. By the late 1600's, astronomers had added small, precise measuring instruments to the telescope's *focal plane,* the point at which the rays of light converge. This improvement allowed scientists to accurately compile dimensions and distances within the known solar system.

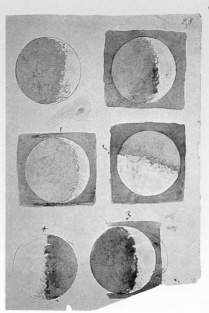

Galileo's sketches of the moon (left). An early telescope built by Galileo (above).

tific method that sought to describe the natural world not through intellectual speculation but through hands-on observation. The assumption underlying this new way of looking at the universe was a new way of thinking about the universe: The more human beings seek, the more they find. Until the invention of the telescope, the number of objects visible in the night sky remained always the same. Armed with the telescope, human beings discovered more and more about the heavens and developed the idea that more surprises were in store.

Astronomers in the 100 years following the invention of the telescope discovered five satellites around Saturn, as well as rings around that planet and spots on the sun. By the end of the 1600's, they referred to the sun, the planets, and moons collectively as a "solar system."

Beyond the solar system

In the 1770's, the German-born, British astronomer William Herschel began an ambitious series of surveys of the so-called stellar "sphere." By counting and classifying the population of stars in various directions, he hoped to provide the kind of three-dimensional view of the universe that previous generations of astronomers had given to the solar system itself. In 1781, during a routine sweep of the sky, he found a new planet, Uranus.

This discovery brought Herschel international renown and the security of a government salary for life, allowing him to build more powerful telescopes.

British astronomer William Herschel (1738-1822) discovered Uranus and observed faint smudges called *nebulae* at the farthest edge of the visible universe. The discovery convinced later astronomers that there were celestial bodies beyond the solar system.

Herschel concluded, after dozens of years and thousands of nights of investigation, that the stars visible from Earth are part of a single *galaxy*, or star system, shaped like a flat, spherical disk that came to be called the Milky Way. Herschel despaired, however, in accomplishing his original intention of surveying the "stellar sphere." No matter how large a telescope he built, no matter how deep into the night sky he probed, he always found more stars.

At the farthest limits of his vision, Herschel also found faint smudges known as nebulae (from the Latin for "clouds"). Were these nebulae located within the Milky Way Galaxy or were they outside it? Throughout the 1800's, astronomers debated the issue. By the early 1900's, most astronomers concluded that the nebulae were part of the Milky Way and that our galaxy was the universe in its entirety.

George Ellery Hale, an American astronomer and visionary, helped astronomers move beyond the edge of the Milky Way. In the early 1900's, Hale raised the funds and oversaw the construction of some of the largest telescopes in the world. The 100-inch (2.5 meter) telescope on Mount Wilson in California was one of these. Using the Mount Wilson instrument in 1923, American astronomer Edwin Hubble proved that at least some nebulae are in fact galaxies entirely separate from, and equal in magnitude to, the Milky Way. This discovery suggested that the universe was swimming with galaxies. In 1929, Hubble made another revolutionary discovery. He found that the galaxies are racing away from one another. The farther apart they are, the faster they appear to be receding. In other words, the universe is expanding.

The big bang

A universe that is getting bigger must be expanding from something. In the 1940's and 1950's, U.S. physicists George Gamow, Ralph Alpher, and Robert Herman used mathematics to work backward through time. They hypothesized the existence of an infinitely dense bundle of energy from which the universe emerged in one monumental expulsion of energy, which came to be called the big bang.

It was a novel theory. The one human perception of the universe that had remained unchanged since the invention of the telescope was that the universe had always looked pretty much the way it does now. According to the big bang theory, however, the universe was more than Newton's clockworklike cosmos, with its gravitational tugs and pulls working together to maintain an intricate and eternal balance. The big bang added the dimension of time to the dimension of distance, which Galileo had shown existed in the solar system, Herschel had found in the galaxy, and Hubble in the universe.

Soon, *cosmologists* (scientists who study the structure and growth of the universe) found they could test the big bang hypothesis, using a new form of astronomy—

The widespread use of the reflecting telescope in the late 1700's allowed astronomers to look beyond the solar system. The reflecting telescope uses a mirror instead of a glass lens, shifting the emphasis of the instrument from magnification to light collection. The more light a telescope collects, the deeper into space an astronomer can look.

In the mid-1800's, telescopes were equipped with photographic equipment. Photographic plates both preserved images—allowing many astronomers to view the image—and collected more light, allowing astronomers to see even deeper into space.

Herschel's drawings of nebulae (left), published in 1814. Herschel's 40-foot (12-meter) reflecting telescope (below).

American astronomer Edwin Hubble (below) made observations of galaxy M31 (right) in 1923 that helped prove some nebulae are galaxies beyond the Milky Way.

6-Oct 1923

nonoptical astronomy. The first types of telescopes were called optical telescopes. They allowed astronomers to see celestial objects that give off rays, or waves, of visible light. In the late 1800's, scientists learned that light waves are just one type of electromagnetic radiation, which consists of waves of electric and magnetic energy. Some waves are long; others, short. The entire range of electromagnetic waves is called the electromagnetic spectrum. The shorter wavelengths of the spectrum are gamma rays, X rays, and ultraviolet light. The longer wavelengths are infrared rays, microwaves, and radio waves. Astronomers then found they could build telescopes that would "see" in other wavelengths of the electromagnetic spectrum.

In the 1930's, radio engineer Karl Jansky made one of the first discoveries in nonoptical astronomy—accidentally. Using a 13-foot (4-meter) antenna to search for the source of annoying static in radio transmissions, Jansky learned that the galaxy is a source of radio waves.

In 1965, American astronomers Arno Penzias and Robert Wilson, using a radio antenna not much taller than Jansky's, found evidence supporting the big bang theory. They discovered diffuse radio waves arriving at Earth from all directions in space. The radio waves, now called the *cosmic microwave background radiation*, were made up of wavelengths corresponding to the cool temperature that theorists expected of the remnants of the big bang. They were seeing leftover radiation from the birth of the universe.

Although radio waves and optical waves penetrate the Earth's atmosphere, other types of radiation—infrared, ultraviolet, X rays, and gamma radiation—do not. Astronomers were able to look at the universe by detecting these other forms of radiation once the space age began. They launched orbiting telescopes that could see in all wavelengths of the electromagnetic spectrum and found very mysterious objects in deep space.

In the 1960's, radio astronomers discovered *quasars* (remote, starlike sources of previously unthinkable levels of energy) and *pulsars* (collapsed stars that rotate dozens and even hundreds of times each second). Studies of X rays from space revealed *black holes* (collections of matter so gravitationally dense that light cannot escape). In the 1990's, astronomers tracking the sources of gamma rays found *hypernovas* (mysterious explosions that momentarily generate more energy than anything in the history of the universe, other than the big bang). Also in the 1990's, amazing images were returned by an orbiting optical telescope, the Hubble Space Telescope. The Hubble Space Telescope found evidence that the universe contains 125 billion galaxies—not 10 billion, as previously estimated.

Closer to Earth, exploration of our solar system was intense during the same period. In 1969, U.S. astronauts landed on the moon. By the late 1900's, robotic spacecraft had landed on Mars and orbited or flown by all the other planets in the solar system except Pluto, the farthest planet from Earth. Space probes and powerful ground-based telescopes detected rings around Jupiter, Uranus, and Neptune; dozens of new moons around planets throughout the solar system; hundreds of icy asteroids in an area beyond Neptune known as the Kuiper belt. And astronomers discovered many single planets around other stars in the galaxy.

In the final decades of the 1900's, a computer innovation called a charge-coupled device (CCD) improved the light-collecting capacity of telescopes from 2 percent of available light to more than 80 percent. Computers also helped revolutionize mirror design, increasing the light-collecting surfaces of ground-based telescopes, and made possible space-based telescopes, including the Hubble Space Telescope.

The Hubble Space Telescope (below).

The Hubble Space Telescope in 1996 revealed the most distant galaxies in the universe (above)—and thus those farthest back in time, because of the time it took for their light to reach us.

American astronomers Arno Penzias (left) and Bob Wilson discovered cosmic background radiation in 1965, providing proof that the universe was formed in an enormous explosion called the big bang.

Questions of cosmic extistence

As astronomy pushed deeper into space—and farther back in time because of the time it takes light from the farthest objects to reach Earth—cosmologists began to address two fundamental questions of cosmic existence: Will the universe end? and what existed before the big bang?

The fate of the universe is of prime interest to cosmologists. Will it expand forever or will it one day collapse back in on itself? In 1998, independent teams of astronomers announced that the universe was expanding, but not in the way they had long assumed it would. They measured the rate of expansion by measuring the distance from Earth to certain bright, exploding stars, called supernovae. They then calculated the speed at which the galaxies where the supernovae reside were moving away from Earth. Instead of the expansion slowing down because of the pull of gravity, the rate of expansion seemed to be speeding up. The accelerating expansion and other factors led astronomers to hypothesize that the universe would continue to expand over time, eventually dwindling away into cold darkness.

Meanwhile, in 1979, U.S. physicist Alan Guth developed a theory that attempted to explain events at the other end of the cosmic timeline—the birth of the universe. According to Guth and other cosmologists, the universe arose out of literally nothing. Such a beginning is possible, according to *quantum physics*

Astronomers, starting with their detection of a mysterious galactic hiss in the 1930's, learned to "see" and interpret the invisible universe—every nonoptical stop along the electromagnetic spectrum: radio, infrared, ultraviolet, X ray, and gamma ray.

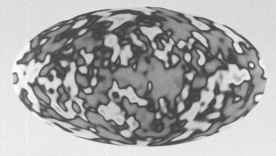

The Cosmic Background Explorer satellite (COBE, left), by detecting radio waves in 1992, made an image of the cosmic background radiation (above), remnants of energy left over from the formation of the universe by the big bang.

(the study of how matter behaves in the unimaginably small world inside the atom and at the high energies that existed when the big bang occurred).

Guth proposed that during the big bang, in the first fraction of a second of the existence of the universe, it underwent a period of "inflation" during which its volume grew trillions upon trillions of times more than it has in the 13 billion years since. As Guth and other physicists developed the idea of inflation, they found compelling evidence to support it in 1992 data from the Cosmic Background Explorer satellite. The data showed subtle irregularities in the temperature of the background radiation that agreed precisely with what astronomers expected from the glow of hot matter in the inflationary universe. Inflation theory led Guth and other cosmologists to another realilzation: The forces that gave rise to our universe may be responsible for the existence of other universes, possibly an infinite number of universes.

Big Bang

Big Bang plus tiniest fraction of a second

Inflation

Big Bang plus 300,000 years

Big Bang plus 1.5 billion years

The new millennium

Astronomers at the end of the 1900's were faced with still another mystery—the mystery of the dark, or missing, matter. Beginning in the 1970's, researchers noticed that the gravitational push and pull of galaxies upon one another did not always correspond with their masses. According to these researchers, quantities of mass were "missing" from the universe. They looked for this missing mass with telescopes that could see the various wavelengths of the electromagnetic spectrum. But they could not find it. In fact, the stars, galaxies, dust, and other matter they could find accounted for only 1 to 10 percent of the universe. Ninety to 99 percent of the universe was "dark" and, therefore, unknown.

So, as astronomers contemplated the new millennium, they took pride in the astonishing changes their profession had wrought, both in humanity's perceptions of the universe and in its conceptions of how the universe works. But they felt humility in the thought that in a universe where 90 to 99 percent of the matter was unknown, their work had only begun. ■ ■ ■

By the end of the second millennium, astronomers believed that the universe exploded into being with the big bang and then expanded rapidly. The hot soup of energy and subatomic particles that was the early universe began to cool and condense, eventually forming galaxies and stars. In 1999, cosmologists were wondering whether ours is the only universe or if many others exist somewhere.

Australia

On Nov. 6, 1999, Australians voted in a referendum on whether the country would remain a constitutional monarchy or become a republic. Australia continued to enjoy prosperity during 1999, despite the economic difficulties of its main Asian trading partners. In June, the Senate passed legislation to introduce Australia's first consumption tax, a 10-percent levy on all goods and services. In September, Australia led an international peacekeeping force into East Timor to try to reestablish order.

The republic question. On November 6, Australians voted in a referendum on a proposal to change Australia, a Commonwealth with ties to the British Crown, into a republic. The Australian Labor Party and much of the Liberal-National Party coalition Cabinet, including Prime Minister John Howard's deputy, Peter Costello, supported the campaign for a yes vote.

Voters were asked whether they supported an act "to alter the Constitution to establish the Commonwealth of Australia as a Republic, with the Queen and Governor General being replaced by a President appointed by a two-thirds majority of members of the Commonwealth Parliament." A voter survey on November 6 showed that 75 percent of the voters who supported a republic wanted a direct vote for a president. Many people disliked the proposed form of government, in which Parliament would choose the president.

Any change to the Australian Constitution requires both the support of a majority of voters in a referendum and the support of a majority of voters in at least four of Australia's six states. In the November referendum, only 45 percent of the voters nationwide and a majority of voters in the state of Victoria supported the change. People in favor of a republic, however, vowed to continue to work for a change in the government.

In March, Prime Minister John Howard, who opposed the proposed change in government, presented a new preamble to Australia's Constitution, which he had worked out with the help of Australian poet Les Murray. The preamble was criticized by Aboriginal groups for failing to acknowledge the "custodianship" of the continent by Australia's original inhabitants. Feminist groups objected to Howard's use of the word *mateship,* and atheists objected to the mention of the word *God.* The final text read as follows:

> With hope in God, the Commonwealth of Australia is constituted as a democracy with a federal system of government to serve the common good.

We the Australian people commit ourselves to this Constitution:
- proud that our national unity has been forged by Australians from many ancestries;
- never forgetting the sacrifices of all who defended our country and our liberty in time of war;
- upholding freedom, tolerance, individual dignity and the rule of law;
- honoring Aborigines and Torres Strait Islanders, the nation's first people, for their deep kinship with their lands and for their ancient and continuing cultures which enrich the life of our country;
- recognizing the nation-building contribution of generations of immigrants;
- mindful of our responsibility to protect our unique natural environment;
- supportive of the achievement as well as equality of opportunity for all;
- and valuing independence as dearly as the national spirit which binds us together in both adversity and success.

Sixty percent of Australia's voters rejected the preamble, a margin even wider than the vote against the republic.

Aborigines. In August, Australia's first inhabitants gained an important new voice in Parliament when Aden Ridgeway, a member of the Australian Democrat Party, took his seat in the Senate. He was only the second Aboriginal Senator to be elected. Senator Ridgeway played an important part in negotiations with John Howard over the wording of a historic statement passed by the Parliament in August. Howard had steadfastly refused

Blackhawk helicopters land Australian troops in East Timor in September. Australians led a multinational United Nations peacekeeping force to halt the violence that broke out following a referendum in which the East Timorese voted overwhelmingly for independence from Indonesia.

to apologize or use the word *sorry* in connection with Australia's past treatment of Aborigines. However, the two men agreed on a declaration of "sincere regret" for past injustices. Many observers saw this compromise as offering hope that white and Aboriginal Australians could reach a final agreement on reconciliation that encompassed both changes of attitude and concrete compensations and reforms that had been discussed for many years.

The economy. Australia's economy hit new records during 1999. On March 23, the country's leading stock indicator, the all ordinaries index,

broke the 3,000 barrier for the first time. Treasurer Peter Costello, in his 1999-2000 budget, forecast an economic growth rate of more than 3.5 percent, inflation below 2 percent, and a large surplus. During 1999, unemployment in Australia dropped to around 7 percent, a 10-year low. The only negative economic indicator was a current account, or trade, deficit as high as 6 percent of the gross domestic product (GDP), as imports continued to exceed exports. GDP is the value of all goods and services produced in a country in a given year.

Early in 1999, a proposed goods-and-services tax (GST), which had been one of the main planks

Members of the Australian House of Representatives

The House of Representatives of the 39th Parliament convened on Nov. 10, 1998. As of Dec. 15, 1999, the House of Representatives consisted of the following members: 66 Australian Labor Party, 64 Liberal Party of Australia, 16 National Party of Australia, 1 independent, and 1 vacancy. This table shows each legislator and party affiliation. An asterisk (*) denotes those who served in the 38th Parliament.

Australian Capital Territory
Annette Ellis, A.L.P.*
Bob McMullan, A.L.P.*

New South Wales
Tony Abbott, L.P.*
Anthony Albanese, A.L.P.*
John Anderson, N.P.*
Peter Andren, Ind.*
Larry Anthony, N.P.*
Bruce Baird, L.P.
Kerry Bartlett, L.P.*
Bronwyn Bishop, L.P.*
Laurie Brereton, A.L.P.*
Alan Cadman, L.P.*
Ross Cameron, L.P.*
Ian Causley, N.P.*
Janice Crosio, A.L.P.*
John Fahey, L.P.*
Laurie Ferguson, A.L.P.*
Timothy Fischer, N.P.*
Joel Fitzgibbon, A.L.P.*
Joanna Gash, L.P.*
Jill Hall, A.L.P.
Michael Hatton, A.L.P.*
Kelly Hoare, A.L.P.
Joe Hockey, L.P.*
Colin Hollis, A.L.P.*
Bob Horne, A.L.P.
John Howard, L.P.*
Kay Hull, N.P.
Julia Irwin, A.L.P.
Jackie Kelly, L.P.*
Mark Latham, A.L.P.*
Tony Lawler, N.P.
Michael Lee, A.L.P.*
Jim Lloyd, L.P.*
Stephen Martin, A.L.P.*
Robert McClelland, A.L.P.*
Leo McLeay, A.L.P.*
Daryl Melham, A.L.P.*
Allan Morris, A.L.P.*
Frank Mossfield, A.L.P.*
John Murphy, A.L.P.
Gary Nairn, L.P.*
Garry Nehl, N.P.*
Brendan Nelson, L.P.*
Tanya Plibersek, A.L.P.
Roger Price, A.L.P.*
Philip Ruddock, L.P.*
Stuart St. Clair, N.P.
Alby Schultz, L.P.
Andrew Thomson, L.P.*
Mark Vaile, N.P.*
Danna Vale, L.P.*

Northern Territory
Warren Snowdon, A.L.P.

Queensland
Arch Bevis, A.L.P.*
Mal Brough, L.P.*
Kay Elson, L.P.*
Craig Emerson, A.L.P.
Warren Entsch, L.P.*
Teresa Gambaro, L.P.*
Gary Hardgrave, L.P.*
David Jull, L.P.*
Robert Katter, N.P.*
De-Anne Kelly, N.P.*
Cheryl Kernot, A.L.P.
Peter Lindsay, L.P.*
Kirsten Livermore, A.L.P.
Ian Macfarlane, L.P.
Margaret May, L.P.
John Moore, L.P.*
Paul Neville, N.P.*
Bernie Ripoll, A.L.P.
Kevin Rudd, A.L.P.
Con Sciacca, A.L.P.
Bruce Scott, N.P.*
Peter Slipper, L.P.*
Alexander Somlyay, L.P.*
Kathy Sullivan, L.P.*
Wayne Swan, A.L.P.
Cameron Thompson, L.P.
Warren Truss, N.P.*

South Australia
Neil Andrew, L.P.*
David Cox, A.L.P.
Alexander Downer, L.P.*
Trish Draper, L.P.*
Martyn Evans, A.L.P.*
Christine Gallus, L.P.*
Christopher Pyne, L.P.*
Rodney Sawford, A.L.P.*
Patrick Secker, L.P.
Andrew Southcott, L.P.*
Barry Wakelin, L.P.*
Trish Worth, L.P.*

Tasmania
Dick Adams, A.L.P.*
Duncan Kerr, A.L.P.*
Michelle O'Byrne, A.L.P.
Harry Quick, A.L.P.*
Sid Sidebottom, A.L.P.

Victoria
Kevin Andrews, L.P.*
Fran Bailey, L.P.*
Phillip Barresi, L.P.*
Bruce Billson, L.P.*
Anna Burke, A.L.P.
Bob Charles, L.P.*
Peter Costello, L.P.*
Simon Crean, A.L.P.*
Michael Danby, A.L.P.
Martin Ferguson, A.L.P.*
John Forrest, N.P.*
Petro Georgiou, L.P.*
Steve Gibbons, A.L.P.
Julia Gillard, A.L.P.
Alan Griffin, A.L.P.*
David Hawker, L.P.*
Harry Jenkins, A.L.P.*
David Kemp, L.P.*
Louis Lieberman, L.P.*
Jenny Macklin, A.L.P.*
Stewart McArthur, L.P.*
Peter McGauran, N.P.*
Peter Nugent, L.P.*
Gavan O'Connor, A.L.P.*
Neil O'Keefe, A.L.P.*
Peter Reith, L.P.*
Michael Ronaldson, L.P.*
Nicola Roxon, A.L.P.
Bob Sercombe, A.L.P.*
Sharman Stone, L.P.*
Lindsay Tanner, A.L.P.*
Andrew Theophanous, A.L.P.*
Kelvin Thomson, A.L.P.*
Gregory Wilton, A.L.P.*
Michael Wooldridge, L.P.*
Christian Zahra, A.L.P.

Western Australia
Kim Beazley, A.L.P.*
Julie Bishop, L.P.
Graham Edwards, A.L.P.
Jane Gerick, A.L.P.
Barry Haase, L.P.
Carmen Lawrence, A.L.P.*
Jann McFarlane, A.L.P.
Judi Moylan, L.P.*
Geoffrey Prosser, L.P.*
Stephen Smith, A.L.P.*
Wilson Tuckey, L.P.*
Mal Washer, L.P.
Kim Wilkie, A.L.P.
Daryl Williams, L.P.*

of the Liberal Party government's platform in the 1998 elections, was in danger of losing in the Senate, where the government did not have a majority. In May 1999, Brian Harradine, an independent Senator from Tasmania, who held the balance of power in the Senate, announced that he could not support the tax. The Australian Democrats had promised to support the GST in general but to oppose a tax on food and books. In negotiations with the governing coalition, Democrat leader Meg Lees worked out a compromise that included books and prepared food as taxable items but excluded fresh food. The compromise gave rise to problems in defining exempt and taxable foods. For example, the final legislation determined that pieces of cooked chicken would be taxed, but whole cooked chicken would not. The Democrats, in return for their support, received the promise of substantial funding for addressing environmental problems. The legislation was passed on June 28 and was scheduled to take effect July 1, 2000. In September 1999, the government backed other proposed changes in taxation laws, including a 50-percent cut in the capital gains tax.

Industry. On September 30, BHP, one of Australia's leading corporations, closed its steel plant in Newcastle, New South Wales, after 84 years. The company blamed low worldwide steel prices. Several hundred of the remaining 1,450 workers were transferred to other plants, and BHP was exploring the conversion of the steel works to a container-shipping facility.

Olympic preparations. The Olympics made headlines as Sydney prepared for the summer games in 2000. On March 6, 1999, the main Olympic venue, Stadium Australia, was inaugurated with two Rugby League football games attended by more than 104,000 people. Spectators pronounced the new stadium a great success. The stadium later hosted a large pop concert, an international soccer match, and a Rugby Union match between Australia and New Zealand. A record crowd of 107,000 people watched the Wallabies defeat the All Blacks and wrest the coveted Bledisloe Cup from New Zealand. In August, the new Olympic swimming pool was tested at the Pan-Pacific Swimming Championships as large crowds watched Australia's latest swimming star, Ian Thorpe, set world records.

The Olympic Games also attracted less favorable publicity in 1999. In February and March, Tom Sheridan, a former auditor general for South Australia, led an inquiry into the methods Sydney used to win its bid for the games. The investigation revealed that before the final vote was taken, the Olympic committee considering Sydney's bid had been promised $2 million to help African athletes. Critics also questioned the conduct of Phil Coles, an Australian representative on the International Olympic Committee (IOC). In February, investigators accused Coles of accepting trips and hospitality from the organizers of the 2002 Winter Games in Salt Lake City, Utah. In March 1999, they accused Coles of accepting expensive jewelry from the organizers of an unsuccessful bid by Athens to host the 1996 games. In May 1999, the IOC criticized Coles for passing information on how fellow IOC members voted to the organizers of the Salt Lake City Winter Games. Although Coles maintained that he had done nothing wrong, he resigned from the Sydney Olympic Games Committee in June. He continued to hold his position with IOC.

In June, the Australian media criticized Ric Birch, the director of the opening ceremony in Sydney in 2000, for inviting marching bands from the United States and Japan in preference to Australian bands. When the Sydney committee withdrew the invitations, U.S. band organizers threatened to sue for damages. The committee compromised by adding musicians from 20 countries on 6 continents to the 1,300 U.S. and 200 Japanese band members and increased Australian participants to 900.

In October 1999, a Sydney newspaper revealed that less than 10 percent of tickets to Olympic events had been made available to the Australian public for many popular events, such as the opening of the games and the swimming and gymnastic meets. The rest had already been set aside for members of the Olympic organization, sponsors, athletes, and wealthy buyers, who were being offered tickets at up to four times the ordinary price.

State elections. Labor premier Bob Carr was reelected as premier of the New South Wales Parliament on March 27 with an increased majority. David Oldfield, a leading member of the One Nation Party, known for its extreme views on race and immigration, was elected to the state's upper house. On September 18, voters in Victoria turned against Premier Jeff Kennett's Liberal-National coalition government. Steve Bracks, leader of Victoria's Labor Party, became premier in October with the support of three independents.

Foreign affairs. In March, Steve Pratt and Peter Wallace, two members of the charity Care Australia, were arrested in the Yugoslav province of Serbia on charges of spying. The president of the charity, former Prime Minister Malcolm Fraser, visited Belgrade twice to try to persuade Serb authorities to release the men, who were sentenced to prison by a military court in May. They were finally released in September.

The first of 4,000 refugees from the Yugoslav province of Kosovo arrived in Sydney in May and were assigned to temporary lodging at several sites, including converted army bases. In June, a group of refugees refused to stay in old army barracks in Singleton, New South Wales, claiming the

A bull on the streets of Sydney, Australia, in November sports a banner protesting the appointment of Prince Charles as British beef ambassador, a position requiring him to lobby against importing Australian beef to Europe. The protest was indicative of efforts made by many Australians in 1999 to break political ties with the British monarchy.

accommodations were substandard. After a cease-fire was concluded in June, most of the refugees returned to Kosovo, although a few stayed until the Australian immigration department in October pressured them to go home and free the space for refugees from East Timor.

In April, Prime Minister John Howard offered Indonesian President B. J. Habibie the use of Australian police to assist with peacekeeping in East Timor in late August when the people of East Timor were scheduled to vote in a referendum on independence from Indonesia. Unarmed police were sent to help supervise the August 30 vote. As returns favoring independence mounted, violence broke out, and many refugees, including Nobel Peace Prize winner Bishop Carlos Belo, fled to Darwin in Australia's Northern Territory. In mid-September, Australia began mobilizing 4,500 troops to lead a peacekeeping force into East Timor. Although the move was approved by both the United Nations and the Indonesian government, Indonesian leaders and protesters criticized Australia for interference in Indonesia's internal affairs.

Drug legislation. Health professionals and drug addicts and their families met with religious and political leaders to discuss Australia's worsening drug problems at a May drug summit in Sydney. The New South Wales state government considered legislation in November that would allow Australia's first legal heroin-injecting room in Kings Cross, an area of Sydney where addicts congregated. The legislation would make it legal to provide a place for addicts to inject themselves but would not provide or legalize the sale of heroin. The aim of the experiment was to determine whether injecting rooms would decrease deaths from overdoses. Victoria's premier, Steve Bracks, promised to conduct a similar experiment.

Storm. On April 14, a freak hailstorm hit parts of Sydney, smashing tile roofs and car windows. Insurers estimated damage at Australian $1.6 billion. Insurance companies handled more than 100,000 vehicle claims and thousands of claims for houses. Many businesses were also damaged.

Illegal immigrants. On March 12, a local news agent alerted authorities that 26 illegal Chinese immigrants had landed near Cairns in northern Queensland. On April 10, a rusting boat with 60 Chinese immigrants ran aground at Scotts Head in New South Wales. On May 9, 69 Chinese were found hidden on a large cargo ship near Jervis Bay in New South Wales. On May 27, 78 Chinese landed from a fishing boat on Cape York in Queensland. On June 4, authorities intercepted a boat carrying 108 Chinese near Broken Bay, north of Sydney. ☐ Brian Kennedy

See also **Asia; Australia, Prime Minister of; Indonesia.**

The Ministry of Australia*

John Howard—prime minister

John Anderson—minister for transport and regional services; deputy prime minister

Peter Costello—treasurer

Mark Vaile—minister for trade

Alexander Downer—minister for foreign affairs

Robert Hill—minister for the environment and heritage; leader of the government in the Senate

Richard Alston—minister for communications, information technology, and the arts; deputy leader of the government in the Senate

Peter Reith—minister for employment, workplace relations, and small business; leader of the House

Jocelyn Newman—minister for family and community services

John Moore—minister for defence

Michael Wooldridge—minister for health and aged care

John Fahey—minister for finance and administration

David Kemp—minister for education, training, and youth affairs; vice president of the Executive Council

Nick Minchin—minister for industry, science, and resources

Daryl Williams—attorney general

Philip Ruddock—minister for immigration and multicultural affairs

Warren Truss—minister for agriculture, fisheries, and forestry

*As of Nov. 1, 1999.

Premiers of Australian states

State	Premier
New South Wales	Bob Carr
Queensland	Peter Beattie
South Australia	John Olsen
Tasmania	Jim Bacon
Victoria	Steve Bracks
Western Australia	Richard Court

Government leaders of Australian mainland territories

Australian Capital Territory	Kate Carnell
Northern Territory	Denis Burke

Australia, Prime Minister of. John Howard, leader of the Liberal-National Party coalition, played an important role on the world stage in 1999. He negotiated with Indonesian President B. J. Habibie to create a ballot measure that would allow people in the Indonesian province of East Timor to vote on independence. When a vote for independence in August resulted in violence, Howard rallied the support of the Australian government to provide troops and resources for a United Nations peacekeeping mission.

Although Howard is a conservative politician opposed to changing the Australian Constitution, he allowed a public referendum on whether the nation should become a republic rather than remain a constitutional monarchy with Queen Elizabeth II of the United Kingdom as head of state. He also proposed a new preamble to the Constitution that recognized the diversity of Australians. Voters rejected both measures.

Howard pursued tax reform in 1999 and won approval for a 10-percent goods-and-services tax (GST), the first consumption tax in Australia's history. In June, Howard and the Australian Democrats, though they held enough votes to pass the legislation, worked out a compromise of the GST bill that exempted fresh food and limited tax rebates on diesel fuel. □ Brian Kennedy

See also **Australia; Indonesia; United Nations.**

Australian rules football. More than 94,000 people watched the 1999 Australian Football League (AFL) grand final between the North Melbourne Kangaroos and the Carlton Blues at the Melbourne Cricket Ground on September 25. The Kangaroos defeated the Blues by 35 points. The Kangaroos scored 19 goals and 10 behinds for 124 points. The Blues finished with 12 goals and 17 behinds for 89 points.

Shannon Grant of the Kangaroos kicked four goals and won the Norm Smith Medal for the best player on the ground. Shane Crawford of Hawthorn captured the Brownlow Medal for the best and fairest player of the 1999 AFL season.

Record breaker. Sydney Swans player Tony Lockett kicked his 1,300th goal on June 6, breaking the AFL all-time goalkicking record. Lockett later announced his retirement and played his last game for the Swans at the Sydney Cricket Ground on August 15.

Local premierships. Port Adelaide won their 36th South Australian premiership, scoring 14.17 (101) over Norwood 14.9 (93). In Western Australia, West Perth 14.13 (97) beat South Fremantle 11.6 (78). In the Tasmanian Football League, Glenorchy 15.9 (99) beat the Northern Bombers 7.11 (53). In New South Wales, Campbelltown 18.5 (113) defeated Balmain 13.13 (99).
□ Brian Kennedy

Austria.

Austria. The extreme right-wing Freedom Party upset political stability in Austria in 1999 when it finished second in a national election on October 3. The result dealt a blow to the Social Democratic Party of Chancellor Viktor Klima and the conservative People's Party, which had dominated Austrian politics since World War II (1939-1945).

Klima's Social Democrats took 65 seats in the 183-seat parliament, the party's worst showing since World War II. Klima refused to form a coalition with the Freedom Party, and political experts predicted it would take the chancellor months to form a new government. The People's Party, which came in third place by just 415 votes, had pledged it would not participate in a coalition government if the party failed to finish second.

The Freedom Party won 52 seats in parliament, the same number as the People's Party. The election results capped a steady rise in support for the Freedom Party throughout the 1990's. Party leader Joerg Haider had stirred controversy by calling Nazi Germany's employment policies "sound." He favored an immigration freeze and sharp tax cuts and opposed the European Union's expansion into Eastern Europe.

Avalanches in the Austrian Alps killed 38 people in 1999 and trapped thousands of tourists for a week in February. □ Tom Buerkle

See also **Europe; Weather.**

Automobile.

Automobile. Cars and light trucks sold at a rapid pace in 1999. Automobile industry analysts predicted in late 1999 that a record 17 million vehicles would be sold on the U.S. market during the year. The previous sales record, 16.1 million vehicles, was set in 1986. Through September 1999, sales of new vehicles totaled 12.9 million units, or about 1.2 million units more than in the same period in 1998. Rising sales helped nearly all automakers. Through the first nine months of 1999, only Mazda and Saturn sold fewer cars than during the same period in 1998. Mazda sales were down about 3,400 vehicles, and Saturn sales were down about 1,360 vehicles.

American motorists in 1999 continued to buy minivans, pickups, and sport-utility vehicles in large numbers. Sales of light trucks totaled 6.2 million by September, 12.1 percent more than for the same period in 1998. Despite the increase, light truck sales still trailed car sales in 1999. Automobile sales totaled 6.7 million through the end of September 1999.

Top sellers. The Toyota Camry led all car sales in 1999 for the third consecutive year. For the 1999 model year, Camry sales reached 476,752 units. Ford Motor Company's F-series truck continued to lead overall vehicle sales. The light truck's sales hit 867,441 units for the 1999 model year.

Part of the Austrian village of Galtur is struck by an avalanche in February. Avalanches in the Austrian Alps in February killed 38 people and trapped thousands of tourists.

Jaguar in 1999 introduced the S-type sedan (foreground), which was styled on a classic Jaguar from the 1960's (background). The 1999 S-type came equipped with a standard 6-cylinder engine and voice-activated audio, phone, and climate controls.

Company news. Ford's sales in the U.S. market grew to 3.1 million units by September 30, 5.2 percent ahead of the same period in 1998. Ford's gain was due in part to better sales from such vehicles as the Mustang, Ranger, and F-series truck.

Ford officials in January 1999 announced plans to buy Volvo Cars, the automotive branch of Volvo AB of Sweden, for $6.4 billion. The acquisition of the Swedish car company boosted Ford's entries in the luxury car market, which included the Lincoln. Automobile analysts in 1999 predicted additional combinations in the auto industry in the 2000's, with smaller automakers becoming part of the industry's leaders.

Volvo's worldwide sales totaled nearly 400,000 units in 1998 compared with Ford's sales of 6.8 million. Through September 1999, Ford reported earnings of $5.4 billion, compared with $4.9 billion in the same period in 1998. In 1999, Ford introduced its new small car, the Focus. Ford also announced it would build a luxury light truck, the Lincoln Blackwood, at a plant near Kansas City, Missouri.

General Motors Corporation (GM) recovered in 1999 from long and costly strikes in 1998. Sales at General Motors rose to 3.8 million units through September 1999, 11.6 percent ahead of the same period in 1998. Popular GM vehicles in 1999 included Chevrolet's Silverado pickup, Buick Century, and Pontiac Grand Prix. GM's sales increases helped boost the company's profits to $4.8 billion through September 30, compared with $1.2 billion for the same period in 1998.

In May 1999, GM spun off its parts-making unit, Delphi Automotive Systems Corporation. Company officials announced that they planned to focus GM's attention on building new cars and trucks. GM's new entries in 1999 included a redesigned Pontiac Bonneville and a Saturn mid-sized sedan and wagon called the L-series.

DaimlerChrysler AG reported high sales in 1999, the first full year of business since the merger of Chrysler Corporation and Daimler-Benz AG in 1998. Sales of the traditional Chrysler lines rose to 2 million units through September 1999, an increase of 7.5 percent from the same period in 1998. Chrysler's Jeep Grand Cherokee and Dodge Durango, both sport-utility vehicles, increased. Mercedes sales rose to 136,962 units through September 1999, a 9.5-percent increase. Through September, DaimlerChrysler AG reported a record net income of $4.9 billion, 12 percent ahead of its income for the same period in 1998.

In November 1999, Chrysler announced that it would close down production of the Plymouth in 2000 and begin to phase out production of the Breeze, Neon, Voyager minivan, and Prowler roadster. Chrysler officials reported that they would focus their attention on their other models.

U.S. CARS GET A NEW LOOK IN 1957

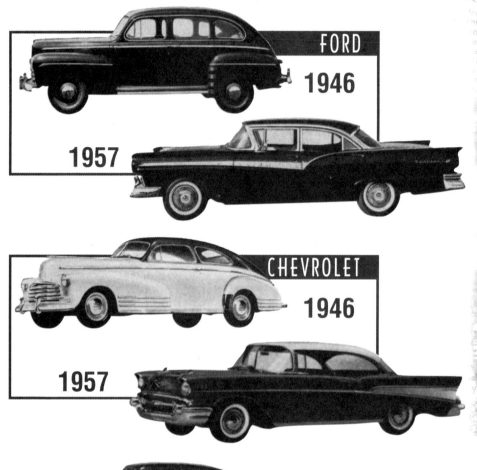

FORD

1946

1957

CHEVROLET

1946

1957

PLYMOUTH

1946

1957

Asian and European automakers. Both Toyota and Honda recorded strong sales increases in the United States in 1999. Toyota's sales through September 30 rose to 1.1 million units, 10.5 percent ahead of sales in 1998. Honda's sales through September 1999 totaled 818,932 units, 7.6 percent ahead of the total for the first nine months of 1998. Increased Camry sales assisted Toyota, while the Odyssey minivan helped Honda.

Honda announced plans in May 1999 to construct a $400-million automotive manufacturing plant in Alabama. In July, Honda unveiled a hybrid car, called the Insight, that used a gasoline engine and an electric motor to get an estimated 70 miles (112 kilometers) per gallon.

Volkswagen's U.S. sales rose to 239,382 units through September 1999, a 40 percent increase from the same period in 1998. The popularity of the Beetle, which was reintroduced in 1998, helped the European automaker.

Labor talks. The United Automobile Workers (UAW) union signed agreements in September and October 1999 with DaimlerChrysler, GM, and Ford. The agreements, which covered more than 400,000 union employees, ran for four years rather than the traditional three years. The contracts provided workers with annual 3-percent wage increases in all four years, a $1,350 signing bonus, and improved cost-of-living adjustments. UAW members at DaimlerChrysler ratified the agreement by an 86-percent majority; GM and Delphi workers by more than a 77-percent majority; and Ford members by an 85-percent majority.

Auto safety. Improving airbag safety continued to be an important issue for automakers and the National Highway Traffic Safety Administration (NHTSA) in 1999. The NHTSA sets and enforces safety requirements for automobiles and related products. On November 2, the NHTSA announced a proposal to ensure that future airbags did not pose an unreasonable risk of serious injury to occupants. The NHTSA reported that new, less-powerful airbags that were first installed in 1998-model cars and trucks had reduced the risk of injury and death. The agency recommended that automakers continue to explore new technologies to control airbag deployments.

The new regulations outlined a list of crash tests and other obstacles that airbags and vehicles would have to pass in order to meet standards. The new airbags would be phased in starting with model year 2003 vehicles and would be required on all model year 2006 cars and light trucks. Automakers in 1999 continued work on so-called "smart systems" that would detect the size of a passenger to properly inflate airbags.

☐ Mike Casey

See also **Transportation.**

Automobile racing. The rivalry between the Indy Racing League (IRL) and Championship Auto Racing Teams (CART) continued in 1999. The rift began in 1995 with the formation of the IRL, which raced under restrictions on cost and other factors that were intended to make less affluent teams more competitive. In its fourth year, the split continued to hurt both organizations, reducing attendance, television ratings, and sponsorship. In June 1999, the two groups held talks to resolve their differences, but few observers predicted that reconciliation was near.

Indianapolis 500. Kenny Brack, an ex-Formula One driver from Sweden, took the checkered flag at the 83rd Indianapolis 500 on May 30. Brack took the lead from Robby Gordon with one lap remaining, when Gordon ran out of fuel. The victory earned Brack's A.J. Foyt-owned team $1.5 million, its share of the $9-million purse.

The 1999 race was also the last Indianapolis 500 for veteran Arie Luyendyk, who had said months beforehand that he would make it his only start of 1999. The two-time Indy champion crashed, without injury, on the 118th lap. Luyendyk retired as the track's career money winner, with nearly $5.6 million.

IRL. Three spectators were killed and eight others were injured on May 1, during the Vision-Aire 500 in Concord, North Carolina, when a wheel and suspension parts flew off a car into the grandstand after a collision. The race was canceled and, in all subsequent IRL races, including the Indy 500, wheels on cars were fitted with synthetic cables designed to prevent similar incidents.

CART. A 20-event schedule of CART races in Canada, Australia, and Hawaii ran from March 21 to October 31. Juan Montoya, a 24-year-old rookie driver from Colombia, and Dario Franchitti of Pompano Beach, Florida, scored 212 points each, but Montoya took the season championship with seven victories to Franchitti's three. Greg Moore, a budding star on the CART circuit, was killed at Fontana, California, on October 31, in the final race of the season when his car veered off the track and struck a retaining wall.

NASCAR. The Winston Cup stock car series expanded from 33 to 34 races during the 1999 season. Jeff Gordon, the three-time Winston Cup champion, finished out of the top 20 in six races during the first half of the season. Gordon began the second half of the season trailing Dale Jarrett by 394 points and never caught up. Jarrett took the series championship with one race to go when he finished fifth in the Pennzoil 400 at Homestead, Florida, on November 14. Jarrett became Ford's first champion since 1992 and the third driver in the 1990's to wrap up the title before the last race of the season.

Formula One. The Grand Prix season consist-

The 1999 NASCAR Winston Cup champion, Dale Jarrett, hoists his championship trophy after the Pennzoil 400 in Homestead, Florida, on November 14. By finishing fifth in the race, Jarrett clinched the Winston Cup series with one race left in the season.

ed of 16 races—11 in Europe and one each in Australia, Brazil, Canada, Malaysia, and Japan. Mika Hakkinen of Finland retained his Formula One world driver's title in the final race of the season, the Japanese Grand Prix in Suzuka. Hakkinen finished the season just two points ahead of his chief rival, Eddie Irvine.

Endurance. Butch Leitzinger, Elliott Forbes-Robinson, Andy Wallace, and team owner Rob Dyson drove a Riley-and-Scott Ford to a rain-soaked victory in the 24 Hours at Daytona on Jan. 31, 1999. The Doyle-Risi team of Max Angelelli, Didier de Radigues, Allan McNish, and Wayne Taylor, driving a Can-Am Ferrari 333SP, swapped the lead with Dyson's team several times during the rainy night but finished second after losing several minutes during a pit stop. The winners covered 2,520.48 miles (4,055.45 kilometers) at an average of 104.9 miles (168.78 kilometers) per hour. On June 13, BMW scored its first victory in the Le Mans 24 Hours, with the driving trio of Pierluigi Martini of Italy, Joachim Winkelhock of Germany, and Yannick Dalmas of France.

Dragsters. The National Hot Rod Association (NHRA) sponsored a 23-race series for the second straight year in 1999. Mike Dunn in the top fuel division, John Force in funny cars, and Warren Johnson in the pro stock division were the season's champions. ☐ Ron Reid

Aviation. Booming airline traffic in 1999 led to overbooked flights, delays, frayed tempers, and even "air rage" assaults on airline staff by disgruntled passengers. In June, major airlines responded to months of U.S. Congressional hearings and the threat of a "passenger bill of rights" by announcing a Customers First program. In this voluntary measure, the airlines pledged to inform passengers of the lowest fares and provide better information about delays and cancellations.

Airlines also responded to public criticism by charging that federal air traffic control policies were responsible for flight delays that annually cost the airlines billions of dollars. In August, the U.S. Federal Aviation Administration (FAA), which regulates the airline industry and controls air traffic, announced a plan to reduce delays by coordinating all air traffic through its national command center in Herndon, Virginia.

American Airlines, based in Fort Worth, Texas, and London-based British Airways reported in July that they had scrapped their 1996 plan to form an alliance. The companies abandoned their plans because the British government demanded that the two companies give up some of their 267 landing slots at London's Heathrow Airport. The airlines did continue a multinational marketing alliance called Oneworld, which began in January 1999.

LINDBERGH'S ATLANTIC CONQUEST. [For] eight days [Charles Lindbergh] waited in New York for favorable weather reports. On May 20, although flying conditions might have been more favorable, he put four sandwiches and a bottle of water in his plane and at 7:52 a.m. stepped aboard. "I feel as though I had just heard the judge pronounce the death sentence," he said, "but when I land in Paris it will be as though I had a pardon from the governor. . . ."

The modest, unassuming youngster, anticipating no riotous interest abroad in his exploit, had secured from influential Americans six letters of identification and introduction to as many people in Paris, in the belief that no one could identify him when he landed. Just 33 hours 29 minutes after leaving New York, during which time he was followed in spirit by the best wishes, prayers, and harassing doubts of hundreds of millions in two continents, he landed, 10:21 p.m., Paris time, May 21, on Le Bourget Flying Field, outside of Paris, 3,610 miles from New York. Here a hundred thousand French people, crazed with joy, gave him a tumultuous welcome.

Charles Lindbergh and his airplane, the Spirit of St. Louis

Competition. Three low-fare airlines—Sunjet International of Orlando, Florida; Winair of Salt Lake City, Utah; and Kiwi International of Newark, New Jersey—declared bankruptcy in 1999. The failure of these airlines and others in recent years led officials at the U.S. Department of Transportation to express concerns that major airlines were protecting their hub airports by aggressively lowering fares to drive small airlines from the market. In May, the U.S. Department of Justice filed an antitrust lawsuit against American Airlines, alleging that the company used such practices at the Dallas-Fort Worth Airport.

In a July 1999 report, the National Research Council, a federal science and technology advisory group in Washington, D.C., proposed measures for ensuring competition. The council recommended eliminating the limits on the number of flights into major airports, because the limits allegedly bar new airlines from the market. The council also suggested that encouraging the use of secondary airports—rather than high-traffic airports—would help small airlines compete. According to the July report, charging high fees to airlines for using congested airports would encourage this transition.

Safety. In March, the U.S. National Transportation Safety Board (NTSB), which makes safety recommendations to the FAA, announced conclusions regarding the 1994 crash of a USAir (later US Airways) Boeing 737 near Pittsburgh, Pennsylvania, which killed all 132 people on board, and the 1991 crash of a United Airlines 737 at Colorado Springs, Colorado, which killed all 25 people on board. The NTSB concluded that in both cases the aircrafts' rudders suddenly moved all the way to one side, possibly opposite to the direction intended, causing the pilots to lose control. After the report, airlines began modifying the rudders on 737's and training pilots in ways to regain control of planes with malfunctioning rudders.

The cause of the September 1998 crash of a Swissair flight near Halifax, Nova Scotia, remained undetermined through 1999. Canadian investigators did determine that the metalized Mylar used as insulation contributed to the spread of the flames on the plane before the crash.

At the time of the Swissair crash, the flight was operating under a "codeshare" agreement with Atlanta, Georgia-based Delta Air Lines, meaning that some passengers held Delta tickets with a Delta flight number. Passengers in these circumstances do not always know they are scheduled to fly on another airline and may assume that a Delta plane ticket guarantees a Delta air safety record. In response to concerns by the U.S. Department of Defense, which purchases thousands of tickets for military personnel, seven major U.S. airlines agreed in August to conduct safety checks on foreign airlines with which they codeshare.

Accidents. Eleven people, including the flight captain, were killed in June when an American Airlines flight skidded off the end of a runway while landing in rain at Little Rock, Arkansas. While the precise cause was not determined, the NTSB noted that pilot fatigue may have contributed to the accident. Both pilots on the flight were close to the 14-hour workday limit when the accident occurred. The deaths were the first in U.S. commercial aviation in about 18 months.

An EgyptAir Boeing 767 plunged into the Atlantic Ocean off the coast of Massachusetts on October 31. All 217 people aboard were killed. Based on flight data and voice recordings, investigators for the NTSB and the U.S. Federal Bureau of Investigation suggested that a copilot may have caused the crash as an act of suicide. Many Egyptians and other Arabs criticized the conclusions as premature and reflecting a Western prejudice against Muslims.

A Federal District Court in Dallas in April fined the pilots' union of American Airlines $45.5 million for failing to force its members to comply with a court order to return to work. In February, more than 2,400 pilots called in sick, protesting the use of nonunion pilots from Reno Air, which American had acquired in 1998. ☐ Ian Savage

See also **Transportation.**

Azerbaijan. On April 17, 1999, the leaders of Azerbaijan, Georgia, and Ukraine inaugurated a new pipeline to carry Azerbaijani oil to Europe while bypassing Russia. The pipeline marked an important step in the development of Caspian Sea oil resources, which experts predicted will eventually be worth billions of dollars to Azerbaijan. In July, the British petroleum company BP Amoco PLC revealed that a natural gas deposit recently discovered in the Caspian Sea contained reserves of more than 15 trillion cubic feet (400 billion cubic meters) of natural gas.

Azerbaijan announced in April that it had withdrawn from the joint defense structure of the Commonwealth of Independent States (CIS). The CIS, created in 1991, had originally linked most of the former republics of the Soviet Union. Azerbaijan joined a new defense alliance with Georgia, Moldova, Ukraine, and Uzbekistan, which is supported by the North Atlantic Treaty Organization (NATO). Azerbaijan's defense minister said that Russia's support of Armenia in the ongoing conflict with Azerbaijan over the disputed region of Nagorno-Karabakh had pushed Azerbaijan closer to NATO. ☐ Steven L. Solnick

See also **Asia.**

Bahamas. See **West Indies.**

Bahrain. See **Middle East.**

Ballet. See **Dance.**

Bangladesh. Political demonstrations disrupted life in Bangladesh throughout 1999. An ongoing rivalry between Prime Minister Hasina Wajed and the prime minister she had replaced three years earlier, Khaleda Ziaur Rahman, known as Begum Zia, fueled the strife. In 1996, Hasina had led agitation that forced elections and brought her Awami League to power. In 1999, Begum Zia's Bangladesh National Party (BNP) led similar demonstrations to overturn Hasina's government.

In February, the BNP called a strike to dramatize its demand for removal of a high election official whom the BNP alleged was biased. The strike paralyzed Bangladesh for several days and sparked violence that left 6 people dead and some 200 injured. In April, the BNP staged another strike to protest shortages and a breakdown in law and order. At least 50 people were injured. In May, three other opposition parties joined the BNP protests, launching another cycle of civil disorder.

India controversy. Government initiatives for joint ventures with India provided more ammunition to the BNP and its allies, who are traditionally cool toward India. In June, Indian Prime Minister Atal Bihari Vajpayee visited Bangladesh's capital, Dhaka, to hold talks with Hasina and open direct bus service between Dhaka and Calcutta.

In late July, Hasina gave her approval for a study of a plan to allow India to transport goods through Bangladesh to India's nearly isolated northeastern provinces. The move led to further clashes between police and demonstrators, which resulted in the injury of at least 70 people.

Resources and economy. Foreign investors advised Petrobangla, Bangladesh's major energy company, to step up gas exploration in 1999. Energy experts speculated that Bangladesh held huge natural gas reserves, and economists noted that Bangladesh could reverse its trade imbalance with energy-hungry India by exporting gas to India. The Bangladeshi government, however, pulled back from a joint venture with India, fearing an attack from the opposition.

Bangladesh's economy grew by 5.2 percent in the fiscal year ending June 30, 1999, according to government estimates. Donors of foreign aid warned, however, that aid might be reduced if economic reforms were not speeded up.

Bumper rice and wheat harvests helped Bangladesh recover from record flooding resulting from the 1998 monsoon, which covered two-thirds of the country. The 1999 floods covered more than the one-third of Bangladesh's land that is normally inundated during the monsoon season.

A ferry boat sank in southern Bangladesh on May 8, killing approximately 200 people. A similar accident had killed 600 people in 1997.

☐ Henry S. Bradsher

See also **Asia; India.**

Traffic struggles through the flooded streets of Dhaka, Bangladesh's capital, after monsoon storms dumped more than 5 inches (128 millimeters) of rain in a 24-hour period in July. The flooding paralyzed Dhaka's transportation systems.

Bank. The Congress of the United States in 1999 overhauled one of the nation's fundamental banking laws. After years of debate and months of negotiations, Congress passed a compromise version of the Financial Services Modernization Act on November 4. President Bill Clinton signed the legislation into law on November 12.

The new law made it easier and cheaper for banks, securities firms, and insurers to enter each other's business. Analysts expected the legislation would speed the already fast pace of mergers and acquisitions among financial institutions.

Proponents of the bill argued that it would promote innovation in financial industries, reduce costs for consumers, and make U.S. financial companies stronger against overseas competitors. Consumer and civil rights groups contended that the new law failed to adequately protect banking customers' privacy or to provide safeguards against unsound banking practices. Community-rights groups also argued that the law weakened the government's ability to enforce fair-lending laws in poor neighborhoods.

Financial analysts noted that the law caught up with what federal banking regulators already permitted on a case-by-case basis. Under the old banking laws, a bank could buy securities firms only if those firms produced no more than 25 percent of the bank's total revenue. For example, federal regulators in 1997 allowed Bankers Trust New York Corpation of New York City to acquire Alex. Brown & Sons Inc., a stock-brokerage firm. In 1998, Citicorp of New York City and Travelers Insurance Group Inc. of Hartford, Connecticut, formed Citigroup Inc., with government approval.

Replacing Glass-Steagall. The new law replaced the Glass-Steagall Act of 1933, the primary law governing the businesses in which U.S. banks may engage. Passed in response to the stock market crash of 1929 and the economic depression that followed, Glass-Steagall prohibited banks from underwriting stocks and bonds or selling insurance policies. Many banks in the 1920's had put depositors' funds into riskier activities—for example, stocks—rather than more traditional mortgages and business loans. When the market crashed in 1929, untold numbers of bank depositors lost their savings.

Banks and other financial firms had contended that Glass-Steagall and the 1956 Bank Holding Company Act prevented them from keeping pace with changes in technology and in the way U.S. citizens save, invest, and borrow. Banks contended that Americans should be able to obtain many types of financial services, including banking, insurance, and investments, from one company. Previous efforts to amend the banking laws had

foundered amid concerns about increasing risks to consumers, resistance from civil rights and community-rights groups, and disputes between competing segments of the financial industry.

CRA controversy. Controversy over the Community Reinvestment Act (CRA) proved to be the biggest obstacle to passage of the new banking act. The CRA, passed in 1977, aimed to ensure that banks made loans in impoverished inner-city areas. Under the law, government regulators had to take a bank's CRA record into account when deciding whether to approve the bank's request to acquire another bank or open new branches.

Many banks complained that the CRA required too much record keeping and that community-rights groups were able to demand financial concessions from banks that were attempting to expand. Community-rights activists countered that without the law, banks would ignore inner-city markets, making it difficult for homeowners and businesses there to obtain credit.

Under the compromise negotiated for the new law, community groups must publicly disclose the ultimate uses of the money that banks make available to them to assist underserved communities in obtaining credit. The new law also eases regulatory scrutiny of smaller banks.

Oversight debate. Regulatory oversight of the banks provided another issue in the debate over the new law. Both the U.S. Federal Reserve System (the Fed), the central bank of the United States, and the Department of the Treasury insisted that they should have primary authority over banks. Under the new law, the Treasury's Office of the Comptroller of the Currency oversees national banks with subsidiaries that underwrite securities. The Fed has authority over bank affiliates that engage in riskier activities, such as insurance underwriting and real estate development. State governments retain

TIME CAPSULE 1933

BANK

FOR ONE WEEK, early in 1933, banking was at a standstill in the United States; no checks could be cashed, no money could be withdrawn, and few bills could be paid. This condition, which had come to a head as President Franklin Roosevelt was inaugurated on March 4, was the final great banking difficulty of the Depression. In spite of the seriousness of the situation, people did not panic, and when . . . the banks were again opened, public confidence was greater than it had been since the beginning of the Depression.

regulatory authority over insurers.

Earnings. A strong U.S. economy kept bank earnings at record levels for most of 1999. In the first six months of the year, the nation's 8,675 banks posted earnings of $34.9 billion, compared to $32 billion for the same period in 1998. The nation's 1,652 savings institutions reported $5.6 billion in earnings in the first half of 1999.

Interest rates. With the United States in its eighth consecutive year of economic expansion, the Fed increased interest rates three times in 1999 in an effort to keep inflation under control. Higher interest rates slow borrowing and economic growth. The Fed raised the federal funds rate, the rate the Fed's member banks charge one another for overnight loans, by one-quarter percentage point in June and another quarter point in August, to 5.25 percent. Although the Fed left the rate unchanged in October, it raised the rate one-quarter percentage point again in November, to 5.5 percent.

Biggest bank. In August, three Japanese banks—Dai-Ichi Kangyo Bank Ltd., Fuji Bank Ltd., and Industrial Bank of Japan Ltd.—announced plans to merge. The assets of the new bank, at least $1.3 trillion, top those of any financial institution in the world. ☐ Paulette Thomas

See also **Economics**.

Baseball. The New York Yankees' second straight sweep of the World Series, record-breaking hitting, and an umpires' strategy that backfired dominated headlines in Major League Baseball (MLB) during 1999. Baseball fans also witnessed thrilling post-season games and the first appearance of Pete Rose in a ball park in 10 years.

Pete Rose took part in an on-field ceremony before Game 2 of the World Series at Turner Field in Atlanta, Georgia, on October 24—the first time Rose had appeared in a ball park since he was banned from baseball in 1989 for betting on games. Rose, the all-time career hits leader, appeared as a member of the 30-man All-Century Team—a group of the greatest baseball players in history as selected by fans and a panel of baseball experts. Rose drew the longest, loudest ovation from fans during the ceremony. However, MLB Commissioner Bud Selig said he had no intention of reinstating Rose into baseball—a move that would be necessary before Rose could be eligible for entry into the Baseball Hall of Fame.

Hit records. Baseball offense surged for the second straight season in 1999 as MLB players—led by Mark McGwire of the St. Louis Cardinals and Sammy Sosa of the Chicago Cubs—hit a record 5,528 home runs, an average of 2.28 homers per game. Records were also set in 1999 for hits, total bases, runs, extra-base hits, singles,

BASEBALL

THE BIGGEST SPORTS HEADLINE of 1948 was the death of George Herman (Babe) Ruth, probably the most famous athlete who ever lived. People from all walks of life—and all nations—mourned when Ruth . . . died at the age of 53 after a lingering illness. Ruth, best described as the "eternal boy," was a hero to both royalty and paupers. His name was recognized by thousands who never had been inside a ball park.

Babe Ruth

and doubles. Critics suggested that hitting increased because baseballs were heavier or wound tighter than in previous years, but MLB officials announced that testing had revealed no statistical difference between 1999 baseballs and those used 10 to 15 years earlier.

Umpires strike out. Twenty-two major league umpires, nearly one-third of the members of the Major League Umpires Association union, lost jobs in 1999 as a result of a failed union strategy. The trouble began in mid-July when union leader Richie Phillips announced that all major league umpires would resign on September 2 unless MLB officials renegotiated the umpires' contract. When MLB officials called the union's bluff, the umpires knuckled under. Those who had not tendered letters of resignation refused to do so, and those who had quit already publicly rescinded their resignations. The MLB officials, however, had hired replacement umpires from the minor leagues and in September accepted the resignations of the 22 umpires from whom they had received letters.

Regular season. The Atlanta Braves won the National League (NL) Eastern Division by compiling the best record (103-59) in the majors for the second time in three seasons. The Arizona Diamondbacks, in only their second season as a MLB franchise, captured the NL Western Division title,

Final standings in Major League Baseball

American League

American League champions—
New York Yankees (defeated Boston, 4 games to 1)
World Series champions—
New York Yankees (defeated Atlanta, 4 games to 0)

Eastern Division	W.	L.	Pct.	G.B.
New York Yankees	98	64	.605	—
Boston Red Sox*	94	68	.580	4
Toronto Blue Jays	84	78	.519	14
Baltimore Orioles	78	84	.481	20
Tampa Bay Devil Rays	69	93	.426	29

Central Division				
Cleveland Indians	97	65	.599	—
Chicago White Sox	75	86	.466	21½
Detroit Tigers	69	92	.429	27½
Kansas City Royals	64	97	.398	32½
Minnesota Twins	63	97	.394	33

Western Division				
Texas Rangers	95	67	.586	—
Oakland Athletics	87	75	.537	8
Seattle Mariners	79	83	.488	16
Anaheim Angels	70	92	.432	25

Offensive leaders

Batting average	Nomar Garciaparra, Boston	.357
Runs scored	Roberto Alomar, Cleveland	138
Home runs	Ken Griffey, Jr., Seattle	48
Runs batted in	Manny Ramirez, Cleveland	165
Hits	Derek Jeter, New York	219
Stolen bases	Brian Hunter, Seattle	44
Slugging percentage	Manny Ramirez, Cleveland	.663

Leading pitchers

Games won	Pedro Martinez, Boston	23
Earned run average (162 or more innings)—		
	Pedro Martinez, Boston	2.07
Strikeouts	Pedro Martinez, Boston	313
Saves	Mariano Rivera, New York	45
Shut-outs	Scott Erickson, Baltimore	3
Complete games	David Wells, Toronto	7

Awards†

Most Valuable Player................Ivan Rodriguez, Texas
Cy Young........................Pedro Martinez, Boston
Rookie of the Year...........Carlos Beltran, Kansas City
Manager of the Year................Jimy Williams, Boston

National League

National League champions—
Atlanta Braves (defeated New York Mets, 4 games to 2)

Eastern Division	W.	L.	Pct.	G.B.
Atlanta Braves	103	59	.636	—
New York Mets*	97	66	.595	6½
Philadelphia Phillies	77	85	.475	26
Montreal Expos	68	94	.420	35
Florida Marlins	64	98	.395	39

Central Division				
Houston Astros	97	65	.599	—
Cincinnati Reds	96	67	.589	1½
Pittsburgh Pirates	78	83	.484	18½
St. Louis Cardinals	75	86	.466	21½
Milwaukee Brewers	74	87	.460	22½
Chicago Cubs	67	95	.414	30

Western Division				
Arizona Diamondbacks	100	62	.617	—
San Francisco Giants	86	76	.531	14
Los Angeles Dodgers	77	85	.475	23
San Diego Padres	74	88	.457	26
Colorado Rockies	72	90	.444	28

Offensive leaders

Batting average	Larry Walker, Colorado	.379
Runs scored	Jeff Bagwell, Houston	143
Home runs	Mark McGwire, St. Louis	65
Runs batted in	Mark McGwire, St. Louis	147
Hits	Luis Gonzalez, Arizona	206
Stolen bases	Tony Womack, Arizona	72
Slugging percentage	Larry Walker, Colorado	.710

Leading pitchers

Games won	Mike Hampton, Houston	22
Earned run average (162 or more innings)—		
	Randy Johnson, Arizona	2.48
Strikeouts	Randy Johnson, Arizona	364
Saves	Ugueth Urbina, Montreal	41
Shut-outs	Andy Ashby, San Diego	3
Complete games	Randy Johnson, Arizona	12

Awards†

Most Valuable Player.................Chipper Jones, Atlanta
Cy Young.................................Randy Johnson, Arizona
Rookie of the Year.............Scott Williamson, Cincinnati
Manager of the Year ....Jack McKeon, Cincinnati

*Qualified for wild-card play-off spot.
†Selected by the Baseball Writers Association of America.

and the Houston Astros won the NL Central Division. The New York Mets qualified for the postseason as a wild-card entry after beating the Cincinnati Reds in a one-game play-off.

The Yankees posted the best record (98-64) in the American League (AL) for the second straight year to win the AL Eastern Division title. The Cleveland Indians blasted through the AL Central Division for the third year in a row, winning the division by 21½ games. The Texas Rangers captured the AL Western crown, and the Boston Red Sox took the AL wild-card slot.

Play-offs. In the first round of the AL play-offs, the Yankees swept the Rangers in three

games, and Boston came back from an 0-2 deficit to beat Cleveland, 3 games to 2. In the NL division series, Atlanta beat Houston, 3 games to 1, and the Mets ousted Arizona by the same margin. New York fans who wanted the 1999 season to end in a "subway series" between the Yankees and Mets cheered when the Yanks defeated Boston for the AL pennant, 4 games to 1. However, their hopes were dashed when the Braves beat the Mets, 4 games to 2, for the NL pennant. Five of the six games in the Braves-Mets contest were decided by one run. In the final game, the Braves scored the winning run on a walk with the bases loaded.

The 1999 World Series opened in Atlanta, where the Yankees took a 4-1 victory. The Yankees' starting pitcher, Orlando "El Duque" Hernandez, struck out 10 and allowed only one hit in seven innings of work. The following night, the Yankees pounded out 14 hits in a 7-2 victory. Back in New York for Game 3, the Yankees rallied from a 5-1 deficit to win, 6-5, in 10 innings.

On October 27, the Yankees captured their 25th World Series championship by finishing off the Braves, 4-1. Yankee pitcher Roger Clemens shut out the Braves into the 8th inning. Mariano Rivera, a relief pitcher who had not allowed a run since July 21, picked up the save and was named the World Series' Most Valuable Player (MVP).

Stars. The Yankees' David Cone pitched a *perfect game* (a game in which the pitcher retires all opposing batters in succession) on July 18, for a 6-0 victory over Montreal. At 36, Cone was the oldest pitcher to throw a perfect game since 37-year-old Cy Young did so in 1904.

Tony Gwynn of the San Diego Padres made history on Aug. 6, 1999, when he became the 22nd major leaguer to achieve 3,000 hits. Gwynn reached the milestone by stroking a single off Montreal's Dan Smith. Although no player had reached the 3,000-hit plateau in 20 years, one night after Gwynn's hit, Tampa Bay's Wade Boggs got his 3,000th hit—a home run—off Cleveland's Chris Haney.

Home run race. Mark McGwire won the home run title for the second straight year in 1999, finishing with 65 homers. Sammy Sosa ended the season with 63 home runs. Each slugger hit one out of Busch Stadium in St. Louis in the season's final game. Sosa was the first player in history to hit 60 home runs in two consecutive seasons.

Hall of Fame. Nolan Ryan, George Brett, and Robin Yount were inducted into the Baseball Hall of Fame in 1999. Ryan's pitching re-

The New York Yankees celebrate their four-game sweep of the Atlanta Braves in the World Series in October 1999. Pitcher Mariano Rivera (center) was named the Most Valuable Player of the series. The victory gave the Yankees their 25th World Series championship of the century.

cords, achieved in a 27-year career, include 5,714 strikeouts and 7 no-hitters. Brett compiled a .305 lifetime batting average during 21 seasons with the Kansas City Royals. Yount played 20 years for the Milwaukee Brewers, winning AL MVP honors in 1982 at shortstop and in 1989 at center field. San Francisco Giants' slugger Orlando Cepeda, umpire Nestor Chylak, manager Frank Selee, and Negro League pitcher Smokey Joe Williams were also inducted in 1999.

International. On March 28, 1999, the Baltimore Orioles beat the Cuban national team, 3-2, in an 11-inning exhibition game in Havana, Cuba. The Orioles were the first MLB team to play in Cuba since the 1959 Communist revolution. Cuba won the rematch, 12-6, on May 3, 1999, at Baltimore's Camden Yards.   □ Ron Reid

See also **People in the news** (Sosa, Sammy).

Where Have You Gone, Joe DiMaggio?

By Donald Liebenson

Many baseball fans and sportswriters consider outfielder Joe DiMaggio, who died on March 8, 1999, at age 84, one of the game's greatest players. He was a near mythic figure of grace on the field and quiet dignity off the field. He had been married briefly to film star Marilyn Monroe. His name turned up in the pages of an Ernest Hemingway novel as the perfect fishing companion. His name evoked a generation's longings for a hero, simple and unsullied. In the song "Mrs. Robinson," written for the film *The Graduate* (1967), songwriter Paul Simon asks, "Where have you gone, Joe DiMaggio? A nation turns its lonely eyes to you." Yet DiMaggio's off-field mystique and pop culture status never overshadowed his skills as a ballplayer. In 1969—baseball's 100th anniversary—fans and the Baseball Writers' Association of America (BBWAA) voted him the game's greatest living player.

DiMaggio was nicknamed "the Yankee Clipper" because of his graceful fielding and "Joltin' Joe" because of his powerful hitting. During 13 seasons with the New York Yankees, DiMaggio set one of baseball's most enduring records—a 56-game hitting streak in 1941. In 1939, 1941, and 1947, he was named the American League's Most Valuable Player. He had a career batting average of .325, hitting 361 home runs while striking out only 369 times in 1,736 games. DiMaggio played in 10 World Series and 11 All-Star Games. In 1955 the BBWAA elected DiMaggio into the National Baseball Hall of Fame and Museum in Cooperstown, New York.

Joseph Paul DiMaggio was born to Italian immigrant parents on Nov. 25, 1914, in the small fishing village of Martinez, California. His love of baseball developed on the streets and sandlots of San Francisco. In 1931, DiMaggio dropped out of Galileo High School and worked at various low-paying jobs. In 1932, he joined his older brother, Vince, on the San Francisco Seals in the Pacific Coast League. Another brother, Dom, later played with the Seals before jumping into the major leagues with the Boston Red Sox.

Following the 1934 season, the Seals sold DiMaggio's contract to the New York Yankees for $25,000 plus five players. As part of the agreement, DiMaggio spent the 1935 season with the minor league Seals before making his major league debut on May 3, 1936. DiMaggio led the American League in hitting in 1939 and 1940. But it was the events of 1941 that turned DiMaggio from a baseball star to national celebrity.

On May 15, 1941, in a game against the Chicago White Sox, DiMaggio hit a single, launching a hitting streak in which he recorded at least one base hit in 56 consecutive games. The legendary hitting streak, a major league record that remains one of baseball's greatest accomplishments, lifted the spirits of a nation weary of the the Great Depression and anxieties of World War II (1939-1945), which the United States was soon to enter. The streak ended on July 17, 1941, when he failed to get a hit in a game against the Cleveland Indians. The next day he started another hitting streak that held through 16 games.

In 1943, DiMaggio enlisted in the U.S. Army. He returned to baseball in 1946 and enjoyed one of his best seasons in 1948, when despite injuries, he hit .320 with 39 home runs and 155 runs batted in. In 1949, he again made baseball history when he became the first player to sign a $100,000-a-year contract. Injuries contributed to his early retirement in 1951.

Despite the adulation of fans, DiMaggio remained an intensely private person. In November 1939, DiMaggio married actress Dorothy Arnold in San Francisco. They divorced in 1943. In 1952, DiMaggio arranged a date with one of the most public figures of the day, Marilyn Monroe. He and Monroe wed in 1954, but the marriage lasted only months. With DiMaggio and Monroe constantly under the glare of the public eye, DiMaggio reportedly became upset by her screen image as a sex symbol. Although he never spoke publicly or wrote about their relationship, he had roses placed at her grave every week for two decades after her death in 1962.

In the 1960's and 1970's, DiMaggio was employed in several roles, including coach with the Oakland Athletics and commercial spokesperson for Mr. Coffee, a manufacturer of coffeemakers. The commercials introduced him to a new generation of fans. Throughout his later life, DiMaggio was vigilant in maintaining his untarnished image. He insisted that he be introduced last at public functions and introduced by the title "greatest living player."

In 1998, DiMaggio underwent surgery for lung cancer. He spent almost 100 days in a Florida hospital, due to health setbacks and complications. In January 1999, a weak DiMaggio returned to his Florida home where he died two months later. He was survived by his son, Joe Jr., his brother Dom, two grandchildren, and four great-grandchildren. In August, his son also died.

DiMaggio once asked Paul Simon if the reference in the song "Mrs. Robinson" was derogatory. Simon assured DiMaggio that the lyrics reflected a new generation's yearning for a hero—a hero who could claim the kind of admiration and carry the same mystique that DiMaggio had earned in the mind of the public.

Joe DiMaggio and film legend Marilyn Monroe were married briefly in 1954.

The author:
Donald Liebenson is a free-lance writer.

Basketball. First-time champions emerged at every major level during the 1998-1999 basketball season. The San Antonio Spurs won the National Basketball Association (NBA) title, ending the three-year reign of the Chicago Bulls. The University of Connecticut won the men's National Collegiate Athletic Association (NCAA) championship for the first time, and Purdue University became the first team from the Big Ten conference to win the women's NCAA championship.

Professional. The 1998-1999 NBA season was derailed before it began when team owners and the players' union failed to reach a new collective bargaining agreement. On July 1, 1998, the owners imposed a lockout, suspending virtually all basketball-related dealings with the players. The lockout lasted 204 days, forcing the league to cancel the first four months of the season as well as the All-Star Game. An abbreviated NBA season began on Feb. 5, 1999, with each team playing 50 games in 89 days. With only two weeks of practice before the start of the season, most teams found themselves ill-prepared to play at such a demanding pace, and the games were characterized by mistakes, poor shooting, and low scoring.

San Antonio and the Utah Jazz were notable exceptions. Although the Spurs and Jazz tied for the best regular-season record (37-13), San Antonio won home-court advantage in the play-offs because they defeated Utah in two of three regular-season games. The Miami Heat (33-17), Indiana Pacers (33-17), and Portland Trail Blazers (35-15) took the other division titles.

San Antonio cruised into the Western Conference championship, dispatching the Minnesota Timberwolves, 3 games to 1, and sweeping both the Los Angeles Lakers and Portland in 4 games. The New York Knicks (27-23), by contrast, barely reached the play-offs but then rumbled to their first Eastern Conference title in five seasons by eliminating the Heat, 3 games to 2, sweeping the Atlanta Hawks in 4 games, and defeating Indiana, 4 games to 2. The Knicks even managed to upset the favored Pacers without Patrick Ewing, the team's star center, who was sidelined after the second game against Indiana by a partially torn Achilles tendon.

Without Ewing, New York faced a formidable task in the NBA Finals—stopping San Antonio's "Twin Towers"—7-foot (2.1-meter) forward Tim Duncan and 7-foot-1-inch (2.2-meter) center David Robinson. After losing the first two games in San Antonio, the Knicks avoided a sweep in Game 3 with an 89-81 victory on their home court in Madison Square Garden. The Spurs, however, came back to win Game 4 and, on June 25, captured their first NBA title in 26 years, with a score of 78-77, in Game 5.

People. After 13 seasons, Chicago Bulls guard

The 1998-1999 college basketball season

College tournament champions

NCAA	(Men)	Division I:	Connecticut
		Division II:	Kentucky Wesleyan
		Division III:	Wisconsin-Platteville
	(Women)	Division I:	Purdue
		Division II:	North Dakota
		Division III:	Washington (Missouri)
NAIA	(Men)	Division I:	Life (Ga.)
		Division II:	Cornerstone Coll. (Mich.)
	(Women)	Division I:	Oklahoma City
		Division II:	Shawnee State (Ohio)
NIT	(Men)		University of California-Berkeley

Men's college champions

Conference	School
America East	Delaware*
Atlantic Coast	Duke*
Atlantic Ten	Rhode Island (tournament)
Eastern Division	Temple
Western Division	George Washington
Big East	Connecticut*
Big Sky	Weber State*
Big South	Winthrop*
Big Ten	Michigan State*
Big Twelve	Texas
	Kansas (tournament)
Big West	New Mexico State (tournament)
Eastern Division	Boise State–New Mexico State (tie)
Western Division	UC Santa Barbara
Colonial	George Mason*
Conference USA	North Carolina (Charlotte)
	(tournament)
American Division	Cincinnati
National Division	Alabama (Birmingham)
Ivy League	Pennsylvania†
Metro Atlantic	Niagara–Siena* (tie)
Mid-American	Kent (tournament)
East Division	Miami (Ohio)
West Division	Toledo
Mid-Continent	Valparaiso*–Oral Roberts (tie)
Mid-Eastern	S. Carolina State–Coppin State (tie)
	Florida A&M (tournament)
Midwestern	Detroit*
Missouri Valley	Evansville
	Creighton (tournament)
Northeast	Maryland (Baltimore Co.)
	Mount St. Mary's (tournament)
Ohio Valley	Murray State*
Pacific Ten	Stanford†
Patriot League	Lafayette*
Southeastern	Kentucky (tournament)
Eastern Division	Tennessee
Western Division	Auburn
Southern	
North Division	College of Charleston*
South Division	Appalachian State
Southland	Southwest Texas State
	Texas-San Antonio (tournament)
Southwestern	Alcorn State*
Sun Belt	Louisiana Tech
	Arkansas State (tournament)
Trans America	Samford*
West Coast	Gonzaga*
Western Athletic	
Mountain Division	Nevada-Las Vegas–Tulsa (tie)
Pacific Division	Utah*

*Regular season and conference tournament champion.
†No tournament played.

Sources: National Collegiate Athletic Association (NCAA); National Association of Intercollegiate Athletics (NAIA); National Invitation Tournament (NIT).

Purdue University forward Katie Douglas (left) and Michele VanGorp of Duke University battle for the ball during the final game of the 1999 NCAA women's basketball championship in March. Purdue won, 62-45, to claim its first national title.

Michael Jordan, whom fans and other observers almost unanimously rate the greatest basketball player of all time, retired from the NBA for the second time, on January 13. Jordan had previously retired in 1993 to play one season of minor league baseball at Birmingham, Alabama, before returning to the NBA in 1995. Without Jordan, and with forward Scottie Pippen and head coach Phil Jackson also leaving Chicago, the six-time champion Bulls turned into an inept team that compiled a 13-37 season record and set an NBA record for lowest point total, in an 82-49 loss at Miami in April 1999.

Karl Malone of Utah was named the NBA's most valuable player for the second consecutive year. Coach of the year honors went to Portland's Mike Dunleavy. Vince Carter of the Toronto Raptors was named the NBA's rookie of the year, and Miami's Alonzo Mourning was the defensive player of the year. The All-NBA First Team included Malone, Duncan, Mourning, Allen Iverson of Philadelphia, and Jason Kidd of Phoenix.

Inductees to the Basketball Hall of Fame in 1999 included former Georgetown University coach John Thompson; ex-Boston Celtics star Kevin McHale; Wayne Embry, the five-time NBA All-Star and the first black general manager in pro sports; Billie Moore, the first women's coach to lead two schools to national titles, and the late Fred Zollner,

the NBA pioneer and Detroit Pistons owner.

Professional women. The Women's National Basketball Association (WNBA) expanded to 12 teams in 1999 and, like the NBA, prefaced its third season with a labor dispute. However, on April 29, the league and players' union signed a four-year contract—the first collective bargaining agreement for a women's sports league in the United States. The quality of WNBA play improved with an influx of talent from the defunct American Basketball League, but the league continued to struggle with poor attendance and low television ratings during the 32-game season. On September 5, the Houston Comets won their third straight WNBA title, defeating the New York Liberty, 59-47, to take the championship series, 2 games to 1.

College men. When the 64-team NCAA tournament began on March 11, Connecticut (28-2), Michigan State University (29-4), Auburn University (27-3), and Duke University (32-1) were the top-seeded teams in their respective regional tournaments. Only Auburn failed to reach the Final Four in St. Petersburg, Florida, on March 27. Ohio State University (23-8), which upset Auburn in the South regional semifinals, 72-64, also advanced to the Final Four.

Connecticut beat Ohio State, 64-58, to reach the championship game for the first time in history. Duke earned a sixth trip to the championship

National Basketball Association standings

Eastern Conference

Atlantic Division

	W.	L.	Pct.	G.B.
Miami Heat*	33	17	.660	—
Orlando Magic*	33	17	.660	—
Philadelphia 76ers*	28	22	.560	5
New York Knicks*	27	23	.540	6
Boston Celtics	19	31	.380	14
Washington Wizards	18	32	.360	15
New Jersey Nets	16	34	.320	17

Central Division

	W.	L.	Pct.	G.B.
Indiana Pacers*	33	17	.660	—
Atlanta Hawks*	31	19	.620	2
Detroit Pistons*	29	21	.580	4
Milwaukee Bucks*	28	22	.560	5
Charlotte Hornets	26	24	.520	7
Toronto Raptors	23	27	.460	10
Cleveland Cavaliers	22	28	.440	11
Chicago Bulls	13	37	.260	20

Western Conference

Midwest Division

	W.	L.	Pct.	G.B.
San Antonio Spurs*	37	13	.740	—
Utah Jazz*	37	13	.740	—
Houston Rockets*	31	19	.620	6
Minnesota Timberwolves*	25	25	.500	12
Dallas Mavericks	19	31	.380	18
Denver Nuggets	14	36	.280	23
Vancouver Grizzlies	8	42	.160	29

Pacific Division

	W.	L.	Pct.	G.B.
Portland Trail Blazers*	35	15	.700	—
Los Angeles Lakers*	31	19	.620	4
Phoenix Suns*	27	23	.540	8
Sacramento Kings*	27	23	.540	8
Seattle Supersonics	25	25	.500	10
Golden State Warriors	21	29	.420	14
Los Angeles Clippers	9	41	.180	26

*Made play-offs

Individual leaders

Scoring

	G.	F.G.	F.T.	Pts.	Avg.
Allen Iverson, Philadelphia	48	435	356	1,284	26.8
Shaquille O'Neal, L.A. Lakers	49	510	269	1,289	26.3
Karl Malone, Utah	49	393	378	1,164	23.8
Shareef Abdur-Rahim, Vancouver	50	386	369	1,152	23.0
Keith Van Horn, New Jersey	42	322	256	916	21.8
Gary Payton, Seattle	50	401	199	1,084	21.7
Tim Duncan, San Antonio	50	418	247	1,084	21.7
Stephon Marbury, New Jersey	49	378	222	1,044	21.3
Antonio McDyess, Denver	50	415	230	1,061	21.2
Grant Hill, Detroit	50	384	285	1,053	21.1

Rebounding

	G.	Off.	Def.	Tot.	Avg.
Chris Webber, Sacramento	42	149	396	545	13.0
Charles Barkley, Houston	42	167	349	516	12.3
Dikembe Mutombo, Atlanta	50	192	418	610	12.2
Jayson Williams, New Jersey	30	147	213	360	12.0
Danny Fortson, Denver	50	210	371	581	11.6
Tim Duncan, San Antonio	50	159	412	571	11.4
Dennis Rodman, L.A. Lakers	23	62	196	258	11.2
Alonzo Mourning, Miami	46	166	341	507	11.0
Shaquille O'Neal, L.A. Lakers	49	187	338	525	10.7
Antonio McDyess, Denver	50	168	369	537	10.7

NBA champions—San Antonio Spurs
(defeated New York Knicks, 4 games to 1)

game by eliminating Michigan State, 68-62. Duke carried a 32-game winning streak into the championship game on March 29, but UConn parlayed impenetrable defense and clutch shooting into a 77-74 victory and its first national title.

Duke University sophomore Elton Brand was the only unanimous choice on the 1998-1999 All-America team. The other First-Team All-America selections were Richard Hamilton of Connecticut, Andre Miller of the University of Utah, Jason Terry of the University of Arizona, and Mateen Cleaves of Michigan State.

College women. The 1998-1999 season ended with a blockbuster upset when the University of Tennessee (28-2), pursuing its fourth straight NCAA championship, lost in the East regional finals to Duke, 69-63. Purdue (28-1), the University of Georgia (23-6), and Louisiana Tech University (26-2) joined Duke in the women's Final Four. Purdue became the NCAA women's champion by defeating Duke, 62-45.

Purdue head coach Carolyn Peck was named coach of the year. The women's All-America First Team included Chamique Holdsclaw and Tamika Catchings of Tennessee, Stephanie White-McCarty of Purdue University, Becky Hammon of Colorado State University, and Dominique Canty of the University of Alabama. □ Ron Reid

Belarus. President Aleksandr Lukashenko made little progress in 1999 toward his goal of re-unifying Belarus with Russia. Successive government reorganizations in Russia repeatedly disrupted negotiations, and opposition to reunification in both countries slowed momentum. In September, Russian Prime Minister Vladimir Putin said he would like to see a Russia-Belarus union completed before the Russian presidential election, scheduled for 2000. Lukashenko, in an October 1999 speech before the Russian parliament in Moscow, said that the time for reunification was "not just ripe, but overripe."

Political repression. Lukashenko's regime continued to repress political opposition within Belarus in 1999. One of Lukashenko's most vocal critics, Viktor Gonchar, mysteriously disappeared on September 16. Gonchar was a member of the Belarusian parliament that had been disbanded by Lukashenko in 1996. Other opponents of Lukashenko also disappeared during 1999, including Tamara Vinnikova, the one-time head of Belarus's national bank, and Yuri Zakharenko, a former interior minister.

Before his disappearance, Gonchar had been a leader of an opposition group that refused to accept the results of a 1996 referendum that extended Lukashenko's presidential term until 2001. Under the terms of Belarus's 1994 constitution, Lukashenko's term was to expire in July 1999. Opposition leaders, including Gonchar, attempted to organize an election to select a "constitutional" successor to Lukashenko. One of the proposed candidates, former prime minister Mikhail Chyhir, was jailed on corruption charges in March before the balloting was due to begin. The initiative collapsed when opposition groups failed to agree on procedures for conducting the balloting.

Foreign affairs. In April, Lukashenko accused the West of "slander" for misrepresenting the political situation in Belarus. Lukashenko's opposition to the 1999 bombing of Serbia by the North Atlantic Treaty Organization (NATO) deepened Belarus's isolation from the West. On April 14, Lukashenko met with President Slobodan Milosevic of Yugoslavia in Belgrade, the Yugoslav capital, as a sign of solidarity. Lukashenko was the first foreign head of state to visit Belgrade after the NATO campaign began on March 24.

In June, the World Bank, a United Nations agency that provides long-term loans to countries for development, reopened its office in Minsk, the capital. The World Bank had closed its offices in Belarus in August 1998 to protest Lukashenko's refusal to implement economic reforms.

□ Steven L. Solnick

See also **Europe; Russia; Yugoslavia.**

Belgium. A food-contamination scare provoked a crisis in Belgium in 1999 that resulted in a dramatic change of government. In national elections on June 13, voters rejected the coalition of Christian Democrats and Socialists that had governed for the past 12 years and elected a government led by the center-right Liberal Party.

The crisis erupted in May when the government of Prime Minister Jean-Luc Dehaene announced that animal feed produced in Belgium had been contaminated with the cancer-causing chemical dioxin. Dehaene imposed a temporary ban on the sale of chicken, eggs, and later, pork products. The government's ministers of health and agriculture resigned after it was disclosed that they had known about the contamination for one month before informing the public and officials of the European Union (EU). The EU regulates agricultural products in Europe.

The crisis was the latest in a series that ranged from kickbacks on defense contracts in 1988 and 1989 to the botched investigation of pedophiles who murdered four girls in 1995 and 1996. The 1999 crisis prompted voters to elect a new coalition led by the country's French- and Dutch-speaking Liberal parties. The Liberals won 41 seats in the 150-seat Chamber of Representatives—up from 39 seats—making the Liberals the largest group in the lower house of Parliament.

Dairy products are removed from Belgian grocery stores when the government reveals in May that animal feed produced in Belgium was contaminated with the cancer-causing chemical dioxin. The resulting scandal brought down the government in June.

Belgium's two Green parties won 20 seats compared with 11 in the old Parliament.

The leader of the Dutch-speaking branch of the Liberal party, Guy Verhofstadt, formed a coalition with the Greens and the Socialist parties and became prime minister on July 12. He promised a new era of clean government and pledged to stimulate the economy and reduce high government debt. The result was a huge defeat for Dehaene's French- and Dutch-speaking Christian Democratic parties. They won only 32 seats—a loss of nine—and found themselves out of government for the first time in 40 years.

In June, the Belgian government ordered a 10-day shutdown of production at two Coca-Cola plants in the country. Hundreds of people had complained of headaches and nausea after consuming the soft drinks. The French government imposed a similar ban on Coca-Cola's plant in Dunkirk, near the Belgian border. The two shutdowns led to the biggest product recall in the company's history. Coca-Cola blamed the problem on defective gas used to carbonate its drinks and the contamination of cans with a chemical used on pallets for transporting.   □ Tom Buerkle

See also **Europe.**

Belize. See Latin America.

Benin. See Africa.

Bhutan. See Asia.

Biology. A team of biologists at the University of Sydney in Australia reported in August 1999 that they had discovered evidence that pushed back the beginning of complex life forms on Earth by at least half a billion years, to 2.7 billion years ago. The scientists found evidence of *eukaryotes,* organisms whose cells have a membrane-covered *nucleus* (a central part containing genetic material), in a shale deposit in northwestern Australia. Eukaryotes make up the diverse group of organisms that includes life forms more advanced than bacteria—everything from protozoa to humans. Simple bacterial life dates to approximately 4 billion years ago.

The Australian team reported that it found chemicals in the shale that could only have been made by eukaryotes. The chemicals were complex *hydrocarbons* (compounds containing only hydrogen and carbon) called steranes. Steranes are the breakdown products of other compounds called sterols, which are components of certain types of living tissues. Cholesterol is an example of such a component. Sterols are only present in the bodies of eukaryotes.

Primordial photosynthesis. The University of Sydney researchers also reported in August that they had detected molecular evidence of ancient cyanobacteria in the same shale deposits in which they had found the sterols. Cyanobacteria are bacteria that, like plants and algae, are capable of *photosynthesis*—the conversion of energy from the sun into chemical energy, with the resulting release of oxygen into the environment. Virtually all the oxygen breathed by animals in the air and sea is produced through photosynthesis. This study indicated that oxygen production began by 2.7 billion years ago—millions of years earlier than scientists had thought.

Largest bacterium. German scientists in April reported the discovery of the largest known bacterium—a monster microorganism that lives in sulfur-containing sediment off the coast of Namibia in Africa. These bacteria reach a diameter of approximately 1/30 of an inch (0.75 millimeter), which is about the size of the period at the end of this sentence. The bacterium is 10 times greater than the diameter of the previously largest known bacterium. The scientists, from the Max Planck Institute for Marine Biology in Bremen, named the microorganism *Thiomargarita namibiensis,* or sulfur pearl of Namibia, because the individual microbes form strands that resemble pearl necklaces.

Researchers are interested in *T. namibiensis,* not because of its size, but because of its ability to remove harmful chemicals from water. The bacterium detoxifies sulfur compounds in the marine sediment called sulfides. In addition, the bacterium breaks down nitrates, nitrogen compounds in agricultural runoff that deplete water of oxygen. Researchers noted that *T. namibiensis* may be used to clean up water pollution.

Animal altruism. Many people admire what appears to be *altruism* (self-sacrificing behavior) in animals. Animal altruism may not be what it seems, however, according to a study of meerkats reported in May by researchers at the University of Cambridge in England, the University of Edinburgh in Scotland, and the University of Pretoria in South Africa.

The meerkat is a type of mongoose that lives in large colonies in the South African desert. One meerkat typically acts as a sentinel, watching for predators, while other members of the group stick their heads underground searching for small mammals to eat. If the sentinels' behavior was an altruistic act, the researchers argued, then those animals should suffer a higher death rate from predation than the other members of the colony.

After more than 2,000 hours of observation, the researchers concluded that the sentinels were never attacked by predators. Instead, once the sentinels sounded an alarm, they were the first to race back into the safety of their burrows. In other words, standing guard gave them extra time for saving themselves. The researchers also found that meerkats would stand sentinel only when they had already had their fill of food.

A genetically altered mouse is tested for learning and memory skills at Princeton University in New Jersey in 1999. Biologists at Princeton announced in September that they had successfully engineered a strain of mice with superior learning and memory skills.

Frog deformities. Evidence reported in April suggested that the parasitic flatworm *Ribeiroia* is one of the culprits responsible for the large numbers of deformities seen in frogs since the mid-1990's. Biologists at Hartwick College in Oneonta, New York, and Claremont McKenna College in Claremont, California, said they had created deformities in frogs similar to those found in nature by infecting the animals with the parasite.

Researchers around the world have found many species of frogs with such deformities as extra limbs. Although scientists are not sure what causes these abnormalities, they have proposed a number of factors—genetic mutations caused by ultraviolet light from the sun; poisoning by industrial chemicals and other pollutants; and infections by *pathogenic* (disease-causing) fungi.

Biologists had previously discounted *Ribeiroia* as a cause of the deformities because healthy frogs seemed to carry as many of the parasites as deformed frogs. The researchers in 1999 demonstrated, however, that if Pacific tree frogs are infected with *Ribeiroia* during the earliest stages of fetal development, they grow extra limbs. On the other hand, if the frogs are infected after their limbs have formed, no problems arise.

The scientists said they did not know why the numbers of *Ribeiroia* parasites have apparently increased sufficiently to cause the problems in frogs. However, they noted that fertilizer runoff from lawns and gardens has made aquatic environments more favorable to algae and the snails that feed on it. Snails function as a host in the parasitic flatworm's life cycle.

Life-saving sperm. When the male rattlebox moth mates with the female, he passes on not only sperm and nutrients for the fertilized eggs but also a chemical that protects the female against being eaten by spiders. This discovery, announced in May by scientists at Cornell University in Ithaca, New York, was the first known example of a sexually transmitted chemical defense in animals.

As a caterpillar, the male rattlebox moth loads up on toxic chemicals called pyrrolizidine alkaloids by eating the rattlebox plant. The chemicals permeate the body of the caterpillar, which is not harmed by them, and remain after the caterpillar becomes a moth. Spiders detest the alkaloids and cut the moths loose from their webs. Female moths also eat the rattlebox plant, but most of the alkaloids they consume go into their eggs, leaving the females themselves at risk.

The Cornell scientists discovered that the weight of the sperm packet donated by the male makes up more than 10 percent of the moth's body mass, and insemination takes as long as nine hours. Chemical analysis revealed that the female's body is immediately permeated with the alkaloids, which protect her for the rest of her 30-day lifespan and add to the protection of her fertilized eggs.

GE corn and caterpillars. Fears that monarch butterflies are harmed by genetically engineered (GE) crops may be unfounded, according to research presented in November at the Monarch Butterfly Research Symposium in Rosemont, Illinois. *Entomologist* (insect expert) John Losey of Cornell University reported in May that, in laboratory experiments, pollen from corn that was genetically modified to be toxic to harmful caterpillars also killed some caterpillars of the monarch butterfly—a well-known, harmless species. This raised the possibility that monarch caterpillars in the field might be killed by toxic corn pollen that blows onto the milkweed plant, the only plant monarchs eat.

However, entomologists from a number of U.S. and Canadian universities announced at the symposium that field tests revealed that only a small amount of corn pollen blows onto milkweed in the wild. This indicated, according to Mark Sears of the University of Guelph in Ontario, Canada, that the risk of GE corn to monarchs is "very minimal." Despite these findings, other scientists said more research was needed to settle the dispute.   □ Thomas H. Maugh II

Boating. The Around Alone race and the Admiral's Cup highlighted competitive sailing in 1999. Selection trials for the 2000 America's Cup yacht race, held off the coast of New Zealand in late 1999, also drew the attention of sailors and fans around the world.

Around Alone. Giovanni Soldini of Italy, aboard the 60-foot (18-meter) yacht *Fila,* won the 27,000-mile (43,400-kilometer) Around Alone race on May 8, becoming a hero in the process. Soldini won the race in a record 116 days, 20 hours, 7 minutes, and 59 seconds, breaking the former record by more than 4 days. He won greater applause, however, for his rescue of Isabelle Autissier, a French rival whose yacht capsized during the third leg of the race in the South Pacific in February. Soldini diverted off course 200 miles (322 kilometers), following satellite and radio tracking reports, to find Autissier's overturned boat. *Somewhere,* skippered by Marc Thiercelin of France, the only other 60-footer among the nine boats in the class to finish, placed second.

The Admiral's Cup. A team from the Netherlands won the Admiral's Cup, regarded as the world championship of off-shore yacht racing, on July 23. Nine international teams, each sailing one big, one mid-sized, and one small boat, started the eight-race competition on June 14, off the English coast. A multinational team from Europe fin-

ished second, and Great Britain placed third. The United States, the defending champion, finished fifth due to lackluster performances from its mid-sized and small boats.

Other sailboat races. *Pyewacket,* a 73-foot (22-meter) sloop skippered by Roy E. Disney, won the Transpacific Yacht Race from Los Angeles to Honolulu, Hawaii, on July 11. The prerace favorite, *Pyewacket* covered the 2,225-mile (3,581-kilometer) distance in 7 days, 11 hours, and 41 minutes—beating its own record by 3 hours.

The Worrell 1000, a 1,000-mile (1,600-kilometer) catamaran race from Ft. Lauderdale, Florida, to Virginia Beach, Virginia, began on May 9, with 13 two-person teams. *Chick's Beach,* sailed by Randy Smyth and Keith Notary, won for the third year in a row, in 97 hours, 58 minutes, and 9 seconds—23 minutes faster than the runner-up.

Powerboats. In Detroit on July 11, Chip Hanauer piloted *Miss PICO* to victory in the Gold Cup race, the showcase event of the American Powerboat Association circuit. Hanauer's average speed of 152.59 miles (245.57 kilometers) per hour helped to end the three-year reign of defending champion Dave Villwock, who placed second in *Miss Budweiser.*   □ Ron Reid

Bolivia. See Latin America.

Books. See Literature, American; Literature, world; Literature for children; Poetry.

Bosnia-Herzegovina. In February 1999, the Bosnian parliament elected Svetozar Mihajlovic as the Serbian co-prime minister and reelected Haris Silajdzic as the Muslim co-prime minister of Bosnia-Herzegovina. (Bosnia's federal government rotates between two prime ministers, a Bosnian Serb and a Bosnian Muslim.) Mihajlovic, a moderate, replaced the more radical Boro Bosic. However, most political developments in Bosnia in 1999 continued to be marked by conflict.

Internal affairs. Carlos Westendorp, the High Representative in Bosnia, removed Nikola Poplasen, president of the Bosnian Serb Republic, from office on March 5. The United Nations and European Union appoint the High Representative to implement the nonmilitary provisions of the 1995 Dayton peace accord, which ended Bosnia's four-year civil war (1992-1995). Poplasen, who was elected in September 1998, had failed to work with the more moderate Bosnian Serb parliament, which had rejected all of his nominees for prime minister.

On March 5, 1999, an international arbitrator removed Brcko, a town captured by Serbs during the war in 1992, from the Serb republic and made it a self-governing neutral district. Brcko occupied a strategic position within a thin strip of territory that comprised the only link between the eastern and western halves of the Serb republic.

The ouster of Poplasen and the Brcko decision triggered protests throughout the Serb republic. Bosnian Serb Prime Minister Milorad Dodik and Zivko Radisic, the Serbian member of Bosnia's three-person federal presidency, threatened to resign in protest. Both men later reconsidered.

On Aug. 3, 1999, Wolfgang Petritsch replaced Carlos Westendorp as High Representative in Bosnia-Herzegovina. Prior to his appointment, Petritsch had served as the Austrian ambassador to Yugoslavia and as the European Union's special envoy for Kosovo.

Economy. Reports surfaced in the international news media in August 1999 that corrupt Bosnian government officials may have diverted as much as $1 billion in Bosnian public funds and foreign aid since 1995. Bosnian leaders worried that the allegations would discourage further foreign aid and investment in the country.

According to a report published by the United Nations, 21,700 refugees from the war in Kosovo had escaped to Bosnia by June 1999. At the time, Bosnia's economy was still struggling under the burden of feeding and housing approximately 800,000 refugees and displaced persons from its own civil war.   ☐ Sharon L. Wolchik

See also **Europe; Yugoslavia; Yugoslavia: A Special Report.**

Botswana. See Africa.

Bowling. Parker Bohn III of Jackson, New Jersey, captured 1999 Player of the Year honors on the men's Professional Bowlers Association (PBA) tour. Aleta Sill of Dearborn, Michigan, became the first player to surpass $1 million in career earnings on the Professional Women's Bowling Association (PWBA) tour.

PBA fans were treated to a year-long duel between Bohn and Jason Couch of Claremont, Florida. Bohn achieved a top-five finish 11 times in 24 PBA events, followed closely by Couch, who tallied 10 top-five finishes in 23 events. Bohn led the PBA in average (228.04) and earnings ($316,495), followed by Couch in both categories. Couch won more than one-third of his season earnings in the World Tournament of Champions in Overland Park, Kansas, on November 17. He claimed a PBA tour-record $100,000 check for a 197-193 victory over Chris Barnes of Wichita, Kansas, in the final match.

Other major PBA events. Pete Weber of St. Ann, Missouri, defeated David Ozio of Vidor, Texas, 277-236, to win the PBA National Championship at Toledo, Ohio, on February 22. Bob Learn, Jr., of Erie, Pennsylvania, beat Couch, 231-215, to take the U.S. Open on August 1 at Uncasville, Connecticut.

PWBA. Wendy McPherson of Henderson, Nevada, a leading candidate for women's bowler of the decade, led the PWBA earnings list with $120,465 and achieved the tour's highest average, 218.85. Kim Adler of Las Vegas, Nevada, also topped $100,000 in earnings. She bowled a league-high three perfect games in 1999 and won the women's U.S. Open at Uncasville, defeating Lynda Barnes of Wichita, Kansas, 213-195, in the final match.

McPherson won the St. Clair Classic in Fairview Heights, Illinois, on May 27, with a 258-180 victory over Leanne Barrette of Pleasanton, California. McPherson also captured the prestigious Sam's Town Invitational on November 6 in Las Vegas, where she fittingly captured the final PWBA title of the 1990's in the 10th frame. McPherson beat Marianne DiRupo of Succassunna, New Jersey, in the title match, 209-195.

Seniors. Dale Eagle of Lewisville, Texas, earned the 1999 Player of the Year title on the PBA Senior Tour. He compiled a 225.28 average and achieved a top-five finish 8 times in 14 events. Dave Soutar of Bradenton, Florida, won the Seniors Tournament of Champions on October 9, 267-196 over John Hricsina of Franklin, Pennsylvania. On October 22, Steve Neff of Homosassa Springs, Florida, won the PBA National Senior Championship in Jackson, Michigan, defeating Bob Glass of Lawrence, Kansas, 236-224.   ☐ Ron Reid

Boxing. Fans who hoped to see boxing become a respectable sport in 1999 were repeatedly disappointed by well-known fighters who performed poorly, by dubious judging, and by bouts that left angry audiences feeling cheated. Former heavyweight champion Mike Tyson returned to the ring in 1999 after a 19-month absence but continued to pay for his hair-trigger temper. Several International Boxing Federation (IBF) officials were indicted in November for allegedly taking bribes to manipulate their rankings of fighters.

Bad bouts. A matchup in New York City's Madison Square Garden between Evander Holyfield and Lennox Lewis on March 13, was supposed to crown an undisputed heavyweight champion. It created a new dispute instead, when the judges called the fight a draw even though Lewis landed almost three punches for every one by Holyfield. The decision allowed Holyfield to retain his World Boxing Association (WBA) and International Boxing Federation (IBF) titles, while Lewis kept his World Boxing Council (WBC) crown.

Fight officials promptly ordered a rematch, which took place on November 13 in Las Vegas, Nevada. This time, although the contest was much closer, Lewis defeated Holyfield in a unanimous decision to become the undisputed world heavyweight champion. Immediately before the bout, however, IBF officials told Lewis's managers that

Lennox Lewis of Great Britain (right) and Evander Holyfield of the United States exchange punches in a heavyweight title bout on November 13. Lewis, the winner, became the first fighter to hold the heavyweight titles of both the World Boxing Association and the World Boxing Council since Riddick Bowe in 1992.

the IBF would not accept the check covering Lewis's sanctioning fee. On November 16, the IBF reported that it had reached an agreement with Lewis over the fee and gave him the IBF belt.

Fans suffered another disappointing bout on September 20, in Las Vegas. Felix Trinidad of Puerto Rico defeated American Oscar De La Hoya in a majority decision. With the victory, Trinidad retained his IBF welterweight championship and won the WBC title as well. However, fans were dismayed by De La Hoya's strategy of avoiding Trinidad rather than attacking him toe-to-toe.

Another bizarre incident in Tyson's career occurred on October 23, when his bout against Orlin Norris was ruled a no-contest at the end of the first round after Tyson dropped Norris with a left hook after the bell. Norris walked back to his corner, then said he could not continue. X rays later revealed that Norris's knee was dislocated. This was Tyson's second bout following the revocation of his boxing license in 1997 for biting off part of Evander Holyfield's ear during an official bout.

Other divisions. WBA and WBC champion Roy Jones, Jr., became boxing's undisputed light-heavyweight champion on June 5, 1999, when he took away Reggie Johnson's IBF title in a unification bout in Biloxi, Mississippi. Jones, widely considered the best pound-for-pound boxer in the game, won a unanimous decision. ☐ Ron Reid

World champion boxers

World Boxing Association

Division	Champion	Country	Date won
Heavyweight	Lennox Lewis	United Kingdom	11/99
	Evander Holyfield	U.S.A.	11/96
Light heavyweight	Roy Jones	U.S.A.	7/98
	Lou Del Valle	U.S.A.	9/97
Middleweight	William Joppy	U.S.A.	1/98
	Julio Cesar Green	U.S.A.	8/97
Welterweight	James Page	U.S.A.	10/98
	Vacant	—	—
Lightweight	Gilbert Serrano	Venezuela	11/99
	Stefano Zoff	Italy	8/99
	Julien Lorcy	France	4/99
	Jean-Baptiste Mendy	France	5/98
Featherweight	Fred Norwood	U.S.A.	5/99
	Antonio Cermeno	Venezuela	10/98
Bantamweight	Paul Ayala	U.S.A.	6/99
	Johnny Tapia	U.S.A.	12/98
Flyweight	Sornpichai Pisnurachank	Thailand	9/99
	Leo Gamez	Venezuela	3/99
	Vacant	—	—

World Boxing Council

Division	Champion	Country	Date won
Heavyweight	Lennox Lewis	United Kingdom	2/97
Light heavyweight	Roy Jones	U.S.A.	8/97
Middleweight	Keith Holmes	U.S.A.	4/99
	Hassine Cherifi	U.S.A.	5/98
Welterweight	Felix Trinidad	Puerto Rico	9/99
	Oscar de la Hoya	U.S.A.	4/97
Lightweight	Steve Johnston	U.S.A.	2/99
	Cezar Bazan	Mexico	6/98
Featherweight	Naseem Hamed	United Kingdom	10/99
	Cesar Soto	Mexico	5/99
	Luisito Espinosa	Philippines	12/95
Bantamweight	Veerapol Sahaprom	Thailand	12/98
	Joichiro Tatsuyoshi	Japan	8/98
Flyweight	M. Lukchaopormasak	Thailand	9/99
	Manny Pacquiao	Philippines	12/98

Brazil. President Fernando Henrique Cardoso of Brazil spent 1999 juggling the demands of the public and those of the International Monetary Fund (IMF), a United Nations agency based in Washington, D.C., that provides short-term credit to member nations. In November 1998, the IMF had pledged $41.5 billion to prop up the Brazilian economy if Cardoso's administration implemented various austerity measures. The people of Brazil complained that they shouldered the major effects of these measures, such as a national unemployment rate of 8.3 percent as of August 1999, the highest in 16 years.

Devaluation. On January 9, Governor Itamar Franco of Minas Gerais state declared a 90-day freeze on repayments of the state's estimated $13.5-billion debt to the federal government. Cardoso countered this threat to economic stability by devaluing Brazil's currency, the real, by more than 8 percent on January 13. He later pledged that the federal government would cover half of Minas Gerais's overdue payments. The devaluation provoked six other governors to join Franco in condemning the federal government's austerity measures as "cruel and unjust."

On January 18, the Brazilian government, which had drawn heavily on its foreign reserves to defend the real's value, lifted exchange-rate controls, allowing the currency to be traded at market value. Economists saw the immediate response as encouraging. The Sao Paulo stock market index, for example, experienced a one-day gain of 33.4 percent as investors rushed to buy stocks at bargain prices. As the fear of hyperinflation subsided throughout 1999, Brazil's central bank cut interest rates 11 times, from 45 percent in late January to 19 percent in late September.

Public protests over IMF demands occurred repeatedly in 1999. In July, Brazil's truck drivers staged a four-day strike that crippled commerce. The truckers ended the strike when the government abandoned a plan to increase taxes on diesel fuel and raise highway tolls. In August, Brasilia, the capital, was the scene of a protest called the March of 100,000. A coalition of left-wing political parties and labor unions demanded an end to the IMF-imposed austerity program and a halt on the privatization of state-owned companies.

Pension reform. In October, President Cardoso won support from state governors for a proposal to reform the government employee pension system. The system, which ran a record $29-billion deficit in 1999, supported more than 905,000 retired civil servants—more than the total number still on the job. In 1999, the retired workers received pensions equal to their highest salaries before retirement. They also received union-negotiated pay increases as if they were still working. The Brazilian governors pledged to

help Cardoso force the proposal through Congress in exchange for federal policies that would ease economic pressures on the states.

Oil discovery. In September, Petroleo Brasileiro (PETROBRAS), Brazil's state-controlled oil company, reported the discovery of an oil field in the Santos Basin off Brazil's southeastern Atlantic coast. PETROBRAS officials estimated that the field was capable of producing 700 million barrels of oil, enough to make Brazil self-sufficient in petroleum production in six years.

Beaches fouled. In April, workers shut down ruptured sewage pipes that carried waste from the city of Rio de Janeiro to a site 3 miles (5 kilometers) out into the Atlantic Ocean. The result was an ecological disaster. Untreated waste was dumped near shore at the rate of 3 tons (2.7 metric tons) per second, fouling such famed Rio beaches as Ipanema and Copacabana.

National mourning. Brazilians observed three days of national mourning, following the death on August 27 of Roman Catholic Archbishop Helder Pessoa Camara at age 90. "Dom Helder," as he was known around the world, had spoken out tirelessly on behalf of the poor.

☐ Nathan A. Haverstock

See also **Latin America.**

British Columbia. See Canadian provinces.
Brunei. See Asia.

Buddhism. On March 10, 1999, Tibetan Buddhists living in exile marked the 40th anniversary of an unsuccessful 1959 revolt against Chinese rule in Tibet. At anniversary commemorations in New Delhi and Dharmsala in India and in Kathmandu, Nepal, thousands of exiled Tibetans condemned Chinese control of Tibetan culture and religion. In the wake of the 1959 revolt, the Dalai Lama, spiritual leader of Tibetan Buddhism, was forced to flee Tibet and was followed into exile by more than 100,000 other Tibetans.

A dispute between Chinese authorities and some Tibetan Buddhists about who should be recognized as the 11th Panchen Lama, a figure of spiritual authority second only to the Dalai Lama, continued in 1999. In June, Gyancain Norbu, a 10-year-old boy appointed to the office by China in 1995, visited Tibet for the first time since his installation. He led more than 16,000 participants in a three-day ritual. Many Tibetan Buddhists did not recognize the authority of China's Panchen Lama. They endorsed the Dalai Lama's choice, Gedhun Choekyi Nyima, also a 10-year-old boy, whom Chinese authorities have held in custody since 1995.

The Dalai Lama became a best-selling author in the United States in 1999 with books that many U.S. readers found to be accessible presentations of Buddhist beliefs and practices. *The Art of Happiness,* which he co-wrote with Howard C. Cutler,

Buddhist monks escort a pagoda housing a tooth believed to have belonged to the Buddha through the streets of Hong Kong in May 1999. The tooth, usually housed in Beijing, was transported to Hong Kong for the province's first official celebration of the Buddha's birthday.

made *The New York Times* best-seller list in January and remained there throughout 1999. The
Dalai Lama's *Ethics for the New Millennium* was
also on the best-seller list for nine weeks in 1999.

Thailand. Phra Dhammachayo, abbot of the
Dhammakaya Temple in Bangkok and one of
Thailand's most influential Buddhist leaders, was
arrested on August 25 in Bangkok on charges of
abusing his authority and embezzling temple
funds. When authorities issued a warrant for
Dhammachayo's arrest, more than 10,000 devo-
tees attempted a blockade of his temple complex.

Falun Gong. An estimated 10,000 members of
the Chinese spiritual movement Falun Gong, or
the Great Wheel of the Law, held a silent vigil in
Beijing on April 25 to protest the movement's lack
of official recognition by the Chinese government.
The movement, which was founded in China in
1992, combines ideas from Buddhism and Taoism
with slow-motion exercise, meditation, and
breathing techniques. By 1999, the sect claimed
more than 70 million members in China and millions more in countries around the world. On July
22, China banned the organization. On October
30, the government passed a law making the
group's activities criminal, and the following day
authorities charged four Falun Gong leaders with
breaking that law.   □ Paul J. Griffiths

See also **China; Human rights.**

Building and construction. The
Seattle Mariners baseball team moved into a new
47,000-seat stadium, named Safeco Field, in July
1999. Safeco Field replaced the Kingdome, the
domed stadium where the team had played since
1977. A series of structural problems with the
roof of the Kingdome convinced Seattle officials
to finance Safeco Field, which, at a cost of more
than $500 million, was the most expensive ball-
park ever built in the United States.

Safeco Field features a retractable roof made
of three fabric-covered panels that move on
tracked rails. Although the complicated structure,
engineered by Skilling Ward Magnusson Bark-
shire Inc., of Seattle, greatly added to the project's cost and engineering time, it enabled the
Mariners to play on a field of natural grass while
shielded from the area's frequent rains. Opening
or closing the 360,000-square-foot (33,400-
square-meter) roof takes from 8.5 minutes (under
normal conditions) to 20 minutes (in high winds).

Under the sod at Safeco Field, irrigation and
drainage lines that were buried in sand and grav-
el are capable of removing 130,000 gallons
(492,000 liters) of water in 45 minutes. Plastic
heating coils were designed to maintain the soil's
temperature at 60 °F (15.5 °C), which helps keep
the turf blend of Kentucky bluegrass and peren-
nial ryegrass in optimum playing condition.

Tallest hotel. The Burj al-Arab ("Arabian
Tower"), the world's tallest hotel, opened in December 1999 in Dubayy, a port and commercial
center in the United Arab Emirates. The hotel rises to a height of 1,054 feet (321 meters). By comparison, the Empire State Building in New York
City is 1,250 feet (381 meters) high. Architect Tom
Wills-Wright of WS Atkins PLC in Epsom, England,
designed the building for Sheik Mohammed bin
Rasheed al Maktoun, the ruler of Dubayy, who
reportedly paid $1 billion for the building.

The hotel is shaped like the sail of a traditional Arab sailing vessel called a *dhow*. This "sail" is
actually a translucent glass and fabric wall, 164
feet (50 meters) wide, which was stretched across
the building's steel framework. The hotel was
built in the Persian Gulf on a small, three-sided,
artificial island, resembling the hull of a dhow.
The island is linked to the mainland by a bridge.

Two guest-room wings spread in a V-shape
from the hotel's central service core. Inside the
hotel, a casino and 201 luxury suites were completed on 55 double-height floors. The building is
topped with observation stations and a helicopter landing pad.

Athens airport. Construction continued in
1999 on Europe's largest airport project, the $2.2-
billion Athens International Airport. The Greek
government began work on the airport in the
early 1980's, but a number of design changes, financial setbacks, and political problems delayed
completion. A group of German contractors took
over the project in 1996 and announced in 1999
that the airport was on schedule to open in
March 2001.

Engineers designed the airport to have a
number of earthquake-resistant features to comply with tough building codes enacted by the
Greek government in 1995. These features included extra steel reinforcement in the foundation of
the main terminal and deep concrete footings.
The airport, located 30 miles (48 kilometers) from
the center of Athens, was designed to accommodate 64 million travelers annually.

Sony Center. The Sony Center, a complex of
offices, shops, residences, and other facilities designed by the German-born U.S. architect Helmut
Jahn, opened in Berlin, Germany, in October
1999. The centerpiece of the triangular complex,
which cost over $1 billion, is a huge, round roof—
made of glass, fabric, and cables—that appears to
hover 246 feet (75 meters) above an elliptical-
shaped grand plaza.

The roof forms a cone, tilted to one side, with
its peak cut off. Spokelike cables radiate from the
roof's hub to its outer ring, which rests on surrounding buildings that are 131 feet (40 meters)
tall. The roof's cables support translucent panels
of Teflon-coated fiberglass.

The $500-million home of the Seattle Mariners baseball team, Safeco Field, which opened in July 1999, features a three-panel retractable roof that moves on tracked rails. The Mariners' old home, the Kingdome (background), was scheduled to be demolished in 2000 to make way for a new football stadium.

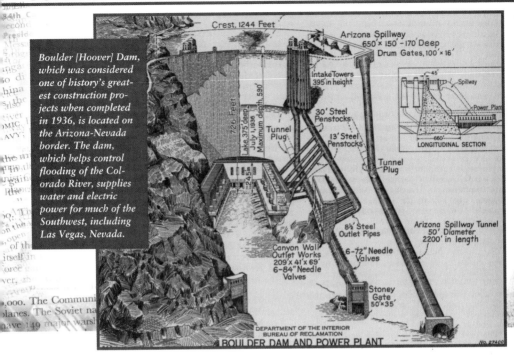

Boulder [Hoover] Dam, which was considered one of history's greatest construction projects when completed in 1936, is located on the Arizona-Nevada border. The dam, which helps control flooding of the Colorado River, supplies water and electric power for much of the Southwest, including Las Vegas, Nevada.

Crest, 1244 Feet

Arizona Spillway
650´ x 150´ - 170´ Deep
Drum Gates, 100´ x 16´

Intake Towers
395´ in height

Spillway

Power Plant

726 Feet

Lake, 375´ deep

July 1, 1936
Maximum depth, 590´

660´

LONGITUDINAL SECTION

30´ Steel
Penstocks

Tunnel
Plug

13´ Steel
Penstocks

Tunnel
Plug

8½´ Steel
Outlet Pipes

Arizona Spillway Tunnel
50´ Diameter
2200´ in length

Canyon Wall
Outlet Works
209´ x 41´ x 69´
6-84˝ Needle
Valves

6-72˝ Needle
Valves

Stoney
Gate
50´x35´

DEPARTMENT OF THE INTERIOR
BUREAU OF RECLAMATION
BOULDER DAM AND POWER PLANT

NO. 27400

Renovated Reichstag. The Sony Center lies to the south of the Reichstag, the German parliament building, built in the 1800's and reopened in April 1999 following an extensive renovation. The renovation included the addition of a transparent glass dome. The Reichstag was partially destroyed in a 1933 fire, which some historians believe was ordered set by Adolf Hitler. British architect Sir Norman Foster designed the dome and supervised the renovation. The Sony Center and Reichstag symbolized the "new Berlin," which in 1999 again became the capital of Germany.

The shape of science. In November, the distinctively shaped Center of Science and Industry, designed by Japanese architect Arata Isozaki, opened in Columbus, Ohio. The museum, which cost $125 million, was designed with arched concrete panels that form a canoelike shape called a *discontinuous clothoid.* The western wall of the building is curved so that it hooks around at the north and south ends, forming hairpin turns.

The structure's geometry was so complicated that only one of several prequalified concrete contractors—Concrete Technology Inc., of Columbus—was willing to undertake the job. The museum formed the centerpiece of a new riverfront park in Columbus. □ Andrew G. Wright

See also **Architecture; Germany; Transportation.**

Bulgaria. The Constitutional Court of Bulgaria ruled in January 1999 that a 1998 law concerning federal officials was unconstitutional. The law had banned former Communist officials and people who had collaborated with Bulgaria's secret police from holding high government offices.

Opinion polls in late March 1999 indicated that most Bulgarians opposed the bombing of Serbia by the North Atlantic Treaty Organization (NATO), which had begun on March 24. On April 28, a stray NATO missile struck a house outside Sofia, the Bulgarian capital. No casualties were reported.

Bulgaria's unemployment rate stood at 12.7 percent in September. The *gross domestic product* (the value of all goods and services produced in a country in a given year) grew by 1 percent during 1999.

Bulgaria and neighboring Macedonia signed a military cooperation pact in March. In February, Bulgaria had officially recognized Macedonian as a separate language, rather than a dialect of Bulgarian. □ Sharon L. Wolchik

See also **Europe; Macedonia; Yugoslavia.**

Burkina Faso. See **Africa.**

Burma. See **Myanmar.**

Burundi. See **Africa.**

Bus. See **Transportation.**

Business. See **Bank; Economics; Labor; Manufacturing.**

Cabinet, U.S. Secretary of the Treasury Robert E. Rubin resigned his Cabinet position in May 1999. He had served in the post since 1995. The announcement occurred as the U.S. economy continued to expand and the stock market continued to rise. Some economists credited Rubin with preserving economic stability in the United States in 1998 and early 1999 despite economic turbulence overseas, particularly in Asia and Russia.

The U.S. Senate in July voted 97 to 2 to confirm Lawrence Summers as Rubin's replacement as secretary of the treasury. Summers, who had been deputy treasury secretary since 1995, vowed to continue Rubin's policies fostering steady U.S. economic growth. Summers, a former Harvard University professor, was regarded as a strong advocate of free trade in a global marketplace.

Holbrooke confirmed. The Senate voted 81 to 16 in August 1999 to confirm Richard Holbrooke as U.S. representative to the United Nations. The confirmation followed a 14-month delay due in part to an ethics investigation, conducted by the State and Justice departments. The eight-month investigation centered on allegations involving Holbrooke's business contacts and speaking fees he received after leaving the State Department in 1996 to become an investment banker. Without admitting wrongdoing, Holbrooke agreed to pay $5,000 to the Justice Department to resolve the allegations.

Holbrooke's confirmation was delayed another six months by a series of parliamentary maneuvers by individual senators, including Charles Grassley (R., Iowa), Trent Lott (R., Mississippi), Mitch McConnell (R., Kentucky), and George Voinovich (R., Ohio). Grassley delayed the confirmation in an attempt to resolve a dispute over the State Department's treatment of an employee.

In 1995, Holbrooke successfully negotiated the Dayton Accords, the peace plan that ended a civil war in Bosnia-Herzegovina. He was named U.S. ambassador to Germany by President Clinton in 1993 and served as assistant secretary of state under President Jimmy Carter.

Secretary of State Madeleine K. Albright in September 1999 helped broker an agreement between Israeli Prime Minister Ehud Barak and Palestinian leader Yasir Arafat. Officials credited the secretary of state with helping to conclude the settlement, called Wye Two, which was designed to renew the stalled Arab-Israeli peace process. □ William J. Eaton

See also **People in the news** (Holbrooke, Richard; Barak, Ehud); **United States, Government of the; United States, President of the; Yugoslavia: A Special Report.**

California. See Los Angeles; San Francisco; State government.

Secretary of the Treasury Robert Rubin (right) talks with Deputy Treasurer Secretary Lawrence Summers (left) and President Bill Clinton following Rubin's announcement in May that he would resign from his post. The U.S. Senate in July voted to confirm Summers as the new secretary.

Cambodia's Prince Sirivudh is carried through the streets of Phnom Penh, Cambodia's capital, on May 3, 1999, for the annual spring plowing ceremony presided over by King Norodom Sihanouk.

Cambodia. The government of Cambodia remained preoccupied in 1999 with the problem of how to deal with participants in the Khmer Rouge terror of 1975-1979, when more than 1.5 million Cambodians died. The Khmer Rouge leader, Pol Pot, died in April 1998. In December, his top deputies Khieu Samphan and Nuon Chea surrendered to the government headed by Prime Minister Hun Sen, a former Khmer Rouge leader.

On March 6, 1999, former Khmer Rouge army chief of staff, Ta Mok, was arrested. Ta Mok's bloody purges in the 1970's had earned him the nickname, "the butcher." In April 1999, a low-level Khmer Rouge official, Kang Kek Ieu, known as "Duch" *(DOOK)*, was found working in Cambodia as a Christian missionary and arrested. Duch had run the Khmer Rouge's Tuol Sleng prison, where thousands were tortured and killed. He said he had accepted Christianity and repented.

Hun Sen opposed a United Nations recommendation that 20 to 30 former Khmer Rouge leaders be tried by an international tribunal. Political experts speculated that the Cambodian prime minister wanted to retain control of any legal action because hundreds of officials in his government might be subject to future charges.

The Cambodian parliament voted on August 11 to extend the period of detention for Khmer Rouge leaders awaiting trial to up to three years.

On September 7, Ta Mok was charged with genocide by a military court. Duch was also charged with genocide, but Khieu Samphan, Nuon Chea, and Ieng Sary, Pol Pot's foreign minister, continued to live freely in western Cambodia.

Army resignation. Hun Sen resigned in January as commander of the army. He said he wanted to demonstrate the political neutrality of the army and counter accusations that he had used it politically.

Foreign relations. The Association of Southeast Asian Nations (ASEAN) granted Cambodia membership on April 30. ASEAN, a regional political and economic association, had previously hesitated to admit Cambodia because of charges that Hun Sen's government was a brutal dictatorship.

Foreign donors resumed aid to Cambodia in 1999. Most donor nations had halted payments in 1997 after many of Hun Sen's political opponents were murdered. Donors sought promises of anti-corruption measures and a reduction in the armed forces' share of Cambodia's budget.

Census. Government officials announced in 1999 the results of the 1998 census, the first in Cambodia in 36 years. The census showed a population of 11.4 million, about twice as many people as in 1962. ☐ Henry S. Bradsher

See also **Asia.**

Canada

No great issues dominated political discussions in Canada in 1999, and the national government did not introduce major policy initiatives during the year. Prime Minister Jean Chretien and his Liberal Party, in power since 1993, remained firmly in control of the national government in 1999. Although the Liberals held only a slight overall majority of 157 members in the 301-seat House of Commons, the party's parliamentary position was stronger than it appeared, because the political opposition was badly divided.

Parliamentary standings. Sectional voting remained a significant factor in Canada's political life. The governing Liberals drew two-thirds of their members from one province, Ontario. Two of the four other parties in the Commons also sprang from narrow regional bases. All 44 members of the separatist Bloc Quebecois (BQ) in the House of Commons, for example, had won election in Quebec. The BQ had a national approval rating of only 8 percent.

All 57 members of Parliament belonging to the right-wing Reform Party, the official opposition, were elected from four western provinces. Although the party's stands on limited government and low taxes appealed to many western voters, Canadians in general considered the party's views on social questions harsh. In 1999, Reform's popular support dropped to 10 percent.

Reform leader Preston Manning spent much of 1999 attempting to forge a coalition of conservative voters. He hoped to draw support from the Progressive Conservative Party (PCP), which was gradually rebuilding itself after a disastrous defeat in the 1993 election. Manning called his new coalition the United Alternative. But PCP leader Joe Clark, a former prime minister, coldly rejected Manning's overtures. In 1999, the PCP had 19 members in the House and attracted 16 percent approval nationwide.

Leaders of the liberal New Democratic Party (NDP), which had 20 members in the House, also found it difficult to widen public support, which fell to 10 percent in 1999. In response, the NDP attempted to remake its image by moving to the center of the political spectrum.

Two members of the House of Commons changed parties in 1999. A PCP member from Newfoundland turned to the Liberals, claiming that he could do more for his fishing constituents as a member of the governing party. An NDP member from New Brunswick abandoned her party to join the PCP. There were also four independent members of the Commons.

Cabinet. Prime Minister Chretien shuffled his Cabinet on August 3, replacing 5 of 28 ministers. The reconfigured team, he said, would carry the government into the next election, which must be called before 2002. Chretien did not change senior ministers.

Quebec debate. Quebec's leaders reacted angrily in November 1999 to Chretien's hard line on the terms for negotiations on Quebec's independence should Quebecers approve sovereignty in a future referendum. Quebecers rejected separation by a razor-thin margin in 1995. In 1998, Quebec Premier Lucien Bouchard said he would hold another vote on separation only if "winning conditions" existed.

Chretien announced in November 1999 that the federal government would not negotiate independence for Quebec unless the margin of victory for sovereignty in a referendum was "much more" than 50 percent and the question on separation was unequivocal. Chretien's statements echoed the Supreme Court of Canada's 1998 ruling on secession. The court ruled that while secession violated "the Canadian legal order," Canadians outside Quebec could not ignore the will of a majority of Quebecers as expressed in a legal referendum.

Bouchard responded to Chretien's tough stance by contending that Quebec might declare its independence without negotiating at all. On Dec. 10, 1999, Chretien tabled draft legislation setting out in law the conditions for the next Quebec referendum on secession. The legislation is based on the 1998 Supreme Court decision. Quebec countered with its own legislation on the issue.

Nunavut. Canada gained a new territory on April 1, 1999, with the creation of Nunavut, the first addition to the Canadian confederation since 1949, when Newfoundland became the 10th province.

Social Union agreement. The government on Feb. 4, 1999, announced new rules regulating the creation and administration of social programs. The rules were enacted to ensure equal access to benefits throughout Canada while giving the provinces and territories more control over federally mandated programs. The Chretien government, 9 of Canada's 10 provincial premiers, and the leaders of 2 territories agreed to the "Framework to Improve the Social Union for Canadians."

Under the three-year agreement, the federal government promised not to launch new health, education, and welfare initiatives without the support of at least six provinces. In return, the pro-

Elaborate snow sculptures from the Canada Snow Sculpture Competition tower over visitors to Winterlude, the winter festival held in Ottawa, Canada's capital, in February.

vinces agreed to scrap policies that limited benefits for new residents.

The accord gave the provinces some control over the design of federally funded social programs and nearly complete control over their administration. The federal government retained the right to set performance standards for continued funding. The national government promised an additional $5 billion in health-care funding over three years to encourage provincial cooperation. (All monetary figures are in Canadian dollars unless otherwise noted.)

Quebec Premier Lucien Bouchard refused to sign the pact. He objected to federal control over

1999 Canadian population estimates

Province and territory populations

Alberta	2,793,425
British Columbia	4,034,403
Manitoba	1,127,318
New Brunswick	747,026
Newfoundland	542,247
Northwest Territories	43,029
Nova Scotia	914,749
Nunavut	26,000
Ontario	11,185,060
Prince Edward Island	137,567
Quebec	7,289,762
Saskatchewan	990,831
Yukon Territory	32,784
Canada	29,821,172

City and metropolitan area populations

	Metropolitan area	City
Toronto, Ont.	4,508,782	2,522,504
Montreal, Que.	3,400,907	1,039,107
Vancouver, B.C.	1,993,350	559,384
Ottawa-Hull	1,055,407	
Ottawa, Ont.		337,710
Hull, Que.		65,110
Edmonton, Alta.	876,123	625,970
Calgary, Alta.	855,901	810,310
Quebec, Que.	688,553	171,412
Winnipeg, Man.	671,221	622,195
Hamilton, Ont.	639,845	330,347
London, Ont.	409,475	334,518
Kitchener, Ont.	400,196	186,459
St. Catharines-Niagara	377,343	
St. Catharines, Ont.		132,662
Niagara Falls, Ont.		77,936
Halifax, N.S.	339,954	116,457
Victoria, B.C.	335,040	76,272
Windsor, Ont.	289,352	205,261
Oshawa, Ont.	288,424	144,188
Saskatoon, Sask.	224,088	198,096
Regina, Sask.	194,816	181,484
St. John's, Nfld.	175,412	102,733
Sudbury, Ont.	162,228	93,057
Chicoutimi-Jonquière	160,166	
Chicoutimi, Que.		62,947
Jonquière, Que.		56,401
Sherbrooke, Que.	151,580	78,971
Trois-Rivières, Que.	142,236	49,207
Thunder Bay, Ont.	125,939	114,003
Saint John, N.B.	125,630	72,451

Source: World Book estimates based on data from Statistics Canada.

performance standards and to the lack of a provision allowing provinces to withdraw from the agreement. Nevertheless, the federal government announced that Quebec would share in the increased funding.

Budget. On February 16, Finance Minister Paul Martin presented what he described as a "health-care budget" for fiscal year 1999-2000 (April 1, 1999, to March 31, 2000). As agreed to during talks on the Social Union, the $156.7-billion budget provided an additional $2 billion in grants to the provinces for health care.

Martin proposed increasing health-care spending by $11.5 billion over the next five years. The increase would push health-care spending to $15 billion by fiscal 2001-2002. This amount would equal the record amount allocated in 1995 before the Liberals initiated spending cuts to erase a $45-billion federal budget deficit.

Martin balanced the budget for the second consecutive year in 1999, the first time a Canadian government had done so since fiscal 1951-1952. The budget offered only limited tax cuts. The most significant was the elimination of a 3-percent surtax on incomes over $65,000. This measure complemented a similar tax cut on incomes below that level announced in the 1998-1999 budget.

Canada's economy registered strong growth during 1999. By midyear, the country had enjoyed 12 months of growth, the longest period of expansion in more than 10 years. Economists expected the 1999 *gross domestic product* (the value of all goods and services produced in a country in a given year) to increase between 3 and 3.5 percent.

Canada benefited from stronger commodity markets and higher commodity prices as the economies of Asian countries revived; from a booming United States economy, the recipient of at least 80 percent of Canadian exports; and from the revival of national consumer and business confidence. The Canadian dollar, which had fallen to unprecedented lows in 1998, regained some ground in 1999. By November, it was trading at about 68 cents U.S., approximately 5 cents higher than November 1998.

The expanding economy created more jobs, especially in manufacturing and construction. The jobless rate fell in October 1999 to 7.2 percent, its lowest point since 1990. Inflation rose slightly from 1998 levels to an annual rate of 2.1 percent.

New governor-general. On Oct. 7, 1999, Canada gained a new governor-general, who symbolized the country's multicultural makeup. Adrienne Clarkson, 60, a well-known broadcaster and publisher, became the first naturalized Canadian named to the largely ceremonial post. The governor-general represents Great Britain's Queen Elizabeth II, Canada's official head of state.

Clarkson, who emigrated with her parents

CANADA welcomed Queen Elizabeth II for a history-making visit in 1959. She took part in ceremonies that officially opened the St. Lawrence Seaway on June 26. . . . The new seaway can accommodate ships 786 feet long and 75 feet wide, carrying loads of up to 25,000 tons. About 80 percent of the world's shipping will be able to pass through the waterway, which has a minimum depth of 27 feet. Most of the seaway locks are equipped to handle two vessels at one time. A ship requires approximately 40 minutes to pass through one of the locks. With the opening of the seaway, total transit time from Montreal to the mouth of Lake Ontario was reduced by 12 to 20 hours.

Two ships navigate Iroquois Lock in the St. Lawrence Seaway following the seaway's opening in 1959. The commercial waterway links the Great Lakes and the Atlantic Ocean.

from Hong Kong at age 3, was recognized as an articulate advocate of Canadian nationalism in culture and economics. She was expected to bring a liveliness to the office not evident for some years.

International affairs. Peacekeeping continued to be a priority for Canada's defense forces during 1999, with about 4,000 Canadian personnel serving on international assignments. In 1999, approximately 2,800 Canadians served in Bosnia-Herzegovina, formerly part of Yugoslavia, and in the Yugoslav province of Kosovo, participating in peacekeeping efforts led by the North Atlantic Treaty Organization (NATO).

The Royal Canadian Air Force also participated in NATO's military action against Serb forces in Kosovo from March to June. In addition, Canada accepted 5,000 refugees from Kosovo.

In October, Canada joined an Australian-led effort to maintain order in the former Indonesian province of East Timor after violence swept the territory following a vote approving independence. Canada contributed 275 troops, 2 Hercules aircraft with 103 personnel, and a supply ship, the *HMCS Protecteur*, to the international force.

These peacekeeping and other military actions placed a severe strain on Canada's defense forces and budget. In November, the government reported that Canadian military efforts in Kosovo had cost $482.5 million.

Since taking office in 1993, the Chretien government had cut defense spending by 23 percent. Some critics charged that the cuts had left Canada's military establishment seriously underfunded. In November 1999, NATO's secretary-general said that Canada needed to increase defense spending and do more to modernize its armed forces. Chretien rejected the suggestion.

Fishery dispute. Disputes between native and nonnative lobster fishermen on the coasts of New Brunswick and Nova Scotia erupted into violence in the wake of a September 17 decision on treaty rights by the Supreme Court of Canada. The court found that a 1760 treaty gave native peoples in those two provinces the right to hunt, fish, and gather year-round and to earn a moderate livelihood from their efforts. The ruling came in a case involving a Mi'kmaq man who had been convicted of fishery offenses for catching and selling eel without a license.

Following the court's ruling, Mi'kmaq Indians in the two provinces immediately began trapping lobster and catching eel even though the lobster season had ended. Nonnative fishermen objected strongly and destroyed 3,700 native-set lobster traps. They also committed acts of vandalism against the Mi'kmaq, especially around Miramichi Bay on New Brunswick's eastern shore.

After federal government intervention, 33 of

Members of the Canadian House of Commons

The House of Commons of the second session of the 36th Parliament convened on Oct. 12, 1999. As of Dec. 15, 1999, the House of Commons consisted of the following members: 157 Liberal Party, 57 Reform Party, 44 Bloc Québécois, 20 New Democratic Party, 19 Progressive Conservative Party, and 4 Independents. This table shows each legislator and party affiliation. An asterisk (*) denotes those who served in the 35th Parliament.

Alberta
Diane Ablonczy, Ref.*
Rob Anders, Ref.*
Leon E. Benoit, Ref.*
Cliff Breitkreuz, Ref.*
Rick Casson, Ref.
David Chatters, Ref.*
Ken Epp, Ref.*
Peter Goldring, Ref.
Deborah Grey, Ref.*
Art Hanger, Ref.*
Grant Hill, Ref.*
Rahim Jaffer, Ref.
Dale Johnston, Ref.*
Jason Kenney, Ref.
David Kilgour, Lib.*
Eric Lowther, Ref.
Preston Manning, Ref.*
Ian McClelland, Ref.*
Anne McLellan, Lib.*
Bob Mills, Ref.*
Deepak Obhrai, Ref.
Charlie Penson, Ref.*
Jack Ramsay, Ind.*
Monte Solberg, Ref.*
Myron Thompson, Ref.*
John Williams, Ref.*

British Columbia
Jim Abbott, Ref.*
David Anderson, Lib.*
Chuck Cadman, Ref.
Raymond Chan, Lib.*
John Cummins, Ref.*
Libby Davies, N.D.P.
Harbance Singh Dhaliwal, Lib.*
John Duncan, Ref.*
Reed Elley, Ref.
Paul Forseth, Ref.*
Hedy Fry, Lib.*
Bill Gilmour, Ref.*
Jim Gouk, Ref.*
Gurmant Grewal, Ref.
Richard M. Harris, Ref.*
Jim Hart, Ref.*
Jay Hill, Ref.*
M. Sophia Leung, Lib.
Gary Lunn, Ref.
Keith Martin, Ref.*
Philip Mayfield, Ref.*
Grant McNally, Ref.
Ted McWhinney, Lib.*
Val Meredith, Ref.*
John Reynolds, Ref.
Nelson Riis, N.D.P.*
Svend J. Robinson, N.D.P.*
Werner Schmidt, Ref.*
Mike Scott, Ref.*
Lou Sekora, Lib.
Darrel Stinson, Ref.*
Chuck Strahl, Ref.*
Randy White, Ref.*
Ted White, Ref.*

Manitoba
Reg Alcock, Lib.*
Lloyd Axworthy, Lib.*

Bill Blaikie, N.D.P.*
Rick Borotsik, P.C.
Bev Desjarlais, N.D.P.
Ronald J. Duhamel, Lib.*
John Harvard, Lib.*
Howard Hilstrom, Ref.
Jake E. Hoeppner, Ind.*
David Iftody, Lib.*
Inky Mark, Ref.
Pat Martin, N.D.P.
Rey D. Pagtakhan, Lib.*
Judy Wasylycia-Leis, N.D.P.

New Brunswick
Gilles Bernier, P.C.
Claudette Bradshaw, Lib.
Jean Dubé, P.C.
Yvon Godin, N.D.P.
John Herron, P.C.
Charles Hubbard, Lib.*
Andy Scott, Lib.*
Greg Thompson, P.C.
Angela Vautour, P.C.
Elsie Wayne, P.C.*

Newfoundland
George S. Baker, Lib.*
Gerry Byrne, Lib.*
Norman Doyle, P.C.
Bill Matthews, Lib.
Fred J. Mifflin, Lib.*
Lawrence D. O'Brien, Lib.*
Charlie Power, P.C.

Northwest Territories
Ethel Blondin-Andrew, Lib.*

Nova Scotia
Scott Brison, P.C.
Bill Casey, P.C.
Michelle Dockrill, N.D.P.
Gordon Earle, N.D.P.
Gerald Keddy, P.C.
Wendy Lill, N.D.P.
Peter MacKay, P.C.
Peter Mancini, N.D.P.
Alexa McDonough, N.D.P.
Mark Muise, P.C.
Peter Stoffer, N.D.P.

Nunavut
Nancy Karetak-Lindell, Lib.

Ontario
Peter Adams, Lib.*
Sarkis Assadourian, Lib.*
Jean Augustine, Lib.*
Sue Barnes, Lib.*
Colleen Beaumier, Lib.*
Réginald Bélair, Lib.*
Mauril Bélanger, Lib.*
Eugène Bellemare, Lib.*
Carolyn Bennett, Lib.
Maurizio Bevilacqua, Lib.*
Raymond Bonin, Lib.*

Paul Bonwick, Lib.
Don Boudria, Lib.*
Bonnie Brown, Lib.*
John Bryden, Lib.*
Sarmite Bulte, Lib.
Charles Caccia, Lib.*
Murray Calder, Lib.*
John Cannis, Lib.*
Elinor Caplan, Lib.
M. Aileen Carroll, Lib.
Marlene Catterall, Lib.*
Brenda Chamberlain, Lib.*
Hec Clouthier, Lib.
David M. Collenette, Lib.*
Joe Comuzzi, Lib.*
Sheila Copps, Lib.*
Roy Cullen, Lib.*
Paul DeVillers, Lib.*
Stan Dromisky, Lib.*
Arthur C. Eggleton, Lib.*
John Finlay, Lib.*
Joe Fontana, Lib.*
Roger Gallaway, Lib.*
John Godfrey, Lib.*
Bill Graham, Lib.*
Herb Gray, Lib.*
Ivan Grose, Lib.*
Albina Guarnieri, Lib.*
Mac Harb, Lib.*
Tony Ianno, Lib.*
Ovid L. Jackson, Lib.*
Jim Jones, P.C.
Joe Jordan, Lib.
Jim Karygiannis, Lib.*
Stan Keyes, Lib.*
Bob Kilger, Lib.*
Gar Knutson, Lib.*
Karen Kraft Sloan, Lib.*
Walt Lastewka, Lib.*
Derek Lee, Lib.*
Rick Limoges, Lib.
Judi Longfield, Lib.
Steve Mahoney, Lib.
Gurbax Singh Malhi, Lib.*
John Maloney, Lib.*
John Manley, Lib.*
Diane Marleau, Lib.*
Larry McCormick, Lib.*
John McKay, Lib.*
Dan McTeague, Lib.*
Peter Milliken, Lib.*
Dennis J. Mills, Lib.*
Maria Minna, Lib.*
Andy Mitchell, Lib.*
Ian Murray, Lib.*
Lynn Myers, Lib.
Robert D. Nault, Lib.*
John Nunziata, Ind.*
Pat O'Brien, Lib.*
John O'Reilly, Lib.*
Gilbert Parent, Lib.*
Carolyn Parrish, Lib.*
Janko Peric, Lib.*
Jim Peterson, Lib.*
Beth Phinney, Lib.*

Jerry Pickard, Lib.*
Gary Pillitteri, Lib.*
David Pratt, Lib.
Carmen Provenzano, Lib.
Karen Redman, Lib.
Julian Reed, Lib.*
John Richardson, Lib.*
Allan Rock, Lib.*
Benoît Serré, Lib.*
Judy Sgro, Lib.
Alex Shepherd, Lib.*
Bob Speller, Lib.*
Brent St. Denis, Lib.*
Paul Steckle, Lib.*
Christine Stewart, Lib.*
Jane Stewart, Lib.*
Paul Szabo, Lib.*
Andrew Telegdi, Lib.*
Paddy Torsney, Lib.*
Rose-Marie Ur, Lib.*
Tony Valeri, Lib.*
Lyle Vanclief, Lib.*
Joseph Volpe, Lib.
Tom Wappel, Lib.*
Susan Whelan, Lib.*
Bryon Wilfert, Lib.
Bob Wood, Lib.*

Prince Edward Island
Wayne Easter, Lib.*
Lawrence MacAulay, Lib.*
Joe McGuire, Lib.*
George Proud, Lib.*

Quebec
Hélène Alarie, B.Q.
Mark Assad, Lib.*
Gérard Asselin, B.Q.*
André Bachand, P.C.
Claude Bachand, B.Q.*
Eleni Bakopanos, Lib.*
Michel Bellehumeur, B.Q.*
Stéphane Bergeron, B.Q.*
Yvan Bernier, B.Q.*
Robert Bertrand, Lib.*
Bernard Bigras, B.Q.
Pierre Brien, B.Q.*
René Canuel, B.Q.*
Serge Cardin, B.Q.
Martin Cauchon, Lib.*
Yvon Charbonneau, Lib.
Jean Chrétien, Lib.*
Jean-Guy Chrétien, B.Q.*
Denis Coderre, Lib.
Irwin Cotler, Lib.
Paul Crête, B.Q.*
Madeleine Dalphond-Guiral, B.Q.*
Pierre de Savoye, B.Q.*
Maud Debien, B.Q.*
Odina Desrochers, B.Q.
Stéphane Dion, Lib.*
Nunzio Discepola, Lib.*
Claude Drouin, Lib.
Antoine Dubé, B.Q.*
Gilles Duceppe, B.Q.*
Maurice Dumas, B.Q.*

Raymonde Folco, Lib.
Ghislain Fournier, B.Q.
Alfonso Gagliano, Lib.*
Christiane Gagnon, B.Q.*
Michel Gauthier, B.Q.*
Jocelyne Girard-Bujold, B.Q.
Maurice Godin, B.Q.*
Monique Guay, B.Q.*
Michel Guimond, B.Q.*
André Harvey, P.C.
Marlene Jennings, Lib.
Francine Lalonde, B.Q.*
René Laurin, B.Q.*
Raymond Lavigne, Lib.*
Ghislain Lebel, B.Q.*
Réjean Lefebvre, Ind.
Clifford Lincoln, Lib.*
Yvan Loubier, B.Q.*
Richard Marceau, B.Q.
Jean-Paul Marchand, B.Q.*
Paul Martin, Lib.*
Réal Ménard, B.Q.*
Paul Mercier, B.Q.*
Gilbert Normand, Lib.
Denis Paradis, Lib.*
Bernard Patry, Lib.*
Gilles-A. Perron, B.Q.
Pierre S. Pettigrew, Lib.*
Pauline Picard, B.Q.*
Louis Plamondon, B.Q.*
David Price, P.C.
Marcel Proulx, Lib.
Lucienne Robillard, Lib.*
Yves Rocheleau, B.Q.*
Jacques Saada, Lib.
Benoît Sauvageau, B.Q.*
Caroline St-Hilaire, B.Q.
Diane St-Jacques, P.C.
Guy St-Julien, Lib.
Yolande Thibeault, Lib.
Stéphan Tremblay, B.Q.*
Suzanne Tremblay, B.Q.*
Daniel Turp, B.Q.
Pierrette Venne, B.Q.*

Saskatchewan
Roy Bailey, Ref.
Garry Breitkreuz, Ref.*
Ralph E. Goodale, Lib.*
Dennis Gruending, N.D.P.
Allan Kerpan, Ref.*
Derrek Konrad, Ref.
Rick Laliberte, N.D.P.
Lee Morrison, Ref.*
Lorne Nystrom, N.D.P.
Jim Pankiw, Ref.
Dick Proctor, N.D.P.
Gerry Ritz, Ref.
John Solomon, N.D.P.*
Maurice Vellacott, Ref.

Yukon Territory
Louise Hardy, N.D.P.

The Ministry of Canada*

Jean Chrétien—prime minister
Lawrence MacAulay—solicitor general of Canada
Don Boudria—leader of the government in the House of Commons
Lloyd Axworthy—minister of foreign affairs
Jane Stewart—minister of human resources development
Arthur Eggleton—minister of national defence
Herb Dhaliwal—minister of fisheries and oceans
Lyle Vanclief—minister of agriculture and Agri-Food
Alfonso Gagliano—minister of public works and government services; deputy leader of the government in the House of Commons
Robert Daniel Nault—minister of Indian affairs and Northern development
David Anderson—minister of the environment
J. Bernard Boudreau—leader of the government in the Senate
Herb Gray—deputy prime minister
Sheila Copps—minister of Canadian heritage
Elinor Caplan—minister of citizenship and immigration
John Manley—minister of industry
Allan Rock—minister of health
Paul Martin—minister of finance
David Michael Collenette—minister of transport
Lucienne Robillard—president of the Treasury Board; minister responsible for infrastructure
Stéphane Dion—president of the Queen's Privy Council for Canada; minister of intergovernmental affairs
Ralph Goodale—minister of natural resources and minister responsible for the Canadian Wheat Board
Anne McLellan—minister of justice; attorney general of Canada
Hedy Fry—secretary of state (multiculturalism/status of women)
Gilbert Normand—secretary of state (science, research, and development)
Ethel Blondin-Andrew—secretary of state (children and youth)
George Baker—minister of veterans affairs; secretary of state (Atlantic Canada Opportunities Agency)
David Kilgour—secretary of state (Latin America and Africa)
Raymond Chan—secretary of state (Asia-Pacific)
Ronald Duhamel—secretary of state (Western economic diversification/Francophonie)
Jim Peterson—secretary of state (international financial institutions)
Claudette Bradshaw—minister of labour
Martin Cauchon—minister of national revenue; secretary of state (Economic Development Agency of Canada for the Regions of Quebec)
Andrew Mitchell—secretary of state (rural development/federal economic development initiative for Northern Ontario)
Pierre Pettigrew—minister for international trade
Maria Minna—minister for international cooperation
Denis Coderre—secretary of state (amateur sport)

*As of Dec. 31, 1999.

Premiers of Canadian provinces

Province	Premier
Alberta	Ralph Klein
British Columbia	Dan Miller
Manitoba	Gary Doer
New Brunswick	Bernard Lord
Newfoundland	Brian Vincent Tobin
Nova Scotia	John Hamm
Ontario	Mike Harris
Prince Edward Island	Patrick George Binns
Quebec	Lucien Bouchard
Saskatchewan	Roy Romanow

Government leaders of territories

Northwest Territories	Jim Antoine
Nunavut	Paul Okalik
Yukon Territory	Piers McDonald

Federal spending in Canada
Estimated budget for fiscal 1999-2000*

Department or agency	Millions of dollars†
Agriculture and agri-food	1,976
Canadian heritage	2,654
Citizenship and immigration	759
Environment	542
Finance	63,716
Fisheries and oceans	1,314
Foreign affairs and international trade	3,388
Governor general	12
Health	2,162
Human resources development	26,264
Indian affairs and northern development	4,524
Industry	3,502
Justice	886
National defence	10,305
National revenue	2,534
Natural resources	713
Parliament	310
Privy Council	271
Public works and government services	3,811
Solicitor general	2,727
Transport	912
Treasury board	1,907
Veterans affairs	1,970
Total	**137,159**

* April 1, 1999, to March 31, 2000.
† Canadian dollars; $1 = U.S. $0.68 as of Oct. 8, 1999.

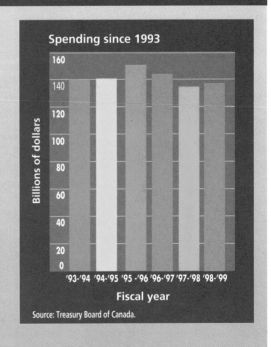

Spending since 1993

Billions of dollars

'93-'94 '94-'95 '95 -'96 '96-'97 '97-'98 '98-'99

Fiscal year

Source: Treasury Board of Canada.

35 native groups agreed on Oct. 10, 1999, to a one-month moratorium on lobster fishing while the government, nonnative commercial fishermen, and native peoples negotiated new fishing regulations. The government allowed the other two nonnative groups to fish for the rest of October, but under strict limits. Commercial fishing in the upper part of the Bay of Fundy opened as scheduled.

Fishery peace. Canada gained a larger share of the salmon catch in the Northwest Pacific Ocean under the terms of a new quota agreement with the United States aimed at restoring the region's seriously diminished salmon stocks. Negotiators hoped the agreement, signed by the two governments on June 30, would end the conflict over the region's fishery that began in 1992 with the expiration of the 1985 Pacific Salmon Treaty.

The new agreement covered coastal areas as well as rivers in Alaska, Oregon, Washington, and British Columbia. Concerns about the implementation of the treaty arose in October 1999, when the Congress of the United States approved only U.S. $10 million of the $60 million requested to finance a fund for salmon conservation, management, and research.

According to the pact, the size of salmon stocks in the region, determined by scientific surveys, are to govern harvest levels. Previously, the

two governments had imposed harvest ceilings before the start of each fishing season. Negotiators said the harvests of some types of salmon may be cut by almost half.

The pact gave fishermen in British Columbia a greater share of the rich run of sockeye salmon, which swim through U.S. waters on their way to the Fraser River. British Columbian fishermen, however, were barred from catching coho salmon, which Alaskan fishermen are allowed to harvest as the coho make their way to British Columbian streams.

Defense curbs lifted. On October 8, U.S. President Bill Clinton and Prime Minister Chretien "agreed in principle" to an agreement to end restrictions on the export of U.S. military and aerospace technology to Canada, imposed in April by the U.S. Congress. The Congress had imposed the restrictions to try to stop merchants of certain technologies from using Canada as a pipeline to avoid U.S. curbs on the transfer of protected technology to other countries.

The U.S. measure had required Canadian firms to obtain export permits from the U.S. government before they could use classified technology in their products. The ruling seriously threatened Canada's defense and aerospace industries, which employ about 73,000 workers and fulfill about $500 million annually in U.S. defense contracts.

In the pact, completed by Clinton and Chretien, the United States agreed to reinstate a 1958 agreement that exempted Canada from technology restrictions. In turn, Canada agreed to establish new export controls similar to those in force in the United States.

Trade disputes and agreements. The $400-billion flow of trade across the Canada-U.S. border—the world's greatest bilateral trade exchange—led to disputes in 1999, particularly over magazines and softwood lumber.

The magazine dispute arose from legislation proposed in Canada's Parliament that would have prevented Canadian advertisers from buying space in U.S. "split-run" magazines. Such magazines are produced in the United States and sold in Canada with little if any change in editorial content for the Canadian market. The United States claimed the measure represented unfair protectionism and threatened to retaliate with high tariff duties on Canadian exports.

After intense negotiations, the two sides compromised on April 25. Publishers of Canadian editions of split-run magazines were allowed to sell up to 18 percent of their advertising to Canadian sources without being required to add new material for the Canadian market. Beyond that limit, they would have to add "a substantial level" of original editorial content for Canadian readers.

Although some Canadians criticized the agreement as an erosion of government protection for Canadian culture, others praised the deal for heading off a costly trade war. Advocates also noted that under the new agreement, the United States, for the first time, had accepted a limited degree of protectionism for Canadian cultural institutions hard-pressed by U.S. competition.

Softwood lumber exports from Canada to the United States remained a point of contention in 1999 despite a 1996 agreement that allowed nearly all soft-lumber (pine and fir) exports to enter the U.S. market tax free. In August 1999, the two countries settled a dispute over British Columbia's June 1998 decision to reduce the fees it charges lumber companies for harvesting timber on public lands. The province had taken the action to stimulate its ailing timber industry. U.S. lumber producers complained that the lowered fees constituted an illegal subsidy.

In a settlement announced on Aug. 23, 1999, Canada agreed to freeze softwood exports from British Columbia to the United States at the average annual volume of trade existing before the province lowered its harvesting fees. All exports above that level would be subjected to a sharply higher entry tax. □ David M. L. Farr

See also **Canada, Prime Minister of; Canadian provinces; Canadian territories; Montreal; Toronto.**

Canada, Prime Minister of. In 1999, Jean Chretien, prime minister since 1993, led a Liberal Party that was confident in its dominant position in Canadian political life. Chretien frequently reminded Canadians that a 1999 United Nations study ranked Canada first for quality of life.

Political observers credited Chretien, who is often referred to as "le petit gar" (the little guy), for a keen political sense derived from 35 years in national politics. Chretien's approval rating remained high—about 65 percent. At the same time, however, public opinion polls indicated 60 percent of Canadians felt it was time for him to step down. But the prime minister made it plain he had no intention of retiring from politics. In August, he announced that he would remain at the helm of the Liberal Party for the next federal election, which must be called by 2001.

Chretien was credited for skillfully managing Canada's relationship with the United States, avoiding charges of overfriendliness that had dogged some previous prime ministers. He recognized the importance of the United States to Canada and developed a good working relationship with U.S. President Bill Clinton. Chretien earned respect, however, for always expressing a distinctly Canadian point of view on the issues concerning the two countries. □ David M. L. Farr

See also **Canada.**

Canadian provinces. Voters in 6 of Canada's 10 provinces went to the polls in 1999 to elect representatives to provincial legislatures. Voters turned three sitting governments out of office and reelected three. The Liberal Party of Prime Minister Jean Chretien, which controlled the federal government in 1999, suffered defeat in two provinces and won only limited support in the others.

Alberta, which enjoyed the healthiest public revenues in 1999 of any Canadian province—thanks to strong oil and gas earnings—moved in March to establish a provincially controlled income tax system with a flat rate of 11 percent. Canada's provinces normally calculate provincial income taxes as a proportion of the federal tax and leave the collection to the national government. Under the new plan, which was announced by provincial Treasurer Stockwell Day in his budget message on March 11, Alberta would impose and collect the tax itself. Day said the new tax system would go into effect by Jan. 1, 2002, if government revenues increase sufficiently to cover the plan's $600-million cost. (All amounts are in Canadian dollars.)

Day's budget for fiscal year 1999-2000 (April 1, 1999, to March 31, 2000) increased spending over the 1998-1999 budget by $1.2 billion, primarily for education and health care. Day forecast a 1999-2000 surplus of $617 million, $463 million of which was to be used to retire the province's net debt. The debt, calculated by the Progressive Conservative Party (PCP) government of Premier Ralph Klein, consisted of the difference between Alberta's total public debt of $22.5 billion in 1993 and its total public assets. Day predicted that the net debt would be eliminated by fiscal year 2001-2002.

British Columbia. Glen Clark, leader of the New Democratic Party (NDP), resigned as premier on Aug. 21, 1999. He was British Columbia's third premier in eight years to be forced from office because of scandal. The resignation followed a revelation, made one day earlier by British Columbia's attorney general, that Clark was under criminal investigation for possible corruption, bribery, and fraud. The Royal Canadian Mounted Police (RCMP) were probing whether Clark had improperly helped a contractor-friend obtain a potentially lucrative casino license in exchange for free renovations at several of Clark's properties. Clark denied any wrongdoing. Dan Miller, Clark's deputy premier, was sworn in as Clark's interim replacement on August 25.

A number of provincial NDP leaders, at a closed meeting in early July, reportedly had called for Clark's resignation because of the probe and because public approval of Clark's NDP administration had fallen to an unprecedented low of 14 percent. On July 22, Clark had shuffled his cabinet after the resignation of two ministers who made it plain that they had lost confidence in the premier.

British Columbia's legislature approved a historic treaty with the Nisga'a, a native people, on April 22. Under the terms of the agreement, the Nisga'a were to receive about 750 square miles (2,000 square kilometers) of land in northwestern British Columbia and the right to limited self-government. Many legislators opposed the treaty, contending it would create a racially based government. Before taking effect, the treaty had to win approval from the federal Parliament.

Manitoba. Canada's longest-serving provincial premier, Gary Filmon, lost office in an election on September 21. The PCP government of Filmon, who had hoped to win his fourth consecutive election victory, was narrowly defeated by the opposition NDP, under former union leader Gary Doer.

The Filmon government went into the election tainted by a scandal involving vote rigging in the 1995 election. In March 1999, a judicial inquiry determined that top PCP officials had illegally financed the campaigns of three First Nations (Native American) candidates. The officials had hoped that the First Nations candidates would divert votes from the more liberal NDP

and help elect PCP candidates. The inquiry exonerated Filmon.

PCP candidates promised in the 1999 election to cut taxes while increasing spending, a plan that many voters believed lacked credibility. The NDP made few campaign promises except to lower the high property taxes in Winnipeg, Manitoba's largest city.

The election gave the NDP 32 seats in the 57-seat legislature. The PCP won 24 seats, and the Liberals took 1 seat. The NDP did well in the north of the province and in urban areas, while the PCP maintained its traditional stronghold in the agricultural south. Filmon resigned as leader of the PCP after the election.

New Brunswick. Bernard Lord, 33, became the youngest premier in New Brunswick's history when his Progressive Conservatives took 44 seats in the 55-seat legislature in provincial elections on June 7. The Progressive Conservatives won 53 percent of the popular vote. Before the election, the party had held only nine seats.

The Liberal Party, which had controlled the province since 1987, won only 10 seats in a bitter defeat for a party which, under former Premier Frank McKenna, had won three elections with landslide majorities. McKenna, however, had retired, and his successor, Camille Theriault, had angered voters by canceling a planned tax cut. Lord had promised to lower the province's tax rate.

Newfoundland. Premier Brian Tobin led his Liberal Party government to a reelection victory on Feb. 9, 1999, only three years into the four-year mandate he won in 1996. Tobin denied speculation that he had called the election early in order to provide himself with strong political backing should Liberal Prime Minister Jean Chretien retire. Tobin claimed he wanted a firm popular mandate before entering into negotiations with Inco Ltd., a Toronto-based mining corporation, over the development of the Voisey's Bay nickel deposit, and with the government of Quebec over the development of a hydroelectric project on Labrador's Lower Churchill Falls.

In the election, the Liberals won 32 of 48 seats in the House of Assembly, 5 fewer than in 1996. The PCP won 14 seats, a gain of 5.

The provincial budget, presented on March 23, 1999, showed that Newfoundland benefited from increased federal transfer payments, which turned a predicted $30-million deficit into a $4.3-million surplus. The surplus, only the second since Newfoundland entered the Canadian confederation in 1947, was used for health and education.

With the cod fishery on the Grand Banks largely shut down, Newfoundland's unemployment rate in 1995 was twice as high as in the rest of Canada. Public sector workers, most of whom had not received a pay raise since 1991, were awarded a modest 7-percent increase over three years.

Nova Scotia. The Liberal government of Premier Russell MacLellan, which had been supported since March 1998 by 13 PCP representatives in Nova Scotia's legislature, lost that support in a fight over the budget for fiscal year 1999-2000. Finance Minister Don Downe's $250-million budget, presented on June 2, 1999, showed a surplus of $1.6 million but included a provision for borrowing $600 million for health care. The government proposed using the money to stabilize the debts of regional health bodies, hire additional nurses, and modernize medical equipment.

The PCP had backed the Liberals on the condition that they present a balanced budget. After a tense two weeks, PCP leader John Hamm announced that his party would no longer back the MacLellan government. He proposed a motion of no confidence, which was carried with the help of the NDP. This action forced the resignation of the government, and an election was scheduled for July 27.

In the subsequent campaign, John Hamm presented himself as an even-tempered moderate who would bring political stability to the Atlantic province. The PCP emerged from the voting with 39 percent of the popular vote and 29 of the 52 seats in the legislature. The NDP took 12 seats, while the Liberals dropped to third place with 11.

Political experts suggested that public perception of Liberal ineffectiveness in dealing with economic problems contributed to the party's defeat. In January, for example, MacLellan had been unable to prevent the federal government from closing one of two federally subsidized coal mines on Cape Breton Island and selling the other. At least 1,000 miners lost their jobs, a devastating economic blow in a region where unemployment ran as high as 25 percent in 1999.

Ontario. After four years in office, the PCP government of Premier Mike Harris swept to victory in elections held on June 3. The PCP win gave Ontario its first back-to-back majority government in 30 years. The Progressive Conservatives captured 59 of 103 seats, many of them in the suburbs around Toronto, and 45 percent of the popular vote. The Liberals took 35 seats, and the NDP won 9.

A booming economy helped propel the PCP to its reelection victory. In 1998, Ontario's *gross domestic product* (the value of all goods and services produced in a given period) had grown by 4.2 percent, double the rate in the rest of Canada. The automotive and telecommunications industries dominated Ontario's economic growth.

The provincial budget, presented on May 4, 1999, just before Harris called the election, contained 30 tax breaks for individuals and families.

The $597-billion budget also contained more money for health care and education.

Finance Minister Ernie Eves promised a balanced budget for fiscal year 2000-2001. Ontario lagged behind other Canadian provinces in accumulating a budget surplus, in part, because of the government's emphasis on personal income-tax cuts.

Prince Edward Island. For the first time in its history, the citizens of Canada's smallest province enjoyed a cut in personal taxes in 1999. Treasurer Patricia Mella announced the 1-percent cut in the tax rate in the provincial budget, introduced on April 6. On total expenditures of $824 million, Mella forecast a $42-million surplus for fiscal 1999-2000. The surplus resulted from a higher-than-expected *equalization grant* (a grant paid by the federal government to ensure a comparable level of health and educational services across Canada). The province used the $55.7-million windfall to pay down its debt and increase funding for health care.

Quebec. The separatist Parti Quebecois (PQ) government, hoping to put the province's financial house in order before a possible referendum on independence in 2000, balanced Quebec's budget on March 31, 1999, the end of the 1998-1999 fiscal year. The balanced budget was Quebec's first in 40 years. An unexpected $1.4-billion windfall in equalization grants helped Quebec achieve the balanced budget.

Although the fiscal 1999-2000 budget, presented on March 9, 1999, contained no relief for Quebec taxpayers, Finance Minister Bernard Landry promised an income tax cut for July 2000. Landry estimated revenue for fiscal 1999-2000 at $45.2 billion, providing a $1.1-billion surplus for the period.

Financial strain on Quebec's health care system led to a 26-day strike by the province's 47,500 hospital nurses. Claiming to be overworked and angry at staff shortages and low salaries, the nurses began 24-hour walkouts on June 26, 1999. They demanded a 6-percent raise over two years and an immediate 10-percent increase to bring their salaries up to the same level as social workers. The government insisted that it could not afford to pay more than 5 percent over three years, a position it had taken with all 400,000 public sector workers in the province.

The nurses returned to work on July 24, when the government agreed to complete by November 15 a comparative study of public sector salaries and workloads and to provide additional funds over the next six months to promote pay equity. The government, however, stuck to its 5-percent pay increase offer.

The nurses enjoyed widespread public sympathy throughout the strike. Political observers expected the labor troubles to damage the popularity of the PQ government, which in the past has counted on the support of the province's public employees.

An avalanche crushed a school gymnasium at Kangiqsualujjuaq, a remote Inuit community in northern Quebec, on January 1, killing 5 children and 4 adults and injuring another 25 people. The victims had been attending a New Year's Eve dance. The community is so isolated that residents were forced to rely on their own efforts to dig through the snow to recover the injured and dead. In a 1995 report on a 1993 avalanche at the same site, an engineering firm had recommended that the school board install steel snow barriers around a hill that overlooks the school.

Saskatchewan. Premier Roy Romanow defied tradition in 1999 by calling an election for September 16, the middle of the harvest season in the agricultural province of Saskatchewan. During the campaign, grain farmers, hurt by spring flooding and low wheat prices, complained that Romanow had not done enough to persuade the federal government to restore grain support programs or take up the question of United States agricultural subsidies with U.S. authorities. They demanded that the premier lead a delegation to the federal capital to argue the case for Saskatchewan farmers.

Although Romanow and his NDP colleagues won the September election, which was their third straight win, the results revealed voter dissatisfaction with the NDP. The NDP captured only 29 seats in the 58-seat legislature, down from the 41 won in 1995. The opposition Saskatchewan Party, a right-wing coalition formed in 1997 by unhappy PCP and Liberal legislators, took 26 seats, up from 10 in 1995. The new party won many of the rural districts in the province. The Liberal Party won 3 seats. The NDP and the Saskatchewan Party won about 38 percent and 40 percent of the popular vote, respectively.

To bolster his position in the legislature, Romanow persuaded two Liberals to enter his cabinet and nominated a third to be speaker of the assembly. The coalition, announced on Sept. 30, 1999, was the first alliance of political parties in Saskatchewan in 70 years.

Saskatchewan's 8,400 nurses began a 10-day strike on April 8, defying back-to-work legislation. The government, recognizing that the nurses enjoyed broad popular support, eventually offered a 13.7-percent salary and benefit increase over the next three years. This was considerably higher than its original offer. The agreement called for the nurses to pay a penalty of $120,000 for their action, with the money being given to a medical charity.   ☐ David M. L. Farr

See also **Canada; Montreal; Toronto.**

Canadian territories. Nunavut, homeland of Canada's Inuit people, officially became a new Canadian territory on April 1, 1999. The Inuit, a native people, began negotiating with the Canadian government in 1976 for their own territory. Nunavut means "our land."

Carved from the Northwest Territories, Nunavut had a 1999 population of about 25,000 people scattered across 770,000 square miles (2.2 million square kilometers). About 85 percent of the residents are Inuit.

Nunavut's new premier, Paul Okalik, warned in his speech at ceremonies marking the creation of the territory that Nunavut must "demonstrate how our [Inuit] society can deal with our problems." The new territory faced formidable challenges, including a 22-percent unemployment rate and high levels of suicide, illiteracy, and drug and alcohol abuse.

Forming the government. Elections were held on February 15 to choose 19 representatives to a Nunavut legislative assembly. The assembly met in the future capital, Iqaluit, on the southern coast of Baffin Island on March 5 and elected Okalik, a 34-year-old lawyer, as the first territorial premier. Most of the new territory's administration was in place by April. Nunavut received its first important visitors on September 5, when Canada's prime minister, Jean Chretien, and the president of France, Jacques Chirac, arrived in Iqaluit for a two-day visit. Chirac reportedly acquired art to add to a personal collection of Inuit artwork.

Northwest Territories. The Giant Mine in Yellowknife, the territorial capital, closed in October, the victim of falling gold prices. The price of gold tumbled from U.S. $500 an ounce in 1987 to U.S. $320 in 1999. The owner of the mine, Royal Oak Mines Inc., of Kirkland, Washington, declared bankruptcy in April. At the height of its production, the Giant Mine employed 1,000 workers. At the time of its closing, the work force had shrunk to less than 300 employees. The Miramar Mining Corporation of North Vancouver, British Columbia, began negotiations in September to take over the Giant Mine. Miramar planned to transport a reduced volume of ore from the mine to its own mill at the Con Mine on the outskirts of Yellowknife.

Diamonds appeared to displace gold as the economic mainstay of the Northwest Territories in 1999. Work continued to progress on the territory's second diamond mine, Diavik, located near the Ekati mine, at Lac de Gras, northeast of Yellowknife. Ekati, which opened in 1998, sent its stones to a diamond sorting and warehousing facility at the Yellowknife airport. The Diavik Mine, which is scheduled to begin production in 2002, signed an agreement in 1999 with Tiffany's, the

Fireworks over the Nunavut capital of Iqaluit on April 1, 1999, (above) celebrate the creation of Canada's new territory, the homeland for the region's native Inuit people. At the center of the Nunavut flag (right) is a representation of an inusuk, a stone monument used as a guide post and marker for sacred places. The star symbolizes the guidance of the North Star and Inuit elders. Blue and gold stand for the earth's riches, while the red refers to Canada.

famed New York City jewelry store, to market the mine's stones.

The Northwest Territories and Nunavut shared a $62-million surplus in 1999. While the money enabled the Northwest Territories to balance its $742-million budget, Finance Minister Charles Dent warned that it was imperative for the territories to secure full management of its resources from the federal government. Ninety percent of the financial benefits from the territories' diamond mines went to the federal government in Ottawa in 1999.

Yukon, Canada's smallest territory in land size, with a population of about 3,200, continued to experience economic problems in 1999. While two lead-zinc mines maintained operations in the Yukon, both were small and unable to make up for the loss of jobs at the large mine at Faro, which closed in 1998. Tourism emerged as the territory's principal employer in 1999, with revenues that topped $125 million.

Premier Piers McDonald, who also served as minister of finance, presented a $479-million budget for fiscal year 1999-2000 on Feb. 22, 1999. For the third consecutive year, the government asked for no tax increases. Funds from a cumulative surplus of $49.3 million were used to make up for a deficit that McDonald estimated would reach $21.4 million. Transfer payments from the federal government represented 71 percent of the territory's budget in 1998-1999. ☐ David M. L. Farr

See also **Canada.**

Cape Verde. See Africa.

Chemistry. Chemist Richard N. Zare of Stanford University in Stanford, California, announced in March 1999 that he had found a solution to a problem involving one of the most basic principles of chemistry—that two chemicals cannot react unless their molecules come into contact with each other. This principle has long been a problem for scientists interested in understanding the details of chemical reactions, in which case chemists need to use very small numbers of molecules. Because these molecules have a difficult time finding each other in the test tubes and other large equipment commonly used in chemistry labs, chemical reactions may not occur.

Zare and his team of researchers created extremely tiny test tubes out of *vesicles.* Vesicles are hollow spheres of fatlike molecules known as phospholipids. Each vesicle was approximately 5 micrometers in diameter—one-fifteenth the width of a human hair. Zare's vesicles were so small that each held as little as one trillionth of a quart.

After putting one kind of molecule in one vesicle and another in a second vesicle, Zare and his colleagues used electric pulses to fuse the two vesicles. The fusion allowed the two small groups of molecules to meet and react. Zare demonstrated this by bringing together molecules of red dye with molecules of green dye to create an orange solution.

The chemists suggested that the tiny test tubes could expand human understanding of *biochemical reactions*—that is, reactions in living cells. Biochemists could use the vesicles to simulate living cells because, like the vesicles, cells are tiny containers with frequent contact between molecules.

Waterproof glue. In July, chemists at the University of California at Santa Barbara reported that they had discovered the chemical ingredient that allows mussels to anchor themselves firmly enough to rocks to resist the powerful action of ocean currents. The chemists also demonstrated that a highly effective waterproof adhesive can be synthesized based on the chemical structure of this natural superglue.

The scientists, led by chemist Timothy J. Deming, found that a modified *amino acid* (building block of protein) called dihydroxyphenylalanine (DOPA) plays a dual role in creating the mussel's tough and waterproof adhesive. DOPA makes the proteins in the mussel glue very sticky and attractive to a variety of materials. In tests, even a small (5 percent) addition of DOPA made protein chains bind much more firmly to aluminum. DOPA also causes the protein chains to set into a tough, rubbery cement. The proteins cross-link, becoming a network of strands, even when they are submerged in water. This helps to perma-

nently tie a mussel to a rock or other convenient surface on the shore.

Practical applications of mussel-glue chemistry may produce several important benefits, especially in the creation of strong, water-resistant adhesives. Because the inside of the human body is a wet environment, such adhesives could be used in dentistry or medicine for suturing a wound or surgical incision.

Carbon dioxide controversy. How much carbon dioxide does Earth absorb? Not enough for a safe environment, according to ecologist Richard A. Houghton of Woods Hole Research Center in Massachusetts. In July, he and his colleagues concluded that the natural "sink" for carbon dioxide in the United States—that is, places where carbon dioxide is removed from the atmosphere and used by trees, other plants, and microorganisms—absorbs only 10 to 30 percent of the carbon dioxide produced in the region.

Many scientists believe that carbon dioxide emissions, generated by the burning of fossil fuels in cars and factories, are increasing the average temperature on Earth by trapping solar heat in the lower atmosphere. However, scientists disagree as to the severity of the problem.

In October 1998, the Climate Modeling Consortium, a group of climate researchers at Princeton University in Princeton, New Jersey, had reported that the carbon dioxide sink of the United States and southern Canada more than offset the annual regional emissions of the gas. The Princeton study made North America appear to be an unusually powerful carbon dioxide sink relative to such regions as Europe and Asia. This surprising finding was difficult to explain and led the Woods Hole researchers to undertake their own study of carbon dioxide in North America.

The Woods Hole scientists used computer simulations to study changes in U.S. forests and fields between 1700 and 1990. The researchers tallied the amounts of carbon dioxide that they believed were absorbed by plants at different times during this period. The numbers they came up with differed dramatically from the Princeton study. Some scientists said the new data implied that the United States needed to act to bring carbon dioxide emissions under control.

The Kyoto Protocol on Climate Change, an agreement made by more than 150 countries in 1997, required developed nations to reduce the amounts of carbon dioxide they release into the atmosphere. Besides curtailing the burning of fossil fuels, nations can fulfill the treaty's requirements by planting trees and increasing crop yields—both of which lead to the absorption of carbon dioxide. In addition, proof that a region is naturally absorbing more of the gas can help a nation meet its treaty obligations.

Both the Princeton and Woods Hole studies used historical data and represented indirect measurements of carbon dioxide absorption. Because of the uncertainties and contradictions in the findings, the two studies pointed to the need for better measurements of carbon dioxide absorption rates.   ☐ Peter J. Andrews

See also **Environmental pollution; Physics.**

Chess. In a giant elimination-format tournament held in Las Vegas, Nevada, from July 30 to Aug. 29, 1999, Alexander Khalifman of Russia emerged as the 14th official World Chess Federation (FIDE) world champion. The contest was the first world championship held in the United States since 1990.

Some of the world's most prominent chess competitors, including Russians Anatoly Karpov, the 1998 FIDE champion, and Garry Kasparov, the World Chess Council (WCC) champion, refused to participate in the FIDE tournament. Karpov claimed that FIDE officials failed to live up to their obligation to allow him to retain his title for two years. Kasparov, whom many experts consider the best player in the world, has not officially defended his title since 1995. As a result, many chess experts noted that Khalifman, who was ranked only 45th in the world, held the FIDE title without any of its usual prestige. The WCC and the FIDE are both official world chess organizations.

Xie Jun of China reclaimed her title as FIDE Women's World Chess champion in August 1999. She defeated Alisa Galliamova-Ivanchuk of Russia in a difficult, three-week match split between the cities of Kazan, Russia, and Shenyang, China.

New grandmaster. On March 15, Maurice Ashley of New York City became the first African American to achieve the title of grandmaster, the highest rank in chess. The title is presented by the World Chess Federation to players who achieve a series of outstanding performances in high-level contests within a certain period.

Tournaments. On March 21, 1999, in Las Vegas, Jaan Ehlvest of Estonia won the National Open. On August 19, Alex Yermolinski, of Euclid, Ohio, won the U.S. Open Championship in Reno, Nevada. In Salt Lake City, Utah, on September 10, Boris Gulko of Fairlawn, New Jersey, won the U.S. Championship. Anjelina Belakovskaia of New York City won the U.S. Women's Championship.

Young champs. Andrew Whatley, 18, of Pike Road, Alabama, won the U.S. Junior Open on July 18 in Tucson, Arizona. Jordy Mont-Reynaud, 16, of Palo Alto, California, won the U.S. Cadet Championship on July 25 in Nashville, Tennessee. Chess teams from three schools in New York City became U.S. scholastic team champions in 1999. On April 11, Stuyvesant High School won the U.S. National High School Championship in Sioux Falls, South Dakota. Hunter College Junior High School took the U.S. Junior High Championship on May 9 in Columbus, Ohio. Dalton School won the U.S. Elementary School Championship on May 16 in Phoenix, Arizona.

☐ Al Lawrence

Chicago. Mayor Richard M. Daley was reelected to his fourth term on Feb. 23, 1999, defeating U.S. Rep. Bobby Rush (D., Illinois) by a margin of more than 2 to 1. Daley has held the office longer than any mayor since his father, Richard J. Daley, who was elected six times between 1955 and 1975.

The mayor's reform of Chicago's schools, which instituted changes ranging from mandatory summer school for failing students to total reorganization of troubled schools, showed mixed results in 1999. Although student scores on standardized tests rose slightly over 1998, 2 out of 3 students continued to read below grade level in May 1999, and more than half of Chicago Public School students tested below grade level in mathematics.

Building and rebuilding. In September, Phillip Jackson, the head of the Chicago Housing Authority (CHA), announced plans to tear down what the agency judged to be the city's worst public housing high-rise buildings, lay off more than one-quarter of the agency's work force by the end of 1999, and privatize thousands of CHA jobs. Jackson proposed to rehabilitate or replace more than 24,000 units in the next 10 years.

A real estate boom in Chicago through much of 1999 helped to revitalize the central city. Conversions of aging office and loft buildings into condominiums brought the population of the Loop, Chicago's central business district, to more

Hey-diddle-diddle jumps over the moon on the plaza of the Wrigley Building on Chicago's Michigan Avenue during the summer of 1999. Some 300 decorated fiberglass cow statues were displayed outdoors or in public buildings during the city's "Cows on Parade" art exhibition.

than 115,000. Married couples with no children at home and young professionals drove sales of condos and townhouses, which surpassed sales of single-family houses in Chicago for the first time.

Two Near North Side landmarks faced possible demolition in 1999—the Medinah Temple, a Moorish revival performance hall, and the adjacent Tree Studios, the oldest existing artists' studio building in the United States. On September 14, the New York City-based World Monuments Fund designated the two buildings among the 100 most endangered structures in the world.

The Chicago City Council approved in September a proposal by developer Scott Toberman to build the world's tallest building in the Loop. Plans called for a slender tower, nearly 1,550 feet (472.4 meters) high, with 112 floors. The building was designed to anchor high-definition television broadcasting antennas that would extend as high as 2,000 feet (609.6 meters).

Cows on Parade, the fourth annual summer public art exhibition and the first to feature Chicago artists, consisted of nearly 300 whimsically decorated fiberglass cows on city streets, in buildings, and in parks. After the display closed on October 31, the cows were auctioned, and proceeds went to the charity of each buyer's choice.

Crime. The U.S. Supreme Court on June 10, 1999, struck down Chicago's 1992 antiloitering law, which had been passed to discourage street gang activity. A majority of the court held that the law gave police officers too much discretion.

Meanwhile, the decrease in crime continued as the city's murder rate hit a 10-year low and sexual assaults, robberies, and burglaries also declined.

Sports. On January 13, Michael Jordan announced his retirement from the Chicago Bulls after leading the team to six National Basketball Association titles. Jordan noted that he had "accomplished everything that I could do as an individual." The Chicago Cubs' Sammy Sosa hit 63 home runs in 1999, becoming the first major-league ballplayer in history to hit more than 60 home runs in two consecutive seasons.

Endings. Carl Fischer Music, a Chicago institution, closed its doors in April after 71 years, when the music publisher discontinued retail sales. Former store employees set up an independent business under the Fischer name.

Deaths. Movie critic Gene Siskel, renowned nationwide for his thumbs-up/thumbs-down reviews with colleague Roger Ebert, died February 20 at age 53. Walter Payton, a star running back for the Chicago Bears professional football team from 1975 to 1987, died on November 1 at age 45.
□ Harold Henderson

See also **Baseball; Basketball; Deaths; People in the news** (Sosa, Sammy); **Supreme Court of the United States.**

Children's books. See Literature for
children.

Chile. No presidential candidate won a majority of votes in the national election on Dec. 11, 1999. Ricardo Lagos of the Socialist-Christian Democratic Party and Joaquin Lavin of the right-wing Union for Chilean Progress were scheduled to face off in a runoff election in January 2000.

Chile's economy went into a severe slump in 1999. A drought led to low water supplies at hydroelectric dams. Power shortages, in turn, triggered low productivity in factories. International prices of copper, Chile's major export, fell from $1.20 a pound (0.45 kilograms) in 1997 to $0.61 a pound in March 1999—the lowest price in 12 years.

A court in London ruled on October 8 that General Augusto Pinochet Ugarte, Chile's dictator from 1973 to 1990, could be extradited to Spain to face charges of human rights violations. Pinochet, who was arrested in England in October 1998, appealed the ruling. During Pinochet's confinement, Chilean authorities arrested 25 military officers on charges of murder, torture, and kidnapping committed during his dictatorship.

On April 9, Chileans mourned the loss of Cardinal Raul Silva Henriquez, who died at the age of 91 in Santiago. As head of Chile's Roman Catholic Church for more than 20 years, Cardinal Silva was a frequent critic of human rights abuses under the Pinochet regime.   □ Nathan A. Haverstock

See also **Latin America.**

China. The Communist Party on Oct. 1, 1999, celebrated the 50th anniversary of the founding of the People's Republic of China. President Jiang Zemin, leader of the Communist Party, presided at an anniversary parade in Beijing, the capital. He was accompanied by Vice President Hu Jintao, who observers believe is likely to be China's next president.

An estimated 500,000 people paraded through Beijing's Tiananmen Square during the celebration. Tanks, missiles, and artillery were on display, and warplanes flew overhead. The parade also featured portraits of Mao Zedong, China's Communist ruler from 1949 to 1976, and Deng Xiaoping, the Chinese leader from 1978 to 1997, who was credited for the economic reforms that increased the nation's prosperity.

Reforms and repression. By mid-1999, about two-thirds of the rural villages in China held open elections to choose leaders of local councils, under a 1998 law that permits a limited form of democracy. In the past, the Communist Party had designated leaders at all levels of government.

The Communist Party, nonetheless, maintained a tight control on political activity in China in 1999. In February, the outlawed Chinese Democracy Party, an opposition party founded in 1998, announced plans to set up a national committee to coordinate political activities. The government responded by arresting dozens of opposition leaders on charges of "subverting state power."

The Chinese government, in an effort to block outside political influences, also interfered with the reception of foreign television broadcasts and limited people's access to the Internet.

Falun Gong. The Chinese government also cracked down on Falun Gong, a spiritual movement that combines slow-motion exercises, meditation, and breathing techniques with ideas from Buddhism and Taoism. Chinese authorities reportedly viewed the movement as a challenge to the Communist Party's influence over the public. Falun Gong claimed more than 70 million members in China in 1999—more than the number of people belonging to China's Communist Party. The government, however, put Falun Gong membership at about 2 million.

Li Hongzhi, who founded Falun Gong in 1992, had been forced by government pressure in 1997 to live in exile. In his absence, the movement continued to grow—almost unnoticed. On April 25, 1999, at least 10,000 followers gathered silently at the residential compound of party leaders in Beijing to seek official recognition.

On July 22, the government banned the group. When members of the movement protested, dozens of people were arrested and charged with "damaging social stability." Communist Party members also burned Falun Gong books in public.

THE CLOSE OF 1949 witnessed the near-completion of one of the greatest political overturns of modern times—the conquest of vast China by the Communists. At the beginning of the year 1949 the Nationalist government, headed by General Chiang Kai-shek, still held the Yangtze River line and important areas north of that great waterway. But before the year had passed the Communist forces had conquered Nanking, Shanghai, and Canton, and all other seaports of importance. They had also taken over the vast northwest provinces, most of Szechwan, and many other tremendous territories into which the Japanese armies were unable to penetrate during eight years of war.

The year's end found General Chiang Kai-shek driven from the mainland of Asia, and holding only the island of Formosa . . .

In a strategic sense the whole balance of the Far East had been upset by the astounding Communist

CHINA'S CAPITAL
Five different cities in turn were the capital of Nationalist China during 1949, as the government fled before Communist forces.

January 25, 1949—the Nationalist government fled from NANKING

CHENGTU abandoned Dec. 8
CHUNGKING abandoned Nov. 30
Shanghai
East China Sea
TAIPEI
FORMOSA
CANTON abandoned Sept. 2
French Indo-China
South China Sea

Five different cities served as the capital of Nationalist China in 1949 as the government fled Communist forces.

sweep southward. The Soviet Union found itself in a place of power and influence never even dreamed of by the czars of Russia. . . . At the close of 1949 the Soviet Union held control of all of Manchuria's 500,000 square miles, controlled the northern half of Korea, and north of Japan, held all of Sakhalin Island and the entire Kuril group.

Economy. China's parliament, the National People's Congress (NPC), focused on economic issues during its session in March. Premier Zhu Rongji said China faced a grim economic outlook in 1999 after enjoying 7.8 percent growth in domestic output in 1998. (Private economists had put the figure at 4 percent.) To achieve a 7-percent growth in 1999, the government promised to boost consumption, increase exports, and continue massive investment for improving the nation's infrastructure.

Economists reported that these steps were needed to counter a fall in prices as people with jobs saved their money rather than buy overstocked, poor-quality manufactured goods. Although unemployment was high—an estimated 10 percent in cities and 30 percent in rural areas—officials closed four plants that were eating up huge government subsidies and failing to repay bank loans. Officials also planned to trim the bloated government bureaucracy in order to reduce deficit financing.

In spite of government efforts to encourage growth, the economic growth rate fell during 1999, according to an October 19 report by China's National Bureau of Statistics. Economists noted that rising exports late in the year failed to offset the dual impact of falling prices and reduced foreign investment.

Free enterprise recognized. The NPC officially acknowledged the importance of free enterprise to China's economy. It amended China's Constitution to declare private business "an important component of the socialist market economy" and incorporated a rule of law intended to give investors protection from Communist Party interference. The amendment marked a significant change from the traditional Communist doctrine that endorses state control of virtually all spheres of the economy. In 1949, the Communist government had crushed private enterprise. By 1999, private business ventures had expanded to one-third of China's economy.

Corruption. Numerous reports of corruption in 1999 threatened government credibility. In January, a corruption probe in Chongqing halted work on 47 local construction projects after a newly built bridge collapsed, killing 40 pedestrians. In June, Auditor-General Li Jinhua reported that $2 billion had been illegally diverted from China's national funds in 1998. In several towns, demonstrations to protest corruption erupted into riots.

Work on the Yangtze River's Three Gorges Dam was delayed in 1999 because of engineering problems attributed in part to corruption. Flooding of the Yangtze in 1999 claimed more than 700 lives and raised questions about corrupt management of the river's dams and dikes.

Chinese police arrest members of the banned Falun Gong movement in Beijing's Tiananmen Square in late Sep-tember. The government tightened security in the capital in preparation for the celebration of 50 years of Communist rule on October 1. Falun Gong is a spiritual movement that combines slow-motion exercises, meditation, and breathing techniques with ideas from Buddhism and Taoism.

Policy changes. In 1999, China moved away from its traditional agriculture policy of providing all of the nation's food needs. The government disclosed in September that it would only grow 95 percent of required grain over the next 10 years, down to 90 percent by 2030. Officials said that capital costs of producing more grain were higher than the cost of importing grain.

In 1999, the government also eased population control measures, long seen as a requirement for maintaining prosperity. Efforts since 1980 to limit families to one child had curbed population growth by 300 million people, according to government claims. In the 1990's, however, the government became concerned that the limits were hurting family life by creating pampered single children—known as "little emperors"—and risking the country's future ability to support an aging population with fewer workers.

Taiwan. China reacted angrily to a statement by President Lee Teng-hui of Taiwan on July 9, 1999, that China and Taiwan should deal with each other as separate, equal states. China, which views Taiwan as a wayward province, repeated threats to conquer the island if it declared independence but promised not to use nuclear arms.

U.S. relations. Official U.S. reports in 1999 claimed that China had systematically stolen nuclear secrets, enabling China to target American cities directly with advanced nuclear missiles by the year 2015. U.S. officials also accused China of illegally trying to import U.S. military equipment and violating human rights agreements.

On May 7, 1999, U.S. warplanes inadvertently bombed China's embassy in Belgrade, Yugoslavia, during the North Atlantic Treaty Organization's campaign to force the Yugoslav army out of the province of Kosovo. The attack killed three Chinese and wounded more than 20 others. The Chinese government rejected the official U.S. explanation that the embassy had been accidentally targeted, and mobs of angry demonstrators attacked and damaged the U.S. embassy in Beijing. On July 30, the two countries agreed to $4.5 million in U.S. compensation for the bombing victims.

Chinese President Jiang Zemin and U.S. President Bill Clinton met in September, agreeing to work for better relations and stronger trade ties.

Hong Kong. In 1999, two years after China took over Hong Kong from Great Britain, controversy arose over Hong Kong residency for children born in mainland China who had at least one parent living in the former colony. In January, Hong Kong's highest court ruled that such children could live in Hong Kong. Fearing a flood of immigrants, the city's government asked the NPC to reinterpret the Chinese government's agreement with Great Britain to grant Hong Kong judicial independence.

The NPC overturned the court's ruling on June 26, raising fears among the people of Hong Kong that its legal system was no longer free.

Macao. On December 20, the government of Portugal turned over Macao, its colony on the southern coast of China, to China. Colonized in 1557, Macao had served as the primary center of trade in Asia for European countries until the 1800's, when British-controlled Hong Kong became a dominant trade center. In the late 1900's, the colony had acquired a reputation as a gambling and gang haven. Edmund Ho, a Macao banker, became the city's first chief executive after the transfer of power.

A separatist movement in the western Chinese province of Xinjiang, led by ethnic Uighurs, who are primarily Muslims, drew worldwide attention in 1999. Amnesty International, a London-based human rights group, reported in June that Chinese officials had executed 190 people in Xinjiang since 1997. Most of those executed were Uighurs who had been convicted of subversion or terrorism. □ Henry S. Bradsher

See also **Asia; Taiwan; United States, Government of the; Yugoslavia: A Special Report.**

Chretien, Jean. See **Canada, Prime Minister of.**

Churches. See **Eastern Orthodox Churches; Protestantism; Roman Catholic Church.**

City. Cities in Asia began to rebound in 1999 from the economic crisis they endured in 1998. Tokyo regained its place as the world's most expensive city in which to live, according to the 1999 city cost-of-living rankings by the Corporate Resources Group (CRG), a consulting firm based in Geneva, Switzerland. During the 1990's, Tokyo had regularly held the top spot as the most expensive city but lost out in 1998 to Hong Kong, which dropped to second place in 1999. The five most expensive cities in 1999, as well as 8 of the 10 most expensive cities, were in Asia.

The CRG annually ranks 150 cities throughout the world by comparing the city-by-city rents and the costs of 145 goods and services. The CRG gives each city a numerical rating compared with New York City, which is assigned a baseline rating of 100. The Tokyo rating in 1999 was 165.5, meaning that it cost almost two-thirds more to live in Tokyo than in New York City. The most expensive cities after Tokyo and Hong Kong (153.3) were Beijing (152.1), Osaka, Japan (144.4), Shanghai (140.3), Moscow (128.3), Guangzhou, China (121.2), London (112.4), Shenzhen, China (109.10), and Seoul, South Korea (107.9).

The least expensive city in the survey was Harare, Zimbabwe (21.7). The growing gap between the most and least expensive cities was very notable in 1999. It was 663 percent more expensive to live in Tokyo in 1999 than in Harare. In 1998, the gap between the most and least expensive cities was only 114 points. In 1999, it had grown to 143.8 points. Analysts attributed this widening gap to the technology-driven economic boom, which was enriching the most developed countries in the late 1990's, while leaving the less developed countries further and further behind.

New York City remained the most expensive city in the United States and ranked 16th in the world in 1999, up five places from 1998. Chicago (85.6), Miami, Florida (85.5), San Francisco (85.3), and Los Angeles (84.6) rounded out the U.S. top five in 1999. Toronto (68.1) continued to be the most expensive city in Canada. After Moscow and London, Europe's most expensive cities were Oslo, Norway (99.3), Paris (97.9), Milan, Italy (92), Frankfurt, Germany (87.2), and Amsterdam, the Netherlands (80.6). Sydney (68.4) remained the most expensive city in Australia.

Residents of Buenos Aires, Argentina (97.6), Sao Paulo, Brazil (95.3), and Rio de Janeiro, Brazil (88.7), had the highest costs of living in Latin America in 1999. Tehran, Iran (97.5), Abu Dhabi, United Arab Emirates (94), and Amman, Jordan (93.6), were the most expensive places to live in the Middle East. Cairo, Egypt (97), and Libreville, Ghana (94.4), were the most expensive cities in Africa.

Thriving U.S. cities. As the U.S. economy boomed during the 1990's, increased revenues combined with innovative local governments placed many U.S. cities on a firm financial footing. The National League of Cities (NLC), a Washington, D.C.-based organization that seeks to improve the quality of life in U.S. cities, reported that 1999 was the sixth straight year in which most U.S. cities reported improved fiscal health. Seventy-five percent of the 317 surveyed cities— each with a population of more than 10,000—reported that they were better able to meet their financial needs in 1999 than in 1998. Sixty-four percent of the cities responded that they expected to be even better off in 2000. In a show of economic assurance, 70 percent of the U.S. cities increased their expenditures in 1999.

The NLC noted that the traditional problems that plagued U.S. cities over the past few decades—crime, unemployment, transportation, and population decline—were less serious in 1999. U.S. Justice Department statistics showed that violent crime in cities dropped 27 percent between 1991 and 1997. The Bureau of Labor reported that unemployment in the 50 largest U.S. cities declined from 6.3 percent in 1990 to 5.4 percent in 1998. The U.S. Congress allocated more money to cities in 1999 to address pressing urban road and rail needs. All major U.S. cities reported that they expected the number of people

50 largest cities in the United States

Rank	City	Population*
1.	New York, N.Y.	7,420,166
2.	Los Angeles, Calif.	3,597,556
3.	Chicago, Ill.	2,802,079
4.	Houston, Tex.	1,786,691
5.	Philadelphia, Pa.	1,436,287
6.	San Diego, Calif.	1,220,666
7.	Phoenix, Ariz.	1,198,064
8.	San Antonio, Tex.	1,114,130
9.	Dallas, Tex.	1,075,894
10.	Detroit, Mich.	970,196
11.	San Jose, Calif.	861,284
12.	San Francisco, Calif.	745,774
13.	Indianapolis, Ind.	741,304
14.	Jacksonville, Fla.	693,630
15.	Columbus, Ohio	670,234
16.	Baltimore, Md.	645,593
17.	El Paso, Tex.	615,032
18.	Memphis, Tenn.	603,507
19.	Milwaukee, Wis.	578,364
20.	Boston, Mass.	555,447
21.	Austin, Tex.	552,434
22.	Seattle, Wash.	536,978
23.	Washington, D.C.	523,124
24.	Nashville, Tenn.	510,274
25.	Charlotte, N.C.	504,637
26.	Portland, Ore.	503,891
27.	Denver, Colo.	499,055
28.	Cleveland, Ohio	495,817
29.	Fort Worth, Tex.	491,801
30.	Oklahoma City, Okla.	472,221
31.	New Orleans, La.	465,538
32.	Tucson, Ariz.	460,466
33.	Kansas City, Mo.	441,574
34.	Virginia Beach, Va.	432,380
35.	Long Beach, Calif.	430,905
36.	Albuquerque, N. Mex.	419,311
37.	Las Vegas, Nev.	404,288
38.	Sacramento, Calif.	404,168
39.	Atlanta, Ga.	403,819
40.	Fresno, Calif.	398,133
41.	Honolulu, Hawaii	395,789
42.	Tulsa, Okla.	381,393
43.	Omaha, Nebr.	371,291
44.	Miami, Fla.	368,624
45.	Oakland, Calif.	365,874
46.	Mesa, Ariz.	360,076
47.	Minneapolis, Minn.	351,731
48.	Colorado Springs, Colo.	344,987
49.	Pittsburgh, Pa.	340,520
50.	St. Louis, Mo.	339,316

*1998 estimates (latest available).
Source: U.S. Bureau of the Census.

50 largest metropolitan areas in the United States

Rank	Metropolitan area	Population*
1.	Los Angeles-Long Beach, Calif.	9,219,257
2.	New York, N.Y.	8,675,158
3.	Chicago, Ill.	7,847,722
4.	Philadelphia, Pa.-N.J.	4,962,840
5.	Washington, D.C.-Md.-Va.-W.Va.	4,687,159
6.	Detroit, Mich.	4,335,435
7.	Houston, Tex.	3,972,235
8.	Atlanta, Ga.	3,777,588
9.	Boston, Mass.	3,275,035
10.	Dallas, Tex.	3,190,842
11.	Riverside-San Bernardino, Calif.	3,183,932
12.	Phoenix-Mesa, Ariz.	2,958,468
13.	Minneapolis-St. Paul, Minn.-Wis.	2,847,756
14.	Orange County, Calif.	2,720,157
15.	San Diego, Calif.	2,711,520
16.	Nassau-Suffolk, N.Y.	2,678,050
17.	St. Louis, Mo.-Ill.	2,566,960
18.	Baltimore, Md.	2,506,386
19.	Pittsburgh, Pa.	2,374,655
20.	Seattle-Bellevue-Everett, Wash.	2,309,061
21.	Oakland, Calif.	2,255,531
22.	Tampa-St. Petersburg-Clearwater, Fla.	2,245,657
23.	Cleveland-Lorain-Elyria, Ohio	2,243,722
24.	Miami, Fla.	2,126,302
25.	Denver, Colo.	1,961,493
26.	Newark, N.J.	1,948,887
27.	Portland, Ore.-Vancouver, Wash.	1,854,600
28.	Kansas City, Mo.-Kan.	1,728,874
29.	San Francisco, Calif.	1,673,159
30.	San Jose, Calif.	1,636,067
31.	Cincinnati, Ohio-Ky.-Ind.	1,622,476
32.	Fort Worth-Arlington, Tex.	1,589,290
33.	Norfolk-Virginia Beach-Newport News, Va.	1,574,324
34.	San Antonio, Tex.	1,552,846
35.	Sacramento, Calif.	1,535,042
36.	Indianapolis, Ind.	1,532,861
37.	Fort Lauderdale, Fla.	1,509,073
38.	Orlando, Fla.	1,492,433
39.	Columbus, Ohio	1,484,552
40.	Milwaukee-Waukesha, Wis.	1,466,414
41.	Charlotte-Gastonia, N.C.-Rock Hill, S.C.	1,382,085
42.	Las Vegas, Nev.-Ariz.	1,370,400
43.	Bergen-Passaic, N.J.	1,322,720
44.	New Orleans, La.	1,322,096
45.	Salt Lake City-Ogden, Ut.	1,273,676
46.	Greensboro-Winston-Salem-High Point, N.C.	1,174,574
47.	Buffalo-Niagara Falls, N.Y.	1,170,544
48.	Nashville, Tenn.	1,167,636
49.	Hartford, Conn.	1,140,381
50.	Austin-San Marcos, Tex.	1,123,056

*1998 World Book estimates based on data from the U.S. Bureau of the Census.

50 largest urban centers in the world

Rank	Urban center*	Population
1.	Tokyo-Yokohama, Japan	29,649,000
2.	Mexico City, Mexico	26,977,000
3.	Sao Paulo, Brazil	24,488,000
4.	Seoul, South Korea	21,325,000
5.	Bombay, India	14,954,000
6.	New York City, U.S.	14,644,000
7.	Osaka-Kobe-Kyoto, Japan	14,241,000
8.	Rio de Janeiro, Brazil	13,867,000
9.	Calcutta, India	13,833,000
10.	Teheran, Iran	13,655,000
11.	Buenos Aires, Argentina	12,769,000
12.	Manila, Philippines	12,515,000
13.	Jakarta, Indonesia	12,434,000
14.	Cairo, Egypt	12,217,000
15.	Lagos, Nigeria	11,870,000
16.	Delhi, India	11,453,000
17.	Moscow, Russia	11,047,000
18.	Karachi, Pakistan	10,850,000
19.	Los Angeles, U.S.	10,653,000
20.	Lima, Peru	8,928,000
21.	Paris, France	8,796,000
22.	London, U.K.	8,637,000
23.	Istanbul, Turkey	8,594,000
24.	Taipei, Taiwan	8,285,000
25.	Bogota, Colombia	7,678,000
26.	Shanghai, China	7,468,000
27.	Bangkok, Thailand	7,383,000
28.	Essen, Germany	7,264,000
29.	Madras, India	7,202,000
30.	Chicago, U.S.	6,562,000
31.	Bangalore, India	6,507,000
32.	Pusan, South Korea	6,487,000
33.	Dhaka, Bangladesh	6,212,000
34.	Santiago, Chile	6,191,000
35.	Beijing, China	5,967,000
36.	Hong Kong, China	5,933,000
37.	Lahore, Pakistan	5,664,000
38.	Kinshasa, Congo	5,380,000
39.	Tianjin, China	5,244,000
40.	Nagoya, Japan	5,243,000
41.	Baghdad, Iraq	5,089,000
42.	Madrid, Spain	5,035,000
43.	Belo Horizonte, Brazil	4,954,000
44.	Milan, Italy	4,830,000
45.	Barcelona, Spain	4,762,000
46.	St. Petersburg, Russia	4,730,000
47.	Ahmadabad, India	4,694,000
48.	Shenyang, China	4,636,000
49.	Hyderabad, India	4,628,000
50.	Ho Chi Minh City, Vietnam	4,390,000

*An urban center is a continuous built-up area, similar to a metropolitan area, having a population density of at least 5,000 persons per square mile (1,900 per square kilometer)
Source: 1999 estimates based on data from the U.S. Bureau of the Census.

living in the downtown area to increase in the early 2000's due to improved schools, declining crime, short commutes, cultural riches, and the many other offerings of large cities.

Economic power. The U.S. Conference of Mayors issued a report in June 1999 on the economic impact of the 317 largest urban areas in the United States. According to the report, these areas produce 84 percent of the nation's *gross domestic product* (the value of all goods and services produced in a country during a given period) and 88 percent of its income.

The report noted that the largest cities in the United States have more economic power than some of the world's most powerful countries. For example, New York City ranked 19th among the world's largest economies in 1999—between the Netherlands and Australia. Los Angeles ranked 25th in economic size, just behind Russia.

Welfare reform in New York. New York City officials reported in early 1999 that the number of city residents on welfare had fallen below 750,000. This figure was down from more than 1.1 million welfare recipients in 1994, when New York City instituted a welfare reform program championed by the city's mayor, Rudolph Giuliani. Giuliani's program required people who were able to work and accepted welfare benefits to work for their benefits. The plan's goal was to move welfare recipients away from their dependency on government aid by first providing them with a part-time city job—such as cleaning parks and streets or working in schools and city offices—and then finding them permanent work after they had developed skills and regular work habits. With the success of New York City's program, a number of other U.S. cities began similar approaches to welfare reform in the late 1990's.

Education reform in Chicago. Officials in Chicago reported in 1999 that test scores in the city's school system had risen in each of the previous three years. In addition, they noted that attendance had increased and the drop-out rate had declined since 1995, when the Illinois legislature granted Chicago Mayor Richard Daley control over the troubled school system. At the time, the system was deeply in debt and well below the national average in achievement. Daley and his officials applied strict standards, fired poor teachers and administrators, balanced the budgets, and sent vast numbers of students to summer school to acquire the requisite skills for promotion. Daley's success surprised many observers, who had thought that inner city schools were an unsolvable problem.

Urban sprawl. In January 1999, U.S. President Bill Clinton proposed a $10-billion program to combat urban sprawl. Most of this money was to be spent on subsidies for public transportation and tax credits to promote the purchase of land and water resources for preservation.

During the 1990's, urban sprawl had become a catch-all phrase for two problems—over-development and traffic congestion. Half of the people in the United States lived in the suburbs in 1999. In 1950, this figure was only 25 percent. As the suburban population increased, houses and roads multiplied, green spaces disappeared, and the number of cars skyrocketed. Many people in 1999 said they worried about the amount of time they spend commuting, the lack of parkland and trees, and the general unattractiveness of recent development.

In November, the Texas Transportation Institute, a research organization at Texas A&M University in College Station, Texas, reported a dramatic rise in the amount of time that Americans spend commuting. Commuters in the Indianapolis, Indiana, area, for example, spent 1000 percent more time driving to and from work in 1997 than they did in 1982. Commuters in Albuquerque, New Mexico, spent 850 percent more time in their cars in 1997 than in 1982. Drivers in Los Angeles had the longest commute, spending, on average, 82 hours a year in traffic jams. The researchers said the increase in commute time was due mostly to sprawl.   □ Robert Messenger

Civil rights. See Human rights.

Classical music. Controversy arose among classical music fans in 1999 about the use of electronic "sound enhancement" systems to improve the acoustical shortcomings of opera houses and concert halls. In August, the management of the New York State Theater, home of the New York City Opera and New York City Ballet, announced it was installing a system of microphones and speakers throughout the 2,700-seat auditorium to enhance the sound of voices and instruments. Although such systems are common in European music halls, no major American opera company had previously used one. The system was in place on an experimental basis for the September opening of the opera company's fall season.

Despite assurances from theater management that the sound system did not amplify voices or instruments, many music professionals and opera buffs remained strongly opposed to the system. They maintained that sound enhancement systems violate a basic tenet of classical music performances—that nothing will be done to alter the natural, acoustical sound produced by the artist. These critics feared that other American opera companies and classical venues in the United States would emulate the respected New York State Theater and install their own sound enhancement systems.

An enormous skeleton, representing the inevitability of death, looms over the 1999 Bregenz Music Festival production of Giuseppe Verdi's opera Un Ballo in Muschera (A Masked Ball). The opera was staged in July from a giant dock, fashioned in the form of a book, set into Lake Constance in Austria.

Musical chairs. An unusually high number of music directorships changed hands in 1999. In June, British conductor Sir Simon Rattle announced he would succeed Claudio Abbado as chief conductor and artistic director of the Berlin Philharmonic Orchestra, beginning with the 2002-2003 season. Rattle became only the second non-German music director in the orchestra's 117-year history. Also in June 1999, Japanese-born conductor Seiji Ozawa announced that he would leave the Boston Symphony Orchestra, which he had directed since 1973, to assume the directorship of the Vienna State Opera in 2002.

The Cleveland Orchestra in June 1999 named the Austrian conductor Franz Welser-Most to succeed Christoph von Dohnanyi as its music director in 2002. Several other major U.S. orchestras shopped around in 1999 for new conductors.

New operas. In October, the Lyric Opera of Chicago gave the first performance of William Bolcom's opera *A View from the Bridge,* based on the 1955 drama about Sicilian immigrants by the American playwright Arthur Miller. Dennis Russell Davies conducted the performance. James Levine led the Metropolitan Opera of New York in December 1999 in the premiere of John Harbison's *The Great Gatsby,* based on the 1925 novel by the American writer F. Scott Fitzgerald.

Grammy Award winners in 1999

Classical Album, *Barber: Prayers of Kierkegaard/Vaughan Williams: Dona Nobis Pacem/ Bartok: Cantata Profana;* Atlanta Symphony Orchestra and Chorus, Robert Shaw, conductor.

Orchestral Performance, *Mahler: Symphony No. 9;* Chicago Symphony Orchestra, Pierre Boulez, conductor.

Opera Recording, *Bartok: Bluebeard's Castle;* Jessye Norman and Laszlo Polgar, singers; Chicago Symphony Orchestra, Pierre Boulez, conductor.

Choral Performance, *Barber: Prayers of Kierkegaard/ Vaughan Williams: Dona Nobis Pacem/ Bartok: Cantata Profana;* Atlanta Symphony Orchestra and Chorus, Robert Shaw, conductor.

Instrumental Soloist with Orchestra, *Penderecki: Violin Con. No. 2 (Metamorphosen);* Anne-Sophie Mutter, violin; Krzystof Penderecki, conductor.

Instrumental Soloist without Orchestra, *Bach: English Suites Nos. 1, 3 & 6;* Murray Perahia, piano.

Chamber Music Performance, *American Scenes (Works of Copland, Previn, Barber, Gershwin);* Gil Shaham, violin; Andre Previn, piano.

Small Ensemble Performance, *Reich: Music for 18 Musicians;* Steve Reich and Musicians.

Classical Vocal Performance, *The Beautiful Voice;* Renee Fleming, soprano.

Classical Contemporary Composition, *Penderecki: Violin Con. No. 2 (Metamorphosen);* Anne-Sophie Mutter, violin; Krzystof Penderecki, conductor.

Classical Crossover Album, *Soul of the Tango— The Music of Astor Piazzolla;* Yo-Yo Ma, cello; Jorge Calandrelli, conductor.

At the renowned Salzburg Festival in Austria in July 1999, the German soprano Hildegard Behrens sang the leading role in the premiere of *Cronaca del Luogo (Chronicle of the Place),* a new opera by Italy's foremost composer, Luciano Berio. Sylvain Cambreling conducted the opera, which explores themes from the Old Testament. The American composer Bernard Rands's *Belladonna,* a tale of journey and discovery inspired by Plato's *Symposium,* was unveiled in July at the Aspen (Colorado) Music Festival. David Zinman conducted the performance.

In April, the Houston Grand Opera added *Resurrection,* by composer Tod Machover, to its long list of premieres of American works. The opera, which weaves electronically generated sounds into its musical fabric, is based on Leo Tolstoy's 1899 novel *Resurrection. Central Park,* an evening-length *trilogy* (group of three related works) of operas by the composers Robert Beaser, Deborah Drattell, and Michael Torke, made its debut in July 1999 at the Glimmerglass Opera in Cooperstown, New York. Broadway playwrights Terence McNally, Wendy Wasserstein, and A. R. Gurney wrote the *librettos* (text) for the three works.

New orchestral and instrumental music. In October, the New York Philharmonic, under conductor Kurt Masur, presented the premiere of two works commissioned by the Walt Disney Company to commemorate the new millennium. Aaron Jay Kernis's *Garden of Light* and Michael Torke's *Four Seasons* are both large-scale choral symphonies for orchestra, chorus, boys choir, and vocal soloists.

At the Salzburg Festival in August 1999, Dennis Russell Davies led the Vienna Symphony Orchestra in the premiere of the epic, 101-minute *Symphony No. 5 (Choral),* by U.S. composer Philip Glass. The symphony reflects Glass's *minimalist* approach to music, characterized by simple harmonies and repeating melodies and rhythms. John Adams, a U.S. composer associated with minimalism until he moved on to a more complex style in the 1980's, had his orchestral work *Naive and Sentimental Music* premiered in February 1999. Esa-Pekka Salonen led the Los Angeles Philharmonic in the performance.

In March, New York City's Eos Orchestra premiered *Dracula,* a spoof of musical cliches in horror films, by the U.S. composer David del Tredici. *Dracula* featured soprano Wendy Hill as one of the vampire's victims. Pianist Emanuel Ax and the New York Philharmonic under the direction of Leonard Slatkin gave the premiere of *Seeing,* a piano concerto by the American composer Christopher Rouse, in May. Reviewers said the work evoked disturbing images of *psychoses* (severe mental disorders). Also in May, composer

A Colombian woman mourns the loss of a granddaughter, who died in an earthquake on January 25. The quake, with a magnitude of 6.0, killed more than 800 people and destroyed two-thirds of Armenia, a city in western Colombia.

Steve Reich's latest chamber work, *Triple Quartet,* was premiered by the Kronos Quartet, at the Kennedy Center Concert Hall in Washington, D.C.

Music Alive. A program to help develop audiences for new symphonic music throughout the United States was announced in September by the American Symphony Orchestra League, a Washington, D.C.-based association of amateur and professional orchestral groups. The program is cosponsored by Meet the Composer, a New York City-based organization that works to increase professional opportunities for composers. "Music Alive: Composers and Orchestras Together" provides orchestras, both large and small, with the funds to finance composers in residence for two to eight week periods. During such residencies, an orchestra performs works written by the composer.

The program was scheduled to begin in early 2000. Music Alive was made possible by a $300,000 gift from the Andrew W. Mellon Foundation, a charitable organization based in New York City. ☐ John von Rhein

See also **People in the news** (Ozawa, Seiji); **Popular music.**

Clinton, Bill. See **United States, President of the.**

Clothing. See **Fashion.**

Coal. See **Energy supply.**

Colombia. An estimated 13 million Colombians participated in a series of protests at some 700 locations throughout the country on Oct. 24, 1999. People carried signs bearing the phrase *No mas* (No more), a call for an end to more than 30 years of civil strife between the government and leftist guerrillas. On that same day, the government began peace negotiations with the Revolutionary Armed Forces of Colombia (FARC), the nation's largest leftist rebel organization.

Violent setbacks. Since taking office in August 1998, President Andres Pastrana Arango had made a number of concessions to rebel leaders in an effort to bring them to the negotiating table. In November 1998, he gave FARC control of a 16,000-square-mile (41,000-square-kilometer) "safe zone." FARC allegedly used the region to reinvigorate its campaign of violence. In July 1999, the rebels launched a well-coordinated, six-day offensive on 20 Colombian towns. In the attack, FARC forces overran an army camp about 25 miles (40 kilometers) south of Bogota, the capital.

On March 12, members of another rebel group, the National Liberation Army (ELN), hijacked a Colombian commercial airliner, taking the 46 passengers and crew members hostage. The ELN kidnapped about 100 people in May during services at a Roman Catholic church in Cali, Colombia's third-largest city.

The United States government provided Colombia with $289 million in military aid in 1999 and sent two high-level missions to Bogota to investigate the country's increasingly precarious situation. After retired U.S. General Barry McCaffrey, director of the U.S. Office of National Drug Control Policy, led a delegation to Colombia in July, he recommended that the U.S. Congress allocate $1 billion in aid to Colombia and neighboring countries to fight drug operations. He earmarked $360 million for rebel-controlled regions of Colombia, where rebels often operate hand-in-hand with drug traffickers. In August, U.S. Undersecretary of State Thomas Pickering and Undersecretary of Defense Brian Sheridan led a second delegation to Colombia to discuss the U.S. role in Pastrana's efforts to control rebel activity and drug trafficking. FARC leaders warned Pastrana that increased U.S. involvement in Colombia would end all hope of peace talks and lead to "a civil war with unforeseen circumstances."

On September 17, Pastrana unveiled a comprehensive three-year plan budgeted at $7.5 billion for achieving "peace, prosperity and strengthening the state." Experts noted that the proposal, Plan Colombia, signaled a shift to a more offensive military strategy against rebel armies and an admission that the government had lost ground in the war against both rebels and drug traffickers. Pastrana claimed that Colombia needed about $3.5 billion in foreign aid to carry out his plan.

Conflict spills across borders. The conflict in Colombia threatened to ignite a regional war, as Colombian rebel armies, drug cartels, and right-wing paramilitary groups began operating in neighboring nations in 1999. On February 17, Jaime Hurtado, the leader of a leftist political party in Ecuador, was assassinated, along with his driver and an aide, in Quito, allegedly by right-wing extremists from Colombia. On March 5, a Venezuelan farmer discovered the bodies of three Americans, allegedly killed by FARC rebels. The victims had worked for environmental protection and civil rights campaigns for native people of the region. On September 11, Colombian rebels abducted 12 foreigners—from Canada, Spain, and the United States—at a site in Ecuador about 20 miles (32 kilometers) from the Colombian border.

An earthquake, with a magnitude of 6.0, struck western Colombia on January 25, killing more than 800 people. Delays in relief efforts led to looting and rioting.   □ Nathan A. Haverstock
See also **Latin America.**

Colorado. See State government.
Common Market. See Europe.
Commonwealth of Independent States. See Asia; Azerbaijan; Belarus; Georgia; Kazakhstan; Russia; Ukraine.
Comoros. See Africa.

Computers. Personal computers (PC's) designed with a new, stylish look and with more user-friendly features went on the market in the autumn of 1999. The new PC's were sleeker than in the past and featured colorful, translucent plastic cases. The designs were modeled on the iMac, a popular desktop computer introduced in 1998 by Apple Computer, Inc., of Cupertino, California. The new PC's were less expensive than the iMac and were designed to use the more popular Windows *operating system* (master control program).

The new-look computers were developed as part of the Easy PC Initiative, a program introduced in 1998 by Microsoft Corporation, the Redmond, Washington-based software manufacturer, and by leading PC hardware manufacturers. Easy PC is a series of design guidelines intended to make PC's easier to set up and use and more appealing to first-time computer buyers.

New iMac. In September 1999, Apple debuted a new generation of iMacs. Seeking to capitalize on the success of the 1998 iMac and its reputation for simple setup and use, Apple priced the base version of the new model at $999. Apple hoped the price would attract first-time computer buyers.

Privacy concerns. In January 1999, Intel Corporation of Santa Clara, California, maker of the world's most popular computer chip, was strongly criticized for building an identification code into its new Pentium III chip. According to Intel officials, the code was intended to verify the computer's identity—to online merchants, for example. Critics noted that the built-in code violated a user's personal privacy by providing a way to track his or her activity on the World Wide Web. Intel promised to provide consumers with free software that would permanently disconnect the feature.

TIME CAPSULE 1954

COMPUTERS

So-called "mechanical brains" held the center of the electronics stage during 1954. Univac, the electronic computer used to predict the election returns, became almost a household word as TV and radio announcers reported its latest findings on election night. Scientists who have developed mechanical brains are confident that they can be made to play such logical games as chess, to supervise the production of standardized articles (correcting mistakes as fast as they are made), and even to read books.

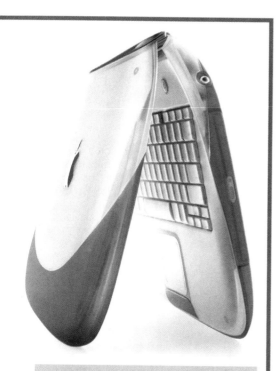

Apple Computer, Inc., of Cupertino, California, unveiled its iBook laptop personal computer in July 1999, available in two colors, blueberry and tangerine. The iBook allowed for such advanced features as wireless technology for networking and Internet access.

The company also pledged to ship future versions of the chip with the identification code disabled unless, to be activated, if wished, by the owner.

Microsoft experienced a similar public-relations problem in March 1999, when an independent programmer discovered that the Windows 98 operating system could be used to gather personal information about computer users without their knowledge. Upon installation, Windows 98 assigned the host computer a unique identifying number that it would automatically attach to certain documents produced on the machine, including items that could contain such personal information as addresses and telephone numbers. Microsoft promised to modify future copies of Windows 98 to fix the problem and make the same repair available to existing customers.

These revelations raised questions about privacy at a time when the computer industry was trying to assure consumers that exchanging personal information electronically over the Internet could be made secure and private.   □ Michael Woods

See also **Internet**.

Congo (Kinshasa). A civil war, which broke out in August 1998 and pitted rebel forces —supported by Rwanda and Uganda—against the forces of Congo President Laurent Kabila and four other African allies, continued in Congo (Kinshasa) through the summer of 1999. In August, all parties to the conflict signed a cease-fire, negotiated in Zambia in July. The continued presence of foreign troops in Congo (formerly Zaire) and disputes between Congo's rebel groups hindered the implementation of the agreement.

Foreign intervention. During the first half of 1999, rebel forces consolidated their grip on huge swaths of territory in northern and eastern Congo. The rebels were backed by troops and equipment from Uganda and Rwanda, which had helped Kabila seize power in 1997. The two countries had turned on Kabila in 1998 because of his failure to stop attacks on Rwanda and Uganda by guerrillas based in eastern Congo.

In response to the rebel successes, Zimbabwe— Kabila's primary foreign backer—stepped up its military operations against Congolese rebel forces. Angola, Namibia, and Chad also provided military assistance to Kabila in 1999. Sudan reportedly contributed soldiers to Kabila's war effort in an apparent attempt to strike at its old enemy, Uganda.

Peace talks. Multiple diplomatic initiatives by leaders in South Africa, other African nations, and various international organizations failed to halt the fighting until fears that the violence in Congo would plunge all of Africa's Great Lakes region into chaos spurred new negotiations. On July 10, the leaders of Congo and the five other nations involved in the war agreed to a peace accord in the Zambian capital, Lusaka. The agreement called for an immediate cease-fire, to be monitored by United Nations observers and African peacekeepers; the withdrawal of all foreign troops; the creation of an army composed of government and rebel forces; and an "open national dialogue" on Congo's future government.

Congo's two main rebel groups initially refused to sign the peace accord. In May, the Rally for Congolese Democracy (RCD), the main rebel movement, had split into two groups—one supported by Rwanda and the other by Uganda. In mid-August, tensions between rival RCD factions erupted into battles for control of Kisangani in Congo's northeast, with Uganda and Rwanda fighting on opposite sides.

Later in August, the two rebel factions announced that they had overcome their differences, and the RCD signed the Lusaka agreement on August 31. The other main rebel group, the Movement for the Liberation of Congo, had signed the accord on August 1.   □ Simon Baynham

See also **Africa; South Africa; Uganda; Zimbabwe**.

Congress of the United States.

The U.S. Senate on Feb. 12, 1999, acquitted President Bill Clinton on impeachment charges passed by the U.S. House of Representatives in December 1998, allowing the president to complete his term. The Senate voted 45 to 55 on one charge of perjury and 50 to 50 on one charge of obstruction of justice. The U.S. Constitution requires that a two-thirds majority of the senators present vote in favor of the charges in order to convict the president and remove him from office.

Clinton was the second U.S. president to be impeached by the House of Representatives. The first was Andrew Johnson in 1868.

The charges against President Bill Clinton stemmed from his denials during sworn testimony that he had had a relationship with Monica Lewinsky, a former White House intern. Republican House members who supported the charges accused Clinton of lying to a federal grand jury in August 1998 and of trying to conceal his relationship with Lewinsky.

During the Senate trial, which began on Jan. 7, 1999, lawyers representing the president argued that Clinton did not give perjured testimony or obstruct justice. The president's lawyers also argued that the alleged offenses were not serious enough to justify Clinton's removal from office.

Funding measures. Congress in 1999 failed to pass 8 of the required 13 spending bills prior to the beginning of fiscal year 2000, which began on Oct. 1, 1999. In order to keep federal agencies functioning during the budget crisis, the House of Representatives and the Senate on September 28 approved a three-week stop-gap spending bill.

Although Congress has passed appropriations bills on time only four times since the 1970's, Republican Congressional leaders had promised to complete the 1999-2000 bills before the start of fiscal year 2000. Republicans had also pledged to keep the spending bills within the limits that Congress had set in 1997 and to refrain from using projected surpluses from the Social Security fund to pay for government operations. Despite failing to pass the appropriations bills on time, the Republicans did not dip into Social Security surpluses.

On Nov. 18, 1999, the House voted 296 to 135 to approve a final version of the 1999-2000 spending bill. The Senate voted 74 to 24 on November 19 to approve five final spending bills that had not yet been approved, totaling about $390 billion of the total $1.8-trillion budget.

The legislation included small budget cuts within the federal government. It required all federal agencies to reduce their budgets by 38 cents out of every $100 for fiscal year 2000. Government officials estimated that the measure would save about $1.3 billion.

Provisions in the spending bills also included funding to hire 100,000 new teachers and 50,000 more police officers nationwide. The measures provided debt relief for low-income nations worldwide and budgeted money to pay $351 million of the $926 million owed in back dues to the United Nations. President Clinton signed the legislation on Nov. 29, 1999.

Test ban treaty. The Senate voted 51 to 48 on October 13 to reject a treaty requiring a ban on all underground nuclear testing. The Comprehensive Test Ban Treaty fell 19 votes short of the two-thirds majority needed for Senate approval. Political experts considered the vote a major defeat for President Clinton. The United States was the first nation with nuclear weapons to reject the 154-nation agreement.

President Clinton criticized the Senate's rejection of the treaty, claiming the vote had been based on politics rather than on issues. Supporters of the ban claimed that the treaty's demise in the United States sent a signal to other nations with nuclear capabilities that underground nuclear testing was an acceptable practice.

Campaign finance reform. In September, the House of Representatives voted 252 to 177 to approve changes in the way candidates for federal office raise money to finance campaigns. The legislation was designed to prohibit the national committees of political parties, as well as their state and local counterparts, from making donations to candidates outside the limits of the Federal Election Campaign Act of 1971. A loophole in that law allowed special interest groups to make unlimited contributions to political parties, which pass the funds on to individual politicians. Many critics viewed the so-called soft-money contributions as a means for special interest groups to gain favor with politicians.

On Oct. 19, 1999, Republican members of the Senate blocked a vote on the legislation to overhaul the campaign finance system, killing debate until at least 2000. The Senate had blocked a vote on the issue each year since 1996.

New House speaker. U.S. representatives elected Dennis Hastert (R., Illinois) speaker of the house on Jan. 6, 1999. Hastert, a former high school teacher and wrestling coach, had served as a U.S. representative since 1986. Hastert held the post of deputy majority whip prior to his selection as speaker. Republican representatives selected Hastert in December 1998 after Robert L. Livingston (R., Louisiana), who had been selected as speaker in November 1998, removed his name from consideration for the Speaker position.

Members of the United States Senate

The Senate of the second session of the 106th Congress consisted of 45 Democrats and 55 Republicans when it convened on Jan. 24, 2000. The first date in each listing shows when the senator's term began. The second date in each listing shows when the senator's term expires.

State	Term	State	Term	State	Term
Alabama		**Louisiana**		**Ohio**	
Richard C. Shelby, R.	1987-2005	John B. Breaux, D.	1987-2005	Mike DeWine, R.	1995-2001
Jeff Sessions, R.	1997-2003	Mary L. Landrieu, D.	1997-2003	George V. Voinovich, R.	1999-2005
Alaska		**Maine**		**Oklahoma**	
Theodore F. Stevens, R.	1968-2003	Olympia Snowe, R.	1995-2001	Don Nickles, R.	1981-2005
Frank H. Murkowski, R.	1981-2005	Susan M. Collins, R.	1997-2003	James M. Inhofe, R.	1994-2003
Arizona		**Maryland**		**Oregon**	
John McCain III, R.	1987-2005	Paul S. Sarbanes, D.	1977-2001	Ron Wyden, D.	1996-2005
Jon Kyl, R.	1995-2001	Barbara A. Mikulski, D.	1987-2005	Gordon Smith, R.	1997-2003
Arkansas		**Massachusetts**		**Pennsylvania**	
Tim Hutchinson, R.	1997-2003	Edward M. Kennedy, D.	1962-2001	Arlen Specter, R.	1981-2005
Blanche Lambert Lincoln, D.	1999-2005	John F. Kerry, D.	1985-2003	Rick Santorum, R.	1995-2001
California		**Michigan**		**Rhode Island**	
Dianne Feinstein, D.	1992-2001	Carl Levin, D.	1979-2003	Jack Reed, D.	1997-2003
Barbara Boxer, D.	1993-2005	Spencer Abraham, R.	1995-2001	Lincoln D. Chafee, R.	1999-2001
Colorado		**Minnesota**		**South Carolina**	
Ben N. Campbell, R.	1993-2005	Paul D. Wellstone, D.	1991-2003	Strom Thurmond, R.	1955-2003
Wayne Allard, R.	1997-2003	Rod Grams, R.	1995-2001	Ernest F. Hollings, D.	1966-2005
Connecticut		**Mississippi**		**South Dakota**	
Christopher J. Dodd, D.	1981-2005	Thad Cochran, R.	1978-2003	Thomas A. Daschle, D.	1987-2005
Joseph I. Lieberman, D.	1989-2001	Trent Lott, R.	1989-2001	Tim Johnson, D.	1997-2003
Delaware		**Missouri**		**Tennessee**	
William V. Roth, Jr., R.	1971-2001	Christopher S. (Kit) Bond, R.	1987-2005	Fred Thompson, R.	1994-2003
Joseph R. Biden, Jr., D.	1973-2003	John Ashcroft, R.	1995-2001	Bill Frist, R.	1995-2001
Florida		**Montana**		**Texas**	
Bob Graham, D.	1987-2005	Max Baucus, D.	1978-2003	Phil Gramm, R.	1985-2003
Connie Mack III, R.	1989-2001	Conrad Burns, R.	1989-2001	Kay Bailey Hutchison, R.	1993-2001
Georgia		**Nebraska**		**Utah**	
Paul Coverdell, R.	1993-2005	J. Robert Kerrey, D.	1989-2001	Orrin G. Hatch, R.	1977-2001
Max Cleland, D.	1997-2003	Chuck Hagel, R.	1997-2003	Robert F. Bennett, R.	1993-2005
Hawaii		**Nevada**		**Vermont**	
Daniel K. Inouye, D.	1963-2005	Harry M. Reid, D.	1987-2005	Patrick J. Leahy, D.	1975-2005
Daniel K. Akaka, D.	1990-2001	Richard H. Bryan, D.	1989-2001	James M. Jeffords, R.	1989-2001
Idaho		**New Hampshire**		**Virginia**	
Larry E. Craig, R.	1991-2003	Robert C. Smith, R.	1990-2003	John W. Warner, R.	1979-2003
Mike Crapo, R.	1999-2005	Judd Gregg, R.	1993-2005	Charles S. Robb, D.	1989-2001
Illinois		**New Jersey**		**Washington**	
Richard J. Durbin, D.	1997-2003	Frank R. Lautenberg, D.	1982-2001	Slade Gorton, R.	1989-2001
Peter Fitzgerald, R.	1999-2005	Robert G. Torricelli, D.	1997-2003	Patty Murray, D.	1993-2005
Indiana		**New Mexico**		**West Virginia**	
Richard G. Lugar, R.	1977-2001	Pete V. Domenici, R.	1973-2003	Robert C. Byrd, D.	1959-2001
Evan Bayh, D.	1999-2005	Jeff Bingaman, D.	1983-2001	John D. Rockefeller IV, D.	1985-2003
Iowa		**New York**		**Wisconsin**	
Charles E. Grassley, R.	1981-2005	Daniel P. Moynihan, D.	1977-2001	Herbert Kohl, D.	1989-2001
Tom Harkin, D.	1985-2003	Charles E. Schumer, D.	1999-2005	Russell D. Feingold, D.	1993-2005
Kansas		**North Carolina**		**Wyoming**	
Sam Brownback, R.	1996-2005	Jesse A. Helms, R.	1973-2003	Craig Thomas, R.	1995-2001
Pat Roberts, R.	1997-2003	John Edwards, D.	1999-2005	Mike Enzi, R.	1997-2003
Kentucky		**North Dakota**			
Mitch McConnell, R.	1985-2003	Kent Conrad, D.	1987-2001		
Jim Bunning, R.	1999-2005	Byron L. Dorgan, D.	1992-2005		

Members of the United States House of Representatives

The House of Representatives of the second session of the 106th Congress consisted of 212 Democrats, 222 Republicans, and 1 independent (not including representatives from American Samoa, the District of Columbia, Guam, Puerto Rico, and the Virgin Islands) when it convened on Jan. 24, 2000. There were 211 Democrats, 223 Republicans, and 1 independent, when the first session of the 106th Congress convened. This table shows congressional district, legislator, and party affiliation. Asterisk (*) denotes those who served in the 105th Congress; dagger (†) denotes "at large."

Alabama
1. Sonny Callahan, R.*
2. Terry Everett, R.*
3. Bob Riley, R.*
4. Robert Aderholt, R.*
5. Bud Cramer, D.*
6. Spencer Bachus, R.*
7. Earl Hilliard, D.*

Alaska
†Donald E. Young, R.*

Arizona
1. Matt Salmon, R.*
2. Ed Pastor, D.*
3. Bob Stump, R.*
4. John Shadegg, R.*
5. Jim Kolbe, R.*
6. J. D. Hayworth, R.*

Arkansas
1. Marion Berry, D.*
2. Vic Snyder, D.*
3. Asa Hutchinson, R.*
4. Jay Dickey, R.*

California
1. Mike Thompson, D.
2. Wally Herger, R.*
3. Douglas Ose, R.
4. John Doolittle, R.*
5. Robert T. Matsui, D.*
6. Lynn Woolsey, D.*
7. George E. Miller, D.*
8. Nancy Pelosi, D.*
9. Barbara Lee, D.*
10. Ellen Tauscher, D.*
11. Richard Pombo, R.*
12. Tom Lantos, D.*
13. Fortney H. (Peter) Stark, D.*
14. Anna Eshoo, D.*
15. Tom Campbell, R.*
16. Zoe Lofgren, D.*
17. Sam Farr, D.*
18. Gary Condit, D.*
19. George Radanovich, R.*
20. Calvin Dooley, D.*
21. William M. Thomas, R.*
22. Lois Capps, D.*
23. Elton Gallegly, R.*
24. Brad Sherman, D.*
25. Howard McKeon, R.*
26. Howard L. Berman, D.*
27. James E. Rogan, R.*
28. David Dreier, R.*
29. Henry A. Waxman, D.*
30. Xavier Becerra, D.*
31. Matthew Martinez, D.*
32. Julian C. Dixon, D.*
33. Lucille Roybal-Allard, D.*
34. Grace Napolitano, D.
35. Maxine Waters, D.*
36. Steven Kuykendall, R.

37. Juanita Millender-McDonald, D.*
38. Steve Horn, R.*
39. Edward Royce, R.*
40. Jerry Lewis, R.*
41. Gary Miller, R.
42. Joe Baca, D.
43. Kenneth Calvert, R.*
44. Mary Bono, R.*
45. Dana Rohrabacher, R.*
46. Loretta Sanchez, D.*
47. C. Christopher Cox, R.*
48. Ronald C. Packard, R.*
49. Brian Bilbray, R.*
50. Bob Filner, D.*
51. Randy (Duke) Cunningham, R.*
52. Duncan L. Hunter, R.*

Colorado
1. Diana DeGette, D.*
2. Mark Udall, D.
3. Scott McInnis, R.*
4. Bob Schaffer, R.*
5. Joel Hefley, R.*
6. Tom Tancredo, R.

Connecticut
1. John Larson, D.
2. Sam Gejdenson, D.*
3. Rosa DeLauro, D.*
4. Christopher Shays, R.*
5. James H. Maloney, D.*
6. Nancy L. Johnson, R.*

Delaware
†Michael Castle, R.*

Florida
1. Joe Scarborough, R.*
2. Allen Boyd, D.*
3. Corrine Brown, D.*
4. Tillie Fowler, R.*
5. Karen Thurman, D.*
6. Clifford B. Stearns, R.*
7. John Mica, R.*
8. Bill McCollum, R.*
9. Michael Bilirakis, R.*
10. C. W. Bill Young, R.*
11. Jim Davis, D.*
12. Charles Canady, R.*
13. Dan Miller, R.*
14. Porter J. Goss, R.*
15. Dave Weldon, R.*
16. Mark Foley, R.*
17. Carrie Meek, D.*
18. Ileana Ros-Lehtinen, R.*
19. Robert Wexler, D.*
20. Peter Deutsch, D.*
21. Lincoln Diaz-Balart, R.*
22. E. Clay Shaw, Jr., R.*
23. Alcee Hastings, D.*

Georgia
1. Jack Kingston, R.*
2. Sanford Bishop, Jr., D.*

3. Mac Collins, R.*
4. Cynthia A. McKinney, D.*
5. John Lewis, D.*
6. Johnny Isakson, R.
7. Bob Barr, R.*
8. Saxby Chambliss, R.*
9. Nathan Deal, R.*
10. Charlie Norwood, R.*
11. John Linder, R.*

Hawaii
1. Neil Abercrombie, D.*
2. Patsy T. Mink, D.*

Idaho
1. Helen Chenoweth, R.*
2. Mike Simpson, R.

Illinois
1. Bobby Rush, D.*
2. Jesse L. Jackson, Jr., D.*
3. William O. Lipinski, D.*
4. Luis Gutierrez, D.*
5. Rod R. Blagojevich, D.*
6. Henry J. Hyde, R.*
7. Danny Davis, D.*
8. Philip M. Crane, R.*
9. Janice Schakowsky, D.
10. John Edward Porter, R.*
11. Gerald Weller, R.*
12. Jerry F. Costello, D.*
13. Judy Biggert, R.
14. J. Dennis Hastert, R.*
15. Thomas W. Ewing, R.*
16. Donald Manzullo, R.*
17. Lane A. Evans, D.*
18. Ray LaHood, R.*
19. David Phelps, D.
20. John Shimkus, R.*

Indiana
1. Peter J. Visclosky, D.*
2. David McIntosh, R.*
3. Tim Roemer, D.*
4. Mark Souder, R.*
5. Steve Buyer, R.*
6. Danny L. Burton, R.*
7. Edward A. Pease, R.*
8. John Hostettler, R.*
9. Baron Hill, D.
10. Julia M. Carson, D.*

Iowa
1. Jim Leach, R.*
2. Jim Nussle, R.*
3. Leonard Boswell, D.*
4. Greg Ganske, R.*
5. Tom Latham, R.*

Kansas
1. Jerry Moran, R.*
2. Jim Ryun, R.*
3. Dennis Moore, D.
4. Todd Tiahrt, R.*

Kentucky
1. Edward Whitfield, R.*
2. Ron Lewis, R.*
3. Anne Northup, R.*
4. Kenneth Lucas, D.
5. Harold (Hal) Rogers, R.*
6. Ernie Fletcher, R.

Louisiana
1. David Vitter, R.
2. William J. Jefferson, D.*
3. W. J. (Billy) Tauzin, R.*
4. Jim McCrery, R.*
5. John Cooksey, R.
6. Richard Hugh Baker, R.*
7. Chris John, D.*

Maine
1. Thomas Allen, D.*
2. John Baldacci, D.*

Maryland
1. Wayne T. Gilchrest, R.*
2. Robert Ehrlich, Jr., R.*
3. Benjamin L. Cardin, D.*
4. Albert Wynn, D.*
5. Steny H. Hoyer, D.*
6. Roscoe Bartlett, R.*
7. Elijah Cummings. D.*
8. Constance A. Morella, R.*

Massachusetts
1. John W. Olver, D.*
2. Richard E. Neal, D.*
3. James McGovern, D.*
4. Barney Frank, D.*
5. Martin Meehan, D.*
6. John Tierney, D.*
7. Edward J. Markey, D.*
8. Michael Capuano, D.
9. John Joseph Moakley, D.*
10. William Delahunt, D.*

Michigan
1. Bart Stupak, D.*
2. Peter Hoekstra, R.*
3. Vernon Ehlers, R.*
4. Dave Camp, R.*
5. James Barcia, D.*
6. Frederick S. Upton, R.*
7. Nick Smith, R.*
8. Debbie Stabenow, D.*
9. Dale E. Kildee, D.*
10. David E. Bonior, D.*
11. Joseph Knollenberg, R.*
12. Sander M. Levin, D.*
13. Lynn Rivers, D.*
14. John Conyers, Jr., D.*
15. Carolyn Kilpatrick, D.*
16. John D. Dingell, D.*

Minnesota
1. Gil Gutknecht, R.*
2. David Minge, D.*
3. Jim Ramstad, R.*
4. Bruce F. Vento, D.*

5. Martin O. Sabo, D.*
6. William P. Luther, D.*
7. Collin C. Peterson, D.*
8. James L. Oberstar, D.*

Mississippi
1. Roger Wicker, R.*
2. Bennie Thompson, D.*
3. Charles Pickering, R.*
4. Ronnie Shows, D.*
5. Gene Taylor, D.*

Missouri
1. William L. (Bill) Clay, D.*
2. James Talent, R.*
3. Richard A. Gephardt, D.*
4. Ike Skelton, D.*
5. Karen McCarthy, D.*
6. Pat Danner, D.*
7. Roy Blunt, R.*
8. Jo Ann Emerson, R.*
9. Kenny Hulshof, R.*

Montana
†Rick Hill, R.*

Nebraska
1. Doug Bereuter, R.*
2. Lee Terry, R.
3. Bill Barrett, R.*

Nevada
1. Shelley Berkley, D.
2. Jim Gibbons, R.*

New Hampshire
1. John E. Sununu, R.*
2. Charles Bass, R.*

New Jersey
1. Robert E. Andrews, D.*
2. Frank LoBiondo, R.*
3. H. James Saxton, R.*
4. Christopher H. Smith, R.*
5. Marge Roukema, R.*
6. Frank Pallone, Jr., D.*
7. Bob Franks, R.*
8. William Pascrell, Jr., D.*
9. Steven Rothman, D.*
10. Donald M. Payne, D.*
11. Rodney Frelinghuysen, R.*
12. Rush Holt, D.
13. Robert Menendez, D.*

New Mexico
1. Heather Wilson, R.*
2. Joe Skeen, R.*
3. Thomas Udall, D.

New York
1. Michael Forbes, D.*
2. Rick Lazio, R.*
3. Peter King, R.*
4. Carolyn McCarthy, D.*
5. Gary L. Ackerman, D.*
6. Gregory Meeks, D.*
7. Joseph Crowley, D.
8. Jerrold Nadler, D.*
9. Anthony Weiner, D.
10. Edolphus Towns, D.*
11. Major R. Owens, D.*
12. Nydia Velazquez, D.*
13. Vito J. Fossella, R.*

14. Carolyn Maloney, D.*
15. Charles B. Rangel, D.*
16. Jose E. Serrano, D.*
17. Eliot L. Engel, D.*
18. Nita M. Lowey, D.*
19. Sue Kelly, R.*
20. Benjamin A. Gilman, R.*
21. Michael R. McNulty, D.*
22. John Sweeney, R.
23. Sherwood L. Boehlert, R.*
24. John McHugh, R.*
25. James Walsh, R.*
26. Maurice Hinchey, D.*
27. Thomas Reynolds, R.
28. Louise M. Slaughter, D.*
29. John J. LaFalce, D.*
30. Jack Quinn, R.*
31. Amo Houghton, R.*

North Carolina
1. Eva Clayton, D.*
2. Bob Etheridge, D.*
3. Walter Jones, Jr., R.*
4. David Price, D.*
5. Richard Burr, R.*
6. Howard Coble, R.*
7. Mike McIntyre, D.*
8. Robin Hayes, R.
9. Sue Myrick, R.*
10. Cass Ballenger, R.*
11. Charles H. Taylor, R.*
12. Melvin Watt, D.*

North Dakota
†Earl Pomeroy, D.*

Ohio
1. Steve Chabot, R.*
2. Rob Portman, R.*
3. Tony P. Hall, D.*
4. Michael G. Oxley, R.*
5. Paul E. Gillmor, R.*
6. Ted Strickland, D.*
7. David L. Hobson, R.*
8. John A. Boehner, R.*
9. Marcy Kaptur, D.*
10. Dennis Kucinich, D.*
11. Stephanie Jones, D.
12. John R. Kasich, R.*
13. Sherrod Brown, D.*
14. Thomas C. Sawyer, D.*
15. Deborah Pryce, R.*
16. Ralph Regula, R.*
17. James A. Traficant, Jr., D.*
18. Bob Ney, R.*
19. Steven LaTourette, R.*

Oklahoma
1. Steve Largent, R.*
2. Tom Coburn, R.*
3. Wes Watkins, R.*
4. J. C. Watts, Jr., R.*
5. Ernest Jim Istook, R.*
6. Frank Lucas, R.*

Oregon
1. David Wu, D.
2. Greg Walden, R.
3. Earl Blumenauer, D.*
4. Peter A. DeFazio, D.*
5. Darlene Hooley, D.*

Pennsylvania
1. Robert Brady, D.*
2. Chaka Fattah, D.*
3. Robert A. Borski, Jr., D.*
4. Ron Klink, D.*
5. John Peterson, R.*
6. Tim Holden, D.*
7. W. Curtis Weldon, R.*
8. Jim Greenwood, R.*
9. E. G. (Bud) Shuster, R.*
10. Donald Sherwood, R.
11. Paul E. Kanjorski, D.*
12. John P. Murtha, D.*
13. Joseph Hoeffel, D.
14. William J. Coyne, D.*
15. Patrick Toomey, R.
16. Joseph Pitts, R.*
17. George W. Gekas, R.*
18. Michael Doyle, D.*
19. William F. Goodling, R.*
20. Frank Mascara, D.*
21. Philip English, R.*

Rhode Island
1. Patrick Kennedy, D.*
2. Robert Weygand, D.*

South Carolina
1. Mark Sanford, R.*
2. Floyd Spence, R.*
3. Lindsey Graham, R.*
4. James DeMint, R.
5. John M. Spratt, Jr., D.*
6. James Clyburn, D.*

South Dakota
†John Thune, R.*

Tennessee
1. William Jenkins, R.*
2. John J. Duncan, Jr., R.*
3. Zach Wamp, R.*
4. Van Hilleary, R.*
5. Bob Clement, D.*
6. Bart Gordon, D.*
7. Ed Bryant, R.*
8. John S. Tanner, D.*
9. Harold E. Ford, Jr., D.*

Texas
1. Max Sandlin, D.*
2. Jim Turner, D.*
3. Sam Johnson, R.*
4. Ralph M. Hall, D.*
5. Pete Sessions, R.*
6. Joe Barton, R.*
7. Bill Archer, R.*
8. Kevin Brady, R.*
9. Nick Lampson, D.*
10. Lloyd Doggett, D.*
11. Chet Edwards, D.*
12. Kay Granger, R.*
13. William Thornberry, R.*
14. Ron Paul, R.*
15. Ruben Hinojosa, D.*
16. Silvestre Reyes, D.*
17. Charles W. Stenholm, D.*
18. Sheila Jackson Lee, D.*
19. Larry Combest, R.*
20. Charlie Gonzalez, D.
21. Lamar S. Smith, R.*

22. Tom DeLay, R.*
23. Henry Bonilla, R.*
24. Martin Frost, D.*
25. Ken Bentsen, D.*
26. Richard K. Armey, R.*
27. Solomon P. Ortiz, D.*
28. Ciro Rodriguez, D.*
29. Gene Green, D.*
30. Eddie Bernice Johnson, D.*

Utah
1. James V. Hansen, R.*
2. Merrill Cook, R.*
3. Christopher Cannon, R.*

Vermont
†Bernard Sanders, Ind.*

Virginia
1. Herbert H. Bateman, R.*
2. Owen B. Pickett, D.*
3. Robert Scott, D.*
4. Norman Sisisky, D.*
5. Virgil Goode, Jr., D.*
6. Robert Goodlatte, R.*
7. Thomas J. (Tom) Bliley, Jr., R.*
8. James P. Moran, Jr., D.*
9. Rick C. Boucher, D.*
10. Frank R. Wolf, R.*
11. Thomas Davis III, R.*

Washington
1. Jay Inslee, D.
2. Jack Metcalf, R.*
3. Brian Baird, D.
4. Doc Hastings, R.*
5. George Nethercutt, Jr., R.*
6. Norman D. Dicks, D.*
7. Jim McDermott, D.*
8. Jennifer Dunn, R.*
9. Adam Smith, D.*

West Virginia
1. Alan B. Mollohan, D.*
2. Robert E. Wise, Jr., D.*
3. Nick J. Rahall II, D.*

Wisconsin
1. Paul Ryan, R.
2. Tammy Baldwin, D.
3. Ron Kind, D.*
4. Gerald D. Kleczka, D.*
5. Thomas Barrett, D.*
6. Thomas E. Petri, R.*
7. David R. Obey, D.*
8. Mark Green, R.
9. F. James Sensenbrenner, Jr., R.*

Wyoming
†Barbara Cubin, R.*

Nonvoting representatives

American Samoa
Eni F. H. Faleomavaega, D.*

District of Columbia
Eleanor Holmes Norton, D.*

Guam
Robert Underwood, D.*

Puerto Rico
Carlos Romero-Barcelo, D.*

Virgin Islands
Donna Christian-Christensen, D.

A patient "bill of rights" passed the House by a vote of 275 to 151 on Oct. 7, 1999. The *bipartisan* (supported by both Democrats and Republicans) bill provided patients a variety of rights, including the right to sue in state courts health insurance plans that cause injury by denying a patient care or by providing insufficient treatment. In July, the Senate passed a similar bill that gave patients a more limited set of rights. The Senate bill, which did not allow individuals to file lawsuits in state courts against health insurance plans, needed to be reconciled with the House bill before the legislation could be presented to President Clinton for approval.

Taxes. Congress in August approved a $792-billion tax cut that would have phased in an across-the-board 10-percent individual income tax rate and increased the standard deduction on tax returns filed by married couples. The measure was also designed to lower taxes on *capital gains* (profit on the sale of assets) and repeal the federal inheritance tax. The measure cleared the House by a vote of 221 to 206 but only narrowly won Senate approval by a vote of 50 to 49.

President Clinton vetoed the bill on September 23, claiming that the tax relief provided by the legislation would be too costly to the federal government. Speaker of the House Hastert pledged that tax relief would be a high priority when the Congress reconvened in 2000.

Lawmakers did pass legislation that extended tax benefits to armed services personnel serving in peacekeeping roles in Yugoslavia. The legislation unanimously cleared the House and the Senate on April 15, 1999. President Clinton signed the measure into law on April 19.

Social Security remained a politically charged issue for Congress through 1999. Lawmakers and President Clinton vowed to ensure the long-term survival of the program but battled over the best way to achieve that goal. The president in September vetoed the tax-cut bill approved by Congress in part because of his belief that budget surpluses should be used to help ensure Social Security's long-term solvency. Republican congressmen responded by asking the Clinton administration to reduce its budget requests in order to ensure excess Social Security revenue would not be spent in fiscal 1999-2000.

The federal government projected a $147-billion Social Security surplus in 2000 and a $235-billion surplus by 2009. However, surpluses were expected to turn into deficits by the 2030's as more Americans reached retirement age.

In March 1999, the trustees of the Social Security and Medicare trust funds reported that the Social Security fund would have adequate revenues until 2034, and the Medicare fund would be able to pay full benefits until 2015.

Education. Congress approved legislation in April 1999 that supporters claimed would improve academic achievement in public schools. The measure, called the Education Flexibility Partnership Act of 1999, popularly known as Ed-Flex, allowed states to grant schools a waiver of some federal requirements. The legislation was approved by the House and the Senate on April 21 and signed by the president on April 29. Prior to passage of the bill, 12 states had participated in a pilot program that similarly waved federal education requirements. Supporters maintained that the program was successfully used in those states to reduce paperwork burdens and expand educational opportunities for students.

Gun control. Lawmakers wrestled with major gun-control legislation throughout the year. The Senate on May 20 approved a juvenile crime bill with a number of gun-control measures, including a requirement that gun dealers sell child safety devices with every handgun and a restriction on the access children under the age of 18 are given to semiautomatic assault weapons. The measure also included provisions requiring mandatory background checks on consumers who buy firearms at gun shows.

The House of Representatives debated similar legislation in June, including the Juvenile Offenders Act. The legislation, approved by the House on June 17, mandated tougher sentences for children who commit crimes involving guns and provided $1.5 billion for combating juvenile crime. By the time the 106th Congress recessed, however, neither the House nor the Senate legislation had been revised.

Environment. Congress approved the Sudbury, Assabet, and Concord Wild and Scenic River Act, designating portions of those Massachusetts rivers as part of the National Wild and Scenic Rivers System. The House approved the bill by a vote of 295 to 22 on February 23. The Senate voted unanimously to pass the measure on March 25. Under the measure, the Department of the Interior, through the National Park Service, would administer the river segments and develop a conservation plan.

The House on April 22 approved the Beaches Environmental Awareness, Cleanup and Health Act of 1999. The act requires states with coastal recreational waters to adopt water quality standards. The legislation also requires the federal Environmental Protection Agency to examine potential health risks from exposure to dangerous materials in coastal waters and to develop methods for monitoring the waters. The Senate Committee on Environment and Public Works began hearings on the measure in July.

Historic preservation. The House voted 394 to 12 on February 23 to increase funding for the

Senator Dianne Feinstein (D., California) displays an AK-47 automatic rifle at a press conference in March 1999, during which she called for a ban on the import of high-capacity ammunition clips for automatic weapons.

New Jersey Coastal Heritage Trail Route, which includes two National Wildlife Refuges, a Civil War-era fort, and historic houses. The increased funding was to be used to complete interpretive exhibits and erect signs. The Senate on March 25 voted unanimously to approve the measure, which was signed into law by President Clinton on April 8.

With little debate, the House on June 30 approved legislation supporters said would help to preserve the cultural resources of the Route 66 corridor. The corridor, which extends from Chicago to Los Angeles, had been the major roadway to the West from the 1930's through the 1960's. The Senate unanimously approved the measure on July 27, 1999. The legislation authorized the Department of the Interior to provide assistance in the preservation and restoration of historic sites along the highway, which was one of the first limited-access interstate roads in the nation. The president signed the bill on August 10.

☐ Geoffrey A. Campbell and Linda P. Campbell
See also **Armed forces; Crime; Democratic Party; Elections; Environmental pollution; Health care issues; People in the news** (DeLay, Tom; Hastert, J. Dennis); **Republican Party; Social Security; Taxation; United States, Government of the; United States, President of the.**

Connecticut. See State government.

Conservation. The wars that ravaged central Africa in the 1990's devastated not only human populations but also threatened the existence of native wildlife. Fighting in the region caused tourism to grind to a halt in 1999.

In March, Hutu tribesmen, refugees from Rwanda living in Congo (Kinshasa), entered Uganda's Bwindi Impenetrable Forest and ambushed a safari party booked for a visit to gorilla country. The ambush killed a game warden and eight foreign tourists, including U.S. and British citizens. Tourism plummeted after the United States and Great Britain responded to the attack by issuing travel advisories warning against visiting the war-torn area.

Bwindi is one of only three places where the endangered mountain gorilla, of which there were about 620 individuals in 1999, lives in the wild. A trek to see the great apes had been a popular tourist attraction in the early 1990's, channeling income to local people.

With the loss of income from tourism, Ugandans in the Bwindi area in 1999 indicated they would return to logging and farming, practices highly destructive to the rain forest, to earn money. This placed the mountain gorilla's habitat and survival in jeopardy. Although the Ugandan government vowed to protect the gorillas, officials acknowledged that this would be a difficult task.

A bald eagle named Challenger perches above an American flag as President Bill Clinton announces a proposal in July 1999 to remove the U.S. national bird from the endangered species list. Wildlife officials said the bald eagle population in the United States had risen from 417 breeding pairs in 1963 to 5,748 pairs in 1999.

Other war pressures on wildlife. In Congo (Kinshasa), Rwanda's Hutu rebels and Congolese Mayi Mayi guerrillas continued to strip Kahuzi-Biega National Park of trees throughout 1999. These forces had been operating in the park since the mid-1990's.

The presence of the rebels in the park aggravated the problem of *poaching* (illegal killing of wildlife). Arrested poachers admitted to killing 20 gorillas and 17 elephants in Kahuzi-Biega between April and July 1999. Park officials estimated that 100 of Kahuzi-Biega's 250 eastern lowland gorillas had been killed since 1996.

The heavily armed rebels and the impoverished local people killed the gorillas for meat, and the elephants for meat and ivory, which fetches a high price on the black market. Gorilla heads were also sold as trophy souvenirs.

Amazon devastation. Brazil's Amazon rain forest is being destroyed at a rate much greater than previously believed, according to research published in April 1999. A team of scientists from Woods Hole Research Center in Massachusetts, the Instituto de Pesquisa Ambiental da Amazonia Campus do Guama in Brazil, and other institutions announced that 15,000 square miles (38,850 square kilometers) of Amazon forest are being destroyed annually—a rate more than double earlier estimates.

The Amazon is home to an incredible variety of animals and plants. Environmentalists also value the Amazon for its ability to absorb vast quantities of carbon dioxide from the atmosphere, reducing the risk of *global warming* (an increase in the average temperature of Earth's surface). Many scientists believe that global warming is caused by the burning of fossil fuels and other human activities that release carbon dioxide and other heat-trapping gases into the atmosphere. Despite these concerns, economic pressures and a growing population have forced many Brazilians to clear the Amazon for farming and timber.

The researchers conducted an in-depth field survey of wood mill operations and forest-burning practices in the Amazon and found that the clearing of forests does not always show up in satellite photographs, the usual method used to evaluate rain-forest loss. The scientists also described how a severe drought in 1998 made 104,250 square miles (270,000 square kilometers) of forest highly vulnerable to fire. The researchers urged the Brazilian government to restrict logging and support improved strategies for preventing forest fires.

The return of the bald eagle. In July 1999, U.S. President Bill Clinton announced a proposal to remove the bald eagle from the Endangered Species List within one year. Officials with the U.S. Fish and Wildlife Service (USFWS) estimated

in mid-1999 that there were 5,748 breeding pairs of bald eagles in the United States. In 1963, there were only 417 breeding pairs of bald eagles in the country.

Conservationists attributed the decline of bald eagles to hunting, loss of habitat, and extensive use of the insecticide dichloro-diphenyl-trichloro-ethane (DDT). DDT entered birds' bodies through fish and other prey that were contaminated with the chemical compound. The insecticide weakened eagle eggshells so that few chicks survived. The United States banned DDT in 1972, and the Endangered Species Act made it illegal to kill listed animals, such as the bald eagle, in 1973.

Peregrine falcons return. United States Secretary of Interior Bruce Babbitt removed the peregrine falcon from the Endangered Species List in August 1999. Like the bald eagle, the peregrine was a victim of DDT. In 1970, the number of peregrine falcons in the United States dropped to 39 breeding pairs. The USFWS estimated that the North American breeding numbers had grown to more than 1,650 pairs by 1999.

Although the peregrine lost some protections when it was removed from the list, it was still covered by the 1918 Migratory Bird Treaty Act. This act makes it illegal to kill the falcon or possess its feathers without a special federal permit.

Second chance for wolves. The USFWS's program to restore Mexican wolves to the American Southwest fared better in 1999 than when it was launched in 1998. The agency hoped to establish a population of 100 Mexican wolves in the wild by 2005. The Mexican wolf had been eradicated from the wild during the 1970's, mainly because ranchers considered it a threat to livestock.

In March 1998, USFWS biologists released 11 wolves into the Blue Range Wolf Recovery Area, which covers 7,000 square miles (18,000 square kilometers) of mountains, forests, and grasslands in Apache National Forest in Arizona and Gila National Forest in New Mexico. By November 1998, all of these animals had either been killed, recaptured, or were missing and presumed dead.

Initially, officials thought that the dead wolves had been shot by ranchers. However, biologists later concluded that hunters, mistaking the wolves for coyotes, probably killed the animals.

The USFWS released several more pairs of wolves between December 1998 and June 1999. By late 1999, two of these wolves had been killed—one was the victim of a collision with a car, while the cause of the other wolf's death was unknown. Biologists said that many of the released wolf pairs produced pups in the wild. By November, there were almost two dozen Mexican wolves in the release area.

Some problems with the wolves did arise in 1999. For example, a small number of cows and calves were found dead, possibly the victims of wolf or coyote attacks. Biologists captured the wolf pack that may have been responsible and planned to relocate it to a site that offered less potential conflict with domestic animals.

Yellowstone bonus. In an August radio address, President Clinton announced a land deal to provide greater protection for Yellowstone National Park, located in the northwest corner of Wyoming and parts of Idaho and Montana. In the deal, the U.S. government purchased the Royal Teton Ranch, 9,300 acres (3,766 hectares) of land on Yellowstone's north border, from the Church Universal and Triumphant. The government paid $13.5 million to the church, which had used the ranch as its headquarters.

The ranch was purchased to preserve the underground supplies of hot water, which, if damaged, could disrupt Yellowstone's geysers and hot springs. The park extension also helps safeguard Yellowstone's bison. Each winter, the bison herd migrates to lower elevations in search of food. If the animals stray across park borders, rangers are required to shoot them because bison may transmit a disease called brucellosis to cattle. This disease can cause cows to suddenly abort. With the additional acreage, bison can safely roam farther. ☐ Eugene J. Walter, Jr.

Costa Rica. See Latin America.

Courts. A California appellate court ruled on Sept. 29, 1999, that gun manufacturers can be sued for promoting a product to criminals that can then be used to commit crimes. The 2-to-1 decision by the First District Court of Appeal in San Francisco was the first ruling in the United States to allow the victims of shootings to sue gun manufacturers for negligence.

More than 20 local governments in the United States, including Chicago, Los Angeles, and San Francisco, filed lawsuits in 1999 against handgun makers and distributors. Officials hoped that the lawsuits would force better control of gun sales and the addition of safety features on weapons. The suits were based upon the claim that companies could make guns safer and should bear some responsibility for those guns that end up in the hands of criminals.

Officials in New Orleans started the legal attack by suing 15 gun manufacturers, several New Orleans-area gun dealers, and three trade associations in 1998. The suits asked for monetary compensation for the costs of dealing with gun violence, such as police, ambulance services, and court time. Officials with the National Association for the Advancement of Colored People (NAACP), a civil rights organization headquartered in Baltimore, sued nearly 100 handgun makers in July 1999 and asked a federal court to order changes

EVOLUTION VERSUS FUNDAMENTALISM. There is among the statutes of Tennessee a law prohibiting the teaching of any theory of the evolution of man from lower forms of life. . . . John T. Scopes, a young teacher, admitted that he taught evolution, and declared that he could not instruct in biology and avoid it. . . . Thus there was begun a legal battle in a little mountain county of Tennessee the like of which had never before been entered upon a docket in any law court of the world. . . . Six days full of dramatic scenes were required to try the cause. Religion and evolution were on trial, rather than Scopes, who was at times quite forgotten during the proceedings. [Defense attorney Clarence] Darrow placed [prosecuting attorney William Jennings] Bryan on the witness stand to disclose weaknesses in his theory of the infallibility of the Bible. . . . The jury . . . quickly returned a verdict of guilty, and the case was appealed at once to the supreme court of the state.

in handgun marketing and distribution practices. The NAACP alleged that gun manufacturers encourage an underground market in illegal handguns. Spokespersons for the gun industry called the lawsuits misguided, and various manufacturers tried to have some state legislatures ban the lawsuits.

Assisted suicide. A Michigan jury in March convicted Jack Kevorkian, a former pathologist, of second-degree murder for the physician-assisted suicide of a 52-year-old man in 1998. In April 1999, a Michigan judge sentenced Kevorkian, 70, to 10 to 25 years in prison. In September 1998, Kevorkian had videotaped the assisted suicide of Thomas Youk, who suffered from amyotrophic lateral sclerosis, known as Lou Gehrig's disease. Kevorkian gave the videotape to the CBS news program "60 Minutes," which later broadcast portions on television.

Wyoming slaying. A Wyoming jury in November 1999 found Aaron McKinney, 22, guilty of felony murder in the 1998 death of Matthew Shepard. Shepard, a 21-year-old gay college student, was severely beaten because of his sexual orientation. He later died from his injuries. A second suspect in the case, Russell Henderson, 22, pleaded guilty in April 1999 to the crime.

Judge Barton Voigt had prohibited defense

attorneys from using a so-called "gay panic" defense in McKinney's trial. The attorneys had argued that McKinney had been the victim of a forced homosexual encounter in his youth. They claimed that a person with latent homosexual tendencies can have a violent, uncontrollable reaction when sexual advances by a person of the same sex are made. Voigt ruled that the strategy was similar to a temporary-insanity defense, which is prohibited under Wyoming state law.

On November 4, Voigt sentenced McKinney to two consecutive life terms in prison. Under an agreement, McKinney waived any rights of appeal or parole in exchange for not receiving the death penalty.

Tobacco litigation. A Florida jury on July 7 ruled that the five largest cigarette makers in the United States should be held liable for knowingly selling a product that causes deadly diseases. The jury decided that monetary damages could be awarded, which could lead to hundreds of thousands of potential claims by current and former smokers.

The U.S. Justice Department on September 22 filed a multibillion dollar federal lawsuit against the tobacco industry, alleging that the industry produces a product that costs taxpayers billions of dollars annually in health-related costs. Justice Department officials also alleged that tobacco companies engaged in consumer fraud by concealing the risks of cigarette smoking.

Linda Tripp on July 30, 1999, was indicted by a Maryland grand jury on two criminal charges of wiretapping. Her taped conversations with Monica Lewinsky, a former White House intern, led to the impeachment trial of President Bill Clinton.

Microsoft lawsuit. On November 5, U.S. District Judge Thomas Penfield Jackson ruled that the Microsoft Corporation of Redmond, Washington, violated federal antitrust laws designed to prevent any one business from developing too much power over competitors. The Justice Department and attorneys general from 20 states sued Microsoft in 1998 for monopolistic practices in the company's marketing of its Windows *operating system* (the master control program that coordinates the operations of a computer) and its Internet Explorer *Web browser* (a program that enables computers to access the World Wide Web).

Same-sex marriage. The Vermont Supreme Court on Dec. 20, 1999, ruled that the state must provide the same benefits to same-sex couples that it does to heterosexual couples. The court directed the Vermont legislature to either legalize same-sex marriages or adopt a domestic partnership law. On December 10, the Hawaii Supreme Court ruled that a 1998 amendment to that state's constitution prohibiting same-sex marriages was legal.

☐ Linda P. Campbell and Geoffrey A. Campbell
See also **Computers; Crime; State government; Supreme Court of the United States.**

and Scotland, which had qualified as the top three sides in the ICC Trophy tournament in Kuala Lumpur, Malaysia, in 1997. The teams were divided into two groups of six, with each side in the two groups playing each of the others. The top three teams in each group then progressed to the Super Six phase, with the top four teams moving on to the semifinals.

Sri Lanka, England, and the West Indies failed to reach the Super Six, as did Bangladesh, Kenya, and Scotland. India, and Zimbabwe, the surprise team in the Super Six phase, failed to reach the semifinals. In the semifinals, Pakistan beat New Zealand by nine wickets, and Australia eliminated South Africa. The Australia-South Africa match was one of the most exciting in World Cup history. Australia batted first, scoring 213. South Africa reached 213 with three balls to spare, but batsman Allan Donald was then run out by nearly 10 yards, and the match was tied. As a result, Australia went to the final due to its superior position in the Super Six standings.

The final match, on the other hand, was an anticlimax. A capacity crowd at Lord's Cricket Ground in London saw Australia defeat Pakistan by eight wickets. This one-sided victory prompted an inquiry into whether certain Pakistani players may have intentionally thrown the match. The charges were later officially withdrawn.

Adam Gilchrist bats for Australia in the final match of the ICC World Cup in London in June 1999. Australia defeated Pakistan by eight wickets to win the world cricket championship for the second time.

Cricket. England hosted the seventh International Cricket Council (ICC) World Cup in May and June 1999. The tournament, which has taken place every four years since 1975, consisted of forty-two 50-over matches. Thirty-eight of the matches were played in England, many at county grounds that had never before staged one-day internationals. Single matches were also played in the Netherlands, Wales, Ireland, and Scotland.

World Cup. Twelve teams took part in the tournament. These included the nine test match-playing teams—Australia, England, India, New Zealand, Pakistan, South Africa, Sri Lanka, West Indies, and Zimbabwe—plus Bangladesh, Kenya,

International cricket. Australia's 1998-1999 test year opened in September 1998 with a tour of Pakistan. Australia won the series, winning one match by an innings, with two draws for their first series win in Pakistan since 1959. In the second test, Mark Taylor scored 334 not out, equaling Sir Donald Bradman's record test score for Australia.

Australia then returned home to defeat England 3-1 with one match drawn. Australia also won the Carlton and United One-day Series, in which Australia and England were joined by Sri Lanka. In February 1999, Taylor retired from test cricket after captaining Australia in 50 tests. Taylor, who many people considered the greatest of modern cricket captains, played in a total of 104 tests and scored 7,525 runs, for an average of 43.49.

The West Indies tour of South Africa from November 1998 through January 1999 was almost canceled due to a dispute about pay and conditions. The row included the dismissal and subsequent reinstatement of West Indian captain Brian Lara and vice-captain Carl Hooper, plus an appeal by the South African president Nelson Mandela for the tour to proceed. Once in South Africa, the West Indies team was outclassed, losing the test series by 5-0 and the subsequent one-day international series by 6-1.

Having been so thoroughly routed, West Indies was all the more impressive in managing a 2-2 draw against Australia, which toured the Caribbean in March and April 1999. The West Indians owed much to the dazzling performance of Lara, who scored three centuries and averaged 91.00. Glenn McGrath was an outstanding bowler for the Australians, taking 30 wickets in the test matches.

New Zealand, an improving side, hosted India in December 1998 and January 1999. India won the series 1-0 with one test drawn and another abandoned. South Africa visited New Zealand in February and March 1999 and beat the host country by 1-0 with two tests drawn. In September 1999, Sri Lanka won in a major upset over Australia 1-0 in a rain-plagued series with two matches drawn. This was Sri Lanka's first series victory over Australia.

Zimbabwe had a good cricketing year in 1998-1999. They won a single test against India at home and, even more remarkably, won their first-ever test series against Pakistan 1-0 with one match drawn and another abandoned. India and Pakistan contested a 2-match series in India in January and February 1999. The series, which was drawn 1-1, was distinguished by India's leg spinner Anil Kumble, who became the second bowler to take 10 wickets in a test match innings. His 10-74 ranked alongside the English bowler Jim Laker, who took 10-53 against Australia in 1956.

England's summer proved a depressing one for cricket fans. After the team's early departure from the World Cup, England lost a test series to New Zealand by 2-1, with one match drawn. As a result, England was unofficially ranked as the worst side playing test cricket. The reason for England's decline was a topic of hot debate. Many observers criticized the domestic County Championship league for a lack of competitiveness. In response, the England and Wales Cricket Board divided the 18 county sides in the first-class County Championship into a first division and a second division. The poorest three sides in the first division are to be demoted and replaced by the top three sides from the second division. Both the board and English cricket fans hoped that this change would raise standards by spurring competition in domestic cricket.   □ Keith Lye

Crime statistics released in November 1999 by the Federal Bureau of Investigation (FBI) revealed that serious crime declined by 11 percent in the first six months of 1999, compared with statistics for the same period in 1998. According to the FBI Uniform Crime Reporting Program, which gathers crime statistics from more than 9,300 law enforcement agencies across the United States, violent crime—murder, robbery, aggravated assault, and rape—dropped by 8 percent nationwide, compared with a 5-percent drop in 1998. Property crime—motor vehicle theft, larceny, and burglary—decreased 10 percent in 1999, compared with 5 percent in 1998.

The FBI reported that the murder rate declined nationwide by 13 percent in the first six months of 1999, compared with 1998 statistics. Rape fell by 8 percent, robbery decreased by 10 percent, assault fell by 7 percent, burglary dropped 14 percent, larceny declined 8 percent, and car theft fell by 12 percent.

The FBI report revealed that declines in crime varied by region. Crime fell by 12 percent in the West, by 11 percent in the Midwest, by 10 percent in the Northeast, and by 7 percent in the South. Crime in cities with a population of more than 1 million people dropped by 6 percent in the first six months of 1999, compared with 1998 statistics. Crime in smaller cities—those with a population of less than 250,000 people—experienced declines between 10 percent and 11 percent in the first six months of 1999.

FBI officials reported that crime rates had dropped each year since 1991. Although law enforcement officials expected a decline in 1999, no one had predicted such a large drop. Officials stated that the decline was the greatest since the bureau began collecting national crime data in 1930. Criminologists speculated that the steep decline could be attributed to a variety of factors. These included the booming U.S. economy, which brought prosperity to large numbers of Americans; the spread of new policing techniques from cities to suburbs; the increasing prison population, which reduces the number of potential criminals; and a decline in the use of illegal drugs—including crack cocaine—which police claim was the impetus behind an increase in urban crime in the 1980's.

Tragedy at Columbine. Two students at Columbine High School in Littleton, Colorado, shot and killed 12 students and a teacher before turning their guns on themselves on April 20, 1999. Police reported that Eric Harris, 18, and Dylan Klebold, 17, were part of a small clique at the school who dressed in black clothing and were obsessed with Nazi Germany. Police reported that Harris and Klebold, dressed in trench coats and ski masks, walked into the school's cafeteria and

People in Atlanta, Georgia, flee from an office complex in July 1999 after a gunman opens fire in a brokerage firm and kills nine people. The gunman, Mark Barton, an independent stock trader upset over unsuccessful investments, later killed himself. Police suspected that he also murdered his wife and children.

began a four-hour shooting spree. Authorities revealed that the teen-agers had apparently planned the attack carefully, going so far as to plant dozens of bombs, most of which did not go off. The violence at Columbine was the worst school shooting incident in U.S. history.

School violence. In the wake of the Columbine shooting, a number of experts questioned the validity of a study published in August 1999 showing that school violence had declined in the 1990's. The Centers for Disease Control and Prevention (CDC) in Atlanta, Georgia, reported that violent acts by U.S. high school students declined between 1991 and 1997. The CDC revealed that the number of students who reported carrying a weapon fell from 26.1 percent in 1991 to 18.3 percent in 1997.

Educators and law enforcement officials argued that the percentages were still unacceptably high. Also, the report stated that incidents such as the shooting at Columbine may result in an increase in students carrying weapons to school.

Racial attacks made news headlines throughout 1999. In July, a 21-year-old man went on a three-day shooting rampage that was apparently racially motivated. The man, Benjamin Smith, on July 2 allegedly shot at but missed six Jewish men who were walking home from Sabbath prayers in a predominantly Jewish neighborhood of Chicago. Later that same day in a Chicago suburb, Smith allegedly shot and killed

Ricky Byrdsong, a former college basketball coach, as Byrdsong was jogging with his children.

On July 3, Smith allegedly shot at various black men and a group of Asian men in downstate Illinois before crossing the state line into Indiana and killing an Asian graduate student outside of a Korean church in Bloomington. Smith reportedly stole a van and shot himself to death following a police chase. Investigators said that Smith was a member of a racist organization that advocates a war against all non-whites and Jews.

Other attacks. An independent stock trader shot and killed nine people in an office complex in Atlanta, Georgia, on July 29, before killing himself. Police reported that Mark Barton, 44, was upset over unsuccessful investments. Police believed Barton also murdered his wife and two children.

On September 15, in Fort Worth, Texas, a man shot seven people and then himself in a Baptist church. Police reported that Larry Ashbrook, 47, burst in on a service for teen-agers gathered to reaffirm their faith and shot 14 people while shouting anti-religious comments. Three teen-agers and three adults died in the church. One girl died the following day. Police could find no motive for the shooting.

☐ Robert Messenger

See also **Human rights; Prison.**

Croatia. President Franjo Tudjman died on Dec. 10, 1999, following a long battle with cancer. Tudjman led Croatia to independence in 1991, but he was widely criticized for his authoritarian style of rule and failure to foster democratic institutions. Many political analysts believed that Tudjman's death would lead to more democratic reforms in Croatia and thus improved relations with the West. Polls in October 1999 indicated that Tudjman's party, the Croatian Democratic Union (HDZ), trailed opposition parties in parliamentary elections scheduled for January 2000. By law, Croatia was required to hold a presidential election within 60 days of Tudjman's death.

Figures released in July indicated that Croatia's *gross domestic product* (the value of all goods and services produced in a country in a given year) had fallen by nearly 2 percent in 1999 from 1998 levels. Unemployment reached 23.4 percent in May 1999.

Officials of the European Union (EU) in October repeated an earlier complaint that Croatia had failed to undertake genuine political reforms. Despite assurances to the EU that it would initiate electoral reforms, Tudjman's government in October passed a law on election procedures that renewed the right of Croats living abroad (who have been strong HDZ supporters in the past) to vote in Croatian elections. ☐ Sharon L. Wolchik

See also **Yugoslavia: A Special Report.**

CUBA underwent sweeping changes in 1959 under Fidel Castro. Castro became premier on February 16. He resigned in July after a disagreement with President Manuel Urrutia Lleo, resumed office a few days later, then smashed an attempted counterrevolution in August. Castro lashed out at the United States when political opposition to his policies mounted in October. He charged the U.S. "countenanced" the bombing of Havana by Cuban-manned planes based in the United States. But he privately admitted the planes had dropped only leaflets. . . .

In an effort to tighten domestic security, Castro placed Major Raul Castro, his younger brother, in charge of the armed forces. Castro also appointed Major Ernesto "Che" Guevara, a suspected Communist sympathizer, to direct the National Bank of Cuba. Major Pedro Luis Diaz, chief of the Cuban air force, fled to the United States, after charging that Communists were gaining control of the government.

Cuba. On Jan. 1, 1999, Cubans celebrated the 40th anniversary of the Communist revolution in Cuba. Government leaders and many citizens noted advances of the past 40 years, including the highest literacy rate and lowest infant mortality rate in Latin America and a free education system that had quadrupled the number of university graduates. Many Cuban Americans marked the anniversary with protests of Cuba's restrictions on civil liberties and a lack of democratic reforms.

Cuban-U.S. relations. About 50,000 people, including Cuban President Fidel Castro, packed the stadium in Havana, the capital, on March 28 to watch Cuba's national baseball team play the Baltimore Orioles, the first major league team from the United States to play in Cuba in 40 years. The Orioles won 3-2. On May 3, Cuban fans were ecstatic when their team beat the Orioles 12-6 in a second game played in Baltimore, Maryland.

The games were part of an increasing number of exchanges between the two nations for athletic events, academic research, and cultural programs after U.S. President Bill Clinton announced on January 5 that the U.S. government would ease some restrictions mandated by the 37-year-old trade embargo against Cuba. The new policy also allowed any U.S. citizen to send $1,200 annually to nongovernmental agencies in Cuba and to any individual in Cuba who was not a high-ranking Com-

Cuban President Fidel Castro (center) meets with members of the Baltimore Orioles baseball team before a game with Cuba's national team in March 1999 in Havana. The two teams competed again in Baltimore in May.

munist official. Such remittances had previously been allowed only between Cuban American families and their Cuban relatives. Cubans in 1999 could buy U.S. food, farm machinery, fertilizers, and pesticides. On August 3, Clinton approved charter flights from New York City and Los Angeles to Havana, making it unnecessary for many U.S. residents to travel to Cuba via third countries or Miami, Florida. Other trade restrictions and a ban on U.S. tourism to Cuba remained in place in 1999.

Custody case. On November 27, the U.S. Coast Guard rescued a boy and two adults off the coast of Florida. The three were the only survivors of a sunken boat that had been carrying Cuban refugees to Florida. The boy's mother drowned in the accident. The boy's father, who remained in Cuba, and the Cuban government demanded the boy's return. The U.S. Immigration and Naturalization Service legally placed the boy with relatives in Miami, pending a decision on his custody by Florida courts.

Four political dissidents, who had called for the end of Cuba's one-party political system, were sentenced on March 15 to jail terms ranging from three and one-half to five years. Many foreign governments and human rights groups had called for the release of the dissidents, who were imprisoned in August 1997.　　　□ Nathan A. Haverstock

See also **Baseball; Latin America.**

Cyprus. See Middle East.

Czech Republic. President Vaclav Havel, who continued to suffer health problems in 1999, consulted with leaders of the minority government over the economic decline and political issues plaguing the Czech Republic.

Domestic affairs. In January, the United States urged Czech leaders to condemn the racial and ethnic animosity among the people of the Czech Republic, especially Czech animosity toward the Roma, a minority ethnic group also known as Gypsies. In reaction to pressure from Romany organizations, the government agreed to restore the condition of a monument to Roma victims of the Holocaust. The government, however, refused to relocate a pig farm adjacent to the monument. The Holocaust was the systematic killing during World War II (1939-1945) of millions of people, including the Roma, considered undesirable by Germany's Nazi government. In 1999 in the city of Usti nad Labem, citizens built a 7-foot- (2-meter-) high wall to separate areas of the city inhabited by Roma from those in which Czechs lived. A Czech government order to tear down the wall met with resistance from local officials.

In February, the Czech parliament defeated an amendment that would have allowed non-Czech citizens to claim restitution from the government for property seized by the former Communist government of Czechoslovakia. (Slovakia and the

Czech Republic became separate countries in 1993.)

An economic recession lasting longer than expected forced the Czech finance ministry to lower its estimates for economic growth in 1999. Analysts expected the country's *gross domestic product* (the value of all goods and services produced in a country in a given year) to drop by 1 percent for the year. In January, the parliament approved a 1999 budget that included a $1-billion deficit. Unemployment reached 9 percent in October, but economists thought that the falling inflation rate would spur the government to lower interest rates, leading to economic growth and more jobs.

Foreign affairs. The Czech Republic joined the North Atlantic Treaty Organization (NATO) on March 12, but polls published in April indicated that only 35 percent of Czech citizens supported the NATO bombing of Serbia, which had begun on March 24.

Relations with Austria were complicated in 1999 by the Czech Republic's decision to complete construction of the Temelin nuclear power plant, which the Austrian government opposed.

Czech and Slovak leaders reached agreement on several major issues in ongoing negotiations involving the division of federal property of the former Czechoslovakia. ☐ Sharon L. Wolchik

See also **Europe; Slovakia.**

Dallas. Dallas/Fort Worth (D/FW) International Airport celebrated its 25th anniversary on Jan. 13, 1999. The celebration, however, was marred by D/FW's decline during the past two years from third to fifth busiest airport in the world in number of passengers served. A legal fight between Dallas and Fort Worth over expanded flight service at Dallas's Love Field continued to delay $2.2 billion in construction work at D/FW Airport in 1999. D/FW's inability to expand permitted other airports to grow more rapidly.

Superintendent appointed. The Dallas school board in May 1999 chose Waldemar "Bill" Rojas, former superintendent of the San Francisco Unified School District, to head the 160,000-student public schools system. The school board set his salary at $260,000, making him one of the highest-paid school administrators in the nation. Rojas pledged to restore credibility to the Dallas school district where school employees had been under federal investigation for criminal wrongdoing for two years.

American Airlines Center. In March 1999, American Airlines announced it had purchased the naming rights to the $300-million sports and entertainment arena under construction on the northwest edge of downtown Dallas. The airline contracted to pay $195 million over the next 30 years for the arena to be named the American Airlines Center. The new facility was scheduled to open in 2001 and to serve as the home of the National Basketball Association Dallas Mavericks and the National Hockey League Dallas Stars.

Stanley Cup win. On June 19, 1999, the Dallas Stars won the Stanley Cup in the National Hockey League championship series against the Buffalo Sabres. Brett Hull's winning score in triple overtime brought the team its first championship since moving to Dallas from Minnesota.

SMU sets new campaign goal. On September 10, Southern Methodist University announced it had surpassed its $350-million campaign goal in gifts and pledges and would try to reach $400 million by the end date in 2002. The money was to be used to construct new buildings, increase student scholarships, hire outstanding professors, and create new academic programs. The fundraising project was the largest ever undertaken by a university in North Texas.

New police chief. On Oct. 1, 1999, Terrell Bolton became Dallas's first African American police chief. Chief Bolton had been with the police force for nearly 20 years when he was named to the post. He succeeded Ben Click, a popular chief who has been credited with improving the Dallas Police Department's public image and reducing major crime during his six-year tenure. The appointment was made by Ted Benavides, who made history in 1998 when the City Council selected him to become Dallas's first Hispanic city manager.

City council member indicted. Longtime Dallas City Council member Albert Lipscomb, 73, was indicted on March 4, 1999, on charges of taking payoffs from a cab company owner. The federal charges accused Lipscomb of using his office to help the Yellow and Checker cab companies receive favorable treatment at city hall. Lipscomb was the second Dallas City Council member to be indicted in the past three years. Former council member Paul Fielding pleaded guilty to extortion charges in 1997.

Mass transit. Completion of the first 20 miles (32 kilometers) of the Dallas Area Rapid Transit (DART) light rail system brought significant economic growth during 1999. New multimillion dollar construction was underway at sites along the rail lines in North Dallas, Oak Cliff, and South Dallas. A study by University of North Texas economist Bernard Weinstein indicated that property values in areas served by DART had increased 25 percent over comparable real estate in other areas. DART received a $333 million U.S. Department of Transportation grant on October 2 to fund extensions into Richardson, Plano, and Garland, suburban communities north of Dallas. ☐ Henry K. Tatum

See also **City.**

Dance. Two major forces in American dance—one an institution, the other a choreographer—celebrated important anniversaries in 1999. The New York City Ballet, founded by George Balanchine in 1948, marked its 50th birthday by presenting an unprecedented 100 ballets during its 1998-1999 winter and spring seasons at the New York State Theater in New York City. The repertory included a tribute to Jerome Robbins, City Ballet's second choreographer-in-residence from 1948 until his death in 1998.

On April 29, 1999, Peter Martins, City Ballet's artistic director, unveiled a new production of *Swan Lake*. Although the choreography greatly resembled that of the 1895 original by Lev Ivanov and Marius Petipa, Martins updated the ballet with new choreography and, more significantly, through his choice of decor. Danish painter Per Kirkeby designed abstract scenery that only vaguely hinted at the ballet's lakeside and ballroom locales. By refashioning the libretto so that love does not conquer all, Martins also gave the ballet a contemporary point of view. Martins's version, however, did not find favor with critics, who judged the decor pallid and the story confusing.

Two City Ballet premieres in June 1999 highlighted jazz. *Duke!*, a tribute to American composer and musician Duke Ellington, featured choreography by modern-dance choreographer Garth Fagan, City Ballet dancer Robert La Fosse, and Broadway's Susan Stroman. *Them Twos* was a series of duets with a score by American trumpeter and composer Wynton Marsalis.

Merce Cunningham, who turned 80 on April 16, proved that he was still the most advanced choreographer of his time. Although Cunningham had used computer programs since 1989 to create dance material, his *Biped*, which premiered April 23, 1999, at Zellerbach Hall in Berkeley, California, took technology to a new level of artistic expression. The dancers moved behind a scrim curtain on which was projected computer-generated images that sometimes hovered over the dancers like friendly ghosts. To achieve these stunning effects, computer experts Paul Kaiser and Shelley Eshkar digitally recorded the movements of three dancers in Cunningham's work and then reconstituted that material into virtual choreography that ran parallel to Cunningham's.

In addition to *Biped*, the Merce Cunningham Dance Company's New York City run in June featured other novelties designed to celebrate Cunningham's birthday. Dance legend Mikhail Baryshnikov appeared with Cunningham in a new duet called *Occasion Piece*. A revival of Cunningham's lyrical *Summerspace* (1958), with American artist Robert Rauschenberg's decor, provided another program highlight.

Dancers from the Kirov Ballet of St. Petersburg, Russia, perform in New York City in June 1999 in a new production of *The Sleeping Beauty* that featured a restoration of the ballet's original choreography, scenery, and costumes from the late 1800's.

Mark Morris, director of the Mark Morris Dance Group, remained on an artistic roll in 1999. *The Argument* premiered with Baryshnikov in a guest appearance on February 25 at Boston's Wang Center for the Performing Arts. Set to Robert Schumann's *Five Pieces in Folk Style* (1851), for cello and piano, the work was graced by the playing of cellist Yo-Yo Ma. Critics hailed the dance, which probes the emotional lives of three couples, as one of Morris's most mature dances.

Dixit Dominus (1701), a sacred vocal piece by George Frideric Handel, provided a springboard for a second Morris premiere at Zellerbach Hall on March 18, 1999. *Sandpaper Ballet,* Morris's commission for the San Francisco Ballet, debuted on April 27. It drew its inspiration from the popular tunes of American composer Leroy Anderson, whose light-hearted music brought out Morris's humor.

Twyla Tharp, like Morris, is known for her musicality and wide-ranging choice of composers. In 1999, Tharp was in a Beethoven phase, and most observers found her choreography equal to the force of the composer. Her troupe, called Tharp!, premiered *Grosse Sonate*, a dance set to the formidable Hammerklavier Sonata, Op. 106, on July 1 at the American Dance Festival in Durham, North Carolina. *Diabelli*, Tharp's second foray into Beethoven—set to his *Diabelli Varia-*

tions (1823)—had its American debut on September 17 at the University of Iowa's Hancher Auditorium in Iowa City.

Diabelli was the first of eight dances cocommissioned by the Hancher Auditorium as part of its Millennium Festival. Hancher's annual arts festival has presented dance since 1977, but the 1999 festival, with a dance budget of nearly $1 million, ranked as the most ambitious to date. The festival presented premieres by some of America's most important dance artists—among them Susan Marshall, Paul Taylor, Lar Lubovitch, and Bill T. Jones.

Farrell and the masters. As part of the millennium season at the John F. Kennedy Center for the Performing Arts in Washington, D.C., Suzanne Farrell, a former City Ballet dancer, created a 16-member troupe to present ballets by Balanchine as well as Robbins and French-born choreographer Maurice Bejart. The program, called "Suzanne Farrell Stages Masters of 20th-Century Ballet," opened at the Center's Terrace Theater on Oct. 21, 1999. Noteworthy in Farrell's venture was the first performance by someone other than Farrell of the female role in the passionate duet *Meditation* (1963). The ballet was a gift to her from Balanchine, whose stormy romance with Farrell in the 1960's made headlines.

The Martha Graham Dance Company suffered more disruption in 1999. To stabilize its long-term finances, the troupe in January sold its New York City home and school of 40 years, where Graham had created all her masterpieces. The sale generated some $3 million, which the troupe used to pay off its debts and establish an endowment. In September, Ron Protas, the group's artistic director since Graham's death in 1991, announced he would step down in July 2000, to be succeeded by former Graham dancer Janet Eilber.

Foreign visitors. Of the many foreign troupes visiting North America in 1999, the Kirov Ballet of St. Petersburg, Russia, brought the most fascinating repertory. For its season at New York City's Metropolitan Opera House in June and July, the Kirov presented *The Sleeping Beauty*, created in Russia in 1890. The heavily researched ballet followed the original as closely as possible, in choreography as well as scenery and costumes.

The Fountain of Bakhchisaria (1934), the most esteemed ballet from the period of the former Soviet Union (1922-1991), proved of little more than historical interest. But the Kirov's final bill, an all-Balanchine program, was smashing. Audiences and critics alike delighted in seeing his works interpreted with genuine enthusiasm by dancers from his homeland. Balanchine left Russia in 1924, and his works rarely have been performed there.　　　　□ Nancy Goldner

See also **Classical music.**

■ Deaths

in 1999 included those listed below, who were Americans unless otherwise indicated.

Adams, Alice (1926–May 27), author of deftly drawn short stories and novels, including *Listening to Billie* (1978) and *Superior Women* (1984).

Adams, Joey (1911–December 2), veteran comedian and *New York Post* columnist.

Ainsworth, Mary D. (1913–March 21), psychologist who promoted the theory that early intimate relationships affect child development.

Bart, Lionel (1930–April 3), British composer, lyricist, and playwright best known for the musical *Oliver!*

Bates, Daisy (1914–November 4), civil rights leader who led the cause to admit black students to Little Rock's Central High School in 1957.

Benzinger, Theodore H. (1905–October 26), researcher who invented the ear thermometer and developed the Planck-Benzinger equation, which modified the second law of thermodynamics.

Bertelli, Angelo (1921–June 26), quarterback dubbed the "T-formation magician" who in 1943 was Notre Dame's first Heisman Trophy winner.

Blackmun, Harry A. (1908–March 4), Supreme Court justice who in 1973 wrote *Roe v. Wade,* which established a woman's right to abortion.

Bogarde, Dirk (1921–May 8), film actor who transformed himself from a British matinee idol into a serious character actor in such films as *Victim* (1961), *The Servant* (1963), and *Darling* (1965).

BoxCar Willie (Lecil Martin) (1931–April 12), country singer known for his "singing hobo" persona.

Bowles, Paul (1910-November 18), novelist, composer, and poet known for *The Sheltering Sky,* a novel set in Africa after World War II.

Gene Siskel, film critic

Charles Conrad, Jr., astronaut

Bradley, Marion Zimmer (1930–September 25), author of the popular "Darkover" novels and the best-selling *The Mists of Avalon.*

Burckhardt, Rudy (1935–July 31), Swiss-born photographer and filmmaker who documented the energy and spontaneity of New York City.

Calhoun, Rory (Francis Timothy Durgin) (1922–April 28), actor best known for his roles in film Westerns and the 1950's television series "The Texan."

Callahan, Harry (1922–March 15), photographer whose sharply contrasting images combined the precision of American photography with the experimentation of modern European art.

Carr, Allan (1939–June 29), producer who moved "camp" into mainstream pop culture with the film *Grease* (1978) and the Broadway musical *La Cage aux Folles* (1983).

Carter, Anita (1933–July 29), singer, stand-up bassist, and member of country music's legendary Carter Family.

Cass, Peggy (1924–March 8), comedian who won a Tony award as the myopic Agnes Gooch in *Auntie Mame* (1956) and who was a frequent guest on "The Jack Parr Show," "To Tell the Truth," and "Password."

Chamberlin, Wilt (1936–October 12), basketball player who set records for most points in a game, highest scoring average in a season, and the most rebounds in a career.

Chaudhuri, Nirad C. (1897–August 1), Indian writer whose *The Autobiography of an Unknown Indian* (1951) was hailed as one of the great works of art to derive from the Indo-English encounter.

Cockerell, Sir Christopher (1910–June 1), British engineer who invented the hovercraft and contributed to the creation of radar.

Harry Callahan, photographer

Walter Payton, football star

Conrad, Charles, Jr., (1930–July 8), astronaut known for his courage and sense of humor. He flew two Gemini missions during the mid-1960's and commanded the 1969 Apollo 12 Moon-landing mission.

Corby, Ellen (1911–April 14), character actress who appeared in dozens of films but was best known as the grandmother on TV's "The Waltons."

Crichton, Charles (1910–September 14), British film director whose classic comedies include *The Lavender Hill Mob* (1951), *The Titfield Thunderbolt* (1953), and *A Fish Called Wanda* (1988).

Crisp, Quentin (1908-November 21), British-born writer and wit who gained fame with his 1968 autobiography, *The Naked Civil Servant.*

Danko, Rick (1942–December 10), bassist and singer who was a member of the rock group The Band in the 1960's and 1970's.

Darrow, Whitney, Jr., (1909–August 10), gently satiric cartoonist for *The New Yorker.*

De Vol, Frank (1911-October 27), composer and arranger who wrote the themes for such TV shows as "The Brady Bunch" and "My Three Sons" and for such movies as *Pillow Talk* (1959) and *The Dirty Dozen (1967).*

DiMaggio, Joe (1914–March 8), legendary center fielder with the New York Yankees. See **Baseball: A Special Report.**

Dmytryk, Edward (1908–July 1), film director— *Murder, My Sweet* (1944), *The Caine Mutiny* (1954), and *The Young Lions* (1958)—and member of the Hollywood 10, who during the McCarthy period of the 1950's were jailed for contempt of Congress.

Ehrlichman, John (1925-February 14), Nixon administration adviser who went to prison for his involvement in Watergate.

Elion, Gertrude Belle (1918–February 21), drug researcher who shared the Nobel Prize in physiology or medicine in 1988 for developing drugs for the treatment of gout, herpes, leukemia, malaria, and immune disorders. Elion also helped develop AZT, the first drug created to treat HIV, the virus that causes AIDS.

John F. Kennedy, Jr., and his wife Caroline Bessette Kennedy

Fadiman, Clifton (1904–June 20), writer, literary critic, and editor who helped establish the Book-of-the-Month Club and moderated the popular 1940's radio program "Information Please."

Farmer, James (1920–July 9), pioneering civil rights activist and a founder of the Congress of Racial Equality, who led the 1961 Freedom Rides.

Feininger, Andreas (1906–February 18), French-born *Life* magazine photographer who captured Chicago and New York cityscapes in the 1940's.

Fish, Hugh (1923–May 26), British environmental engineer who helped restore the Thames River.

Forrest, Helen (1917–July 11), World War II-era big-band singer.

Fuchs, Sir Vivian (1908–November 11), British geologist and Antarctic expert who led the first known team to cross Antarctica.

Funt, Allen (1914–September 5), creator and original host of TV's "Candid Camera," which featured practical jokes.

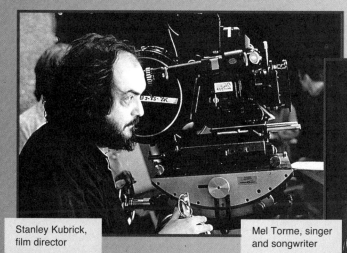

Stanley Kubrick, film director

Mel Torme, singer and songwriter

DeForest Kelley, actor

Gertrude Belle Elion, Nobel Prize-winning scientist

Gorbachev, Raisa (1932–September 20), Russian first lady who broke Kremlin traditions to share the spotlight with her husband, former Soviet President Mikhail Gorbachev.

Gould, Sandra (1926-July 20), television character actress best known for her role as nosy Gladys Kravitz on the TV series "Bewitched."

Greenfield, Meg (1930–May 13), Pulitzer Prize-winning editor of the *Washington Post* editorial page and *Newsweek* magazine columnist.

Hall, Huntz (1919–February 2), actor who was best known for portraying a dumb, good-natured adolescent in more than 80 "Dead End," "Bowery Boys," and "East Side Kids" motion pictures of the 1930's, 1940's, and 1950's.

Hassan II (1929–July 23), king who ruled Morocco for 38 years and played an important role as mediator between Israel and the Arab nations of the Middle East.

Heller, Joseph (1923–December 13), author whose World War II novel *Catch-22* provided a catch phrase that became part of American culture.

Herlihy, Ed (1909–February 2), radio and television announcer known for his deep voice.

Herzberg, Gerhard (1904–March 3), German-born Canadian physicist who received the 1971 Nobel Prize in chemistry for determining the electronic structure of molecules.

Hirt, Al (1922–April 27), jazz trumpeter, called the "Round Mound of Sound," who became a symbol of New Orleans.

Horst, Horst P. (1906-November 18), German-born fashion photographer whose photos evoked drama and glamor.

Hume, Basil Cardinal (1923–June 17), leader of the Roman Catholic Church in England and Wales for 23 years and an influential moralist.

Hunter, James "Catfish" (1946–September 9), Hall-of-Fame baseball pitcher who led the Oakland A's to three World Series titles and helped the New York Yankees win three pennants.

Hustead, Ted (1903–January 13), pharmacist whose Wall Drug Store came to attract some 2 million visitors a year to a small South Dakota town.

Wilt Chamberlain, basketball star

Jackson, Milt (1923–October 9), vibraphonist known for his warm, rich sound who played with Charlie Parker, Dizzy Gillespie, and the Modern Jazz Quartet.

Kahn, Madeline (1942-December 3), actress, comedian, and singer who starred in Mel Brooks farces and won a Tony Award in 1993 for her role as a ditzy matron in *The Sisters Rosensweig.*

Kanin, Garson (1912–March 13), author of the prize-winning play *Born Yesterday* (1946), who with his wife, actress Ruth Gordon, also wrote *Adam's Rib* (1949) and *Pat and Mike* (1952) for Katharine Hepburn and Spencer Tracy.

Kelley, DeForest (1920–June 11), actor who played Doctor Leonard "Bones" McCoy in the original "Star Trek" television series and six films.

Kendall, Henry W. (1926–February 2), physicist who shared the 1990 Nobel Prize for physics for proving the existence of the quark.

Kennedy, John F., Jr., (1960-July 17), publisher and editor-in-chief of *George* magazine and son of the late U.S. President John F. Kennedy.

Kiley, Richard (1922–March 5), versatile stage, screen, and television actor who won a Tony Award in 1966 for his starring role in the musical *Man of La Mancha.*

Killanin, Lord (1914–April 25), Irish journalist, film producer, author, and business executive who served as the president of the International

George C. Scott, actor

Olympic Committee from 1972 to 1980.

Kirkland, Lane (1922–August 14), labor leader who was president of the AFL-CIO from 1979 to 1995.

Kleitman, Nathaniel (1895–August 13), Russian-born physiologist who demonstrated that sleep includes rapid eye movements (REM's).

Kraus, Alfredo (1927–September 10), Spanish lyric tenor who was widely admired for his musical intelligence and the taste and style he brought to his roles in the bel canto repertory.

Kubrick, Stanley (1928–March 7), director of such classic films as *Dr. Strangelove* (1964), *2001: A Space Odyssey* (1968), and *The Shining* (1980).

Lewin, Lord Terrence (1920–January 23), a former First Sea Lord of the Royal Navy and Great Britain's overall military chief who planned the British victory over Argentina in the 1982 Falklands War.

Llewelyn, Desmond (1914–December 19), British actor who played gadget expert Q in James Bond films.

Lortel, Lucille (1900–April 4), theater patron whose promotion of innovative playwrights and cutting-edge stage productions earned her the title "Queen of Off-Broadway."

Mars, Forrest (1904–July 1), candy company magnate who created M&M's and the Milky Way bar.

Mature, Victor (1913–August 4), film actor as well known for serious performances in such films as *My Darling Clementine* (1946) and *Kiss of Death* (1947) as he was for his work in such "costume epics" as *Samson and Delilah* (1949) and *Demetrius and the Gladiators* (1954).

Mayfield, Curtis (1942–December 26), soul singer and songwriter of the 1960's who introduced the politics of race and equality to pop music.

Mellon, Paul (1907–February 1), philanthropist who donated more than 900 works of art to the National Gallery of Art in Washington, D.C., and funded the gallery's East Wing.

Menuhin, Yehudi (1916–March 12), legendary violinist who debuted as a soloist at the age of 7 and grew gracefully from child prodigy to respected artist and conductor.

Mills, Donald (1915–November 13), last surviving member of the Mills Brothers, the singing goup of the 1930's, 1940's, and 1950's whose hit songs included "Up a Lazy River" and "Glow Worm."

Miranda, Altina Schinasi (1907–August 19), artist and window display designer who in the late 1930's created the Harlequin eyeglass frame.

Montagu, Ashley (1905-November 26), anthropologist who wrote popular nonfiction books on topics ranging from the reasons why people cry to the history of swearing.

Moore, Brian (1921–January 11), novelist born in Northern Ireland whose acclaimed works include *The Lonely Passion of Judith Hearne* (1956), *Black Robe* (1985), and *No Other Life* (1993).

Moore, Clayton (1914–December 28), actor who portrayed the "Lone Ranger" on television and in two movies and made innumerable personal appearances as the "kemo sabe" (trusty scout).

Morita, Akio (1921–October 2), Japanese businessman who co-founded the Sony Corporation and led Japan's entry into the world economy.

Motley, Marion (1920–June 27), Cleveland Browns fullback who rushed for 4,720 yards and 31 touchdowns between 1946 and 1953.

Murdoch, Iris (1919–February 8), English writer whose philosophical novels included *A Fairly Honorable Defeat* (1970) and *The Sea, the Sea* (1961), for which she won the Booker Prize.

Murray, Kathryn (1906–August 6), dance-studio executive who, with her husband Arthur, hosted TV's "Arthur Murray Party" in the 1950's.

Newley, Anthony (1931–April 14), British actor, singer, and composer who co-wrote *Stop the World—I Want to Get Off* (1961) and the musical's hit song "What Kind of Fool Am I?"

Norvo, Red (Kenneth) (1908–April 6), jazz master who pioneered the drummerless band and the use of the xylophone and vibraphone in jazz orchestrations.

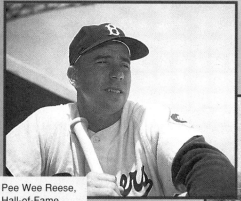

Pee Wee Reese, Hall-of-Fame baseball player

Shel Silverstein, author and cartoonist

Nyerere, Julius Kambarage (1922–October 14), founding father of Tanzania who served as president from 1964 until 1985.

Paterson, Jennifer (1928–August 10), British chef, food critic, and columnist who co-starred with Clarissa Dickson Wright on the British cooking show "Two Fat Ladies."

Patterson, Louise (1901–August 27), civil rights advocate who became a force in the Harlem Renaissance, the black artistic and literary movement in New York City in the 1920's and 1930's.

Payton, Walter (1954–November 1), former Chicago Bears running back (1975-1987) who set a career rushing record of 16,726 yards.

Peck, Bob (1945–April 4), British stage, film, and television actor best known for his portrayal of a detective on the television thriller "Edge of Darkness."

Plato, Dana (1964–May 8), former child star who appeared on television's "Diff'rent Strokes" from 1978 to 1984.

Pritzker, Jay (1922–January 23), Chicago billionaire who founded Hyatt hotels and endowed the Pritzker Architectural Prize.

Puzo, Mario (1920–July 2), author of *The Godfather* (1969).

Ramsey, Sir Alf (1920–April 28), British soccer manager who in 1966 coached the British national team to its only World Cup championship.

Peggy Cass, actress and game show panelist

Dirk Bogarde, film actor

Red Norvo, jazz musician

Raymond, Arthur (1899–March 22), aeronautical engineer who designed the DC-3. His career stretched from World War I-era biplanes to the NASA Apollo and Gemini missions, on which he played key roles.

Redington, Joe (1917–June 24), cofounder of Alaska's Iditarod Trail Sled Dog Race.

Reed, Oliver (1938–May 2), stocky English actor known for his tough-guy roles in such films as *Oliver!* (1968) and *Women in Love* (1969).

Reese, Pee Wee (1918–August 15), Hall-of-Fame shortstop and captain for the Brooklyn Dodgers who played on seven pennant-winning teams in the 1940's and 1950's. Reese promoted tolerance toward Jackie Robinson when Robinson joined the Dodgers in 1947, integrating baseball.

Richardson, Elliot (1920–December 31), former U.S. attorney general who resigned in 1973 rather than carry out President Richard Nixon's order to fire the special prosecutor investigating the Watergate scandal.

Ripken, Cal, Sr., (1935–March 25), baseball coach and manager who was the only person ever to manage two sons, Cal Jr. and Billy, on the same major league team, the Baltimore Orioles.

Robertson, Betty (1911–May 18), runner who in 1928 became the first woman to win an Olympic gold medal in track and field.

Roman, Ruth (1923–September 9), actress who played wholesome characters in such films as *Beyond the Forest* (1949) and *Strangers on a Train* (1951).

Rossington, Norman (1928–May 21), British stage, film, and TV character actor who appeared in the "Carry On" comedy films, *Lawrence of Arabia*, *A Hard Day's Night*, and *I, Claudius*.

Sarazen, Gene (Eugene Saraceni) (1902–May 13), golfer who won all four major golf championships in the 1930's. Sarazen also invented the sand wedge.

Sayao, Bidu (1902–March 12), Brazilian soprano who was a favorite with opera audiences from the 1930's to the 1950's.

Schawlow, Arthur (1921–April 28), physicist who received the 1981 Nobel Prize for physics for coinventing the laser.

Scott, George C. (1927–September 22), intense and versatile film and stage actor most celebrated for his film portrayals of generals—Buck Turgidson in *Dr. Strangelove* (1964) and George S. Patton, Jr., in *Patton* (1970).

Seaborg, Glenn (1912–February 25), Nobel Prize-winning chemist and nuclear physicist who headed the team that discovered plutonium, the element used in the atomic bomb dropped on Nagasaki in 1945. In addition, Seaborg directed research that resulted in the creation of nine artificial elements.

Semon, Waldo (1898–May 26), B. F. Goodrich research director who invented vinyl and supervised the development of synthetic rubber.

Senor Wences (Wenceslao Moreno) (1896–April 20), Spanish-born ventriloquist whose hand puppet Johnny delighted "Ed Sullivan Show" audiences during the 1950's.

Shaw, Robert (1916–January 25), music director and conductor known for his work with the Atlanta Symphony choruses, the Collegiate Chorale, and the Robert Shaw Chorale.

Sidney, Sylvia (1910–July 1), stage and film actress of 70 years best known for playing victims in Depression-era, social realism films, such as *City Streets* (1931), *Fury* (1936), and *Dead End* (1937).

Silverstein, Shel (1932–May10), cartoonist and poet whose best-selling children's books included *Where the Sidewalk Ends* (1974) and *A Light in the Attic* (1981).

Siskel, Gene (1946–February 20), *Chicago Tribune* film critic who starred with critic Roger Ebert in the TV show "Siskel & Ebert at the Movies."

James Farmer, civil rights activist

Snow, Hank (1914–December 20), Canadian-born country star who sang "I'm Movin' On."

Sopkoski, J. John, Jr., (1948–May 1), University of Chicago paleontologist who pioneered the use of quantitative library and computer research to trace large-scale patterns of evolution and extinction in nature.

Springfield, Dusty (Mary Isabel Catherine Bernadette O'Brien) (1939–March 2), English torch singer and pop star whose hits included "Wishin' and Hopin'" (1964), "The Look of Love" (1967), and "Son of a Preacher Man" (1969).

Stader, Maria (1911–April 27), Hungarian-born lyric soprano who was considered a leading interpreter of Mozart operas.

Stears, John (1934–June 28), British-born Oscar-winning special effects artist who created James Bond's Aston Martin, the Jedi Knights' light sabers, and *Star Wars* robots R2-D2 and C-3PO.

Steinberg, Saul (1914–May 12), artist whose *New Yorker* magazine illustrations are credited with transforming comic illustration into fine art.

Stewart, Payne (1957–October 26), professional golfer who won the United States Open for the second time in 1999.

Strasberg, Susan (1938–January 21), actress who starred in the original Broadway staging of *The Diary of Anne Frank* (1955). She was the daughter of the Actors Studio director Lee Strasberg.

Strickland, David (1969–March 22), an actor on the TV situation comedy "Suddenly Susan."

Torme, Mel (1925–June 5), pop-jazz singer dubbed the "velvet fog" for the smooth timbre of his voice. A child star, Torme eventually earned distinction as an actor, writer, band leader, arranger, and composer.

Tudjman, Franjo (1922–December 10), president of Croatia. A one-time Communist general, Tudjman became a nationalist and led Croatia to independence from Yugoslavia.

Washington, Grover, Jr., (1943–December 17), saxophonist who fused jazz and soul music.

Watson, Bobs (1930–June 26), child film actor who played Pee Wee in *Boys Town* (1938).

Whitelaw, Lord William (1918–July 1), prominent British Conservative and a principal lieutenant of Prime Minister Margaret Thatcher, for whom he served as home secretary and leader of the House of Lords.

Yehudi Menuhin, violinist

Whyte, William H. (1917–January 12), social analyst who in his 1956 bestseller *The Organization Man* warned of the dangers of corporate conformity.

Williams, Joe (1918–March 29), legendary blues singer who played Grandpa Al on television's "The Cosby Show" in the 1980's.

Woolf, Sir John (1913–June 28), British producer whose Romulus Films won 13 Academy Awards for such movies as *The African Queen* (1951), *Beat the Devil* (1954), and *Oliver!* (1968).

Wynn, Early (1920–April 4), Hall-of-Fame pitcher for the Washington Senators, Cleveland Indians, and Chicago White Sox.

Zoll, Paul (1911–January 5), heart specialist who invented the cardiac pacemaker, defibrillator, and monitor.

Payne Stewart, professional golfer

Democratic Party. A split developed within the Democratic Party in 1999 over the choice of a presidential nominee in 2000 after former U.S. Senator Bill Bradley (D., New Jersey) challenged Vice President Al Gore for the nomination.

President Bill Clinton supported Vice President Gore in his bid throughout 1999. However, many political experts maintained that the president's influence had been weakened by the revelation in 1998 of a sexual relationship Clinton had had with a former White House intern and by subsequent impeachment proceedings. Experts also theorized that the apparent disarray in Vice President Gore's campaign helped Bradley's underdog campaign.

Vice President Gore formally announced his bid for the Democratic presidential nomination on June 16. He vowed to continue President Clinton's economic policies, which had contributed to record prosperity throughout the 1990's. While attempting to identify himself with the president's economic policies, the vice president also tried to distance himself from the presidential scandal and Clinton's impeachment by stressing moral leadership, personal responsibility, and family life. He also criticized the president's personal behavior.

Vice President Gore announced his candidacy in Carthage, Tennessee, near the family farm where he spent summers as a young boy. He also moved his campaign headquarters from Washington, D.C., to Tennessee to reduce costs and, some experts maintained, to distance himself from the image of being a Washington insider.

First Lady Hillary Rodham Clinton shakes hands with supporters in Binghamton, New York, in July 1999. On November 23, Clinton announced her intention of running for the U.S. Senate in 2000.

While the vice president led in national polls and fund-raising throughout much of 1999, political analysts predicted that he could still be vulnerable despite the backing of most of the Democratic leadership.

Opposition. Bradley formally declared his candidacy for the Democratic nomination on September 8, in his hometown of Crystal City, Missouri. Although regarded as a moderate during his three terms in the Senate, many Democratic leaders in 1999 viewed Bradley as a more liberal alternative to the vice president. Bradley's supporters, including Senator Daniel Patrick Moynihan (D., New York), maintained that Vice President Gore could not win in 2000 against a strong Republican opponent. In late 1999, Texas Governor George W. Bush, son of former President George Bush, was the front-runner for the Republican presidential nomination.

While Gore campaigned heavily on his record as vice president, Bradley relied on his tenure in the Senate and also on his celebrity as a former basketball star. Bradley was a former professional basketball player with the New York Knicks and a member of the Basketball Hall of Fame. In November, Bradley hosted a political fund-raiser in which he raised some $1.5 million for his campaign. More than 7,000 supporters paid between $100 and $1,000 per ticket for the chance to watch Bradley and about 20 Hall of Fame basketball players, including Julius Erving and Bill Russell, relive memories.

The campaign for the Democratic presidential nomination began earlier than usual in 1999 because many key primaries were scheduled in the opening months of 2000. Most analysts expected that the outcome would be known by March 2000, when voters in California and New York were scheduled to cast ballots in primary elections.

Senator Clinton? Following months of speculation, First Lady Hillary Rodham Clinton announced on June 4, 1999, that she planned to form an exploratory committee to help her decide whether she would seek the U.S. Senate seat in New York being vacated by Moynihan. Moynihan was scheduled to retire when his term expired in 2001. Clinton's announcement came one day after U.S. Representative Nita Lowey (D., New York) decided to seek reelection to the House, rather than seek the senatorial post.

On Nov. 23, 1999, Hillary Rodham Clinton told the United Federation of Teachers that she intended to seek Moynihan's seat and planned to formally announce her candidacy in 2000.

Acquittal. The Senate on Feb. 12, 1999, acquitted President Clinton on impeachment charges passed by the House of Representatives in 1998. All 45 Democrats and 10 Republicans voted to acquit Clinton on one charge of perjury while 45 Democrats and 5 Republicans voted for acquittal on an obstruction of justice charge. The charges against President Clinton stemmed from his denials during sworn testimony that he had had a sexual relationship with Monica Lewinsky, a former White House intern.

Fund-raising. The Federal Election Commission (FEC) in September 1999 reported that the Democratic Party had raised $38.1 million in contributions in the first six months of the year, compared with $66.4 million raised by the Republican Party. Democrats raised $26.4 million in soft money, compared with $30.9 million raised by the Republican Party. Soft money refers to individual contributions made to political parties that are not subject to the same stringent restrictions placed on contributions to candidates.

□ William J. Eaton

See also **Congress of the United States; Elections; People in the news** (Bradley, Bill; Bush, George W.); **Republican Party; State government; United States, President of the.**

Denmark. The economy of Denmark slowed significantly during 1999, arousing concern that the country was suffering because of its decision not to join the single European currency, the euro. The Danish government predicted that *gross domestic product* (the value of all goods and services produced in a country in a given year) would grow by 1.6 percent in 1999—well below the 2.1-percent average growth of the 15 countries of the European Union (EU).

The slowdown triggered concern that Denmark was losing its competitiveness because Danish wages were rising faster than those of other EU countries and interest rates were higher than rates in the 11 EU countries that joined the euro. Most Danish business leaders supported adopting the single currency. Prime Minister Poul Nyrup Rasmussen announced in August 1999 that his ruling Social Democratic Party would not decide whether to hold a referendum on adopting the euro until September 2000.

Link to Sweden. Workers installed the last section of a bridge-and-tunnel link between Copenhagen and the Swedish city of Malmo in August 1999. The 10-mile- (16-kilometer-) long Oresund Fixed Link, named after the strait that separates Denmark and Sweden, was scheduled to open in mid-2000. □ Tom Buerkle

See also **Europe.**

Disabled. The United States Supreme Court substantially narrowed the scope of the 1990 Americans with Disabilities Act in June 1999. The court ruled in three cases that people with correctable conditions—such as vision problems that can be improved with eyeglasses or high blood pressure that can be treated with medication—cannot be considered disabled under the law.

The Supreme Court ruled in March that public schools must provide disabled students with assistance during the school day, as long as the assistance can be given by someone other than a physician. The ruling was issued to resolve the question of whether nursing services for a paralyzed student attending high school should be paid for by his family or by the school district.

In June, the U.S. Senate unanimously passed the Work Incentives Improvement Act, a bill allowing people with disabilities to retain their Medicare or Medicaid coverage after they return to work. The bill was expected to help hundreds of thousands of people with such chronic or degenerative conditions as AIDS, multiple sclerosis, and Parkinson disease. The House of Representatives approved the bill in October. However, disagreements about how to fund the bill delayed its final passage until November.

□ Kristina Vaicikonis

See also **Supreme Court of the United States.**

Disasters. The deadliest disasters of 1999 included an earthquake that ravaged Turkey in August, killing more than 17,000 people; and torrential rains in Venezuela, causing mudslides and floods that may have killed as many as 25,000 people. Disasters that resulted in 25 or more deaths during 1999 include the following:

Aircraft crashes

February 24—Wenzhou, China. All 61 passengers and crew members aboard a China Southwest Airlines flight die when the Russian-made jet crashes while making its descent into Wenzhou, a port city on the East China Sea. Airport officials report more casualties on the ground.

August 31—Buenos Aires, Argentina. Sixty-four of the 95 passengers and 5 crew members aboard a Boeing 737 and 10 people on the ground die when an Argentina LAPA airliner skids off a runway during takeoff, crashes through a fence, and crosses a busy road, striking cars and heavy machinery. The jet rolls onto a golf course before exploding.

October 31—East Coast, United States. EgyptAir Flight 990, traveling from New York City to Cairo, plunges into the Atlantic Ocean near Massachusetts. All 217 passengers and crew members die in the crash. After analyzing voice and data recorders salvaged from the wreckage, U.S. investigators suspected that a pilot may have forced the plane to dive into the ocean.

December 11—Azores Islands. A Portuguese passenger flight crashes into a mountain, killing all 35 people on board.

Earthquakes

January 25—Western Colombia. An earthquake measuring 6.0 kills at least 830 people and injures 3,000 in a mountainous region that is the center of Colombian coffee cultivation. Two-thirds of the buildings in the city of Armenia are rendered uninhabitable. Officials describe the quake as the worst in Colombia since 1875.

June 15—Oaxaca, Mexico. A powerful earthquake, registering 6.7, rocks central Mexico, and 25 people are killed under falling debris. While the quake's epicenter is near Huajuapan de Leon in Oaxaca, damage in the nearby state of Puebla is worse. Destruction is severest in the city of Puebla, where many churches and colonial-era buildings are damaged in the town's center.

August 17—Turkey. More than 17,000 people are killed and thousands more injured in western Turkey in an earthquake registering 7.4 in magnitude. The quake's epicenter is near Izmit, 56 miles (90 kilometers) east of Istanbul.

September 7—Athens, Greece, is shaken by a 5.9 magnitude earthquake, the strongest to hit the city in 100 years. Toppled buildings kill more

Residents of Golcuk, Turkey, survey the damage from the Aug. 17, 1999, earthquake that left more than 17,000 people dead and tens of thousands homeless. A second quake in Turkey on November 12 killed at least 450 people.

than 135 people and leave 60,000 homeless.

September 21—Taiwan. An earthquake registering 7.6 rocks Taiwan, killing more than 2,300 people and destroying thousands of buildings, including a 12-story hotel in Taipei, the capital. Approximately 4,000 people are injured and 100,000 left homeless.

November 12—Turkey. The second major earthquake to hit Turkey since August strikes Bolu, a hilly northwestern province. The 7.2-magnitude quake kills at least 450 people and injures more than 3,000.

Explosions and fires

May 24—Ukraine. A methane gas explosion in a coal mine in western Ukraine kills 39 of the 131 miners working below ground.

September 26—Central Mexico. A fireworks warehouse explodes in Celaya, a city 120 miles (193 kilometers) northwest of Mexico City. Blasts kill at least 50 people and injure more than 75.

Shipwrecks

February 6—West Kalimantan, Indonesia. The Harta Rimba, a 100-foot (30-meter) ferry, sinks in rough seas off the port of Pontianak, on Borneo. More than 300 of the 325 passengers drown.

April 1—Nigeria. At least 200 people die when a ferry capsizes in a tropical storm off Nigeria's

southern coast. Officials believe the ferry, made to hold 150 passengers, was carrying 300 people.

May 8—Southern Bangladesh. A ferry with about 300 people aboard capsizes in the Meghna River 60 miles (104 kilometers) south of Dhaka in a storm. At least 200 passengers drown.

November 25—China. A Chinese ferry burns and breaks apart in frigid seas about 25 miles (40 kilometers) off China's northeastern coast. Most of the 318 people on board drown.

December 23—Cebu, the Philippines. Approximately 550 people drown when a passenger ship sinks on a trip between the central islands.

Storms and floods

February 23—Galtuer, Switzerland. Thirty-eight people die in an avalanche in the Austrian ski resort of Galtuer during a blizzard that produced more than 16 inches (41 centimeters) of snow and winds of 175 miles (282 kilometers) per hour. A series of massive snowfalls have set off avalanches in Austria, France, and Switzerland.

May 20—Gharo, Pakistan. At least 400 people are killed when a cyclone with winds of 170 miles (274 kilometers) per hour produces giant tidal waves that crash into fishing villages about 25 miles (40 kilometers) east of Karachi, the capital.

July 23—India. The monsoon-swollen waters of the Yamuna River flood low-lying areas of New Delhi, India's capital, killing more than 250.

August 3—Manila, the Philippines. More than 75 people are killed and thousands evacuated from Manila, capital of the Philippines, when torrential rains from tropical storm Olga trigger flash floods and the collapse of whole hillsides, burying residents in their houses.

August 3—South Korea. Heavy rains from tropical storm Olga swell rivers in South Korea to overflowing, flooding more than 8,500 houses and killing at least 50 people. In Choonchon City, 90 miles (145 kilometers) northeast of Seoul, the capital, a tour bus is swept into a flooded river, drowning 5 passengers and injuring 30.

August 5—China. The death toll from summer flooding in the Yangtze River Valley hits 725. At least 5.5 million people have been evacuated from 23 provinces since June. The flooding was triggered by overflow from the Yangtze River, swollen to its highest level in recorded history.

August 16—India. The death toll from flooding during the 1999 monsoon season, which began in July, hits 330. Floods in the Indian state of Bihar have killed 221 people and disrupted the lives of nearly 5 million others.

September 16—East Coast, United States. Hurricane Floyd hits land at Cape Fear on the North Carolina coast and drops 19 inches (48 centimeters) of rain in Wilmington, North Carolina, before moving to the northeast. Massive flooding from North Carolina to New England kills at least 40 people and causes billions of dollars in damage. In North Carolina, state agriculture officials estimate as many as 110,000 hogs and more than 1 million chickens and turkeys drown in floods.

September 24—Japan. More than 25 people are killed and nearly 450 injured when a typhoon hits southern Japan with wind gusts clocked as high as 148 miles (238 kilometers) per hour.

October 6—Nigeria. The National Electric Power Authority, overwhelmed by rising waters on the Niger River, opens floodgates on two dams approximately 300 miles (500 kilometers) north of Lagos, the capital, flooding 400 villages. The News Agency of Nigeria estimates that 500 people are dead and 300,000 homeless.

October 7—Mexico. Days of ceaseless rain trigger flooding and mudslides in nine Mexican states, driving hundreds of thousands of people from their homes. About 350 people are killed, including dozens buried under mudslides in a mountainous stretch about 100 miles (160 kilometers) east and northeast of Mexico City.

October 29—India. An extremely powerful cyclone hits Orissa, a state on the northeastern coast of India. The cyclone reaches wind speeds of 160 miles (260 kilometers) per hour and drives tidal waves as high as 15 feet (5 meters) into In-

dia's shore. The storm leaves more than 1 million people homeless. Nearly 10,000 people are killed.

December 17—Venezuela. Flooding and mudslides caused by three days of intense rain leave more than 15,000 people dead.

December 26 and 28—Western Europe. More than 100 people die in France and other areas of Western Europe in two storms with hurricane-force winds of more than 100 miles (161 kilometers) per hour.

Train crashes

March 24—Kenya. Thirty-two people are killed and more than 100 injured when a runaway train derails some 200 miles (322 kilometers) from Nairobi, at Man-eaters Junction in the Tsavo East National Park game reserve.

April 27—Jhukia, India. At least 45 people die when a bus carrying more than 70 wedding guests hits the engine of a train about 270 miles (440 kilometers) southeast of New Dehli, India.

August 2—Eastern India. More than 285 people die and hundreds more are injured when two trains collide head-on near the border of West Bengal and Assam in eastern India. The trains, the Awadh-Assam Express and Brahmaputra Mail, carried approximately 2,000 passengers.

October 5—London, England. A high-speed express, en route to London's Paddington Station

TIME CAPSULE 1937
DIASTERS

THE GERMAN DIRIGIBLE *Hindenburg* was destroyed by fire and explosion on May 6 at Lakehurst, N.J., resulting in 35 deaths, including that of Captain Ernst A. Lehmann. On its first 1937 voyage, the giant Zeppelin was demolished in 32 seconds, just as it was being pulled to the mooring mast following a severe thunderstorm. The basic cause of the worst disaster in commercial aviation history was the highly flammable hydrogen gas, which is to be displaced by non-flammable helium.

The Hindenburg explodes at Lakehurst, New Jersey.

with 500 passengers, plows into a smaller train filled with morning commuters. More than 30 people are killed and 175 injured when the front cars ignite after jackknifing into the air.

Other disasters

January 14—Pamba, India. More than 30 people are trampled to death in a stampede of thousands of pilgrims near the Sabarimala Shrine in Pamba in southern India. The incident was triggered by the collapse of a hill, which the throng had clambered up, hoping to see a celestial light that was reported to surround the Hindu shrine.

March 24—Chamonix, France. A fire aboard a truck loaded with flour and margarine turns the 7-mile (11-kilometer) Mont Blanc highway tunnel, which connects France and Italy under the highest peak in the Alps, into an inferno that causes 328 feet (100 meters) of the tunnel's ceiling to collapse. More than 30 vehicles are destroyed, and 35 people are killed.

April 29—New Delhi, India. At least 75 people die when temperatures in New Delhi, the capital, climb to 109 °F (43 °C).

May 30—Minsk, Belarus. At least 40 people are killed and 100 wounded when part of a crowd of 10,000 people, attending a traditional beer festival in Minsk, Belarus, stampede in an underground passage near a subway entrance.

Drug abuse.
Although the overall number of Americans who used illegal drugs remained unchanged from 1997 to 1998, illegal drug use among children ages 12 to 17 declined, according to an annual United States-government survey of drug abuse released in August 1999. At the same time, the 1998 National Household Survey on Drug Abuse found that new users of cocaine between the ages of 18 and 25 rose to the highest level since 1989. The survey, published by the U.S. Department of Health and Human Services, also found that this age group was using hallucinogens at the highest level ever recorded. Surveyers interviewed 25,500 Americans age 12 and older about their illegal drug use. Overall, an estimated 13.6 million Americans—6.2 percent of the population age 12 and older—reported using illegal drugs at least once in the month prior to the survey.

Teen-agers. According to the survey, an estimated 9.9 percent of children age 12 to 17 used illegal drugs in 1998, compared with an estimated 11.4 percent in 1997. Teen use of inhalants declined significantly in 1998. In addition, fewer teen-agers reported using marijuana—8.3 percent, compared with 9.4 percent in 1997.

Young adults. The rate of young adults age 18 to 25 reporting the use of illicit drugs rose to an estimated 16 percent in 1998 from 14.7 percent in 1997. Young adults also reported a significantly increased rate of cocaine use—2 percent, up from 1.2 percent in 1997.

Marijuana continued to be the most frequently used illegal drug. According to the survey, an estimated 60 percent of all users of illegal drugs reported using only marijuana. Overall, an estimated 11 million Americans—5 percent of the population age 12 and older—used marijuana in 1998, a figure unchanged from 1997.

Alcohol. The survey also estimated that 10.4 million Americans age 12 to 20 used alcohol regularly in 1998. Of this group, 5.1 million (48.5 percent) engaged in binge drinking, and 2.3 million (21.9 percent) regularly drank heavily. These numbers were unchanged from 1997.

Treatment. Addiction to opiates, primarily heroin, surpassed cocaine addiction as the second most common reason for admission to a U.S. substance abuse treatment program, according to a government survey reported in August 1999. The survey, by the Substance Abuse and Mental Health Services Administration, showed that by 1997 heroin accounted for 16 percent of the 1.5 million reported treatment admissions, while cocaine accounted for 15 percent. Of the heroin admissions, 28 percent were for heroin inhalation, up from 19 percent in 1992. Alcohol abuse continued to rank first (48 percent) among causes of admission for treatment.   □ David C. Lewis

Drugs.
A new drug to kill germs that cannot be destroyed by any other antibiotic won approval by the United States Food and Drug Administration (FDA) in September 1999. Synercid, manufactured by Rhone-Poulenc Rorer, Inc., of France, was the first antibiotic alternative in 30 years to vancomycin, long used as the antibiotic of last resort when all other drugs had failed.

Bacteria develop resistance to drugs through exposure. Since the late 1980's, scientists have noted an increase in the number of disease-causing bacteria that are resistant to existing antibiotics, including vancomycin. More than 16,000 patients in U.S. hospitals are annually infected with vancomycin-resistant *Enterococcus faecium* (VREF), the leading cause of surgical-wound infections.

The FDA reported that Synercid was tested on 1,222 patients with VREF, and the drug killed the germs in 52 percent of the patients. The agency said the drug was also effective for some cases of skin and soft-tissue infections caused by *Staphylococcus* and *Streptococcus* bacteria.

While the FDA urged physicians to limit the use of Synercid, experts predicted it would be only a matter of time before bacteria developed resistance to the new drug. Scientists continued in 1999 to conduct research into several other vancomycin alternatives.

Injected polio vaccine safer. Children should be given the polio vaccine exclusively through injections, according to a June recommendation by an advisory panel of the United States Centers for Disease Control and Prevention (CDC) in Atlanta, Georgia. Most children in the 1990's received either four oral doses of the vaccine or two oral and two injected doses. Epidemics of poliomyelitis, or polio, a viral infection that may cause paralysis and death, swept the United States and many other countries before development of polio vaccines in the 1950's.

The CDC panel noted that 8 to 10 children in the United States contract polio annually as a result of the oral vaccine, which contains live but weakened polio virus. The injected vaccine is made from killed polio virus. United States physicians were expected to begin using only the injected vaccine, except in rare circumstances, in January 2000.

New treatments for flu. An inhaled antiviral drug to treat influenza in people aged 12 and older was approved by the FDA in July 1999. Zanamivir, sold under the brand name Relenza by Glaxo Wellcome, Inc., of Research Triangle Park, North Carolina, was the first new flu treatment since 1993.

The FDA said Relenza is effective in patients who start treatment within two days of symptoms. Patients take the drug by inhaling it in powdered form through the mouthpiece of a plastic inhaler device. In September 1999, researchers led by respiratory-illness expert Frederick Hayden at the University of Virginia School of Medicine in Charlottesville reported that Relenza also appears to reduce transmission of the flu between family members.

In October, the FDA approved the first pill, called Tamiflu, to treat types A and B influenza. Research indicated that Tamiflu, manufactured by Hoffmann-LaRoche, Inc., of Nutley, New Jersey, reduced the duration of flu symptoms by approximately one day.

Better drug labels. In March, the FDA announced new regulations requiring more consumer-friendly labels on about 100,000 drug products sold without a prescription. Under the regulations, manufacturers must use a standardized label with bigger type and clearer instructions on pain relievers, heartburn remedies, anti-itch ointments, and other over-the-counter (OTC) drugs. The FDA said the changes, which were scheduled to take effect by 2004, would reduce misuse of OTC drugs.

While acknowledging that nonprescription drugs are safe if used correctly, the agency noted that consumers sometimes take the wrong drug or the wrong dose. Medical statistics indicate that misuse of OTC drugs sends about 170,000 people to the hospital each year in the United States. Larger print was expected to make it easier for older people and other individuals with less-than-perfect vision to read product labels. The labels were also to feature more prominent information for children's dosages.

All labels were to have easy-to-understand instructions under the headings "Warnings" and "Directions" and information about harmful interactions with other drugs under "Do Not Use."

Online pharmacies. A new effort to stop illegal marketing of prescription drugs on the Internet was announced in July 1999 by the FDA. Although the agency said that online drug sales by reputable pharmacies with World Wide Web sites can benefit consumers, it expressed concern about Web sites that illegally sell prescription drugs without a valid prescription from a physician. Patients often get a prescription drug from such sites after simply filling out a basic health questionnaire.

People who take a prescription drug with no direct physician contact face risks of dangerous side effects and other problems, the FDA said. In the new program, the FDA planned to take legal action against unlicensed online drug merchants and work with state agencies to better enforce drug laws. ☐ Michael Woods

See also **AIDS; Drug abuse; Medicine.**

Eastern Orthodox Churches. On

June 15, 1999, Patriarch Pavle and the Holy Synod of the Serbian Orthodox Church called for the resignation of Yugoslav President Slobodan Milosevic "in the interest of the people and their salvation." The church leaders condemned atrocities carried out by the Yugoslav military under Milosevic's leadership against the ethnic Albanian civilians in the Serbian province of Kosovo. The ethnic Albanians of Kosovo are primarily Muslims.

Patriarch Pavle condemned Milosevic's government again on June 28 at the Gracanica monastery in Kosovo, where the Serbian Orthodox Church holds an annual commemoration of the defeat of Serbs by the Muslim forces of the Ottoman Empire in 1389. Denouncing the ethnic cleansing in Kosovo, Pavle stated, "If the only way to create a greater Serbia is by crime, then I do not accept that, and let that Serbia disappear."

Russian Orthodox Church. On July 21, 1999, the Holy Synod of the Russian Orthodox Church removed Bishop Nikon of Yekaterinburg after six months of appeals by local clergy and lay people who charged him with corruption and immoral behavior. He was replaced by Bishop Vikenty, a scholar known for improving the conditions of poor people near Russia's border with Mongolia.

Patriarch Alexie II, head of the Russian Orthodox Church, announced in May that he supported moving the remains of Communist leader V. I. Lenin from a mausoleum in Moscow's Red Square to a cemetery.

Pope John Paul II, leader of the Roman Catholic Church, visited Romania in May 1999 at the invitation of the Romanian government and the Romanian Orthodox Church. Many religious leaders heralded the visit, the first ever by a pope to a predominantly Orthodox country, as the beginning of better relations between the two churches.

Greek Orthodox Church in America. A two-year struggle between Archbishop Spyridon of the Greek Orthodox Archdiocese of America and his opponents in the U.S. church intensified in 1999, when the six senior *Metropolitans* (bishops) of the archdiocese called for his removal. They accused Spyridon of making decisions without consulting other church leaders.

Spyridon, who was appointed in 1996, resigned on Aug. 19, 1999, under pressure from the Ecumenical Patriarchate of Constantinople (Istanbul, Turkey), upon which the Archdiocese of America is dependent. On the same day, Patriarch Bartholomew and the Holy Synod of Constantinople elected Metropolitan Demetrios Trakatellis of Greece as the new archbishop. Trakatellis's appointment appeared to have ended the escalating divisions in the archdiocese.　　□ Stanley Samuel Harakas

See also **Yugoslavia: A Special Report.**

Economics. The world economy during 1999 did not go into a recession following the global financial crisis in 1998, as economists had feared. Instead, the world economy grew so strongly that many nations attempted to slow growth to avoid the risk of inflation.

Robust consumer spending in the United States pulled vast amounts of goods into the United States from other countries, spurring economic recovery in the smaller Asian nations that had suffered two years of sharp decline. Japan began to pull out of its recession in 1999. European economies initially slowed but averted a downturn. By late 1999, they were again solidly growing. Large parts of Latin America slid into recession in 1999, but the broader global rebound helped that region avoid the more extreme collapse that had swept Asia in 1998.

Y2K. Businesses and government agencies scrambled in 1999 to make sure that computer software would not be affected by a computer glitch known as Y2K (for Year 2000). Much computer software still in use by some companies at the end of the 1900's was originally programmed to read only the last two digits of a year. As a result, computer engineers worldwide expected computers equipped with such software to misread the year 2000 as 1900 and not function properly.

ECONOMICS

THE STORY OF BUSINESS in 1931 is best epitomized by the single word, contraction. Feeling the pinch of the Depression, people found they could eat less, wear less, and spend less generally than they had thought possible in the boom years. Health statistics show that people found less occasion to visit the doctor and the dentist; and while it would probably be technically correct to say that the public is healthier in a depression . . . many simply let aches and ills go rather than spend the money to overcome them.

Where owners of motor cars had been in the habit of trading them for new ones at the end of two years' use, many found a way to run their old cars another year; householders put up with their old buildings; women found they could do their own manicuring, men their own shaving; many who had used chauffeurs for years found they could drive their own cars, and others put their cars in the garage and became streetcar patrons.

The risk that older computer codes could cause malfunctions forced businesses and agencies to spend billions of dollars to replace or reprogram their computer systems. The changes led many companies to have employees learn new ways to use the improved computer systems. Concern over potential Y2K hazards also led some industries to increase their inventories of an array of goods as a precaution against possible supply interruptions, which also served as a short-term boost to the economy.

New economic era. In 1999, economists and financial publications increasingly accepted the idea that the U.S. economy, the strongest in the world, had entered a long-lasting "new era" during the 1990's in which the interactions of business output, labor supply, and raw materials were fundamentally more efficient than in most of the years following World War II (1939-1945).

This new era appeared to be characterized by a much calmer pace of price inflation even when economic growth was rapid. Many economists and government policymakers had thought strong growth would predictably push inflation higher. An era of growth without inflation had tremendous implications for economic policy, as some of the world's *central banks* (government agencies that control the money supply and interest rates) realized they could achieve more hearty growth without higher inflation rates.

While strong worldwide demand in 1999 drove up some prices, the price of crude oil doubled in 1999 only after oil-producing nations cut output and the global economy improved. Food prices remained so low that the federal government gave special aid to U.S. farmers.

Currency turmoil. Traders on the world's currency markets began 1999 concerned about how the currencies of Brazil, Europe, and Japan would perform. Brazil was the initial test case of whether the global financial-market crisis of 1997 and 1998 could be halted or would move into another dangerous phase.

In Brazil, Latin America's largest economy, the government in January 1999 lifted exchange-rate controls, allowing Brazil's currency, the real, to be traded at market value. The Brazilian government had drawn heavily on its foreign reserves to defend the real's value. Although Brazil, Argentina, and some smaller Latin American nations were in a recession during 1999, their economies did improve during the year. The other regional power, Mexico, showed solid growth amid active trade with the United States and with Canada under the North American Free Trade Agreement (NAFTA).

The problem with the Japanese currency, the yen, in 1999 was the opposite of what it had been throughout 1998. Rather than prop up the yen in 1999, the Japanese government sold yen in currency markets to decrease its value. The Japanese government feared that an unchecked yen would raise the price of Japanese goods in foreign markets and hurt the country's export-fueled growth prospects.

The euro, a new common currency of 11 western European Union nations—Austria, Belgium, Finland, France, Germany, Ireland, Italy, Luxembourg, the Netherlands, Portugal, and Spain—had a weak start following its January 1 launch. During much of 1999, the euro's value fell against the U.S. dollar and the yen, as investors saw better returns from the surging U.S. economy or Japan's recovery.

Germany, Europe's largest economy, began 1999 near recession. The European Central Bank cut interest rates in the spring to spur growth, and growth in Germany, as well as in France, was strong enough by autumn for the bank to increase rates.

While Europe was still easing credit, the U.S. Federal Reserve System (the Fed), the central bank of the United States, increased short-term interest rates on June 30, from 4.75 percent to 5 percent. On August 24, the Fed increased the interest rate to 5.25 percent and also increased the

Selected key U.S. economic indicators

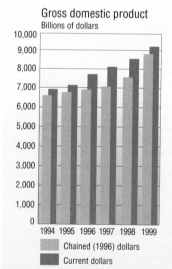

Gross domestic product
Billions of dollars

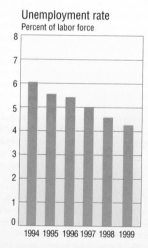

Unemployment rate
Percent of labor force

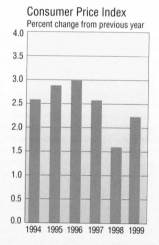

Consumer Price Index
Percent change from previous year

Chained (1996) dollars

Current dollars

Sources: U.S. Department of Commerce and U.S. Department of Labor, except 1999 figures, which are estimates from The Conference Board.

The gross domestic product (GDP) measures the value in current prices of all goods and services produced within a country in a year. Many economists believe the GDP is an accurate measure of the nation's total economic performance. Constant dollars show the amount adjusted for inflation. The unemployment rate is the percentage of the total labor force that is unemployed and actively seeking work. The Consumer Price Index measures inflation by showing the change in prices of selected goods and services consumed by urban families and individuals.

federal funds rate, the interest commercial banks are charged when borrowing from the Federal Reserve, from 4.5 percent to 4.75 percent. On November 16, the Fed raised short-term interest rates another one-quarter of a percent to 5.5 percent. The Fed announced that the increases were made to reduce economic inflationary pressures.

Growth rates. Despite the rate hikes, the U.S. economy grew at a 5.5-percent annual rate in the July-September quarter. Economists expected growth for the full year to meet or exceed the 4.2-percent pace realized in 1998. The prosperity in the United States fueled a budget surplus for fiscal year 1998-1999. The budget surplus prompted a national debate in 1999 over possible tax cuts versus paying down the national debt and placing Social Security on a firm financial foundation, but the year ended with no final agreement on either choice.

The International Monetary Fund (IMF)—a United Nations-affiliated organization, located in Washington, D.C., that provides short-term credit to member nations—estimated in September that world economic growth for 1999 would hit 3 percent, up from 2.5 percent in 1998. The IMF predicted that global growth could reach 3.5 percent in 2000. □ John D. Boyd

See also **Brazil; Europe; International trade; Japan; Manufacturing.**

Ecuador. President Jamil Mahuad Witt of Ecuador closed the nation's banks for five working days beginning March 8, 1999. He made the move to preserve the banks' reserves, which were being depleted by withdrawals made by nervous depositors. Ecuadorans had lost half the value of their savings since the government devalued the sucre, the national currency, on February 12.

Protests. While the banks were closed, Mahuad announced additional austerity measures, including a doubling of gasoline prices and a 5-percent hike in the sales tax. In response, angry protesters in Quito, Ecuador's capital, blocked intersections with their vehicles, hung Mahuad in effigy, and threw rocks at soldiers. Nineteen people were injured in the protests.

International loans. On April 30, the World Bank, a United Nations agency based in Washington, D.C., and other international financial institutions agreed to provide Ecuador with a $500-million loan to help stabilize the country's banks. On September 25, Mahuad announced that Ecuador would default on repayments of its foreign debt. Mahuad hoped to pressure the International Monetary Fund, an international credit organization based in Washington, D.C., to reduce Ecuador's debt and negotiate a new aid package. □ Nathan A. Haverstock

See also **Latin America.**

Education. The number of students attending elementary and secondary schools in the United States reached a record 53.2 million in September 1999—a half-million increase over 1998—while U.S. college enrollment rose to an all-time high of 14.9 million. The U.S. Department of Education predicted enrollment would continue to rise until 2008, when 54.3 million children were expected to be attending U.S. schools.

Public opinion polls in 1999 showed that Americans ranked education among their top concerns. Polls also indicated that many Americans were displeased with the quality of public schools. This displeasure inspired experiments with alternate ways of running schools, such as public vouchers, private vouchers, charters, and education management companies.

Public vouchers. In June, Florida Governor Jeb Bush signed the first statewide law in the country to enact public vouchers, a system that allows children to attend private schools, including religious schools, at public expense. The Florida vouchers are available to children who attend public schools that have failed to meet minimum state requirements in standardized test scores. The vouchers provide the parents of a child with funds for private school tuition equal to the amount the state would pay to send the child to public school for a year—approximately $4,000.

Children in two schools in Pensacola, Florida, were the only students eligible for the vouchers in 1999, because Florida had only recently begun giving grades to its schools. However, researchers at Florida State University in Tallahassee expected that as many as 65,000 children in 80 schools might be eligible for the vouchers in 2000.

Confusion in Cleveland. The status of a voucher program in Cleveland, Ohio, was thrown into confusion in August 1999, when a federal district judge, Solomon Oliver, blocked the program just days before school was to begin. Oliver concluded that the vouchers probably violated the constitutional guarantee of separation of church and state. Following a public outcry, the judge said he would allow the voucher program to continue for the 3,200 children who had attended private and religious schools in 1998 on publicly funded vouchers but not for the more than 700 children who were new to the program. In November 1999, the U.S. Supreme Court overruled Oliver's decision and allowed the Cleveland program to continue on a temporary basis for all of the students, while a federal Circuit Court of Appeals pondered its ruling on the matter.

Private vouchers, scholarships given by businesses and individuals to low-income students to enable them to attend the schools of their choice, received a boost in April, when Theodore Forstmann, a Wall Street financier, and John Walton, the heir to the discount-store chain Wal-Mart, announced the 40,000 recipients of the Children's Scholarship Fund. The students were picked at random from 1.25 million applicants. Forstmann and Walton had announced the formation of the Children's Scholarship Fund in June 1998, to be financed with $100 million of their own money and millions more raised from other business people.

CEO America, a Bentonville, Arkansas-based umbrella group for private voucher plans, reported that there were 68 private voucher programs in U.S. cities in the 1999-2000 school year and that they paid for scholarships for 48,000 children. CEO America said at least 1 million students were on the waiting list for scholarships.

Charter schools. Researchers at the Center for Education Reform, a Washington, D.C.-based advocacy group, reported in 1999 that 350,000 children had enrolled in 1,684 charter schools in 36 states and Washington, D.C., at the beginning of the 1999-2000 school year. Charter schools are publicly funded schools that are not part of school district systems. Because of their independence from school districts, charter schools are free to experiment with new approaches to education. Many parents and legislators viewed charter schools, which had grown significantly in number since the early 1990's, as much-needed competition for district public schools.

Public schools began to fight back in the late 1990's against the loss of students to charter schools. School districts in some states sought to duplicate creative charter programs, such as environmental science education, in their own schools. However, experts noted that few districts felt pressure to make major changes, because charter enrollments remained small compared to district enrollments.

Education management organizations (EMO's), for-profit companies that manage public schools, also grew in popularity in 1999. Although there were fewer than two dozen EMO's in the United States, some stock market analysts predicted in 1999 that EMO's would grow into a major force in school management over the next 10 to 15 years. The largest EMO, Edison Schools, Inc., of New York City, operated 77 schools with 37,000 students in 1999. In many cases, EMO's operate like charter schools, receiving an allocation from the state or local school district for each child they enroll. A number of charter schools, which are usually operated by parent, teacher, or civic groups, began contracting with EMO's in the late 1990's.

ESEA. The U.S. Congress began work in 1999 to reauthorize the 1965 Elementary and Secondary Education Act (ESEA), which—with an annual budget of about $14 billion—is the federal government's largest education program. ESEA's biggest program, called Title 1, distributes about $8 billion a year to school districts that have high percentages of poor families.

ESEA must be reauthorized every five years, but it has so many individual programs—from teacher training to technology—that Congressional passage usually takes two years. Democrats in 1999 used the ESEA debate to promote President Bill Clinton's plans to hire 100,000 additional teachers, fund after-school tutoring programs, and require schools to improve student performance or face sanctions. Republicans used the debate to push for programs that would give school districts greater freedom to spend federal education dollars as they see fit.

School shootings. Schools across the United States added new security measures, such as metal detectors and security cameras, in 1999 following several incidents in which students killed or injured classmates with firearms. The worst such incident occurred on April 20, when two students at Columbine High School in Littleton, Colorado, killed 12 classmates and a teacher before shooting themselves. In contrast to the rash of school shootings, federal education and health officials reported in 1999 that violence had declined in U.S. schools in recent years.   □ June Kronholz

See also **Crime; State government.**

Egypt. Egyptian President Hosni Mubarak won his fourth six-year term in a referendum on Sept. 26, 1999. The Interior Ministry reported that 94 percent of the votes cast approved of Mubarak's continued rule. Egypt does not have multiparty presidential elections. In June, the Egyptian parliament, which is heavily dominated by Mubarak's supporters, had selected Mubarak as the sole presidential candidate. Voters had a choice of either "yes" or "no" as to whether Mubarak should serve another term.

Dissent. In May, the Egyptian Organization for Human Rights and other human rights groups criticized the Egyptian parliament for enacting a law granting the government broad new powers over private organizations. The law permitted the government to disband boards and regulate outside funding of many private groups. It also banned political activity by such groups.

Opposition groups criticized Mubarak in 1999 for refusing to repeal a 1981 law that restricted political activity and regulated the media. The emergency law had been enacted after Islamic militants assassinated Mubarak's predecessor, President Anwar Sadat, after he signed a peace treaty with Israel. Government officials argued that the law was necessary to curb the continued activity of Islamic extremists, who declared war on the government in 1992.

Attack on Mubarak. On Sept. 6, 1999, Mubarak received a minor wound when a man attacked his motorcade as it traveled through the coastal town of Port Said. Mubarak's bodyguards killed the attacker, leaving it unclear whether he was an Islamic extremist or mentally disturbed. Nevertheless, the attack led to a further crackdown on suspected Muslim activists. The attack occurred the day after Mubarak helped mediate a new agreement between the Palestinians and Israel.

EgyptAir crash. The crash of EgyptAir flight 990 after it took off from Kennedy International Airport in New York City on October 31 led to tensions between the United States and Egypt. Egyptian officials objected to U.S. reports that an Egyptian co-pilot deliberately caused the crash, which killed all 217 people on board.

Tourists return. Tourism rebounded in Egypt in 1999, following a decline caused by the massacre in 1997 of 58 foreign tourists by Islamic militants. The Egyptian government staged several lavish events next to the Great Pyramids of Giza to attract tourists, including an open-air production of Giuseppe Verdi's opera *Aida* and a New Year's Eve millennium celebration that was to be broadcast worldwide.   □ Christine Helms

See also **Israel; Middle East; Middle East: A Special Report.**

Elections. Both Democrats and Republicans claimed trend-setting victories at state and local levels in 1999 during off-year elections on November 2. One of the most historic changes occurred in Virginia, where the Republican Party won control of both houses of the legislature for the first time in that state's history. The victory ended more than 100 years of Democratic control of the state legislature. When the state legislature met in 2000, the Republican Party controlled 52 seats in the 100-member House and 21 seats in the 40-member Senate.

Gubernatorial races. Democrats in Mississippi were forced to wait until January 2000 to see whether they had captured the governorship. Lieutenant Governor Ronnie Musgrove, a Democrat, led Republican Mike Parker, a former U.S. congressman, by approximately 8,000 votes in the November 1999 election. However, Musgrove failed to get a majority of the popular vote. For the first time in Mississippi history, an electoral vote by the state legislature would decide the governor's race.

Kentucky Democratic Governor Paul Patton easily won a second term, defeating the Republican candidate Peppy Martin, and the Reform Party candidate, Gatewood Galbraith. Patton was the first governor in Kentucky since 1800 who was not constitutionally prohibited from seeking

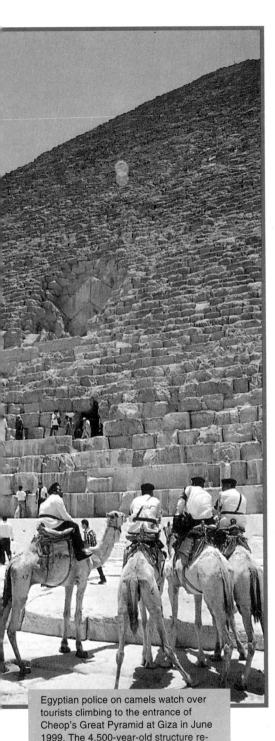

Egyptian police on camels watch over tourists climbing to the entrance of Cheop's Great Pyramid at Giza in June 1999. The 4,500-year-old structure reopened in 1999 after a major restoration, which included the installation of new lighting and ventilation systems.

a second consecutive term. Voters in 1992 had changed the Kentucky state constitution to allow governors to serve successive terms beginning with the 1999 election.

In Louisiana, Governor Mike Foster, a Republican, defeated U.S. Representative William J. Jefferson, a Democrat, and 10 other challengers for the office of governor in an open primary election on October 23. Foster, who captured more than 60 percent of the vote, was not required to face a challenger in a runoff election in November. It was the first time since 1983 that a Louisiana governor had avoided a runoff.

Mayoral races. Democrats placed great importance on mayoral victories in the November 1999 election, particularly in Indianapolis and Columbus, where decades of Republican leadership ended. In Indianapolis, Democrat Bart Peterson defeated Indiana Secretary of State Sue Anne Gilroy, a Republican. Peterson became the first Democrat to hold the mayor's title since 1963. He succeeded Mayor Stephen Goldsmith, who became chief domestic adviser for Texas Governor George W. Bush's presidential campaign.

In Columbus, City Council President Michael Coleman, a Democrat, defeated Dorothy Teater, a former teacher who was the Republican candidate. Coleman's victory ended 28 years of Republican dominance. Coleman was the first African American to hold the mayor's office in Columbus.

In Philadelphia, Democrat John F. Street narrowly defeated Republican challenger Sam Katz in a city where Democrats outnumbered Republicans by four to one. Street, the second African American to be elected mayor of Philadelphia, won with about 51 percent of the vote.

In San Francisco, Mayor Willie Brown, a Democrat, was forced into a December 14 run-off election against Tom Ammiano, the president of the city's board of supervisors, who ran a last-minute write-in campaign. Brown won the election.

In Baltimore, voters elected Democrat Martin O'Malley mayor. Voters in Houston reelected Democratic Mayor Lee Brown to a second term in office. Democrat Ross "Rocky" Anderson won a nonpartisan mayoral election in Salt Lake City, Utah.

Chicago Mayor Richard M. Daley defeated U.S. Representative Bobby Rush (D., Illinois) on Feb. 23, 1999, to win a fourth term (third full 4-year term) in office. Daley, who was first elected in 1989, defeated Rush by a nearly 2-to-1 margin. Daley has held the office longer than any other Chicago mayor since his father, Richard J. Daley, who was elected six times between 1955 and 1975.

In a runoff election on June 8, 1999, voters in Las Vegas, Nevada, elected Oscar Goodman mayor. Goodman captured 64 percent of the

ELECTIONS

HARRY S. TRUMAN was elected President of the United States in 1948. Few political observers had expected him to keep the high office to which he had been elevated from the vice-presidency on the death of Franklin D. Roosevelt. But Truman himself seemed confident of victory throughout his campaign. His election was called one of the great political upsets in American history.

President Harry Truman enjoys a mistake in the Chicago Tribune *the morning after his election.*

vote to defeat Arnie Adamsen, a 12-year city councilman. Controversy had surrounded Goodman's campaign because as a defense attorney, he had defended people with ties to organized crime.

Congressional elections. On February 23, voters in Georgia's 6th Congressional District chose Republican Johnny Isakson, a state legislator, to succeed Newt Gingrich as their representative in Congress. Gingrich stepped down as Speaker and resigned from the House in 1998. On May 29, 1999, former longtime Louisiana state representative David Vitter, a Republican, narrowly defeated former lieutenant governor David Treen to succeed Republican Robert Livingston as representative from Louisiana's 1st Congressional District. Vitter won 51 percent of the vote. Livingston left Congress in 1999.

Ballot initiatives. Maine voters on November 2 rejected a proposed ban on late-term abortions and approved the use of marijuana for medical purposes. San Francisco voters banned fees for using automatic teller machines.

☐ William J. Eaton

See also **Chicago; Congress of the United States; Democratic Party; Republican Party; San Francisco; State government; United States, Government of the.**

Electric power. See Energy supply.

Electronics. The Secure Digital Music Initiative (SDMI), an affiliation of home electronics and recording companies, in June 1999 announced an agreement on new design standards for portable music players that store music as computer files. The agreement, which was designed to eventually stop the illegal distribution of copyrighted music over the Internet, ended several months of concern about the economic impact of new digital music formats.

The controversy erupted in 1998, when Diamond Multimedia Systems, Inc., of San Jose, California, announced its intention to market a portable player called Rio. The Rio played music recorded in a digital format known as MP3 (MPEG 1, Audio Layer 3). This format was an evolution of existing MPEG (Moving Pictures Experts Group) standards for compressing audio and video information into files that were small enough to conveniently store, distribute, and play recorded music without a significant loss of sound quality.

By 1999, thousands of sites on the World Wide Web featured music coded as MP3 files (or similar formats) that had been copied from compact discs (CD's). Individuals could download these files—often without the consent of the artist or record company—to their personal computers. The emergence of portable digital audio devices like the Rio threatened to increase the spread of illegal copies. Music industry representatives objected to the practice, calling it "piracy" because people who downloaded the unauthorized copies made no payment to the artist or recording company, a violation of existing copyright laws.

Under the agreement, the SDMI standards would be adopted in two phases. In the first phase, the recording industry agreed to drop its lawsuits against manufacturers of portable digital devices. In return, the manufacturers agreed to design players in such a way that they could be modified at a later date, after the second phase goes into effect. In the second phase, which was tentatively scheduled to begin in 2001, all new music CD's would include a special digital code designed to limit the number of copies that could be made from the disc. Older digital music players would be unable to play these encoded CD's without accepting the modification that restricts copying.

Super CD's. A new generation of CD's that delivers superior sound quality debuted in late 1999. The manufacturers, Sony Electronics of Park Ridge, New Jersey, and Philips Electronics North America of New York City, began selling the Super Audio Compact Disc (SACD) in October. SACD technology provides much richer, truer sound than conventional CD's. Sony and Philips, which codeveloped the original audio CD in 1982, predicted that SACD's would eventually replace traditional CD's.

A competing format, known as DVD-Audio, also appeared in late 1999. It was created by a consortium of companies calling themselves the DVD Working Group. An offshoot of the DVD video format already used to present feature films, DVD-Audio also promised high-quality sound but presented music in up to six channels of surround-sound rather than traditional, two-channel stereo. The two formats were not compatible, but players of both types would also play existing CD's.

Molecular computer. In July 1999, researchers at the University of California at Los Angeles and Hewlett Packard Laboratories in Palo Alto, California, announced progress in their efforts to develop a molecular-electronic computer. The researchers used chemical processes to create simple switches using a group of molecules. With circuits hundreds of times smaller than those on modern silicon chips, molecular computers would operate 100 billion times faster than today's fastest commercial chips. In 1999, researchers demonstrated for the first time that the switches, known as molecular-based logic gates, can work better than traditional silicon-based logic gates.   □ Michael Woods

See also **Computers; Popular music.**

El Salvador. Francisco Guillermo Flores Perez of the conservative Nationalist Republican Alliance (Arena) was sworn in on June 1, 1999, for a five-year term as president of El Salvador. Flores Perez had earned a reputation as a consensus builder while presiding over the National Assembly from 1994 to 1997. He pledged to reduce poverty and crime, increase foreign investment, and reduce government's role in business affairs.

El Salvador experienced high unemployment in 1999 and a slowdown of the economy. A 7-percent shortfall in coffee production in 1999 and falling world prices resulted in a 40-percent decline in annual earnings from coffee.

El Savaldor's government continued to privatize state-owned businesses in 1999. Duke Energy Corporation based in Charlotte, North Carolina, announced on August 2 that it was acquiring two Salvadoran power plants—Generadora Acajutla and Generadora Salvadorena—for $125 million.

On March 8, Raul Ernesto Cruz Leon, a Salvadoran, admitted before a tribunal in Havana, the capital of Cuba, that he had been responsible for a 1997 series of bombings in Cuba, which killed 1 person and wounded 11 others. Cruz was sentenced to death.   □ Nathan A. Haverstock

See also **Latin America.**

Employment. See Economics; Labor.

Endangered species. See Conservation.

Great Empires of the

illennium

Much of the world's history has been shaped by nations' imperial ambitions, but the age of empires may be over.

By David Dreier

E mpires have existed throughout recorded history. They have risen and fallen like shifting desert dunes. In ancient times, the Egyptians, the Assyrians, and the Persians all acquired empires. By the dawn of the First Millennium (A.D. 1 to A.D. 1000), the Western world was ruled by Rome, which founded the mightiest, most influential empire the world had ever known. At its height in the A.D. 100's, the Roman Empire encompassed all the lands around the Mediterranean Sea and extended westward to the British Isles.

During the Second Millennium (A.D. 1001 to A.D. 2000), other empires rose and fell. Some were short-lived. Others endured for centuries. By the year 1000, the Roman Empire had long since dis-

1000	1100	1200	1300	1400

Byzantine Empire

Holy Roman Empire

Mongol Empire

Ottoman Empire

Aztec Empire

integrated in the west, but its eastern half (created by a division of the Roman domains in A.D. 395) continued as the Byzantine Empire. Between the 1600's and the mid-1900's, the British Empire became the most far-flung empire of all time, on which, Britons were fond of declaring, the sun never set. As the Second Millennium drew to a close, that proud empire, too, was gone, and the very concept of empire was in question.

The birth and death of empires

The term *empire* generally refers to a group of regions or nations under the rule of a more powerful nation. Most empires have been won through military conquest. Throughout history, military commanders have won power, glory, and usually, wealth by marching armies into and subduing foreign lands. The desire for wealth was the motivating force behind nearly all efforts to establish empires. An imperial power could amass riches by looting subjugated lands of valuable resources. If a conquered people were prosperous, they could be made to pay tribute. New lands also served imperial nations as sources of raw materials and markets for finished goods.

While an empire is at its peak, the controlling nation tends to become immensely wealthy. But all empires come to an end, usually because the empire becomes more trouble than it's worth to the controlling nation. Historically, empires were maintained with a large force of soldiers and bureaucrats at a cost that eventually became intolerable. This was especially the case if the subject peoples demanded their freedom or if the borders of the empire had to be defended against another expanding power. Every empire's story is unique, but the final chapter could always be entitled "Decline and Fall."

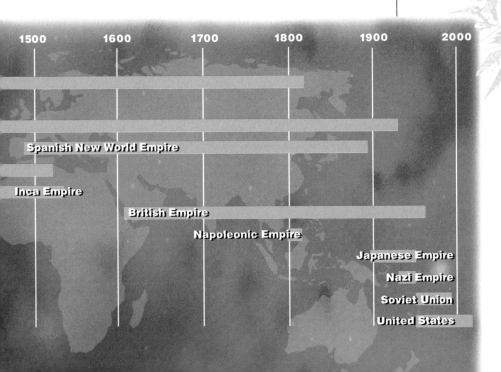

| 1500 | 1600 | 1700 | 1800 | 1900 | 2000 |

Spanish New World Empire

Inca Empire

British Empire

Napoleonic Empire

Japanese Empire

Nazi Empire

Soviet Union

United States

Emperor Constantine IX and Empress Zoe, rulers of the Byzantine Empire from 1042 to 1054, flank Christ in a mosaic in Hagia Sophia, a museum built in the 530's as a cathedral in Constantinople (modern Istanbul), capital of the Byzantine Empire.

The Byzantine Empire in the year 1000.

The author:
David Dreier is a *World Book* managing editor.

The Byzantine Empire

In the year 1000, the Byzantine Empire was the world's greatest power. It began in A.D. 330, when the Roman Emperor Constantine I founded a new capital of the Roman world on the site of the ancient Greek city of Byzantium, where the Mediterranean meets the Black Sea. Constantine had converted to the Christian religion, and in A.D. 313, he elevated Christianity from cult status to the official religion of the empire. His new capital, named Constantinople in his honor, was a center of Christian worship from the start. In that respect it differed profoundly from Rome, which still had many adherents of pagan religions.

Paganism eventually died out in the Western world, and for centuries there was a single Christian church. However, differences between Christians in the East and West grew over church doctrine and the authority of the pope in Rome. In 1054, a split, or schism, divided the church. The Roman Catholic Church remained dominant in the West, and the Eastern Orthodox Churches, ruled over by the patriarch of Constantinople, became dominant in the Byzantine Empire.

The Byzantine Empire was rich and powerful for most of its history. It expanded and prospered particularly after A.D. 476, when Rome fell and Western Europe went into a long decline. Under the Emperor Justinian, who ruled from 527 to 565, the empire encompassed Southern and Eastern Europe as well as parts of North Africa and the Middle East. After Justinian's death, tribes of barbarians and the Persians attacked the empire. In the 630's, Byzantine territories were assailed by Arab invaders carrying the banner of Islam, a religion established a few years earlier. The Arabs conquered much of the Middle East, including Palestine (the Holy Land) and the city of Jerusalem.

In the 800's, the Byzantine Empire regained its strength and retook much of its former holdings. The revival was, however, short-lived. In the mid-1000's, a militantly Islamic people known as the Seljuk Turks stormed out of central Asia, posing one of the greatest dangers that the empire had ever faced. In 1071, the Seljuks annihilated a huge Byzantine army at the Battle of Manzikert in Armenia. The Seljuks took control of the Holy Land and harassed Christians attempting to make pilgrimages there. Anxious to counter the Seljuk menace, the Byzantine emperor, Alexius I Comnenus, asked Pope Urban II in Rome to send a military force of Christian knights to help fight the Turks. The pope agreed. The result was the Crusade of 1097, the first of eight major crusades.

The crusaders won control of the Holy Land. During the same period, the Byzantine Empire reconquered some of its former lands from the Turks. These successes were only temporary, however. Islam was ascendant in the Near East and was threatening to push westward into Europe. (Muslims from North Africa, called Moors, had already penetrated into Spain.) In 1204, the Byzantine Empire was dealt a severe blow by its fellow Christians. The knights of the Fourth Crusade, diverted from their trip to the Holy Land, sacked Constantinople and established their own kingdom. The Byzantine Empire never recovered from the catastrophe. The Byzantines regained control of Constantinople in 1261, but the empire was fatally weakened and survived for less than 200 more years.

The Holy Roman Empire

The Byzantine Empire was a continuation of the Roman Empire, but it was not the only Second Millennium empire to consider itself a successor to Rome. The Holy Roman Empire claimed to have revived Rome's western empire. Some scholars trace the beginnings of the Holy Roman Empire to the Frankish King Charlemagne (Charles the Great), who in the late 700's conquered and unified an expanse of Europe that included modern-day Belgium, France, Luxembourg, the Netherlands, and part of Germany. To honor the illustrious monarch, Pope Leo III in 800 crowned Charlemagne Emperor of the Romans.

Charlemagne's empire broke apart after his death in 814. Although anarchy soon engulfed the continent, the idea of a unified Christian empire persisted. In 961, King Otto I of Germany crossed the Alps and put down an uprising in Rome. In 962, a grateful pope crowned Otto emperor of a combined German and Italian realm.

King Otto I of Germany (below) was crowned emperor of a combined German and Italian realm—the Holy Roman Empire—by Pope John XII in 962. Although the name Holy Roman Empire lasted until 1806, it was, as the French writer Voltaire pointed out in the 1750's, "neither Holy, nor Roman, nor an Empire."

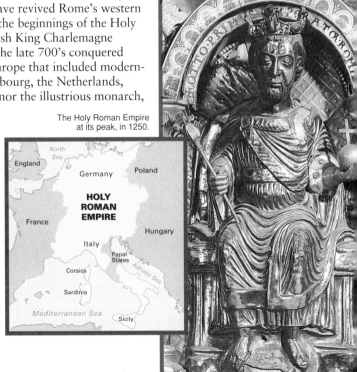

The Holy Roman Empire at its peak, in 1250.

The coronation was the true beginning of the Holy Roman Empire, though that term was not used until the 1200's.

The Holy Roman Empire was essentially German and bore little relationship with the ancient Roman Empire. Nonetheless, it had great prestige and, for a while, great power. From the 900's to the 1300's, the empire and the Roman Catholic Church were the two most important institutions in Europe, both vying for preeminence in European affairs. By the 1400's, however, the empire had been reduced to Germany alone, and the emperor was powerless beyond his own realm.

The Habsburgs, one of Europe's oldest royal families, gained control of the empire in 1438 and held it for nearly 400 years. Under the Habsburgs, the empire grew ever weaker, especially with the Protestant Reformation of the 1500's, which divided Germany into Catholic and Protestant factions. In 1806, Emperor Francis II declared that the Holy Roman Empire was at an end.

The Mongol Empire

No empire of the Second Millennium was forged with as much bloodshed as that of the Mongols. The Mongols were a nomadic people who lived in what is now Mongolia, Manchuria, and Siberia. In the late 1100's, a great leader, who became known as Genghis Khan, organized the Mongol tribes into a fierce military force and set out to conquer China, central Asia, and parts of Eastern Europe. People had never encountered anything like these merciless mounted warriors who descended on unsuspecting nations like swarms of locusts and defeated every army they encountered. Well-trained in both horseback fighting and siege warfare, the Mongols left desolation wherever they roamed.

A 1590 painting (below) depicts a bloody battle between Mongol forces under Genghis Khan and Persian tribes. The Mongols, who lived in what is now Mongolia, Manchuria, and Siberia, conquered vast territories in Asia and Eastern Europe in the 1200's (below, right).

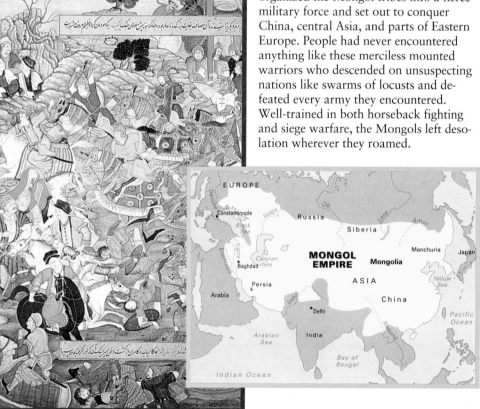

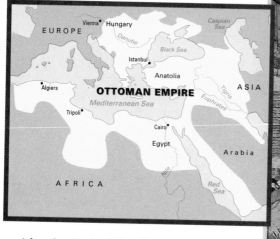

After the death of Genghis Khan in 1227, the conquests were continued by his sons and grandsons. One grandson, Batu, ravaged Poland and Hungary in 1241. Another grandson, Kublai Khan, subdued all of China in 1279 and established the Yuan Dynasty, which ruled for 89 years. Kublai Khan was of a somewhat milder temperament than his predecessors and actually encouraged contact with Europeans. The Italian adventurer Marco Polo visited China during the reign of Kublai Khan and returned with tales of fabulous wealth, which inspired later generations of European explorers.

The entire realm of Kublai Khan stretched from China to the Byzantine Empire on the Mediterranean Sea, constituting the largest land empire the world had ever known. It was, in fact, too large to hold together and began splintering in Kublai's own time. After his death in 1294, the empire split into four parts. Mongol rule, however, continued for centuries in several regions. A group of Mongols called the Golden Horde controlled Russia until the late 1400's. In India, another Mongol tribe, called the Mughuls, held power until the 1700's.

The Ottoman Empire

By the middle of the Second Millennium—the 1500's and 1600's—the Ottoman Turks controlled the world's most powerful empire. The Ottomans, a Turkish people from central Asia, established a small state in Anatolia (modern-day Turkey) in the late 1200's. Like the Seljuk Turks before them, the Ottomans had adopted the Islamic religion. In quest of new lands, the Ottomans in the 1300's began encroaching on the remaining territory of the Byzantine Empire, which at the time consisted of little more than Constantinople. In 1453, a new Ottoman *sultan* (absolute ruler), Muhammad II, advanced on Constantinople with an army of more than 100,000 men. The Byzantine Emperor, Constantine XI Palaeologus, was able to muster fewer than 10,000 defenders. On May 29, the Turks overran the city after a 40-day siege. Emperor Constantine died in the thick of the fighting. The victorious Turks made Constantinople their own capital and renamed it Istanbul.

Defenders of Belgrade, in what is now Yugoslavia, bow and surrender to Suleiman the Magnificent, ruler of the Ottoman Empire, in 1521 (above). The Ottoman Empire (above, left) peaked under Suleiman, who controlled much of southwestern Asia, southeastern Europe, and northern Africa.

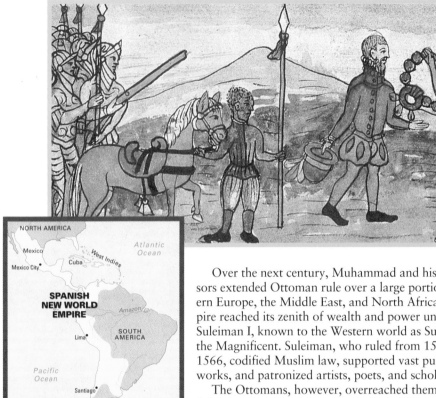

The Spanish explorer Hernando Cortes is greeted by representatives of the Aztec leader Montezuma in 1519 (top). Cortes conquered the Aztec Empire, in what is today central and southern Mexico, in 1521. By the mid-1500's, Spain controlled large areas of the Americas (above).

Over the next century, Muhammad and his successors extended Ottoman rule over a large portion of Eastern Europe, the Middle East, and North Africa. The empire reached its zenith of wealth and power under Sultan Suleiman I, known to the Western world as Suleiman the Magnificent. Suleiman, who ruled from 1520 to 1566, codified Muslim law, supported vast public works, and patronized artists, poets, and scholars.

The Ottomans, however, overreached themselves. Suleiman conquered the eastern third of Hungary in 1526, but failed three years later to take Vienna, Austria. With this defeat, the seemingly unstoppable Turkish advance into the heart of Europe ground to a halt, and the Ottoman Empire went into a slow decline. In World War I (1914-1918), the Ottoman Empire fought on the side of Germany. After Germany's defeat, the empire was occupied by Allied forces, and in 1922 it was dissolved and replaced the following year by the Republic of Turkey.

Empires of the "New World"

The discovery of the Americas by Europeans presented new opportunities for empire building during the second half of the Second Millennium. In 1492, the Spanish rulers Ferdinand and Isabella—having finally rid Spain of the Moors—agreed to finance a voyage proposed by a young Italian seafarer named Christopher Columbus. Columbus argued that he could reach Asia by sailing west across the Atlantic Ocean, thereby opening a new trade route to the riches of the Far East. In October 1492, after 70 days at sea, Columbus did find land. Although he encountered no Asian merchants on any of his four expeditions, he died believing that he had sailed to Asia. It soon became obvious, however, that Columbus had discovered previously unknown lands—a vast New World waiting to be claimed and exploited.

In the early 1500's, Spain settled Cuba and other parts of the West Indies, and Spaniards intent on making their fortunes flocked to the mainland of the Americas. They had heard tales from coastal tribes about advanced Indian civilizations in the interior that were awash in silver and gold. The stories were true. Although the great Maya culture of Central America had fallen into decay, the Aztecs in Mexico and the Incas in Peru ruled great empires.

The Aztec Empire was located in the Valley of Mexico. The Aztecs had subdued several other Indian groups in the 1300's and early 1400's, and by 1450 they ruled all of central Mexico from their capital, Tenochtitlan. The empire was at its height of wealth and power when the Spanish arrived. The Spanish adventurer Hernando Cortes overthrew the Aztecs in 1521.

A similar fate befell the Inca Empire, which extended along the western coast of South America from present-day Colombia to Argentina, including parts of present-day Ecuador, Peru, Bolivia, and Chile. Just before the Spanish arrived, civil war broke out between followers of two rivals for the title of emperor. The civil war so weakened the empire that it fell easily in 1532 to the Spanish explorer Francisco Pizarro.

By the mid-1500's, Spain controlled Mexico, Central America, most of the West Indies, much of western South America, a large chunk of what is now the Southwestern United States, and all of present-day Florida. Mexico, renamed New Spain, was the center of the Spanish New World empire. The empire's capital, Mexico City, grew atop the rubble of Tenochtitlan, which Cortes had leveled.

The growing Spanish Empire in the 1500's was not confined to the Americas. Spain held territories in Europe, including present-day Belgium and the Netherlands, and gained control of the Philippines. A failed attempt to invade and conquer England in 1588—the defeat of the Spanish Armada—followed by a series of wars with France and other European nations in the 1600's left Spain in a weakened state with a ruined economy. By the 1690's, France had eclipsed Spain as the greatest power on the European continent, and England became France's bitter rival as the two nations battled for supremacy in Europe and the New World.

Compared with Spain, France and England were late-comers to the Americas. Their first tentative investigations of the New World began in the early 1500's. During the 1600's, French and English explorers and settlers planted their nations' flags throughout much of the vast North American wilderness.

The French laid claim to a large portion of present-day Canada and all the land drained by the Mississippi River. The latter territory, a vast area stretching westward to the summit of the Rocky Mountains, was named Louisiana in honor of France's King Louis XIV. The combined regions were called New France, which the rulers of France envisioned becoming a great New World empire. Meanwhile, England staked rival claims in much of eastern Canada and established settlements along the Atlantic Coast of North America—as did the Netherlands and Sweden. The coastal settlements were all under the control of England by 1664 and became the Thirteen American Colonies. Both France and England also established colonies in the West Indies.

France and England competed for the New World's lucrative fur trade and challenged each other's territorial claims west of the Appalachian Mountains. From 1689 to 1763, France and Great Britain fought four wars in Europe and North America. The last and most important was the French and Indian War, so-called because both sides made heavy use of American Indian allies. Although the immediate cause of the war was a dispute over ownership of the Upper Ohio River valley, the overriding issue was which of the two nations was to dominate North America. The conflict began in America in 1754 and spread to Europe two years later, where it became known as the Seven Years' War.

The war ended in a British victory in 1763. In the Treaty of Paris, France ceded to Great Britain its territories on the North American mainland east of the Mississippi River, including Canada. The year before, King Louis XV of France had secretly transferred all of Louisiana west of the Mississippi to Spain to compensate Spain for its military aid and territorial losses during the war. As a result, France was left with virtually no New World possessions except for a few West Indian islands.

Great Britain's triumph over the French marked the beginning of its ascendance as the world's greatest power. Britain's formidable navy and growing industrial might made it the strongest and wealthiest nation in the world by the end of the 1700's. However, Britain's expanding colonial empire, coming at the end of a string of costly wars, put a heavy economic burden on the treasury. To improve the nation's financial situation and defray the expense of guarding the western frontier of its American lands, the British Parliament adopted policies aimed at squeezing revenue from the colonies. The colonists' protests against these highly unpopular measures were answered with acts limiting their political rights.

The situation grew explosive, and in 1775 Britain's King George III was faced with a revolution in his American Colonies. In 1776, the colonies declared their independence as the United States of America. With French aid, the new nation prevailed against Great Britain.

After crowning himself emperor of France, Napoleon Bonaparte in 1804 crowns his wife, Josephine, empress (below). Through military conquest, Napoleon built an empire that covered much of Europe by 1812 (below, right). The empire was to be short-lived, however, and ended with Napoleon's defeat at Waterloo in 1815.

France (red) and Napoleon's empire (yellow) in 1812.

While the defeat was unexpected and a setback, it did little to slow Britain's march toward a global empire. Nor was this march stopped by a series of costly wars that Britain was forced to wage in the early 1800's against the France of Napoleon Bonaparte.

The Emperor Napoleon

Revolution swept over France in 1789. The French Revolution degenerated into a Reign of Terror in which nearly 20,000 people, including France's King Louis XVI, were executed. In 1799, after the revolution had run its course, the French people wanted a strong leader, a dictator. A brilliant French general, Napoleon Bonaparte, took charge of the government. In 1802, Napoleon assumed dictatorial powers, and in 1804, the French Senate and the citizens of France approved a proposal making him emperor.

An emperor needs an empire, and Napoleon acquired one. Through years of almost perpetual warfare, he brought nearly all of Western Europe under his sway. In 1806, he refused to acknowledge the existence of the Holy Roman Empire, an act that prompted Francis II to declare that the empire was at an end.

Napoleon's expansive realm soon followed the Holy Roman Empire into oblivion. France was surrounded by enemies, who were determined to rid the continent of the Bonaparte yoke. In April 1814, Napoleon abdicated after suffering two severe military defeats and was exiled to the island of Elba, off the coast of Italy. The following February, he escaped, returned to France, and raised a new army. It was to be his last hurrah. In June, he was defeated by British and Prussian forces at the Battle of Waterloo in Belgium. This time, the emperor was packed off to the remote island of St. Helena in the South Atlantic Ocean. There he spent the remaining six years of his life, insisting to the last that he be addressed as "Your Majesty."

King George V and Queen Mary of Great Britain, who presided over the most far-flung empire of all time, visit India in 1911 (top). In the early 1900's, the British Empire included colonies or dependencies on every continent (above), allowing Britons to declare, "The sun never sets on the British Empire."

The British Empire

When the Napoleonic Wars finally ended in 1815, Great Britain held colonial possessions that stretched from Canada and the Caribbean to Australia and India, which became the crown jewel of the British Empire. There had been a British presence in India since the 1600's, when England's East India Company, which was founded to open trade with Eastern nations, received permission from the Mughal emperor to do business in India. As Mughal power declined in the 1700's, the East India Company acted more like a government entity and less like a business concern. It collected taxes in some regions and used force against local rulers who opposed company policies. In 1784, the British Parliament passed the India Act, which gave the government increased power over the East India Company. In 1858, the British government decided to govern most of India directly, creating what was known as the British raj, a word in India's Hindi language meaning rule or administration.

In the late 1800's and early 1900's, Great Britain and other European powers—including France, Germany, Belgium, and the Netherlands—also carved out colonial empires in Africa and Southeast Asia. Africa had earlier been a source of slaves for the lucrative slave trade in the Americas. Both Africa and Asia became places for business investment, sources of raw materials for European factories, and markets for manufactured goods. Although the British Empire would survive through two world wars, it was, like all empires, destined to fall.

The Nazi empire and imperial Japan

From 1914 to 1918, Europe was engulfed in the first conflict ever to be called a world war. World War I severely weakened Russia, which suffered more than 6.5 million casualties, a situation that led to the overthrow of the Russian czar and the imposition of a Communist dictatorship. The Treaty of Versailles, which ended the war, imposed extremely harsh penalties on Germany and set in motion a series of events culminating in the rise of Adolf Hitler and the Nazi Party in the 1930's.

Hitler and the Nazis had a deadly agenda—to rid Europe of Jews and other peoples they considered inferior and to gain "living space" by conquering neighboring lands. The Nazis gained control of Germany in 1933 and established the Third Reich, the beginning of an empire that Hitler predicted would last a thousand years. His regime plunged Europe into another world war in 1939 when his armies invaded Poland. German forces went on to defeat and occupy most of Europe. In 1941, Hitler disregarded a nonaggression pact with Soviet leader Joseph Stalin and invaded the Soviet Union, the first step in the fall of the Third Reich.

The war machine of Nazi Germany brought most of Europe under its sway in the early stages of World War II (1939-1945). Territory controlled by Germany or its Axis partner Italy in 1942 extended from Norway to northern Africa and from France to the Soviet Union.

Axis countries (red) and Axis-occupied areas (yellow) in 1942.

Before the Nazis gained power in Germany, the government of Japan, which had fallen into the hands of an army clique, was laying plans to enlarge its already sizable empire, which included Korea and a number of Pacific islands. The goal was to create a

"Greater East Asia Co-Prosperity Sphere," an economic association of Asian nations under the leadership of Japan. The benevolent-sounding proposal was little more than a cover for Japanese imperial aims. Japan planned to replace European colonial rule in much of Asia with its own and help itself to the resources of the "liberated" nations.

Japan's aggressive agenda became clear in 1931, when it occupied Manchuria, and again in 1937, when it launched a major attack against China. The Chinese army was unable to withstand the Japanese onslaught, and by the end of 1938 Japan controlled most of eastern China. In 1941, Japanese forces entered French Indochina (Cambodia, Laos, and Vietnam). The United States tried unsuccessfully to persuade Japan to withdraw from China and from Southeast Asia.

The United States had eyed Japan warily for years. In the 1920's, the U.S. military recognized that war with Japan was a serious possibility and formulated a strategy for defeating the Japanese Empire. Nonetheless, the United States was caught unaware on Dec. 7, 1941, when Japanese planes attacked the U.S. naval base at Pearl Harbor in Hawaii. Because Japan was an ally of Germany, the United States was soon at war in both Europe and the Pacific.

World War II, the greatest military conflict in history, resulted in the death of 50 million people, including some 11 million who perished in the Nazi death camps. By 1945, Japan and Germany had been defeated utterly—their armies destroyed, their cities in ruins. The final act in this most terrible of wars came in August 1945, when Hiroshima and Nagasaki, Japan, were incinerated with the newly invented atomic bomb.

From empires to superpowers

In the years after World War II, the Asian and African colonial empires of the European powers, including that of the once mighty Great Britain, soon fell apart. Nationalism was on the march. Peo-

Japanese troops celebrate capturing U.S. artillery on the Bataan Peninsula in the Philippines in 1942 (top). The Japanese Empire reached its greatest extent in 1942 (above), covering parts of China and Southeast Asia and spreading across much of the Pacific Ocean.

The Soviet Union (yellow) and its satellites (red) in the late 1940's.

After World War II, the Soviet Union under dictator Joseph Stalin (above), organized East Germany, Poland, Bulgaria, Czechoslovakia, Hungary, and Romania into a group of "satellite" nations with Soviet-controlled Communist governments (above, right). The Soviet Union during the same period exercised great influence in Yugoslavia and Albania.

ple around the world refused to be ruled by foreigners. In 1947, Britain granted independence to India, and by the mid-1960's nearly all the nations under colonial rule in Africa and Asia had won their freedom.

The post-war world gave rise not to more traditional empires, but to a new concept altogether—the superpower. Two superpowers, the United States and the Soviet Union, emerged from the war, and they faced off in a long, grim confrontation known as the Cold War.

The Cold War grew out of the situation in Europe after the war. The leading Western Allies (Britain, France, and the United States) assumed jurisdiction over western Germany and western Berlin. The Soviet Union, also a member of the Allied forces, controlled eastern Germany and eastern Berlin. The Soviet Union was also left in possession of several Eastern European nations—Bulgaria, Czechoslovakia, Hungary, Poland, and Romania. In 1948, the Soviet holdings were organized into an Eastern bloc of Soviet-controlled nations with Communist governments.

Fearing that the Soviet Union was a threat, the United States, Canada, and 14 other Western nations in 1949 formed a military alliance called the North Atlantic Treaty Organization. In response, the Soviet Union and its Eastern European "satellites" formed their own alliance, the Warsaw Pact, in 1955.

In 1947, the United States adopted the policy of "containment" to counter the influence of the Soviet Union and resist the spread of Communism around the world. The policy led the United States into war in Korea in June 1950, when North Korean forces invaded South Korea. The northern part of Korea had been occupied by Soviet troops after World War II and had become a Communist state. The United States and other members of the newly established United Nations intervened and were on the verge of winning the war when hundreds of thousands of troops from China, which had itself become a Communist nation the year before, poured into North Korea to join the fighting. The conflict was brought to a negotiated end in 1953, with Korea still divided.

The Korean conflict was a war without victory, a new experience for the United States. The experience would be repeated in the Vietnam War (1957-1975), waged in an unsuccessful attempt to prevent a Communist takeover of the former French colony.

These "hot wars" were played out against the backdrop of the Cold War, which held great peril for humanity. With the United States and the Soviet Union eventually armed with thousands of nuclear missiles capable of turning the Earth into a radioactive wasteland, both sides knew that an all-out war would be a disaster beyond comprehension. For the first time in history, a rivalry between two powerful empires threatened the entire world.

The Cold War dragged on until the late 1980's, when the Eastern European nations broke free of Soviet rule. In 1991, the Soviet Union, which for years had been slowly disintegrating, simply went out of business. Russia and many of the former republics of the Soviet Union became independent nations. As the millennium ended, the United States remained the world's only superpower.

The worldwide renown of The Coca-Cola Company and other large U.S. corporations symbolizes the global dominance of the U.S. economy in the year 2000.

Empires of the Third Millennium

What is the future of empire? In a 1943 address at Harvard University, Britain's Prime Minister Winston Churchill predicted, "The empires of the future are empires of the mind." Churchill was undoubtedly referring to the competition of ideologies for people's minds, as was then occurring between the competing Communist and democratic systems. But his prediction could also apply to the situation at the beginning of the Third Millennium. Some observers think we may be witnessing the beginnings of a global culture in which people around the world are linked together by telecommunications and the Internet. This global community is dedicated to the free exchange of information and ideas—certainly an empire of the mind.

The emerging global society is also devoted to the pursuit of wealth, the nonstop electronic movement of money, and consumerism. Much of the latter was based on American popular culture, which—like an expanding empire of old—appeared to be taking over the planet. A world given over to capitalist enterprise and the good life might be less colorful than one dominated by the march of empires. But it probably would be a more peaceful one.

■ ■ ■

Energy supply. Petroleum supplies figured prominently in the world economy in 1999. At the beginning of the year, analysts speculated that the world surplus of oil that was believed to exist in 1998 would continue throughout 1999. By the spring of 1999, however, perceptions of an oil glut began to fade as leading oil exporters, such as Saudi Arabia, Venezuela, and Mexico, moved to prop up depressed prices by cutting their petroleum production.

The Organization of Petroleum Exporting Countries (OPEC), an association of 11 oil-producing nations, showed its strength in 1999 by implementing further output cuts totaling more than 1 million barrels of oil a day. (A barrel of oil contains 42 gallons, or 159 liters.) Although similar OPEC cuts in 1998 had little effect on the market, the 1999 cuts, along with new growth in the world's demand for energy, drove up oil prices.

Petroleum use up. Thriving economies in the United States and parts of Europe, some economic recovery in Asia, and expanding numbers of vehicles pushed up consumption of petroleum in 1999. According to the Paris-based International Energy Agency (IEA), an association of major oil-consuming nations, the world's rate of petroleum consumption increased more than 1 percent in 1999, to 75.3 million barrels per day. This was more than double the growth rate of 1998.

The IEA estimated that world oil consumption would average a record 77.1 million barrels a day in 2000. With the world's oil inventories continuing to shrink, some analysts in 1999 were concerned that oil shortages could develop in 2000 unless petroleum-producing countries increased their output. OPEC's ministers were scheduled to meet in March 2000 to decide on production quotas for the remainder of 2000.

Petroleum prices up. Oil prices, which had dropped sharply in 1998 because of the perceived glut, made a big recovery in 1999. The price of petroleum more than doubled from less than $12 a barrel in early 1999 to beyond $25 by late 1999—the highest level in three years.

In late November, oil prices briefly jumped to nearly $28 a barrel—the highest level in almost nine years—when Iraq cut off most of its oil exports in a dispute with the United Nations (UN). Iraq, which remained under UN economic sanctions in 1999 because of its 1990 invasion of Kuwait, had been allowed to sell $5.2 billion worth of oil every six months to buy humanitarian supplies. Iraq cut its exports in a protest against a UN Security Council decision to extend the "oil-for-food" program for only two weeks while the council negotiated a new Iraqi policy.

The 1999 jump in crude oil prices had an impact on the costs of other energy. In the United

The nuclear reactor from the Trojan Nuclear Power Plant near Rainier, Oregon, is loaded onto a barge in August 1999 for transport to the Hanford Nuclear Reservation in Washington state, where it was later buried. The Trojan plant shut down in 1993 because of technical problems.

States, the retail price of gasoline, which had averaged approximately $1 a gallon for the regular grade during much of 1998, surged in 1999. Gasoline prices reached $1.35 a gallon by November. Fuel oil used for home heating and other purposes also rose sharply in price in 1999.

Economists noted that rising energy prices may have contributed to increases in inflation and interest rates in the United States in 1999. Although inflation remained relatively low in the United States, the *Consumer Price Index* (a statistical measurement of changes in the prices of goods and services in the United States) rose 0.4 percent in September—the biggest increase in five months. Interest rates on U.S. treasury bonds surged more than 1 percent late in 1999, with some economists attributing the change to higher petroleum prices.

Petroleum predictions. In late 1999, observers of world oil markets debated the future direction of petroleum prices. Various factors, including concerns about volatile regions of the Middle East, diminishing oil stockpiles, growing world economies, and the approaching winter months (when petroleum demand makes a seasonal upswing), led some energy forecasters to predict that the price of crude oil would go beyond $30 a barrel, if only for a short period. Other industry observers, however, looked for petroleum prices to flatten out in 2000, possibly at lower levels. Ahmed Zaki Yamani, the former oil minister of Saudi Arabia, suggested in September 1999 that oil markets were overheated. Yamani said, ". . .most likely, after March [2000], the market and price will slow down."

Other fossil fuels. The Washington, D.C.-based Energy Information Agency (EIA), an agency of the U.S. Department of Energy, estimated that coal production for the first 10 months of 1999 was approximately 919 million tons (834 million metric tons)—1.5 percent less than during the same months in 1998. Electric-utility coal consumption in the United States during the first six months of 1999 totaled 432 million tons (392 million metric tons)—a 1.6-percent decrease compared with the first half of 1998.

The EIA estimated that Americans burned 17.59 trillion cubic feet (502.5 billion cubic meters) of natural gas in the first 10 months of 1999—slightly more than the amount used in the same months of 1998. Natural gas production through October 1999 was down by more than 1 percent compared to the same period in 1998, according to the EIA.   □ James Tanner

See also **Iraq; Saudi Arabia.**

Engineering. See Building and construction.

England. See United Kingdom.

Environmental pollution. Efforts to reduce the emissions of greenhouse gases, which many scientists blame for causing *global warming* (a gradual warming of Earth's surface), continued in 1999. Greenhouse gases, such as carbon dioxide, are generated by the burning of fossil fuels. A number of scientific studies in the 1990's indicated that these gases were accumulating in the atmosphere, where they trap heat much like a greenhouse. Scientists fear that this warming might disrupt climate and cause glaciers to melt, leading to rising sea levels and coastal flooding.

In September 1999, the leaders of the Alliance of Small Island States, an association of several dozen small island nations, voiced their concerns about greenhouse gases before the United Nations (UN) General Assembly. They noted that if global warming is not abated, their nations would bear the brunt of rising seas and increasingly violent weather.

The island leaders urged the United States and the world's other industrial nations to ratify the Kyoto Protocol, a UN treaty negotiated in 1997. The treaty requires participating countries to reduce their greenhouse gas emissions by an average of 5 percent below 1990 levels in the years between 2008 and 2012. Because the United States is one of the leading emitters of greenhouse gases, the treaty required the United States to reduce its emissions by 7 percent.

Although Clinton administration officials representing the United States signed the Kyoto Protocol in 1998, many members of the U.S. Congress said they feared the treaty would hurt the U.S. economy. Congress had not yet ratified the treaty by the end of 1999.

Private industry initiatives. The Worldwatch Institute, an environmental research group based in Washington, D.C., announced in August that global emissions of carbon dioxide declined 0.5 percent during 1998. The institute attributed the decline partly to voluntary initiatives by private industry. The chemical-industry giant E. I. DuPont DeNemours and Company of Wilmington, Delaware, for example, had invested $50 million in equipment to reduce greenhouse gas emissions since 1991.

A number of corporate executives in 1999 endorsed a bill before the U.S. Congress that would grant "pollution credits" to companies that curtail emissions of greenhouse gases. Under this legislation, the U.S. government would guarantee that companies would receive credits for any emission reductions they achieve before the Kyoto treaty, if ratified, becomes effective in 2008. The companies could then use these credits to satisfy their reduction requirements in the future or sell them to other companies that are unable to meet their reduction requirements.

Biologist Rachel Carson, in her book *Silent Spring*, took up the cudgels for birds and wildlife lovers, and brought down upon her gentle head the united wrath of the chemical industry and the commercial farmers.

Miss Carson began her book with a vivid description of a spring ". . . unheralded by the return of birds, and the early mornings, once filled with the beauty of bird song, are strangely silent." She then cited examples of how insecticides, herbicides, and fungicides had been misused and how they threatened human as well as plant and animal life. Cancer-inducing chemicals, she contended, remain as residues in nearly everything we eat or drink. . . .

At least partly in response to the furor caused by her book, the federal government initiated a review of its pesticide programs by a committee of the Federal Council of Science and Technology.

Everglades restoration. The Clinton administration in July 1999 presented to Congress a program to restore the natural ecology of the Everglades, a large area of wetlands in southern Florida. In the late 1940's, the U.S. Army Corps of Engineers began to install a system of canals, levees, and pumps to control flooding and provide drinking and irrigation water for southern Florida's expanding population. The system reduced the natural flow of water in the Everglades, altering plant and animal communities. The ecology of the Everglades was also adversely affected by runoff polluted with fertilizers and pesticides from nearby agricultural areas.

The 20-year, $7.8-billion project required the Army Corps to restore much of the Everglades' natural waterflow. This involved punching holes in levees and highways that impede the flow, creating underground reservoirs to capture water that is presently channeled to the sea, and using nearby marshland to filter chemical contaminants from the water. As part of the plan, Congress approved $80 million in November 1999 to purchase land to be used for the restoration.

Clean air vs. clean water. The U.S. Environmental Protection Agency (EPA) proposed in July 1999 that Congress no longer require oil companies to add an ingredient to gasoline that helps make the air cleaner. The agency said the ingredient, methyl tertiary butyl ether (MTBE), posed a serious danger as a water pollutant.

Under the EPA's urging, Congress in 1990 required MTBE to be added to gasoline because of the chemical's ability to cut toxic emissions, such as carbon monoxide, benzene, and toluene. However, researchers have since found that MTBE is a possible *carcinogenic* (cancer-causing) substance that can flow into drinking-water wells when fuel leaks from underground tanks or pipelines.

SUV's and smog. In May 1999, the EPA announced regulations to reduce the emission of smog-causing chemicals by sport-utility vehicles (SUV's), light trucks, and cars. The EPA said the new standards would reduce respiratory illness by cutting emissions of nitrogen oxides and other pollutants by 75 to 95 percent.

Under the regulations, which were to be phased in gradually between 2004 and 2009, SUV's and trucks weighing less than 8,500 pounds (3,859 kilograms) were to be held to the same strict pollution standards as automobiles for the first time. The regulations also required the oil industry to cut the content of smog-causing sulfur in gasoline by 90 percent.

In October 1999, the EPA extended the tough emission requirements to "super-large" SUV's and heavy-duty trucks—those weighing more than 8,500 pounds.

Pesticide safety. Environmentalists criticized the EPA in 1999 for its slower-than-expected action on the 1996 Food Quality Protection Act. The act required that the agency by 2006 reassess the safety levels of 9,700 pesticides based on risks to children. The EPA had set an August 1999 goal for completing analysis of the riskiest chemicals, but it was behind in meeting that goal.

On August 2, EPA Administrator Carol Browner announced the first results of the reassessment. She said that, starting in early 2000, the widely used pesticide methyl parathion would be banned on a variety of fruits and vegetables. She noted that animal tests indicated that the pesticide could cause nerve damage in children.

Following this announcement, agriculture industry groups sued the EPA, alleging that it failed to use sound science in the evaluation of the pesticide. Environmental groups also sued the EPA, seeking to force the agency to take more aggressive action against pesticides.

EPA rebuked by court. In May 1999, the EPA found its regulatory authority challenged when a three-judge panel of the U.S. Circuit Court of Appeals in Washington, D.C., invalidated two rulings the agency made in 1997. One of these rulings had tightened the standards for air pollutants that contribute to smog. The other ruling had set new limits on microscopic respiratory irritants called particulates, which are generated in certain industrial processes. The EPA had established the regulations to protect people with asthma and lung disease.

The court struck down both laws on the grounds that the EPA failed to establish clear criteria for determining what level of health protection was provided by the standards. The court also said the EPA's move amounted to an unconstitutional transfer of power from the Congress to the EPA. To work around the rulings, EPA Administrator Carol Browner resurrected two-year-old petitions from several Northeast states requesting relief from pollution caused by out-of-state sources. Browner hoped to use the petitions to impose controls on Midwest power plants, whose pollution drifts to the Northeast.

Power plant suits. In September 1999, New York State notified coal-fired power plants in Indiana, Kentucky, Ohio, Virginia, and West Virginia that it intended to sue them for violations of the 1970 Clean Air Act. The attorney general of Connecticut announced identical intentions in November 1999. Also in November, the U.S. Justice Department began enforcement actions under the Clean Air Act against 32 coal-fired plants from Florida to Illinois. ☐ Andrew Hoffman

See also **Conservation.**
Equatorial Guinea. See **Africa.**
Eritrea. See **Africa.**

Estonia. Voters in Estonia elected a new parliament on March 7, 1999. Economic issues dominated the campaign. Despite a sharp decline in Estonia's economic growth since August 1998, a coalition of proeconomic reform parties won 53 of the 101 seats in the legislature. On March 25, 1999, Mart Laar became prime minister. Laar had served as Estonia's prime minister from 1992 to 1994.

Estonia continued to make progress toward integration into Europe and the world economy in 1999. In October, Estonia joined the World Trade Organization (WTO), the arbiter of trade disputes among member countries. The European Union (EU) reported in October that Estonia remained high on its list of countries being considered for EU membership. The EU expressed concern, however, over an Estonian "language law" that required persons offering services in the private sector to be fluent in the Estonian language.

In May, the defense ministers of Estonia, Latvia, and Lithuania met in Estonia to discuss closer cooperation in defense matters. In October, the commanders of the armed forces of the three Baltic nations agreed to establish a joint Baltic Sea training center in Latvia.

☐ Steven L. Solnick

See also **Europe; Latvia; Lithuania.**
Ethiopia. See **Africa.**

The freighter New Carissa burns as it lies grounded off the coast of Coos Bay, Oregon, in February 1999. After efforts to refloat the ship failed, the U.S. Coast Guard set the ship's fuel afire to save the area's beaches from a dangerous fuel oil spill.

Europe

Instability caused by the breakup of the former Yugoslavia returned to haunt Europe in 1999. Serbia's attempt to crush an independence movement in its Kosovo province led to civilian massacres, prompting the United States and its Western European allies in the North Atlantic Treaty Organization (NATO) to intervene. NATO's bombing campaign against Serbia marked the first time the alliance had attacked a sovereign nation and set a precedent to justify the use of armed force to protect human rights.

The conflict in Kosovo. Tensions between Serbia and Kosovo had been growing since Slobodan Milosevic became president of Serbia in 1989. Milosevic had secured power by rescinding Kosovo's *autonomy* (limited self-government) and promising to promote the interests of the minority Serb population. Serbs, who are mostly Orthodox Christians, made up 10 percent of Kosovo's population of 2.2 million in the early 1990's. Ethnic Albanians—mostly Muslims—made up 90 percent.

The situation deteriorated in 1997, when Serbian police used force to break up demonstrations against the Serb government in Kosovo. The Kosovo Liberation Army (KLA), which sought independence for the province, retaliated by attacking Serbian security forces. A peace agreement brokered by the United States and five European countries in late 1998 failed.

Fearing that tensions could escalate into civil war throughout the Balkans, the United States and its European allies held peace talks in France in March 1999. Serbia, however, refused to accept any plan that included autonomy for Kosovo and increased its attacks on the KLA. NATO began bombing Serb forces on March 24, hoping to force Serbia to sign a peace agreement. Nearly 800,000 ethnic Albanians fled Kosovo for refugee camps in Montenegro, Albania, and Macedonia.

The bombing campaign threatened the unity of NATO and strained relations between the alliance and Russia, which historically had close ties to Serbia. Several NATO members were reluctant to use force, including center-left coalition governments in Germany and Italy. Most Greeks, who like the Serbs are Orthodox Christians, opposed the intervention. The campaign also posed a challenge to governments in Poland, Hungary, and the Czech Republic, which had joined NATO in early March. They found themselves involved in a war less than two weeks later. Several bombing accidents also provoked public criticism, including a mistaken attack on a refugee convoy that killed at least 75 ethnic Albanians in April. The accidental bombing of the Chinese Embassy in the Yugoslav capital, Belgrade, in May, killed three Chinese nationals.

In May, NATO persuaded Russia to endorse a peace plan demanding that Serbia withdraw from Kosovo and allow the refugees to return under the protection of a NATO-led peacekeeping force. On June 3, President Martti Ahtisaari of Finland and Russian envoy Viktor Chernomyrdin convinced Milosevic to agree to the plan. NATO halted its bombing on June 10. Under the accord, Kosovo remained a province of Yugoslavia, and most ethnic Albanian refugees returned to Kosovo. Nearly 200,000 Serbs fled the province for Serbia and Montenegro out of fear of retaliation.

NATO expanded into Eastern Europe in 1999 as Poland, Hungary, and the Czech Republic became members on March 12. The countries had been among the first formerly Communist nations to embrace democracy and free-market economics. They regarded NATO membership as a

TIME CAPSULE 1943
EUROPE

POSSESSED OF MANY EXCELLENT air bases in Tunisia . . . the Allies prepared for the invasion of Sicily. . . . The main seaborne American force—the Seventh Army under the command of Lieutenant General George S. Patton—put ashore near Licata. It fought its way rapidly westward along the shore road and captured Porto Empedocle, Agrigento, and other towns farther west. It met with no very serious resistance. Many of the Sicilians, remembering their relatives in the United States, actually welcomed the American soldiers as liberators. Even the Italian troops, whose morale was very low, began to surrender in large numbers. The American troops then fanned out inland and within [two weeks] had occupied the whole western half of the island. They were welcomed into Palermo, a city of 400,000, and the capital of Sicily, on July 23.

They at once took measures to feed the population, replace Fascist officials, and install the Allied Military Government.

An ethnic Albanian woman pleads with Macedonian police to allow 10,000 Kosovar refugees to cross the border into Macedonia in April 1999. The Kosovars were fleeing Serbian forces attempting to crush an independence movement in Serbia's Kosovo province.

way to guarantee their independence and ensure close ties with the West. In April, NATO marked its 50th anniversary at a summit meeting in Washington, D.C. Celebrations were muted because of the war in Kosovo. The alliance postponed decisions about admitting new members to avoid increasing tensions with Russia.

European defense. European nations took steps to improve their own defense in 1999. European countries carried out few bombing missions during the Kosovo conflict because they lacked precision-guided munitions and planes that could fly in all weather conditions. The 15-member European Union (EU) hoped that closer cooperation would help the EU catch up to the United States in military capability and enable Europe to intervene in future conflicts even if the United States were unwilling to do so. In June, EU leaders appointed Javier Solana, then secretary general of NATO, as head of EU foreign and security policy. In December, EU leaders agreed to form a rapid reaction force of some 50,000 troops by 2003.

Country	Population	Government	Monetary unit*	Foreign trade (million U.S.$)	
				Exports[†]	Imports[†]
Albania	3,624,000	President Rexhep Mejdani; Prime Minister Ilir Meta	lek (131.95 = $1)	205	788
Andorra	67,000	Co-sovereigns bishop of Urgel, Spain, and the president of France; Prime Minister Marc Forne Molne	French franc & Spanish peseta	47	1,000
Austria	8,148,000	President Thomas Klestil; Chancellor Viktor Klima	schilling (12.88 = $1)	60,955	66,450
Belarus	10,069,000	President Aleksandr Lukashenko	ruble (244,000.00 = $1)	7,016	8,509
Belgium	10,248,000	King Albert II; Prime Minister Guy Verhofstadt	franc (37.76 = $1)	185,409	172,244 (includes Luxembourg)
Bosnia-Herzegovina	4,330,000	Chairman of the collective presidency Zivko Radisic	marka (1.83 = $1)	152	1,100
Bulgaria	8,756,000	President Petar Stoyanov; Prime Minister Ivan Kostov	lev (1.82 = $1)	4,449	4,512
Croatia	4,433,000	President Franjo Tudjman*	kuna (7.15 = $1)	4,546	8,384
Czech Republic	10,346,000	President Vaclav Havel; Prime Minister Milos Zeman	koruna (34.31 = $1)	26,416	28,917
Denmark	5,207,000	Queen Margrethe II; Prime Minister Poul Nyrup Rasmussen	krone (6.96 = $1)	46,532	44,738
Estonia	1,495,000	President Lennart Meri; Prime Minister Mart Laar	kroon (14.65 = $1)	3,129	4,611
Finland	5,201,000	President Martti Ahtisaari; Prime Minister Paavo Lipponen	markka (5.57 = $1)	42,963	32,301
France	59,024,000	President Jacques Chirac; Prime Minister Lionel Jospin	franc (6.14 = $1)	305,470	286,794
Germany	81,700,000	President Johannes Rau; Chancellor Gerhard Schroeder	mark (1.84 = $1)	540,588	467,344
Greece	10,573,000	President Konstandinos Stephanopoulos; Prime Minister Konstandinos Simitis	drachma (307.28 = $1)	8,656	27,718
Hungary	9,940,000	President Arpad Goncz; Prime Minister Viktor Orban	forint (240.52 = $1)	18,613	20,652
Iceland	282,000	President Olafur Grimsson; Prime Minister David Oddsson	krona (71.11 = $1)	2,050	2,489
Ireland	3,689,000	President Mary McAleese; Prime Minister Bertie Ahern	pound (punt) (0.74 = $1)	64,331	44,222
Italy	57,254,000	President Carlo Azeglio Ciampi; Prime Minister Massimo D'Alema	lira (1,812.56 = $1)	242,554	215,793 (includes San Marino)
Latvia	2,471,000	President Vaira Vike-Freiberga; Prime Minister Andris Skele	lat (0.58 = $1)	1,811	3,191
Liechtenstein	33,000	Prince Hans Adam II; Prime Minister Mario Frick	Swiss franc	2,470	917

*Died Dec. 10, 1999

European Union crisis. The EU was shaken in 1999 by allegations of corruption at its executive agency, the European Commission. The European Parliament ordered an investigation of the agency after a commission auditor complained of fraud, mismanagement, and *nepotism* (showing favor to relatives or friends by those in power). The investigators' report strongly criticized the commission and its president, Jacques Santer, for allowing nepotism and failing to oversee EU spending programs properly. All 20 members of the commission resigned on March 16. The clash strengthened the role of the European Parliament in EU affairs and led national governments to demand more openness and accountability in the commission, an unelected body with broad powers over EU policy.

On March 24, EU leaders appointed Romano Prodi, the former Italian prime minister, to succeed Santer. Prodi and a new team of commissioners took office on September 15. In December, the commission unveiled plans for reforms that included organizational restructuring, merit reviews, and improved financial management.

Country	Population	Government	Monetary unit*	Foreign trade (million U.S.$) Exports[†]	Imports[†]
Lithuania	3,692,000	President Valdas Adamkus; Prime Minister Andrius Kubilius	litas (4.00 = $1)	3,711	5,794
Luxembourg	425,000	Grand Duke Jean; Prime Minister Jean-Claude Juncker	franc (37.76 = $1)	185,409 (includes Belgium)	172,244
Macedonia	2,247,000	President Boris Trajkovski	denar (56.49 = $1)	1,147	1,627
Malta	377,000	President Guido De Marco; Prime Minister Eddie Fenech Adami	lira (0.40 = $1)	1,820	2,685
Moldova	4,510,000	President Petru Lucinschi; Prime Minister Dumitru Braghis	leu (8.32 = $1)	650	1,081
Monaco	34,000	Prince Rainier III	French franc	no statistics available	
Netherlands	15,995,000	Queen Beatrix; Prime Minister Wim Kok	guilder (2.06 = $1)	198,514	184,428
Norway	4,427,000	King Harald V; Prime Minister Kjell Magne Bondevik	krone (7.79 = $1)	39,649	36,196
Poland	38,786,000	President Aleksander Kwasniewski; Prime Minister Jerzy Buzek	zloty (4.09 = $1)	25,751	42,308
Portugal	9,807,000	President Jorge Sampaio; Prime Minister Antonio Guterres	escudo (187.67 = $1)	24,218	37,046
Romania	22,607,000	President Emil Constantinescu; Prime Minister Mugur Isarescu	leu (16,632.00 = $1)	8,300	11,821
Russia	145,552,000	Acting President Vladimir Putin	ruble (25.82 = $1)	71,800	58,500
San Marino	27,000	2 captains regent appointed by Grand Council every 6 months	Italian lira	242,554 (includes Italy)	215,793
Slovakia	5,468,000	President Rudolf Schuster; Prime Minister Mikulas Dzurinda	koruna (40.69 = $1)	10,667	12,956
Slovenia	1,945,000	President Milan Kucan; Prime Minister Janez Drnovsek	tolar (184.09 = $1)	9,048	10,098
Spain	39,848,000	King Juan Carlos I; President of the Government (Prime Minister) Jose Maria Aznar	peseta (155.76 = $1)	109,240	133,164
Sweden	8,972,000	King Carl XVI Gustaf; Prime Minister Goran Persson	krona (8.16 = $1)	84,739	68,420
Switzerland	7,494,000	President Ruth Dreifuss	franc (1.49 = $1)	75,439	73,885
Turkey	67,748,000	President Suleyman Demirel; Prime Minister Bulent Ecevit	lira (466,085.00 = $1)	25,938	45,369
Ukraine	50,974,000	President Leonid Kuchma	hryvna (4.52 = $1)	11,300	13,100
United Kingdom	59,032,000	Queen Elizabeth II; Prime Minister Tony Blair	pound (0.61 = $1)	271,853	314,036
Yugoslavia	10,696,000	President Slobodan Milosevic; Prime Minister Momir Bulatovic	new dinar (10.95 = $1)	2,604	4,622

*Exchange rates as of Oct. 8, 1999, or latest available data.   †Latest available data.

Control of the parliament shifted from the political left to the right as the European People's Party (EPP), which consists of mainly Christian Democratic parties in the EU, defeated the Socialist bloc in elections held in June. The EPP won 233 seats in the 626-seat parliament, up from 201 seats in the last election in 1995. The Socialists came in second with 180 seats, down from 214. The result was considered a protest vote against center-left parties that controlled most national governments, particularly in Germany and Great Britain, rather than a demand for policy changes.

EU enlargement. At the March 1999 meeting, EU leaders agreed to a budget plan designed to finance the entry of new members from Eastern Europe. The plan, which set spending targets for the years 2000 to 2006, imposed a limit on EU farm subsidies in order to free up money to finance enlargement. The plan sought to ensure that the six countries that began membership negotiations in late 1998—Poland, Hungary, the Czech Republic, Slovenia, Estonia, and Cyprus—could join the EU by 2006. In December 1999, EU leaders agreed to begin membership negotia-

TIME CAPSULE 1944

EUROPE

BATTLE OF THE BULGE. The speed and success with which the Allies had liberated France, taking more than 700,000 German prisoners, created an unjustified optimism as to the early end of the war with Germany. This optimism received a rude shock on December 16 when [German General Carl Gerd] Von Rundstedt made a powerful surprise thrust through the Allied line into the Ardennes in southern Belgium and northern Luxemburg. He had gathered an unexpectedly large number of first-class divisions, superior in quality to the middle-aged Nazi troops in France, where many of the German prisoners turned out to be not Germans but satellite troops and captives whom the Nazis had forced to fight in their ranks.

Von Rundstedt's armored divisions slashed 40 miles westward until they were stopped within a few miles of the Meuse by American and British troops rushed to the spot. His break-through created a dangerous bulge in the Allied line and compelled [U.S. General George] Patton to pull back his forces from the Saar front. Field Marshal Bernard L. Montgomery, at once put in command of all the Allied forces north of the Belgian Bulge, then began to press upon the northern German flank.

Meanwhile an American garrison in Bastogne on the southern German flank held out with great heroism, until joined by some of Patton's Third Army. This Bastogne wedge into the German line threatened to pinch off Von Rundstedt's advanced columns from their line of communications. Within two weeks Von Rundstedt, pressed on both flanks, began to withdraw his advanced spearhead.

On December 31, 1944, the Allied front ran from the mouth of the Rhine eastward to the bridge near Arnhem, then southward between Aachen and Duren to the Belgian Bulge.

tions with six more countries—Slovakia, Bulgaria, Romania, Latvia, Lithuania, and Malta—and acknowledged Turkey as a potential member.

Europe's economy slowed early in 1999 because of weakness in global markets caused by Russia's debt default in August 1998. Growth picked up later in 1999 but was uneven. The economies of Germany and Italy remained relatively sluggish while smaller economies, such as those of Spain and the Netherlands, prospered. The European Commission forecast that growth across the 15-nation EU would average 2.1 percent in 1999, down from 2.9 percent in 1998. Unemployment was expected to fall to 9.2 percent in 1999 from 9.9 percent a year earlier.

Euro launched. The slower growth posed a challenge for the single European currency, the euro, launched on January 1. Many investment advisers had predicted that strong demand for a new currency and high expectations for Europe's economy would drive the value of the euro high in 1999. But after rising strongly against the dollar on its opening day of trading to $1.18, the euro declined steadily during much of the year. Its value stood at $1.02 by early December.

The European Central Bank, which opened in 1998 to manage the single currency, did little to stop the currency's decline. Instead the bank focused on the outlook for growth and inflation in the 11 countries that adopted the euro. In April 1999, the central bank cut its key short-term interest rate by one-half percentage point to 2.5 percent, a record low in Europe, in an attempt to stimulate the economy. After growth began to accelerate again, the central bank raised rates to 3 percent in November.

Merger activity. European companies continued to engage in an unprecedented spree of mergers and takeovers in 1999 in order to gain the size needed to compete with global rivals and take advantage of the new possibilities for European business created by the euro. European companies were involved in mergers worth a total of more than $1.2 trillion during 1999, double the total for 1998. There was also a rise in so-called hostile takeovers in 1999, where companies are acquired by others against the will of management rather than through agreed deals.

There were a number of mergers among European telecommunications firms, particularly in the area of mobile telephones, where European usage exceeded that of the United States and Asia. In November, Vodafone AirTouch PIC, a British mobile telephone company, made an offer of $147 billion in stock and assumed debt to buy Mannesmann AG, a German company with the largest mobile-phone business in continental Europe. The deal was the largest takeover offer ever made in Europe, but the management of Mannesmann rejected it as too low. The company's unions also opposed it. The contest turned political when German Chancellor Gerhard Schroeder declared that hostile takeovers posed a threat to Germany's corporate tradition of consensus between management and workers. Mannesmann shareholders were to decide on the bid in early 2000.

Olivetti SpA acquired Italy's national telephone company, Telecom Italia, in May 1999 in a debt-financed transaction that imitated tactics used in the United States in the 1980's. France also experienced hostile takeover battles, including a bank struggle that the government tried but failed to mediate. Banque Nationale de Paris S.A., the country's biggest bank, acquired Paribas S.A. in August 1999 for $19 billion but failed to win its main target, Societe Generale S.A., France's second-largest bank. In September, Total Fina S.A. agreed to acquire Elf Aquitaine S.A. for $48 billion, creating the world's fourth-largest oil company.

Efforts to form an all-European stock exchange floundered in 1999. The London and Frankfurt stock exchanges, which formed an alliance in 1998, invited six other exchanges—Paris, Amsterdam, Brussels, Milan, Madrid, and Zurich—to develop a common trading system. However, the alliance could not agree on whose technology it would use to handle the trades. In November 1999, the U.S.-based Nasdaq exchange announced a rival plan to set up a computerized exchange in Europe to focus on new high-technology companies. The Frankfurt exchange announced in December that it would move ahead with its own plans to launch an all-European trading system.

EU-U.S. trade. The United States won two long-running trade disputes with the EU in 1999. In April, the Geneva-based World Trade Organization (WTO) ruled that EU quotas on banana imports discriminated against fruit grown by U.S. companies in Central America. The WTO authorized the United States to impose tariffs on $191 million worth of imports from the EU as compensation. In July, the WTO authorized the United States to impose similar tariffs on $117 million worth of imports from the EU in retaliation for Europe's refusal to buy American beef from cattle treated with growth hormones.

Storms. Two storms with hurricane-force winds of 100 miles (161 kilometers) per hour barreled across France and parts of Belgium, Switzerland, and Germany on December 26 and 28, killing more than 100 people. □ Tom Buerkle

See also **International trade;** and the various European country articles.

A parade in Paris on the first business day of the year, Jan. 4, 1999, celebrates the launch on January 1 of the euro, the European Union's new currency. The value of the euro declined against the U.S. dollar and Japanese yen through much of 1999.

Fashion. The fashion industry's primary concern in 1999 was on mergers and acquisitions, rather than traditional style elements, such as hem lengths and colors. As recently as the 1980's, most fashion firms were relatively small and flexible enough to quickly capitalize on the newest fashion trends. In the 1990's, however, fashion firms increasingly became big corporate enterprises, strong enough to make their mark on the global market.

The French conglomerate LVMH Moet Hennessey-Louis Vuitton, the world's largest luxury products group, triggered the biggest merger story in fashion in 1999 when it attempted to take over Gucci Group, the spectacularly successful Italian design company. LVMH, headed by Bernard Arnault, already controlled the fashion houses of Givenchy, Christian Lacroix, and Kenzo. Gucci managed to fend off Arnault's bid, selling out instead to the French company Pinault-Printemps-Redoute, which promised Gucci more independence.

The acquisitions movement refused to be squelched, however. In the United States, apparel-maker Kasper of New Jersey bought New York City-based Anne Klein Company, one of the leaders in the sportswear industry. Cosmetics giant Estee Lauder of New York swept up Stila, a small but rapidly growing California-based cosmetics business.

Sportswear rules. Sportswear, or casual dress, remained the dominant fashion trend everywhere in 1999. Some sportswear designers promoted dressier looks, but they enjoyed only modest success. Fitted shirts, made with stretch yarns that held them close to the body, won a certain acceptance. Women often wore fitted shirts as a jacket over T-shirts or tank tops, giving the shirts more formality, while jeans sprouted embroidery and other decorative details.

Accessories. Although women retained their fondness for casual, comfortable clothes, they took to colorful accessories, such as brightly colored handbags, glittering hair ornaments, and

By the end of the century, the formality of the business suit—a uniform that had changed little through much of the 1900's—appeared to be coming to an end in offices across the United States, a victim of the comfort and economy of "business casual" clothing.

some jewelry, including bracelets and arm bands.

The pashmina shawl, made from the finest quality cashmere, in bright pastel shades, became a big success in 1999. Women wore the shawl over casual clothes as well as evening clothes. Prices of the shawls usually topped three figures, but as a touch of luxury on otherwise practical clothes, they won widespread acceptance.

Evening wear. Despite sportswear's unshakable hold on the fashion business, many designers, inspired by the expected profusion of turn-of-the-millennium parties, increased their collections of evening wear. The dresses were slithery, came in all lengths, and were made from fanciful fabrics. They were decorated with beads, embroidery, and appliques.

Decline of the supermodel. The waning of the supermodel became a most significant fashion trend in 1999. Some models, like Naomi Campbell and Kate Moss, still appeared on fashion runways, where they were almost guaranteed a place in newspaper and TV reports.

Hollywood stars, such as Gwyneth Paltrow and Nicole Kidman, took the place of supermodels as fashion icons. Driven by the interest in celebrities, general interest magazines as well as fashion magazines prominently featured the clothes these actresses wore at the Academy Awards ceremony and other gala events.

Hot trends. With the world's economy on the upswing, certain pockets of fashion showed growth. Swimsuit sales were up, based on the variety of styles offered. Bikinis dominated, but they were not exclusively the tiny, three-handkerchief variety. Some offered more coverage. The tankini, with its covered top and bikini bottom, was also popular in 1999.

Attractive underwear was in demand, including body-slimming styles and lounge or sleep designs. Sweaters, ranging from heavy, bulky styles to snugly fitted twin sets, were seen everywhere. And the new prominence of women's soccer and basketball may point to sports clothing that is not just casual but athletically oriented as well.

☐ Bernadine Morris

Finland played an active role in international affairs in 1999. The government held the presidency of the 15-nation European Union (EU) for a six-month term, from July through December, for the first time since it joined the economic and political bloc in 1995. The government focused on developing closer economic and political relations between the EU and Russia, which it believed would strengthen the hand of democratic, market-oriented politicians in Russia.

Finland also sought to improve cooperation between EU countries on foreign policy and defense matters. Although the EU was formed primarily as an economic trading bloc, governments sought to increase defense cooperation because of frustration at their inability to stop the recurring conflicts in the former Yugoslavia during the 1990's. At a summit meeting in Helsinki in December 1999, EU leaders agreed to form a rapid-reaction force of 50,000 troops by 2003. The force would intervene in European conflicts.

Finland stirred controversy during its presidency when it decided to use only the English, French, and Finnish languages at informal working meetings, pointing out that the size and cost of interpreting services had mushroomed as the EU admitted more countries. The 11 languages of the EU nations continued to be used during formal meetings. Germany and Austria boycotted several meetings to protest the decision, claiming that Finland was breaking precedent. Other countries supported Finland's move.

Diplomacy. Finns took pride in the role Finland's president, Martti Ahtisaari, played in negotiations to resolve the conflict over the Serbian province of Kosovo in 1999. Ahtisaari, a career diplomat before becoming president in 1994, became involved in the negotiations at the request of the United States and Russia. In the Yugoslav capital, Belgrade, on June 3, 1999, Ahtisaari presented Western demands for the withdrawal of Serbian troops from Kosovo and obtained the agreement of Yugoslav President Slobodan Milosevic, which brought an end to the conflict.

The economy continued to grow in 1999, driven largely by the success of such high-technology industries as mobile telephones. Finland boasted the world's highest percentage of owners of mobile telephones and use of the Internet, with more than half of the population using both. Finland's *gross domestic product* (the value of all goods and services produced in a country in a given year) was expected to increase by 3.9 percent in 1999, down from 5.6 percent in 1998 but still well above the EU average. Unemployment was projected to decline to 10.4 percent from 11.4 percent in 1998. ☐ Tom Buerkle

See also **Europe; Yugoslavia: A Special Report.**

Food safety continued to be a concern in the United States in 1999. In September, the U.S. Centers for Disease Control and Prevention (CDC) in Atlanta, Georgia, released a report that estimated that 76 million cases of food poisoning occur each year in the United States. This figure was more than twice as high as previous estimates. The CDC reminded the public that many cases of food-borne illness can be prevented by thorough cooking of meat, frequent washing of hands and cutting boards, and prompt refrigeration of perishable items.

Listeriosis, a food-borne illness caused by the bacterium *Listeria monocytogenes,* broke out in the United States in August 1998. The outbreak, which spread through 22 states and lasted into March 1999, was linked to more than 100 cases of food poisoning, including at least 15 adult deaths and 6 miscarriages.

Investigators traced many of the incidents to sliced chicken breast and hot dogs that had been processed at a plant in Zeeland, Michigan, owned by Sara Lee Corporation of Chicago. The plant voluntarily closed in December 1998. Jane E. Henney, commissioner of the U.S. Food and Drug Administration (FDA), said in July 1999 that prevention of future listeriosis outbreaks depended largely upon increased anticontamination efforts in the processed-food industry.

Salmonella. The rate of contamination of meat and poultry products with *Salmonella* bacteria is declining, according to an October report by the Food Safety and Inspection Service (FSIS), a division of the U.S. Department of Agriculture, in Washington, D.C. Officials credited the reductions partly to the implementation in January 1998 of the Hazard Analysis and Critical Control Point (HACCP) inspection system. This system requires meat and poultry processors to focus their efforts on potential trouble points in order to head off *Salmonella* contamination.

The FSIS data came from the sampling of broiler carcasses, swine, ground beef, and ground turkey at 200 large plants. The data showed large decreases in the rate of *Salmonella* prevalence in all four food items since the HACCP system went into effect.

Eggs. In July 1999, the FDA and FSIS proposed new measures to reduce illnesses and deaths associated with *Salmonella enteritidis* in eggs. Food scientists noted that 2.3 million eggs are contaminated each year with *S. enteritidis*, which causes abdominal pain, diarrhea, vomiting, and in some cases, death. The FDA estimated that the measures would prevent as many as 66,000 illnesses and 40 deaths per year.

The regulations required that eggs be kept at a temperature no greater than 45 °F (7 °C) when being transported, stored in warehouses, or sold in retail establishments. The regulations also required that egg cartons be labeled with safe-handling instructions.

Company mergers. An explosion of merger-related activity, involving both retail and wholesale grocery companies, continued in 1999. As a result, some of the industry's largest companies gained even more market power. In May, Kroger Company, Inc., of Cincinnati, Ohio—the largest grocery chain in the United States—purchased Fred Meyer Stores, Inc., of Portland, Oregon. In June, Albertson's, Inc., of Boise, Idaho—the second-largest grocer in the United States—purchased American Stores Company, Inc., of Salt Lake City, Utah. The number-three U.S. grocery chain—Safeway, Inc., of Pleasanton, California—took over Carr-Gottstein Foods Company of Anchorage, Alaska, in April, and Randall's Food Markets, Inc., of Houston in September.

Future leader? While some grocery chains grew in 1999 through consolidation, food-industry observers noted that the supermarket division of Wal-Mart Stores, Inc., based in Bentonville, Arkansas, grew in market importance by adding new locations. Observers expected that Wal-Mart, which was building as many as 150 new stores each year in the late 1990's, would become the grocery industry's volume leader by 2002.

☐ Bob Gatty

Football. Computers continued to influence college football in 1999 and had a surprisingly good effect on a season in which no genuinely great team stood out. Professional football was brightened in January by the Denver Broncos' second consecutive Super Bowl victory, then enlivened later in the year when teams that had rarely come close to a championship suddenly turned into Super Bowl contenders.

College. The National Collegiate Athletic Association (NCAA) adopted the Bowl Championship Series (BCS) in 1998 to determine a football national champion. The BCS uses data from several computer ranking services, two national media and coaches' polls, strength-of-schedule factors, and other variables to decide which teams will play for the national championship. In the BCS's first match-up, the University of Tennessee defeated Florida State University, 23-16, at the Fiesta Bowl in Tempe, Arizona, on Jan. 4, 1999.

Fans who favored a postseason play-off series complained that the BCS system was too complicated. However, the system delivered a great title match-up in 1999 between top-ranked Florida State University and second-ranked Virginia Tech University. Each team had a record of 11-0 and were the only unbeaten teams in the six major conferences. The teams were scheduled to play for the national title in the Sugar Bowl on Jan. 4, 2000, in New Orleans, Louisiana.

Virginia Tech had been outranked through most of the season by Pennsylvania State University and the University of Nebraska. But Penn State, unbeaten and ranked second on Nov. 1, 1999, closed out its schedule by losing three straight games, to finish with a 9-3 record. It was the first time since 1914 that Penn State ended a season with three consecutive losses. Unbeaten Nebraska fell out of contention on October 23, in a 24-20 loss to the University of Texas, and failed to improve its position later in the season despite winning its next five games to finish 11-1.

Notre Dame University lost three of its first four games and closed with four straight losses to end up with a 5-7 record, its first seven-loss season since 1963. Ohio State University and the University of Arizona also disappointed their fans in 1999. Ohio State failed to qualify for a bowl game for the first time in 11 seasons after finishing a mediocre 6-6. Arizona, a nearly unanimous choice as a top-five team in the preseason polls, also finished 6-6 and stayed home during bowl season.

Bonfire collapse tragedy. Eleven Texas A&M University students and one graduate died and 28 others were injured when a 55-foot (17-meter) log pile collapsed on November 18. The accident occurred as students were stacking hundreds of large logs for a traditional pep-rally bonfire. A flaw in the construction led to the collapse. The

Running back Ron Dayne of the University of Wisconsin poses with the 1999 Heisman Trophy on December 13. Dayne rushed for 6,397 yards, a new collegiate record.

National champions

NCAA Div. I-A*	Florida State	46	Virginia Tech	29
NCAA Div. I-AA	Georgia Southern	59	Youngstown State	24
NCAA Div. II	NW Missouri State	58	Carson-Newman	52
NCAA Div. III	Pacific Lutheran	42	Rowan	13
NAIA	NW Oklahoma State	34	Georgetown (Ky.)	26

Bowl games

Bowl	Result			
Alamo	Penn State	24	Texas A&M	0
Aloha	Wake Forest	23	Arizona State	3
Citrus	Michigan State	37	Florida	34
Cotton	Arkansas	27	Texas	6
Fiesta	Nebraska	31	Tennessee	21
Gator	Miami	28	Georgia Tech	13
Holiday	Kansas State	24	Washington	20
Humanitarian	Boise State	34	Louisville	31
Independence	Mississippi	27	Oklahoma	25
Insight.com	Colorado	62	Boston College	28
Las Vegas	Utah	17	Fresno State	16
Liberty	Southern Mississippi	23	Colorado State	17
MicronPC.com	Illinois	63	Virginia	21
Mobile Alabama	Texas Christian	28	East Carolina	14
Motor City	Marshall	21	Brigham Young	3
Music City	Syracuse	20	Kentucky	13
Oahu	Hawaii	23	Oregon State	17
Orange	Michigan	35	Alabama	34
Outback	Georgia	28	Purdue	25
Peach	Mississippi State	17	Clemson	7
Rose	Wisconsin	17	Stanford	9
Sugar*	Florida State	46	Virginia Tech	29
Sun	Oregon	24	Minnesota	20

* Championship decided in the Sugar Bowl on Jan. 4, 2000.

Conference Champions
NCAA Division I-A

Conference	School
Atlantic Coast	Florida State
Big East	Virginia Tech
Big 10	Wisconsin
Big 12	Nebraska
Big West	Boise State
Conference USA	Southern Mississippi
Mid-American	Marshall
Mountain West	Utah—Colorado State—Brigham Young (tie)
Pacific 10	Stanford
Southeastern	Alabama
Western Athletic	Texas Christian—Fresno State—Hawaii (tie)
Independents	Louisiana Tech

NCAA Division I-AA

Conference	School
Atlantic 10	James Madison—Massachusetts (tie)
Big Sky	Montana
Gateway	Illinois State
Ivy League	Brown—Yale (tie)
Metro Atlantic	Duquesne
Mid-Eastern	North Carolina A&T
Northeast	Robert Morris
Ohio Valley	Tennessee State
Patriot	Colgate—Lehigh (tie)
Pioneer	Dayton
Southern	Georgia Southern—Appalachian State—Furman (tie)
Southland	Troy State—Stephen F. Austin (tie)
Southwestern	Southern

All-America team (as picked by AP)

Offense
Quarterback—Joe Hamilton, Georgia Tech
Running backs—Ron Dayne, Wisconsin; Thomas Jones, Virginia
Wide receivers—Peter Warrick, Florida State; Troy Walters, Stanford
Tight end—James Whalen, Kentucky
Center—Ben Hamilton, Minnesota
Other linemen—Jason Whitaker, Florida State; Chris Samuels, Alabama; Chris McIntosh, Wisconsin; Cosey Coleman, Tennessee
All-purpose player—Dennis Northcutt, Arizona
Place-kicker—Sebastian Janikowski, Florida State

Defense
Linemen—Corey Simon, Florida State; Courtney Brown, Penn State; Corey Moore, Virginia Tech; Casey Hampton, Texas
Linebackers—LaVar Arrington, Penn State; Mark Simoneau, Kansas State; Raynoch Thompson, Tennessee; Brandon Short, Penn State
Backs—Deltha O'Neal; California; Mike Brown, Nebraska; Tyrone Carter, Minnesota; Brian Urlacher, New Mexico
Punter—Shane Lechler, Texas A&M

Player awards
Heisman Trophy (best player)—Ron Dayne, Wisconsin
Bronko Nagurski Trophy (best defensive player)—Corey Moore, Virginia Tech
Lombardi Award (best lineman)—Corey Moore, Virginia Tech

---

pep rally was to have preceded the 106th game between Texas A&M and the University of Texas. The November 26 game, which produced both boisterous cheering and solemn silence, was a thriller that A&M won, 20-16, in the final seconds.

Records and achievements. On October 16, Mount Union College beat Otterbein College, 44-20, for its 48th consecutive victory, breaking the former collegiate record set by the University of Oklahoma in 1957. Mount Union's winning streak ended at 54 when it lost, 24-17, to Rowan College on December 11.

On December 11, Ron Dayne of the University of Wisconsin won the Heisman Trophy in a landslide. The Badgers running back received 2,042 votes to 994 for Georgia Tech University quarterback Joe Hamilton, the runner-up. Dayne broke the major college career rushing record set in 1998 by Ricky Williams of Texas, improving the record to 6,397 yards.

Professional. The 1998-1999 National Football League (NFL) season ended in triumph for John Elway, who finished his 16th and final season as quarterback of the the Denver Broncos by being named the Most Valuable Player of Super Bowl XXXIII. Elway retired the following April. In contrast to 1998, when the Broncos made the play-offs as a wild-card entry and competed as an underdog in every contest that followed, the

National Football League final standings

American Conference

Eastern Division

	W.	L.	T.	Pct.
Indianapolis Colts*	13	3	0	.813
Buffalo Bills*	11	5	0	.688
Miami Dolphins*	9	7	0	.563
New England Patriots	8	8	0	.500
New York Jets	8	8	0	.500

Central Division

	W.	L.	T.	Pct.
Jacksonville*	14	2	0	.875
Tennessee*	13	3	0	.813
Baltimore	8	8	0	.500
Pittsburgh	6	10	0	.375
Cincinnati	4	12	0	.250
Cleveland	2	14	0	.125

Western Division

	W.	L.	T.	Pct.
Seattle*	9	7	0	.563
Kansas City	9	7	0	.563
San Diego	8	8	0	.500
Oakland	8	8	0	.500
Denver	6	10	0	.375

*Made play-offs

National Conference

Eastern Division

	W.	L.	T.	Pct.
Washington Redskins*	10	6	0	.625
Dallas Cowboys*	8	8	0	.500
New York Giants	7	9	0	.438
Arizona Cardinals	6	10	0	.375
Philadelphia Eagles	5	11	0	.313

Central Division

	W.	L.	T.	Pct.
Tampa Bay Buccaneers*	11	5	0	.688
Minnesota Vikings*	10	6	0	.625
Detroit Lions*	8	8	0	.500
Green Bay Packers	8	8	0	.500
Chicago Bears	6	10	0	.375

Western Division

	W.	L.	T.	Pct.
St. Louis Rams*	13	3	0	.813
Carolina Panthers	8	8	0	.500
Atlanta Falcons	5	11	0	.313
San Francisco 49ers	4	12	0	.250
New Orleans Saints	3	13	0	.188

*Made play-offs

Team statistics

Leading offenses (yards gained)

	Total	Per game
Indianapolis	5,726	357.9
Oakland	5,693	355.8
Jacksonville	5,586	349.1
Buffalo	5,333	333.3
Kansas City	5,321	332.6

Leading defenses (yards allowed)

	Total	Per game
Buffalo	4,045	252.8
Baltimore	4,222	263.9
Jacksonville	4,334	270.9
Miami	4,044	275.3
Denver	4,753	297.1

Team statistics

Leading offenses (yards gained)

	Total	Per game
St. Louis	5,972	398.1
Washington	5,695	379.7
Minnesota	5,414	360.9
Carolina	5,331	355.4
Chicago	5,226	351.1

Leading defenses (yards allowed)

	Total	Per game
Tampa Bay	4,023	268.2
Dallas	4,460	297.3
St. Louis	4,491	299.4
New York Giants	4,544	302.9
Atlanta	4,717	314.5

Individual statistics

Leading scorers, touchdowns

	TD's	Rush	Rec.	Ret.	Pts.
Edgerrin James, Indianapolis	17	13	4	0	102
Eddie George, Tennessee	13	9	4	0	78
James Stewart, Jacksonville	13	13	0	0	78
Marvin Harrison, Indianapolis	12	0	12	0	74

Leading scorers, kicking

	PAT att./made	FG att./made	Longest FG	Pts.
Mike Vanderjagt, Indianapolis	43/43	34/38	53	145
Olindo Mare, Miami	27/27	39/46	54	144
Todd Peterson, Seattle	32/32	34/40	51	134
Mike Hollis, Jacksonville	37/37	31/38	50	130

Leading quarterbacks

	Att.	Comp.	Yds.	TD's	Int.
Peyton Manning, Indianapolis	533	331	4,135	26	15
Rich Gannon, Oakland	515	304	3,840	24	14
Ray Lucas, N.Y. Jets	272	161	1,678	14	6
Mark Brunell, Jacksonville	441	259	3,060	14	9
Elvis Grbac, Kansas City	499	294	3,389	22	15

Leading receivers

	Passes caught	Rec. yards	Avg. gain	TD's
Jimmy Smith, Jacksonville	116	1,636	14.1	6
Marvin Harrison, Indianapolis	115	1,663	14.5	12
Tim Brown, Oakland	90	1,344	14.9	6
Keyshawn Johnson, N.Y. Jets	89	1,170	13.1	8

Leading rushers

	Rushes	Yards	Avg.	TD's
Edgerrin James, Indianapolis	369	1,553	4.2	13
Curtis Martin, N.Y. Jets	367	1,464	4.0	5
Eddie George, Tennessee	320	1,304	4.1	9
Ricky Watters, Seattle	325	1,210	3.7	5
Corey Dillon, Cincinnati	263	1,200	4.6	5

Leading punters

	Punts	Yards	Avg.	Longest
Tom Rouen, Denver	84	3,908	46.5	65
Josh Miller, Pittsburgh	84	3,795	45.2	75
Tom Tupa, N.Y. Jets	81	3,659	45.2	69
Darren Bennett, San Diego	89	3,910	43.9	60

Individual statistics

Leading scorers, touchdowns

	TD's	Rush	Rec.	Ret.	Pts.
Stephen Davis, Washington	17	17	0	0	104
Cris Carter, Minnesota	13	0	13	0	78
Emmit Smith, Dallas	13	11	2	0	78
Isaac Bruce, St. Louis	12	0	12	0	74

Leading scorers, kicking

	PAT att./made	FG att./made	Longest FG	Pts.
Jeff Wilkins, St. Louis	64/64	20/28	51	124
Brett Conway, Washington	49/50	22/32	51	115
Ryan Longwell, Green Bay	38/38	25/30	50	113
Martin Gramatica, Tampa Bay	25/25	27/32	53	106

Leading quarterbacks

	Att.	Comp.	Yds.	TD's	Int.
Kurt Warner, St. Louis	499	325	4353	41	13
Steve Beuerlein, Carolina	571	343	4436	36	15
Jeff George, Minnesota	329	191	2816	23	12
Brad Johnson, Washington	519	316	4005	24	13
Charlie Batch, Detroit	270	151	1957	13	7

Leading receivers

	Passes caught	Rec. yards	Avg. gain	TD's
Muhsin Muhammad, Carolina	96	1,253	13.1	8
Cris Carter, Minnesota	90	1,241	13.8	13
Bobby Engram, Chicago	88	947	10.8	4
Marshall Faulk, St. Louis	87	1,048	12.0	5

Leading rushers

	Rushes	Yards	Avg.	TD's
Stephen Davis, Washington	290	1,405	4.8	17
Emmitt Smith, Dallas	329	1,397	4.2	11
Marshall Faulk, St. Louis	253	1,381	5.5	7
Duce Staley, Philadelphia	325	1,273	3.9	4
Charlie Garner, San Francisco	241	1,229	5.1	4

Leading punters

	Punts	Yards	Avg.	Longest
Mitch Berger, Minnesota	61	2,769	45.4	75
Toby Gowin, Dallas	81	3,500	43.2	64
Mark Royals, Tampa Bay	90	3,882	43.1	66
John Jett, Detroit	86	3,637	42.3	62

1999 Broncos lost only twice in 19 games.

In the American Football Conference (AFC) wild-card play-offs in the first weekend of January 1999, the Miami Dolphins beat the Buffalo Bills, 24-17, and the Jacksonville Jaguars bested the New England Patriots, 25-10. The next weekend, the New York Jets defeated Jacksonville, 34-24, to advance to the AFC title game for the first time in 30 years, and Denver routed Miami, 38-3. The Broncos won the AFC championship on January 23, beating the Jets, 23-10.

In the first round of the National Football Conference (NFC) play-offs, the Arizona Cardinals upset the Dallas Cowboys, 20-7, and the San Francisco 49ers nipped the Green Bay Packers, 30-27. The Minnesota Vikings, whose 15-1 record was the NFL's best, beat Arizona, 41-21, a week later while the Atlanta Falcons edged San Francisco, 20-18. The Falcons won the NFC title and reached their first Super Bowl with a 30-27 upset of the Vikings.

On January 31, the Broncos won the Super Bowl for the second straight season with a 34-19 rout of the Falcons. Elway completed 18 of 29 passes for 356 yards, throwing for one touchdown and running for another in what would be the final game of his Hall-of-Fame career.

Milestones. All-pro defensive end Reggie White retired on February 15, after 14 years in the NFL in which he set a league record for career sacks, with 192½. White began his professional career with the Philadelphia Eagles before joining the Green Bay Packers in 1993.

In March 1999, NFL owners voted to reinstate instant replay on a trial basis for the 1999-2000 season. The league had stopped using instant replay in 1992 because it slowed the pace of games. However, a number of controversial calls in previous seasons persuaded many owners to change their minds. The new system, however, was subject to far more restrictions than in the past.

The Cleveland Browns returned to the NFL in 1999, after a three-year absence, as an expansion team. This raised the number of NFL teams to 31, which created a scheduling problem that the league solved by assigning a week off to at least one team each week during the season.

The 1999-2000 season. Injuries to crucial players and the surprising success of emerging stars created an extraordinary power shift in the NFL, soon after the season started. The once-lowly St. Louis Rams led the league in scoring, thanks to the stellar play of new quarterback Kurt Warner, a former Arena Football League player. Similarly, the Indianapolis Colts won their division on the performances of second-year quarterback Peyton Manning, wide receiver Marvin Harrison, and rookie running back Edgerrin James.

Denver and Atlanta hardly resembled the teams that had played in the Super Bowl just sev-

en months earlier. The Broncos offense collapsed when injuries took Terrell Davis, the NFL's rushing leader of 1998, and tight end Shannon Sharpe out of the lineup that no longer included Elway. Atlanta lost Jamal Anderson, the key element in its rushing attack. The Jets, an expected Super Bowl contender, saw their hopes fade when quarterback Vinny Testaverde suffered a season-ending injury in the season's opening game.

The Detroit Lions became a surprise play-off contender despite losing running back Barry Sanders, who unexpectedly announced his retirement, after 10 seasons, on July 28, 1999. Sanders needed only 1,458 yards to surpass Walter Payton to become the NFL's all-time rushing leader.

Other leagues. The Hamilton Tiger-Cats won the 87th Canadian Football League (CFL) Grey Cup championship with a 32-21 victory over the Calgary Stampeders on November 28, in Vancouver, British Columbia. Hamilton quarterback Danny McManus completed 22 of 34 passes for 347 yards and 2 touchdowns and was named the game's Most Valuable Player.

NFL Europe's season ran from April to June 1999. The Frankfurt Galaxy became the first team to win two NFL Europe championships by beating the Barcelona Dragons, 38-24, in the World Bowl on June 27 in Dusseldorf, Germany. ☐ Ron Reid

See also **Deaths.**

France endured a year of political turmoil and scandal in 1999 that tarnished several of the country's major parties. The worst incident occurred in November when Finance Minister Dominique Strauss-Kahn was forced to resign because of allegations of fraud. Magistrates investigated charges that a health insurance fund closely related to the governing Socialist Party had paid Strauss-Kahn $96,000 for fictitious legal work in the mid-1990's. Strauss-Kahn resigned on Nov. 2, 1999, to defend himself. Christian Sautter, the budget minister, replaced Strauss-Kahn as finance minister.

The resignation was a severe blow to the Socialist government of Prime Minister Lionel Jospin. The incident damaged the government's reputation for integrity and removed one of Jospin's most important ministers. Strauss-Kahn had played a key role in reducing government intervention in industry and the economy, policies that helped to reassure the business community and promote economic growth.

The Socialist Party's main political rival, President Jacques Chirac's Rally for the Republic Party, was also tainted by allegations of corruption in 1999. A special prosecutor investigating charges that the party took kickbacks from contractors in the early 1990's placed Paris Mayor Jean Tiberi under investigation in June. Tiberi, who denied the accusations, was a close associate of Chirac.

Tainted blood. Former Prime Minister Laurent Fabius was acquitted of charges in March 1999 over the deaths of hundreds of people who contracted AIDS from tainted blood transfusions in the 1980's. The jury acquitted Fabius and another former minister of having knowingly delayed the testing of blood for the AIDS virus for commercial reasons. However, the jury found a former health minister guilty of negligence for failing to destroy untreated blood when the risk of contamination became known.

Party splits. Chirac's party suffered from a serious rift among its leaders in 1999. Charles Pasqua, a former interior minister, had left Chirac's Rally for the Republic Party in December 1998. Pasqua formed a nationalist party that campaigned against greater French involvement in the 15-nation European Union (EU) in elections for the EU parliament in June 1999. Pasqua's party, the Rally for France, came in second place behind the Socialists, winning 13 percent of the vote, compared with 12.8 percent for Chirac's Rally for the Republic.

The far-right National Front Party was also split in 1999 by a disagreement between founder Jean-Marie Le Pen, and his deputy, Bruno Megret. Megret wanted to moderate the National Front's image to appeal to more voters. The National Front, which campaigned primarily against immigrants, won 5.7 percent of the vote in the June election, well below the 15 percent Le Pen polled in the 1995 presidential election. Megret's new National Movement won 3.3 percent.

Economy. France enjoyed another year of solid economic growth in 1999. The economy was helped by the low interest rate policies of the European Central Bank, which managed the single currency adopted by France and 10 other EU countries in 1999, as well as by strong demand from French consumers. France's *gross domestic product* (the value of all goods and services produced in a country in a given year) was expected to increase by 2.5 percent in 1999. Unemployment declined for the second consecutive year to around 11.1 percent from 11.7 in 1998.

Corporate takeovers. France experienced a surge of corporate takeovers in 1999 as French companies sought to position themselves as key players in European and global markets. The most dramatic incident involved a battle for supremacy between three of the country's leading banks. In February, Societe Generale S.A., France's second-largest bank, offered to acquire Paribas S.A. for $18 billion. Banque Nationale de Paris S.A. (BNP), which feared the proposed merger would threaten its position as France's largest bank, then offered to buy both Societe Generale and Paribas for $37 billion. After the banks lobbied investors and the government tried to mediate an agreement, BNP won control of Paribas in August but was rejected by shareholders of Societe Generale. The result failed to create a dominant French bank and left both BNP and Societe Generale subject to takeover.

Total Fina S.A., one of France's leading oil companies, agreed to acquire its rival, Elf Aquitaine S.A., in September for $48 billion. The

---

TIME CAPSULE 1940

FRANCE

FROM [DUNQUERQUE] and its flat sandy beaches more than 300,000 . . . soldiers were rescued by British vessels of all sizes and protected valiantly by the Royal Air Force. . . . This evacuation from Dunquerque, from May 29 to June 4, under fire from German guns in the rear, from German planes in the air, and from German ships in the [English] Channel, was one of the most remarkable amphibious operations in the history of warfare, and did much to hearten the British in the hour of disaster.

merger created the world's fourth-largest oil company. Retailer Carrefour S.A. acquired rival Promodes S.A. in September for $17 billion to create the world's second-largest retailer after U.S.-based Wal-Mart Stores, Incorporated.

Renault S.A., the French automaker, agreed in March to acquire 37 percent of Japan's Nissan Motor Company for $5 billion. Although Nissan was considerably larger than Renault, the Japanese company had run up debts of about $40 billion. Renault appointed Carlos Ghosn, an executive renowned for cutting costs, to manage Nissan. The acquisition marked a turnaround for Renault, which had nearly collapsed in the 1980's.

Defense. French aerospace company Aerospatiale Matra S.A. agreed in October 1999 to merge with the aerospace division of Daimler-Chrysler AG of Germany, creating European Aeronautic, Defense and Space Company.

Disasters. An Alpine avalanche killed 12 people near the ski resort of Chamonix in February. Forty people were killed in March when a fire broke out on a truck and spread to other vehicles inside the Mont Blanc Tunnel. More than 100 people died in Europe when storms with winds of 100 miles (161 kilometers) per hour swept across France and parts of Belgium, Germany and Switzerland on December 26 and 28.   □ Tom Buerkle

See also **Europe; Germany; Sports.**

TIME CAPSULE 1940
FRANCE

ON JUNE 17 [French Premier Henri Philippe Petain] announced that he had asked Hitler . . . to put an end to hostilities. . . .

After delays and negotiations, the armistice with Germany was signed on June 22. The ceremony took place in the same historic railway car and in the same Forest of Compiegne where Germany had been compelled to sign the armistice which ended . . . World War I. According to the terms, German troops were to remain in occupation of northern and western France until a final peace should be signed. . . . The Petain government was to remain in control of "Unoccupied France," but subject to a great many German regulations. . . .

General Charles de Gaulle and many other Frenchmen who had fled abroad refused to recognize the armistice. They represented "Free France," organized a government on English soil, and later won some of the French colonies in West Africa to their cause.

Charred automobiles and trucks line the Mont Blanc Tunnel between France and Italy after a fire on a truck spread to other vehicles on March 26, 1999, killing 40 people. The tunnel, which runs under the Alps and is one of the busiest routes between France and Italy, was shut down for the remainder of the year.

Gardening. Gardeners across the United States faced ecological problems in 1999. Drought damaged trees in the Western states, and wildfires broke out in Florida after a prolonged dry season. The hurricane season brought flooding from South Carolina to New Jersey, leaving sodden oaks and other hardwood trees susceptible to root rots and cankers. In the Northeast, ash trees weakened by drought succumbed to a disease called ash yellows.

Invading pests. The President's Council on Invasive Species met in Washington, D.C., on July 22 for the first time to address the growing problem of invading species, including plants as well as insects and other animal pests.

Asian long-horned beetles, first imported in wood packing material from China, continued to be a problem in 1999 as new sites of infestation appeared in Chicago and New York City. In California, ambrosia beetles infested and killed thousands of oak trees.

Commemorating landscape design. The American Society of Landscape Architects celebrated its 100th anniversary in 1999 as participating members completed and donated 100 new park designs to the organization. One of the new designs was to be created on the Omaha Indian Reservation in Nebraska. The U.S. Postal Service issued a stamp honoring Frederick Law Olmsted, the premier American landscape artist, whose best-known work is New York City's Central Park.

Gardening trends. Balcony and rooftop gardens burgeoned in 1999 as city dwellers embraced new lightweight synthetic containers, often available from specialty garden shops. Other trends included low-voltage outdoor lighting and automatic watering systems for gardens on high-rise balconies as well as for spacious lawns.

Veteran gardeners, as well as affluent homeowners who longed for romantic gardens but had limited gardening skills, enhanced their gardens with such ornaments as stone "ruins," sculpturelike sprinklers, and statuary, which were highly popular in 1999. Even plastic pink flamingos enjoyed a comeback as more gardeners dared to be whimsical.

Decorative vegetables were also a popular choice in 1999. Gardeners tried such unusual plants as cardoons, tall ornamentals related to artichokes.

Stolen ornaments. A 1998 investigation that uncovered a ring of thieves stealing graveyard statuary from cemeteries in New Orleans broadened in 1999 as New Orleans police and the U.S. Federal Bureau of Investigation managed to recover more than $1 million in stolen statuary. Many decorative pieces, which were highly sought after by gardeners, were recovered locally, but by year's end, the investigation reached from coast to coast.

Garden history emerged as a field of study in 1999 with the installation of several period landscapes. The new owners of Thornewood Castle, a Victorian mansion in Tacoma, Washington, recreated its original sunken garden. In Boston, the Society for the Preservation of New England Antiquities presented a historical exhibit in June, "Lost Gardens of New England."

Individual gardeners also delved into the history of gardening by experimenting with heirloom plants. Old varieties of flowers, vegetables, and shrubs, grown from seed through many generations, were available through specialized nurseries and seed companies.

New public gardens. Callaway Gardens in Pine Mountain, Georgia, opened its Callaway Brothers Azalea Bowl on March 29. From a bridge, pedestrians could view a reflecting pond surrounded by 40 acres of spring blossoms.

A performance by cellist Yo-Yo Ma launched The Toronto Music Garden on June 10. The new Canadian park, a landscape interpretation by designer Julie Moir Messervy of the First Suite for Unaccompanied Cello by Johann Sebastian Bach (1685-1750), featured a garden to accompany each movement of the piece.   □ Carol Stocker

Gas and gasoline. See **Energy supply.**

Genetic engineering. See **Agriculture; Biology; Medicine.**

Geology. In 1999, carbon dioxide and other so-called greenhouse gases that trap solar heat in the atmosphere were at their highest atmospheric concentration of the last 420,000 years, according to a report published in June by an international team of researchers led by geologist Jean R. Petit of the Laboratory of Glaciology and Geophysics of the Environment in France.

The team studied the gas content of air bubbles in an ice core from the East Antarctic icecap. The ice was laid down over a 420,000-year period that included four ice ages and four *interglacial periods* (the warmer eras between ice ages). The scientists found that present levels of greenhouse gases are at an all-time high for that time span. The discovery lent strong support to the idea that greenhouse gases have been building up in the atmosphere during recent centuries as a result of the burning of *fossil fuels* (oil, coal, and natural gas) and the destruction of forests.

A group of scientists at the Physics Institute in Bern, Switzerland, and the University of California at San Diego reported a similar conclusion in March. That team examined air bubbles in an Antarctic ice core containing ice from all of the past 11,000 years—the present interglacial period. They found that concentrations of atmospheric carbon dioxide in 1999 were the highest they have ever been during that entire period.

Mantle "lava lamp." During the 1960's and 1970's, lava lamps were highly popular novelty items. In lava lamps, colorful fluids of different densities rise and fall without mixing in response to heating from below and cooling from above. In March 1999, geophysicists in the United States and elsewhere reported that lava lamps may provide a fairly close simulation of what is happening within the Earth's *mantle* (the part of the planet below the crust). Studying the movement of earthquake waves through the Earth's mantle, the researchers discovered a boundary at a depth of about 1,000 miles (1,600 kilometers) that may be the base of Earth's "lava lamp."

Scientists at the University of California at Davis reported that mantle rock below the 1,000-mile boundary is about 4 percent denser than the overlying mantle. This dense layer acts as a barrier to great slabs of ocean-floor rock that descend into the Earth at subduction zones, places where 2 of some 30 plates that make up the Earth's *lithosphere* (crust and upper mantle) meet. At these zones, the edge of one plate slides under the other and dives deep into the Earth.

Data published by scientists at the Massachusetts Institute of Technology in Cambridge showed that subducted slabs penetrate the mantle easily until they reach the 1,000-mile-deep boundary, where they appear to break apart and melt. The melted rock then moves back toward the Earth's surface—much like the rising fluid of a lava lamp—eventually emerging from volcanoes. Researchers at the Tokyo Institute of Technology in Japan and the University of Bristol in the United Kingdom made similar findings.

Archean molecular fossils. The discovery of fossilized molecules left by organisms that lived during the Archean Eon, some 2.7 billion years ago, was reported in August 1999 by geologist Jochen J. Brocks at the University of Sydney, Australia, and his colleagues at the Australian Geological Survey. The fossils, mostly of fatlike compounds called lipids, were found in deposits of shale in northwestern Australia. The fossils are about 1 billion years older than previously discovered fossil molecules. Their discovery provided evidence for the existence of oxygen-producing microorganisms called cyanobacteria during the Archean Eon. The find sheds light not only on the evolution of the first life on Earth but also on the evolution of the planet's atmosphere.

Oxygen, which makes up 21 percent of Earth's atmosphere, is produced by organisms—including cyanobacteria and many kinds of plants—that use sunlight to produce carbohydrate compounds from carbon dioxide and water. Oxygen is a by-product of this process, called photosynthesis. The finding that cyanobacteria existed on Earth as early as 2.7 billion years ago means that

Earth's atmosphere may have been sufficiently rich in oxygen to allow the evolution of oxygen-breathing organisms by the end of the Archean Eon, about 2.5 billion years ago.

Squeeze play in L.A. The Earth's crust in the Los Angeles area is being compressed in a north-south direction at a fairly high rate, according to a report published in August 1999 by geologist Donald F. Argus and his colleagues at the California Institute of Technology in Pasadena.

Along most of its length, the San Andreas Fault in the Los Angeles area is a strike-slip fault, along which two lithospheric plates grind past each other. Usually, the plates are locked together. But when sufficient pressure builds up, they slip into new positions, causing an earthquake.

In a portion of the San Andreas fault where the fault bends, the plates are pushing directly against each other and compressing. Argus's team used the satellite-based Global Positioning System to measure the rate of this compression. The scientists found that downtown Los Angeles and the San Gabriel Mountains are converging at the rate of 0.24 inch (6 millimeters) a year. As a result, the crust in that area is thickening. This finding indicates that Los Angeles is susceptible to thrust-fault earthquakes, caused when the edge of one plate is forced over the edge of an opposing plate. □ Henry T. Mullins

Georgia. In May 1999, security forces foiled a conspiracy to assassinate Georgian president Eduard Shevardnadze. Attempts on his life were also made in 1995 and 1998. The latest plot was part of a planned *coup* (overthrow). Shevardnadze blamed Russia for supporting the conspiracy and attempting to destabilize Georgia. Shevardnadze's ruling Citizens' Union bloc preserved its majority in the first round of voting in parliamentary elections held on Oct. 31, 1999.

For much of 1999, Georgia struggled to diminish Russian influence over its affairs. Russia maintained four military bases in Georgia, as well as peacekeeping troops in the breakaway region of Abkhazia. On October 3, Abkhazians approved a constitution that formally defined Abkhazia as an independent state.

In April, Georgia withdrew from the joint security alliance of the Commonwealth of Independent States (CIS). The CIS, founded in 1991, is a loose economic and military alliance of former Soviet republics. Georgia joined Azerbaijan, Moldova, Ukraine, and Uzbekistan in 1999 in a security alliance that excluded Russia. On April 17, Azerbaijan, Georgia, and Ukraine opened a new pipeline that allowed Caspian oil to bypass Russia on its way to export in the West. □ Steven L. Solnick

See also **Asia; Azerbaijan; Russia.**

Georgia. See **State government.**

Germany experienced both economic and political difficulties in 1999. A sluggish economy and near-record unemployment levels contributed to dissent in Chancellor Gerhard Schroeder's coalition government.

A decline in exports because of the economic troubles of such trading partners as Russia and Eastern Europe caused German growth to slow early in 1999. Growth later increased, but the European Union's (EU) Executive Commission forecast that Germany's *gross domestic product* (GDP —the total of all goods and services produced in a year) would rise by only 1.7 percent in 1999, one of the slowest growth rates in the 15-nation EU. The unemployment rate, which hit a post-World War II (1939-1945) high of 13 percent in 1998, fell to 10 percent in 1999 but remained in double digits for the fourth straight year.

Government. The slow economy caused tremendous difficulties for Chancellor Schroeder, who was elected in September 1998 after promising to revive growth and safeguard Germany's welfare system. Schroeder's government initially pursued an economic program devised by Finance Minister Oskar Lafontaine, which called for cuts in personal income taxes and increases in corporate taxes. Business leaders protested that the tax changes would increase costs—already among the highest in Europe—and make German industry less competitive, worsening unemployment problems. The criticism damaged Schroeder, who had won election in part by promising to adopt probusiness policies.

The economic troubles provoked an early political crisis for the government. In February 1999, Schroeder's Social Democratic Party lost the election in the state of Hesse. As a result, the party lost its majority in the Bundesrat, or upper house of the national parliament. The loss meant

TIME CAPSULE 1930
GERMANY

IN THE REICHSTAG election of September 14, the Fascists, popularly known as "Nazis," declared themselves . . . against the Jews and against political rights for women. Their opposition to the Versailles peace treaty . . . and to the reparations settlement, appealed to the youth and to the new voters of Germany. . . . In a flamboyant and violent speech . . . Hitler boasted of what his Fascists would do some day to avenge Germany's participation in the war settlement, and said, "Heads will roll in the sand!"

TIME CAPSULE 1938
GERMANY

ANTI-SEMITISM. A wave of destruction, looting, and incendiarism began to sweep over Germany about 2 a.m. on November 10. Bands of men, wearing Nazi boots and moving in organized groups, set fire to or otherwise sought to destroy all Jewish synagogues throughout the Reich. They also toured the streets, smashing the windows of Jewish shops and hurling furniture, typewriters, and all sorts of property onto the sidewalk. Thousands of Jews were arrested and hustled to prison or concentration camps.

Schroeder needed the support of the opposition Christian Democratic Party to pass major legislation. One month later, Lafontaine resigned after Schroeder publicly criticized his policies.

Schroeder appointed a moderate ally, Hans Eichel, to replace Lafontaine. Eichel made deficit reduction his top priority, announcing in April $1.6 billion in cuts in government spending to reduce the 1999 budget deficit to $30.6 billion. In June, Eichel announced plans to reduce corporate taxes and to cut spending by $16 billion in 2000, including cuts in welfare and retirement benefits. Schroeder said the reforms were necessary to restore competitiveness and create jobs. The policy change failed to halt the government's growing unpopularity. In September and October 1999, the Social Democrats lost five out of seven state elections, an unprecedented number for a party in national power for only one year.

Elections in the former East Germany reflected strong discontent over the region's slow growth and an unemployment rate of nearly 20 percent. The former Communist Party surpassed the Social Democrats and finished second behind the Christian Democrats in the eastern states of Thuringia and Saxony.

Former chancellor Helmut Kohl, who was defeated by Schroeder in 1998, admitted using secret bank accounts to finance his Christian Democratic Union party during the 16 years he was in power. Kohl disclosed the practice in November 1999 to a parliamentary committee investigating a $520,000 donation made by an arms dealer in 1991. Kohl denied that the gift helped influence a government decision at the time to sell 36 tanks to Saudi Arabia, but the revelation raised the possibility of legal action and threatened to tarnish the reputation of the leader who reunified Germany.

Nuclear power. The government in 1999 backed away from promises to begin shutting down the country's 19 nuclear power stations.

Members of the lower house of Germany's parliament, the Bundestag, gather in the renovated Reichstag in the new capital, Berlin, in April 1999. German officials decided to move the government from Bonn, which became the capital in 1949, to Berlin after the 1990 unification of East and West Germany.

The closures had been a main goal of the Green Party, which participated in the coalition government with Schroeder's Social Democrats. However, the electrical industry objected that the shutdowns would be too costly and that Germany lacked sufficient alternative energy sources.

Move to Berlin. The German government in 1999 moved from Bonn, which had served as the nation's capital since the founding of the Federal Republic in 1949, to the previous capital, Berlin. Germany's postwar leaders had chosen Bonn as the new capital to break with the country's Nazi past, but the government decided to move back to Berlin after the unification of East and West Germany in 1990. In a speech in April 1999 inaugurating the renovated Reichstag, the new home of the parliament, Schroeder said democracy and freedom were firmly established and pledged that modern Germany would remain a dependable ally to its European Union partners and the United States.

Citizenship. The parliament in May changed the country's citizenship laws, making it easier for Germany's foreign workers to become German citizens. Since 1913, Germany had limited citizenship to ethnic Germans. The new law granted automatic citizenship to anyone born in Germany who had had at least one parent living in the country for eight years.

Children of foreign workers who qualify under the new law are allowed to hold dual nationality until the age of 23, when they must decide between being German or another nationality. Nearly 7 million foreign workers, most of whom are from Turkey, lived in Germany in 1999.

Germany in Kosovo. Schroeder's government overcame dissent from passivist elements of the Social Democratic Party and its coalition partner, the Green Party, to support a North Atlantic

Treaty Organization (NATO) campaign in Yugoslavia in 1999. NATO conducted bombing raids from March to June to protect the ethnic Albanian province of Kosovo from Serbian attacks. The Greens had long opposed the use of armed force abroad because of Germany's militaristic past, but Green Party member and Foreign Minister Joschka Fischer argued that Germany must be prepared to use military force in the pursuit of humanitarian aims. Germany deployed several thousand peacekeeping troops to Kosovo, and in October, a German general took over the command of the NATO-led peacekeeping force.

Breaking with the past. Germany took several steps in 1999 to address its Nazi past. In June, the parliament agreed to construct a national memorial in central Berlin to the 6 million Jewish victims of the *Holocaust* (the systematic killing during World War II of Jews and other people considered undesirable by Germany's Nazi government). The 5-acre (2-hectare) memorial was to consist of a field of more than 2,000 stone pillars and a building of remembrance.

The German government and the country's largest companies agreed in December to pay $5.2 billion in compensation to hundreds of thousands of people, mostly living in Eastern Europe, who were forced into slave labor by the Nazi regime during World War II. Under the agreement, the government and a group of 65 major companies and banks will each pay $2.6 billion into a compensation fund. The settlement came after lawyers for the victims had sued the companies in U.S. courts. Since World War II, the German government has paid more than $60 billion in reparations to Jews and other victims of the Nazis.

Industry. German companies played an active role in the wave of restructuring that swept European industry in 1999. The biggest move came in the aerospace industry, where the aero-

TIME CAPSULE 1989

GERMANY

EAST GERMANY. What may have been the most dramatic political event since World War II (1939-1945) occurred on the night of Nov. 9, 1989, when East Germany suddenly and unexpectedly opened the Berlin Wall. The world was gripped by emotional pictures of East Berliners streaming West—older people reunited with relatives they had not seen for nearly 40 years and young people sightseeing in the well-stocked stores of West Berlin.

space division of DaimlerChrysler AG agreed in June to acquire Construcciones Aeronauticas SA, Spain's aerospace company. In October, the division merged with Aerospatiale Matra SA of France. The new company, called European Aeronautic, Defense and Space Company, ranked as the third-largest aerospace company in the world after Boeing Corporation and Lockheed Martin Corporation of the United States. □ Tom Buerkle

See also **Europe.**

Ghana. See Africa.

Golf.
Superb competition and thrilling finishes produced a captivating year of golf in 1999. Fans were amazed when Payne Stewart won the U.S. Open with a 15-foot (4.5-meter) uphill putt on the final hole and impressed when Tiger Woods survived the challenge of Sergio Garcia to win the PGA Championship. Golf fans worldwide, however, were shocked and saddened by the deaths of Stewart and five other people in a mysterious plane crash in October.

In 1999, Eldrick "Tiger" Woods, 23, was voted the Professional Golfers Association (PGA) Player of the Year for the second time. He boosted his career earnings by more than $6 million in 20 PGA Tour events, winning 8 events, including the Buick Invitational, the Memorial and Western Open tournaments, the PGA Championship, and the Tour Championship. Woods also played on the U.S. Ryder Cup team and defeated David Duval on August 2, in an 18-hole, match-play event created for television. Woods earned $1.1 million for beating Duval.

Grand Slam. Jose Maria Olazabal of Spain won the Masters for the second time on April 11 at Augusta, Georgia. Olazabal shot a final-round 71 to finish with an 8-under-par 280. Davis Love III was two strokes behind in second place and one ahead of Greg Norman, who finished third.

Stewart won the 99th U.S. Open by one stroke over Phil Mickelson at Pinehurst, North Carolina, on June 20. Combating incredible pressure with steely putting, Stewart made amends for his one-stroke loss in the 1998 Open. Woods and V. J. Singh of Fiji tied for third place at 281.

Scotland's Paul Lawrie captured the 128th British Open on July 18, 1999, after the biggest collapse in golfing history. Down by 10 strokes when the final round began at Carnoustie Golf Links in Carnoustie, Scotland, Lawrie prevailed when Jean Van de Velde of France butchered his final round. Van de Velde started the final round with a five-stroke lead and needed to finish the 18th hole in six strokes to win the tournament. But he shot a triple-bogey 7 to wind up in a play-off with Lawrie and Justin Leonard. Lawrie birdied the last two play-off holes to become the first Scot since 1931 to win the British Open in Scotland.

Woods beat Sergio Garcia, 19, by one stroke to win the PGA Championship on Aug. 15, 1999, at Medinah, Illinois. Woods fired an even-par 72 in the final round to finish with an 11-under 277. Garcia shot a 71 and might have won his first major but missed a critical, 6-foot (2-meter) putt that enabled Woods to save par on the 17th hole.

Seniors. Bruce Fleischer pressed Hale Irwin throughout the season in the battle for top honors on the senior tour. Fleischer finished the season first in earnings with $2.5 million and seven victories. Irwin won six tournaments and placed second in earnings with $2.02 million.

Women. Juli Inkster won her 20th try at the U.S. Women's Open by five strokes with a tournament record 16-under-par 272 on June 6, at West Point, Mississippi. Three weeks later, Inkster became the second woman in modern Ladies Professional Golf Association (LPGA) history to complete a career Grand Slam by winning the LPGA Championship in Wilmington, Delaware. The Grand Slam took Inkster 15 years to complete. (She had won the du Maurier Classic and the Dinah Shore tournament in 1984.) On Sept. 26, 1999, Inkster won the LPGA Golf Championship in Portland, Oregon. This netted her enough career points to qualify for induction into the LPGA Hall of Fame.

Team. The United States rebounded from a four-point deficit to capture the Ryder Cup, 14½ to 13½, on September 26. The implausible comeback included Justin Leonard's 45-foot (14-meter) putt on the 17th hole of the 11th match. Olazabal missed a 30-foot (9-meter) birdie putt to tie but won the 18th hole to halve the match, which was enough to give the Americans the win. A spontaneous celebration by the U.S. players following Leonard's putt infuriated the Europeans. This breach of golf etiquette forced Olazabal to wait before putting at the 17th hole. □ Ron Reid

See also **Deaths.**

Great Britain. See United Kingdom.

A Kurdish demonstrator sets himself on fire in Athens, Greece, in February to protest the arrest of Abdullah Ocalan, the leader of the Kurdish movement for *autonomy* (self-rule), which began in 1984.

Greece in 1999 was dominated by changing relations with its neighbor and Aegean rival, Turkey. The government of Greek Prime Minister Costas Simitis was shaken in February by the arrest by Turkey of Abdullah Ocalan, the leader of the Kurdish movement for *autonomy* (self-rule) which began a guerrilla war with Turkey in 1984. Ocalan had been smuggled into Greece by Greek sympathizers to the Kurdish cause who sought to help him evade arrest by Turkish authorities. Fearing a clash with Turkey over Ocalan, the Greek government sent the rebel leader to the Greek embassy in Kenya, but Turkish commandos seized Ocalan in Nairobi on February 15. The attempt to hide Ocalan humiliated the Greek government and forced Simitis to dismiss three cabinet ministers and the chief of intelligence.

Earthquakes later in the year led to improved relations between Greece and Turkey. An earthquake that struck northwestern Turkey on August 17 killed more than 17,000 people and triggered a wave of sympathy and aid from Greece. The Greek government sent rescue teams to Turkey, and a Greek naval vessel docked in a Turkish port for the first time in more than 25 years. Similarly, Turkey sent rescue teams to Greece after an earthquake struck near Athens on September 7, killing more than 140 people and leaving 100,000 homeless.

Amid the wave of sympathy that followed the Turkish quake, the Greek government announced in September that it would no longer block Turkey's application for membership to the European Union (EU). Greece had vetoed Turkey's EU membership for years because of a long-running dispute over Cyprus, a predominantly ethnic-Greek island that Turkey invaded in 1974. Talks to resolve the Cyprus dispute failed to make significant progress during 1999.

Economy. The Simitis government made progress during 1999 in preparing Greece to join the euro. The European Commission, the executive agency of the EU, projected that the Greek budget deficit would decline to 2.1 percent of *gross domestic product* (GDP, the value of all goods and services produced in a country in a given year) in 1999. In the early 1990's, Greece's budget deficit stood at more than 10 percent of GDP, the highest of any EU country.

Greece's rate of inflation—which was also once the highest in Europe—was projected to fall to 2.5 percent in 1999. The improvement kept Greece on track toward joining the euro in 2001. Greece's improved finances helped the economy expand strongly, with GDP expected to grow by 3.4 percent in 1999. ☐ Tom Buerkle

See also **Europe; Turkey.**

Grenada. See **Latin America.**

Guatemala. Alfonso Portillo of the conservative Guatemalan Republican Front was elected president of Guatemala on Dec. 26, 1999. Portillo promised health, education, and land reforms to assist poor and working-class people. His opponents criticized his ties to Efrain Rios Montt, a Guatemalan dictator in the early 1980's.

On Feb. 25, 1999, the Historical Clarification Commission, an international panel, released a 3,600-page report on human rights abuses in Guatemala during the country's 36-years of civil war, which ended in 1996. The commission estimated that more than 200,000 people, most of whom were civilians, had been killed in the war. More than 90 percent of some 42,000 documented human rights violations were attributed to the Guate-malan army and paramilitary groups. U.S. President Bill Clinton, visiting Guatemala on March 10, 1999, formally apologized for U.S. support of the military regime during the long conflict.

On May 16, Guatemalan voters rejected 47 constitutional changes that would have provided more rights for native people. Observers attributed the failure of the referendum, which had the support of all major political parties, to low voter turnout.   □ Nathan A. Haverstock

See also **Latin America.**

Guinea. See Africa.

Haiti. President Rene Preval of Haiti announced on Jan. 11, 1999, that he would rule by decree. He dissolved a deadlocked parliament, which had left Haiti without a fully functional government since June 1996. The political stalemate had made it impossible for Haiti to avail itself of $500 million in loans from international agencies and to address the nation's dire circumstances, such as the 60-percent unemployment rate.

Preval's assumption of dictatorial power in 1999 sparked violence. The day after he took power, gunmen wounded his sister, Marie-Claude Calvin, and killed her driver. On March 1, Jean-Yvon Toussaint, a senator of the leftist Struggling People's Organization party, was assassinated in a suburb of Port-au-Prince, the capital.

In November, the United Nations proceeded with plans to end its mission in Haiti despite a warning from UN Secretary General Kofi Annan that the withdrawal of the remaining 279 UN-sponsored police officers might undermine Haiti's stability "at a particularly sensitive stage." The United States proceeded with plans to withdraw 480 troops by January 2000—the last of more than 20,000 U.S. troops that had occupied Haiti since September 1994.   □ Nathan A. Haverstock

See also **Latin America.**

Harness racing. See Horse racing.

Hawaii. See State government.

Health care issues. Efforts by the United States Congress to reform Medicare, the federal program that pays for many health expenses of the elderly, failed in 1999. The reform attempts were aimed at expanding coverage of Medicare and saving the system from bankruptcy, which some experts feared might occur soon after 2011, when *Baby Boomers* (people born between 1946 and 1964) begin retiring and become eligible for the program.

In March 1999, the National Bipartisan Commission on the Future of Medicare, a congressional commission that had been trying to develop a reform plan for Medicare, disbanded after failing to agree on a plan. In June, President Bill Clinton unveiled his own proposal for Medicare reform, the centerpiece of which was a new prescription drug benefit. Under Clinton's plan, each of the 39 million Medicare beneficiaries would have the option, beginning in 2002, of paying a $24-per-month premium and receiving a federal subsidy for drug costs up to $2,000 per year. Over time, the premium and subsidy would increase.

Although most Democrats supported Clinton's proposal, Republicans criticized it as being too expensive. Congress was expected to reconsider Medicare reform in 2000.

Managed care controversy. The managed care form of health insurance generated additional political debate in 1999. Managed care is a type of health insurance in which costs are controlled by offering incentives to health providers to practice more conservative care. Health maintenance organizations (HMO's) are a type of managed care plan.

More than 100 million of the nation's 274 million people belonged to HMO's or other forms of managed care plans in 1999. Some physicians and patients involved in these plans complained that managed care often reduced patients' access to needed health care by restricting which physicians patients can see and denying patients certain medical procedures.

The Republican-controlled U.S. Senate passed a "patients' rights" bill in July to address some of these concerns. However, Democrats condemned the bill as insufficient. In the U.S. House of Representatives in August, a *bipartisan* (supported by both Democrats and Republicans) bill was introduced by Representatives John Dingell (D., Michigan) and Charles Norwood (R., Georgia). This bill, which was also supported by President Clinton, was approved by the House in October 1999.

The Dingell-Norwood bill contained provisions to give patients more power in dealing with managed care companies, including allowing patients to file lawsuits in state court against these companies if medical procedures were denied or delayed. Negotiations were needed to reconcile the House bill with the Senate bill, which did not allow such lawsuits, before the legislation could be presented to Clinton for his signature.

Americans without health insurance. The U.S. Census Bureau reported in October that the number of U.S. citizens without health insurance rose by 833,000 in 1998, to 44.3 million people. This figure represented more than 16 percent of the total population of the United States.

The National Governors' Association, consisting of the governors of the 50 U.S. states and 5 U.S. territories, announced in March 1999 that 828,000 children had obtained health insurance through the State Children's Health Insurance Program (SCHIP). Congress had established SCHIP in 1997 to aid the estimated 10 million U.S. children who did not have health-care coverage.

Kevorkian convicted. Jack Kevorkian, a retired Michigan pathologist who claimed to have helped at least 130 people suffering from disease commit suicide, was convicted of second-degree murder in March 1999. In September 1998, Kevorkian had injected a man suffering from amyotrophic lateral sclerosis (Lou Gehrig's disease), an incurable disease of the nervous system, with lethal chemicals at the man's request. Kevorkian's conviction was based on a videotape he made of the event. □ Emily Friedman

See also **Medicine; Public health and safety.**

Hinduism.
The Hindu Nationalist Bharatiya Janata Party (BJP) softened many of its Hindu-centered goals in 1999 during its campaign for seats in India's lower house of Parliament. In the campaign, the BJP issued a manifesto that did not mention the party's traditional goal of giving Hindu ideology a larger role in Indian life. Instead, it called for "a moratorium on contentious issues" to promote political stability. Party leaders endorsed this statement to reassure India's 120 million Muslims and 23 million Christians. Nonetheless, some journalists reported that BJP party leaders were divided between pursuing religious goals, such as having all schoolchildren recite a daily prayer to a Hindu goddess of learning, and more pragmatic goals, such as promoting India's economic growth.

Religious attacks. In January, Indian Prime Minister Atal Behari Vajpayee condemned attacks on Christian places of worship in India and the killings of an Australian missionary and his two young sons. The missionary and his sons were burned alive in their van on January 23 in the eastern state of Orissa as a mob chanting Hindu slogans circled them.

Vajpayee also called for a national debate on religious conversions. Hindu militants have accused Christian missionaries of converting Hindus through bribes and intimidation.

Tragic pilgrimage. More than 60 people died in a stampede of Hindu pilgrims in January on a mountain in the Indian state of Kerala. The stampede occurred where thousands of pilgrims had crowded to watch what the faithful believe is the celestial light on a route leading from a shrine at Sabarimala. At Sabarimala, millions of pilgrims climb the mountain to worship at a temple to the god Ayappa, culminating 40 days of penance.

Alaskan temple. More than 40 Hindu pilgrims traveled to Anchorage, Alaska, in June for the opening of Sri Ganesha Mandir, Alaska's only Hindu temple. Native American chiefs met with the pilgrims and honored the Hindu community with chants and sacred drumming.

Fiji election. Mahendra Chaudhry, an ethnic Indian, was elected Fiji's first Hindu prime minister in May. Hindus make up approximately 44 percent of Fiji's population and are mostly ethnic Indians. In 1987, Fiji elected a coalition government that was dominated by Indians, but it was almost immediately ousted by a coup that ushered in 12 years of Fijian-majority ethnic domination under a Constitution that barred Indians from major political posts and from holding a majority of seats in Parliament. □ Brian Bouldrey

See also **India.**

Hobbies. See Toys and games.

Hockey.
The retirement of superstar Wayne Gretzky and the Dallas Stars' first Stanley Cup championship were the headline stories of the 1998-1999 National Hockey League (NHL) season. The Stars defeated the Buffalo Sabres, 2-1, on June 20, 1999, when Brett Hull scored a controversial goal after 14 minutes and 51 seconds of the third overtime period at Buffalo.

Hull's goal ended the second-longest finals game in NHL history and clinched the series, 4 games to 2. It also set off a controversy when video replays revealed that Hull's left skate was inside the goal crease when he made the winning shot, arguably a rules violation. Sabres fans were infuriated that the goal was not disallowed.

Season. Over the 82-game regular season, the Dallas Stars led the NHL with 51 victories and 114 points. The New Jersey Devils once again led Eastern Conference teams with 105 points, 2 points more than the Ottawa Senators, the only other division champion to top 100 points. Carolina, Colorado, and Detroit also won division titles.

Play-offs. The Stars reached the Stanley Cup finals for the first time since 1991, when the franchise was known as the Minnesota North Stars. Along the way, Dallas swept Edmonton in four first-round games, beat St. Louis, 4 games to 2, and took the Western Conference title from Colorado, 4 games to 3.

Western Conference

Central Division

	W.	L.	T.	Pts.
Detroit Red Wings*	43	32	7	93
St. Louis Blues*	37	32	13	87
Chicago Blackhawks	29	41	12	70
Nashville Predators	28	47	7	63

Northwest Division

	W.	L.	T.	Pts.
Colorado Avalanche*	44	28	10	98
Edmonton Oilers*	33	37	12	78
Calgary Flames	30	40	12	72
Vancouver Canucks	23	47	12	58

Pacific Division

	W.	L.	T.	Pts.
Dallas Stars*	51	19	12	114
Phoenix Coyotes*	39	31	12	90
Anaheim Mighty Ducks*	35	34	13	83
San Jose Sharks*	31	33	18	80
Los Angeles Kings	32	45	5	69

Eastern Conference

Northeast Division

Ottawa Senators*	44	23	15	103
Toronto Maple Leafs*	45	30	7	97
Boston Bruins*	39	30	13	91
Buffalo Sabres*	37	28	17	91
Montreal Canadiens	32	39	11	75

Atlantic Division

New Jersey Devils*	47	24	11	105
Philadelphia Flyers*	37	26	19	93
Pittsburgh Penguins*	38	30	14	90
New York Rangers	33	38	11	77
New York Islanders	24	48	10	58

Southeast Division

Carolina Hurricanes*	34	30	18	86
Florida Panthers	30	34	18	78
Washington Capitals	31	45	6	68
Tampa Bay Lightning	19	54	9	47

*Made play-offs

Stanley Cup champions—Dallas Stars
(defeated Buffalo Sabres, 4 games to 2)

Leading scorers

	Games	Goals	Assists	Pts.
Jaromir Jagr, Pittsburgh	81	44	83	127
Teemu Selanne, Anaheim	75	47	60	107
Paul Kariya, Anaheim	82	39	62	101
Peter Forsberg, Colorado	78	30	67	97
Joe Sakic, Colorado	73	41	55	96

Leading goalies (26 or more games)

	Games	Goals against	Avg.
Ron Tugnutt, Ottawa	43	75	1.79
Dominik Hasek, Buffalo	64	119	1.87
Ed Belfour, Dallas	61	117	1.92
Byron Dafoe, Boston	68	133	2.00
Nikolai Khabibulin, Phoenix	63	130	2.13

Awards

Adams Trophy (coach of the year)—Jacques Martin, Ottawa
Calder Trophy (best rookie)—Chris Drury, Colorado
Hart Trophy (most valuable player)—Jaromir Jagr, Pittsburgh
Jennings Trophy (team with fewest goals against)—Ed Belfour, Roman Turek, Dallas
Lady Byng Trophy (sportsmanship)—Wayne Gretzky, N.Y. Rangers
Pearson Award (best player as voted by NHL players)—Jaromir Jagr, Pittsburgh
Masterton Trophy (perseverance, dedication to hockey)—John Cullen, Tampa Bay
Norris Trophy (best defenseman)—Al MacInnis, St. Louis
Ross Trophy (leading scorer)—Jaromir Jagr, Pittsburgh
Selke Trophy (best defensive forward)—Jere Lehtinen, Dallas
Smythe Trophy (most valuable player in Stanley Cup)—Joe Nieuwendyk, Dallas
Vezina Trophy (best goalkeeper)—Dominik Hasek, Buffalo

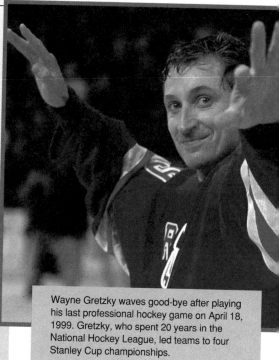

Wayne Gretzky waves good-bye after playing his last professional hockey game on April 18, 1999. Gretzky, who spent 20 years in the National Hockey League, led teams to four Stanley Cup championships.

The Buffalo Sabres swept Ottawa in four games, ousted Boston, 4 games to 2, and beat Toronto in the Eastern Conference final, 4 games to 1. The team's Stanley Cup finals appearance was its first since 1975 and only the second in its history.

Wayne Gretzky, who set 61 records during 20 seasons, played the last game of his career at Madison Square Garden in New York City on April 18, 1999. "The Great One" retired at age 38 on a high note. On March 29, he scored his 1,072nd professional goal to pass hockey legend Gordie Howe as the game's top goal scorer. The Hockey Hall of Fame Selection Committee waived the customary three-year waiting period and inducted Gretzky on November 22.

Women's hockey. On March 14, Canada's women's national hockey team avenged its 1998 Olympics loss by beating the United States, 3-1, at Espoo, Finland, for the Canadian team's fifth straight world championship.

International. The Czech Republic men's team won its second world championship in four years on May 16, 1999, at Lillehammer, Norway. Winger Jan Hlavac scored the winning goal 17 minutes into overtime in the second game of the two-game final series. ☐ Ron Reid

Honduras. See **Latin America.**

Charismatic (right), a 31-1 long shot, races to victory at the 125th Kentucky Derby on May 1, 1999. Menifee (left) placed second. Charismatic went on to win the Preakness Stakes but failed to capture the Triple Crown because it lost the Belmont Stakes.

Horse racing. Charismatic, a horse with a modest pedigree and a 31-1 long shot, won the 1999 Kentucky Derby and the Preakness Stakes. He fell short of becoming history's 12th Triple Crown winner on June 5, when he finished third in the Belmont Stakes behind Lemon Drop Kid, a 29-1 long shot. Charismatic was the third horse in three years to win the Derby and Preakness before failing in the 1½-mile Belmont Stakes.

On December 13, Panamanian-born jockey Laffit Pincay broke the legendary Bill Shoemaker's record for most victories by a jockey. Pincay captured his 8,834th victory aboard Irish Nip in the sixth race at Hollywood Park in Inglewood, California. Shoemaker's record of 8,833 victories had stood since 1970.

Three-year-olds. Charismatic won the 125th Kentucky Derby at Churchill Downs in Louisville, Kentucky, on May 1, 1999. A crowd of 151,051 people watched Charismatic, ridden by Chris Antley, hold off a late charge by Menifee to win by a neck. Charismatic took the winner's purse of

$886,200 and paid $67.60 to win, the third-largest payoff in Derby history.

Two weeks later, Charismatic captured the 124th Preakness Stakes at Baltimore's Pimlico Race Course to advance to the brink of the Triple Crown. Antley brought Charismatic off the final turn to finish 1½ lengths ahead of Menifee. Badge, a non-Derby starter, ran third.

Charismatic's Triple Crown bid ended in the 131st running of the Belmont Stakes on June 5, at Elmont, New York. Lemon Drop Kid took the lead in the final furlong and beat Vision and Verse, another long shot (54-1), by a head, with Charismatic 1½ lengths back.

Harness racing. On August 7, Self Possessed recorded the fastest trotting mile in history when he won the $1-million Hambletonian final in 1:51.3 at Meadowlands race track in East Rutherford, New Jersey. Blissfull Hall won the Cane Pace, Little Brown Jug, and Messenger Stakes to become pacing's ninth triple-crown winner in 1999. The horse earned $195,615 for the Messenger, plus a $250,000 bonus for winning the triple crown.

International. On March 27 in the United Arab Emirates, Almutawakel won the $5-million, 1¼-mile Dubayy World Cup, the world's richest horse race. Silver Charm, who won at Dubayy in 1998, finished sixth in a field of eight.

Irish-trained Bobbyjo won the $350,000 Grand National Steeplechase at Liverpool, England, by 10 lengths on April 10, 1999. Blue Charm came in second and Call It a Day third over the 4½-mile course. Bobbyjo, a 9-year-old horse, was ridden by Paul Carberry, the son of Bobbyjo's trainer, Tommy Carberry. □ Ron Reid

Hospital. See Health care issues.

Housing. See Building and construction.

Major horse races of 1999

Thoroughbred racing		Value to
Race	Winner	Winner
Atto Mile (Canada)	Quiet Resolve	$630,000
Belmont Stakes	Lemon Drop Kid	$600,000
Blue Grass Stakes	Menifee	$465,000
Breeders' Cup Classic	Cat Thief	$2,080,000
Breeders' Cup Distaff	Beautiful Pleasure	$1,040,000
Breeders' Cup Filly & Mare Turf	Soaring Softly	$556,400
Breeders' Cup Juvenile	Anees	$556,400
Breeders' Cup Juvenile Fillies	Cash Run	$520,000
Breeders' Cup Mile	Silic	$520,000
Breeders' Cup Sprint	Artax	$624,000
Breeders' Cup Turf	Daylami	$1,040,000
Canadian International Stakes	Thornfield	$936,000
Derby Stakes (United Kingdom)	Oath	$982,417
Dubai World Cup (United Arab Emirates)	Almutawakel	$3,000,000
Gallery Furniture.com Stakes	Stephen Got Even	$450,000
Haskell Invitational Stakes	Menifee	$600,000
Hollywood Gold Cup Stakes	Real Quiet	$600,000
Irish Derby (Ireland)	Montjeu	$583,779
Jockey Club Gold Cup Stakes	River Keen	$600,000
Kentucky Derby	Charismatic	$886,200
Kentucky Oaks	Silverbulletday	$341,620
King George VI and Queen Elizabeth Diamond Stakes (United Kingdom)	Daylami	$539,950
Oaklawn Handicap	Behrens	$450,000
Pacific Classic Stakes	General Challenge	$700,000
Preakness Stakes	Charismatic	$650,000
Prix de l'Arc de Triomphe (France)	Montjeu	$815,000
Santa Anita Derby	General Challenge	$450,000
Santa Anita Handicap	Free House	$600,000
Stephen Foster Handicap	Victory Gallop	$512,895
Travers Stakes	Lemon Drop Kid	$600,000

Harness racing		Value to
Race	Winner	Winner
Cane Pace	Blissfull Hall	$220,461
Hambletonian	Self Possessed	$550,000
Kentucky Futurity	Self Possessed	$187,770
Little Brown Jug	Blissfull Hall	$127,834
Meadowlands Pace	The Panderosa	$508,750
Messenger Stakes	Blissfull Hall	$195,615
Woodrow Wilson	Richess Hanover	$312,500
Yonkers Trot	CR Renegade	$159,679

Sources: The Blood Horse Magazine and U.S. Trotting Association

Houston voters overwhelmingly reelected Mayor Lee Brown to a second two-year term on Nov. 2, 1999. Brown, who became the city's first African American mayor in 1997, received 67 percent of the vote. His opponents, newspaper publisher Jack Terence and a wrestling promoter named Outlaw Josey Wales IV, collected 23 percent and 10 percent of the vote, respectively.

Arena rejected. While reelecting Brown, voters in Houston and surrounding Harris County rejected a bond issue strongly backed by the mayor for a new $160-million basketball arena. The proposed downtown arena was to replace the 25-year-old Compaq Center as the home of the Rockets of the National Basketball Association and the Comets of the Women's National Basketball Association. The Rockets' owners had argued that the Compaq Center was too outmoded to remodel with such revenue-enhancing options as luxury boxes. Opponents contended that the plan, which required the city to buy the land for the new center, was a bad deal for taxpayers.

Football franchise. Houston football fans cheered on October 6, when National Football League (NFL) team owners voted to award the league's 32nd franchise to Houston businessman Bob McNair. The city had been without an NFL team since Houston Oilers owner Bud Adams moved the team to Tennessee in 1997.

McNair's total investment in the franchise surpassed the record $800 million paid for the NFL's Washington Redskins franchise in May 1999. McNair paid $700 million for the franchise itself and pledged $115 million toward a new $310-million, retractable-roof football stadium to be built beside the Astrodome. Houston's new NFL team was scheduled to begin playing in 2002.

Astros leave Astrodome. The Astros, the city's Major League Baseball team, closed out its 35-year stay at the Astrodome, the first domed, all-purpose athletic stadium, at the close of the 1999 baseball season. The Astros played their final regular-season home game in the Astrodome on October 3, defeating the Los Angeles Dodgers, 9-4.

The Astrodome, which opened in 1965, drew tourists from around the world and hosted a wide range of events. Its future remained uncertain at the end of 1999. There was even talk of demolishing it once Enron Field, the Astros' new $250-million baseball stadium, opened in 2000.

Comets. The Houston Comets of the Women's National Basketball Association experienced a bittersweet season in 1999. On September 5, they won their third-straight league championship. But they did so without the help of feisty point guard Kim Perrot, who died of cancer in Houston on August 19.

Led by guards Cynthia Cooper and Sheryl

Swoopes, the Comets finished with a regular-season record of 26 wins and 6 losses. The team beat the Los Angeles Sparks, 2 games to 1, in the first round of the play-offs before winning the championship by beating the New York Liberty, 2 games to 1.

Charges dropped. In May, a federal judge dismissed charges of bribery and conspiracy against Houston City Council members John Castillo and Michael Yarbrough, and former council member John Peavy, Jr. They had been among a group of Houston officials indicted in July 1997 as the result of a sting operation conducted by the Federal Bureau of Investigation (FBI). The judge dismissed the charges after two separate trials for Castillo, Yarbrough, and Peavy resulted in hung juries.

The government alleged that former council member Ben Reyes and former Port Commissioner Betti Maldonado bribed Castillo, Yarbrough, and Peavy to help a company obtain city contracts. The FBI charged that Reyes received kickbacks in exchange for contracts.

Reyes and Maldonado were convicted of bribery and conspiracy charges. On Feb. 24, 1999, a judge sentenced Reyes to a nine-year prison term. Maldonado was sentenced to serve four years and three months. □ Burke Watson

See also **City; Dallas.**

Human rights.
On April 23, 1999, the 53-nation United Nations Human Rights Commission failed to pass a United States-sponsored measure to censure China for its human rights record. The failed motion cited "continuing reports of violations of human rights and fundamental freedoms in China," as well as restrictions on the cultural, religious, and civil freedoms of the people of Tibet, which China invaded in 1950.

On July 22, 1999, China outlawed Falun Gong, or the Great Wheel of the Law, a spiritual movement that combines ideas from Buddhism and Taoism with slow-motion exercise, meditation, and breathing techniques. China labeled Li Hongzhi, the founder of the sect, an "evil" person and a threat to the Chinese government. Protests against the ban broke out in cities across the country, and thousands of Falun Gong followers were arrested.

The International Criminal Tribunal in The Hague, the Netherlands, indicted Yugoslav President Slobodan Milosevic on May 27 for crimes against humanity in connection with the persecution, deportation, and deaths of thousands of ethnic Albanians in Kosovo, a Serbian province. The tribunal indicted Milosevic and four other Yugoslav leaders in absentia.

Holocaust victims. The International Commission on Holocaust Era Insurance Claims announced on May 6 that families of Holocaust victims would be paid the real value of life insurance policies in order to compensate for changes in the value of currency after World War II (1939-1945). The Holocaust, the Nazi persecution of Jews and others, resulted in the deaths of more than 6 million people. Large numbers of European Jews bought life and property insurance prior to the war, but most insurers refused to honor the policies after the war. In August 1999, five European insurance companies set up a $100-million fund to cover the claims.

Rosa Parks on June 15 received the Congressional Gold Medal, the highest civilian honor granted by the U.S. Congress. On Dec. 1, 1955, Parks was arrested when she refused to give up her seat to a white person on a bus in Montgomery, Alabama. Her arrest prompted a 382-day boycott, led by civil rights leader Martin Luther King, Jr., of Montgomery buses. It fueled other civil rights protests throughout the United States.

Death penalty. Nebraska Governor Mike Johanns on May 26, 1999, vetoed legislation for a two-year moratorium on executions in the state, labeling the measure "poor public policy." Under the ban, death sentences could have been issued, but no executions would have taken place while the state conducted an investigation on whether minorities and poor people were more likely than most whites to receive a death sentence. The legislature did not overturn the veto but did allocate funds for the study.

Racial profiling. On April 20, New Jersey Governor Christine Todd Whitman and State Attorney General Peter G. Verniero said some state troopers used race as a criteria for traffic stops and searches. A two-month study of vehicle stops revealed that minorities made up 77 percent of all drivers who were asked to consent to searches.

The Supreme Court of Vermont ruled unanimously on December 20 that the state of Vermont must guarantee that homosexual couples receive the same benefits and protections as married heterosexual couples. The court directed the state legislature either to legalize same-sex marriages or pass a domestic partnership law.

Confederate flag protest. In early July, the National Association for the Advancement of Colored People, which is based in New York City, called for a boycott against South Carolina to protest the state legislature's refusal to remove the Confederate flag from the capitol. The flag was adopted by Southern slave states that seceded from the Union in 1861, setting off the U.S. Civil War (1861-1865). In late July 1999, two civil rights organizations—the National Urban League based in New York City and the Southern Christian Leadership Conference in Atlanta, Georgia—joined the protest by canceling plans to hold conventions in Charleston, South Carolina.

HUMAN RIGHTS

Jesse Jackson (left), Martin Luther King, Jr. (center), and Ralph Abernathy stand on the balcony of a Memphis motel where King would be assassinated the next day, April 4, 1968.

THE ASSASSIN'S BULLET was the most oppressive force in the civil rights arena in 1968. Two leaders deeply involved in the civil rights movement, Martin Luther King, Jr., and Robert F. Kennedy, were murdered. King was felled in Memphis, on April 4, as he lingered on his motel balcony before supper. He was in Memphis to support a local strike of black garbage workers and was seeking to forestall a takeover of their cause by black militants.

In stressing brotherhood and nonviolence, King was the bridge between black and white America. But, in recent years, the violence of the cities was sweeping aside his doctrines. His murder was viewed by many as a final refutation of his nonviolent philosophy. Violence and riots erupted in 126 cities following his assassination.

An assassin again achieved momentary triumph, on June 5, when Senator Robert F. Kennedy was struck down in Los Angeles after an important election victory in California's presidential primary. As much as any other national politician, Kennedy had been involved in the civil rights movement.

Police brutality. A federal jury in New York City found police officer Charles Schwartz guilty on June 8 of violating the federal civil rights of Haitian immigrant Abner Louima. Schwartz and officer Justin Volpe had been charged for the August 1997 assault of Louima, who had been arrested after an altercation outside a nightclub. In May 1999, Volpe pleaded guilty. Officers Thomas Bruder and Thomas Wiese were found not guilty of beating Louima, and Sergeant Michael Bellomo was found not guilty of covering up the incident.

On April 28, New York City agreed to pay $2.75 million to Harold Dusenbury, who had been beaten by several police officers in 1996, as he was walking to work. Police were looking for a suspect described as a "black male in T-shirt and jeans" who had been seen with a knife. Officers allegedly stopped Dusenbury, beat him, and directed racial slurs at him. In a subsequent investigation, city officials concluded that the officers had made a mistake but did not reprimand them.

Hate crimes. A Texas jury on Feb. 25, 1999, sentenced John William King to death for the 1998 murder of James Byrd, Jr. King was one of three white men accused of chaining Byrd, who was black, to the bumper of a pickup truck and dragging him to death. Lawrence Russell Brewer was sentenced to death on Sept. 23, 1999, for his role in the murder. The third defendant, Shawn Berry, received a life sentence on October 18.

On April 5 in Laramie, Wyoming, Russell Henderson pleaded guilty to first-degree murder charges for the 1998 kidnapping and murder of Matthew Shepard, a gay college student. Shepard was allegedly killed because of his sexual orientation. Aaron McKinney, a codefendant in the case, was found guilty on Nov. 3, 1999. Both defendants were sentenced to two consecutive life terms without a possibility of parole.

Buford O'Neal Furrow shot two adults and three children on August 10 at the North Valley Jewish Community Center in Los Angeles. Furrow also shot and killed a Filipino American postal worker, reportedly because of his race. Burrow, who confessed to the shootings, said his action was "a wake-up call to America to kill Jews." Authorities filed the charges of murder and attempted murder as hate crimes.

Benjamin Smith allegedly targeted racial minorities in July on a three-day, seven-city shooting spree in Illinois and Indiana. One black man and one Korean man were killed. Four other blacks, six Jews, and one Taiwanese man were injured. Smith, who had belonged to a white supremacy group, committed suicide after a police chase.

☐ Geoffrey A. Campbell and Linda P. Campbell

See also **China; Courts; Crime; Human Rights: A Special Report; Yugoslavia.**

A Century of Civil Rights

A century of crusaders demanding changes expands the civil rights of all Americans.

By Jay Lenn

In 1900, African American scholar W. E. B. Du Bois declared that the problem of the new century was "the problem of the color line." At that time, most white Americans—through laws, traditions, and beliefs—had drawn a very distinct line between themselves and people of color. Du Bois believed that the greatest challenge to the United States would be bringing about the political and social changes that could erase that line. Du Bois's proclamation proved prophetic. Throughout the 1900's, the "color line"—as well as other lines of division—demanded national attention.

The civil rights movement in the United States is the story of individuals and organizations that used the courts and democratic processes to change the practices, laws, and attitudes that had led to the segregation of blacks and whites, prevented women from voting, denied accommodations to Jews, disregarded the religious practices of Native Americans, and threatened the lives of people who differed from the majority. Although the history of the civil rights movement is a complex catalog of events, certain pivotal moments of the 1900's introduced far reaching legal changes that expanded the civil liberties of all Americans.

A Political Voice for Women

How it was:

In the early 1900's, various policies and laws denied women admission to many colleges and universities, barred them from juries in most states, and excluded them from professions in law and medicine. Most married women could not own property, and single women who could own property could not vote on the levying of property taxes. Many women considered *suffrage* (the right to vote) the most important right and a necessary first step in the pursuit of other rights.

Forces for change:

The suffragists paraded and rallied to protest the widespread arguments that men could represent women better than women could represent themselves. In 1917, several suffragists were arrested for picketing outside the White House in Washington, D.C., and they later staged hunger strikes in prison. The public outcry about the treatment of the protesters helped change the course of the suffrage movement.

Constitutional amendment:

In 1919, the U.S. Congress passed a constitutional amendment, stating that the right to vote could not "be denied or abridged by the United States or by any state on account of sex." In 1920, Tennessee became the 36th state to ratify the measure that became the 19th Amendment to the U.S. Constitution.

Impact of the change:

The 19th Amendment granted suffrage to approximately half of the entire population of the United States and opened all aspects of American politics to women. In the presidential election of 1996, a higher percentage of women voted than men. By 1999, women held 12 percent of the seats in the U.S. Congress, 6 percent of the state governorships, and 28 percent of elected state offices.

How it was:

In 1896, the U.S. Supreme Court ruled that "separate but equal" public facilities for blacks and whites did not violate the rights of African Americans. In practice, separate schools for blacks and whites were far from equal. Textbooks in black schools were often used and damaged, black teachers made significantly less money than white teachers, and many school buildings for black students were substandard.

Forces for change:

In the 1930's, the National Association for the Advancement of Colored People (NAACP), a civil rights organization founded in 1909, filed numerous suits in state and federal courts to improve conditions in black schools, gain equitable pay for black teachers, and force state universities either to open institutions for black students or to integrate student populations.

Supreme Court decision:

In 1951, Thurgood Marshall, a leading NAACP attorney who later became a Supreme Court justice, took up the case of Oliver Brown, who had tried to enroll his daughter Linda in an all-white school in Topeka, Kansas. When the case, *Brown v. Board of Education of Topeka,* reached the U.S. Supreme Court in 1953, it was combined with similar cases. The justices ruled unanimously that "separate educational facilities are inherently unequal."

Impact of the ruling:

The ruling led to the desegregation of public schools, a slow and difficult task. In 1957, President Dwight D. Eisenhower sent U.S. Army troops to Arkansas to protect and escort nine African American students after Governor Orval Faubus tried to bar them from the all-white Little Rock Central High School. Nonetheless, the court's ruling on *Brown* set a precedent for further court action to force the desegregation of schools. In the 1970's, the U.S. Supreme Court ordered school districts to bus students to different neighborhoods in order to integrate public schools.

How it was:

Discrimination based on race, ethnicity, and religion was the norm in one form or another in both the North and the South as late as the 1960's. Separate theaters, drinking fountains, restrooms, and waiting rooms for blacks and whites were common. Restaurants and hotels could deny accommodations to African Americans, Jews, and other minorities. Racial discrimination abounded in the job market. White supremacy groups regularly lynched black males with impunity.

COLORED WAITING ROOM

PRIVATE PROPERTY NO PARKING Driving through or Turning Around

Forces for change:

In 1957, Rosa Parks was arrested in Montgomery, Alabama, for refusing to give up her seat on a city bus to a white passenger. Her protest launched a 382-day bus boycott that encouraged hundreds of marches, lunch counter sit-ins, and other demonstrations.

On Aug. 28, 1963, more than 200,000 people attended a march in Washington, D.C., to demand civil rights legislation. In an impassioned speech to the crowd, civil rights leader Martin Luther King, Jr., captured the essence of the civil rights movement by proclaiming his dream of a country without prejudice, hatred, and discrimination.

Civil rights legislation:

President Lyndon B. Johnson signed into law the Civil Rights Act of 1964, the most sweeping civil rights legislation ever passed in the United States. It bans discrimination in nearly every arena of public life because of a person's color, race, national origin, religion, or sex.

Impact of the legislation:

The desegregation of public accommodations and the elimination of discrimination from the U.S. work force did not occur overnight. Nevertheless, the 1964 law gave African Americans, women, and members of numerous minority groups leverage for securing their rights through the nation's court systems. It also provided the legal foundation and inspiration for the modern women's rights and gay rights movements.

How it was:

In the 1960's, many Southern states required people to pass a literacy or "character" test or to pay a poll tax before they could vote. Consequently, most blacks and some poor whites were barred from voting. In many Southern states, white people used violence and intimidation to prevent blacks from registering to vote.

Forces for change:

Several civil rights volunteers risked their lives to conduct voter registration campaigns in Southern states. In 1964, three volunteers—James Chaney, Andrew Goodman, and Michael Schwerner—were murdered in Mississippi. In 1965, state and local law enforcement officers in Selma, Alabama, used tear gas, clubs, and cattle prods to break up a peaceful demonstration against voter discrimination.

Constitutional and legislative changes:

The 24th Amendment, ratified in 1964, abolished poll taxes as a requirement for voting. The continued discrimination and violence in the South caused a public outrage that led to more comprehensive reforms. The Voting Rights Act of 1965 abolished literacy tests and other discriminatory practices, authorized federal officials to register voters, and gave the federal government the right to oversee changes in local and state election laws.

Impact of the changes:

By the end of the 1960's, more than 60 percent of the blacks who were old enough to vote had registered. The reforms also allowed for the election of more African Americans to public office. By 1997, black politicians held 40 seats in the U.S. Congress, 585 elected state offices, and 387 mayoralties.

How it was:

Discrimination in housing based on race, ethnicity, and religion was a problem throughout America. Landlords often refused to rent apartments to blacks, Jews, Irish Catholics, and other people. Banks denied mortgages on the basis of ethnicity and race, and real estate agents influenced who moved into a neighborhood. The result was highly segregated cities and vastly different housing conditions.

Forces for change:

In 1966, Martin Luther King, Jr., began a campaign in Chicago that focused on discrimination in housing and the conditions of slums. The campaign was not successful in changing policies, but did expose widespread racism in the North. Legislation to ban housing discrimination failed in the U.S. Congress in 1966 and 1967. On April 4, 1968, King was assassinated. Subsequent riots in cities across the nation added political pressure to housing reform efforts.

Federal legislation:

The Fair Housing Act of 1968 was signed on April 11, seven days after King's assassination. The law bans discrimination in the sale, rental, and advertisement of most housing, based on race, color, religion, or national origin. It also forbids banks and other institutions from discriminatory lending practices.

Impact of the legislation:

Blacks, Jews, and other minorities, for the first time in U.S. history, could rent or buy housing of their choice in whatever neighborhood they chose. The Fair Housing Act did not solve all of the inequities in housing in the United States, but did allow people to use the courts to challenge unfair practices and resistance to integrated neighborhoods. The act later provided some of the legal groundwork for demands of protection in the housing market for homosexuals.

How it was:

Between 1897 and 1934, Native Americans lost more than 90 million acres (36 million hectares) of reservation land through federal policies and actions of various presidential administrations. During the same period, most Indian children were forced to attend boarding schools, where they could not speak their native languages and were taught to abandon cultural traditions. On the reservations, tribal governments lost their authority, and most Native American religious ceremonies were prohibited.

Forces for change:

During the 1960's and 1970's, Native Americans frequently protested the abuse of their civil rights as individuals and their sovereign rights as tribal nations. In 1973, a demonstration at Wounded Knee, South Dakota, on the Pine Ridge Indian Reservation, escalated into an armed stand-off between members of the American Indian Movement and federal law enforcement agents. The Wounded Knee incident, which gained nationwide attention, was symbolically important to American Indians because it was the site of a brutal massacre of Indians in 1890.

Federal and legislative policy changes:

The Indian Self-Determination and Education Assistance Act of 1975 grants tribes the right to manage their own community development, education, health, housing, and law enforcement programs. The American Indian Religious Freedom Act of 1978 declares that Indians should have the right to the free exercise of religion. During the 1970's, the federal government began returning land to some tribes.

Impact of the changes:

Native Americans won advances in civil and sovereign rights relatively slowly, one court case at a time, because much of the early legislation was difficult to enforce. In the 1990's, for example, American Indians gained some protections for sites they held sacred, such as Devils Tower in Wyoming. The U.S. Supreme Court compelled several state governments to recognize the sovereignty of Native American tribal nations and the legitimacy of federal treaties with tribes.

How it was:

During World War II (1939-1945), several million women entered the work force to help with the war effort. After the war, American society encouraged women to stay at home and discouraged them from pursuing careers. Few women earned advanced degrees, and most women could not take out loans to purchase a house. They were rarely promoted to managerial positions. Throughout the 1960's and 1970's, the average income of women employed in full-time jobs was about 60 percent of the average income of men.

Forces for change:

In 1963, Betty Friedan published *The Feminine Mystique,* in which she described cultural expectations of feminine behavior and called for the breakdown of dehumanizing sexual stereotypes. Her book helped launch the modern women's movement. Women's rights activists founded several organizations—including the National Organization of Women, the National Women's Political Caucus, the Women's Equity Action League, and the Women's Legal Defense Fund—that led the campaign to gain legal protection against sex-based discrimination and to support women in leadership and professional roles.

Women's rights legislation:

Several pieces of legislation helped women to combat discrimination. The Equal Pay Act of 1963 requires equal wages for women and men doing the same work. Title VII of the Civil Rights Act of 1964 bans work-place discrimination based on sex. Title IX of the Education Amendments of 1972 bans discrimination on the basis of sex by schools and colleges receiving federal funds. The Equal Credit Opportunity Act of 1975 prohibits banks and other organizations from discriminating on the basis of sex or marital status in making loans or granting credit.

Impact of the legislation:

By the 1990's, opportunities for women had improved. Average incomes increased as managerial and professional jobs opened up for women. By 1998, the average income for women was 76 percent of the average income for men. Between 1972 and 1992, the number of businesses owned by women expanded by an average of 15 percent a year. By the mid-1990's, more women than men enrolled in both undergraduate and graduate degree programs.

Hungary. On March 12, 1999, Hungary officially joined the North Atlantic Treaty Organization (NATO), and Hungarian officials agreed to make the country's air space and military airfields available to NATO forces during the alliance's bombing campaign in neighboring Yugoslavia. Fearing Yugoslav reprisals against the ethnic Hungarian population in Vojvodina, a region of Yugoslavia, Hungarian officials did not allow Hungarian forces to participate in the NATO strikes.

In February, Hungary's Constitutional Court struck down a slate of laws designed to cripple organized crime. The Hungarian parliament had passed the laws in 1998 by a simple majority instead of the required two-thirds majority. Following the court's decision, President Arpad Goncz returned the legislation to parliament for reconsideration.

Hungary's inflation rate stood at 10 percent in July 1999 and was widely expected to drop by the end of the year. Unemployment fell to 6.8 percent in August.

In March, eastern Hungary experienced its most severe flooding in at least 100 years. Record amounts of snow, which had fallen in early February, melted rapidly, triggering flooding that the government estimated caused more than $3 million in damage. □ Sharon L. Wolchik

See also **Europe; Yugoslavia.**

Ice skating. Russians dominated competitive figure skating in 1999, winning every medal at the European championships and then taking every gold medal at the World Championships. Russia became the first country to win every event in the World Championships since ice dancing was added to the competition in 1952. Alexsei Yagudin, 18, successfully defended the World and European titles he captured in 1998.

European championships. In January 1999, at the European championships in Prague, Czech Republic, Yagudin followed a disastrous fall in the short program with a dazzling long program that included a quadruple toe-loop and seven triple-jumps. Yevgeny Plushenko, 16, placed second, and Alexsei Urmanov, the 1994 champion, finished third, completing a Russian men's sweep.

Mariya Butyrskaya defended her European title with a long program that included seven triple jumps. Julia Soldatova, 17, and Viktoria Volchkva, 16, took the silver and bronze medals, respectively, for a Russian women's sweep. The Russian team of Mariya Petrova and Alexei Tikhonov won the pairs gold, as did Russian ice dancers Angelika Krylova and Oleg Ovsiannikov.

U.S. championships. Michelle Kwan, 18, won her third U.S. championship in Salt Lake City, Utah, on Feb. 13, 1999. Michael Weiss, 22,

Russia's Mariya Butyrskaya wins the women's title at the 1999 World Figure Skating Championships in Helsinki, Finland, in March. Her performance in the free skate included seven triple jumps. At age 26, Butyrskaya became the oldest women's world champion in skating history.

who barely missed the gold medal in two previous attempts, fell early in his long program while attempting a quadruple toe-loop but landed eight triple jumps cleanly.

At the World Championships in Helsinki, Finland, Yagudin won the men's title on March 25, 1999, with an extraordinary long program performance that included eight triple jumps. The silver medal went to Plushenko while Weiss completed the best season of his career by taking the bronze. On March 27, Butyrskaya upset Kwan for the women's gold medal, with a remarkable free program that included seven triple jumps. At 26 years and 272 days, Butyrskaya was the oldest women's champion in history, as well as the first Russian to win the title. The pairs gold medal went to Russia's Yelena Berezhnaya and Anton Sikharulidze. Krylova and Ovsiannikov were the ice dancing champions.

Speed skating. Gunda Niemann-Stirnemann of Germany gained the 16th World Cup championship of her remarkable career when she won the season's overall title for the 1,500 meters on March 7, at Inzell, Germany. Bart Veldkamp, of the Netherlands, competing for Belgium, won gold in the 5,000 and 10,000 meters. ☐ Ron Reid

Iceland. See Europe.

Idaho. See State government.

Illinois. See Chicago; State government.

Immigration. The U.S. Supreme Court ruled unanimously on May 3, 1999, that foreign citizens in the United States were not eligible for protection as refugees if they had committed a "serious nonpolitical crime" in their own country. The court held that commission of such a crime was sufficient reason to deny admission, even if a person seeking asylum in the United States faced political persecution at home. The high court's opinion supported a Clinton administration decision to deport a Guatemalan who had been a student activist before coming to the United States. Juan Annibal Aguirre-Aguirre, who entered the United States illegally in 1993, admitted that as a student he had burned buses and attacked passengers to protest high bus fares and government policy toward students.

1996 Immigration Act. On March 8, 1999, the Supreme Court let stand lower court rulings that allowed aliens who have committed crimes to receive a court review of deportation orders issued under provisions of the 1996 Immigration Act. Activists regarded the ruling as a major victory for immigrant rights because the 1996 act deprived anyone classified as a "criminal alien" of the right to appeal to federal courts to reverse Immigration and Naturalization Service (INS) deportation orders.

In a related action, the INS on May 12, 1999, freed five Cuban-born prisoners who had committed serious crimes and were being detained under the 1996 immigration law. Because of the lack of diplomatic relations between the United States and Cuba, the five men could not be deported after serving their sentences and were being held indefinitely by the INS.

Refugees. The INS on May 20, 1999, eased its application rules for permanent resident status for some refugees from Central America and the countries of the former Soviet Union. The ruling allowed about 300,000 illegal immigrants, who were primarily Guatemalans and Salvadorans, to remain in the United States while they applied for permanent resident status. The immigrants, most of whom had fled repressive, right-wing governments during civil wars in the 1980's and 1990's, did not have to prove that they would suffer extreme hardship if forced to return to their home countries.

Welfare. A study by the Urban Institute, a Washington, D.C., policy research group, concluded in March that the percentage of immigrants receiving welfare payments from 1994 to 1997 fell at a far faster rate than the percentage of U.S. citizens receiving the same benefits. The study indicated a 35 percent decline in the use of benefits by immigrants, compared to a 15 percent drop for citizens. ☐ William J. Eaton

India. Parliamentary elections in 1999 returned Prime Minister Atal Behari Vajpayee to office at the head of a 24-party National Democratic Alliance (NDA). Vajpayee led the coalition in an election campaign that climaxed in five rounds of polling over a four-week period beginning September 5. Indian voters—more than 350 million in all—chose members for the Lok Sabha, India's lower house of parliament. The Lok Sabha selects India's prime minister and cabinet.

Vajpayee's party, the Hindu nationalist Bharatiya Janata Party (BJP), won 182 of the Lok Sabha's 543 seats. In all, the NDA coalition won about 300 seats, enough for a parliamentary majority. The main opposition group, the Congress Party and its allies, won 134 seats.

Vajpayee had governed India in a smaller alliance with 17 other parties since coming to power on March 19, 1998. The BJP suffered embarrassing losses, however, in state assembly elections late in 1998, and Vajpayee had difficulty keeping the NDA's Lok Sabha coalition together.

In April 1999, the BJP's largest partner, a regional party from Tamil Nadu state headed by a former movie actress, Jayalalitha Jayaram, withdrew from the NDA coalition. Indian President K. R. Narayanan then asked the NDA to prove it still had a majority in the Lok Sabha. The coalition failed by one vote, 269-270.

Vajpayee stayed on as head of a caretaker government. In the meantime, leaders of the Congress Party, which had governed India for 45 of the nation's 52 years of independence, attempted to form an alternative government. When they were unable to put together a coalition with a Lok Sabha majority, President Narayanan called new elections to be held after the 1999 monsoon rains.

NDA manifesto. In the campaign, the BJP issued a joint manifesto with its NDA allies. The manifesto did not mention the party's traditional goal of giving Hindu ideology a larger role in Indian life. Instead, it called for "a moratorium on contentious issues" to promote political stability. Party leaders endorsed this statement to reassure India's 120 million Muslims and 23 million Christians as well as many low-caste Hindus, who reportedly felt that the BJP worked mainly for an upper-caste elite. Nonetheless, some journalists reported that BJP party leaders were divided between pursuing religious goals, such as having all school children recite a daily prayer to a Hindu goddess of learning, and more pragmatic goals, such as promoting India's economic growth.

Congress Party. Sonia Gandhi, the widow of former Prime Minister Rajiv Gandhi, led the Congress Party in the election campaign. Early in the campaign, the Congress Party leader from Maharashtra state, Sharad Pawar, and two other senior party leaders questioned whether a foreign-born person should lead India. In response, Gandhi, an Italian-born Roman Catholic who acquired Indian citizenship in 1983, resigned as Congress president. After an outcry in the party, she returned to the party leadership. Pawar and the other two leaders then formed a splinter party, robbing the Congress Party of vital support in Maharashtra and other areas.

In the elections, Gandhi won a Lok Sabha seat from a south Indian constituency despite a strong campaign against her by a BJP candidate who focused on Gandhi's foreign birth. However, the Congress Party, on the whole, did poorly in the elections. The party won fewer Lok Sabha seats than in any previous election.

Several states elected legislatures during the parliamentary voting in 1999. In India's eastern state of Andhra Pradesh, the leader of a regional party, Chandrabadu Naidu, retained control of the government despite warning voters not to expect the kind of subsidies on public utilities that had been promised by the local Congress Party. For years, politicians in many Indian states had prevented governments from raising prices on such necessities as electricity and irrigation water. Selling energy and water below the cost of production cut deeply into state budgets, re-

Shattered rail passenger cars litter tracks near a station in eastern India after the head-on collision of two express trains in August 1999. The accident killed more than 300 people injured hundreds of others.

A ballistic missile with nuclear capabilities is paraded through the streets of New Delhi, the Indian capital, on Republic Day, January 26. India, which declared itself a nuclear power in 1998, conducted tests in 1999 of missiles with nuclear capabilities.

stricting states' ability to improve education, health services, and other programs.

Relations with Pakistan continued to pose a difficult challenge to India's leaders in 1999 and became a major theme of parliamentary elections. Pakistan and India have been bitter enemies since their creation by partition in 1947. The two countries fought three wars, two of them over Jammu and Kashmir, a mountainous Indian state with a Muslim majority. Hindu India eventually held most of the Kashmir region, which Muslim Pakistan wanted. In 1949, the United Nations arranged a cease-fire and established a "line of control" that separated the two armies. During the 1990's, Pakistani-backed guerrillas and terrorists attempted to shake India's hold on Kashmir's most populous area, the Srinagar Valley, resulting in the deaths of between 24,000 and 70,000 people, according to varying estimates. In 1998, India and Pakistan escalated hostilities by testing nuclear devices near each other's borders.

Leaders of India and Pakistan made a brief attempt at reconciliation in early 1999. On February 20, officials opened the first commercial bus service between India's capital, New Delhi, and Pakistan's northern city of Lahore. Indian Prime Minister Vajpayee rode the inaugural bus to Pakistan's border, where he met with Pakistani Prime Minister Nawaz Sharif. After talks in Lahore, the two leaders announced that they had agreed to work for better relations. However, they settled nothing about Kashmir, the two countries' thorniest issue. Later, India accused Pakistan of acting deceitfully in the February talks, by participating in discussions of peace while planning an attack on Indian-held Kashmir.

Renewed conflict in Kashmir. As mountain snows began to melt in April, about 600 heavily armed and well-trained troops seized mountaintop positions 3.7 miles (6 kilometers) on India's side of the Kashmir line of control. They began firing down at an important Indian highway near the towns of Dras and Kargil.

Pakistan said that the men were Muslim rebels with local support in Kashmir. India charged they were mostly Pakistani troops supported by Pakistan's army. Bitter fighting continued for two months. India claimed that its army and air force lost 486 soldiers while killing some 700 invaders. Pakistan countered that the rebels lost only 187 men while killing up to 1,700 of the Indian forces.

Amid fears of a general war between India and Pakistan, the conflict generated worldwide pressure for a settlement. After failing to win support from Pakistan's longtime friend, China, Pakistani Prime Minister Sharif abruptly flew to Washington, D.C., to talk on July 4 with U.S. Pres-

INDIA

IN EARLY 1948, the world was shocked by the death of Mohandas K. Gandhi. He was assassinated by one of his own people during a prayer service on the evening of January 30. . . . Gandhi was a martyr to the violence between Muslims, Sikhs, and Hindus, whose way of life had been interrupted by the partition of their country. It was a sad story of cruelty such as India had not known for hundreds of years.

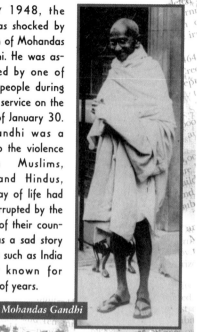
Mohandas Gandhi

ident Bill Clinton, who urged Sharif to end the fighting. A week later, Pakistan agreed to withdraw the forces across the line of control. Most of them were out of India by July 17. However, Indian officials estimated in mid-August that more than 2,000 Pakistani-backed militants were sporadically attacking Indian security forces inside Indian-held Kashmir.

Missiles amplify nuclear threat. On April 11, India announced that it had tested a ballistic missile capable of carrying a nuclear warhead. Pakistan fired a missile with nuclear capabilities three days later. Both countries had tested nuclear devices in 1998.

In August 1999, India's National Security Advisory Board made public a draft doctrine on nuclear weapons. It said that while India would never use such weapons first, it needed to have a "credible minimum deterrence" against attack. The draft called for land-based nuclear missiles and weapons deployed at sea and in aircraft.

Plane shot down. An Indian fighter plane shot down an unarmed Pakistani naval aircraft flying along the India-Pakistan border near the Arabian Sea on August 10. All 16 crew members were killed.

Attacks on Christians. More than 30 attacks on Christians and their churches and schools were carried out in Gujarat, a western state, in early 1999. Responsibility was not clearly established, but some observers blamed the BJP for failing to stop the attacks.

In January, a mob in India's eastern state of Orissa trapped a Christian missionary from Australia and his two young sons in a car and then burned them to death. Although Indian police initially blamed a group associated with the BJP, a government-sponsored judicial inquiry ultimately held a Hindu activist responsible. BJP opponents labeled the finding a "whitewash." In early September, a mob in another Orissa village killed a Roman Catholic priest with bows and arrows.

Separatist rebels kept parts of northeastern India in turmoil throughout 1999. Two guerrilla groups carried out sporadic attacks in the states of Assam and Nagaland. The Assam fighting spilled over into the adjacent nation of Bhutan, where some rebels had established illegal camps in the jungles.

In India's northeastern state of Bihar, upper-caste landlords and low-caste laborers clashed repeatedly in 1999. Landlord armies shot workers to keep others in line. In retaliation, Communist resistance groups beheaded upper-caste villagers.

India's population, growing at a rate of 1.6 percent a year, reached 1 billion in August, according to several estimates. The population of India more than tripled between 1947, when the country gained independence, and 1999.

India's economy grew in 1999 with the help of a summer harvest that was 9.4 percent larger than in 1998. Industrial production rose, and exports grew by 9 percent, with textiles, garments, jewelry, and computer software in the lead. India continued to attract new computer-related industries as companies sought out its well-educated, English-speaking workers whose salary expectations were low by Western standards.

The use of satellite communications enabled companies in India to handle computer-processing work for businesses throughout the world. India's domestic output grew at a rate of nearly 6 percent in 1999, and inflation held at 1.2 percent, a 17-year low.

Train wreck. Two express trains traveling more than 50 miles (80 kilometers) per hour crashed head-on near the border of West Bengal and Assam on August 2. The collision killed more than 300 people and injured hundreds.

Cyclone. On October 29, a cyclone hit Orissa, on the northeastern coast, with winds of 160 miles (260 kilometers) per hour driving tidal waves as high as 15 feet (5 meters). The storm destroyed hundreds of villages, killed nearly 10,000 people, and left 1 million people homeless.

☐ Henry S. Bradsher

See also **Asia; Pakistan; Terrorism.**

Oglala Lakota Sioux Indians perform a ceremony to honor the bison in February 1999 at Yellowstone National Park in Wyoming. Some of the participants traveled on foot from South Dakota to protest the slaughter of bison that wander from the park.

Indian, American. An ongoing controversy regarding how the United States government manages trust-fund accounts for Native Americans grew more complicated in 1999. In January, Paul Homan, who was appointed in 1995 to correct past problems and develop an efficient fund-management system, resigned. Homan accused Secretary of the Interior Bruce Babbitt, who oversees U.S. policy regarding Native Americans, of depriving Homan of the authority and resources he needed to fulfill his responsibilities.

In the 1800's, the U.S. government began leasing Indian property to businesses, such as oil or mining companies, and promised to turn over the fees to the owners of the property or to their descendants. A 1994 audit of the previous 20 years of transactions revealed that the Bureau of Indian Affairs (BIA), a division of the Department of the Interior, could not account for $2.4 billion.

The trust-fund controversy in 1999 also figured in an ongoing lawsuit. Several Native Americans filed the lawsuit in 1996, seeking a court order to compel the Department of the Interior to fix the system. In February 1999, presiding U.S. District Judge Royce Lamberth cited Babbitt, Treasury Secretary Robert E. Rubin, and BIA director Kevin Gover for contempt of court for a "flagrant disregard" of orders to turn over relevant documents to the court. In December, Lamberth ruled that the government had violated its duty, calling the mismanagement "fiscal and governmental irresponsibility in its purest form." Lamberth ordered that the lawsuit remain pending for five years, during which time the government must remedy problems and provide the court with quarterly reports demonstrating progress.

The Pecos and Jemez Pueblo Indians of New Mexico held traditional burial services in May 1999 for the remains of nearly 2,000 Pueblo ancestors that had been in museums in Massachusetts—at Harvard University in Cambridge and Phillips Academy in Andover. The remains were buried at a site sacred to the Pueblo in the Pecos National Historic Park. The return of the remains and numerous artifacts was the largest of such efforts since the passage of the Native American Graves Protection and Repatriation Act of 1990.

A groundbreaking ceremony was held on Sept. 29, 1999, for a new National Museum of the American Indian to be built on the last available space on the National Mall in Washington, D.C. The museum was scheduled for completion in 2002. Its design included innovative features, such as windows that would allow sunlight to illuminate sacred objects at the winter and summer solstices. The solstices, the shortest and longest days of the year, are sacred in many Indian religions.

Ceremony honoring bison. In February 1999, about 100 Native Americans gathered in Yellowstone National Park in Wyoming to participate in a traditional ceremony honoring bison, which were essential to the livelihood of the Great Plains Indians before the 1900's. The ceremony participants protested the slaughter of bison that wander from the park. Ranchers claim the bison can tranfser disease to cattle. Some Oglala Lakota Sioux had traveled 500 miles (800 kilometers) on foot or horseback from the Pine Ridge Indian Reservation in South Dakota to join in the ceremony.

The Cherokee Nation in Oklahoma inaugurated Chad Smith as its new principal chief on Aug. 14, 1999. The inauguration marked the end of four years of political strife for the second-largest group of American Indians. Many Cherokee voters criticized Smith's predecessor, Joe Byrd, who took office after a disputed 1995 election, for unconstitutional practices. When Byrd left office, he faced charges of misappropriating tribal funds. Chief Smith claimed that the primary agenda of his administration would be to bring "healing" to the Cherokee Nation.

U.S. President Bill Clinton visited Pine Ridge Indian Reservation in July 1999, while on a tour of impoverished regions of the United States. Clinton pledged to introduce incentives that would encourage private investors to create job opportunities on Pine Ridge. Clinton was the first U.S. president to visit a reservation since President Franklin Delano Roosevelt traveled to a reservation in North Carolina in 1934. ☐ Jay Lenn

Indiana. See **State government.**

Indonesia. The People's Consultative Assembly named Abdurrahman Wahid president of Indonesia on Oct. 20, 1999. With Wahid's support, the assembly elected Megawati Sukarnoputri vice president. Megawati is the daughter of Sukarno, Indonesia's first president.

The assembly, composed of a newly elected parliament and 200 people appointed by regional parliaments and the election commission, chose Wahid by 373 to 313 votes. The vote followed President B. J. Habibie's decision to withdraw his name from consideration after the assembly voted no confidence in his 17-month administration.

On June 7, Indonesians voted for the bulk of the People's Consultative Assembly in the first free election in 44 years. Megawati's Indonesian Democratic Party for Struggle won 34 percent of the vote. Habibie's Golkar Party, long Indonesia's ruling party, took 22 percent. Wahid's National Awakening Party ranked third, with 11 percent.

Wahid, a respected moderate Muslim leader, had suffered several strokes and was nearly blind at the time he was elected president. His fragile health amplified the importance of Megawati's selection as vice president. Political analysts characterized Megawati as politically inexperienced, noting that she had let the presidency slip away by refusing to participate in political bargaining prior to the vote. However, she had a loyal following among the public, and her party held the largest block of assembly seats.

President Wahid proceeded to name a "national unity cabinet," which embraced all major political factions, including the discredited Golkar Party. In a departure from past governments, Wahid named a civilian to the post of defense minister. He attacked corruption, pursuing investigations against officials of previous regimes as well as three of his own cabinet members.

East Timor, a predominantly Roman Catholic enclave of 800,000 people on Timor Island, gained independence from Indonesia in 1999 after a long, bloody struggle that drew United Nations (UN) peacekeeping forces and administrators into the conflict. Indonesia had seized the region in 1975 after Portugal abandoned colonial rule there. The Indonesian army had fought a guerrilla movement in East Timor for more than 20 years, a conflict that cost some 200,000 lives.

In January 1999, President Habibie indicated to the United Nations that he was willing to allow a vote on the future status of East Timor, either as an *autonomous* (semi-independent) region within Indonesia or as an independent nation. The UN scheduled a referendum for August. Indonesia's army, which bitterly opposed independence for East Timor, responded by organizing and arming anti-independence militias.

An Indonesian student burns the United Nations flag outside a UN office in Jakarta, Indonesia, in September to protest international intervention in East Timor. The UN sent peacekeepers into East Timor in 1999 to halt the violence of anti-independence militias allegedly supported by elements within the Indonesia military.

Referendum. On August 30, more than 99 percent of registered East Timor voters cast ballots in the UN-sponsored referendum. More than 78 percent voted for independence. Almost immediately, the anti-independence militias went on a rampage, killing East Timorese and driving thousands from their residences. According to observers, the Indonesian army and police did little to stop the violence.

On September 12, President Habibie yielded to intense international pressure and invited the UN to send peacekeeping troops to East Timor. An Australian-led UN force began arriving on September 20 and gradually halted the violence.

The UN voted on October 25 to replace the peacekeepers with a more permanent force of about 9,000 UN troops and an administrative team. An East Timor guerrilla leader who had been living in exile, Jose "Xanana" Gusmao, returned to participate in the task of building a new government.

Other separatist agitation. After the last of the Indonesian forces withdrew from East Timor on October 30, Indonesian army officials insisted that independence for East Timor did not set a precedent for independence for other provinces. Some observers accused the Indonesian army of attempting to destroy East Timor as an example to separatists in other areas.

In early November, half a million people demonstrated for independence in Banda Aceh, capital of Aceh province. Acehnese separatists had agitated for independence for years. The dispute was partly cultural. The Acehnese practice a far stricter form of Islam than most Muslims in Indonesia. The Indonesian army had launched a crackdown in Aceh in the early 1990's, which continued until August 1999. According to human rights groups, more than 6,000 people had died or disappeared in Aceh during the years of army repression.

Civic strife wracked two other areas in Indonesia in 1999. On Ambon Island, clashes between Muslims and Christians left more than 350 people dead and caused thousands to flee the area. In West Kalimantan, Muslim Malays, animist Dayaks, and Confucian Chinese united to drive out settlers from another Indonesian island, Madura. More than 200 people were killed in February and March on West Kalimantan, where severed heads were displayed openly.

Indonesia's economy improved slightly in 1999 from the severe recession that began in 1997. In 1998, Indonesia's domestic output had shrunk 16 percent, according to some estimates, while inflation escalated to 66 percent.

□ Henry S. Bradsher

See also **Asia; Australia; United Nations.**

International trade flourished during 1999. A robust economy in the United States led consumers to increase purchases from other regions, which played a key role in helping foreign economies avert a general recession. In 1999, China and the United States reached an agreement that experts maintained would pave the way for China to enter the world's international trading community. Other Southeast Asian nations, aided by foreign sales and domestic demand, began to recover from an economic crisis that had spread across the area in 1997 and 1998. Although European economies stumbled in 1999, they were able to stabilize later in the year. One of the most dramatic protests surrounding international trade occurred in November and December, when demonstrations turned violent at a World Trade Organization (WTO) meeting in Seattle.

Asian nations made greater contributions to international trade in 1999 than they had during most of the late 1990's. In Japan, which had been in the midst of a severe economic contraction in 1998, regional trade grew in 1999 as economic recovery continued in such neighboring Southeast Asia nations as South Korea. Increased government spending and loans by the government of Japanese Prime Minister Keizo Obuchi also supported the economy and bolstered trade.

In November 1999, negotiators from China and the United States reached a landmark deal designed to open the economy of China to foreign competitors. Under the trade pact, China agreed to reduce *tariffs* (taxes charged on imports or exports) on agricultural and industrial products and to lift bans that hampered U.S. companies from expanding their investments in China. In return, U.S. officials agreed to support China's entry into the WTO, the Geneva, Switzerland-based arbitrator of trade disputes among member countries. The WTO also sets the rules for international commerce.

During 1999, China resisted devaluing its currency, the yuan, despite weakness in its trade sector. Devaluation would have made it easier to sell more Chinese goods abroad but would most likely have had a negative effect on the currencies of other Asian countries.

Euro launch. Eleven western European countries—Austria, Belgium, Finland, France, Germany, Ireland, Italy, Luxembourg, the Netherlands, Portugal, and Spain—forged stronger economic ties and became a more solid force in global trading as they launched a new currency, the euro, on January 1. The 11 countries were all part of the European Union (EU—an organization of 15 European nations). Officials in three other EU nations—the United Kingdom, Sweden, and Denmark—opted not to participate in the euro's launch. Greece, the EU's weakest economy, did not qualify for participation in the Euro.

The euro nations managed their money supply under a combined European Central Bank, rather than each continuing to manage money and currency values separately. However, Europe's growth slowed so much in late 1998 and early 1999 that many economic experts feared a recession. The European economy sustained a mild growth pace through the remainder of the year and did not contribute greatly to the trade surge that kept the world economy on track.

The fast-growing U.S. economy served as the main engine of international trade growth in 1999 as it pulled in imports from other countries eager to rebuild weak economies. The growth continued throughout the year, despite pressure from some U.S. businesses that complained of unfair competition from those imports.

Such imports brought an extra benefit to the U.S. economy in the form of falling prices for imported goods that helped keep U.S. inflation low for many years. When the currencies of such nations as Brazil, Japan, and Russia plunged during the late 1990's, the price of goods they sent abroad automatically dropped. When many currencies strengthened in 1999, global prices of both raw commodities and finished goods rose.

Trade deficits. The government's commitment to keep the United States open to imports was evident in a monthly increase in the U.S. trade deficit for goods and services in 1999. A trade deficit is the shortfall between the value of a country's exports of goods and services and the value of its imports. During the first eight months of 1999, the U.S. trade deficit reached $167.2 billion. In August the monthly deficit hit $23.5 billion, a decrease from the July level of $24.9 billion. The U.S. Department of Commerce reported that September's trade deficit hit $24.2 billion.

The U.S. monthly trade deficit with Japan hit $6.8 billion in July 1999, even though the United States was pushing Japan to open its own economy to foreign goods and to increase Japanese economic growth. The U.S. shortfall in trade with China reached nearly $6.9 billion in September, a reflection of U.S. policies to maintain low overall tariff barriers to many Chinese goods, even though China was not a member of the WTO. The United States maintained large monthly trade deficits with leading continental economies, despite Europe's slow rate of growth and high unemployment. The United States also sustained sizable monthly deficits with its border partners of Canada and Mexico in the North America Free Trade Agreement.

Trade recovery. With global recovery under way, major oil-producing nations curbed output in the spring of 1999 and increased prices from their lowest levels in decades. As a result, consumers were hit with large price increases. However, the price hikes stabilized an important global sector by restoring revenues for oil-producing nations and for energy producers in some oil-importing countries, including the United States. Many economists, however, also blamed the increases in the price of oil for the swelling of the U.S. trade deficit.

With domestic steel producers hurt by the flood of cheaper imports during 1998, both the United States and Europe fought back with a mix of negotiated curbs, pressures, and legal remedies to curb those flows during 1999. Among the nations affected by such measures were economically ravaged Russia, recession-struck Brazil, and economically recovering South Korea and Japan.

Protests turned violent during a WTO conference in Seattle, where members met, beginning on November 29, to discuss dropping trade barriers. Police and protesters clashed in the streets, leading to a dusk-to-dawn curfew to curb looting of area businesses. Many protesters peacefully tried to express concern over various issues, including the possibililty that China, if admitted to the WTO would not adhere to global stardards of trade, labor practices, or environmental protections.   ☐ John D. Boyd

See also **Economics; Manufacturing.**

Stamps.com, a U.S. Postal Service-regulated Web site, which debuted in 1999, enables users to purchase stamps over the Internet. After paying the postage fee and a service charge, the user downloads digitized "stamps," which can be printed onto an envelope by a standard laser or inkjet printer.

Internet. The Internet came into its own in 1999, not only as a novel means of communication and a tool for scientists and educators, but also as a commercial medium. A strong economy, plummeting prices for personal computers, and growing familiarity with the Internet by consumers combined to fuel the explosive growth of electronic commerce, or "e-commerce." Forrester Research, a market research firm in Cambridge, Massachusetts, estimated that 7 million Internet users made their first online purchase in 1999, helping push Internet retail sales in the United States to more than $20.2 billion. Jupiter Communications, a New York City-based Internet commerce market researcher, estimated that consumers would spend approximately $6 billion online in November and December. Books, compact discs, airline tickets, and toys were among the most popular items purchased online. Online supermarkets also gained popularity, with companies filling their customers' online grocery orders for home delivery.

Internet-related companies seemed intent on repealing conventional laws of economics in 1999—the more money they lost, the higher their stock price went. Indeed, the roller-coaster ride on Wall Street in 1999 was due in large part to the wild fluctuations in the prices of Internet stocks. In this topsy-turvy world, profit was seen as less important than "branding," the notion that huge future payoffs were in store for companies willing to establish their presence on the Internet now.

E-commerce takes root. The two-way nature of an e-commerce transaction enabled innovative approaches for selling products and services. One of the hottest new ways of doing business in 1999 was the online auction. Activity at sites such as eBay of San Jose, California, increased significantly, as people logged on to bid on items ranging from collectibles and baseball tickets to used cars. Another novel technique was the "name your price" system offered by companies like Priceline.com, based in Stamford, Connecticut. Visitors to Priceline.com entered the amount of money they would be willing to pay for a product or service, such as airline tickets or long-distance telephone service. Priceline.com subsequently informed the consumer when a merchant visiting the Web site accepted the offer.

E-trading. The trading of stocks and other securities hit the Internet in a big way in 1999. Traditional brokerage companies had been reluctant to offer their services over the Internet, but the success of small, upstart discount brokerages persuaded most established firms to offer e-trading. Individuals who established Internet accounts at brokerage companies were able to buy and sell shares through their computers, bypassing brokers, which significantly reduced transaction fees. Some investors began trading stocks many times over the course of a day in an attempt to squeeze profits out of the daily price fluctuations of the stock market. Investment experts warned that most of these so-called "day traders" actually lost money in the long run.

Other services. While most e-commerce still consisted of electronic order-taking, a number of companies offering Net-based services emerged in 1999. For example, the popular Yahoo! Web site offered registered users free access to a calendar program that kept track of appointments and sent reminders. While the program itself ran on the provider's system, users could enter, store, and update the information over the Net. Such Net-based services were useful to people who traveled frequently, since they were accessible from any computer with an Internet connection.

Another Net-based service, i-drive of San Francisco, enabled users to store computer files, such as backup copies of data. Instead of saving files on local disks, users could transfer files to i-drive's computers using the Net. Although such services were free of charge in 1999, they served as examples of how Net-based service providers could generate revenue in the future.

The Net also continued to grow in 1999 as a reference source. The contents of *The World Book Encyclopedia* became available as World Book Online, first for schools and libraries and later for individual consumers.

In October 1999, *Encyclopaedia Britannica* made the contents of its encyclopedia available on the Web at no charge. Britannica hoped to make money on the venture through paid advertisements on its Web site. Internet users deluged the Britannica Web site, jamming it for days. Britannica officials soon increased the site's resources to handle the load.

Better access. While most home computer users still accessed the Net through ordinary telephone lines in 1999, a growing number of residential users began to enjoy the benefits of high-speed access. The two most popular methods were cable modems, which transfer data over the same coaxial cables that deliver cable TV signals, and digital subscriber lines (DSL), which use special hardware to squeeze greater amounts of information through standard telephone lines. Both of these technologies provided an "always on" Internet connection at home that did not interfere with traditional telephone use. This promised to make household use of the Internet more routine and less disruptive. □ Herb Brody

See also **Computers; Electronics; Telecommunications.**

Iowa. See **State government.**

Iran. A bitter struggle for political power between religious conservatives and reformers continued in Iran in 1999. The power struggle began in the presidential election of 1997, when moderate cleric Mohammed Khatami won an upset victory, with 70 percent of the vote, against a conservative candidate. Iran's conservatives, many of whom supported Ayatollah Ali Khamenei, Iran's supreme leader, opposed the pace of political reform promised by Khatami. Khatami was hampered because Khamenei controlled Iran's military, security, and intelligence forces, as well as the courts and clerical institutions. In addition, the Iranian parliament was headed by Ali Akbar Nateq-Noori, an ally of Khamenei.

Reformist-conservative tensions increased in February 1999, when moderates scored an overwhelming victory in municipal elections. The moderates won most of the seats in city councils across the nation, including all the seats in the city council of Teheran, Iran's capital.

Demonstrations. Several days of violent demonstrations were touched off on July 7, 1999, after conservatives banned the liberal Islamic newspaper *Salam* and enacted a law to curb freedom of the press. Students at Teheran University began the demonstrations as peaceful protests for cultural freedom. However, the protests soon spread to 18 other cities and became violent after police and Islamic paramilitary groups attacked the Teheran students in their dormitories on July 8, killing at least two students.

The demonstrations ended abruptly on July 13. Many observers believed that the student reformers refrained from further demonstrations out of fear that conservatives would blame the violence on Khatami's efforts to allow greater cultural freedom. On July 14, Iranian conservatives rallied hundreds of thousands of supporters in a counter-protest.

Reformist found guilty. A clerical jury in November found Abdollah Nouri, a prominent reformist cleric, politician, and newspaper director, guilty of publishing sacrilegious articles and insulting the government. Nouri was sentenced to five years in prison and banned from running in upcoming elections. In December, the court said it would allow Nouri to appeal.

Khatami's travels. Khatami, seeking foreign investment and an end to Iran's international isolation, visited Italy in March. He was the first Iranian leader to visit a Western nation since the 1979 Islamic Revolution, in which Islamic radicals overthrew the pro-West shah of Iran. In October 1999, Khatami visited France for high-level talks.

U.S. relations. In May, the United States again included Iran in its annual report of countries that sponsor state terrorism, though the report dropped Iran's 1998 designation as the "most active state sponsor of terrorism." Also in May 1999, the United States eased trade sanctions against Iran to permit the sale of some medicine and food to the country. Despite these moves, U.S. Secretary of Defense William Cohen stated publicly in October that Iran remained a threat to regional security. Analysts noted that more concrete steps, such as increased Iranian efforts to reduce terrorism and a lifting of all U.S. sanctions against Iran, were needed before U.S.-Iranian ties could improve. Analysts, however, warned that further efforts to improve relations with the United States would place Khatami at great political risk with Iranian conservatives.

In October, Iran rejected a request by U.S. President Bill Clinton to provide information about Iranian suspects in the 1996 bombing of an apartment complex in Khobar, Saudi Arabia, which killed 19 U.S. troops. Iran denied involvement in the bombing.

Spy case. Iranian officials announced in June 1999 that several Iranians, including 13 Jews, had been arrested earlier in the year for spying for the United States and Israel—charges the United States and Israel denied. Since 1979, more than 15 Jews had been executed for spying in Iran.

☐ Christine Helms

See also **Israel; Middle East; Middle East: A Special Report.**

IRAN

IRAN became the storm center of the Middle East in 1979 and designated an old ally, the United States, as the enemy. A yearlong popular revolution reached its goal on January 16, when Shah Mohammad Reza Pahlavi left the country with his family on a "vacation" that ended his 38-year rule. . . .

Behind him, the shah left a nation in turmoil. The Ayatollah Ruhollah Khomeini, chief religious leader of the Iranian Shiite Muslim sect . . . returned from 15 years in exile on February 1, to become the de facto head of state. . . .

The gulf between the real and ideal widened rapidly after Khomeini's return as the Iranian revolution took on more and more the coloration of the bloody French Revolution. A wave of executions, initially of agents of Savak (the shah's secret police) but later broadened to include military and business leaders and even some opponents of the shah, had claimed at least 600 victims by October.

A Teheran University student throws stones at Iranian police in July 1999. Violent demonstrations erupted in Iran on July 7, when conservatives enacted a law to curb freedom of the press. The student protesters supported the cultural reforms of moderate Iranian President Mohammed Khatami.

Iraq repeatedly charged in 1999 that ongoing bombing raids by the United States and Great Britain in northern and southern Iraq had killed scores of civilians. Since the early 1990's, U.S. and British aircraft had patrolled northern and southern "no-fly zones" in Iraq, which were established by the United States after the Iraqi military put down uprisings in the areas following the end of the Gulf War in 1991. In December 1998, the United States and Britain began a bombing campaign in the zones after Iraqi President Saddam Hussein expelled UN inspectors who were monitoring Iraqi weapons programs.

Although the United States and Great Britain maintained that they were justified in bombing Iraqi air defenses and radar sites, Iraq claimed that many civilian sites were hit in the thousands of bombing raids that were carried out in 1999. A number of countries, including France and Qatar, that had supported the United States in the ouster of Iraqi troops from Kuwait in 1991, criticized the raids as exceeding the original intent of the no-fly zones.

Sanctions. In October 1999, UN Secretary General Kofi Annan accused the United States and Great Britain of blocking contracts that would approve the sale of medicine, food, and other humanitarian supplies to Iraq. The two Western nations denied the charge. The UN "oil-for-food" program required that a UN sanctions committee approve contracts for the export of humanitarian goods to Iraq, which paid for the goods with oil revenues. UN sanctions were first imposed on Iraq after its 1990 invasion of Kuwait.

The UN Security Council remained deadlocked throughout most of 1999 over a new resolution concerning the sanctions on Iraq. On December 17, the Security Council voted to suspend the sanctions if Iraq fully cooperated with a new team of weapons inspectors. However, Russia and China, both of which wanted a quicker end to sanctions, as well as France and Malaysia, abstained from voting. Iraq rejected the resolution, saying it would not allow new inspectors into the country unless the sanctions were first lifted.

UNICEF, the United Nations Children's Fund, warned in August that the UN sanctions were contributing to a "humanitarian emergency" in Iraq. The warning was based on a UNICEF survey of child *mortality* (death rate) in Iraq.

According to UNICEF, the death rate for children under 5 years of age in southern and central Iraq—where 85 percent of Iraq's population lives—more than doubled since the sanctions were imposed. Between 1984 and 1989, 56 children died per every 1000 live births. Between 1994 and 1999, 131 children died per every 1000 live births. *Infant mortality* (the death rate of children in their first year) climbed in the same

period from 47 deaths to 108 deaths per 1000 live births.

The UNICEF report cited a number of factors for the mortality increase, including the UN sanctions, two recent wars in Iraq, a collapsed economy, and mismanagement within the Iraqi government. The UN organization recommended that Iraq implement better nutrition programs for children and provide more food for pregnant and nursing mothers. UNICEF also pleaded for more international relief, including food and medicine.

Opposition. Approximately 300 Iraqi opposition figures—including some who lived in Iraq and others living in exile—concluded a four-day meeting in New York City on Nov. 1, 1999. The U.S.-financed gathering, known as the Iraqi National Council, met in an attempt to unite the various Iraqi opposition groups, such as Kurds, Shiite Muslims, and monarchists. However, certain prominent opposition leaders refused to attend the meeting, arguing that the strong U.S. presence discredited it.

Thomas Pickering, a U.S. Undersecretary of State, told the council that the United States would "protect and help" any Iraqis seeking to oust Saddam. Pickering also said the United States continued to pursue means to indict Saddam and other Iraqi officials for war crimes. The United States announced in October that it was donating $2 million in office supplies to the opposition groups and planned to offer four opposition figures a 10-day training course in military-civilian relations. Critics charged that U.S. aid fell far short of a 1998 offer to provide $97 million in support, including military equipment, to opposition forces. ☐ Christine Helms

See also **Energy supply; Middle East; Middle East: A Special Report; United Nations.**

IRAQ

SADDAM HUSSEIN, the secretary-general of the ruling Baath Party and chairman of the Revolutionary Command Council (RCC), succeeded President Ahmad Hasan al-Bakr, who retired for health reasons on July 16, 1979. Within days, the new president moved against a "vile conspiracy" against his regime that involved several RCC members plus a number of senior military commanders. Some 250 people were arrested and 21 executed as the Iraqi leader quickly asserted his authority over the country.

Ireland. The economy of Ireland continued to boom in 1999. And while Ireland's public life pulsed with a new economic and artistic vitality, the government became mired in 1999 in accusations of corruption.

Economy. Ireland continued in 1999 to experience stronger economic growth than most other countries in the European Union. The Central Bank of Ireland forecast that the country's *gross domestic product* (the value of all goods and services produced in a country in a given year) would fall, but only slightly, from 8 percent in 1998 to 6.5 percent in 1999. In October, unemployment in Ireland fell to 5.7 percent, and Martin Kohlhaussen, president of the German Banking Association, described Ireland as "the European success story of the decade." In 1993, unemployment in Ireland stood at 15.9 percent.

Government analysts attributed the economic boom to a plentiful labor supply (the high birth rate before 1980 resulted in a great number of people entering the work force in the 1990's); an increase in women in the work force; an increase in the education level of the work force; foreign investment, especially from the United States; and an economic policy in which trade unions agreed to lower their wage demands in return for higher economic growth. One of the most noticeable features of the Irish boom was the number of people moving to Ireland—including Irish nationals returning to their country—attracted by the new economic opportunities. For much of its modern history, Ireland had been a land of emigrants.

Government scandal. Taoiseach (prime minister) Bertie Ahern, who led a coalition government made up of his Fianna Fail Party, the Pro-gressive Democrats, and some independents, continued to be embarrassed by corruption allegations against the former Fianna Fail taoiseach, Charles Haughey. Haughey was accused in 1997 of obstructing an investigation into charges that he had used public money to fund a lavish lifestyle while in office from 1988 to 1992. Ahern, who had been minister of finance under Haughey, was asked in July 1999 to explain why he had signed blank checks for Haughey's use.

In another ongoing investigation, property developer Tom Gilmartin revealed in January that he had presented a donation for Fianna Fail in 1989 to Padraig Flynn, the Irish representative to the European Union's Executive Commission. In 1989, Flynn was Fianna Fail's treasurer and environment minister. The money never reached the party, leading to allegations of corruption. The revelation almost toppled the government, when Fianna Fail's coalition partner, the Progressive Democrats, expressed outrage.

Finally, a commission investigating tax evasion by leading political and business figures found that as many as 120 prominent Irish citizens had hidden accounts in a Cayman Island bank founded by an assistant of Haughey. Ahern's hold on power was aided by the improved prospects for peace in Northern Ireland.   ☐ Rohan McWilliam

See also **Europe; Northern Ireland.**

Islam. In 1999, numerous Muslims awaited the new millennium with concern and expectation, even though 2000 is the year 1420 in the Islamic calendar. Sheik Nazem Rabbani Haqani predicted that the new millennium would bring an era of natural disasters, the return of Jesus, whom Muslims regard as a prophet, and the establishment of a kingdom of justice. Nazem is a Sufi, a Muslim mystic, belonging to a religious order known as the Naqshbandi. His followers live throughout the Middle East, Europe, the United States, and Southeast Asia. His followers in Beirut, the capital of Lebanon, rented houses in the Denniyeh Mountains in 1999 in preparation for a "catastrophe" that they expected in 2000.

A number of Muslim clerics reacted to Nazem's predictions with harsh criticism. Taha Sabunji, a Lebanese Muslim official of the Sunni sect, to which most Muslims belong, denounced the "superstitions" and called on the faithful not to follow people "who pretend to know the future."

Sheik Hisham Kabbani, a Naqshbandi Sufi leader in the United States, created a storm of protest in January 1999, when he declared at a U.S. State Department forum in Washington, D.C., that many U.S. Muslim leaders were "extremists." Kabbani also stated that Islamic fundamentalists threatened Sufis in Eastern Europe and central Asia with violence for their beliefs. He

---

TIME CAPSULE   **1949**

IRELAND

EIRE celebrated Easter Monday, April 18, 1949, as the day on which it became the fully independent Republic of Ireland. This was the 33rd anniversary of the Easter revolt against the British in 1916.

Former Prime Minister Eamon de Valera refused to take part in the celebration because Northern Ireland had not joined the new republic. Northern Ireland had shown by a large majority vote in February that it wished to remain part of the United Kingdom.

claimed that examples of such extremism could be seen in the United States and accused Muslim student associations on U.S. university campuses of being "brainwashed" by extremist ideas.

U.S. Muslim organizations condemned Kabbani's statements, claiming that they reinforced stereotypes of Muslims as terrorists and fanatics. Kabbani's followers defended his position, describing him as an inspired spiritual master who seeks to challenge fundamentalist beliefs and promote what he perceives as the true teachings of Islam.

Internet access became available in Saudi Arabia in 1999. For Muslim women who work, the Internet provided important opportunities. Travel restrictions, a ban on women's driving, and other legal limitations—based on interpretations of Islamic teachings—make it difficult for women to work in the private sector. The Internet allowed them to conduct business without meeting clients face to face.

Most of the 3,000 Saudi women who owned private businesses in 1999 worked in the fashion industry. Through the Internet, they visited fashion shows and purchased goods from around the world. In 1999, two-thirds of Internet users in Saudi Arabia were women. Business analysts expected that the Internet would allow the number of Saudi businesswomen to grow by 200 percent over the next five years.   □ Vincent J. Cornell

TIME CAPSULE 1948

ISRAEL

AT MIDNIGHT on May 14, 1948, the Jews in Palestine proclaimed the new state of Israel. The new nation began its life with territory whose boundaries were hotly disputed. The Jewish part of its population—or Israeli—increased in numbers with every ship's arrival, and much of the Arab part of it was fleeing. . . .

Great Britain formally gave up its mandate over Palestine on May 14. Immediately David Ben-Gurion, as provisional Prime Minister, proclaimed the existence of the state of Israel. Three councils of government were set up to act until elections could be held and a constitution drafted and adopted.

The United States and the Soviet Union recognized Israel. But the United States granted only *de facto* recognition—recognizing that a government had in fact been established but withholding approval of it as a lawful and rightful government. Great Britain and the Arab states refused to recognize Israel.

Israel. Ehud Barak, the most decorated soldier in Israeli history, was elected prime minister of Israel in May 1999. Barak, the leader of One Israel (a reconstituted and expanded version of the Labor Party), won 56 percent of the vote. Prime Minister Benjamin Netanyahu, of the Likud Party, captured 44 percent of the vote. Barak pledged to restart the peace process with Palestinian leader Yasir Arafat and Syrian President Hafez al-Assad. The peace process had stalled under Netanyahu, whose government included conservative Jewish groups opposed to granting concessions to Palestinians or trading land to Syria in exchange for peace.

Barak's coalition. The 26 seats that the One Israel party captured in the *Knesset* (Israeli parliament) in 1999 were not enough to control the 120-seat chamber, and Barak formed a seven-party coalition government. The coalition, which controlled 75 of the Knesset's 120 seats, represented diverse and sometimes conflicting interest groups. These included Jewish settlers of the West Bank (territory captured by Israel in the 1967 Six-Day War), Israelis opposed to West Bank settlements, *secular* (nonreligious) leftists, and ultra-Orthodox Jewish parties. Shas was the most prominent of the ultra-Orthodox parties. Barak included Shas in his coalition only after its controversial leader, Aryeh Deri, was forced to quit the

party following his conviction on corruption charges in March 1999.

Peace initiatives. On September 5, Barak and Arafat recharged the peace process by signing an agreement that laid out a schedule for final peace negotiations. According to the schedule, Israeli and Palestinian negotiators would draw up an outline of a final peace settlement by February 2000, and the final peace agreement would be ready to be signed by September 2000. Many observers believed that this timetable was overly ambitious, considering the many unresolved issues that separated Israelis and Palestinians. These issues included conflicting claims to the control of Jerusalem; the possibility of an independent Palestinian state in the West Bank and Gaza Strip (territory controlled by Palestinian authorities); the return of more than 3 million Palestinian refugees from Jordan and other countries; and the sharing of water resources.

A few days after signing the agreement with Arafat, Barak released 200 Palestinian prisoners and transferred 7 percent of Israeli-occupied West Bank territory to Palestinian civilian control. Israel planned additional transfers that would place more than 40 percent of the West Bank under Palestinian control by January 2000. In October 1999, Barak opened a "safe-passage" corridor that stretched for 28 miles (45 kilometers) between the West Bank and Gaza Strip for Palestinians with Israeli-issued permits.

Lebanon and Syria. Barak pledged in 1999 that he would withdraw Israeli troops from a "security zone" in southern Lebanon by mid-2000. Israel had established the zone in 1985 as a buffer against attacks on northern Israel by the Islamic guerrilla group Hezbollah. Since that time, Israeli troops in the zone had come under increasing attack by the guerrillas. In February 1999, a bomb killed Israeli General Erez Gerstein, the highest-ranking Israeli officer to be slain in the zone.

In December, Israel and Syria resumed peace talks that had been suspended in 1996. Many differences remained between the two nations. Syria wanted the return of the Golan Heights, territory captured by Israel in the 1967 war. However, many Israelis wanted to keep the Golan Heights for security reasons.

Millennial cults. In October 1999, Israeli authorities ordered the deportation of 20 members of two extreme Christian cults. The authorities suspected that the cult members, who were from the United States and Great Britain, might commit violent acts at the end of 1999 to mark the end of the millennium.   □ Christine Helms

See also **Lebanon; Middle East; Middle East: A Special Report; People in the news** (Barak, Ehud); **Syria**.

Italy. Italian industry in 1999 was caught up in the wave of mergers that had swept Europe since the mid-1990's. The takeover spree began in February 1999 when Olivetti SpA, a former typewriter company that diversified into telecommunications, made a $58-billion offer to acquire a majority of Telecom Italia, the country's main telephone company. The offer was one of the largest hostile takeover attempts in Europe.

Olivetti was less than one-fifth the size of Telecom Italia and planned to finance the acquisition with Europe's biggest bond issue. Telecom Italia, which had been privatized by the government in 1997, waged a three-month battle to defeat Olivetti. Telecom Italia proposed to merge with the German phone company Deutsche Telekom AG in a deal valued at $80 billion. But a majority of Telecom Italia shareholders agreed to accept Olivetti's offer in May 1999.

Gucci Group NV, the Italian fashion and luxury goods company, fought off an $8.7-billion takeover attempt by French rival LVMH Moet Hennessy Louis Vuitton SA. Gucci sold a 42-percent stake in the company in March to Pinault-Printemps-Redoute SA, a French department store company that supported Gucci's ambition of developing new brands to compete with LVMH. In November, Gucci brought the French fashion house Yves Saint Laurent for $1 billion.

Supporters of Ehud Barak, the One Israel/Labor Party candidate for Israeli prime minister, celebrate his election on May 17, 1999, in a landslide victory over Prime Minister Benjamin Netanyahu of the Likud Party. Barak's election jump-started both Arab-Israeli peace negotiations and Syrian-Israeli peace talks.

Merger activity also shook Italy's banking and insurance industries, which were attempting in 1999 to strengthen their position in expectation that the euro, the European single currency, would bring greater competition in financial services across Europe. In June, Banca Intesa SpA agreed to acquire a majority of Banca Commerciale Italiana SpA for $10 billion in a deal that created Italy's largest bank. In November, after a two-month battle, Assicurazioni Generali SpA, the country's largest insurer, acquired rival Istituto Nazionale delle Assicurazioni SpA, or INA, for $12 billion.

Economy. Despite the corporate activity, Italy's economy remained one of the most sluggish in the European Union (EU). Italy's *gross domestic product* (GDP—the value of all goods and services produced in a country in a year) was projected to grow by 1.1 percent, compared with an EU average of 2.1 percent. Unemployment remained high at 11.7 percent of the labor force, the second-highest rate in the EU.

Tax increases and government spending cuts that were imposed to reduce the budget deficit and qualify Italy for the single European currency had slowed the Italian economy for the last several years. Prime Minister Massimo D'Alema continued that policy by presenting a budget in September for the year 2000 that contained spending cuts of almost $6 billion. The measures were designed to reduce Italy's deficit to 1.5 percent of GDP, a level Italy had promised its EU partners it would achieve.

Politics. D'Alema's center-left coalition government was weakened in 1999 when an attempt to transform Italy's relatively unstable political system—which has about 40 political parties—into a two-party system failed. The government and the main opposition parties had agreed on a proposed constitutional amendment to abolish proportional representation, which allots one-quarter of seats in the Chamber of Deputies, or lower house of Parliament, to political parties according to their percentage of the vote. The practice has allowed numerous small parties to gain seats in Parliament and a disproportionate level of power to bring down a government. Ninety-one percent of voters who participated in an April 18 referendum supported the change, but the turnout was too low for the result to be valid.

After months of disputes inside the government coalition over pension reform and funding for religious schools, D'Alema resigned on December 18 when two of the nine parties in the coalition withdrew their support. D'Alema quickly reformed a new coalition, but its ability to govern effectively was uncertain.

TIME CAPSULE 1932
ITALY

Benito Mussolini

THE 10TH ANNIVERSARY of the Fascist revolution was celebrated by the dedication of numerous public works, monuments, and other undertakings of the regime. On October 27, the archaeological excavations of the Capitol Hill in Rome were opened by Mussolini. The theater of Marcellus, long covered with earth and buildings, was restored. Among the notable improvements inaugurated on this occasion in the city of Rome was a broad avenue linking the Colosseum with Piazza Venezia, the heart of modern Rome. . . .

Like the Caesars and Pharaohs of old, the dictator who brought about these notable changes is being immortalized in numerous monuments.

In Rome there is a Mussolini forum with an athletic stadium, all of marble. In time this is expected to be one of the largest sport centers of the world, symbolic of Mussolini's efforts to encourage physical prowess among his people. In the midst of this forum rises the Mussolini obelisk, a single piece of Carrara marble 54 feet high and weighing 313 tons. Turin inaugurated, at a cost of $500,000 another stadium dedicated to Mussolini. There is a town called Mussoliniana in Sardinia situated in the heart of what was once a swamp.

President Jiang Zemin of China waves from a gondola in Venice's Grand Canal in March 1999. Zemin's trip to Italy opened a three-nation European tour in which he attempted to expand trade ties and deflect criticism of China's human rights record.

On May 13, the two houses of Parliament elected Carlo Ciampi, the Treasury minister and former prime minister, as Italy's new president. Ciampi, who helped Italy to qualify for the single currency, was elected on the first ballot, a sign of widespread respect.

Mafia trial. Giulio Andreotti, who was Italian prime minister seven times, was acquitted in September of conspiring with the Mafia in the 1979 murder of a journalist. The case raised questions about how Andreotti's Christian Democratic Party managed to govern for almost 50 years before collapsing over corruption scandals in the early 1990's. In October 1999, Andreotti was acquitted in a separate case on charges of having been the Mafia's chief protector in government.

Cable-car disaster. Italians were outraged in March 1999 when a United States military jury acquitted a U.S. Marine pilot of manslaughter in a ski-lift accident that killed 20 people in the Italian Alps in February 1998. The Marine was piloting a jet on a low-altitude training run when it severed the cable of a ski lift, sending a gondola plunging more than 300 feet (100 meters) to the ground. The Marine Corps dismissed the flight's navigator after he pleaded guilty to obstructing justice by destroying a videotape he shot during the flight.

☐ Tom Buerkle

See also **Europe.**

Japan. Workers at a uranium processing plant accidentally triggered a chain reaction on Sept. 30, 1999. The accident, the worst ever to occur in Japan's nuclear power industry, took place at Tokaimura, about 85 miles (138 kilometers) northeast of Tokyo. Technicians released 35 pounds (15.9 kilograms) of uranium, seven times the specified amount, into a purification tank containing nitric acid, setting off a chain reaction. Accompanied by a flash of blue light, the out-of-control chain reaction exposed 35 people in the plant to high levels of radioactivity.

Three workers were hospitalized, and more than 50 plant employees and nearby residents were treated for radiation exposure. The government confined more than 300,000 people within a 6-mile (10-kilometer) radius to their residences for 24 hours.

Although Japanese nuclear plants had experienced accidents before—including another accident at the Tokaimura facility in 1997—the latest incident exposed fundamental problems with Japan's nuclear power policies. According to nuclear power experts, Tokaimura employees had not received adequate training nor appropriate warnings about the dangers of their work. The plant lacked critical equipment and plans for dealing promptly and effectively with a nuclear emergency.

JAPAN

HIROSHIMA, a military base and city of about 343,000 on Honshu, one of the Japanese homeland islands, was struck by the world's first atomic bomb on August 6, 1945. Up to this time, the patient Japanese civilians believed they were winning the war. Americans described the sight by saying, "It was hard to believe what we saw." The bomb was released at 9:15 a.m. from an altitude of 20,000-30,000 feet, and two minutes later the entire area was covered by a column of black smoke—20,000 feet high with a 10,000-foot diameter base. Down below, many people were in the streets, when suddenly a brilliant flash lighted the sky above them, searing everything on the ground. So powerful was the blast that each person thought he had been struck by an individual bomb. The terrible impact was felt for miles around. Not one building remained intact. Hiroshima, 60 percent destroyed, became the world's most damaged city. American investigators reported 68,000 buildings destroyed and damaged. A Japanese report said 60,000 to 100,000 people were killed and 75,000 to 200,000 injured.

A mushroom cloud rises over Hiroshima, Japan, following the detonation of an atomic bomb on Aug. 6, 1945.

Nuclear power and weapons remained a sensitive subject with the Japanese, the only people ever to experience a nuclear attack. On Oct. 19, 1999, a deputy vice minister of defense, Shingo Nishimura, stated publicly that since other countries marked Japan as a possible target for attack, the Japanese parliament should "consider the possibility that Japan would be better off if it armed itself with nuclear weapons." The statement challenged Japan's long-standing renunciation of nuclear weapons, and Nishimura was forced to resign the following day.

Prime Minister Keizo Obuchi reshuffled his cabinet in October and promised to concentrate on revitalizing Japan's sluggish economy. The revamped government was based on an expanded coalition of political parties that gave Obuchi working majorities in both houses of Japan's parliament, the Diet. Obuchi's Liberal Democratic Party (LDP) had lost a majority in the upper house of the parliament in a 1998 election that weakened the party and forced his predecessor, Ryutaro Hashimoto, to resign. The LDP retained control of the lower house, which dominates the Diet.

On Jan. 14, 1999, the LDP completed an alliance with the Liberal Party led by Ichiro Ozawa. A former LDP boss, Ozawa had left the LDP in 1993 to lead an opposition group. His return to the governing coalition improved Obuchi's working majority in the lower house but left the coalition still short of an upper house majority.

In October 1999, Obuchi secured a working majority in the upper house by bringing two more parties—the Reformers Network and the larger New Komeito, backed by Soka Gakkai, Japan's second-largest lay Buddhist organization—into the governing coalition.

In exchange for his support of the LDP, Ozawa demanded that the number of seats in the lower house be reduced from 500 to 450, a change that would have enhanced the Liberal Party's position. The new coalition compromised by agreeing to reduce proportional representation by 20 seats in the near future and by an additional 30 seats sometime later.

LDP shutout in local elections. Obuchi's parliamentary success followed a dismal showing by the LDP in local elections on April 11. Other parties also did poorly, as independents won many *prefectural* (provincial) and municipal assembly seats. The election of Shintaro Ishihara, an independent, as governor (mayor) of Tokyo proved a major LDP defeat. Ishihara, who had risen to fame a decade earlier as the author of an anti-American book, campaigned on a platform to get the United States to quit using Tokyo's Yokota Air Base.

Obuchi's legislative successes. Obuchi's majorities in both houses of parliament enabled him to pass legislation that had long been considered too controversial to become law. One of the most controversial designated the *Hinomaru*, or rising sun flag—a red disk on a white field—and the *Kimigayo* anthem, "His Majesty's Reign," as legal symbols of the nation. The flag, in common use since the 1600's, had been banned by the United States during U.S. occupation of Japan after World War II (1939-45). The flag and the anthem were seen as symbols of Japan's militarism in the 1930's and wartime aggression.

Japanese conservatives, arguing that a normalized Japan had overcome postwar timidity and shame, had long sought to have the flag and anthem legally recognized. They also wanted to require use of these symbols in schools. The national teachers' union opposed this, claiming that it infringed on students' constitutional rights. The legislation provoked a battle among politicians and intellectuals over the nation's postwar identity and direction. But the lower house finally passed it, 403 to 86, and the upper house followed by a vote of 166 to 71.

The parliament also passed a law, long sought by conservatives, allowing police to tap telephones in criminal investigations.

The influence of conservatives in Japan in 1999 was also demonstrated by the refusal of a Japanese publisher to put out a local edition of a book by a Chinese-American author on Japanese atrocities in China in 1937 without making major changes. The book, *The Rape of Nanjing,* had been widely hailed abroad for its documentary account but was attacked by Japanese right-wingers as twisted and exaggerated.

Warning shots. On March 24, 1999, Japanese warships fired guns, actually warning shots, for the first time since World War II. They shot at two ships believed to be North Korean vessels trying to drop off or pick up agents in Japan or to smuggle ashore drugs made in North Korea to raise money for its impoverished regime. The vessels escaped capture.

Japan also worried about a missile attack from North Korea, which had fired a missile over Japan in August 1998. Japan warned North Korea against repeated firings and discussed with the United States the creation of a missile defense system.

Japan's economy showed signs of breaking out of a decade of troubles and 15 months of recession, growing by 0.9 percent in the first half of the year, according to official figures. In 1998, domestic output had fallen 2.8 percent. Industrial production rose in 1999, and new housing starts, down for 27 months, were up 7.3 percent in June from a year earlier.

Unemployment, however, reached 4.9 percent in June and declined only slightly later in 1999. Consumers remained hesitant about buying, and many economists considered the 1999 growth rate a temporary result of government deficit spending. Later figures suggested lower growth rates than early in the year.

Deficit spending to stimulate the economy at the rate in 1999 of 13 percent of the economy's total value—one of the highest levels of any industrial nation—pushed Japan's national debt to 120 percent of the value of annual domestic output, one of the world's highest debt ratios. This left little room for priming the economy through deficit financing. Public resistance to deficit financing grew in 1999 as well, especially for construction projects used to sustain employment and to reward companies supporting the LDP.

The burdens of even greater national debt loomed if the government were forced to bail out Japanese banks and insurance companies with assets grossly overvalued as a result of a late-1980's bubble in property prices. On Aug. 20, 1999, three troubled Japanese banks agreed to combine into the world's largest financial institution.

Both Japan's stock market and the value of its currency, the yen, rose in 1999 amid new hopes for the economy. □ Henry S. Bradsher

See also **Asia.**

Jordan. Heads of state and leaders representing 75 nations attended the funeral of Jordan's King Hussein on Feb. 8, 1999. Tens of thousands of Jordanians lined the streets of Amman, the capital, during the funeral procession. Hussein, who died on February 7 at the age of 63, had ruled Jordan for 47 years. He had survived tumultuous Middle East politics and weathered the criticism of many of his own subjects for signing a peace treaty with Israel in 1994. He had also endured the anger of Western leaders for his perceived support of Iraq after Iraqi troops invaded Kuwait in 1990. United States officials viewed Hussein as a major supporter of a comprehensive Arab-Israeli peace agreement.

The king's death stunned many Jordanians, though palace officials had announced in 1998 that Hussein was receiving chemotherapy treatments in the United States for lymphatic cancer. On Jan. 19, 1999, Hussein returned to a triumphant welcome in Jordan after announcing that he was "fully recovered." However, his health declined rapidly after his return.

Succession surprise. On January 25, King Hussein surprised Jordanians by announcing that he was appointing his eldest son, Abdullah, as his heir. Hussein made the announcement one day after press reports described a highly critical letter from the king to his brother Crown Prince

Pallbearers carry the coffin of Jordan's King Hussein, who ruled for 47 years, in a procession from Raghadan Palace, where the monarch had lain in state, to the Royal Guards Mosque in February 1999. The procession included many heads of state and political leaders, including U.S. President Bill Clinton and British Prime Minister Tony Blair.

Hassan, who had been groomed for 34 years to succeed Hussein. Some observers speculated that Hussein was concerned that the right of succession would not revert to his sons. The letter also criticized Hassan's supporters for their treatment of Hussein's U.S.-born fourth wife, Queen Noor.

King Abdullah II. Upon the king's death, Abdullah—the 37-year old son of Hussein's second wife, the British-born Princess Muna—ascended to the throne. Abdullah, the fourth member of the Hashemite family to rule Jordan, previously headed an elite unit of army commandos.

Bold new leadership. After becoming king, Abdullah moved swiftly on several fronts. In March, he reopened Jordan's embassy in Kuwait. Relations between the two countries had been broken during the 1990-1991 Persian Gulf crisis. In August 1999, Abdullah closed the Jordanian offices of Hamas, a militant Palestinian group, and ordered four of the group's leaders arrested. Hamas had long opposed an Arab-Israeli peace settlement and had claimed responsibility for a number of terrorist bombings in Israel. Some analysts interpreted the move against Hamas as an attempt to secure Western financial aid. Abdullah inherited a $7-billion national debt, owed mainly to Western creditors. ☐ Christine Helms

See also **Israel; Middle East; Middle East: A Special Report; People in the news** (Abdullah II).

Judaism. The year 1999 was characterized in world Jewish life by a return to centrism on many fronts. Renewed efforts to establish peace in the Middle East, a resurgence of anti-Semitism, and developments within Judaism's religious movements all pointed away from polarization and toward an emphasis on cooperation.

Israel. Israel's government, formed by the new prime minister, Ehud Barak, in July, included political parties with varying religious outlooks, including the secular Meretz party and the fervently religious Shas party. Religious divisions threatened the coalition from the start, but compromises were made. As the year ended, a compromise was being sought on a proposal to change the "Law of Return," a provision of the Israeli Constitution guaranteeing that most Jews may immigrate to Israel if they choose. Orthodox Jews expressed concern that many of those claiming Israeli citizenship under the law were actually non-Jews of Jewish descent who actively practiced Christianity.

World. The war in Yugoslavia and continued unrest in Ethiopia affected the fate of Jews in 1999. The American Jewish Joint Distribution Committee, a relief organization, created a refuge in Hungary, for Jewish refugees from Yugoslavia. Some of the refugees went on to Israel. More than 1,800 Jews from embattled regions of Ethiopia also arrived in Israel between July and November.

The deportations and mass-murders perpetrated against ethnic Albanians in Kosovo rekindled in many Jews in 1999 memories of the Nazi Holocaust that killed 6 million Jews during World War II (1939-1945). Jews responded generously to appeals for aid to Kosovo, quickly raising more than $4 million. A coalition of 42 different Jewish organizations helped to provide humanitarian relief.

United States. The American Jewish community was particularly shaken by the wave of hate crimes that occurred in the United States in 1999. On June 18, three synagogues in Sacramento, California, were damaged in arson attacks. In July, a member of a white supremacy group went on a shooting spree targeting minority groups in Illinois and Indiana, including Jews in a predominantly Jewish neighborhood in Chicago. In August, a gunman opened fire in a Los Angeles Jewish preschool, injuring five people. A shooting at Columbine High School in Littleton, Colorado, in April, coincided with the birthday of Adolf Hitler. Many Jews considered these attacks a wake-up call that highlighted the persistence of anti-Semitism.

The U.S. Jewish community moved to effect greater unity during 1999. Three major Jewish philanthropic organizations—the Council of Jewish Federations, the United Jewish Appeal, and the United Israel Appeal—merged in April to create the United Jewish Communities.

Reform Judaism, the liberal movement embracing more than 40 percent of religiously identifying American Jews, adopted in May a new, more traditional "Statement of Principles." Among other provisions, the statement called for increased study of *Torah* (the teachings of Judaism) and observance of commandments. While the statement was nonbinding, it indicated an effort by Reform leaders to reinvigorate abandoned traditions.

Edah, a two-year-old organization representing Orthodox Judaism's more liberal wing, held a large national conference in New York City in February aimed at strengthening what many of its members called "Modern Orthodoxy." It sought to counter a perceived rightward turn in Orthodoxy, away from modernity.

The Jewish community, however, displayed growing political diversity on such issues as public school vouchers, abortion, and Middle East peace. Leaders of the New York and Chicago Jewish communal federations, in letters sent in June and August, urged that secular matters such as these should be removed from the communal agenda, in order to focus on core issues relating to survival of the Jewish people and faith.

☐ Jonathan D. Sarna and Jonathan J. Golden
See also **Israel; Middle East.**

Kampuchea. See **Cambodia.**

Kansas. See **State government.**

More than 250,000 Orthodox Jews participate in a rally in Jerusalem in February 1999 to protest against Israel's Supreme Court, which they perceive as predominantly liberal and a threat to Orthodox authority over religious matters in Israel.

Kazakhstan. President Nursultan Nazarbayev was reelected on Jan. 10, 1999, in a vote held nearly two years ahead of schedule. After becoming president in 1991, Nazarbayev steadily strengthened his grip on power in Kazakhstan by systematically eliminating political opposition. By 1999, he had gained control of the national media and enjoyed virtually unlimited campaign funding. International observers condemned the 1999 election, which Nazarbayev won with 80 percent of the vote. The U.S. State Department described it as having "tarnished Kazakhstan's reputation." Nazarbayev's chief rival, former prime minister Akezhan Kazhegeldin, had been disqualified from the race in November 1998 for attending a meeting of an unregistered political group.

International criticism had little effect on the parliamentary elections held in September and October 1999. At the request of the Kazakh government, opposition leader Kazhegeldin was briefly arrested in Russia in September for tax violations and his Republican People's Party of Kazakhstan boycotted the election. However, the Communist Party did make modest gains at the polls, as voters reacted to an economic recession triggered by the steep decline of Kazakhstan's currency, the tenge, in April.   □ Steven L. Solnick

See also **Europe.**

Kentucky. See State government.

Kenya continued to experience grave economic problems in 1999. In June, Vice President Saitoti reported that the country's economic growth rate had fallen to 1.8 percent in 1998 from 2.4 percent in 1997. Per capita income fell 1.6 percent in 1998, in part because of a lack of foreign investment. International lending agencies have reduced aid to Kenya since the mid-1990's because of the government's failure to curb widespread official corruption and inefficiency.

The vice president also reported in June 1999 that revenues from tourism were down 23 percent in the previous 12 months. Saitoti attributed the decline to international publicity about tribal and political violence; the 1998 terrorist bombing of the United States embassy in Nairobi, Kenya's capital; and the poor condition of Kenya's roads.

Cabinet changes. President Daniel arap Moi renamed Saitoti vice president on April 2, 1999, filling a vacancy that had existed since Saitoti's demotion from the post after the 1997 presidential election.

Simeon Nyachae, finance minister since January 1998, resigned on Feb. 19, 1999, shortly after being transferred to the industrial development ministry by Moi during a Cabinet shakeup. Moi's move stunned the international donor community, which viewed Nyachae as a key figure in efforts to address Kenya's economic crisis.

Nyachae charged that his removal from finance had resulted from his "unwavering" battle against corruption. In July, Moi named Richard Leakey, renowned director of the Kenya Wildlife Service and a long-time political opponent, head of the civil service. Observers saw the move as a response to foreign appeals for official reform.

Political protest. On June 10, riot police injured scores of proreform protesters outside the National Assembly in Nairobi. The demonstrators were protesting Moi's decision to grant parliament, where his ruling Kenya African National Union has a clear majority, the sole right to review Kenya's Constitution. Before the 1997 elections, Moi had promised to establish a commission to recommend constitutional reforms. Opposition parties expressed concern that parliament would amend the Constitution to allow Moi to seek a sixth term. Under the current Constitution, Moi must relinquish his office in 2002.

Student protest. The government temporarily closed Nairobi University on Feb. 1, 1999, following three days of student rioting in which hundreds of demonstrators and policemen were injured. The students were protesting the destruction of a section of the protected Karura forest, north of Nairobi, for the development of housing.   □ Simon Baynham

See also **Africa.**

Korea, North. The North Korean Food Damage Rehabilitation Committee released in 1999, the fifth year of food shortages in North Korea, the first official estimate of deaths from starvation and malnutrition. According to the report, about 220,000 North Koreans died from malnutrition between 1995 and 1998.

In late 1999, foreign experts released estimates that between 1.5 million and 3 million people, out of a population of 25 million, had died in the first four years of food shortages. These estimates were based on sample surveys revealing high infant mortality rates and eyewitness accounts of people eating weeds and bark from trees.

At least 100,000 people escaped North Korea's tight police system in 1999 to enter China. Chinese officials returned many of these to North Korea to avoid encouraging a flood of refugees.

The famine began in 1995 with severe floods that damaged the inefficient agricultural organization of the Communist regime. Subsequent years of poor weather combined with economic mismanagement kept food production low. A drought in the spring of 1999 followed by floods in August prolonged the famine.

The economy. With industrial production low and the economy depressed, North Korea attempted to raise money in 1999 in a variety of ways. It sold missiles and other weapons to such

South Korean honor guards, in traditional costumes, bow to Dennis Blair, commander in chief of the U.S. Pacific Fleet, during an inspection ceremony in Seoul, South Korea, in March 1999. The United States has been South Korea's staunchest ally since the Korean War (1950-1953).

nations as Iran and Iraq and charged high prices to South Korean tourists traveling on tightly controlled tours. According to Western sources, including the U.S. State Department, North Korea also forged U.S. $100 bills and manufactured narcotics, which it smuggled abroad.

Despite famine and economic distress, North Korea's "great leader," Kim Chong-il, spent $100 million on an elaborate celebration of his 57th birthday on February 16. While relying on outside aid to feed his people, the reclusive dictator also maintained a huge military force and spent money to develop new weapons systems.

International relations. Dictator Kim, exploiting foreign concern over North Korea's missile and nuclear programs, demanded $300 million in 1999 to allow U.S. inspectors to check if he had adhered to a 1994 agreement not to make nuclear arms in return for economic aid. He eventually agreed to an inspection in return for agricultural assistance.

North Korea continued in 1999 to obstruct talks with South Korea, China, and the United States to seek an official end to the 1950–1953 war.

On Sept. 12, 1999, the United States agreed to expand trade with North Korea after the North agreed to freeze its missile testing program.

◻ Henry S. Bradsher

See also **Asia; Japan; Korea, South.**

Korea, South. South Korea's economy returned in 1999 to strong growth, ending a sharp recession that had begun in 1997. Domestic output, which had fallen 5.8 percent in 1998, grew more than 8 percent in 1999.

Economists attributed the recovery to reforms instituted by President Kim Dae-Jung. Kim, however, was criticized for failing to bring down unemployment to prerecession levels. Unemployment remained at about 6 percent in 1999, three times the 1997 level. Some foreign economists also questioned whether the strong performance of the economy in 1999 was sustainable.

The chaebols. Kim focused on problems of big family-owned conglomerates known as chaebols in 1999. Encouraged by previous regimes to lead South Korea's industrial growth with government-directed credit, the chaebols had come to dominate the economy. Many economists believed that the chaebols over time had diversified into too many industries and built factories too large for potential sales. The government accused the five leading chaebols of making investment decisions that eventually triggered South Korea's 1997 financial crisis.

Kim had tried in 1998 to persuade the chaebols to sell off some businesses and reduce their debts, but they resisted. On Aug. 15, 1999, Kim declared that he was determined to accomplish corporate reforms. The next day the government announced plans to restructure the second-largest chaebol, Daewoo, which had refused to divest its money-losing affiliates and pay down its $50-billion debt. South Korea's four other leading chaebols owed more than $160 billion in debt.

On August 25, the government announced a package of measures intended to reduce family control of the chaebols and bring in more professional management. The government attempted to salvage Daewoo, which employed some 2.5 million people, rather than close it because it feared that closures would lead to strikes.

The government's effort to reform the chaebols apparently did not shrink their size and power in 1999. According to a Korea Stock Exchange analysis made public on September 20, the chaebols had actually increased their linked holdings during the previous 12 months.

President Kim tightened his political control on July 21 when Prime Minister Kim Jong Pil agreed to accept delay of a promised constitutional reform. In the 1997 presidential election, Kim Jong Pil's United Liberal Democrats had made an alliance with Kim Dae-Jung's National Congress for New Politics, while extracting a promise that the prime minister's power would increase at the expense of the president's power. The two leaders agreed in 1999, however, that such constitutional revision would be too difficult to tackle in the near future.

The agreement reflected fears that the opposition Grand National Party might win parliamentary elections in April 2000. The party won two by-elections in June 1999.

Nevertheless, the parties of the two Kims retained a tight grip on parliament. In early January, they passed 66 bills in 15 minutes over the opposition's protest. In a May session, they passed six bills in quick succession.

South Korea's relations with North Korea remained tense through 1999. On June 15, naval vessels of the two countries exchanged fire in the Yellow Sea. South Korea accused the North of intruding into South Korea's waters. Talks to improve relations between the two Koreas accomplished nothing in 1999.

Amnesty. On February 25, President Kim marked his first anniversary in office by granting amnesty to 8,800 people, including 17 long-term political prisoners. One prisoner, Woo Yong Gak, had been captured on a North Korean commando mission to the South in 1958 and held for 41 years in solitary confinement. Another 56 political prisoners were given amnesty in August 1999.

□ Henry S. Bradsher

See also **Asia; Korea, North.**

Kuwait. See Middle East.

Kyrgyzstan. See Asia.

Labor and employment. Labor prospered in the United States in 1999 as the U.S. economy continued to expand. The U.S. Department of Labor reported in December that the national unemployment remained at 4.1 percent in November, its lowest level since 1970. Unemployment rates, however, varied from state to state. Rates in New Hampshire dropped to as low as 2.2 percent, while unemployment in New Mexico remained as high as 6.4 percent in 1999. More than 2.5 million jobs were created in the United States in 1999, and by November, 133.9 million people were employed.

The Labor Department reported in November that 5.8 million people in the United States were looking for, but not finding, work. The unemployment rates for various groups varied widely. The jobless rate for adult men was 3.3 percent and 3.6 percent for adult women. The 1999 unemployment rate was 3.5 percent for whites; 6 percent for Hispanics; 8.1 percent for blacks; and 14.1 percent for teen-agers.

Wages and salaries of workers rose 3.3 percent the first nine months of 1999, a slight drop from the 4-percent increase for the same period in 1998, according to the U.S. Bureau of Labor Statistics (BLS). Economists who have argued for a "new economic paradigm," in which pay could rise indefinitely without price inflation received what some considered an economic warning in 1999. The BLS Consumer Price Index increased 2.8 percent in the first nine months of 1999, compared with 1.6 percent in the same period in 1998 and 1.7 percent for the same period in 1997.

Postal settlement. The largest postal union in the United States, the American Postal Workers Union, ratified a two-year contract with the U.S. Postal Service in January 1999. The agreement provided a 6.75-percent pay increase over the course of the contract. Members of the National Postal Mail Handlers Union also ratified a two-year wage agreement with the Postal Service in January. The agreement provided union members with pay increases up to 7 percent over the course of the contract. In September, the Postal Service and the National Association of Letter Carriers agreed on a three-year contract that included a wage increase of up to 2 percent for employees.

Airline industry. In February, 3,600 pilots at Federal Express, an international package delivery service headquartered in Memphis, Tennessee, approved a five-year agreement by an almost 9-to-1 margin. The pact provided a 5-percent pay increase in the first year of the contract and a total pay increase of 17 percent.

Pilots from American Airlines of Fort Worth, Texas, and the Allied Pilots Association (APA), the

Changes in the United States labor force

	1998	1999*
Civilian labor force	137,673,000	139,206,000
Total employment	131,463,000	133,285,000
Unemployment	6,210,000	5,921,000
Unemployment rate	4.5%	4.3%
Change in real weekly earnings of production and nonsupervisory workers (private nonfarm sector)†	2.7%	1.2%
Change in output per employee hour (private nonfarm sector)	2.8%	2.5%

*All 1999 data is through the third quarter of 1999 (preliminary data).
†Real weekly earnings are adjusted for inflation by using constant 1982 dollars.
Source: U.S. Bureau of Labor Statistics.

union that represents the airline's pilots, battled in 1999 over 300 pilots at Reno Air, a small airline that American Airlines purchased in 1998. The pilots demanded that management pay the pilots at Reno Air at the same scale as American pilots. The pilots feared that the acquisition of Reno was a ploy to lower pay rates at American. In early February 1999, hundreds of American Airlines' pilots began calling in sick, forcing American Airlines to cancel thousands of flights. U.S. District Judge Joe Kendall on February 10 ordered the pilots to return to work, which prompted some 2,400 pilots to call in sick in protest. On April 15, Kendall fined the APA $45.5 million for defying his back-to-work order and to compensate the airline for losses caused by the walkout.

In April, the International Association of Machinists (IAM) reached agreements for service employees with USAir, headquartered in Arlington, Virginia, and with Chicago-based United Airlines. The USAir pact provided 6,000 fleet service employees with a pay raise of nearly 13 percent over the course of the agreement and new provisions covering overtime assignments that went into effect on December 31. The United Airlines agreement, which covered 20,000 passenger service employees, included a 5.5-percent general wage boost and elimination of the lower-tier pay structure. In May, 70 percent of voting IAM members ratified the United agreement. In July, however, 75 percent of the union members rejected the USAir settlement.

In early May, a difficult bargaining round between America West Airlines, headquartered in Tempe, Arizona, and the Association of Flight attendants ended when the union members ratified a 5-year contract with the company. The union had rejected a 1998 pact. The 1999 agreement provided pay and compensation increases that raised top pay for attendants flying more

than 75 hours a month from $25,000 to $32,200.

American Airlines and the Association of Professional Flight Attendants reached a six-year pact in May, which the membership overwhelmingly rejected in September. The members's main objection to the plan was the substitution of a guaranteed general wage and benefit package for a profit-sharing plan. The flight attendants and the airlines had not reached a new settlement by the end of 1999.

Aerospace industry. Lockheed Martin Corporation of Calabasas, California, and the IAM reached an agreement in March on a three-year contract covering more than 6,000 employees at Lockheed Martin plants in Marietta, Georgia, and Palmdale, California. The contract provided a 9-percent wage increase over three years and a $600 lump-sum payment.

In September, IAM members ratified a three-year agreement with Boeing, Inc. of Seattle. The contract covered more than 44,000 workers. Under terms of the agreement, Boeing agreed to increase pay 4 percent in each of the first two years of the contract and 3 percent in the third year of the contract. Upon contract ratification of the agreement, workers received a pay bonus equal to 10 percent of their gross earnings in the 12 months prior to Sept. 1, 1999.

Teamster negotiations. Representatives from the International Brotherhood of Teamsters and employees at 17 U.S. trucking companies that haul new cars to automobile dealers across the country reached a 4-year agreement in June. The agreement provided a wage boost of 5 percent in the first year and 4 percent in each of the next three years.

The car-haulers agreement was the first negotiated by James P. Hoffa, who was inaugurated Teamster president in May. Hoffa is the son of James R. Hoffa, who led the union from 1957 to 1971 and who mysteriously disappeared in 1975.

Automobile industry. In September 1999, the United Automobile Workers (UAW) and automobile manufacturer DaimlerChrysler, headquartered in Auburn Hills, Michigan, reached a contract agreement covering 75,000 employees. The four-year agreement provided annual 3-percent wage increases, a $1,350 bonus for approving the contract, and a company promise of neutrality at nonunion DaimlerChrysler facilities. A 86-percent majority of UAW members at DaimlerChrysler ratified the agreement.

The DaimlerChrysler automotive settlement provided a pattern for the rest of the U.S. automotive industry in 1999. In late September, the UAW and General Motors (GM) reached an agreement on a four-year contract that covered 143,000 workers. A similar contract covered

LABOR AND EMPLOYMENT

END OF THE 12-HOUR DAY. For years various agencies have labored to put an end to a workday of 12 hours in the steel mills. Most industries may close down at the end of 8 hours, suspending all operations until the morrow, but in steelmaking some of the operations must continue 24 hours every day. . . . In August, abandonment of the 12-hour day in the steel mills was begun, resulting in a demand in that industry for possibly 55,000 additional employees.

45,000 workers at GM's parts-production unit, Delphi Automotive Systems, which GM had spun off as a separate company in May. More than 77 percent of GM and Delphi workers ratified the agreement.

The final major contract in the 1999 automotive bargaining round involved employees at Ford Motor Company, headquartered in Dearborn, Michigan. The four-year pact covered more than 100,000 employees and featured similar terms to those reached at DaimlerChrysler and GM. An 85-percent majority of UAW members at Ford ratified the settlement.

Chain-store agreements. The United Food and Confectionery Workers Union conducted bargaining sessions across the United States during 1999. In May, the union approved an agreement with Meijer Inc., a retail and food store headquartered in Grand Rapids, Michigan. The agreement covered more than 31,000 Meijer employees.

In August, the union reached an agreement with the drugstore chain, Rite Aid Corporation of Shiremanstown, Pennsylvania. The agreement covered 6,800 technical workers and retail pharmacy clerks.

Union merger. In January, delegates to simultaneous conventions of the United Paperworkers International Union and the Oil, Chemical, and Atomic Workers International Union approved a merger of the two unions into a 320,000 member PACE (Paper, Allied-industrial, Chemical and Energy Workers) International Union.

Overseas unemployment. In 1999, many of the world's industrialized nations continued to experience unemployment rates higher than the United States. Unemployment rates in the major industrialized countries—including Canada, France, Germany, Japan, Sweden, the United Kingdom, and the United States—averaged 8.1 percent in September, according to preliminary data gathered by the Organization for Economic Cooperation and Development (OECD), a Paris-based multinational association working to promote economic and social welfare. Unemployment rates in these countries remained steady through the first nine months of 1999.

The OECD reported that Mexico had the lowest average unemployment rate at 3 percent. Japan reported a 4.3 percent unemployment rate. Some European countries reported considerably higher rates. Unemployment averaged 11.7 percent in France in 1999 and 9.3 percent in Germany, the OECD reported. France and Germany are the two biggest economies of western Europe.

Unemployment in Germany remained steady at 9.1 percent from June through September, dropping only slightly to 9 percent in October. Unemployment rates in Sweden rose from 6.8 percent in May to 7.1 percent by September. Unemployment in Canada reached 7.5 percent in September, down from 8.1 percent in May.

The International Labor Organization of the United Nations, which estimates global employment and unemployment, estimated that 1 billion persons worldwide were either unemployed or underemployed in 1999.

Muscular-skeletal injuries. In January 1999, the Department of Labor's Occupational Safety and Health Administration (OSHA) announced that it would seek input from labor and business groups on ways to establish workplace standards to prevent muscular-skeletal injuries, such as carpal tunnel syndrome. Carpal tunnel syndrome is a disorder of the hand that is caused by pressure on the median nerve as the nerve passes through a canal called the carpal tunnel. The tunnel is formed by the bones and ligaments in the wrist. A variety of conditions, including repetitive wrist motions, may cause the carpal tunnel to narrow and put pressure on the median nerve.

The topic of *ergonomics* (designing workplace tools and workplaces in ways to prevent worker injury) had been widely discussed in the 1960's and 1970's but disappeared from public discourse as global competition and industry downsizing hit U.S. industry in the 1980's and 1990's. The emergence of computer-related ergonomic injuries, such as carpal tunnel syndrome and various types of back and eye strain injuries, gave the establishment of workplace standards new impetus in 1999.

☐ Robert W. Fisher

See also **Economics; Manufacturing.**

Laos. See Asia.

Latin America

Latin America passed a demographic milestone in 1999. According to a September report by the United Nations (UN), the women of Latin America at the end of the century bore on average 2.7 children. In 1965, the women of Latin America had borne more than 6 children on average. These figures represented a landmark change in social attitudes within the rising generation, as did the UN finding that in 1999 two-thirds of married women in Latin America regularly used contraceptives.

Smaller families. The trend toward smaller families was particularly pronounced in the cities, where Latin America's growing middle class lived, and in Mexico. In 1999, women in Mexico bore on average 2.5 children, compared with an average of 7 children in 1965. Population experts attributed the drop in family size in Mexico to an intensive government-supported program, begun in 1974, that encouraged family planning.

Experts attributed the trend toward smaller families throughout Latin America to numerous privately sponsored programs, some of them funded in part by United States foreign-aid programs. Profamilia in Colombia, established in 1965, pio-

Severe flooding on Peru's Rimac River, caused by heavy rains in the central Andes Mountains, washes out a bridge at Santa Eulalia in February 1999. The floods isolated many rural Peruvian communities.

Facts in brief on Latin America

Country	Population	Government	Monetary unit*	Foreign trade (million U.S.$) Exports†	Imports†
Antigua and Barbuda	68,000	Governor General James B. Carlisle; Prime Minister Lester Bird	dollar (2.70 = $1)	38	326
Argentina	36,648,000	President Fernando de la Rua	peso (1.00 = $1)	25,227	31,402
Bahamas	295,000	Governor General Orville Turnquest; Prime Minister Hubert Ingraham	dollar (1.00 = $1)	181	1,662
Barbados	268,000	Governor General Sir Clifford Husbands; Prime Minister Owen Arthur	dollar (2.00 = $1)	283	996
Belize	245,000	Governor General Sir Colville Young; Prime Minister Said Musa	dollar (2.00 = $1)	167	298
Bolivia	8,329,000	President Hugo Banzer Suarez	boliviano (5.84 = $1)	1,103	1,983
Brazil	175,825,000	President Fernando Henrique Cardoso	real (1.94 = $1)	51,120	57,550
Chile	15,311,000	President Eduardo Frei Ruiz-Tagle	peso (531.03 = $1)	14,895	18,828
Colombia	37,822,000	President Andres Pastrana	peso (1,994.50 = $1)	11,522	15,378
Costa Rica	3,798,000	President Miguel Angel Rodriguez	colon (292.74 = $1)	5,511	6,230
Cuba	11,385,000	President Fidel Castro	peso (1.00 = $1)	2,015	3,205
Dominica	71,000	President Crispin Anselm Sorhaindo; Prime Minister Edison James	dollar (2.70 = $1)	53	125
Dominican Republic	8,495,000	President Leonel Fernandez Reyna	peso (15.89 = $1)	882	4,821
Ecuador	12,646,000	President Jamil Mahuad	sucre (14,600.00 = $1)	4,141	5,503
El Salvador	5,980,000	President Francisco Flores Perez	colon (8.76 = $1)	1,263	3,112
Grenada	101,000	Governor General Daniel Williams; Prime Minister Keith Mitchell	dollar (2.70 = $1)	23	171
Guatemala	12,222,000	President Alvaro Arzu Irigoyen	quetzal (7.78 = $1)	2,344	3,852
Guyana	718,000	President Bharrat Jagdeo	dollar (177.30 = $1)	643	629
Haiti	7,959,000	President Rene Preval; Prime Minister Jacques-Edouard Alexis	gourde (16.82 = $1)	175	800
Honduras	6,485,000	President Carlos Roberto Flores Facusse	lempira (14.48 = $1)	1,533	2,500
Jamaica	2,543,000	Governor General Sir Howard Cooke; Prime Minister P. J. Patterson	dollar (38.78 = $1)	1,304	3,003
Mexico	102,410,000	President Ernesto Zedillo Ponce de Leon	new peso (9.46 = $1)	65,583	76,746
Nicaragua	5,169,000	President Arnoldo Aleman Lacayo	gold cordoba (12.13 = $1)	704	1,532
Panama	2,856,000	President Mireya Elisa Moscoso	balboa (1.00 = $1)	784	3,074
Paraguay	5,613,000	President Luis Gonzalez Macchi	guarani (3,311.50 = $1)	1,089	3,403
Peru	26,082,000	President Alberto K. Fujimori	new sol (3.46 = $1)	6,814	10,263
Puerto Rico	3,522,000	Governor Pedro Rossello	U.S. dollar	30,300	21,800
St. Kitts and Nevis	41,000	Governor General Cuthbert Montraville Sebastian; Prime Minister Denzil Douglas	dollar (2.70 = $1)	36	148
St. Lucia	152,000	Governor General Perlette Louisy; Prime Minister Kenny Anthony	dollar (2.70 = $1)	61	332
St. Vincent and the Grenadines	117,000	Governor General David Jack; Prime Minister James F. Mitchell	dollar (2.70 = $1)	50	193
Suriname	447,000	President Jules Wijdenbosch	guilder (809.50 = $1)	549	552
Trinidad and Tobago	1,380,000	President Arthur Napoleon Raymond Robinson; Prime Minister Basdeo Panday	dollar (6.27 = $1)	2,542	2,990
Uruguay	3,274,000	President Julio Maria Sanguinetti	peso (11.44 = $1)	2,769	3,808
Venezuela	24,170,000	President Hugo Chavez Frias	bolivar (630.13 = $1)	21,067	14,573

*Exchange rates as of Oct. 8, 1999, or latest available data.   †Latest available data.

neered the use of radio announcements to promote contraceptive use. The program also created a national network of trained volunteers who provide contraceptives and birth-control information door to door, even in remote areas.

Some experts attributed the drop in average family size in Brazil to the popularity of soap operas, called telenovela, which run all day long. These top-rated shows offered Brazilians glimpses into the lifestyles of families that are small enough to participate as active consumers in the economy.

Women in politics. Mexico City inaugurated its first female mayor in 1999. On September 29, the city council selected Rosario Robles Berlanga of the Democratic Revolutionary Party to fill the term of Mayor Cuauhtemoc Cardenas Solorzano, who resigned to run for the presidency. Robles had served as the secretary of government in the Cardenas administration.

Mireya Elisa Moscoso de Grubar of the conservative Arnulfista Party, Panama's first woman president, was sworn in on September 1. On December 14, she presided over a ceremonial transfer of the Panama Canal from U.S. to Panamanian control. Moscoso was the sixth woman to lead a Latin American nation.

New presidents. Seven other Latin American nations—Argentina, El Salvador, Guatemala, Guyana, Paraguay, Uruguay, and Venezuela—elected or inaugurated new presidents in 1999. President Janet Jagan of Guyana, the first elected U.S.-born leader of a Latin American nation, resigned from office on August 11 because of poor health. She was succeeded by Finance Minister Bharrat Jagdeo, who at age 35 was the youngest head of state in the Western Hemisphere in 1999.

Political observers considered Argentina's presidential election in October the biggest political upset in Latin America in 1999. Fernando de la Rua of the center-left Alliance coalition defeated Eduardo Duhalde of the conservative Peronist Party, which had dominated Argentine politics during the 1990's.

In Venezuela, Hugo Chavez Frias, a former army colonel who had attempted a military *coup* (takeover) in 1992, was sworn in as a civilian president on Feb. 2, 1999. In a move that Chavez said was necessary to end government corruption, he supplanted the legislature with a popularly elected National Constituents Assembly, which was charged with writing a new constitution. Chavez's political opponents feared that the proposed constitutional changes would allow the new president to assume dictatorial power.

Revisiting dictatorships of the past. A British court in London ruled in October that General Augusto Pinochet Ugarte, Chile's dictator from 1973 to 1990, could be extradited to Spain to face 34 charges of torture and a single charge of conspiracy to torture. Pinochet, who had been under house arrest in England since October 1998, appealed the ruling.

Human rights activists, encouraged by the prospect that Pinochet might be tried in court, re-examined a 1,500-page archive about Operation Condor, a secret pact begun in 1975 among six South American governments. The archive, which was found in Paraguay in 1993, contains records of how police forces collaborated across borders to monitor and capture people believed to be involved in Communist organizations.

In November 1999, Spanish magistrate Baltazar Garzon, seeking Pinochet's extradition, issued international arrest warrants for 98 Argentinians on charges of human rights abuses. Human rights activists in 1999 accused Bolivia's incumbent president, Hugo Banzer Suarez, of being responsible for the disappearance of 200 Bolivian dissidents between 1971 and 1978, when Banzer was dictator in Bolivia. The activists based their accusations on evidence from the Operation Condor archive.

Corruption was exposed at the highest levels of government and society in several Latin American countries in 1999. In Mexico, Raul Salinas de Gortari, brother of a former president, was convicted on January 21 on charges of orchestrating the 1994 assassination of a prominent member of the ruling political party. Fabian Alarcon Rivera, who served as Ecuador's interim president from February 1997 to August 1998, was arrested in March 1999. He was charged with padding the government payroll with more than 1,000 nonexistent employees during his tenure as the leader of Ecuador's legislature in 1996. In July 1999, a court in The Hague, the Netherlands, sentenced Desi Bouterse, former military dictator of Suriname, to 16 years in prison and fined him $2.18 million. Bouterse, who never appeared before the court, was convicted of complicity in smuggling 2 tons (1.8 metric tons) of cocaine seized at Dutch and Belgian ports from 1989 to 1997.

Drug traffickers arrested. On Oct. 13, 1999, the U.S. Justice Department announced the arrest of 31 people in Mexico and Colombia on drug trafficking charges. Among those apprehended were Alejandro Bernal Madrigal, head of Colombia's largest cocaine ring, and Fabio Ochoa, a member of Colombia's Medellin drug cartel. Colombian authorities pledged to extradite suspects to the United States.

In August and September, U.S. authorities arrested 74 people, most of whom were airline employees at the Miami (Florida) International Airport, on charges of smuggling drugs into the United States from Latin America. The airline employees allegedly used their security clearances to smuggle drugs for payments of $3,000 to $5,000 per delivery.

The Colombian government's conflict with leftist rebels and drug traffickers developed into a regional problem in 1999. Most Colombians were apprehensive about traveling through areas of the country where rebel armies, drug cartels, regular military forces, and paramilitary units operated freely. Many Colombians fled to neighboring Panama and Venezuela to avoid violence at home. In the northern Colombian province of Cordoba, all 2,500 members of an Embera-Katio Indian village applied to Spain for political asylum.

Recession and devaluation. The economies of most Latin American countries were in recession in 1999. Three countries—Brazil, Colombia, and Ecuador—were forced to devalue their currencies. In September, Ecuador defaulted on a $6-billion debt to international lenders.

The region as a whole was expected to have a negative economic growth rate of one-tenth of 1 percent in 1999, according to estimates in June by Bear, Stearns & Co. Inc., a New York City securities firm. Mexico, however, was expected to record a 3-percent economic growth rate.

Unemployment reached severe levels in several nations of Latin America. Observers attributed high unemployment in part to an 18-percent drop in Latin America's automotive production. In Argentina, auto sales plummeted 43.5 percent to the lowest level since 1995. In Brazil, international automakers put their plans for investment on hold.

Economic analysts noted another trend in Brazil in 1999. An estimated 40,000 Brazilians of Japanese descent traveled to Japan in search of jobs in the second half of 1999—twice the number of people who had sought work in Japan in the same period of 1998. In the first half of 1999, Brazilians working in Japan sent home about $1.09 billion.

U.S. investments. The rate at which U.S. companies bought up Latin American businesses increased in 1999. In the first half of the year, Dole Food Company, Inc., based in Westlake Village, California, bought four of Colombia's largest flower growers. Those companies, which together account for one-quarter of the country's flower exports, did about $555 million in export sales in 1998.

In September 1999, Morgan Stanley Dean Witter & Company, an investment firm in New York City, paid $100 million for a minority stake in Latin America's largest provider of Internet service, Universo Online of Sao Paulo, Brazil, which has more than 500,000 subscribers.

Anheuser-Busch Companies Inc. of St. Louis, Missouri, reported that an aggressive advertising campaign for Budweiser beer in Argentina had resulted in a 61-percent increase in sales during the first quarter of 1999. Anheuser-Busch, which has a 2-percent share of Latin America's beer market, planned to boost its presence by creating partnerships with local bottlers and distributors and by acquiring exclusive sponsorship rights to popular sporting events, such as soccer games.

In June, Brazil ended its government monopoly on oil production at a two-day auction of offshore exploration licenses. Among those bidding a total of $181 million to explore for oil off Brazil's Atlantic coast were Exxon Corporation based in Irving, Texas; Texaco Incorporated based in White Plains, New York; and Unocal Corporation based in El Segundo, California. The Brazilian government predicted that oil exploration would lead to foreign investments of $15 billion and the creation of 300,000 jobs.

Stock exchanges. U.S. investments and buyouts in Latin America led to a sharp increase in the number of shares of Latin American companies traded on the New York Stock Exchange in 1999. From July 1997 to July 1999, the average daily trading volume on the exchange in Sao Paulo, Latin America's largest securities market, fell by 75 percent, according to figures complied by Economatica, a Sao Paulo economic research firm. In Mexico City, trading fell by 48 percent; in Lima, Peru, by 69 percent; in Buenos Aires, Argentina, by 37 percent; and in Bogota, Colombia, by 74 percent.

Mercosur-European Union. The nations of the South American Common Market (Mercosur)—Argentina, Brazil, Chile, Paraguay, and Uruguay—sought to offset the growing U.S. dominance in the region by improving commercial relations with Europe during 1999. On February 21, Brazil's President Fernando Henrique Cardoso urged business executives attending the first meeting of the Mercosur-European Union Business Forum in Rio de Janeiro, Brazil, to strive for better balance in trade regulations and tariffs among Latin American and European nations.

On June 25, Rio de Janeiro hosted a follow-up Latin American-European Summit. Delegates from 33 Latin American and 15 European nations established a "strategic partnership" to begin negotiations on tariff issues by July 2001.

Language extinction. Linguists in 1999 lamented the extinction of many languages in South America. In the Peruvian Amazon, for example, where some 100 to 150 languages were once spoken, only 57 survived in 1999. According to linguist Mary Ruth Wise of the Summer Institute of Linguistics based in Dallas, 25 of those languages would become extinct within a generation. Doug Whalen of Yale University in New Haven, Connecticut, noted that linguists were still discovering previously unknown languages among isolated populations. But the discovery of "new" languages, he asserted, "immediately endangers them." □Nathan A. Haverstock

See also articles on the individual nations; **People in the news** (Chavez, Hugo; Moscoso, Mireya).

Latvia. The Latvian parliament elected Vaira Vike-Freiberga as the nation's new president on June 17, 1999. Although born in Latvia, Vike-Freiberga, a linguist and psychologist, was a citizen of Canada until four days before her election.

Vike-Freiberga won on the sixth ballot, after three different candidates backed by Prime Minister Vilis Kristopans failed to garner sufficient support to win the presidency. On July 5, Kristopans resigned. On July 16, the parliament elected People's Party leader Andris Skele prime minister. Skele, who previously had served as prime minister from 1995 to 1997 and left office amid a corruption scandal, formed a coalition government.

On July 8, 1999, the parliament passed a language law that mandated the use of the Latvian language on signs, in public meetings, and in the workplace. International organizations like the European Commission, the administrative arm of the European Union (EU), objected to such attempts to regulate language use in the private sector. President Vike-Freiberga vetoed the bill, sending it back to parliament for revision. In October 1999, the European Commission invited Latvia to apply for membership in the EU in 2000.

☐ Steven L. Solnick

See also **Europe.**

Law. See **Courts; Human rights; Supreme Court of the United States.**

Lebanon. Israeli Prime Minister Ehud Barak, who assumed office in July 1999, declared in September that he would withdraw 1,500 Israeli troops stationed in southern Lebanon by July 2000. Israel had established a security zone in southern Lebanon in 1985 to deter cross-border attacks on northern Israel by the pro-Iranian Islamic group Hezbollah. Hezbollah later began attacking Israeli troops in the zone and members of the South Lebanon Army (SLA), which was allied to the Israeli military to defend Israel's border.

In response to Barak's announcement, Lebanese Prime Minister Salim al-Huss said that, without a peace agreement, the Lebanese army could not guarantee an end to cross-border attacks by Hezbollah following an Israeli pullback. In December 1999, after the unexpected resumption of peace talks between Israel and Syria, prospects arose that Lebanon might be included in peace negotiations with Israel in 2000.

SLA leaves Jezzin. Some 200 members of the SLA withdrew in June 1999 from the mountain town of Jezzin, the northernmost point controlled by the SLA, to the Israeli-controlled south. Many Lebanese hoped this marked the beginning of an Israeli-SLA withdrawal.   ☐ Christine Helms

See also **Israel; Middle East; Middle East:** A Special Report; **Syria.**

Lesotho. See **Africa.**

Library. The British Library in London completed construction of its new facility in June 1999 with the opening of the science reading rooms. Since the new library opened its doors in April 1998, the number of people requesting access to the library's reading rooms increased by 60 percent. Most library patrons praised the new facility, but the new automated book-request system was not able to fill most requests in less than 30 minutes, the initial goal of the library's director.

The Royal Library in Copenhagen, Denmark, reopened in a new facility in September 1999. The 430,000 square-foot (40,000 square-meter) black granite building was designed to resemble an open book with the binding facing up. The Royal Library directors hoped the new facility would help the institution redefine itself as a major cultural and research center.

Library funding. The Carnegie Corporation of New York, a charitable foundation established in New York City in 1911 by industrialist Andrew Carnegie, announced in June 1999 that it was awarding a total of $15 million to 25 urban libraries. Carnegie Corporation President Vartan Gregorian called the grants a "vote of confidence" in the future of books and added, "No search engine can replace the library or the librarian."

In the tradition of Andrew Carnegie, who financed the construction of libraries around the world, Bill Gates, chairman of Microsoft Corporation of Redmond, Washington, invested in public libraries in 1999. The Bill and Melinda Gates Foundation, through a program called the Gates Library Initiative, made grants totaling $38.5 million to underserved public libraries for the purchase of computers, software, and technical training to provide public access to the Internet. The grant money was distributed to public library programs operated in eight states: California ($11-million), Florida ($5 million), Montana ($1 million), New York ($7.7 million), South Carolina ($4.3 million), Oklahoma ($2.5 million), Tennessee ($4 million), and Virginia ($3 million).

Scholarships. In September, the Bill and Melinda Gates Foundation pledged $1 billion over the next 20 years to provide college scholarships to at least 20,000 minority students. The scholarships were expected to include assistance to students pursuing graduate studies in library science.

The Chicago-based American Library Association (ALA) awarded 50 scholarships of $5,000 through its Spectrum Initiative, which was implemented in 1998. The program provided scholarships for graduate study in library sciences to African American, Asian, Hispanic, and other minority students in the United States and Canada. Many accredited graduate library education programs matched the Spectrum Scholarships.

Literacy. At a March 1999 literacy summit at Southern Illinois University in Carbondale, former U.S. Senator Paul Simon unveiled an action plan to combat illiteracy in the United States. Simon called on the library director of the largest community in every U.S. county to convene educators, business leaders, and social service providers in a community effort to determine how to solve the problem of adult illiteracy. Simon, who introduced the National Literacy Act of 1991, had hoped to eliminate illiteracy in the United States by 2000. "We are far from that goal," he concluded in a written statement. "But with creative, practical people working at it, we can build substantially on the gains we have made."

Arthur. The ALA and public television station WGBH in Boston announced in February 1999 a library outreach initiative designed around the popular children's television show "Arthur." The animated program about an aardvark named Arthur is based on a series of books by Marc Brown.

The ALA and WGBH awarded grants to 10 public libraries to create and implement programs that use the appeal of the Arthur books and TV series to attract a new group of readers to libraries. The ALA planned to use ideas from the test sites to help other public libraries develop effective outreach programs.   □ Peggy Barber

Libya. Libyan leader Muammar Muhammad al-Qadhafi took steps in 1999 to end both his political isolation and the United Nations (UN) sanctions imposed against Libya in 1992. The UN had instituted the sanctions to pressure Libyan officials into turning over for trial two Libyans accused of the 1988 terrorist bombing of Pan Am flight 103 over Lockerbie, Scotland. The sanctions included a ban on sales to Libya of certain equipment needed for that country's oil industry, a freeze on some overseas Libyan assets, and a ban on flights to and from Libya.

Qadhafi surrendered the suspects in April 1999. The UN immediately suspended the sanctions, though it announced that the measures would be permanently lifted only after Libya demonstrated complete cooperation during the trial, scheduled for May 2000.

European relations. Libya's admission of "general responsibility" for the 1984 killing of a British policewoman outside the Libyan embassy in London led to the restoration of diplomatic relations with Britain in 1999. In July, Libya paid France $31 million to be distributed to the relatives of passengers killed in the 1989 explosion of a French airliner.   □ Christine Helms

See also **Africa; Middle East; Middle East: A Special Report.**

Liechtenstein. See **Europe.**

Literature, American. A debate raged in 1999 over the future of the book. For years, computer experts had predicted that people would soon do most of their reading on computer screens. Then, in August, Terry Teachout asserted in *The Wall Street Journal* that movies had replaced books as the cultural currency of Americans. While best-selling novels usually sell 1 million to 2 million copies, popular movies are seen by tens of millions of people. In predicting that the movie would succeed the book as the central literary form, Teachout cited two factors—computers, videocassette recorders, and other devices that allow people to watch movies at home and the emergence of technology that allows movies to be reproduced and distributed cheaply.

The assault on books was not well received. In the November *Harper's Magazine,* novelist William Gass noted, "We shall not understand what a book is, and why a book has the value many persons have, and is even less replaceable than a person, if we forget how important to it is its body, the building that has been built to hold its lines of language together through many adventures and a long time. Words on screen have visual qualities, to be sure, and these darkly *limn* (illuminate) their shape, but they have no materiality, they are only shadows, and when the light shifts they'll be gone." Nobel Prize-winning novelist Saul Bellow, discussing the possible replacement of books by newer media in *The New York Times,* responded to Teachout, saying that readers are still out there, and "They want more than they are getting."

Oprah Winfrey's television book club provided another strong argument that literature published in book form remained healthy in 1999. Winfrey had chosen 28 books since starting her televised book club in 1996, and all of them became bestsellers. The National Book Awards honored Winfrey's commitment to literature with a special citation in 1999. Many publishers interpreted Winfrey's power to create bestsellers as a reflection of a large reading public that was more strongly influenced by television than by such literary media as newspapers or magazines.

The 1999 National Book Award in fiction went to Chinese American author Ha Jin for *Waiting.* The novel tells the story of Lin Kong, a physician in the Chinese army trapped by an arranged marriage. When Lin falls in love with a nurse, he repeatedly attempts to persuade his wife to agree to a divorce. Without her consent and constrained by China's Cultural Revolution and by ancient tradition, the lovers discover how a relationship changes over many years.

Four other books were nominated for the fiction award. Kent Haruf's *Plainsong* is a quiet tale of life in a small Colorado town. Haruf's novel weaves together the lives of a high school teacher, a pregnant 17-year-old girl, and a pair of elderly bachelor farmers all struggling to cope with family and life. *House of Sand and Fog,* by Andre Dubus III, is the story of an ambitious Iranian immigrant, whose attempts to maintain the status and dignity of his family, place them on the road to disaster. Jean Thompson's collection of short stories, *Who Do You Love,* details the disappointments of love and people's inherent loneliness. Patricia Henley's first novel, *Hummingbird House,* is both the story of a compassionate American woman in Central America in the late 1980's and a political commentary about U.S. intervention in the region.

The New Yorker magazine's summer fiction issue caused a stir in the literary world in 1999 with its focus on what the magazine's fiction editor, Bill Buford, called the "twenty best young fiction writers in America." ("Young" was defined as being under the age of 40.) The 20 writers chosen by *The New Yorker* were George Saunders, David Foster Wallace, Sherman Alexie, Rick Moody, A. M. Homes, Allegra Goodman, William T. Vollmann, Antonya Nelson, Chang-rae Lee, Michael Chabon, Ethan Canin, Donald Antrim, Tony Earley, Jeffrey Eugenides, Junot Diaz, Jonathan Franzen, Edwidge Danticat, Jhumpa Lahiri, Nathan Englander, and Matthew Klam. Buford described them as a "highly accomplished group of writers robustly taking on the stories of their Americanness."

Five of the writers chosen by *The New Yorker* published books in 1999. A. M. Homes's *Music for Torching,* her fourth novel, is a black comedy that describes a suburban couple in the throes of absolute misery. Nathan Englander's *For the Relief of Unbearable Urges,* his first book, is a collection of stories about a variety of people, from a Jewish writer in the Soviet Union to a Park Avenue lawyer. Englander's great strength is depicting how religion clashes with modern life. Jhumpa Lahiri's collection of stories, *Interpreter of Maladies,* is also her first book. Lahiri, an American writer whose family is Indian, writes about Indian immigrants and the difficulties faced by modern Indian women. Chang-rae Lee's second novel, *A Gesture Life,* tells the story of Franklin Hata, a perpetual outsider first as a Korean in wartime Japan then as a postwar immigrant to the United States. David Foster Wallace's *Brief Interviews with Hideous Men,* a collection of stories displaying his usual verbal and intellectual pyrotechnics, is his first work of fiction since the mammoth *Infinite Jest.*

Second novels. Ralph Ellison's (1914-1994) incomplete second novel, *Juneteenth,* was published in 1999. Ellison's first novel, *Invisible Man* (1952), is considered one of the most significant books ever written by an American novelist. At his death, Ellison left behind 2,000 pages of

MOST CRITICS agreed that the outstanding fiction work of the year was Ernest Hemingway's short but magnificent *The Old Man and the Sea,* an epic story of an old Cuban fisherman and his coming to grips with the savage forces of nature. It missed a top spot on the best-seller list because a national magazine printed it in its entirety in one issue, before book publication.

Novelist Ernest Hemingway

manuscript, fragments of an epic story that he had worked on for nearly 40 years. His literary executor extracted from the many drafts and revisions a smaller tale of two men in the 1950's—a "white" racist senator, who is the son of a mixed marriage, and a black minister who is a key to the senator's past. Parts of *Juneteenth* display the verbal artistry, often likened to jazz with words, that made *Invisible Man* so electrifying, but on the whole, the book does not hold together.

Claire Messud's second novel, *The Last Life,* provided one of the literary sensations of 1999. Set in the 1960's, it tells the story of the LaBasse family from Algeria, who live on the southern French coast. In a poignant tale of loneliness and displacement, the narrator, 14-year-old Sagesse, watches the family disintegrate in France.

The National Book Award in nonfiction went to John Dower's *Embracing Defeat: Japan in the Wake of World War II.* The follow-up to his landmark study of the Pacific War, *War Without Mercy* (1986), *Embracing Defeat* confirms Dower's reputation as a leading scholar in the field.

Other Book Award nominees included Natalie Angier's eloquent exploration of female physiology, *Woman: An Intimate Geography;* Mark Bowden's account of the U.S. military intervention in Somalia, *Black Hawk Down: A Story of Modern War;* John Philip Santos's poetic exploration of his family's Mexican heritage, *Places Left Unfinished at the Time of Creation;* and Judith Thurman's nuanced portrait of French novelist Colette, *Secrets of the Flesh: A Life of Colette.*

Two of the most anticipated books of 1999, Edmund Morris's *Dutch* and Frank McCourt's *'Tis,* were not nominated. Morris spent 14 years writing *Dutch,* the authorized biography of former President Ronald Reagan. The book was heavily criticized because Morris created a fictional character, whom he named after himself and interwove through Reagan's life, breaking the boundaries between nonfiction and fiction. *'Tis* is McCourt's follow-up to *Angela's Ashes,* his 1996 bestseller. Many reviewers found the new book which describes McCourt's life as an immigrant in America, less touching than *Angela's Ashes.*

Authors. The year 1999 was the 100th anniversary of the birth of American novelist Ernest Hemingway (1899-1961), who was honored with the publication of several books. Patrick Hemingway, the novelist's son, edited Ernest Hemingway's Africa writings, published in 1999 under the title *True at First Light.*

Joseph Heller, author of the 1961 novel *Catch-22,* died Dec. 12, 1999, at age 76. Heller's fiction showcased his fascination with the absurd.

       □Robert Messenger

See also **Literature for children; Poetry.**

Literature, World.

The 1999 Nobel Prize for literature was awarded to Gunter Grass, who joined fellow German Nobel laureates Heinrich Boll (1917-1983), Herman Hesse (1877-1962), and Thomas Mann (1875-1955). Grass is perhaps best known for his novel *The Tin Drum,* about a boy who refuses to grow and protects himself with a toy drum. Throughout his literary career, Grass has explored the effects of war and progress through the 1900's, especially in his homeland. Like Grass, many writers of fiction, poetry, and essays published in 1999 focused on the assessment of changes and events through the past 100 years.

In 1999, popular Irish writer Roddy Doyle published *A Star Called Henry,* the first of a projected series, "The Last Roundup," that would chronicle Ireland in the 1900's through the eyes of Henry Smart, an orphan who becomes a hit man for Irish Republican militants.

Canadian writer Wayne Johnston published the highly praised *The Colony of Unrequited Dreams.* This deceptively simple fictionalized history of Joseph Smallwood, the first premier of the newly created Canadian province of Newfoundland, is a study of history as the accumulation of many people living their lives.

Award-winning works. South African writer J. M. Coetzee won the 1999 Booker Prize for his novel *Disgrace,* the story of an aging professor at a second-rate university in Cape Town who is dismissed after seducing one of his students. (The Booker Prize recognizes writers from the Commonwealth and other former British colonies.) Other novels shortlisted for the award included Colm Toibin's *The Blackwater Lightship,* the story of estranged family members who gather when a son falls ill with AIDS, and Anita Desai's *Fasting, Feasting,* a novel about a family dominated by like-minded parents whose plans for their children have unforeseen consequences.

The 1998 Whitbread Book of the Year prize—the top honor of the prestigious annual awards for works published in the United Kingdom and Ireland—was awarded posthumously in January 1999 to Ted Hughes for *Birthday Letters,* his collection of poems about his marriage to American poet Sylvia Plath, who committed suicide in 1963. It was his third consecutive Book of the Year award. The Best Novel award went to Justin Cartwright for *Leading the Cheers,* the story of a British American who returns to the United States for his high school reunion to make some interesting discoveries. The Best First Novel prize was given to Giles Foden for *The Last King of Scotland,* a dark comedy about Ugandan dictator Idi Amin. Awards for books published in 1999 were to be announced in January 2000.

Also in 1999, Scottish poet Jackie Kay won the Author's Club First Novel Award for her 1998 novel, *Trumpet,* a story about a mixed-race jazz trumpeter who was posthumously revealed, by his wife, to be a woman. The novel explores the consequences of this revelation for his family, admirers, and colleagues.

Other notable works that were published in the United Kingdom in 1999 included Penelope Lively's *Spiderweb,* Pat Barker's *Another World,* and John Berger's *King: A Street Story.*

India and the subcontinent. Two heavyweight authors from India who write in English, Vikram Seth and Salman Rushdie, produced large novels in 1999, both addressing the theme of music. Salman Rushdie's *The Ground Beneath Her Feet* is the story of a very popular Indian pop star and her disappearance in an earthquake. Vikram Seth's *An Equal Music* concerns an unhappy violinist in London who meets a pianist he loved and lost years before in Vienna.

Recently, English-speaking readers have discovered writers from India and Pakistan and other subcontinental countries. Among the favorites of 1999 was Amit Chaudhuri's *Freedom Song,* three short novels that echo India's distinguished poet and philosopher Rabindranath Tagore (1861-1941) in their simplicity and delicate handling of domestic drama.

Writer Gertrude Stein

THE LITERARY MINDED, who may have heard much of Gertrude Stein and her startling manner of writing, will find that this frequently unintelligible author can produce perfectly straight English when she is so inclined. Her autobiography, which masquerades under the title of *The Autobiography of Alice B. Toklas*, is a fluent, and at times striking, record of a life of remarkable influence. Stein, who is a woman of . . . intellect, with a great capacity for friendship, an ardent preoccupation with art and literature, and a personality so individual as to have established her as an almost legendary figure both in Paris, where she lives, and in America, where she was born, has just entered the dramatic field with the opera, *Four Saints in Three Acts.*

Translations of past writers. The task of translating and selecting the works of Argentine writer Jorge Luis Borges (1899-1986) was finished with the publication of three volumes: *Collected Fictions, Selected Poems,* and *Selected Non-Fictions.* Borges, known for his cerebral inventiveness, also wrote widely on cultural and literary topics and had a special love for the childlike inventiveness of fairy tales, which can be seen in his own work.

The posthumous writings of famed Italian writer Italo Calvino (1923-1985) continued to be collected and translated, notably with the publication of *Why Read the Classics?* in 1999. This collection of essays by the exhaustively inventive author spans his entire literary career, from his assessment of American writer Ernest Hemingway to his essay on Borges, who was also interested in fairy tales and inventive constructions. (Calvino's novel *Cosmicomics* plays with science fiction, and *The Castle of Crossed Destinies* is told through Tarot cards.)

New lucid translations of works by Franz Kafka (1883-1924)—*The Castle,* translated by Mark Harman, and *The Trial,* translated by Breon Mitchell—were especially notable because they were based on restored texts. *The Castle* was never finished, and *The Trial* was edited from an unfinished manuscript. These end-of-the-century editions were timely, as the novels were published in the first decade of the 1900's and are considered to have launched the modernist movement.

Zbigniew Herbert (1924-1998), one of the distinguished Polish literary figures of the 1900's, was celebrated in 1999 with a collection entitled *King of the Ants: Mythological Essays.* Known best for his poetry, Herbert wrote a series of sometimes satirical essays that takes apart the classic myth stories and reexamines their meaning.

Translations of modern works. Several fine novels from France became available in English-language translations in 1999. These include *The Palace,* by Lisa St. Aubin de Teran, the story of an Italian soldier who, while in prison, reinvents himself as a gentleman gambler with the goals of building a palace and marrying a woman from a wealthy family.

The premise of Laurence Cosse's *A Corner of the Veil* is the discovery by an order of priests of the absolute proof of the existence of God. The consequences of this proof constitute the plot of the novel. The provocative writer Marie Darrieussecq's second book, *My Phantom Husband,* explores the emotional states of a woman whose husband suddenly disappears.

Eastern European writers continued to offer new works in English translation. Highlights of 1999 included the English publication of Balkan writer Aleksander Tisma's *The Book of Blam,* set in the Yugoslavia of Tito's time. Andrei Makine's *The Crime of Olga Arbyelina,* his most recent novel, is about a Russian princess who flees to Paris during the revolution. Makine is best known for *Dreams of My Russian Summers.* Makine himself left Russia for Paris and writes in French.

Japan's wealth of fine writers was best represented in 1999 by two small collections of short stories. Yasunari Kawabata's *First Snow on Fuji* was made available in English translation for the first time in 1999. Kawabata (1899-1972) was known for his simplicity and for echoing the Japanese tradition of haiku imagery. His style conveys a wide range of emotional states with delicacy and silence. Contemporary writer Haruki Murakami, after the success of his large and complex 1998 novel *The Wind-Up Bird Chronicle,* produced a simpler, purer *South of the Border, West of the Sun,* an investigation into the life of an ordinary Japanese man who reencounters a first love.

Israeli writer Amos Oz published in 1999 *The Story Begins: Essays on Literature,* a series of essays that looks carefully at the opening pages of several classical stories and novels and considers the idea of beginnings and their importance to readers. ☐ Brian Bouldrey

See also **Literature, American; Literature for children; Nobel Prizes; Poetry.**

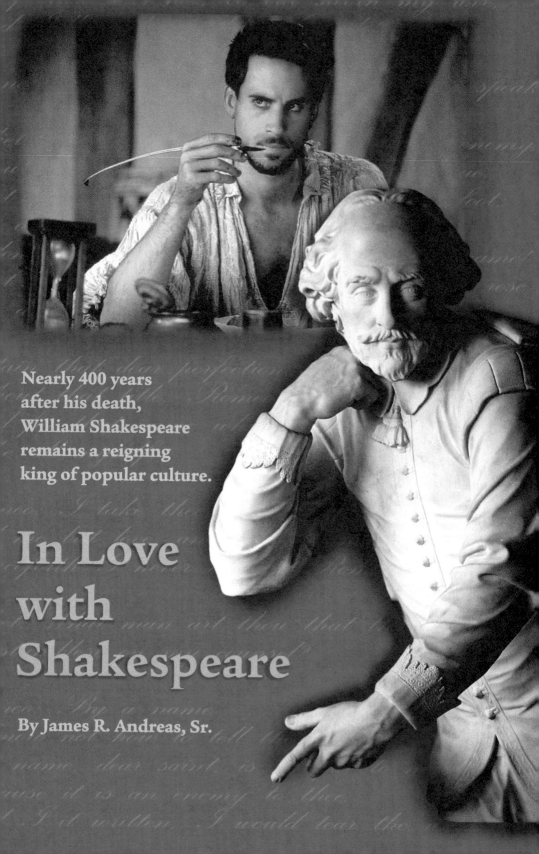

Nearly 400 years
after his death,
William Shakespeare
remains a reigning
king of popular culture.

In Love
with
Shakespeare

By James R. Andreas, Sr.

Harold Bloom, a literature professor at Yale University in New Haven, Connecticut, argues in his 1998 best seller, *Shakespeare: The Invention of the Human,* that William Shakespeare was the world's first writer to portray characters as realistic human beings who are capable of change. According to Bloom, Shakespeare's characters, after nearly four centuries, continue to generate as much popular appeal as they do scholarly interest. Another literary scholar, Jan Kott, refers to Shakespeare as "our contemporary" because his plays never go out of style. The plays of Shakespeare have been in almost continuous production, in one form or another, since the author's death in 1616. This four-century run keeps William Shakespeare as much a king of contemporary popular culture today as he was in his own time.

In March 1999, *Shakespeare in Love,* a fictional portrayal of the playwright, won seven Academy Awards, marking the culmination of a decade of successful film productions based on his works and life. These films were created by a who's who of Hollywood actors, directors, and writers. The costumers and set designers for these films re-created a variety of settings representing everything from Shakespeare's own age to present-day Seattle. The Shakespearean blockbusters of the 1990's, director Oliver Parker's *Othello* (1995) and director Baz Luhrmann's *Romeo and Juliet* (1996), starred Laurence Fishburne as the tormented Othello and Leonardo DiCaprio and Claire Danes as the "star-cross'd lovers." Actor and director Kenneth Branagh's *Much Ado About Nothing* (1993) and *Hamlet* (1996), director Trevor Nunn's dark interpretation of *Twelfth Night* (1996), and director Michael Hoffman's *A Midsummer Night's Dream* (1999) were also well-received films of the decade. More Shakespeare films were scheduled for 2000, including a musical adaptation of *Love's Labour's Lost* set in the 1930's and a futuristic version of the thriller *Titus Andronicus.*

The popularity of Shakespeare at the end of the century was not limited to the screen, however. He remained a favorite of intellectuals, who often refer to him as the Bard, the greatest of master poets. Shakespeare's plays continued to be a mainstay of literature curriculums in secondary schools and were constantly produced on the local theater scene. In the 1990's, Shakespeare festivals and theater companies around the world drew millions of people to hundreds of productions annually. A replica of Shakespeare's own Globe Theatre opened in 1997 on the original site in London. Since the new Globe's first season, hundreds of thousands of people have trooped to this open-air theater to experience Shakespeare's panorama of human comedy and tragedy performed within the theatrical conventions he helped to create.

Shakespeare's popularity in his own age

Evidence of the original success of Shakespeare's plays appears in the court records of Queen Elizabeth I, who reigned in England from 1558 to 1603, and in the diaries of Philip Henslowe,

Opposite page:
Joseph Fiennes portrays William Shakespeare in *Shakespeare in Love,* the 1999 Academy Award-winning film based loosely on the life of the playwright.

an Elizabethan theater manager. Historical documents, however, reveal few details about Shakespeare himself, except that he was raised in the small town of Stratford-on-Avon, England, lived most of his adult life in London, worked as an actor, and wrote poetry for rich patrons. This lack of information led a number of scholars to question whether a lowly actor could have written so knowledgeably about subjects as lofty as royalty and the law, but most experts dismiss these doubts. Almost all literary scholars agree that William Shakespeare produced the most impressive body of dramatic writing in the history of world literature.

The sketchy biographical details about Shakespeare's life allowed the writers of *Shakespeare in Love*, Tom Stoppard and Marc Norman, to improvise. They present a young Will suffering from an unlikely bout of writer's block after some early successes with such comedies as *The Two Gentlemen of Verona*. But Viola, a young noblewoman who violates class and gender conventions by pursuing a dream to act in a London theater company, provides the romantic inspiration for Shakespeare's first tragedy and the most famous love story ever written, *Romeo and Juliet*.

In spite of the fictional premise of *Shakespeare in Love*, the film is based on either generally accepted assumptions about the playwright's life or well-documented details about Elizabethan theater. The movie refers to Shakespeare's probable alienation from his wife, Anne Hathaway, the shameful reputation of London's theater district, Shakespeare's competition with the successful playwright Christopher Marlowe, and the Puritans' criticism of the "immoral" theater. The film also captures the immense popularity of Shakespeare's plays and of the Globe Theatre. The innovative design of the Globe allowed audience members to see and hear easily. Three stories of balconies wrapped around the stage and a ground-level, open-air "pit" where patrons stood. Although the theater held an estimated 3,500 people, no member of the audience was more than about 55 feet (17 meters) from the performance space. During Shakespeare's association with the Globe, when London had a population of only about 250,000 people, nearly 1 million patrons attended productions at the theater. Aristocracy and royalty also patronized Shakespeare's plays at the royal palaces of Whitehall and Hampton Court.

The author:
James R. Andreas, Sr., is a professor of English at Clemson University in South Carolina and director of the Clemson Shakespeare Festival.

The Bard for all time

Ben Jonson, a rival playwright in the Elizabethan theater, declared Shakespeare the "soul of the age" and "wonder of our stage." Jonson compared Shakespeare favorably to the great poets and playwrights of ancient Greece—Euripides, Sophocles, and Aristophanes—as well as to England's own Geoffrey Chaucer (1340?–1400), author of *The Canterbury Tales*, and Edmund Spenser (1552?–1599), author of *The Faerie Queen*. Jonson also claimed that Shakespeare was "not of an age but for all time." The rival playwright's assessment proved to be accurate.

Shakespeare's importance and the strength of his popular appeal can be measured, in part, by how often people turned to his plays for inspiration and ideas—even when they did not entirely approve of his creations. In every period since Shakespeare's death, his plays have been excerpted, spoofed, "fixed," or otherwise amended. Writers have even supplied the tragedies with happy endings. In the late 1600's, British playwright James Howard reconceived *Romeo and Juliet* as a comedy, keeping the lovers alive at the end of the play. In the early 1800's, Thomas Bowdler "sanitized" the plays in a volume called *The Family Shakespeare*. Bowdler changed or omitted words that he believed were inappropriate for children. This kind of editing, or "bowdlerization," as it came to be known, was never popular with scholars, but it did have the beneficial effect of extending the audience of Shakespeare.

Michelle Pfeiffer as the fairy Queen Titania and Kevin Kline as Bottom the Weaver succumb to fanciful spells in the 1999 film production of *A Midsummer Night's Dream*.

Musicians borrowed from the playwright's work and, in turn, contributed to his popularity. Composers transformed his poetic language into scores for operas, ballets, and orchestral music. Other composers used Shakespeare's poetry and the songs he wrote for some of his plays as the lyrics of short recital pieces.

An evolving popularity

Shakespeare's enduring popularity is also apparent in how well his work weathered the evolving conventions of theater and the shifting expectations of the public. During some periods, people venerated him as the greatest writer who ever lived. During other times, he was attacked as a "natural," but ungainly genius whose plays failed to conform to standards of decency and good taste. No matter how much the public opinion varied, however, people found they could not ignore Shakespeare's work.

When England's Puritan-controlled government displaced the monarchy in 1649, London's theaters were shut down and remained closed until the restoration of the king in 1660. Nevertheless, underground performances of Shakespeare "skits" were commonplace during the period of Puritan rule. In the 1700's, female actors, rather than young boys, were allowed for the first time to perform women's roles, a circumstance that considerably boosted the popularity of Shakespeare's plays, particularly among male patrons.

Intellectuals of the 1700's criticized Shakespeare's work as being "rude" or "vulgar"—not because of his themes—but because his plots did not follow the popular doctrine of the "classical unities." According to this literary convention, the playwright should restrict the action of a play to a single place and time period. The romantic poets of the early 1800's, on the other hand, celebrated Shakespeare's relatively humble origins and idolized him as the natural, unschooled, and spontaneous genius of romantic lore. Their praise helped transform the playwright into an "author," and many people came to regard the plays primarily as texts rather than scripts for dramatic performances.

Changes in British theater productions also contributed to the perception of Shakespeare as an author. In the 1800's, plays were not performed in open-air theaters, but in large halls similar to modern theaters. In these new settings, playwrights of the time created dramatic spectacles that relied on elaborate and cumbersome sets. In order to produce Shakespeare plays that met the prevailing taste of theatergoers, directors stripped down Shakespeare's original dialogue. As a result, the complex characters and poetic language were overshadowed by spectacular sets depicting, for example, the military skirmishes in *Henry V* or the naval battle in *Antony and Cleopatra*.

The theater conventions of the 1800's ultimately affected public perception of Shakespeare in two ways. The "special effects" robbed the plays of their rich language, so that audience members did not need to be actively engaged in listening and responding to the players on stage. Also, the high price of spectacle resulted in the staging of fewer Shakespeare plays and higher ticket prices, restricting attendance to more affluent audiences. The spectacle, consequently, relegated the playwright's words to the printed page and cost Shakespeare his popularity among the common people.

Shakespeare and the scholars

Intellectuals began to consider his work "theater of the mind" rather than of the stage. They deemed *King Lear* and other plays unperformable and accessible only through the written word. With this change in thinking, British scholars in the second half of the 1800's transformed Shakespeare—the highly popular, but rude, scandalous, and even "vulgar" playwright—into an elite cultural icon. They held up the image of Shakespeare the author as an authority in all matters literary, cultural, and moral. They used his plays to promote British culture and the English language throughout the world.

For the essayist and historian Thomas Carlyle (1795-1881), Shakespeare was a British hero worthy to be "worshipped." For the poet Matthew Arnold (1822-1888), the Bard was the token of the highest "seriousness," for which British culture yearned. The great Shakespearean scholar of that period, A. C. Bradley (1845-1933), wrote *Shakespearean Tragedy*, in which he extols the high virtue and irreproachable morality of Shakespeare's tragic heroes. Bradley's book, which remains required reading in most modern Shakespeare courses, overlooks the

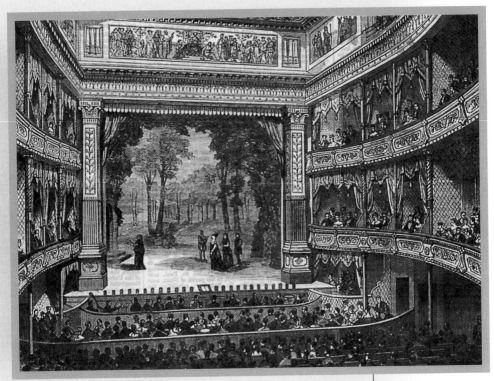

An engraving from the mid-1800's depicts a production of Shakespeare's *A Winter's Tale* at The Prince's Theatre in Manchester, England.

various heroes' heinous crimes in favor of their courage and resolve to overcome all obstacles to their ambitions.

During this period, Shakespeare's plays and poetry entered the curriculum of most English-speaking schools around the world. According to Shakespeare scholar Charles Frey of the University of Washington in Seattle, teachers for more than 100 years offered Shakespeare as the definitive model of correct English, effective public speaking, and high morals. Some educators used abridged collections of his plays, such as *Tales from Shakespeare* (1807) by Charles and Mary Lamb, to supply young people, especially girls, with properly edifying instruction. This approach resulted in "Shakespearophobia," the fear of Shakespeare experienced by many English-speaking schoolchildren. Even in the 1990's, *Romeo and Juliet, Julius Caesar, Macbeth*, and *Hamlet*—tragedies that emphasize the "high seriousness" of literature—remained the plays most often studied in middle and high schools.

State-of-the-art Shakespeare

In spite of Shakespeare's uncertain reception in the classroom through much of the 1900's, performances of his plays experienced a revival as new technologies—motion pictures, radio, television, computers, and the Internet—led to breakthroughs in artistic expression. Shakespeare's work was easily translated into silent films because the plays had been produced through much of the 1800's as visual spectacles. Filmmakers created scores of adaptations from a wide range of the plays, most no-

tably a silent *Othello* (1922), starring Academy Award-winner Emil Jannings, and a *Hamlet* (1920), starring female Danish film star Asta Nielsen in the male role of the

Shakespeare adapted well to the movies. Francis X. Bushman and Beverly Bayne (above) portray Shakespeare's "star-cross'd lovers" in a 1916 silent film version of *Romeo and Juliet.* Claire Danes and Leonardo DiCaprio (above right) introduced a new generation of moviegoers to the same characters in the 1996 film version of the play.

melancholy Dane. Radio performances and sound recordings of the plays were commonplace until the rise in popularity of television in the mid-1900's. Television producers in the 1950's stripped down and adapted Shakespeare's plays to fit the format and time limitations of commercial television. Notable TV productions included the "Westinghouse Theatre" presentation of *The Taming of the Shrew,* featuring actor Charlton Heston as Petruchio, and the "Hallmark Hall of Fame" presentation of *The Tempest,* starring Lee Remick, Roddy McDowell, and Richard Burton.

In the 1990's, the computer proved to be a viable medium for enhancing Shakespeare's popularity and even the next staging ground for his plays. Discussion groups on his life and work sprouted online, and Web sites cropped up on every conceivable Shakespearean subject—his life, the Globe Theatre, staging conventions, and research about what works were the actual creations of Shakespeare. Other sites offered production schedules for the many Shakespeare festivals around the world. Production companies, such as Castle Rock Entertainment and New Line Cinema, successfully generated interest in Shakespeare films with online presentations of film trailers, summaries of the plays, interactive features, and biographical information about Shakespeare geared toward younger audiences. The theatrical and academic possibilities for the new medium represented what Shakespeare himself might have called a "sea change" in the way people consume and digest theater and literature. A perfect example of new theatrical forms and media influencing the performance of Shakespeare's plays is Luhrmann's slick repackaging of *Romeo and Juliet* as an action film and the release of the movie trailer as a rock video on MTV.

Shakespeare's plays have in many ways lent legitimacy to these new media. Film, radio, television, and the Internet have, in turn, helped restore the plays to the author's original intention—that the words be spoken and heard, not just read. Ralph Cohen of James Madison University in Harrisonburg, Virginia, describes Shakespeare's language as "ear candy." The plays were written for audiences—that is listeners—not merely for spectators. Radio broadcasts, records, cassettes, and CD's of Shakespeare's plays, not to mention "talkie" films and television, helped restore the public's appetite for live performances of the plays. Even though the dialogue is written in verse and the vocabulary of Elizabethan English, the beauty of the language is irresistible to most audiences. As a result, most filmmakers retained Shakespeare's original words, even if they shortened the text or adapted the story to a modern setting.

The Bard for all people

Beyond the brilliance of the language, the plays remained popular because Shakespeare filled the stories with characters whom people have loved, admired, pitied, and despised for centuries. In some eras, a favorite play emerged to represent the prevailing tastes and the social and political circumstances of the age. In the late 1600's and early 1700's, when the institution of slavery existed through much of the Western world, the most popular Shakespeare play was *Othello,* a story of an African man who rises to prominence in a white man's world. The romantics of the early 1800's favored Hamlet—brooding, shrewd, and melancholy. In the late 1800's and early 1900's, when the British Empire was at its height, the public preferred *Henry V,* which displayed the pageantry of a king who united the various peoples of Great Britain and extended imperial domains beyond its shores. In the late 1900's, Shakespeare's most popular play was the comedy *A Midsummer Night's Dream,* perhaps because of its grotesque humor and sexual ambiguities.

The celebrity of most Shakespeare plays, however, was never confined to a particular era because the playwright carefully chose stories with long-lasting appeal. He rifled through famous literary sources—the plays of Euripides and Sophocles, Geoffrey Chaucer's *The Canterbury Tales,* the 100 stories of the *Decameron* by Italian writer Giovanni Boccaccio (1313?-1375)—as well as "news" stories of the 1500's and 1600's. From these materials, Shakespeare created stories and characters that address issues as relevant to current audiences as they were to the theatergoers of Elizabethan England.

In *Romeo and Juliet,* the young characters discover the perils of love in a world dominated by the concerns of adults. Racism motivates, at least in part, Iago's plot to destroy the title character in *Othello.* In *Measure for Measure,* a moralizing ruler demands sexual favors from a young woman in exchange for her brother's life—a circumstance that people today identify as sexual harassment. Through the title character of *King Lear*, Shakespeare explores the tyranny of self-serving authority and the potentially disastrous expectations of parents and children toward one another. *The Tempest*, in which a shipwrecked man rules over the inhabitants of an enchanted island, addresses issues that include the politics of empire and colonial control. In all of these cases, Shakespeare's characteristic refusal to arrive at firm or satisfying solutions perpetuates the appeal of the plays.

Even the lighter fare of Shakespeare's plays continue to be relevant. The 1999 film version of *A Midsummer Night's Dream* aptly underscored the play's theme, articulated by actor Kevin Kline in the role of Bottom the Weaver: "to say the truth, reason and love keep little company together now-a-days." Two pairs of lovers, one of whom is played by Calista Flockhart of television's "Ally McBeal," run off into the woods near Athens, the citadel of reason, to escape the stern influence of parents and society. They are subjected to the fancy of the fairy king and become—as Puck, the fairy trickster, exclaims—the "fools" of the immortals. The play is updated to Tuscany, Italy, in the 1800's, and the addition of bicycles multiplies the confusion that love introduces to young people on their own in the world for the first time.

Shakespeare's themes endured through the ages. Irene Jacob and Laurence Fishburne portray Desdemona and Othello in the 1995 film version of Shakespeare's *Othello*. The actors won critical praise for performances that captured the jealousy, envy, and prejudices that destroy the characters' lives.

Universal Shakespeare

Because of the relevance of these themes, Shakespeare's work is generally regarded as "universal"—that is, his plays are for all people in all times. Most contemporary scholars, however, prefer to characterize his plays as durable, versatile, and widely applicable. Like all great writers, Shakespeare chose story lines with themes that translate well into cultural contexts other than his own. This adaptability made possible director Richard Locraine's chilling film rendition of *Richard III* (1995). Locraine uses the original language of the play but recasts the English monarch of the 1400's as a Nazi leader in a fictional England of the 1930's. In *Looking for Richard* (1996), actor and director Al Pacino interprets the monstrous monarch as a forerunner of the modern mafia boss. The durability, versatility, and applicability of Shakespeare's work also allowed authors Toni Morrison and Gloria Naylor to successfully appropriate *The Tempest* in their novels *Tar Baby* and *Mama Day*. These qualities allowed Jane Smiley to re-create the story of *King Lear* in her 1992 Pulitzer

Prize-winning novel *A Thousand Acres*. Because Shakespeare's themes translate into other cultural context, Kate and Petruchio from *The Taming of the Shrew* still rage against and tame each other in a Seattle high school in the film *10 Things I Hate About You* (1999), and actor Ethan Hawke discovers there is something as rotten in New York City as there ever was in Denmark in an updated *Hamlet* scheduled for 2000.

Romantic poet John Keats (1795-1821) claimed that Shakespeare's definitive talent was "negative capability." He had the ability to suppress his own individuality in order to see the world as each of his characters might see it. In the 1990's, a new generation of actors assumed these roles, and audiences discovered not only the distinct voice of each character, but a voice for their own time. To the latest generation of teen-agers, Romeo became a teen idol in the person of Leonardo DiCaprio. For people who learned to view the world differently after decades of challenges to racial prejudices, Laurence Fishburne became the definitive Othello. For people perplexed by the challenges of modern relationships, Calista Flockhart embodied the confusion and comedy of romantic endeavors as Helena in *A Midsummer Night's Dream*. These and Shakespeare's other extraordinary characters continue to reveal the author's genius and justify his renown as the greatest and most popular writer of the millennium. ■ ■ ■

Ian McKellen plays the title role in a 1995 film production of *Richard III* that sets the story of an English monarch from the 1400's in a fictional Nazi state in the England of the 1930's.

Additional information:

Books

Bloom, Harold. *Shakespeare: The Invention of the Human.* Riverhead Books, 1998.

Coursen, H. R. *Shakespeare in Production: Whose History?* Ohio University Press, 1996.

Schoenbaum, Samuel. *Shakespeare's Lives.* Oxford University Press, 1991.

Taylor, Gary. *Reinventing Shakespeare: A Cultural History from the Restoration to the Present.* Oxford University Press, 1989.

Web sites

Shakespeare at Clemson University—http://www.clemson.edu/shakespeare. (This site includes a virtual tour of the Globe Theatre.)

The Complete Works of William Shakespeare—http://www.tech.mit.edu/Shakespeare/works.html.

Literature for children.
Fantasy books and picture books proved especially popular in 1999. Some of the outstanding children's books of 1999 included the following:

Picture books. *Raising Sweetness* by Diane Stanley, illustrated by G. Brian Karas (Putnam). When the kindly sheriff, who adopted eight orphans, gets a letter he cannot read, Sweetness takes over. Ages 4 to 8.

The Memory Coat by Elvira Woodruff, illustrated by Michael Dooling (Scholastic). Rachel's family brings her orphaned cousin Grisha with them to America, but will he pass the medical exam at Ellis Island? Ages 5 to 9.

Blue Willow by Pam Conrad, illustrated by S. Saelig Gallagher (Philomel). Haunting pictures illuminate the traditional legend of tragic lovers depicted on the blue willow plate. Ages 8 to 12.

Harry and Lulu by Arthur Yorinks, illustrated by Martin Matje (Hyperion). Lulu wants a real dog, but the stuffed one her parents give her instead takes her on an adventure. Ages 4 to 8.

A Symphony of Whales by Steve Schuch, illustrated by Peter Sylvada (Harcourt Brace). When Glashka finds hundreds of whales trapped in an inlet, she and her village help to save them. Ages 6 and up.

Basket Moon by Mary Lyn Ray, illustrated by Barbara Cooney (Little, Brown). A backwoods boy goes to town with his basket-making father, where a snide comment almost ruins the trip. Ages 4 to 8.

Tough Cookie by David Wisniewski (Lothrop, Lee & Shepard). Tough Cookie, who lives in a jar with friends, vows to stop Fingers, their enemy, in a parody of a "hard-boiled" detective story filled with puns. Ages 6 and up.

Toestomper and the Caterpillars by Sharleen Collicott (Houghton Mifflin). Rude, crude Toestomper has similar friends until caterpillars enter his life. Ages 4 to 8.

Poetry. *The Bookworm's Feast: A Potluck of Poems* by J. Patrick Lewis, illustrated by John O'Brien (Dial). A gentleman bookworm and his guests eat their way through a library in a series of nonsense poems. Ages 4 to 8.

I Am the Cat by Alice Schertle, illustrated by Mark Buehner (Lothrop). Intriguing cat poems are accompanied by paintings featuring hidden animals. All ages.

Laugh-eteria by Douglas Florian (Harcourt Brace). Fun and nonsense on a variety of silly subjects are presented in 150 poems, illustrated with the author's black line drawings. Ages 5 to 9.

The Gargoyle on the Roof by Jack Prelutsky, illustrated by Peter Sis (Greenwillow). Werewolves, trolls, ogres, and other monsters carouse in a variety of poems. Ages 6 and up.

Fiction. *Bluish* by Virginia Hamilton (Blue Sky/Scholastic). Dreenie makes friends with the new girl in her fifth-grade class, Bluish, who is fighting to recover from leukemia. Ages 8 to 11.

Oh No, It's Robert by Barbara Seuling, illustrated by Paul Brewer (Front Street/Cricket). Struggling third-grader Robert wants to win the class achievement contest, but he earns a different kind of reward instead. Ages 6 to 9.

Looking for Alibrandi by Melina Marchetta (Orchard Books). In an Australian award-winner, Josephine Alibrandi's Italian heritage and illegitimate birth create problems until she learns more about her family and herself. Ages 12 and up.

The Way to Schenectady by Richard Scrimger, illustrated by Linda Hendry (Tundra). When Jane and her family set out from Toronto to New England, Jane smuggles a homeless man into their van, and the romp begins. Ages 8 to 11.

I Miss You, I Miss You by Peter Pohl & Kinna Gieth (R & S Books). An identical twin must come to terms with the sudden death of her sister in this Swedish award-winner. Ages 12 and up.

Child Bride by Ching Yeung Russell (Boyds Mills). Ying, 11, who lives in China in the 1940's, must leave her ailing grandmother for an arranged marriage. Ages 8 to 12.

Ramona's World by Beverly Cleary, illustrated by Alan Tiegreen (Morrow). In the first new book in this series in 15 years, Ramona, entering fourth grade, worries about spelling, her new baby sister, and her old friend Danny, known as Yard Ape. Ages 8 and up.

A Face in Every Window by Han Nolan (Harcourt Brace). When JP's grandmother dies, the family falls apart. As JP's mother takes charge, JP learns to accept change. Ages 12 and up.

Jason's Gold by Will Hobbs (Morrow). Jason sets out to find his brothers in the Klondike gold fields of the 1890's. During the harsh Yukon winter, a dog Jason rescued from an abusive master helps him survive. Ages 12 and up.

Fantasy. *The Cure* by Sonia Levitin (Harcourt Brace). It's 2407, and Gemm 16884's love of music, which is banned, sends him back to 1348 as the son of a Jewish money-lender at the start of the plague. Ages 12 and up.

A Hive for the Honeybee by Soinbhe Lally (Arthur A. Levine/Scholastic). Thora, a worker bee in this Irish allegory, ponders her role in the life of the hive as the bees await the birth of a new Queen and worry about the approaching winter and a war with the wasps. Ages 11 and up.

Gypsy Rizka by Lloyd Alexander (Dutton). The townspeople look down on Rizka because of her gypsy heritage. But as she awaits her father's return, Rizka's hilarious solutions to her troubles help her gain acceptance. Ages 11 and up.

The Banished by Betty Levin (Greenwillow). Young Siri and her people must deliver a live polar bear to their king to end their banishment. The furfolk help them, but treachery awaits. Ages 10 and up.

The Taker's Stone by Barbara Timberlake Russell (DK Ink). Shy, 14-year-old Fischer steals special stones, setting off a conflict between good and evil in himself and others. Ages 12 and up.

Skellig by David Almond (Delacorte). Michael, lonely and unhappy in a new house and worried about his seriously ill baby sister, finds Skellig, a mysterious part-human creature who eats spiders and flies. As Michael and his friend Mina help keep Skellig alive, they discover what he is. Ages 8 to 12.

Harry Potter and the Chamber of Secrets and *Harry Potter and the Prisoner of Azkaban* by J. K. Rowling (Levine/Scholastic). The orphaned Harry continues his studies at the Hogwarts School for Witchcraft and Wizardry, where disaster strikes during his second year. Then Harry's life is endangered by an escapee from the wizard prison of Azkaban. All ages.

Informational books. *The Magic School Bus Explores the Senses* by Joanna Cole, illustrated by Bruce Degen (Scholastic). Mr. Wilde, the new assistant principal, accidentally sets the school bus in motion and drives Ms. Frizzle's class to another fact- and fun-filled adventure. Ages 6 to 9.

The Perilous Journey of the Donner Party by Marian Calabro (Clarion). An original letter written by 12-year-old Virginia Reed is the basis for a story about the tragic wagon train journey to California. Ages 12 and up.

Bizarre Birds by Doug Wechsler (Boyds Mills). The unusual physical appearances and habits of some of the world's strangest birds are highlighted in close-up photos and text. Ages 8 to 12.

Gorilla Walk by Ted and Betsy Lewin (Lothrop, Lee & Shepard). The authors describe their journey through the tropical rain forest of Uganda to see gorillas and how their encounter with the creatures has affected their lives. Ages 6 and up.

Kids on Strike! by Susan Campbell Bartoletti (Houghton Mifflin). Photographs, newspaper sto-

A wide audience of both children and adults made J. K. Rowling's Harry Potter and the Prisoner of Azkaban one of the best-selling books of 1999. The book continues Rowling's tales of an English orphan and his adventures at the Hogwarts School for Witchcraft and Wizardry.

ries, and journal entries reveal the harsh and unjust treatment of working children that led to violence and strikes, and finally, union shops, better wages, and safer working conditions. Ages 10 and up.

The 1999 Newbery Medal went to Louis Sachar for *Holes*. The award is given by the American Library Association (ALA) for "the most distinguished contribution to children's literature" published the previous year. The ALA's Caldecott Medal for "the most distinguished American picture book" was awarded to Mary Azarian for *Snowflake Bentley*. □ Marilyn Fain Apseloff

Lithuania. Prime Minister Gediminas Vagnorius resigned on May 3, 1999, after President Valdas Adamkus sharply criticized him in a nationwide broadcast. Adamkus accused Vagnorius of ruling in an authoritarian manner and ignoring the country's economic stagnation.

On May 18, the parliament confirmed Rolandas Paksas as the new prime minister. Paksas, the mayor of Lithuania's capital, Vilnius, and a member of the ruling Conservative Party, left the previous cabinet largely intact. Paksas stunned the country on October 27 when he too resigned in protest over the privatization of Lithuania's oil industry. Andrius Kubilius, the deputy speaker of the parliament, replaced Paksas on November 2.

In March, the Constitutional Court upheld a 1998 law barring former KGB agents from holding posts in "strategic" industries, as well as courts of law and the diplomatic corps. (The KGB was the intelligence service of the Soviet Union, of which Lithuania was a republic.) Adamkus, who opposed the law, had appealed to the court to overturn it.

In October 1999, the European Union (EU) invited Lithuania to apply for EU membership in 2000. Leaders in Lithuania were upset when Estonia, a neighboring Baltic nation that also had been occupied by the Soviet Union, was invited to apply to the EU in 1997.   □ Steven L. Solnick

See also **Estonia; Europe; Latvia.**

Los Angeles. Voters on June 8, 1999, approved a plan to reform Los Angeles's 74-year-old city charter to streamline city government and shift more power to the mayor's office. The new charter was scheduled to become fully effective July 1, 2000. Experts said that the majority of the changes implemented by the charter, such as the creation of new city departments, mainly would affect the way the city government operated.

Budget approval. On May 17, 1999, the Los Angeles City Council approved a $2.8-billion general fund budget. The balanced budget reflected increased spending for police, fire stations, libraries, and parks—without raising taxes—largely because tax revenues and fees increased as a result of a booming economy. The Los Angeles County Board of Supervisors on June 21 approved a $15-billion budget. A growing economy, aided by rising property taxes, enabled the supervisors to add 5,000 county employees, repair county buildings, and provide funds for the construction of new fire stations and libraries.

Staples Center, a 20,000-seat, state-of-the-art arena located in the center of downtown Los Angeles, opened in October 1999 with a Bruce Springsteen concert. Some 200 annual events were scheduled to take place in the $375-million sports and entertainment complex, which was to be home to the Los Angeles Kings of the Na-

A new Los Angeles subway station at Hollywood and Vine is decorated in movie-industry themes, with support columns sprouting palm leaves and a ceiling from which film reels are suspended. The Los Angeles County Metropolitan Transportation Authority opened the station in June.

tional Hockey League and both the Los Angeles Lakers and the Los Angeles Clippers of the National Basketball Association. The Arena Football League's new franchise, the Los Angeles Avengers, was scheduled to begin play at the center in April 2000. The center, with nearly 1 million square feet (90,000 square meters) of arena and office space, was constructed on 10 acres (4 hectares).

Military simulations. The University of Southern California (USC), located in South Central section of Los Angeles, and the U.S. Army announced plans in August 1999 to establish the Institute for Creative Technologies at USC. The institute was part of a five-year, $45-million contract to allow the Army to create training simulations that rely on virtual reality, artificial intelligence, and other cutting edge technologies. The entertainment industry was also expected to use the institute to improve movie special effects, develop more realistic video games, and create new simulation attraction for virtual reality arcades.

Trade. Improved economies in Asia and Latin America in 1999, which spurred tourism in Los Angeles, also provided the Ports of Los Angeles/Long Beach with an optimistic outlook for international trade. The Los Angeles Economic Development Corporation projected in July that the total value of two-way trade at the Los Angeles Cus-

toms District, which includes all the ports and airports in the Los Angeles metropolitan area, would increase 1.9 percent in 1999 to $312.1 billion.

Economy. The Los Angeles County Economic Development Corporation projected in July 1999 that industrial job growth in the Los Angeles metropolitan area would increase by 2.1 percent in 1999. Economists said the growth would produce 84,300 jobs. The economists noted that certain industrial sectors in the city would continue to be sluggish into 2000. The economy of Los Angeles never fully recovered from major defense cutbacks and aerospace mergers that occurred during the 1980's and early 1990's.

Subway system. The Los Angeles County Metropolitan Transportation Authority in June 1999 extended its MetroRail subway service to the famous intersection of Hollywood and Vine streets. The line was scheduled to extend 6.3 miles (10 kilometers) from Hollywood into North Hollywood by mid-2000. On Nov. 4, 1999, the California Transportation Commission approved $83.2 million to begin a $683 million light-rail line linking downtown Los Angeles and the city of Pasadena by 2003.

☐ Margaret A. Kilgore

See also **City.**

Louisiana. See **State government.**
Luxembourg. See **Europe.**

Macedonia. Boris Trajkovski was elected president of Macedonia in a runoff election in November 1999. Trajkovski, a moderate, won 53 percent of the vote. His opponent, Social Democrat Tito Petkovski, complained of widespread election fraud, and Trajkovski agreed to repeat balloting in December in some polling stations. Trajkovski won again, by a similar margin.

Some 250,000 ethnic Albanian refugees from the Yugoslav province of Kosovo fled to Macedonia in 1999, as a result of Serbian ethnic cleansing campaigns. Officials in Skopje, the Macedonian capital, accused Yugoslavia of trying to destabilize Macedonia by flooding the country with refugees. On April 7, U.S. officials learned that Macedonia had forcibly shipped some 30,000 to 45,000 refugees to Albania, Greece, Turkey, and other locations and warned Macedonia about mistreating the Kosovars.

The United Nations (UN) ended its peacekeeping mission in Macedonia on March 1. UN troops had been deployed in Macedonia since the start of Yugoslavia's civil war in 1992. When China vetoed a motion to extend the mission, analysts suggested that the Chinese were retaliating for Macedonia's establishment in January of diplomatic relations with Taiwan, which China considered a renegade Chinese province.   ☐ Sharon L. Wolchik

See also **Yugoslavia: A Special Report.**

Magazine. The magazine industry in the United States experienced a major increase in advertising income during the first half of 1999, the Magazine Publishers of America (MPA), a trade group in New York City, reported in July. The MPA said that magazine advertising revenue rose to $7.23 billion, an increase of 10.5 percent over the same period in 1998.

Ethical standards. In August 1999, the U.S. Senate passed legislation that would impose new restrictions on magazine publishers and other companies sponsoring sweepstakes as a way of selling their products. The Senate bill mandated "clear and conspicuous" statements on sweepstakes advertisements that warn consumers that winning a prize was not automatic and buying a magazine or other product would not improve the chances of winning a prize. The bill, which was not passed by the House of Representatives in 1999, would also require sweepstakes promotions to list the odds of winning the prizes.

In February, attorneys general and other representatives from 25 states held public hearings on alleged deceptions in sweepstakes promotions. Also in February, the MPA announced new voluntary guidelines for sweepstakes advertisements.

Webzine. After less than one year as one of the Internet's few paid subscription "magazines," *Slate* in February announced that it would be available online free of charge. The magazine, published by Microsoft Corporation, the Redmond, Washington-based software manufacturer, focused on popular culture and politics. Publisher Scott Moore said that *Slate* had signed up only about 20,000 subscribers at $19.95 annually.

Brown's latest. Tina Brown, former editor of *The New Yorker* and *Vanity Fair,* launched a new consumer magazine, *Talk,* in August. The magazine was a joint venture by Miramax Films, a division of the Walt Disney Company of Burbank, California, and Hearst Magazines of New York City.

Time Inc. Health, part of Time Inc., a New York City-based publisher, announced in August its purchase of the trademark and subscription list of *American Health* magazine from The Reader's Digest Association, Inc., of New York City. Time Inc. Health owns *Health,* a leading consumer health magazine. The company said it would stop publication of *American Health* in November.

George. Frank Lalli, a former managing editor of *Money* magazine, took over as editor-in-chief of *George* magazine on November 29. Lalli replaced John F. Kennedy, Jr., who died in a plane crash in July. The survival of *George,* which suffered from declining advertising revenues and poor circulation, had been in doubt after Kennedy's death. □Michael Woods

Maine. See State government.
Malawi. See Africa.

Malaysia. The National Front coalition headed by Prime Minister Mahathir bin Mohammad won parliamentary elections on Nov. 29, 1999. The victory gave Mahathir, who had led Malaysia for 18 years, another five-year mandate. He announced that the term in office would be his last.

The Front won 148 of the 193 seats in parliament, retaining the two-thirds majority needed to override political opposition. The coalition's share of the popular vote fell, however, from 65 percent in the previous election in 1995 to 56 percent. Mahathir's party in the coalition, the United Malays National Organization, lost 16 seats in the 1999 election, while opposition parties doubled their number of seats by winning 45.

The opposition Islamic Party of Malaysia (PAS) won 27 seats with the support of many ethnic Malays, Mahathir's traditional constituency. Mahathir, therefore, was more dependent on votes from ethnic Chinese and Indians. PAS won control of the governments in two northern states.

Anwar Ibrahim was sentenced on April 14 to six years in prison on corruption charges and went on trial again in June on charges of sexual misconduct. Anwar had been deputy prime minister and Mahathir's apparent successor until the two leaders clashed in 1998 over economic policy. Anwar was arrested in September 1998 for interfering with an investigation into his alleged homosexual activities. The arrest touched off huge protests in Malaysia and drew sharp international criticism.

Anwar's wife, Wan Azizah Ismail, led a new protest group, the Justice Party, to win five seats in the 1999 parliamentary elections.

Economic progress. Malaysia emerged in 1999 from its worst recession in 42 years of independence. After a 7.5-percent decline in output in 1998 and a 1.3-percent decline during the first three months of 1999, the Malaysian economy grew 4.1 percent in the quarter beginning in April.

In response to the recovery, the Malaysian government on September 1 lifted most of the controls that it had imposed in 1998 on international capital movement—the transfer of assets into and out of Malaysia. The controls were intended to insulate Malaysia from the economic turmoil then affecting East Asia. Foreign economists criticized the controls for hampering trade, but by late 1999 many economists acknowledged their success.

New capital. Prime Minister Mahathir moved his office in June to a new capital city, Putrajaya, under construction south of the old capital, Kuala Lumpur. The $5.8-billion complex is scheduled for completion in 2005. □Henry S. Bradsher

See also **Asia.**

Maldives. See Asia.
Mali. See Africa.
Malta. See Europe.
Manitoba. See Canadian provinces.

Fireworks light up the Petronas Twin Towers in Kuala Lumpur on Aug. 31, 1999, in celebration of Malaysia's independence day and the official opening of the 1,480-foot (542-meter) structures, which are recognized as being the world's tallest buildings.

Ford Motor Company's River Rouge complex in Dearborn, Michigan, catches fire on Feb. 1, 1999, killing an employee in the power plant. The giant complex, begun in 1915, covers 1,100 acres (450 hectares) and encompasses all basic steps of auto production.

Manufacturing. The United States manufacturing industry gained strength in 1999 as factories recovered from a worldwide economic crisis in 1998. During 1999, many factories consolidated in an effort to achieve greater efficiency. Manufacturers also faced an end-of-year deadline to prepare for possible computer disruptions in 2000.

Increased demands for goods followed a long-awaited rebound in foreign economies in 1999, especially in those Southeast Asian nations hit hard by financial crisis in 1997 and 1998. Increased demand triggered higher prices of the raw materials used by factories, which raised factory costs. However, foreign markets that had shrunk in the 1990's absorbed more U.S. products in 1999.

In the United States, manufacturers in 1999 found that the supply of available labor was growing increasingly tighter. This forced some increase in compensation for workers and, at times, crimped production or expansion plans as some companies could not find enough employees to fill jobs. Yet the tight labor market meant that more people were employed and could buy goods. Strong consumer demand in 1999 led many economists to predict that the economy would remain strong into 2000.

The rising costs of materials and the tighter labor market worried economists, however. The U.S. Federal Reserve System (the Fed), the central bank of the United States, increased short-term interest rates in June 1999 by one-quarter of a percentage point to remove some of the money it had pumped into the economy during 1998's credit-market meltdown. In August 1999, the Fed increased short-term interest rates by another one-quarter of a percentage point. In November, the Fed increased the rate another one-quarter of a percentage point to 5.5 percent. The Fed had hoped that the increases would head off the threat that the U.S. economy would overheat, producing inflation.

Computer problems. Manufacturers in 1999 were faced with the problem of modernizing some computer equipment to solve a computer glitch known as Y2K (for Year 2000). Much outmoded computer software still in use at the end of the century was originally programmed to read only the last two digits of a year. As a result, many computer engineers expected computers equipped with the software to misread the year 2000 as 1900 and not function properly.

Although solving the Y2K problem forced manufacturers to spend money beyond their normal business needs, it also forced them to adopt newer technology on a massive scale. This laid the basis for productivity gains in 1999 as industries learned new ways to use the improved computer systems they were forced to install.

New-era economic issues. The Y2K problem underscored an important feature of the U.S. economy, which had so embraced high-technology by 1999 that many economists and business executives believed the United States had moved into a new industrial era. This new-era economy, some experts claimed, allowed stronger growth with lower inflation.

As economists debated whether this trend would continue in the 2000's, the manufacturing of new-era goods, for example, cellular telephones and computers, became such a powerful economic segment that the U.S. Commerce Department revised years of economic data to better reflect the high-technology output. The new data revealed that the U.S. economy was stronger and more efficient in the 1990's than economists had previously thought.

The biggest of the new-era manufacturers, Microsoft Corporation of Redmond, Washington, the world's largest creator of computer software, slipped in its long-running battle against the U.S. Justice Department. The Justice Department had charged that Microsoft Corporation violated federal antitrust laws and unfairly benefited from monopolistic practices. On Nov. 5, 1999, U.S. District Judge Thomas Penfield Jackson ruled that Microsoft was a monopoly, a finding that raised questions about whether the computer company would negotiate a settlement that could shave its dominance or even split off some of its operations.

New-era technology of another sort affected manufacturing of crop seeds and food products. A wave of European protests against genetically modified organisms, such as plant seeds with new genes for producing natural pesticides, caused most major U.S. food or seed exporters to curb use of such products to retain European markets. The European protests grew even louder when Coca-Cola in June was forced to recall products in some European countries after Belgian and French consumers became sick from drinking Coke products.

The U.S. steel industry rebounded during 1999. Less-expensive imports from weakened foreign economies in 1997 and 1998 had taken more of the domestic market away from U.S. steel producers. As a result, some steel companies were forced into bankruptcy, while others cut costs and profits to keep operating. As economic conditions improved in 1999, worldwide demand for steel began to rebound. As a result, most U.S. steel companies began regaining business.

Industrial rebound. Monthly measurements of U.S. industrial activity showed that the factory sector grew steadily throughout 1999. The upturn was a relief for many industry leaders who had feared that slumping industrial activity and financial-market crises in many Asian economies might spread elsewhere in the world.

In January, the National Association of Purchasing Management (NAPM) index reading stood at 49.5 percent, which was the lowest reading of the first 10 months of 1999. By June, the NAPM reading had increased to 57 percent, and in October it hit 56.6 percent. The NAPM polls more than 300 U.S. manufacturers monthly about new orders, employment, cost of materials, delivery problems, and other factors. Index values above 50 percent mean a growing economy. Index values below 50 percent indicate that the factory sector is contracting.

Gross domestic product. The U.S. *gross domestic product* (GDP—the total value of goods and services produced in the United States in a year) grew at a quarterly rate of 3.7 percent between January and the end of March 1999. The increase surprised some economists who had predicted that the GDP would slow in 1999. However, low inflation and unemployment levels helped the growth rate remain steady. The GDP slowed in the April-June quarter to 1.9 percent, which many experts attributed to a decrease in government and consumer spending. The GDP improved to a 5.5 percent growth rate in the July-September quarter. ☐ John D. Boyd

See also **Economics; International trade.**

Maryland. See **State government.**
Massachusetts. See **State government.**
Mauritania. See **Africa.**

Mauritius. In 1999, Prime Minister Navinchandra Ramgoolam and his Labor Party, elected in 1995, maintained a firm grasp on the government of Mauritius. Labor held 38 of 66 elected seats in the National Assembly, the Mauritian parliament. In January 1999, the country's main opposition parties, the Militant Socialist Movement (MSM), led by former Prime Minister Sir Aneerood Jugnauth, and the Militant Mauritian Movement (MMM), led by Paul Berenger, formed a coalition. Jugnauth started the MSM in 1983 after breaking with the MMM.

Under the coalition agreement, Jugnauth, who had served as prime minister from 1982 to 1995, became the official leader of the opposition. The agreement also stipulated that Jugnauth would become prime minister, with Berenger serving as his deputy, if the coalition won the next general election, scheduled for December 2000 or early 2001.

Riots broke out in Port Louis, Mauritius's capital, and nearby towns on Feb. 21, 1999, following the death in police custody of a popular Mauritian singer. The singer, Joseph Reginald Topize, known as Kaya, had been arrested for smoking marijuana at a rally held in support of efforts to decriminalize the drug. In four days of rioting, at least three people were killed and many more injured as hundreds of demonstrators ransacked police stations, blocked highways, and burned more than 100 vehicles. The riots also sparked clashes between the country's Hindu majority and the underprivileged, racially mixed minority.

Recognizing the economic tensions that lay behind the disorders, President Sir Cassam Uteem requested that the government implement antipoverty measures as quickly as possible. He also promised a judicial inquiry into Kaya's death.

A soccer match between a primarily Muslim team and a primarily Hindu team exploded into violence and arson on May 23. The rioters destroyed a stadium, attacked buildings in Port Louis, and hurled bombs at a casino, killing dozens of people. The rioting, which was followed by rumors of death squads allegedly set up to defend the Hindu community, caused widespread alarm.

Economy. The government, already contending with a deteriorating economy from a severe drought and lower earnings from the key textile and sugar industries, feared that the unrest in 1999 would further lower revenues from tourism and foreign investment.

Foreign affairs. Mauritius hosted the first Organization of African Unity (OAU) Ministerial Conference on Human Rights from April 12-16. Delegations from 47 OAU member-nations attended the historic meeting. □ Simon Baynham

See also **Africa.**

Medicine. Officials with the Human Genome Project (HGP), an international, government-supported effort to decode the human *genome* (total amount of genetic information), announced in March 1999 that a "working draft" of the genome would be completed by early 2000.

The HGP's goal was to determine the makeup and sequence of the 3 billion molecular subunits, called nucleotides, that constitute the human genome. Nucleotides are the building blocks of genes, which determine most of an organism's characteristics, including how a person looks and how the body functions. Biologists estimate that every human has somewhere between 60,000 and 120,000 genes. The completed sequence was expected to revolutionize medicine by enabling a better understanding of genetically influenced diseases. Scientists hoped that this would lead to improved diagnosis, treatment, and prevention of these diseases.

Francis S. Collins, director of the National Human Genome Research Institute, the division of the National Institutes of Health (NIH) that oversees the role of the United States in the HGP, noted that the draft would be somewhat less complete and less accurate than the final version, targeted for 2003.

Smallpox virus saved. In April 1999, U.S. President Bill Clinton announced that the United States would not destroy its stock of the smallpox virus, despite pleas to do so from the World Health Organization (WHO), a United Nations agency based in Geneva, Switzerland. Clinton's decision was based on a recommendation made in March by the U.S. Institute of Medicine (IOM) in Washington, D.C. The IOM concluded that the smallpox samples might prove valuable in future research on the immune system. The agency also noted that, in the event of a terrorist attack using smallpox, the virus samples would be needed to make a protective vaccine.

Smallpox, a highly contagious disease that caused scarring and sometimes blindness and death, was eradicated throughout the world by 1980. Samples of the virus are held in laboratories in two known locations—one in the United States and the other in Russia.

Ovary transplant. Surgeons transplanted tissue from an ovary into the body of a 30-year-old woman who had previously had both ovaries removed, according to a September 1999 announcement by New York Methodist Hospital in New York City. The surgery was the first successful transplant of ovarian tissue.

The New York physicians, led by Kutluk Otkay, used ovarian tissue that had been removed from the woman in 1998 for an undisclosed medical reason. Otkay transplanted the tissue, which had been preserved in a frozen condition, into the woman's body in February 1999. Beginning in June, the woman was able to *ovulate* (produce eggs) when given fertility hormones.

The surgery indicated that women who are about to undergo radiation therapy or chemotherapy for cancer could have their ovaries removed to prevent them from being damaged by the treatment. After the cancer therapies were completed, physicians could transplant the ovaries back into the women's bodies.

Cervical cancer treatment. The NIH's National Cancer Institute (NCI) in Bethesda, Maryland, recommended in February that physicians add chemotherapy to the standard treatment for women with invasive cervical cancer. This is a type of cancer that spreads inside the *cervix* (the opening of the uterus) or to other structures inside the pelvis. Most women with invasive cervical cancer are treated with radiation therapy or surgery. The NCI noted that five major NCI-sponsored clinical trials indicated that chemotherapy reduced the risk of death by 30 to 50 percent, compared with radiation or surgery alone.

Cancer rates decline. Cancer death rates and the number of new cancer cases in the United States declined every year between 1990 and 1996, according to an April 1999 report by the NCI, the Atlanta, Georgia-based American Cancer Society, and the Atlanta-based U.S. Centers for Disease Control and Prevention. The study found that cancer death rates fell by an average of 0.6 percent annually. Cancer incidence rates—the number of new cancer cases per 100,000 population—fell by an average of 0.9 percent each year.

The study concluded that part of the decrease resulted from a decline in cigarette smoking and lung cancer, which causes more deaths than any other form of the disease. Earlier diagnosis and better treatment also contributed to the lower rates, the report stated.

Animal-test alternative. A U.S. government panel of scientists concluded in May that a test not involving the use of laboratory animals can accurately determine whether a chemical compound is likely to burn or corrode the human skin. The test, called Corrositex, was the first nonanimal test to gain the approval of the Interagency Coordinating Committee on the Validation of Alternative Methods (ICCVAM). The ICCVAM is a group of 14 government agencies established in 1977 to evaluate alternative methods of testing the toxicity of compounds used in medications and cosmetics. The scientists said Corrositex, in which scientists observe the effects of chemicals on a type of artificial skin, can replace a method in which chemicals are tested on laboratory animals. □Michael Woods

See also **Drugs; Public health and safety.**

TIME CAPSULE 1955
MEDICINE

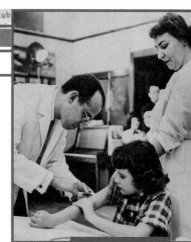

Jonas Salk injects a schoolgirl with the polio vaccine.

POLIO. The Salk vaccine in 1955 proved to be an effective weapon in the fight against polio. Scientists at the University of Michigan, a center for compiling data, announced on April 12 that the vaccine had passed its 1954 field tests with flying colors. As the evaluators put it themselves, "The vaccine works."

With this announcement, the National Foundation for Infantile Paralysis promptly began a mass inoculation program. The program ran into trouble when several children given the vaccine contracted polio. But scientists and health authorities quickly solved the unexpected problems. By the end of the year, doctors throughout the nation were giving thousands of schoolchildren their second round of shots.

The United States Public Health Service announced in January 1956, that polio cases dropped sharply in 1955. Preliminary figures showed there were 29,270 cases during the year, compared with 38,400 in 1954. The polio death rate fell about 40 percent. The Salk vaccine accounted for about 25 percent of the reduction in cases.

The announcement that Dr. Jonas E. Salk's antipolio vaccine had proved effective became one of the biggest news stories of 1955. Doctors, parents, and health authorities welcomed the report.

Mental health. United States Surgeon General David Satcher issued a "call to action" in July 1999 to prevent suicide, the ninth leading cause of death in the United States. About 31,000 people committed suicide in 1996, compared to 20,000 victims of homicide. In addition, more than 500,000 Americans annually were reported to need hospital treatment for suicide attempts.

Satcher issued recommendations for increasing public awareness about suicide, increasing research, and encouraging physicians and mental health personnel to intervene with people at high risk for suicide. His advice was based on findings of a national conference of experts in Reno, Nevada, in October 1998. The panel concluded that people with undiagnosed and untreated psychological disorders, such as severe depression and substance abuse, face the highest risk of suicide.

The panel's list of 81 recommendations ranged from increasing biomedical research on the causes of suicide to having more open discussion by parents, teachers, and physicians. The panel emphasized the need for understanding that suicide is a serious public health problem, that people with clinical depression are at high risk, and that many suicides could be prevented through better diagnosis and treatment of depression by primary-care physicians.

Dispelling myths. U.S. President Bill Clinton in June 1999 announced a new national public education campaign to fight the stigma often associated with mental illness. The president said that people in many communities still have negative attitudes about forms of mental illness, including the attitude that mental illness is a personal weakness or failure, rather than a physical disease. President Clinton also announced that he would issue an order eliminating the federal government's stricter standards for hiring and promoting people with mental illness.

Shyness drug. The U.S. Food and Drug Administration in May approved the first drug for social anxiety disorder, an excessive form of shyness that affects an estimated 10 million Americans. People with social anxiety disorder so fear interactions with other people that they are unable to participate in business meetings, make new friends, or talk to strangers. The drug Paxil, sold by SmithKline Beecham Corporation of Philadelphia, had been previously approved for several other conditions, including severe depression. About 69 percent of extremely shy patients who took Paxil in clinical trials reported lower anxiety levels and better ability to function.

Prescribing psychologists. A study reported by the U.S. General Accounting Office (GAO) in June 1999 concluded that specially trained military clinical psychologists can safely and effectively prescribe antidepressants and other medications used to treat mental conditions.

The study came during a continuing debate on whether psychologists in civilian health care should be allowed to prescribe drugs. Although psychologists and psychiatrists treat many of the same illnesses, only psychiatrists, who are practicing physicians, can prescribe drugs.

In the study, GAO checked the performance of 10 graduates of a training program started in 1991 in the military health care system. After training, the psychologists were allowed to prescribe medication in military hospitals and clinics. GAO concluded that the psychologists performed well and had a positive effect on the quality of health care. However, the special training was discontinued in 1997 because it proved more costly than traditional staffing with a mix of psychiatrists and nonprescribing psychologists.

Exercise therapy. Exercise is an effective but underused treatment for mild-to-moderate depression, a group of Canadian researchers from the University of Manitoba in Winnipeg reported in June 1999. The study reviewed results of all major research done since 1981 on exercise and mental illness. It found strong evidence that regular exercise can reduce the symptoms of severe depression and may help in the treatment of schizophrenia, alcohol and tobacco dependence, anxiety, and other conditions. Schizophrenia is a severe, disabling form of mental illness that affects about 1.5 million Americans.

Prison population. The first comprehensive study on mental illness in correctional facilities reported in July 1999 that 16 percent of the prison population, or about 283,000 people, had some form of mental illness. The study, conducted by the U.S. Department of Justice, disclosed that an additional 547,800 mentally ill people were on probation.

Schizophrenia model. Scientists at the University of North Carolina at Chapel Hill and Duke University in Durham, North Carolina, announced in August 1999 that they had developed the first animal model for schizophrenia. The animal model is a laboratory mouse genetically engineered to have a biochemical defect in nerve-cell receptors for a substance called NMDA, which affects cell function. The receptors are areas on the surface of nerve cells to which NMDA molecules can attach.

The genetically engineered mice showed symptoms that included repeated actions, antisocial behavior, and neglect of their young. The researchers believed that decreased function of NMDA receptors could be a key factor in schizophrenia. They expected that the mice would be important in testing new drugs to treat schizophrenia. □ Michael Woods

Local people view one of the mudslides caused by torrential rains in the state of Puebla in southeastern Mexico in October 1999. The massive flooding and mudslides claimed the lives of more than 300 people and left thousands homeless.

Mexico. Mexicans in 1999 experienced a presidential election campaign that resembled a political campaign in the United States, complete with party primaries, nationally televised debates, and unprecedented spending on TV advertising. The presidential election was scheduled for July 2000.

The Institutional Revolutionary Party (PRI), which had dominated Mexican politics since 1929, held its first primary election to choose a presidential candidate in November 1999. Previously, the incumbent PRI president had chosen a successor. Francisco Labastida Ochoa, the interior minister from 1995 to May 1999, was elected to be the PRI candidate.

In October, the leading opposition parties, the conservative National Action Party (PAN) and the center-left Revolutionary Democratic Party (PRD), failed to reach an agreement on how to select a single opposition candidate. Consequently, political observers expected Labastida to face two principal challengers—the PAN's Vicente Fox Quesada, a former governor of the state of Guanajuato, and the PRD's Cuauhtemoc Cardenas Solorzano, who resigned as mayor of Mexico City in September.

Corruption. Federal authorities in Mexico issued a warrant for the arrest of Mario Villanueva Madrid on drug trafficking charges on April 6, the day after his term as governor of the state of Quintana Roo ended. Villanueva, who had claimed immunity from charges as governor, was the highest-ranking elected official in Mexico ever to be investigated for drug trafficking. He reportedly went into hiding in March.

In several surveys in 1999, Mexicans accorded President Ernesto Zedillo Ponce de Leon high marks for his efforts to curtail illegal government intervention in the political process, but corrupt practices were still reported. Mori International, an independent research firm based in London, announced the results of a survey conducted after the July 4 gubernatorial elections in the state of Mexico. According to the survey, one-third of the state's voters received groceries, lottery tickets, crop payments, scholarships, or other gifts from the PRI-dominated federal government in the days before the balloting. The PRI candidate won the election. Observers noted that the survey demonstrated PRI efforts to circumvent election reforms that had been adopted in the late 1990's.

Landmark sentence. On Jan. 21, 1999, Raul Salinas de Gortari, the brother of a former Mexican president, was sentenced to 50 years in prison for ordering the 1994 assassination of Jose Francisco Ruiz Massieu, a prominent PRI official. Although the sentence was reduced on appeal to 27½ years in July 1999, political observers regarded Salinas's conviction as a landmark in judicial history, marking the end of the Mexican elites' enjoyment of immunity from prosecution.

The Bank Savings Protection Institute, a federal bank-insurance agency, began operating on May 21. The agency assumed the debts from failed banks that the government began to rescue in 1994. The total cost to taxpayers of the controversial bailout program was estimated in 1999 to be from $71 billion to $105 billion.

Chiapas massacre. In September, Jacinto Arias Cruz, a former mayor in the state of Chiapas, and 23 of his supporters were sentenced to 35 years in jail for their part in the massacre of 45 unarmed Tzotzil Indians on Dec. 22, 1997. The Indians were allegedly killed for being sympathetic to leftist rebels of the Zapatista National Liberation Army.

The National Museum of Anthropology in Mexico City, which opened its doors in 1964, underwent the first phase of a $13-million facelift in 1999. The museum houses a world-renowned collection of Latin American treasures that predate the arrival of Europeans in the New World in the late 1400's. In deference to U.S. visitors, the museum added English translations to the Spanish-language descriptions of the exhibits in the newly renovated galleries. □ Nathan A. Haverstock

See also **Latin America.**

Miami officials allegedly defrauded bondholders in 1995 by concealing a financial crisis the city was going through at the time, according to a September 1999 complaint by the United States Securities and Exchange Commission (SEC). The SEC charged that Miami misled investors about $116.5 million worth of tax-exempt bonds issued to finance city pensions, sewer construction, and a public building project. The regulators said Miami did not inform the investors that its financial state was so poor that it might not be able to cover its operating expenses or pay the interest on its outstanding bonds. Although the SEC did not seek to impose any financial penalties on Miami, it asked a federal judge to require the city to produce accurate financial reports in the future.

Drug smuggling. Thirteen workers and two other suspects were arrested at Miami International Airport on September 9 on charges of conspiracy to import cocaine into the United States with the intent to distribute it. The airport employees were arrested after allegedly diverting what they thought was cocaine past customs agents and into the hands of federal agents posing as drug smugglers.

The workers were the latest of 74 suspected drug smugglers arrested at the airport since August 25 in a two-year federal sting operation. Federal agents said the suspects moved more than 115 pounds (52 kilograms) of fake cocaine hidden in luggage, food carts, and garbage bags through the airport between October 1997 and September 1999. The agents had planted the substance on flights from the Caribbean and South America. Following the arrests, Miami-Dade County officials enhanced security at the airport.

Hunger strike. In May, the U.S. Immigration and Naturalization Service (INS) released five Cuban immigrants, three of whom had been held in the Krome Detention Center, which is located in the Miami metropolitan area. The release followed a 47-day hunger strike staged outside the Krome Center by the men's parents.

The Cubans had been held by the INS—some for as long as three years—since being released from U.S. prisons, where they had served time for a variety of felonies. The INS detained the ex-convicts under the 1996 Immigration Reform and Immigrant Responsibility Act, which ordered the deportation of noncitizens who had been imprisoned in the United States for committing felonies. The Cubans could not be deported, however, because of the lack of diplomatic relations between the United States and Cuba.

The hunger strike prompted a review of the Cubans' cases by the INS, which concluded that the men no longer posed a threat to society and should be released. The INS also said it would institute regular reviews of more than 4,000 other detainee cases that came under the 1996 act.

Firearms lawsuit. In December 1999, a Florida judge dismissed a lawsuit that Miami-Dade County had filed against 25 firearms manufacturers and trade associations in January. Officials had sought to recover hundreds of millions of dollars in costs absorbed by the county as the result of shooting deaths and injuries. However, the judge stated that gun makers were not responsible for the criminal or reckless use of guns.

Indian site. A Florida circuit judge ruled in June that Miami-Dade County could legally take possession of private property where an ancient stone formation known as Miami Circle had been carved by Tequesta Indians. Archaeologists discovered Miami Circle in late 1998, just months before landowner Michael Baumann was to begin construction of an apartment complex on the site. The circle consists of a ring of carvings 38 feet (12 meters) wide made in the limestone bedrock approximately 2,000 years ago.

In late November 1999, county officials paid Baumann $26.7 million for the property. To help finance the purchase, the county accepted an $8.7-million loan from The Trust for Public Land, a nonprofit conservation organization based in San Francisco. □ Al Smuskiewicz

See also **City.**

Michigan. See **State government.**

Middle East

Major issues in the Middle East in 1999 included an attempt by the United States to apprehend a suspected terrorist, new hope for the peace process between Israelis and Palestinians, a warning about water scarcity, and political liberalization in Morocco.

Osama bin Laden. The United States attempted in 1999 to secure the arrest of Osama bin Laden, a millionaire Saudi exile accused of masterminding the 1998 bombings of two U.S. embassies in Africa. The bombings killed more than 200 people. Bin Laden opposed U.S. influence in the Middle East. Since 1996, he had been living in Afghanistan under the protection of the Taliban, an Islamic militia that ruled 90 percent of the country.

In November 1999, the United Nations (UN) Security Council—at the urging of the United States—imposed economic and air-travel sanctions on Afghanistan because of the Taliban's refusal to turn over bin Laden to the United States. The United States also offered a $5-million reward in 1999 for bin Laden's capture, barred U.S. investment and trade with Afghanistan, and lobbied the United Arab Emirates to halt its alleged financial dealings with bin Laden.

Palestinan issues. On November 8, Palestinian and Israeli negotiators began in-tensive talks on unresolved issues in an effort to conclude a final peace treaty by September 2000. The talks were characterized by a number of disagreements.

The chief Palestinian negotiator, Yasir Abed Rabbo, complained about an Israeli building boom in the area of Jerusalem, Israel's capital. The final status of Jerusalem—whether it

The funeral procession of King Hassan II of Morocco leaves the Royal Palace in the capital, Rabat, on July 25, 1999. King Hassan died after 38 years on the throne.

Facts in brief on Middle Eastern countries

Country	Population	Government	Monetary unit*	Foreign trade (million U.S.$) Exports†	Imports†
Bahrain	633,000	Amir Hamad bin Isa Al Khalifa; Prime Minister Khalifa bin Salman Al Khalifa	dinar (0.38 = $1)	3,269	3,463
Cyprus	777,000	President Glafcos Clerides (Turkish Republic of Northern Cyprus: President Rauf R. Denktash)	pound (1.81 = $1)	1,062	3,687
Egypt	69,146,000	President Hosni Mubarak; Prime Minister Kamal Ahmed al-Ganzouri**	pound (3.41 = $1)	3,130	16,166
Iran	74,644,000	Supreme Leader Ayatollah Ali Hoseini-Khamenei; President Mohammed Khatami-Ardakani	rial (1,750.00 = $1)	22,391	16,274
Iraq	23,753,000	President Saddam Hussein	dinar (0.31 = $1)	5,000	3,000
Israel	6,062,000	President Ezer Weizman; Prime Minister Ehud Barak	new shekel (4.27 = $1)	22,100	26,100
Jordan	4,746,000	King Abdullah II; Prime Minister Abdur-Rauf Rawabdeh	dinar (0.71 = $1)	1,749	3,829
Kuwait	1,818,000	Amir Jabir al-Ahmad al-Jabir Al Sabah; Prime Minister & Crown Prince Saad al-Abdallah al-Salim Al Sabah	dinar (0.30 = $1)	9,646	8,003
Lebanon	3,289,000	President Emile Lahud Prime Minister Salim al-Huss	pound (1,501.00 = $1)	716	7,063
Oman	2,626,000	Sultan Qaboos bin Said Al Said	rial (0.39 = $1)	7,630	5,026
Qatar	605,000	Amir Hamad bin Khalifa Al Thani; Prime Minister Abdallah bin Khalifa Al Thani	riyal (3.64 = $1)	3,752	2,868
Saudi Arabia	21,257,000	King & Prime Minister Fahd bin Abd al-Aziz Al Saud	riyal (3.75 = $1)	62,381	28,742
Sudan	32,079,000	President Umar Hasan Ahmad al-Bashir	pound (2,568.00 = $1)	596	1,915
Syria	17,329,000	President Hafez al-Assad; Prime Minister Mahmud Zubi	pound (46.25 = $1)	3,916	4,028
Turkey	67,748,000	President Suleyman Demirel; Prime Minister Bulent Ecevit	lira (466,085.00 = $1)	25,938	45,369
United Arab Emirates	2,603,000	President Zayid bin Sultan Al Nuhayyan; Prime Minister Maktum bin Rashid al-Maktum	dirham (3.67 = $1)	42,666	32,250
Yemen	17,051,000	President Ali Abdallah Salih; Prime Minister Abd al-Karim al-Iryani	rial (159.44 = $1)	2,504	2,014

*Exchange rates as of Oct. 8, 1999, or latest available data. **Succeeded by Atef Mohammed Obeid on October 5.
†Latest available data.

would be under the exclusive control of Israelis or under joint control with Palestinians—had not yet been determined. Rabbo also complained about the continued development of Jewish settlements in the West Bank (Arab territory captured by Israel in 1967). Israeli chief negotiator Oded Eran insisted that Jerusalem would remain the undivided capital of Israel and that some West Bank settlements were necessary to preserve Israel's security.

The negotiations were also to cover the borders of any future Palestinian state; whether Palestinians who were displaced by Arab-Israeli

wars in 1948 and 1967 would return to such a state; and the sharing of dwindling water resources. Negotiators hoped to draw up the outline of a final agreement by February 2000.

Water. An international panel of scientists warned in March 1999 that Israeli, Palestinian, and Jordanian authorities must cooperate over the use of scarce water resources in order to maintain a decent quality of life for the region's 12 million people. The scientists, from the U.S. National Academy of Sciences in Washington, D.C., and Israeli, Palestinian, and Jordanian science institutions, noted that high population growth rates and depletion of underground aquifers had become major threats to regional stability.

The scientific panel pointed out that farms, rather than households, were the biggest consumers of fresh water in Israel and Jordan. The panel said that although agriculture was responsible for 57 percent of Israel's water consumption, it provided only 3 percent of Israel's *gross domestic product (GDP)*—the value of all goods and services produced in a country in a given period. In Jordan, agriculture consumed 72 percent of the water supply but contributed just 6 percent to the country's GDP.

The scientists suggested that Israelis, Palestinians, and Jordanians jointly manage their watersheds to make the most efficient use of water resources. They also recommended that fresh water be reserved for household use, while farms and industries restrict themselves to using treated waste water or salt water.

Morocco. King Mohammed VI of Morocco pledged to support political liberalization when he ascended to the throne in July upon the death of his father, King Hassan II, who had ruled Morocco for 38 years. A number of the new king's initial acts indicated a possible new era of political freedom in Morocco.

In Mohammed's first act as king, he released nearly 8,000 prisoners, many of whom were held for political activities, and he reduced jail terms for another 38,000 prisoners. Mohammed also allowed many political exiles to return home and lifted a ban imposed in 1986 against a popular television political commentator who was critical of the government. In addition, Mohammed pledged to reduce social inequalities and Morocco's high unemployment rate.

In November, Mohammed dismissed Driss Basri, the Minister of the Interior in charge of security and intelligence. Critics had often accused Basri of abuse of power and opposition to democracy since he became minister in 1981.

Western Sahara. Mohammed committed himself in a November 1999 speech to a UN-sponsored referendum concerning the disputed Western Sahara. The referendum, delayed repeatedly since 1992, was to determine whether Western Sahara would become independent or remain a part of Morocco. Morocco annexed the territory in the 1970's. In 1991, Morocco agreed to a UN-sponsored cease-fire with Algerian-backed rebels seeking independence for the area.

Mohammed's speech on the referendum followed the suppression by Moroccan police of prodemocracy demonstrators in the Sahara in October 1999. Many observers believed that Driss Basri, whom Mohammed had dismissed a week after the speech, had ordered the crackdown on the demonstrators.

UN Secretary General Kofi Annan said in October that the referendum, which was scheduled for July 2000, would likely be delayed because of a dispute over voter eligibility.

Turkish-Greek relations. Centuries-old animosities between Turkey and Greece eased in 1999 following devastating earthquakes that rocked both countries. Greece provided humanitarian aid to Turkey in August, after northwestern Turkey was hit with a 7.4-magnitude quake that killed more than 17,000 people, and again in November, when another earthquake killed hundreds more in northwestern Turkey. Turkey sent aid when a powerful earthquake struck Greece in September.

A potential crisis between Turkey and Greece was averted in February, when Greece ordered the expulsion of Kurdish rebel leader Abdullah Ocalan from the Greek embassy in Nairobi, Kenya, where Ocalan had been granted *asylum* (shelter for political reasons). Ocalan's group, the Marxist Kurdish Workers Party, began a militant campaign for Kurdish independence from Turkey in 1984. Kurds are an ethnic group that originated in southwestern Asia. After his expulsion, Ocalan was captured by Turkish commandos. In June 1999, a Turkish court sentenced Ocalan to death for treason.

The first high-level talks in five years between Turkey and Greece began in June. The two nations remained split over many issues, including the status of Cyprus, which was divided into Turkish- and Greek-controlled regions.

In December, the European Union, an economic and political alliance of Western European nations, agreed to make Turkey a candidate for membership after Greece dropped its previous objections.

EgyptAir crash. On Oct. 31, 1999, EgyptAir flight 990 crashed into the Atlantic Ocean after taking off from Kennedy International Airport in New York City en route to Cairo, Egypt. The crash killed all 217 passengers and crew members. Speculation by U.S. officials that an Egyptian co-pilot had deliberately crashed the plane led to intense anti-American feelings in the Arab world. □ Christine Helms

See also **Afghanistan; Disasters; Middle East: A Special Report; United Nations;** and the various Middle Eastern country articles.

Mining. See Energy supply.

Minnesota. See State government.

Mississippi. See State government.

Missouri. See State government.

Moldova. See Europe.

Mongolia. See Asia.

Montana. See State government.

A Century of Struggle

Although the 1900's were a time of endless problems for the people of the Middle East, hope for peace remained alive as the troubling century closed.

By Christine Helms

The winds of history and change continued to blow over the ancient lands of the Middle East in 1999 as the region's two longest reigning rulers passed from the scene. The death in February of King Hussein, who led Jordan for 47 years, was followed by the death in July of King Hassan, who reigned in Morocco for 38 years. Both monarchs claimed direct descent from the prophet Muhammad, who delivered the message of Islam to the Arabs in the 600's. King Hussein's family, the Hashemite dynasty, assumed power in Jordan after World War I (1914-1918). King Hassan's Alawi dynasty has ruled Morocco since the 1600's. These royal families and the other people of the Middle East played important roles in some of the most dramatic events of the past century. Fights against foreign domination, repeated wars between Arabs and Jews, battles over conflicting ideologies, and deep problems caused by poverty and population growth all made the 1900's a century of struggle for the Middle East.

Conditions in the Middle East were turbulent from the outset of the 1900's. The mainly Arab Middle East had been controlled since the 1500's by the Ottoman Empire, which was ruled by a Turkish Muslim dynasty. By 1900, the empire was eroded by corruption, internal dissent, and European encroachment into its lands. Great Britain and France, increasingly interested in exploiting the economic and strategic potential of the Middle East, began to assert their interests in the late 1800's, mainly by establishing *protectorates* (countries that are partially controlled by and dependent upon stronger countries) in parts of the weakened empire. Although the Ottomans still maintained authority over

most of the Middle East in 1900, the British had established power in Egypt and parts of the Arabian Peninsula, while the French had moved into northwest Africa.

In 1908, a group of young Turkish military officers, united by patriotism and a desire to halt the dwindling power of the empire, forced the Ottoman leader, Sultan Abdul-Hamid, to make political reforms. The people in outlying areas of the empire—particularly in North Africa and the Arabian Peninsula, where the Arab Muslims deeply resented Turkish control—hoped that this "Young Turk" revolution would grant them more control over their own affairs. They were soon disappointed.

In 1914, the eve of World War I, *Sherif* (Muslim leader) Hussein of Mecca—the great-grandfather of King Hussein of Jordan—asked Great Britain if it would support an Arab revolt against Ottoman rule. Two years of negotiations led to the

Arab guerrillas organized by British officer T. E. Lawrence (Lawrence of Arabia) ride into battle against the Ottoman Turks in 1917. The British supported the Arab struggle for independence but joined France to take control of the Arab lands after the Ottoman Empire collapsed at the end of World War I (1914-1918).

Major ethnic groups of the Middle East

- **Arabs**, the overwhelming majority of people in the Middle East, are descended from ancient people of the Arabian Peninsula and are bound by the common language of Arabic.
- **Jews** trace their lineage to an ancient Middle Eastern people called Hebrews.
- **Persians** make up the majority of Iran's population and form smaller groups in other countries. They are descended from an ancient Asian people called Aryans.
- **Turks** are descendants of an ancient people that lived in central Asia and make up the majority of the population in Turkey.
- **Kurds** are people of a mountainous region in southwest Asia that extends over parts of Armenia, Iran, Iraq, Syria, and Turkey.
- **Berbers** live in northwest Africa and the Sahara region and speak a wide variety of Berber dialects.
- **Nubians** are people of mixed African, Arab, and Mediterranean ancestry. They live along the Nile River in southern Egypt and in Sudan.

The author:

Christine Helms is a free-lance writer and Middle East analyst.

British-supported Arab Revolt, which began in June 1916. During the revolt, the Arabs mounted successful guerrilla raids against Turkish forces in the Arabian Peninsula and elsewhere.

The Arabs finally won their freedom from the Ottomans at the end of World War I in 1918. However, their hopes for self-rule were soon dashed. Great Britain and France had made a secret deal during the war to *partition* (divide) the Arab territories of the Ottoman Empire into countries that would be under British or French control. By 1920, Great Britain and France agreed upon the division of the spoils, and the League of Nations (a pre-United Nations association of countries created to maintain peace) granted them *mandates* (commissions) to rule the region.

European colonialism

France added the newly created nations of Syria and Lebanon to its previous interests in the Middle East—Algeria, Morocco, and Tunisia. The French had a reputation for harsh colonial rule, especially in Algeria, where 1 million French immigrants supplanted native people in administering the country's government and economy.

The British took control of Iraq, Transjordan (present-day Jordan), and Palestine (roughly present-day Israel). The British considered these lands vital to the protection of the Suez Canal in the Sinai Peninsula of Egypt. British shipping trade between the Mediterranean Sea and Britain's rich empire in India and the East depended upon the canal. Great Britain used Transjordan as a land and air corridor to link Egypt to Iraq. To strengthen the Iraq-Transjordan bond and calm Arab anger, Britain installed members of the Sherif Hussein's Hashemite family as hereditary rulers in both Iraq and Transjordan.

British concerns in Palestine dated to a 1917 document, the Balfour Declaration, in which British Foreign Secretary Arthur

Balfour announced that his government supported the establishment of "a national home for the Jewish people" in Palestine. In 1917, the majority of Jewish people lived in Eastern Europe and North America. Many Jews longed for the creation of a Jewish state in Palestine, the location of the Biblical lands of Israel and Judah, or Judea. The Balfour Declaration was designed, in part, to ensure Jewish support for Great Britain in World War I. However, Arabs, who made up approximately 90 percent of Palestine's estimated 700,000 people, opposed the declaration.

Only three remote Arab regions escaped colonial domination—Oman, northern Yemen, and the desert interior of the Arabian Peninsula (what would later become Saudi Arabia). Western interest in central Arabia did not grow until the development of the region's oil reserves in the 1930's. The non-Arab, Middle Eastern nation of Persia (later to be known as Iran) also remained independent in the post-World War I era, though its government and economy were heavily influenced by Great Britain and Russia.

Arab nationalism and Zionism

Arab opposition to colonialism began immediately after the League of Nations mandates were granted. Arabs took little comfort in the installation of Arab rulers hand-picked by European overlords. Arabs also found the Balfour Declaration's clause that "nothing shall be done which may prejudice the civil and religious rights of existing non-Jewish communities in Palestine" at odds with the declaration's commitment to a Jewish homeland. Some groups of Arabs rallied around Islamic calls for self-rule, while others united around Arab *nationalism* (a people's sense of belonging together as a nation), which soon evolved into a powerful political force.

Events prior to World War II (1939-1945), as well as the war itself, marked the beginning of the end of European colonialism in the Arab world. Great Britain slowly came to realize that it was impossible to honor the conflicting commitments that the Balfour Declaration made to Arabs and Jews. *Zionism* (the movement to establish a Jewish state in Palestine) and growing Arab resentment against both British rule and increasing Jewish immigration to Palestine led to violent clashes, which British

Various religions of the Middle East

- **Islam** is the religion revealed by the prophet Muhammad in the A.D. 600's. Its followers, called Muslims, make up more than 90 percent of the Middle East's population. The religion has two main branches—Sunni Islam, to which the majority of Muslims in the Middle East belong, and Shiah Islam.

- **Judaism** is the religion of the Jews. Nearly all Jews in the Middle East live in Israel.

- **Christianity** is a religion based on the life and teachings of Jesus Christ. The largest Christian groups in the Middle East are Coptic Christians, an ancient sect in Egypt; Maronite Christians, who live mostly in Lebanon; and Eastern Orthodox Christians, who live in various Middle Eastern countries.

- **The Druse religion** is related to Islam but has many secret doctrines that are known only to the elite of the faith. Its followers are found mainly in Syria and Lebanon.

- **The Baha'i Faith** is based on the teachings of a Persian prophet named Baha'u'llah (1817-1892). This group forms one of the largest religious minorities in Iran.

- **The Yazidi religion**, often mistakenly called Devil worship, is based on the denial of the existence of evil. The religion, centered in northern Iraq, combines elements of several other religions.

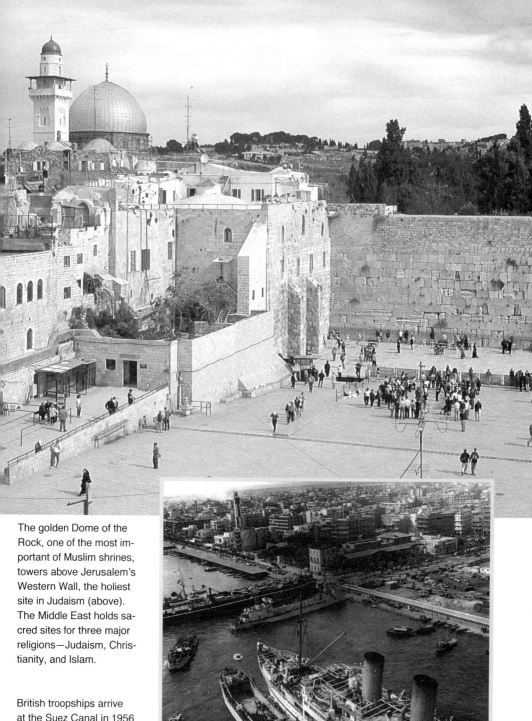

The golden Dome of the Rock, one of the most important of Muslim shrines, towers above Jerusalem's Western Wall, the holiest site in Judaism (above). The Middle East holds sacred sites for three major religions—Judaism, Christianity, and Islam.

British troopships arrive at the Suez Canal in 1956 (right) with forces attempting to retake from Egypt control of the canal, which was crucial to British shipping.

Western interest in central Arabia grew with the development of the region's vast oil reserves in the 1930's. As more oil deposits were discovered, the strategic value of the Middle East to the world's industrial nations increased.

authorities found impossible to control.

In August 1929, nearly 250 people were killed in fighting between Arabs and Jews in Palestine. The violence intensified during the 1930's as Nazi persecution of European Jews hastened immigration to Palestine. The number of Jews in Palestine increased from 85,000 in 1914 to 400,000 in 1936.

Arabs leaders met in Cairo, Egypt, in 1944 to discuss colonialism and the situation in Palestine. Independence from Great Britain and France was a major demand. They also declared that the plight of the Palestinian Arabs was of grave concern to Arabs throughout the Middle East. In 1945, a group of seven Arab nations formed the Arab League, which immediately voiced opposition to a Jewish state and recognized the Arab character of Palestine.

When the extent of the *Holocaust* (the murder of millions of Jews by the Nazis) became known at the end of World War II, the United States pressured Great Britain to allow unlimited Jewish immigration to Palestine. In 1947, Great Britain, frustrated by worsening violence in Palestine as well as growing international opposition to colonialism, referred the entire problem to the newly formed United Nations (UN). The UN General Assembly voted to partition Palestine, ceding 56 percent of the land west of the Jordan River for a Jewish state. The Zionists welcomed the vote. The Arabs, who made up about 66 percent of the nearly 2 million people in the designated area, opposed it.

A civil war broke out almost immediately, with Arabs from other regions of the Middle East fighting alongside the Palestini-

The evolution of the Middle East

In the Middle East during the 1900's, there were a number of different political divisions and colonial rulers before countries in the region achieved independence and self-determination.

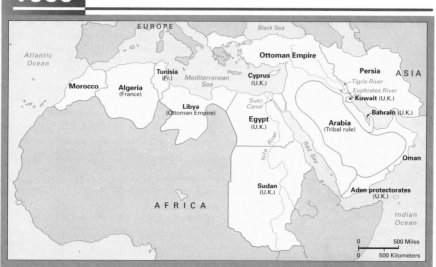

In 1900, the Ottoman Empire, ruled by a Turkish Muslim dynasty, dominated a large part of the Middle East.

ans. In May 1948, Zionists, having seized control of key towns, declared the birth of a new nation, Israel. The fighting between Israelis and Arabs lasted until July 1949, by which time the victorious Israelis held 80 percent of Palestine.

The creation of a Jewish nation rallied Arabs throughout the Middle East to the Palestinian cause and to the wider cause of Arab nationalism, which grew throughout the 1950's. In 1952, a military coup in Egypt ousted the country's monarchy—a legacy of British rule that Great Britain had established 30 years earlier. The Arab nationalist Gamal Abdel Nasser, one of the leaders of the military coup, became Egypt's president in 1956. In 1954, Arab rebels attacked French authority in Morocco, Tunisia, and Algeria. France granted independence to Morocco and Tunisia in 1956, but insisted on holding onto Algeria. After a bloody war of liberation that lasted several years, Algeria became independent in 1962.

In July 1956, President Nasser of Egypt *nationalized* (brought under the control of the government) the Suez Canal one month after British forces had withdrawn from the canal zone and Sinai Peninsula. In October, Israel, concerned about Egyptian control over a major strategic and economic asset, launched a surprise attack against Egyptian forces, inflicting heavy damage. This prompted Great Britain and France, which had jointly controlled

1923

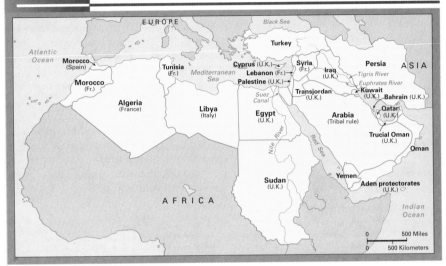

With the collapse of the Ottoman Empire after World War I, Great Britain and France carved up much of the Middle East into nation-states, which the two Western powers ruled as colonies.

In 1999, the Middle East was composed of independent nations, most of which gained their independence after World War II (1939-1945).

1999

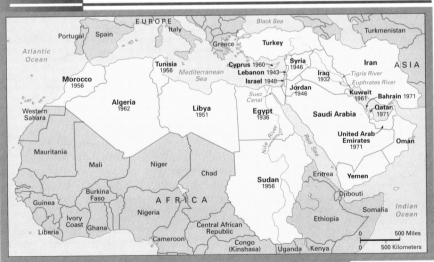

The boundaries of the Gaza Strip, West Bank, and Golan Heights are shown adjacent to Israel.
Southern Yemen (Aden), which became independent in 1967, merged with northern Yemen in 1990.

Middle East timeline

- **1916:** Arab Revolt begins against Ottoman Empire.
- **1917:** Great Britain pledges support in Balfour Declaration for Jewish "national home."
- **1918:** Ottoman Empire is defeated in World War I (1914-1918), paving the way for European powers to establish colonial control in Middle East.
- **1933:** Petroleum industry develops in Saudi Arabia.
- **1945:** The Arab League is founded to promote closer relations among member states.
- **1948:** The state of Israel is established, leading to first Arab-Israeli war.
- **1952:** Egyptian army officers overthrow King Faruk.
- **1956:** Egypt nationalizes Suez Canal, leading to second Arab-Israeli war.
- **1958:** Revolution ousts King Faisal of Iraq.
- **1967:** Third Arab-Israeli war (Six-Day War).
- **1973:** Fourth Arab-Israeli war (Yom Kippur War).
- **1978:** Israel and Egypt make peace through the Camp David Accords.
- **1979:** Islamic revolution in Iran creates Islamic republic.
- **1980-1988:** War between Iran and Iraq.
- **1991:** U.S.-led coalition forces Iraqi troops out of Kuwait, in Persian Gulf War.
- **1993:** Israel and the Palestinians move toward peace by signing the Oslo Accords.
- **1999:** Israel and the Palestinians agree to reach final peace settlement by September 2000.

the canal through the Suez Canal Company, to deploy troops to retake control. However, diplomatic pressure from the United States and Soviet Union—new world superpowers that took a dim view of any colonial vestige that might undermine their own interests in the strategically important, oil-rich region—forced Israel, Great Britain, and France to withdraw their forces.

In 1958, a popular revolution in Iraq toppled the British-installed Hashemite monarchy. The revolution's leader, Abdul Karim Kassem, became Iraq's premier. Arabs across the Middle East hailed the revolutions in Iraq and Algeria as great victories for the cause of Arab nationalism.

More Arab-Israeli wars

Although Arab nationalism was triumphant in these countries, the Arab dream of controlling the Holy Land was not to be. Repeated clashes between Israeli forces and those of Egypt, Jordan, and Syria erupted into war in 1967. The so-called Six-Day War began on June 5, when Israel attacked Arab forces on three fronts, winning major victories before the United Nations imposed a cease-fire on June 11. Egypt lost the Sinai Peninsula and the Gaza Strip, a small area along the Mediterranean coast, to Israel. Israel also captured eastern Jerusalem and the West Bank (land on the west bank of the Jordan River) from Jordan and the Golan Heights from Syria.

This crushing Arab defeat fueled a growing Palestinian guerrilla movement against Israel. The Palestine Liberation Organization (PLO) was formed in 1964 and quickly gained preeminence among the various guerrilla groups. Under Yasir Arafat, who was elected chairman of the PLO in 1969, terrorist attacks against Israel began in earnest. Israel responded with attacks against the PLO in Jordan, the group's largest base of operation. These attacks threatened to destabilize the government of King Hussein. In what became known to Arabs as Black September, King Hussein's army ousted the guerrillas from Jordan in September 1970.

On Oct. 6, 1973, Syrian President Hafez al-Assad and Egyptian President Anwar el-Sadat launched a surprise attack on Israel on the Jewish day of atonement, Yom Kippur. The attack was initially successful, but ultimately resulted in the loss of more Arab territory.

Moves toward peace

In November 1977, President Sadat, realizing that Egypt had been drained by 30 years of war and enticed by hopes of U.S. financial aid, made a historic trip to Israel, where he told the Israeli parliament that peace was dependent on ending mutual fears. In March 1979, Sadat and Israeli Prime Minister Menachem Begin signed a U.S.-brokered peace treaty known as the Camp David Accords in Washington, D.C. In exchange for Egypt's recognition, Israel agreed to withdraw its forces from the Sinai Peninsula. Other Arab states and the PLO condemned the treaty. In October 1981, Islamic extremists opposed to the peace process assassinated Sadat during a military parade.

Another Arab-Israeli crisis arose when Israel invaded southern Lebanon in June 1982. Israel hoped that by dislodging PLO guerrillas from the area, a peace treaty could be signed with Lebanon's Christian-led government. However, strong Lebanese opposition to the Israelis ended such hopes. Most Israeli forces retreated in June 1985, but some troops remained in the south to patrol a 9-mile- (14-kilometer-) wide security zone.

Arab grievances against Israeli occupation of the West Bank and Gaza Strip fueled the start in December 1987 of the *intifada*—an uprising that took the form of widespread, often violent, demonstrations by young Palestinians living in the occupied lands. King Hussein, concerned about the worsening violence, renounced Jordan's claims to the West Bank and eastern Jerusalem in July 1988. This move helped open the door to direct talks between the Palestinians and Israelis.

In 1993, the PLO and Israel revealed that they had secretly concluded an initial agreement of mutual recognition. The agreement, known as the Oslo Accords, was signed in September by Arafat and Israeli Prime Minister Yitzak Rabin. It outlined a plan in which the Israeli government would transfer control of the Gaza Strip and the West Bank town of Jericho to Palestinians over a five-year period. Then, in 1994, Jordan concluded a peace treaty with Israel.

A second Israeli-Palestinian agreement in 1995 was meant to expand Palestinian self-rule. However, growing opposition to the details of the accords among both Arabs and Jews put peace proponents on the defensive. A series of Palestinian suicide bombings exacted a high toll in Israel and caused many Israelis to oppose further moves toward peace. In addition, the assassination of Prime Minister Rabin in November 1995 by a right-wing Jewish extremist underscored deep divisions within Israeli society.

The 1999 election of the highly decorated military hero and moderate Labor Party leader Ehud Barak as Israeli prime minister fostered new hope for peace. In September 1999, Barak's government and the Palestinians agreed to return to the bargaining table to hammer out a final peace settlement by September 2000.

Political Islam

The troubled Arab-Israeli peace process of the 1990's was the latest of the many frustrating problems faced by people in the

High annual popula-
tion growth rates in
many Middle Eastern
countries in the late
1990's put increased
pressure on econo-
mies, environments,
and existing social
divisions.

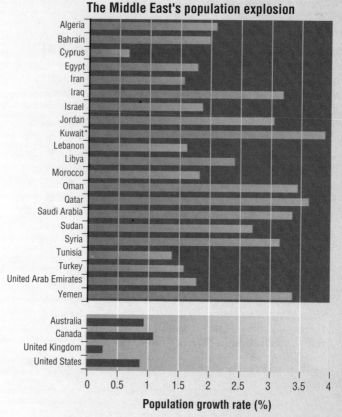

The Middle East's population explosion

Algeria, Bahrain, Cyprus, Egypt, Iran, Iraq, Israel, Jordan, Kuwait*, Lebanon, Libya, Morocco, Oman, Qatar, Saudi Arabia, Sudan, Syria, Tunisia, Turkey, United Arab Emirates, Yemen

Australia, Canada, United Kingdom, United States

0   0.5   1   1.5   2   2.5   3   3.5   4

Population growth rate (%)

*Figure for Kuwait reflects
continued return of expatriates
after 1990-1991 Persian Gulf War.
Source: *The World Factbook* 1999,
U.S. Central Intelligence Agency.

Middle East during the 20th century. In the early 1970's, unemployment, poverty, and other societal problems combined with
Israel's repeated military victories over the Arab states to cause a
growing number of Arabs to turn to a new ideology called *political Islam*, a political movement based on Islamic fundamentalism. Similar movements began forming in the non-Arab states of
Turkey and Iran.

By the late 1970's, political Islam was a rallying cry in a number of Middle Eastern nations for opposition groups demanding
social, economic, and political reform. Nearly all of these movements condemned the United States for its support of Israel and a
perceived anti-Muslim bias.

While many Islamic fundamentalists tried to work through
social and professional organizations or seek elective office, a
number of radical Islamic groups preached violence. The violence
took many forms. A civil war in Lebanon between various Christian and Muslim groups over the sharing of power devastated the
country between 1975 and 1990. In 1979, Islamic militants
seized the Great Mosque in Mecca to protest the rule of the pro-

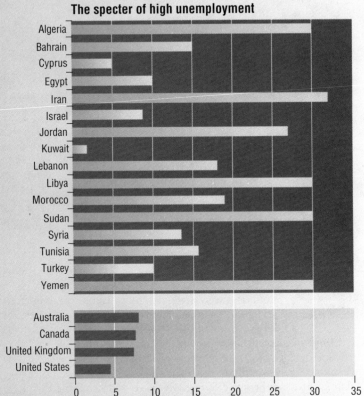

The specter of high unemployment

Unemployment in Middle Eastern countries in the late 1990's grew in relation to the population.

No unemployment data is available for Iraq, Oman, Qatar, Saudi Arabia, or United Arab Emirates.
Source: *The World Factbook* 1999, U.S. Central Intelligence Agency.

Unemployment rate (%)

U.S. Saud dynasty, the founding family of Saudi Arabia. Soon after the intifada began in the Israeli-occupied territories in late 1987, a group of Palestinians once loyal to the PLO formed Hamas, a militant Islamic group that fought for improved economic conditions for Arabs.

The most significant event shaped by political Islam occurred in 1979, when Islamic fundamentalists in Iran overthrew the pro-U.S. Shah of Iran. The revolution, led by the religious authority Ayatollah Khomeini, grew out of disappointment with the economic performance of the Shah's government. Mass demonstrations were fueled by the conservative Shiite Muslim clergy, who blamed U.S. meddling and Westernization for Iran's problems.

The Islamic revolutionaries established a *theocracy* (a government ruled by religious authorities) in Iran. The Shiite *mullahs* (Muslim scholars) clamped down on opposition groups, restricted personal freedoms and women's rights, and supported the export of Islamic militancy to the Arab world. Iran also promoted terrorist activities directed against the United States and other Western powers.

Palestinians line up to fill bottles with water during a drought in 1999 (above left). Periodic droughts worsened the chronic water shortage faced by most of the Middle East in the 1900's.

Children play in garbage-strewn streets in a poor part of Cairo, Egypt (above right). Poverty continued to threaten the stability of many Middle Eastern nations in 1999.

By the 1990's, the governments of all Arab countries were struggling with Islamic militancy. In Egypt, a violent campaign by militants targeted government officials, security personnel, Coptic Christians, and foreign tourists. The most deadly violence growing out of Islamic extremism began in Algeria in 1992, when the Algerian military canceled an election that the radical Islamic Salvation Front (FIS) was poised to win. An armed wing of FIS and other Islamic groups then unleashed a civil war that left an estimated 100,000 people dead by 1999.

Saddam Hussein

Islamic militancy was also an issue when, in September 1980, Iraqi President Saddam Hussein ordered his nation's troops to invade Iran. Saddam—as he became known to the world—succeeded to the presidency in 1979 after rising through the ranks of the Arab *Baath* (Renaissance) Socialist Party, a *secular* (nonreligious), Arab-nationalist political organization. Many observers in the West blamed Saddam for starting the war for territorial gain. Most Arab observers recognized that despite long-term territorial disputes between Iran and Iraq, the main factor behind the war was Iraq's desire to prevent Iran from exporting Islamic revolution to Iraq's secular state. Both Iran and Iraq sustained hundreds of thousands of casualties and suffered severe damage to oil facilities and other economically important sites. The war ended in a cease-fire after eight years.

In 1990, Iraq, laying claim to a contested oil field, invaded Kuwait. It was the first time in the history of the Arab League that one Arab state had invaded another, and the invasion deeply divided the Arab world. The United States, concerned about its oil interests, led a large international force that ousted Iraqi troops from Kuwait in 1991. The coalition received military support from Saudi Arabia, Egypt, and Syria. Jordan, Yemen, and the Palestinians expressed either sympathy for Iraq or a desire that the conflict be resolved peacefully.

Many Western policymakers expected these divisions to lead to the demise of Arab nationalism. This was not to be. Although divisions in the Arab world lingered after the Gulf War, tough U.S.-led economic sanctions and repeated bombings of Iraq long after the war ended fueled popular Arab support for Iraq. This was true even in those states that had joined the military coalition against Iraq.

The hope of Western governments that the devastation sustained by Iran during the Iran-Iraq War would diminish the appeal of political Islam also was not realized. Political Islam continued to spread throughout the Arab world as a result of both the stalemated Arab-Israeli peace process and internal problems unique to each country.

A new pragmatism

By the late 1990's, most governments in the Middle East were responding to Arab nationalism and political Islam by devoting more of their attention to practical solutions of internal problems. Population growth was the most serious of these problems. In some Arab countries in 1999, population growth rates were so high that as much as 70 percent of the population was under 17 years of age. As a result, unemployment rates, especially among the young, grew dramatically.

Population growth and industrial development also contributed to environmental pollution and a scarcity of water throughout the Middle East. Most nations in the Middle East suffered severe water shortages in the 1990's, requiring the rationing of drinking water.

By the end of the century, many of the region's governments found themselves in serious economic trouble resulting from expensive welfare and employment programs created to ease or prevent social unrest. Widespread government corruption also hampered efforts at finding workable solutions to economic problems.

As the 1900's closed, higher literacy rates and modern communication technologies, such as the Internet, placed growing pressure on Middle Eastern governments to make both economic and political reforms. Further pressure for reform came from various non-Arab groups. The Berbers of northern Africa and the Kurds of mountainous southwest Asia, for example, demanded greater rights.

Despite the daunting problems remaining from the 1900's, the future of the Middle East held promise at the dawn of the 21st century. A number of rulers in the region were aging, and aging rulers meant that many states—like Jordan and Morocco in 1999—would soon have a new and younger generation at the helm. The disappointments and unrealized dreams experienced by the older generation led many younger people in the Middle East to hope their new leaders would follow more pragmatic policies to solve the region's economic and social ills. ∎∎∎

Montreal lost its longest-serving mayor on Aug. 12, 1999, with the death of Jean Drapeau at age 83. Elected to the office eight times, Drapeau served as mayor from 1954 to 1957 and from 1960 until his retirement in 1986. During his 29-year tenure, the colorful mayor brought Montreal international recognition with his ambitious projects, including the world's fair, Expo 67; the 1976 Summer Olympic Games; the introduction of a major-league baseball team, the Montreal Expos; and the construction of a subway system.

More than 5,000 people attended Drapeau's funeral on Aug. 16, 1999. In September, Montreal's City Council renamed the Parc des Iles to honor the former mayor. The new Parc Jean Drapeau was the site of Expo 67.

Stadium woes. The problem-plagued Olympic Stadium, home of the Montreal Expos, experienced the latest in a long history of potentially dangerous incidents on Jan. 18, 1999. Five people were slightly injured when an avalanche of snow crashed through the stadium's new $37-million roof onto the stadium floor, where workers were setting up an auto show. (All monetary amounts are in Canadian dollars unless noted.)

The Olympic Installations Board, the agency that runs the stadium, filed a $4.1-million lawsuit in August against the roof's contractor, Birdair Incorporated of New York City. Birdair had won a contract in 1998 to replace the stadium's old retractable roof with a fixed roof.

The Molson Centre, home of the Montreal Canadiens hockey team, was put up for sale on Sept. 2, 1999, only three years after it opened. Molson, Inc., the Toronto-based brewing company that owns the Centre and the Canadiens, cited lackluster revenues from the sports and entertainment arena and the stadium's $9-million annual property tax bill as factors in its decision to sell. Molson President James Arnett assured Montrealers that the Canadiens team itself was not for sale and would continue to play at the Centre regardless of who owned the arena.

Arnett also introduced Pierre Boivin as the Canadiens' new president on September 2. Boivin replaced Ronald Corey, who stepped down on May 31 after 18 years at the helm of the franchise.

Theme park. A $900-million high-tech indoor amusement park, scheduled to open in 2002 near the Port of Montreal, was announced in April 1999 by Heathmount A.E. Corporation of Toronto. The park, called Destination: Technodrome, was expected to employ 7,000 permanent workers and attract 500,000 visitors annually to Montreal.

Film. A new $25-million film production studio opened at a converted air force base in suburban Saint-Hubert, south of Montreal, in March. The 61,500-square-foot (5,700-square-meter) Cine Cite Montreal was constructed with five indoor studios.

Television and motion picture production in the Montreal area totaled $694 million in 1998.

Bullfight dispute. Montreal's first bullfight since 1973, held on Aug. 21, 1999, pitted animal rights activists against fans, as well as matadors against bulls. At least 200 protesters marched outside Olympic Stadium, where 10,000 spectators watched Portuguese-style bullfighting. Portuguese bullfighting differs from Spanish bullfighting in that the bulls are generally not killed. In the Montreal bullfights, the bulls were prodded with padded poles. The Montreal chapter of the Society for the Prevention of Cruelty to Animals and the Global Action Network, a Montreal-based animal protection organization, maintained, however, that the bulls suffered during the fights.

Business news. Montreal's Quebecor Printing, Inc., became the world's largest commercial printer on August 20, when it acquired Connecticut-based World Color Press, Inc., in a $2.7-billion (U.S.) deal.

Saputo Group, Inc., a Montreal cheese producer, paid $280 million for legendary Quebec baker Culinar, Inc., in September in order to prevent the takeover of Culinar by a U.S. firm. In 1999, Culinar controlled from 85 to 90 percent of the snack-cake market in Canada.   □ Mike King

See also **Canada; Canadian provinces; City.**

Morocco. See **Middle East.**

Motion pictures. A note of artistic hope surfaced at the end of the 1999 motion picture season, promising new challenges for filmmakers and new pleasures for audiences. After a series of formulaic summer movies that often found viewers several steps ahead of the storylines, a healthy crop of unconventional films, many coming from major mainstream studios, made strong impressions on moviegoers at year-end.

Critics cited two reasons for this emergence of free-thinking films. Studio heads noted the reception afforded independent films in 1998 and wanted to apply some of that anarchic spirit to their own films. Warner Brothers, for example, hired David O. Russell to direct its Persian Gulf War (1991) action-comedy, *Three Kings,* on the strength of his irreverent independent features, *Spanking the Monkey* (1994) and *Flirting With Disaster* (1996).

Many new filmmakers were also inspired by films made in the late 1960's and early 1970's, when cinema cliches often were cast aside, resulting in such landmark films as *Bonnie and Clyde* (1967), *Midnight Cowboy* (1969), *Easy Rider* (1969), and *M*A*S*H* (1970).

Russell captured the spirit of Robert Altman's Korean War comedy *M*A*S*H* with *Three Kings,* while adding his own touches to embellish the tale of four burnt-out soldiers trying to find a rumored cache of Iraqi gold. Many critics also viewed the film as the vehicle to turn television star George Clooney into a major movie personality.

Big splashes. The director of one of the most highly praised films of 1999 moved directly from the theater to make the acclaimed *American Beauty*. Sam Mendes had directed Nicole Kidman in the play *The Blue Room* (1998) and Dame Judi Dench in *The Cherry Orchard* (1989). Like Russell, Mendes viewed the late 1960's and early 1970's as the most fruitful period of American filmmaking.

American Beauty featured Kevin Spacey and Annette Bening in vivid, richly textured performances as an ineffectual husband and his overbearing wife whose pursuit of the American dream turns into a nightmare. The idea of a suburban paradise camouflaging misplaced passions was not new, but Mendes and screenwriter Alan Ball put new twists on a familiar story. *American Beauty* boasted an energy absent from mainstream U.S. filmmaking until the resurgence in the late 1990's.

David Fincher's *Fight Club* was another film that made a big impression in 1999. Brad Pitt lures Edward Norton into joining a club where discontented yuppies vent their anger with barefisted fights in which they beat their opponents to dangerous extremes.

Director Frank Darabont, absent from the screen following the success of his prison drama *The Shawshank Redemption* (1994), returned to a setting of incarceration with his widely anticipated version of horror writer Stephen King's series of novelettes, *The Green Mile*. Popular film actor Tom Hanks portrays a death row guard in the Depression era South. The character discovers that an African American inmate may have healing powers.

Tim Burton, who put unconventional spins on such familiar genre films as *Batman* (1989) and *Ed Wood* (1994), directed a new version of Washington Irving's literary classic, *The Legend of Sleepy Hollow,* released in 1999. The story's fussy schoolteacher, Ichabod Crane, was changed to a fussy detective, played by Johnny Depp. The title was shortened to *Sleepy Hollow,* and Burton's camera savored the spectacle of the story's headless horseman.

Music video veteran Spike Jonze, one of the stars of *Three Kings,* made a strong directorial debut in 1999 with *Being John Malkovich.* The movie was a wild fantasy in which an inept file clerk, played by John Cusack, discovers a portal that leads directly to the consciousness of eccentric actor John Malkovich. Cameron Diaz played Cusack's spacy wife, in what many movie critics considered a bold career move following the actress's success

TIME CAPSULE 1941
MOTION PICTURES

THE INDUSTRY found itself embattled, but very much on its toes during 1941. From any standpoint, its offerings proved noteworthy . . . .

The outstanding motion picture of the year was both experimental and excellent. Orson Welles turned out a brilliant screen biography in *Citizen Kane.* Its savage delineation of a tycoon publisher was close enough to recognizable figures to be the record of an American type and an American era. In this, his first film, Welles contrived to violate conventions so expertly that the photoplay will unquestionably stand as a landmark in the history of the medium.

Since Welles himself gave a truly great performance as the overween-ing publisher who was able to buy everything but affection and friendship, *Citizen Kane* took on an added quality of compulsion. With splendid actors from the New York theater (relatively unknown to film audiences) in supporting roles, it had a freshness of performance which gave it great bite and insight. This picture fused a great many aspects of technique and treatment into an enduring screen composition.

Orson Welles produces, directs, and stars in the landmark film Citizen Kane *(1941).*

in *There's Something About Mary* (1998).

Other well-received releases in late 1999 followed more traditional lines. Jodie Foster starred in *Anna and the King,* an elaborate nonmusical version of *The King and I,* the story of a British governess hired by the king of Siam (present-day Thailand) to teach his children. Action hero Arnold Schwarzenegger returned to form in *End of Days,* in which he battles Satan, who plans to take over the world for the new millennium. Pierce Brosnan retreaded his suave James Bond impersonation in *The World Is Not Enough.*

Animated films gained more attention with the release of Disney Studio's *Tarzan* in the summer of 1999. The film displayed an abundance of verve and creativity. *Princess Mononoke,* a spectacular animated film that had broken attendance records in Japan in 1997, drew additional raves with its 1999 U.S. debut. *Princess Mononoke* set a new standard for animation with hand-drawn and computer-generated images depicting both mystical and stark images of nature.

A phantom menace. Audiences in early 1999 eagerly awaited the release of *Star Wars: Episode I—The Phantom Menace,* the prequel to *Star Wars* (1977). *The Phantom Menace* traced the early years of Anakin Skywalker, a character who in the original film had become the villainous Darth Vader. With curiosity whetted by the 1997 reissue of *Star Wars* and its sequels, *The Empire Strikes Back* (1980) and *Return of the Jedi* (1983), fans in some cities camped outside theaters for several weeks prior to the opening of *The Phantom Menace* on May 19, 1999.

Many movie studios scheduled their summer releases so they would not collide with the opening of the film. But such precautions proved unnecessary. Although the film was a huge box-office draw, earning $28.5 million opening day and $205 million in less than two weeks, it failed to dominate the summer movie season in the same way as the wildly successful *Titanic* (1998).

Public and critical opinions of the film were mixed. Many people enjoyed director George Lucas's in-depth creation of a galactic universe but found most of the characters too simplistic and lacking in depth. One of the film's computer-generated creations, a chatterbox amphibian named Jar Jar Binks, was singled out for derision.

Summer successes. Despite mixed reviews, *The Phantom Menace* became the summer's most successful film. It earned $421 million between its May 19 opening and Labor Day. The summer movie season overall broke box-office records, with film receipts totaling $2.9 billion between Memorial Day and Labor Day.

Julia Roberts scored in two romantic comedies in 1999. *Runaway Bride,* which contained a surprising comic performance by Richard Gere, and

Notting Hill with Hugh Grant. Although the humor of many of the summer's comedies was geared toward younger audiences, particularly adolescent boys, such films as *Austin Powers: The Spy Who Shagged Me,* starring Mike Myers, and *Big Daddy,* starring Adam Sandler, were among the year's most popular films.

The Sixth Sense, a supernatural thriller starring Bruce Willis, was also well-received by audiences. The movie's impact was partly due to its surprise ending, and many viewers returned for additional screenings to study the hints that lead to the film's final revelation.

The Blair Witch Project, an inexpensive independent film budgeted at approximately $600,000, became one of the surprise hits of 1999 and one of the most profitable films ever produced. The film earned about $1.5 million in its opening weekend in July.

Written and directed by Daniel Myrick and Eduardo Sanchez, the film avoided special effects in favor of jerky camera movements, forcing viewers to rely on their imaginations in the absence of on-screen violence. The movie told the fictional story of three filmmakers who disappear while tracing the legend of a witch who lives in remote woods in Maryland. The filmmakers presented the tale in documentary fashion, and many audiences were convinced that it was fact rather than fiction.

The Internet was extensively used in promoting *The Blair Witch Project.* Such heavy reliance on cyberspace for publicity was a first, but it turned out to be a successful move. Scores of fans visited the film's highly popular Web site. The Internet's impact on moviegoing, however, was mixed. Many film industry heads criticized the use of the Internet and the practice of audience members who attend previews of works-in-progress and then give their opinions of unfinished films.

Despite the film's financial success, some critics and audience members criticized *The Blair Witch Project* for containing too little substance. Others complained that the jerky camera movements caused headaches and nausea for some audience members.

Violent entertainment was scrutinized in 1999 following accusations that portrayals of violent acts in movies and on television were partly responsible for shootings by students at a number of high schools in 1999. On June 9, President Bill Clinton announced that members of the National Association of Theater Owners, which controls about two-thirds of all movie screens in the United States, agreed to require photo identification before a younger-looking person could be admitted to an R-rated film. Films rated R by the Motion Picture Association of America require anyone under the age of 17 to be accompanied

Best actress Gwyneth Paltrow (from left), best supporting actress Dame Judi Dench, best supporting actor James Colburn, and best actor Roberto Benigni, display their Oscars on March 21, 1999, following the Academy Awards ceremonies.

by a parent or adult guardian. Critics questioned whether theater box office employees would enforce the requirement.

Overseas successes. Hollywood films dominated the global film market in 1999, with most U.S. features grossing more money overseas than in the United States. *Star Wars: Episode I—The Phantom Menace* was a notable exception. It earned only $26.7 million in 24 countries following its overseas premiere in July. In Mexico, the animated film *Tarzan* earned $3 million during opening weekend, which was a record amount for the film's distributor, Buena Vista International.

Top Italian film. *Life Is Beautiful* became the highest-grossing foreign language film ever released in North America, earning nearly $21.9 million by February. The film starred Italian director and comic actor Roberto Benigni as a concentration camp inmate who tries to convince his young son that their efforts to survive the Holocaust—the systematic extermination of some 6 million people by Nazi Germany during World War II (1939-1945)—is only a game.

See also **People in the news** (Benigni, Roberto; Dench, Dame Judi; Paltrow, Gwyneth).

☐ Philip Wuntch

Mozambique. See **Africa.**
Music. See **Classical music; Popular music.**

Academy Award winners in 1999

The following winners of the 1998 Academy Awards were announced in March 1999:

Best Picture, *Shakespeare in Love*

Best Actor, Roberto Benigni, *Life Is Beautiful*

Best Actress, Gwyneth Paltrow, *Shakespeare in Love*

Best Supporting Actor, James Colburn, *Affliction*

Best Supporting Actress, Judi Dench, *Shakespeare in Love*

Best Director, Steven Spielberg, *Saving Private Ryan*

Best Original Screenplay, Marc Norman and Tom Stoppard, *Shakespeare in Love*

Best Screenplay Adaptation, Bill Condon, *Gods and Monsters*

Best Cinematography, Janusz Kaminski, *Saving Private Ryan*

Best Film Editing, Michael Kahn, *Saving Private Ryan*

Best Original Dramatic Score, Nicola Piovani, *Life Is Beautiful*

Best Original Music or Comedy Score, Richard Warbeck, *Shakespeare in Love*

Best Original Song, Stephen Schwartz, "When You Believe" from *The Prince of Egypt*

Best Foreign-Language Film, *Life is Beautiful* (Italy)

Best Art Direction, Martin Childs and Jill Quetierer, *Shakespeare in Love*

Best Costume Design, Sandy Powell, *Shakespeare in Love*

Best Sound, Gary Rydstrom, Gary Summers, Andy Nelson, and Ronald Judkins, *Saving Private Ryan*

Best Sound Effects Editing, Gary Rydstrom and Richard Hymns, *Saving Private Ryan*

Best Makeup, Jenny Shircore, *Elizabeth*

Best Visual Effects, *What Dreams May Come*

Best Animated Short Film, *Bunny*

Best Live-Action Short Film, *Election Night*

Best Feature Documentary, *The Last Days*

Best Short Subject Documentary, *The Personals: Improvisations on Romance in the Golden Years*

Myanmar. The State Peace and Development Council, a 21-man military group that ruled Myanmar—formerly known as Burma—argued in 1999 that the armed forces were the only institution able to keep the nation stable. The regime clamped down on Rangoon and other cities to prevent demonstrations that exiles had called for on September 9, a date that many Burmese believed to be auspicious.

Amnesty International, a London-based human rights organization, issued a report in June accusing the regime of torturing and killing members of ethnic minorities. The report also alleged that Myanmar used forced labor drawn from ethnic groups, including child labor.

Myanmar authorities refused to allow British scholar Michael Aris to visit his wife, democracy leader Daw Aung San Suu Kyi, before he died on March 27. Suu Kyi, a 1991 Nobel Peace Prize winner, did not want to risk leaving Myanmar for fear that the government might bar her return.

The government published no economic data in 1999. Foreign economists speculated that Myanmar's rulers wanted to hide signs of an ailing economy. □ Henry S. Bradsher

See also **Asia.**

Namibia. See **Africa.**

Nebraska. See **State government.**

Nepal. See **Asia.**

Netherlands. Dissension grew among the partners of Prime Minister Wim Kok's coalition government in 1999 and cast doubt on its ability to remain in power to the end of its term in 2002. The government was criticized for its response in March 1999 to the world's worst outbreak of *Legionnaire's disease* (a bacterial infection named after the 1976 American Legion convention in Philadelphia, where the disease first surfaced). The Netherlands' outbreak, which began in February 1999 at a flower exhibition, killed 28 people. In April, a parliamentary committee investigating the 1992 crash of an El Al cargo plane into an Amsterdam apartment building criticized several government ministers, as well as Kok. The committee said the ministers had failed to properly investigate the accident and health complaints among residents near the crash site.

On May 19, 1999, the government resigned in a dispute over a bill to allow Dutch voters to overturn some government decisions by referendum. The bill was a longtime goal of the Democrats 66 party, the smallest member of the country's three-party coalition government. The referendum bill was blocked in the upper house of parliament when a member of the Liberal Party, another coalition member, voted against it. After further negotiation, the coalition agreed to a watered-down version of the bill and reestab-

A Kurdish woman in The Hague, the Netherlands, protests the arrest in February 1999 of Abdullah Ocalan, leader of the Kurdish autonomy (self-rule) movement. Ocalan's arrest in Kenya by Turkish agents sparked massive demonstrations across Europe.

lished the government under Kok, whose Labour Party is the country's largest political party.

Economy. The Dutch economy in 1999 remained one of the strongest in Western Europe. The *gross domestic product* (GDP—the value of all goods and services produced in a country in a given year) was expected to increase by about 3 percent for the fourth straight year. Unemployment declined to less than 3.5 percent—the lowest level since the 1960's—largely because of a strategy of curbing wage increases in exchange for more jobs and shorter working hours.

Euthanasia. The Dutch government announced in July that it would propose legislation to decriminalize euthanasia for terminally ill patients. In 1993, the government had decided to tolerate euthanasia for people who suffer unbearable pain and repeatedly request assisted suicide, but the practice remained officially illegal and left doctors liable to prosecution. About 3 percent of all deaths in the Netherlands in 1999 were recorded as mercy killings. □ Tom Buerkle

See also **Europe.**

Nevada. See State government.
New Brunswick. See Canadian provinces.
New Hampshire. See State government.
New Jersey. See State government.
New Mexico. See State government.
New York. See State government.

New York City. A controversial art exhibit at the Brooklyn Museum touched off a legal battle in 1999 over free speech, freedom of expression, and public funding for the arts. The show—"Sensations: Young British Artists from the Saatchi Collection"—opened October 2 and featured a painting of a black Madonna decorated with elephant dung.

New York Mayor Rudolph Giuliani labeled the exhibit "sick" and "offensive" and withdrew $7.2 million in subsidies from the museum—a third of its budget. He also threatened to evict the museum from public property. Lawyers representing the mayor's administration argued that the museum violated its lease by displaying art "unsuitable for children and objectionable to many New Yorkers." On November 1, Federal Judge Nina Gershon ruled that the city was in violation of the First Amendment to the U.S. Constitution and ordered the restoration of all funds. The judge compared the mayor's action to an attack on a public library with unpopular books.

Public health. A rare African viral infection killed four elderly New Yorkers, two suburban residents, and a Canadian who was visiting the city. The disease was first diagnosed as St. Louis encephalitis. Following an investigation by Tracey McNamara, a Bronx Zoo veterinarian, health specialists identified West Nile virus as the source of

The Empire State Building, now nearing completion (in 1930), is indisputably the tallest of all tall buildings, measuring by number of stories as well as by height of structure. It has 85 stories above the street, and the height to the top of the 85th is 1,043 feet. The mooring mast for airships brings the total height to 1,243 feet. This is 219 feet above the height at the top of the Eiffel Tower flagpole.

The Great Hall of ancient Greek art at New York City's Metropolitan Museum of Art reopens in April 1999. The gallery, including its barrel-vaulted skylights, which had been blacked out during World War II (1939-1945), was restored to conform closely to the architects' original 1912 plans.

the infection. The virus is transmitted to humans by mosquitoes that have bitten infected birds.

Law enforcement. Amadou Diallo, an immigrant from West Africa, was killed February 4 in the vestibule of his Bronx building. Four police officers mistook Diallo for a man wanted on rape charges and fired 41 shots at him. The shooting led to civil rights protests and the redeployment of the 380-member street unit to the city's eight regional commands. The four officers were indicted on murder charges.

In another case, Police Officer Justin Volpe interrupted his trial on May 25 to plead guilty to torturing Haitian immigrant Abner Louima in a Brooklyn holding cell on Aug. 9, 1997. Volpe faced a sentence of 30 years to life in prison. Four officers had testified against him. Mayor Giuliani described the testimony as a crack in the department's "blue wall of silence."

Education. On Sept. 1, 1999, schools Chancellor Rudy Crew announced an end to social promotion, the promotion of failing students to the next grade. Of the 35,344 students required to attend summer school in 1999, more than 21,000 students in grades 3, 6, and 8 were held back. Under the new policy, outlined to parents in November, students to be promoted are required to have a 90-percent attendance record, fulfill homework requirements, and perform at a satisfactory level on standardized tests.

Civil rights. Sixteen Ku Klux Klan members, in robes but without hoods, demonstrated at the U.S. Courthouse in Manhattan on October 23, after U.S. Supreme Court Justice Ruth Bader Ginsberg upheld a 154-year-old city law prohibiting masked gatherings.

Transportation. The Metropolitan Transportation Authority on September 29 authorized building the Second Avenue Subway, New York City's first subway expansion in more than 60 years. Engineers expected the $3.6-billion line, which was to run between 125th Street and 63rd Street, to take at least 10 years to build.

Real estate. On September 28, developer Donald Trump won approval from the New York Board of Standards and Appeals to construct a 90-story condominium building two blocks from the United Nations. A number of civic groups objected to the skyscraper, which will be the world's tallest residential structure when completed.

City government. Voters on November 2 rejected changes in the City Charter, one of which mandated a special election within 60 days if the mayor should leave office early. Under the present charter, Public Advocate Mark Green, a political foe, would become mayor if Mayor Rudolph Giuliani, a probable senatorial candidate against First Lady Hillary Rodham Clinton in 2000, should be elected and vacate the post. □ Owen Moritz

New Zealand. Voters entered polling booths on Nov. 27, 1999, facing the prospect of another coalition government and uncertain about the voting system they had adopted in 1996. The first government crafted under the system, also a coalition, had collapsed in 1998, leaving the National Party to govern with the support of minor parties. As preelection polling predicted, neither the National Party nor the main opposition Labour Party obtained an outright majority, and Helen Clark of the Labour Party was expected to govern with the support of minor parties.

A citizen's referendum held in conjunction with the general election proposed that the number of seats in Parliament, which had increased under the new proportional system, be reduced from 120 to 99. Opponents of the reduction claimed that it would decrease the representation of smaller parties and minority populations.

International relations. The Asia-Pacific Economic Co-operation (APEC), chaired by New Zealand Prime Minister Jenny Shipley, met in Auckland in September 1999 to discuss trade liberalization within the region. The meeting of leaders of 21 Asian and Pacific Rim countries supported a three-year round of global talks starting with a November meeting in Seattle, Washington, of the World Trade Organization (WTO), which arbitrates trade disputes among member nations. APEC also called for removing food export subsidies and agreed to develop banking standards for the region. U.S. President Bill Clinton, Chinese President Jiang Zemin, and South Korean President Kim Dae-Jung remained in New Zealand for state visits following the meeting.

In September, New Zealand announced that it would commit troops to a United Nations peacekeeping force in the Indonesian territory of East Timor, where violence had broken out following an independence vote in August. East Timor had been under Indonesian control since 1976. A battalion of New Zealand soldiers, air force helicopters, transport aircraft, and two navy ships were deployed to East Timor in September and October.

Economy. New Zealand reported a deficit of NZ$6.3 billion (U.S.$3.3 billion) for the six months ending in June 1999. Overall, the economy shrank by 0.3 percent. The outlook for exports was optimistic, however, with expected growth of 3 percent in the remainder of 1999 and 4 percent in 2000.

Defense. The government announced in July 1999 the lease of 28 F-16 fighters from the United States to replace aging A4 Skyhawks. The 10-year agreement was to cost more than NZ$350 million (U.S.$185 million). □ Gavin Ellis

See also **Indonesia; Pacific Islands; United Nations.**

Newfoundland. See **Canadian provinces.**

■ News bytes

Balloon quest successful. A flurry of attempts in recent years to make the first successful flight around the world in a balloon finally culminated in success in March 1999. Bertrand Piccard, a Swiss psychiatrist, and Brian Jones, a British balloonist and former Royal Air Force pilot, accomplished one of the last major challenges in aviation on March 20, when their balloon, *Breitling Orbiter 3,* crossed the latitude of 9 degrees, 27 minutes west, to complete the first successful balloon journey around the world. Piccard and Jones landed on March 21, approximately 300 miles (480 kilometers) southwest of Cairo, Egypt. During their trip, they had also set new ballooning records for duration—19 days, 21 hours, and 55 minutes—and for distance traveled—29,054.6 miles (46,758.8 kilometers).

Piccard was born into a family of scientist-explorers. His grandfather, Auguste Piccard, invented a pressurized cabin for use with high-altitude balloons and designed a deep-sea diving vessel called a bathyscaph. In 1960, Bertrand Piccard's father, Jacques Piccard, and Lieutenant Don Walsh of the U.S. Navy set a manned deep-sea diving record in a bathyscaphe, the *Trieste.*

London celebrates the Millennium. The British and their guests celebrated the dawn of the new century and the third millennium aboard the largest Ferris wheel ever constructed and at a grand, World's Fair-style event under one of the world's largest domes.

The celebration in England was inspired in part by the role played by Greenwich, England, in international timekeeping. From 1675 to 1948, Greenwich was the site of the Royal Greenwich Observatory. The Greenwich Meridian (also called the "prime meridian") is an imaginary north-south line crossing Greenwich at the observatory site, which in 1884 was designated 0 degrees longitude, with all other meridians of longitude numbered east or west of it. Since 1884, Greenwich Mean Time (GMT) has been used as a standard time reference between different time zones.

To celebrate the new millennium and century, British officials chose Greenwich as the site of the Millennium Dome, an immense structure with 1 million square feet (93,000 square meters) of covered space, large enough to contain 117 tennis courts or 12 football fields. The Dome was built around 14 themed pavilions dealing with the mind, the body, the environment,

The balloon Breitling Orbiter 3, piloted by Bertrand Piccard of Switzerland and Brian Jones of Great Britain, on March 20, 1999, became the first balloon to fly around the world. The balloon also set records for duration of flight and distance traveled.

The Millennium Dome (below), located in Greenwich, England, near London, opened to visitors on Dec. 31, 1999. The Dome, large enough to hold the Great Pyramid of Giza, contained 14 world's fair-style pavilions with exhibits on themes concerning humanity in the present and future. The 450-foot (145-meter) Millennium Wheel (right), an attraction built on the River Thames across from the Houses of Parliament, also debuted as a celebration of the start of the new century.

and other aspects of human life in the present and the future. The exhibition also featured a spectacular, 28-minute live performance featuring acrobats, musicians, and visual effects in a sunken arena that holds an audience of 12,000. Britain's Queen Elizabeth II officially opened the Dome on Dec. 31, 1999. The British Tourist Authority expected 12 million people, including 2.5 million international visitors, to come to the Millennium Dome during the year 2000.

On Oct. 17, 1999, British workers raised the Millennium Wheel, London's newest landmark. Standing 450 feet (145 meters) tall, the $33-million Ferris wheel, located on the south bank of the River Thames opposite the Houses of Parliament, was in 1999 the fourth-tallest structure in the British capital, towering over Big Ben. At the wheel's opening on "Millennium Eve," Dec. 31, 1999, 800 passengers at a time took 30-minute rides in 32 glass and steel gondolas. Whether the Millennium Wheel would become a permanent part of London's cityscape remained undetermined at year end.

Explorer's body found on Everest. In May 1999, an expedition of U.S. mountain climbers solved the 75-year-old mystery of what became of George Mallory. In 1924, Mallory, a British schoolteacher and adventurer, and Andrew Irvine, a British student, disappeared while attempting to complete the first ascent to the top of Mount Everest, the world's tallest peak at 29,028 feet (8,848 meters) above sea level. (Sir Edmund Hillary of New Zealand and Tenzing Norgay of Nepal, who climbed Everest in 1953, are considered the first people to reach the summit.)

The disappearance of Mallory and Irvine intrigued mountaineers for many years, because it was possible that the two men had managed to reach the summit and perished while on their way down. In 1933, climbers on Everest discovered an ice axe that they believed belonged to one of the men. A Chinese climber reported finding what he called an "old English dead" on Everest in 1975, but the climber died in an accident before he could report the location of the body.

The U.S. group, called the Mallory and Irvine Research Expedition, found Mallory's body on May 1, 1999, about 2,000 feet (610 meters) below the summit. The body, well preserved by the extreme cold and lack of moisture near the peak, bore Mallory's name on a tag on his clothing. The U.S. climbers were unable to determine whether Mallory had reached the summit before his death. The team performed a committal ceremony and buried Mallory's body on the mountain. They did not find Irvine's remains.

Rescue from Antarctica. On Oct. 15, 1999, the crew of a New York Air National Guard LC-130 Hercules airplane made a daring rescue at Amundsen Scott South Pole Station, a scientific research facility in Antarctica operated by the United States. The crew's mission was to pick up Jerri Nielson of Youngstown, Ohio, the station's physician, who required treatment for breast cancer. Nielson had detected a lump in her breast in June but was unable to leave the station because of the extreme winter conditions at the South Pole. Temperatures dipping to −100 °F (−73 °C) make it impossible for aircraft to reach the South Pole safely between mid-February and mid-October.

After self-diagnosing breast cancer in June, Nielson began communicating with cancer specialists in the United States, primarily through e-mail. With their advice, Nielson began treating herself with cancer-fighting drugs that were flown to Antarctica and airdropped near the station. It eventually became evident to her doctors that Nielson needed to be hospitalized. After several days of waiting for a break in the frigid weather, the National Guard aircraft took off from the U.S. Antarctic base at McMurdo Sound for the 1,600-mile (2,600-kilometer) journey to Amundsen Scott South Pole Station.

The plane landed despite white-out conditions caused by strong winds and blowing

Former crew members return to the battleship USS Missouri in January 1999, for a ceremony to dedicate the ship as a World War II memorial in Hawaii's Pearl Harbor. The Japanese surrendered to the United States aboard the Missouri on Sept. 2, 1945, ending the war.

The last total solar eclipse of the 20th century, viewed over the Blue Mosque in Istanbul, Turkey, occurs on Aug. 11, 1999. It was visible to observers in England, France, Germany, Eastern Europe, Turkey, Iran, Pakistan, and India.

snow. To minimize the danger to the plane and crew after landing, the plane could spend no more than three minutes on the ground to retrieve Nielson and drop off a replacement physician for Amundsen Scott Station. The pickup was successful, and Nielson returned to the United States, where she was evaluated and treated by cancer specialists at Indiana University Hospital in Indianapolis.

Monroe auction. In October 1999, a two-day auction of personal effects belonging to the film star Marilyn Monroe garnered more than $11 million, 37 years after her death. The most sought-after item—the flesh-colored dress Monroe wore when she sang "Happy Birthday" to U.S. President John F. Kennedy on May 19, 1962—fetched a record $1,267,500. The high bid came from the owners of a New York City memorabilia store. The previous record sale price for a dress at auction, $222,500, was paid in June 1997 for a gown belonging to Britain's Princess Diana.

Monroe literally had to be sewn into the semitransparent, silk gauze dress, which was embroidered with some 6,000 rhinestone sequins. She wore it once, during the few minutes it took her to sing to the president at New York City's Madison Square Garden.

Other items sold at the auction included a 35-diamond platinum ring, which sold for $772,500, given to Monroe by baseball legend Joe DiMag-

gio after their 1954 wedding; a white grand piano that Monroe inherited from her mother, which brought $662,500; and a traveling case and makeup, which sold for $268,800. Monroe's 1956 California temporary driver's license fetched $162,550.

The Big Top Returns. Forty-two years after Ringling Bros. Barnum & Bailey Circus folded its tents for what the circus assumed to be the last time "the greatest show on Earth" again began to perform under a tent. "Barnum's Kaleidoscope," a small-scale show with one ring instead of three, debuted Feb. 26, 1999, in Austin, Texas. It then traveled to California and staged shows in the Western United States through the end of the year.

Ringling Bros. officials said the new show was not intended to replace the company's two indoor touring companies, which annually attract some 11 million spectators in 90 cities. Instead, the smaller show allowed the company to bring the circus to smaller cities and towns. Since the new show traveled by

Workers unveil "Il Cavallo," the world's largest equestrian statue, in Milan, Italy, in September 1999. The bronze sculpture, inspired by a Leonardo da Vinci design, stands 24 feet (7.3 meters) tall. It was created by American sculptor Nina Akamu.

truck instead of by train, it could reach places not served by a railroad line. In addition, circus officials expected many people to be drawn by the nostalgic appeal of an old-time circus, staged beneath a big top with music from a live orchestra.

The new tent, which seated just 1,680 spectators, is much smaller than the previous big top, which could hold as many as 16,000 spectators. The new tent was made of fireproof polyvinyl, instead of canvas. In 1944, a Ringling Bros. canvas big top burned in Hartford, Connecticut, killing 168 spectators.

Record-setting row. Tori Murden on Dec. 3, 1999, became the first woman and the first American to cross an ocean alone in a rowboat, using only human power. The first person to accomplish such a feat was John Fairfax of Great Britain, who rowed across the Atlantic in 1969.

Murden, a 36-year-old attorney from Kentucky, completed her 82-day, 3,000-mile (4,800-kilometer) odyssey by reaching the French Caribbean island of Guadeloupe, after setting out from Tenerife, the Canary Islands, off the northwest coast of Africa, on September 13.

Rowing 12 to 14 hours each day, Murden lived on energy bars and freeze-dried meals and drank ocean water purified by a solar-powered desalinating pump. She slept below deck on a hammocklike cloth. The solar panels also powered a portable computer and satellite telephone, which she used for communication.

Murden's previous attempt to cross the Atlantic ended in September 1998, when she nearly died after being caught in the path of Hurricane Danielle. Her 1999 attempt was nearly derailed in November by Hurricane Lenny. Upon returning to dry land for the first time in almost three months, Murden quipped, "Next time, the Concorde."   □ Peter Uremovic

Newspaper. Mike Gallagher, a reporter who was fired in 1998 by *The Cincinnati Enquirer* after illegally accessing voice-mail messages at Chiquita Brands International, testified on April 5, 1999, that a former lawyer for the Cincinnati-based fruit company, George Ventura, helped him obtain access to the voice mail system. Gallagher used the voice-mail messages to document an 18-page article that questioned business practices at Chiquita. He further testified that he had promised Ventura that he, Gallagher, would go to jail rather than reveal his source for the article.

Journalists jailed. A federal district judge in June 1999 jailed Kathy Scruggs and Ron Martz, two reporters for *The Atlanta* (Georgia) *Journal-Constitution,* after they refused to reveal their source for a 1996 story about the bombing at the Summer Olympic Games in Atlanta. The reporters wrote a story claiming that a part-time security guard was the focus of a federal investigation into the bombing.

Reporters fired. The publisher of *The Owensboro* (Kentucky) *Messenger-Inquirer* fired a reporter on May 10, 1999, after the newspaper discovered that she had fabricated stories published as fact. The reporter, Kim Stacy, wrote a series of newspaper columns about her battle with brain cancer. She later told editors that she had acquired immune deficiency syndrome (AIDS). In an interview published on May 14, Stacy admitted that she was not sick and had lied about the cancer and about having AIDS.

Editors at the *Arizona Republic* fired columnist Julie Amparano on August 21 after they were unable to verify quoted sources and the existence of several people interviewed for her stories. Amparano said that the sources were real.

Editors from *The Indianapolis* (Indiana) *Star* and *The Indianapolis News* on August 27 suspended Steve Hall, a television columnist, for submitting an article editors said was *plagiarized* (copied from another's work and claimed as one's own) from a television critic at another newspaper. The editors fired Hall on September 7 after uncovering other incidents of plagiarism.

Newspaper closings. The *Chattanooga* (Tennessee) *Times* shut down on January 4 after 120 years of publication, following its sale to the owners of a rival newspaper, *The Chattanooga Free Press. The Indianapolis News* closed on October 1 after 130 years of publication. Like many afternoon newspapers, *The Indianapolis News* had experienced declining circulation in recent years. The *Honolulu* (Hawaii) *Star-Bulletin,* another afternoon paper with declining circulation, closed on October 31 after 117 years.

□ Mark Fitzgerald

Nicaragua. See **Latin America.**
Niger. See **Africa.**

General Abdulsalam Abubakar (right), Nigeria's military dictator, relinquishes power to newly elected President Olusegun Obasanjo at an inauguration ceremony on May 29 in Abuja, the Nigerian capital. Obasanjo was Nigeria's first civilian leader in 15 years.

Nigeria. In 1999, Nigeria's military regime, headed by General Abdulsalam Abubakar, fulfilled its promise, made in 1998, to restore civilian rule to the country. The May 29, 1999, inauguration of President Olusegun Obasanjo, who was elected in February, ended more than 15 years of continuous military dictatorship in Africa's most populous country. However, economic worries and allegations of electoral fraud overshadowed the transition to democracy.

Civilian elections. Abubakar's regime organized a series of elections in January and February, including a vote for seats in the National Assembly, Nigeria's parliament. The People's Democratic Party (PDP), which had dominated previously held state and local elections, won 59 of 109 seats in the Senate and 208 of 360 seats in the House of Representatives.

In the final election, held on February 27, Obasanjo, the leader of the PDP and Nigeria's military ruler from 1976 to 1979, won the presidency with 63 percent of the vote. Former United States President Jimmy Carter, speaking for several international monitoring groups, noted that there were many serious discrepancies in the balloting. Nigeria's Independent National Elections Commission nevertheless accepted the result.

The Commonwealth of Nations, an association of states that have lived under British law

and government, agreed on April 4, 1999, to allow Nigeria to rejoin the organization. The decision ended years of isolation for Nigeria, which was suspended from the Commonwealth in 1995 for the human rights abuses under Abubakar's predecessor, Sani Abacha, who died in June 1998.

Economic corruption. Between the February 1999 elections and the May transition to civilian rule, Nigeria's military regime was widely accused of awarding members and cronies lucrative business contracts. As a result, Obasanjo's government inherited a $2.5-billion deficit. On May 31, Obasanjo suspended all contracts and agreements made by the outgoing government in 1999.

The new administration faced a major challenge in turning around Nigeria's ailing economy, a legacy of decades of mismanagement and institutional corruption. The economy continued to bear the burden of the largest foreign debt in Africa, estimated at some $34 billion in 1999.

Truth panel. In mid-August, a seven-member panel, headed by Nigeria's most respected judge, began hearings into murders and other human rights abuses carried out by the country's military regimes since 1976. At the same time, the government announced a plan to reduce the size of the armed forces by half. □ Simon Baynham

See also **Africa; People in the news** (Obasanjo, Olusegun).

Nobel Prizes in literature, peace, the sciences, and economics were awarded in October 1999 by the Norwegian *Storting* (parliament) in Oslo and by the Royal Swedish Academy of Sciences, the Karolinska Institute, and the Swedish Academy of Literature in Stockholm. Each prize was worth about $960,000.

The 1999 Nobel Prize for literature went to German author Gunter Grass. Grass is perhaps best known for his 1959 novel *The Tin Drum,* the story of an articulate but perpetually 3-year-old boy named Oskar who overpowers other people with a toy drum. In Grass's 1961 novel *Cat and Mouse*, a boyhood friendship is destroyed when a war game turns into real combat. Both novels capture the brutal events that occurred in Germany during and after the Nazi regime of World War II (1939-1945). *My Century,* a novel published in 1999, balances the tragedy of the war years with great enthusiasm for the discoveries and developments of the late 1900's.

The 1999 Nobel Peace Prize was awarded to the organization Doctors Without Borders, or *Medecins Sans Frontieres.* The group, which has members from many countries, was founded in France in 1971. Doctors Without Borders was honored for "the organization's pioneering humanitarian work on several continents."

Doctors Without Borders has operated on the principle that all victims of disaster—whether natural or man-made—have a right to efficient and quick professional assistance. National boundaries and political circumstances, such as wars, do not influence who receives humanitarian aid from the group. Through its rapid intervention in war-torn and impoverished places, Doctors Without Borders has called public attention to catastrophes and human rights abuses and helped to focus international opposition to violations and abuses of power.

The 1999 Nobel Prize for physiology or medicine went to cell and molecular biologist Gunter Blobel, a German-born scientist at Rockefeller University in New York City. Blobel discovered that proteins contain "signals that govern their transport and localization in the cell."

A large number of proteins perform different functions within each human cell. These proteins must be transported out of the cell or to different compartments within. Blobel learned how signals within each protein direct newly made proteins to their correct locations. He discovered that the principles governing these movements are the same in both plant and animal cells. Blobel's research has helped scientists understand the molecular mechanisms behind many inherited diseases and contributed to the development of useful drugs to correct misdirected proteins.

The 1999 Nobel Prize for economics was awarded to Canadian-born Robert A. Mundell, a professor at Columbia University in New York City, for his contributions to current international economic theories. Mundell constructed theories that help economists develop financial policies for free-market economies. Mundell's work, which was largely done in the 1960's at the University of Chicago, has proven both prophetic and useful as new currencies, such as the European Union's euro, introduced in 1999, are established. Mundell's theories have been applied to such monetary issues as finding ways to link national money policies to international policies and helping governments decide whether or not to fix the exchange rate of currency.

The 1999 Nobel Prize for chemistry was awarded to Egyptian American chemist Ahmed H. Zewail of the California Institute of Technology in Pasadena for developing a technique that has been called "the world's fastest camera." With this method, called femtosecond spectroscopy, Zewail captured the movements of atoms in a molecule during a chemical reaction.

While some chemical reaction take place over a long period, others appear to be instantaneous. Zewail's technique uses a laser flash that matches the time scale at which the fastest chemical reactions occur—a femtosecond, or 0.000000000000001 of a second. Zewail's contribution to *femtochemistry* (the chemistry of reactions that occur in extremely small fractions of a second) in the late 1980's has helped scientists study delicate mechanisms in life processes and improve the way medicines are produced.

The 1999 Nobel Prize for physics was awarded to Dutch physicists Gerardus 't Hooft, of the University of Utrecht in the Netherlands, and Martinus J. G. Veltman, retired from the University of Michigan in Ann Arbor, for work that helped explain the behavior of subatomic particles. The researchers developed a mathematical foundation for the electroweak theory. That theory, developed in the 1960's, revealed an underlying unity between electromagnetism—a force common to everyday experience—and the weak force, which governs some nuclear reactions.

One mathematical technique developed by 't Hooft and Veltman, called renormalization, enables physicists to formulate new variations of equations to eliminate the infinities that sometimes result from calculations. They also developed a mathematical technique known as non-Abelian gauge theory. The new methods pioneered by the two physicists led to the prediction of two previously unknown subatomic particles—the W and Z particles—and explained the properties of the then-undiscovered top quark, a high-energy particle created only in particle accelerators.

☐ Brian Bouldrey

Northern Ireland. The optimism that accompanied the signing of the Good Friday peace agreement in 1998 gave way to dismay in 1999, as difficulties in carrying out the terms of the agreement arose. The British Parliament finally transferred authority for local affairs to the new Northern Ireland Assembly on December 2, more than 19 months after the Good Friday agreement.

The Good Friday agreement sought to end years of conflict between unionists, who favored the union of Northern Ireland with Great Britain, and nationalists, who favored the union of Northern Ireland with Ireland. Under the agreement, Northern Ireland was to remain part of the United Kingdom unless a majority of Northern Ireland's people voted for a change. Ireland was to play a role in the north's affairs by sending representatives to a newly created Northern Ireland Assembly. Unofficial military groups, including the Irish Republican Army (IRA)—which sought to unite Northern Ireland with Ireland—were to surrender weapons within two years.

A youth in Portadown, Northern Ireland, throws rocks during a riot in March 1999, following the funeral of a Catholic human rights lawyer murdered by a Protestant. The violence erupted as disagreements over terms stalled the Good Friday peace accord.

Decommissioning. In 1999, the decommissioning, or surrender, of weapons was a stumbling block in the peace effort. The IRA and its political wing, Sinn Fein, refused to set a date for the decommissioning. The Ulster Unionist Party—Northern Ireland's largest political party—refused to allow Sinn Fein to take its seats in the Northern Ireland Assembly until the IRA had given up its weapons. Mo Mowlam, the British Secretary of State for Northern Ireland, delayed the opening of the assembly several times in an attempt to break the deadlock. The Unionists became increasingly distrustful of Mowlam, who had been praised for her earlier role in the cease-fire.

Gridlock breaks. Annual summer marches by members of the Orange Order, a 200-year-old Protestant organization, through Roman Catholic neighborhoods in Belfast and other areas were conducted with relatively little violence in July. In an attempt to renew the peace process, British Prime Minister Tony Blair replaced Mowlam with Peter Mandleson in October. Former United States Senator George Mitchell, who had chaired the earlier talks that led to the cease-fire in 1998, returned for further talks.

On Nov. 16, 1999, Sinn Fein accepted decommissioning as a key to the peace process. The next day, the IRA promised to begin turning over its weapons once the new assembly was created. On November 27, the Ulster Unionist Party abandoned its insistence that the IRA decommission before Sinn Fein could join the assembly. A cabinet for Northern Ireland was elected November 29, and a ceremony marking the transfer of power took place on December 2.   □Rohan McWilliam

See also **Ireland; United Kingdom.**

Northwest territories. See **Canadian territories.**

Norway struggled in 1999 to cope with the worldwide move toward a global economy. Kvaerner ASA, one of Norway's largest companies, announced in April that it would sell its shipbuilding business and other unprofitable operations and reduce its work force by one-third, or 25,000 workers. The restructuring was one of the largest ever announced by a European company and was intended to restore profitability at Kvaerner, which had struggled with heavy debts since acquiring the British shipbuilding company Trafalgar House Plc in 1996.

The government of Norway tried to protect major Norwegian companies from foreign take-overs in 1999. Norsk Hydro ASA and Statoil, Norway's state-owned oil companies, agreed in June to buy the private company Saga Petroleum ASA for $4.9 billion after Elf Aquitaine SA of France bid for Saga. In September, the government stated it may oppose a $3.1-billion takeover offer from MeritaNordbanken Oyj, a Finnish-Swedish bank, for Christiania Bank, Norway's second-largest bank. The ownership of Christiania was to be resolved in 2000. In December, a proposed merger of the state-owned telephone company, Telenor, with Telia, the telephone company of Sweden, collapsed over disagreements on the location of the new company's headquarters.

Norway's economy slowed sharply during 1999, because of $1.7 billion in tax increases and spending cuts designed to prevent inflation. The country's gross domestic product (the value of all goods and services produced) was expected to grow by just 0.5 percent in 1999.   □ Tom Buerkle

See also **Europe.**

Nova Scotia. See Canadian provinces.
Nuclear energy. See Energy supply.
Nutrition. See Food.

TIME CAPSULE   1940

NORWAY

THERE WERE A FEW NORWEGIANS, but only a few, who sought personal advancement by conspiring with the Nazis. One of these was Major Vidkun Quisling, who came back from Germany to Norway just before the invasion. He organized a tiny pro-Nazi party, called *Nasjonal Samling*, and was rewarded for his treachery by being made political leader in the Nazi administration of the country.

Ocean. The tropical Pacific Ocean temperatures in 1999 remained relatively stable, though somewhat on the cool side, compared with the El Niño and La Niña years of 1997 and 1998. El Niño is a warming of tropical Pacific waters, which occurs every three to seven years. La Niña is the periodic cooling of the same waters.

Missing icebergs. A possible sign of global warming was reported in July 1999 by the International Ice Patrol (IIP), part of the United States Coast Guard. The IIP announced that it had detected no icebergs in the Grand Banks shipping lanes, which located just south of Newfoundland, Canada, for the first time in 85 years. This area, known as "Iceberg Alley," is normally studded in July with icebergs that drift south from the Arctic.

Global warming is an increase in the average temperature of Earth's surface. Many scientists believe that such an increase is being caused by human activities, particularly the burning of fossil fuels, which release *greenhouse gases* into the atmosphere. These gases, most notably carbon dioxide, trap solar heat near the planet's surface.

Seas are less salty. In another possible sign of global warming, oceanographers at the Antarctic Cooperative Research Center and University of Tasmania, both in Hobart, Australia, reported in July that seawater in the Indian and Pacific oceans between 1,600 and 3,300 feet (500 and 1,000 meters) deep had become less salty since the late 1970's. Most climate-change models predict that atmospheric warming will result in more rain and snow at *high latitudes* (areas closer to the planet's poles). This increased precipitation would dilute the surface waters, which would eventually sink and spread toward the equator, making the seas less salty.

The Australian researchers claimed their studies provided the first clear evidence that greenhouse gases were seriously affecting the cycle of water on Earth. Other scientists countered that the factors found by the Australian researchers could be the result of natural climate variation.

Coral bleaching. Ove Hoegh-Guldberg, director of the Coral Reef Research Institute at the University of Sydney in Australia, warned in July 1999 that coral bleaching events, in which corals turn white and die, were likely to occur annually in most tropical oceans by 2030. Hoegh-Guldberg further predicted that coral reefs "could be eliminated from most areas by 2100" due to rising sea's surface temperatures.

Corals are limestone formations made by millions of tiny animals, called coral polyps, which depend on food manufactured and released by algae called zooxanthellae. Scientists believe that increased water temperatures can kill zooxanthellae, resulting in coral bleaching.

Jesse Owens of the United States turns in the outstanding performance of the 1936 Olympic Games, held in Germany. Owens won the 100-meter dash, the 200-meter dash, the broad jump, and the final leg of the winning 400-meter relay race.

Scientists have used satellite observations since the early 1980's to document rising sea temperatures. This data showed that sea surface temperatures in 1998 were the highest yet recorded.

A number of other scientists remained skeptical about Hoegh-Guldberg's conclusions. They believed that coral animals can probably adapt to warmer conditions. Nonetheless, even these scientists agreed that 1998 was the worst year yet for coral bleaching.

A landmark conference of marine scientists—the First International Conference on the Ocean Observing System for Climate—was convened in October 1999 in St. Raphael, France. Scientists at the meeting discussed an international project underway in 1999 to establish a worldwide system of satellites, ships, and floating sensors to collect a constant stream of data on temperature, currents, and other factors from the world's oceans. When the system is completed in the early 2000's, it will enable oceanographers to collect near "real-time" data on global ocean conditions—much like meteorologists collect information on weather conditions from a worldwide system of weather-reporting stations.

□ Arthur G. Alexiou

Ohio. See State government.
Oklahoma. See State government.
Old age. See Social security.

Olympic Games. On Jan. 24, 1999, a panel of inquiry formed by the International Olympic Committee (IOC) voted to expel six delegates who had accepted more than $440,000 in bribes and illicit gifts in exchange for awarding the 2002 Winter Olympics to Salt Lake City, Utah. The scandal—the biggest in the 105-year history of the IOC—first broke in December 1998. While an additional three members resigned in the wake of the scandal, sports writers familiar with IOC procedures did not expect the committee to make meaningful reforms. After the scandal initially broke in the press, additional reports surfaced of the bribing of IOC members by representatives of other cities, including Nagano, Japan, which hosted the 1998 Winter Olympics, and Sydney, Australia, site of the 2000 Summer Games.

In June 1999, the IOC turned down a bid by Sion, Switzerland, the perceived leading candidate to host the 2006 Winter Olympics, and awarded the 2006 games to Turin, Italy. Some observers suggested that the IOC's decision was colored by the fact that it had been a Swiss IOC member who first blew the whistle on the bribing of IOC members. □ Ron Reid

Oman. See Middle East.
Ontario. See Canadian provinces.
Opera. See Classical music.
Oregon. See State government.

Pacific Islands. In September 1999, the United Nations (UN) admitted the Pacific Island nations of Kiribati, Nauru, and Tonga as member states. The new members increased Pacific Islands representation in the UN to 11 nations.

South Pacific Games. The 11th South Pacific Games were held in Guam in May and June. Twenty-one island countries and territories competed for 14 days. The French territory of New Caledonia captured the most medals, a total of 170. Tiny Nauru, which won all 27 of its gold medals in weightlifting categories, placed third in total number of gold medals. The next games were scheduled to be held in Fiji in 2003.

Fiji. In May 1999, Fiji voters cast their ballots in the first general election since a new constitution went into effect in 1997. The Fiji Labour Party won a majority of seats in parliament, and Ma-

hendra Chaudhry, the party's leader, was chosen prime minister. Chaudhry, a grandson of indentured laborers from India, became the first Indo-Fijian prime minister in the nation's history.

Solomon Islands. Ethnic conflicts troubled the Solomon Islands throughout 1999. A militant group called the Guadalcanal Revolutionary Army —composed of members of Guadalcanal Island's native ethnic group—used violence to drive ethnic Malaitans from their homes. The Malaitans, in search of better jobs, began immigrating to Guadalcanal in the 1960's from Malaita, one of the nation's largest islands. The militants perceived the Malaitans as a threat to their land, traditions, and economic opportunities. Violence in 1999 caused the death of at least 10 people and forced more than 10,000 Malaitans to flee Guadalcanal.

In June 1999, the Commonwealth of Nations

 Facts in brief on Pacific Island countries

Country	Population	Government	Monetary unit*	Foreign trade (million U.S.$) Exports†	Imports†
Australia	19,222,000	Governor General William Deane; Prime Minister John Howard	dollar (1.52 = $1)	55,896	64,668
Fiji	845,000	President Ratu Sir Kamisese Mara; Prime Minister Mahendra Chaudhry	dollar (1.95 = $1)	589	965
Kiribati	87,000	President Teburoro Tito	Australian dollar	7	37
Marshall Islands	63,000	President Imata Kabua	U.S. dollar	18	72
Micronesia, Federated States of	144,000	President Leo A. Falcam	U.S. dollar	73	168
Nauru	12,000	President Rene Harris	Australian dollar	25	21
New Zealand	3,759,000	Governor General Sir Michael Hardie-Boys; Prime Minister Helen Clark	dollar (1.94 = $1)	12,074	12,499
Palau	19,000	President Kuniwo Nakamura	U.S. dollar	14	72
Papua New Guinea	4,809,000	Governor General Sir Silas Atopare; Prime Minister Sir Mekere Morauta	kina (2.89 = $1)	1,667	1,189
Samoa	222,000	Head of State Malietoa Tanumafili II; Prime Minister Tuila'epa Sailele Malielegaoi	tala (3.03 = $1)	15	97
Solomon Islands	444,000	Governor General Father John Lapli; Prime Minister Bartholomew Ulufa'alu	dollar (5.06 = $1)	184	151
Tonga	107,000	King Taufa'ahau Tupou IV; Prime Minister Baron Vaea	pa'anga (1.60 = $1)	12	79
Tuvalu	10,000	Governor General Sir Tomasi Puapua; Prime Minister Ionatana Ionatana	Australian dollar	1	4
Vanuatu	192,000	President Father John Bani Prime Minister Donald Kalpokas	vatu (127.33 = $1)	35	94

*Exchange rates as of Oct. 8, 1999, or latest available data.
†Latest available data.

U.S. Marines raise the American flag on Iwo Jima in 1945, after retaking the island from the Japanese in one of the fiercest battles of World War II.

ter Luagalau Levaula Kamu was assassinated at the 20th anniversary celebration of the governing Human Rights Protection Party. The son of the previous Public Works Minister Leafa Vitale was arrested, convicted, and sentenced to death for the murder.

Prime Minister Tuila'epa Sailele Malielegaoi reported that budget and taxation measures appeared to be spurring economic growth after years of deficits. The policies were initiated when he was finance minister under former Prime Minister Tofilau Eti.

Tuvalu. Prime Minister Bikenibeu Paeniu was ousted by a no-confidence vote in Parliament on April 13. Disappointment over the failure of an Internet deal, which had been expected to bring millions of dollars to Tuvalu, contributed to the ouster. On April 26, Parliament elected Ionatana Ionatana as the new prime minister.

Marshall Islands. After five years of experimental pearl oyster farming, a private firm, Black Pearls of Micronesia, announced in August that it had succeeded in producing black pearls of high quality and would begin commercial production. The firm planned to develop a multimillion-dollar pearl industry with hundreds of employees, like that of French Polynesia.

☐ Eugene Ogan

Painting. See Art.

appointed Sitiveni Rabuka, the former prime minister of Fiji, as an envoy to the Solomon Islands. (The Commonwealth is an association of states that have lived under British law and government.) Rabuka negotiated a peace pact that was signed by the representatives of the militants, the national government, and the provincial governments of Guadalcanal and Malaita. Peacekeeping forces from Fiji and Vanuatu moved into the Solomons in October to speed disarmament.

Papua New Guinea. Sir Mekere Morauta took office as prime minister of Papua New Guinea on July 14. Michael Somare, the country's first prime minister, regarded Sir Mekere's long experience in banking and finance as an important asset in accomplishing financial reforms. Despite Papua New Guinea's rich natural resources, especially minerals, the country experienced serious financial problems in 1999. The national currency, the kina, dropped to its lowest level in history, inflation climbed to 22 percent, and domestic debt was an estimated Australian $1.2 billion.

The peaceful restoration of government and public service proceeded slowly in 1999 on the island of Bougainville, where a peace accord signed in 1998 remained in effect. Objections to a copper mine on the island had led to attempts to secede from Papua New Guinea and to armed conflict.

Samoa. On July 16, 1999, Public Works Minis-

Pakistan. General Pervez Musharraf, chief of the army, seized power in Pakistan in a bloodless *coup d'etat* (overthrow) on Oct. 12, 1999. In a TV broadcast, the general said that Prime Minister Nawaz Sharif, in office for 31 months, had tried to politicize the armed forces and "systematically destroyed" the country's other institutions. Musharraf named himself "chief executive" and set up a National Security Council of generals and civilians to rule with him. He placed Prime Minister Sharif under house arrest.

"State of emergency." Musharraf declared a "state of emergency" on October 15, suspending the constitution and dismissing the parliament. He promised to pursue those "guilty of plundering and looting the national wealth."

Musharraf's government published lists of prominent Pakistanis who owed large sums of money on government-sponsored loans and imposed a mid-November deadline for repayment. Bankers later reported that of the $4.2 billion owed to the government or in default, borrowers had repaid only 1 percent. On November 17, the government arrested 21 prominent citizens on corruption charges.

On November 19, authorities charged Nawaz Sharif with treason, hijacking, and conspiracy to commit murder. Musharraf alleged that the prime minister had tried to hinder the landing of a plane on which the general and others were returning from Sri Lanka on October 12.

Relations with India. Days after seizing power, General Musharraf announced a new policy of military de-escalation along the border with India. The pullback did not extend to the disputed "Line of Control" that separates Pakistani- and Indian-held areas in Kashmir.

Fierce fighting occurred in Kashmir in mid-1999 between Indian troops and Muslim forces that India claimed were backed by Pakistan. Under international pressure in July, Sharif agreed to a withdrawal of the Muslim forces from Indian-held areas. Domestic critics called Sharif's action a "sellout."

Economy. According to Finance Minister Shaukat Aziz, Pakistan in 1999 paid 57 percent of its budget to service its debt and most of the rest on defense. Musharraf's government promised to make debt reduction its highest priority.

Benazir Bhutto, a former prime minister of Pakistan who was removed from office twice on corruption charges, was convicted in absentia on April 15 of taking kickbacks and sentenced to five years in prison. Her husband, already in jail in Pakistan, was similarly convicted and sentenced. Benazir Bhutto, who lived outside Pakistan, denied the charges. □ Henry S. Bradsher

See also **Asia; India.**

Paleontology.
Scientists reported several new discoveries from the ancient lake-bed sediments of the Yixian Formation at Liaoning, China, in 1999. Since the mid-1990's, these sediments have yielded fossil remains of what may have been feathered dinosaurs, primitive birds, and one of the world's oldest flowering plants.

Yixian deposits dated. In July 1999, geologist Carl Swisher of the Berkeley Geochronology Center in California and four Chinese colleagues clarified the age of the Yixian fossil deposits. The researchers used *radioisotope analysis,* a dating method based on the rate of decay of the *isotope* (form of a chemical element) potassium 40, to date volcanic ash beds in the deposits from 120 to 125 million years ago. The deposits originated in the early Cretaceous Period (138 million to 65 million years ago), a time later than expected by some paleontologists. The primitive nature of the Liaoning fossils had led some scientists to suspect that the deposits dated from the late Jurassic Period (205 million to 138 million years ago).

Oldest mammal. In March, paleontologists reported that they had found a beautifully preserved mammal fossil in the Yixian beds. The specimen was at least 120 million years old, making it the oldest-known complete skeleton of a mammal. Researchers Ji Qiang and Ji Shu-An of the National Geological Museum of China, and

University of Chicago paleontologist Paul Sereno unveils the model of a newly discovered dinosaur, *Jobaria tiguidensis,* in November at the National Geographic Society headquarters in Washington, D.C. The *Jobaria,* named after a mythical Nigerian monster, was 70 feet (21 meters) long. A plant eater, it could rear up on its hind legs to eat treetop leaves.

Luo Zexi of the Carnegie Museum of Natural History in Pittsburgh, Pennsylvania, said the animal, dubbed *Jeholodens jenkinsi*, was the size of a rat, with straight, mammallike forelegs and *splayed* (spread to the sides), reptilian hind legs.

More feathered dinosaurs? A number of dinosaur fossils with impressions resembling feathers were reported from Liaoning in 1999. In May, a research team led by paleontologist Xu Xing of China's Institute of Vertebrate Paleontology and Paleoanthropology published a report on *Beipiaosaurus inexpectus*, a small, plant-eating dinosaur. The *Beipiaosaurus* specimen showed frilly, filamentlike projections arising from the dinosaur's body. These projections may have been an early type of feather. In September, Xu and his colleagues described another dinosaur from Liaoning—*Sinornithosaurus millenii. Sinornithosaurus* had what looked like short, downy feathers and a birdlike skeleton. Paleontologists believed that the rudimentary nature of the feathers on *Beipiao-saurus* and *Sinornithosaurus* probably prevented these dinosaurs from flying.

In October, a group of paleontologists that included Philip Currie of the Royal Tyrrell Museum in Canada reported on a Liaoning dinosaur that may have been able to fly. The dinosaur, *Archaeoraptor liaoningensis,* had forearms resembling wings with a full set of feathers. The animal also had a birdlike shoulder girdle and breast bone.

Warm-blooded vs. cold-blooded. The best preserved dinosaur fossil ever found, *Scipionyx samniticus*, revealed new information in 1999 in the long-standing debate over whether dinosaurs were warm-blooded or cold-blooded. Warm-blooded animals, like mammals and birds, have complex lungs and are able to control their body temperature regardless of the outside temperature. Cold-blooded animals, like reptiles and amphibians, have simple lungs, and their body temperature is dependent on the outside temperature. *S. samniticus* was found in Italy in the 1980's, but it was not identified until 1998.

Researchers led by respiratory physiologist John Ruben of Oregon State University in Corvallis announced in January that they had studied the *Scipionyx* specimen using ultraviolet (UV) light. The UV light allowed the scientists to view the preserved outlines of internal organs in the 100-million-year-old fossil. The researchers observed that the lungs were simpler than those of birds and other warm-blooded animals, supporting the theory that dinosaurs were cold-blooded. However, the scientists also found that *Scipionyx* had a large liver that was attached by a muscle to its *pelvis* (hip bone).

Ruben and his colleagues concluded that this arrangement of organs probably enabled the liver to act as a pump piston, drawing rapid bursts of air into the lungs. While the lungs were simple compared with those of birds, they may have been capable of pulling in enough oxygen to maintain bursts of intense activity. This new twist on the warm-blooded-cold-blooded debate implied that dinosaurs may have had a unique physiology with elements of each of the two basic types common in animals today.

Prehistoric insects and climate. One of the first attempts to relate prehistoric climate to interactions between plants and insects was reported in June. Paleobiologists Peter Wilf and Conrad LaBandeira of the Smithsonian Institution in Washington, D.C., examined hundreds of fossil leaves preserved in Wyoming lake sediments for evidence of insects, such as bite marks. The sediments dated from the late Paleocene Epoch (65 million to 58 million years ago) to the early Eocene Epoch (58 million to 38 million years ago), during a time of gradual warming in Earth's climate.

The scientists found a greater number and variety of insect attacks on the leaves from the warmer period than on those from the cooler period. This evidence appeared to support the theory that there is a direct correlation between a warming of climate and an increase in the population of insects. ☐ Carlton E. Brett

See also **Biology.**

Pan American Games.
Winnipeg, Canada, hosted the 13th Pan American Games from July 23 through Aug. 8, 1999. The games were the largest sporting event ever held in Canada. More than 5,000 athletes from Central America, the Caribbean, and North and South America competed in 330 events.

The United States team led the games with 106 gold medals, nearly one-third of the number awarded, and topped the overall medal total with 296. Canada won 196 medals, including 64 golds, while Cuba took 69 gold medals among 156 overall. The Games turned into a major embarrassment for Cuba when 11 athletes, a softball coach, and a journalist from the island nation defected, all seeking political asylum.

Seven athletes tested positive for banned drugs at Winnipeg. The most prominent was Cuba's Javier Sotomayor, the world record holder in the high jump (8 feet, ½ inch [2.48 meters]) and the only high-jumper ever to clear 8 feet (2.44 meters). Officials said Sotomayor tested positive for cocaine after he had cleared 7 feet, 6½ inches (2.3 meters) to become the first athlete to win an event in four consecutive Pan American Games. Sotomayor, who claimed to be the victim of an attempt to disgrace the government of Cuba, had his medal taken from him. ☐ Ron Reid

See also **Sports; Track and field.**

The United States, which operated the Panama Canal for 85 years, transferred control of the canal and U.S. military bases along the waterway to Panama on Dec. 31, 1999, following a ceremonial transfer on December 14. The U.S. government began construction of the Panama Canal in 1903.

Panama.

Panama. On Sept. 1, 1999, Mireya Elisa Moscoso de Grubar of the conservative Arnulfista Party was sworn in for a five-year term as Panama's president. She was the first woman to lead the nation. In her inaugural address, Moscoso pledged that her administration would manage the Panama Canal in such a way as to benefit all Panamanians, especially the poor.

Panama Canal transfer. On December 31, the United States transferred to Panama the ownership and operation of the Panama Canal. The United States also relinquished property worth $4 billion that had been used for the operation and defense of the canal. The United States had taken control of an area called the Panama Canal Zone in 1903, when construction began on the 50-mile

(80-kilometer) waterway linking the Pacific Ocean and the Gulf of Mexico. In a 1977 treaty between the two nations, the United States agreed to relinquish its claims on the Canal Zone in 1979 and to hand over the canal itself in 1999.

On December 14, former U.S. President Jimmy Carter, whose administration negotiated the treaty, attended the ceremonial transfer of the canal. President Moscoso used the occasion to assure the United States that the canal would "continue offering safe, efficient, and competitive services to the international maritime community."

Plans to develop the Canal Zone. Throughout 1999, Panamanian authorities developed ambitious plans for the Canal Zone to make up for the loss of an estimated annual revenue of $350

million from U.S. military bases. In December, the Sol Melia, a 310-room hotel, opened its doors in the facilities formerly occupied by the School of the Americas, where the U.S. government trained military officers from Latin America.

Work was also under way on the Gamboa Tropical Rainforest Resort, a 91-acre (37-hectare) complex about midway along the canal on the banks of the Chagres River. Scheduled to open in 2000, the $25-million facility was designed to include a 100-room hotel, a marina for fishermen, rain forest trails, and tours for bird-watching enthusiasts.

Visa scheme. In June 1999, Panama's government dismissed Intelligence Chief Samantha Smith after U.S. authorities alleged that she had sold Panamanian visas for as much as $15,000 apiece to Chinese citizens seeking illegal entry into the United States. The visas allowed the Chinese to travel north through Central America and enter the United States unlawfully. Smith claimed that she had acted under direct orders from outgoing President Ernesto Perez Balladares. In November, U.S. authorities revoked Balladares's visa to visit the United States.   □ Nathan A. Haverstock

See also **Latin America; People in the news** (Moscoso, Mireya).

Papua New Guinea. See Asia; Pacific Islands.

Paraguay. On March 28, 1999, Luis Gonzalez Macchi, head of Paraguay's senate, was sworn in as president after several days of violence and political unrest. On March 23, Vice President Luis Maria Argana and his driver were killed by gunmen in Asuncion, the capital. Argana, a political rival of President Raul Cubas Grau, had condemned the president's pardon of General Lino Cesar Oviedo, who had been sentenced in 1998 to 10 years in prison for an attempted military takeover in 1996.

The day after Argana's assassination, the Paraguayan Congress voted to begin impeachment proceedings against the president. On March 28, 1999, Cubas Grau resigned, bowing to the demands of angry mobs in Asuncion and diplomatic pressure from the ambassadors of Brazil, the United States, and the Vatican in Rome.

Oviedo, who Paraguayan officials believed was behind Argana's assassination, was granted political asylum in Argentina, where he remained for more than eight months despite repeated Paraguayan demands for his extradition to stand trial. Oviedo secretly returned to Paraguay in December. From an undisclosed location, he vowed to clear his name and to campaign for the presidency in 2003.   □ Nathan A. Haverstock

See also **Latin America.**

Pennsylvania. See Philadelphia; State government.

■ People in the news

in 1999 included those listed below, who were all Americans unless otherwise indicated.

Abdullah II (1962–) became king of Jordan on Feb. 7, 1999, after the death of his father, King Hussein. Two weeks earlier, the late king had removed his brother, Prince Hassan, from the line of succession and named Abdullah, his eldest son, heir to the throne.

Abdullah was among a handful of younger Western-educated, technology-oriented Arab leaders to come to power in the late 1990's. In the first month of his reign, the Jordanian king reshuffled his cabinet, appointing ministers known for backing market reforms and Middle East peace efforts. He sought aid and debt reduction among wealthy nations, including the United Kingdom and the United States.

Political observers noted that Abdullah demonstrated concern for his subjects, many of whom suffered the hardships of a debt-burdened economy. On several occasions, he reportedly donned disguises and went out among the people to see their condition for himself.

Abdullah bin Al-Hussein was born on Jan. 30, 1962, to King Hussein and his second, British-born wife, Antoinette Gardiner, who is known as Princess Muna. Abdullah was educated in Great Britain and the United States. As a career officer in the Jordanian army, he held the rank of major general. The king is married to Queen Rania.

See also **Jordan.**

Armstrong, Lance (1971–), won the 86th Tour de France, the world's most prestigious cycling competition, on July 25, 1999. Armstrong was only the second American to win the 2,290-mile (3,690-kilometer) race.

Armstrong's victory completed a comeback from a near-fatal bout of cancer. In 1996, doctors told Armstrong that he had advanced testicular cancer that had spread to other organs. He underwent brain and lung surgery and 12 weeks of intensive chemotherapy. A year later, tests showed no signs of cancer, and physicians pronounced Armstrong cured. The young athlete founded the Lance Armstrong Foundation to promote cancer awareness and provide support to cancer survivors.

Armstrong was raised in the Dallas, Texas, area. He began his amateur athletic career competing in triathlons, combination races that include swimming, cycling, and running. He captured the U.S. junior triathlon sprint title at age 16. He eventually turned to regular cycling competition. Armstrong won the U.S. amateur cycling title in 1991 and the world road-racing championship in 1993.

See also **Sports.**

King Abdullah II
of Jordan

Barak, Ehud

Barak, Ehud (1942–), head of Israel's Labor Party, was elected prime minister of Israel on May 17, 1999, defeating Prime Minister Benjamin Netanyahu of the conservative Likud Party. Barak took office on July 7.

Israel's new prime minister was born Ehud Brog on a *kibbutz* (collective farm) near Tel Aviv, Israel, on Feb. 12, 1942. His parents had fled persecution in Eastern Europe in the 1930's. Ehud, during his childhood, developed a reputation as an avid reader, a serious piano student, and a gifted mechanic. In 1959, he joined the Israeli Army and took the last name of Barak, which means *lightning* in Hebrew. Later, Barak earned degrees at Hebrew University in Jerusalem and at Stanford University in Stanford, California.

Barak rose quickly through the ranks of the Israeli Army, specializing in commando raids, such as a 1972 assault on Palestinian hijackers at the Tel Aviv airport. In 1991, he was appointed chief of staff of the Israeli Army. Sponsored by the late Prime Minister Yitzhak Rabin, Barak entered politics in the mid-1990's. After Labor's 1996 defeat, Barak took control of party leadership.

According to political observers, Barak faced a twofold challenge: to bring together the polarized Israeli public and to safeguard Israeli security while pursuing peace. He met Arab leaders at the funeral of Morocco's King Hassan in July and set a 15-month timetable for working out an Israeli-Palestinian peace plan. Barak also resumed peace negotiations with Syria, which had been stalled since the 1996 election of Netanyahu.

See also **Israel; Middle East; Syria.**

Benigni, Roberto

Benigni, Roberto (1952–), won the Academy Award for best actor and for best foreign-language film in 1999 for *Life Is Beautiful (La Vita e bella)*. Benigni co-wrote, directed, and starred in the film, a bittersweet comedy about an Italian Jewish family's struggle to survive in a Nazi concentration camp during World War II (1939-1945). Benigni also won the Screen Actors Guild Award and other prestigious film awards throughout the world for his role in the film. In 1998, *Life Is Beautiful* captured the Cannes Film Festival Grand Prix.

Benigni gained celebrity status in Italy in the early 1990's, but *Life Is Beautiful* made him an international sensation. The movie achieved the biggest box-office success of any Italian-language film ever released in the United States.

Benigni was born on Oct. 27, 1952, in the Tuscany region of Italy. When he was a boy, his family sent him to a seminary in Florence to prepare for the Roman Catholic priesthood, but he ran away and joined a circus. Later in his teens, he joined a comedy troupe in Rome. Benigni began making movies in the late 1970's, appeared on Italian TV, and became known to the Italian public as a master of comedy.

See also **Motion pictures.**

Bradley, Bill

Bradley, Bill (1943–), a former United States senator, declared his candidacy for president on Sept. 8, 1999. His entry into the race placed him in competition with Vice President Al

U.S. presidential candidate Bill Bradley

Eileen Collins, space
shuttle commander

Gore for the Democratic nomination.

Bradley represented New Jersey in the U.S. Senate for 18 years, beginning in 1979. Political observers credited Bradley for helping to enact the Tax Reform Act of 1986, which sharply reduced tax rates and eliminated most tax shelters. Bradley resigned from his Senate seat in 1996, declaring politics "broken." In Bradley's presidential bid, he pledged to work for government reforms, including changes in campaign financing regulations.

William W. Bradley grew up in Crystal City, Missouri, excelling in academics and basketball. He graduated with honors from Princeton University in 1965, the same year he was named College Player of the Year by the National Association of Basketball Coaches. Bradley then accepted a Rhodes scholarship to study at Oxford University in England. In 1967, he joined the New York Knicks basketball team, which won two National Basketball Association championships during his career. Bradley retired from professional sports in 1977. He wrote several books, including a memoir of his career in professional basketball.

See also **Democratic Party.**

Bush, George Walker (1946–), announced his candidacy for the Republican nomination for president on June 12, 1999. Bush, the oldest son of former President George Bush and Barbara Bush, assumed front-runner status for the nomination soon after his landslide reelection as Texas governor in November 1998.

In his first term as governor, George W. Bush and the Democratic-controlled legislature cooperated to pass a major legislative program. Bush signed into law a bill for *tort reform* (a revision of the rules for bringing lawsuits in court), a welfare reform act, a measure to give more authority to local school systems, and a tougher juvenile justice law. In his reelection bid, Governor Bush received endorsements from many Democratic state officials, including the lieutenant governor.

Bush was born in New Haven, Connecticut, but grew up in Texas, where his family moved when he was 2 years old. He graduated from Yale University in New Haven, Connecticut, in 1968 and served in the Texas Air National Guard. Bush entered the Texas oil business in the mid-1970's. In 1989, he became a partner in the Texas Rangers professional baseball team but sold his share before beginning his first term as governor in 1994.

See also **Republican Party.**

Chavez, Hugo (1954–), was sworn in as president of Venezuela on Feb. 2, 1999, after winning a landslide victory in December 1998. From 1992 to 1994, Chavez, a former army colonel, had been imprisoned for staging a *coup* (overthrow) against the Venezuelan government.

During the presidential campaigns of 1998, Chavez called for sweeping constitutional reforms. After taking office, he led Venezuela into what many observers considered a constitutional crisis. In April 1999, voters approved Chavez's referendum calling for a revision of the Constitution. In July, voters elected the 131-member National Constituent Assembly, a strongly pro-Chavez group, to rewrite the Constitution.

The new assembly met in early August, and Chavez retook his presidential oath, reportedly to underline the authority of the office. A power struggle developed between the assembly and the existing congress, which functioned under provisions of the 1961 Constitution. In quick succession, the National Constituent Assembly established control over the courts and greatly reduced the independence and powers of Congress. Venezuel's voters approved a new Constitution on Dec. 15, 1999.

Hugo Rafael Chavez Frias was raised in the Venezuelan state of Barinas. He graduated from the Venezuela Military Academy in 1975. In 1982, he founded the Bolivarian Revolutionary Movement, which participated in the 1992 coup attempt.

See also **Latin America; Venezuela.**

Collins, Eileen (1956–), commanded the space shuttle Columbia in July 1999. She was the first woman to command a shuttle mission for the National Aeronautics and Space Administration (NASA). The mission accomplished its primary

goal—to place the $1.5-billion Chandra X-ray telescope into orbit around the Earth.

Eileen Collins grew up in Elmira, New York. As a teen-ager, she worked part-time jobs to save money for flying lessons. Collins earned a math degree at Syracuse University in Syracuse, New York, in 1978, intending to teach high school. Her career plans changed when she was accepted into the U.S. Air Force pilot training program. In 1979, Collins became the first female flight instructor in the U.S. Air Force. She taught mathematics at the Air Force Academy in Colorado Springs, Colorado, from 1986 to 1989.

Collins was selected to enter NASA's astronaut program in 1990. In 1995, she became the first woman to pilot a space shuttle. In 1997, she piloted the shuttle Atlantis on its mission to link up with the Russian space station, Mir.

See also **Space exploration.**

DeLay, Tom (1947–), a Texas congressman and the majority whip of the United States House of Representatives, became, according to political observers, the most powerful Republican in the U.S. Congress in 1999. Although DeLay's position in the House made him second in the ranks of House Republican leaders, he was often perceived as a stronger force than the first-ranked Republican, Speaker of the House Dennis Hastert.

In late 1998, DeLay survived political upheavals that brought down other Republican leaders—most notably, former Speaker Newt Gingrich. In December 1998, DeLay led the Republican majority in the House toward an impeachment vote against President Bill Clinton, even though his par-

U.S. Speaker of the House Dennis Hastert

ty had suffered losses in the November election. In April 1999, DeLay led a Republican majority vote against President Clinton's policy on military action in the Serbian province of Kosovo—a policy that Speaker Dennis Hastert had supported.

Thomas D. DeLay was born in Laredo, Texas. He earned a biology degree from Houston University in 1970 and ran a pest-control business for many years. DeLay served in the Texas Legislature from 1978 to 1984. Since his election to the U.S. Congress in 1984, DeLay has held conservative positions on such issues as federal regulations of commerce, environmental protection, welfare reform, gun control, and defense spending.

See also **Congress of the United States; Republican Party; United States, President of the.**

Dench, Dame Judi (1934–), won the Academy Award for best supporting actress in 1999 for her portrayal of Queen Elizabeth I in *Shakespeare in Love.* She also received the 1999 Antoinette Perry (Tony) Award for best actress in the Broadway production of *Amy's View,* a play by David Hare.

Dench was born in York, England, and attended the Central School of Speech and Drama in London. Her acting career on stage, film, and television has spanned more than 40 years. In 1957, she made her stage debut at the Old Vic theater in London as Ophelia in Shakespeare's *Hamlet.* Dench eventually performed in stage and film productions of most of Shakespeare's plays. She also

Judi Dench, actress

played many classic stage roles in the works of such playwrights as Anton Chekhov (1860-1904), Oscar Wilde (1854-1900), and Noel Coward (1899-1973). She performed in numerous contemporary plays, including Hugh Whitemore's *Pack of Lies* (1983) and a 1995 revival of Stephen Sondheim's *A Little Night Music* (1973). Her TV career included the British situation comedies "A Fine Romance" and "As Time Goes By."

Dench has garnered many acting awards, including five presentations of the London stage's Laurence Olivier Award. She received a Golden Globe award for best actress in a drama and an Academy Award nomination for her portrayal of Queen Victoria in the film *Mrs. Brown* (1997). She was made a Dame Commander of the British Empire in 1988.

See also **Motion pictures; Theater.**

Richard Holbrooke, U.S. representative to the United Nations

Ecevit, Bulent (1925–), of the Democratic

Left Party, became prime minister of Turkey in January 1999 after nearly a 20-year absence from power. Ecevit had resigned the office in 1979 after serving three times as prime minister. In January 1999, Turkish President Suleyman Demirel, a political rival, asked Ecevit to form a *caretaker government,* a parliamentary group that governs until elections can be held. In April, voters upheld Ecevit's governing coalition in the Turkish Parliament.

Initially, Ecevit enjoyed high approval ratings. His government restored public confidence in the wake of scandals that had toppled former Prime Minister Mesut Yilmaz in late 1998. Ecevit, who strongly opposes political *autonomy* (self-rule) for the Kurdish region of Turkey, benefited politically when Turkish agents captured Abdullah Ocalan, a Kurdish rebel, in February 1999. Ecevit's government came under severe criticism, however, for its handling of emergency relief after a devastating earthquake struck western Turkey on August 17. In that disaster, more than 17,000 Turks perished and as many as 600,000 were left homeless.

Ecevit is a published poet, journalist, essayist, and translator. He has written many books on Turkish politics and has translated Hindu and British literature into Turkish.

See also **Greece; Middle East; Turkey.**

Hastert, J. Dennis (1942–), an Illinois

congressman, was sworn in as speaker of the United States House of Representatives on Jan. 6, 1999. Hastert was elected to the speakership in late 1998 after the resignations first of Speaker Newt Gingrich and then of his designated replacement,

Representative Robert L. Livingston of Louisiana.

Hastert held the post of deputy majority whip, the third-ranking party leader, prior to his selection as speaker. In recent years, he had worked closely with Tom DeLay, the majority whip who, according to many political observers, is the most powerful Republican in Congress. Some House Republicans expressed concern that, as speaker, Hastert would function only as a *figurehead* (head in name only). Other members believed Hastert's nonconfrontational style would heal divisions in the Republican Party.

In 1999, some political observers blamed Hastert for the failure of the Congress to support U.S. military intervention in the Serbian province of Kosovo and the failure of the Congress to pass meaningful handgun legislation. House Republicans praised Hastert, however, for securing party unity during budget negotiations.

Hastert earned a bachelor's degree in 1964 from Wheaton College in Wheaton, Illinois, and a master's degree in 1967 from Northern Illinois University in DeKalb. He taught high school and coached athletics before entering politics in 1980. He served three terms in the Illinois legislature before becoming a U.S. representative in 1987.

See also **Congress of the United States; Republican Party.**

Holbrooke, Richard (1941–), won con-

firmation from the United States Senate on Aug. 5, 1999, to serve as the U.S. representative to the United Nations (UN). The vote ended a 14-month confirmation battle between the Senate and the Clinton administration.

According to UN experts, U.S. prestige at the world organization was at an all-time low when Holbrooke assumed his position. The U.S. Congress continued to withhold $1 billion in U.S. dues. UN officials also criticized the United States for allegedly side-stepping UN authority in such crisis spots as Kosovo and Iraq. UN observers noted that Holbrooke's first challenge was to address the ill will generated by these developments.

Holbrooke graduated in 1963 from Brown University in Providence, Rhode Island. As a White House staff member during the Johnson administration in the mid-1960's, Holbrooke authored a volume of the *Pentagon Papers,* an encyclopedic document about the causes of the Vietnam War. In 1968, he went to Paris as a U.S. delegate to peace negotiations to end the Vietnam War (1957-1975). Holbrooke served in the State Department from 1977 to 1981 during the Carter administration and returned to government service when President Bill Clinton took office in 1993. In 1995, Holbrooke led negotiations in Dayton, Ohio, that ended the civil war in Bosnia-Herzegovina.

See also **Cabinet, U.S.; United Nations; Yugoslavia: A Special Report.**

Martin, Ricky (1971–), a popular Latin music singer, consolidated his superstar status in the United States when he performed at the Grammy Awards ceremony in Los Angeles on Feb. 24, 1999. Martin, whom critics and fans variously compared to Elvis Presley and Frank Sinatra, created a sensation at the ceremony with his energetic performance of "La Copa de la Vida" ("The Cup of Life"). On the same evening, Martin received the Grammy award for best Latin pop performance for his song "Vuelve" ("Return"). During 1999, his first English-language album hit number one on U.S. song charts, he appeared on the covers of *Time* and *TV GUIDE* magazines, and he made guest appearances on many TV shows.

Martin was born Enrique Jose Martin Morales IV in San Juan, Puerto Rico. He began performing in TV commercials at the age of 6. At age 12, he joined the internationally popular teen singing group, Menudo. Before turning 20, Martin launched a successful stage, TV, and film career in Mexico. In 1994, he landed a role in the ABC daytime drama, "General Hospital." Martin made his Broadway theater debut in 1996 in the musical *Les Miserables* (1985).

See also **Popular music.**

Moscoso, Mireya (1946–), of the conservative Arnulfista Party, was elected president of Panama in May 1999. Moscoso, the widow of former President Arnulfo Arias, defeated Martin Torrijos of the ruling Revolutionary Democratic Party (PRD). Torrijos's father had helped oust Arias in a 1968 *coup* (military takeover).

Moscoso, who was sworn in for a five-year term on Sept. 2, 1999, became the first woman to serve as Panama's head of state. On Dec. 14, 1999, she presided over the ceremonial

Ricky Martin, singer

turnover of the Panama Canal from the United States to Panama.

Moscoso promised during her presidential campaign to reduce the nation's poverty and unemployment. Observers noted, however, that her hands would be tied by Panama's national debt, the PRD-dominated legislature, and her own inexperience in politics.

Mireya Elisa Moscoso de Grubar grew up in poverty in a small Panamanian town. She married President Arias in 1967 and lived with him in exile in Miami, Florida, after the 1968 coup that toppled his government. After Arias's death in 1988, Moscoso returned to Panama and served in several government positions. She became head of the Arnulfista Party in 1991.

See also **Latin America; Panama.**

Obasanjo, Olusegun (1937–), took office as president of Nigeria on May 29, 1999, after winning a February election that was marred by irregularities. Obasanjo's inauguration marked the end of 16 years of military rule in Africa's most populous nation.

A former military ruler, Obasanjo had yielded power in 1979 to a democratically elected leader. He was the only military ruler in the country's history to do so voluntarily. When Obasanjo took office in 1999, Nigeria's economy was in shambles. Although the nation is a major oil producer, it experienced chronic fuel shortages. Supplies of water and electricity were undependable. Political observers credited President Obasanjo for beginning to root out corruption that reportedly caused the shortages.

Seiji Ozawa, conductor

Obasanjo was born in the city of Abeokuta on March 5, 1937, when Nigeria was still a British colony. He joined the Nigerian army in 1958 and rose quickly in the ranks. He became military leader of Nigeria after the assassination of General Murtala Mohammed in 1976. Obasanjo's peaceful transition to civilian rule in 1979 earned him both praise and condemnation among the various ethnic groups in Nigeria. From 1995 to 1998, he was imprisoned for criticizing the regime of Nigerian dictator General Sani Abachi.

See also **Africa; Nigeria.**

Ozawa, Seiji (1935–), artistic and music director of the Boston Symphony Orchestra (BSO), announced in 1999 that he would leave the orchestra in 2002 to assume the post of music director of the Vienna State Opera. Ozawa had held Boston's podium since 1973, longer than any other conductor of a major symphony orchestra.

Seiji Ozawa is credited with expanding the repertoire of the Boston Orchestra from a traditional French emphasis to include more German works and compositions of many contemporary composers. Under his direction, the BSO incorporated the works of Bohemian-born composer Gustav Mahler (1860-1911) into its programs and performed music of such modern Japanese composers as Toru Takemitsu. Born in the Chinese province of Manchuria, Ozawa was raised and educated in

President Mireya Moscoso of Panama

his parents' native Japan. In 1959, he went to Europe to study with the Austrian conductor Herbert von Karajan (1908-1989). Ozawa became assistant conductor of the New York Philharmonic in New York City in 1961. From 1965 to 1969, he conducted the Toronto Symphony Orchestra. From 1968 to 1976, he served as music director of the San Francisco Symphony Orchestra. Ozawa was named artistic director of Tanglewood, the summer festival of the BSO, in 1970 and director of the BSO in 1973.

See also **Classical music.**

Paltrow, Gwyneth (1972–), won the

Academy Award, the Golden Globe Award, and the Screen Actors Guild Award for best actress for her performance in the 1998 movie *Shakespeare in Love.* Paltrow tearfully accepted her Academy Award in Los Angeles on March 21, 1999.

Gwyneth Paltrow is the daughter of actress Blythe Danner and TV producer Bruce Paltrow. Gwyneth Paltrow's interest in acting began at an early age. When she was 2 years old, she reportedly memorized her mother's lines for a play. By her mid-20's, Paltrow had appeared in several movies and a TV miniseries, *Cruel Doubt* (1992), starring opposite her mother. Paltrow received critical acclaim for her portrayal of a young Texas con artist in *Flesh and Bone* (1993) and of the prickly heroine of *Emma* (1996), a film based on the novel by Jane Austen (1775-1817).

Born in Los Angeles, Paltrow grew up for the most part in New York City. She briefly attended the University of California at Santa Barbara before embarking on her acting career. Her film awards include the Golden Satellite Award for Best Motion Picture Actress in 1996 for *Emma* and the Special San Diego Film Critics Award for Consistent Acting Excellence in 1998.

See also **Motion pictures.**

Sosa, Sammy (1968–), an outfielder for the

Chicago Cubs, made headlines for the second year in a row in 1999, competing with Mark McGwire of the St. Louis Cardinals for most home runs during the regular season. In 1998, both players exceeded Roger Maris's 1961 record of 61 home runs in a single season. Sosa hit 66 home runs in 1998 and 63 in 1999. His 60th home run on September 18 made him the first player in history to hit 60 home runs in two consecutive seasons. McGwire hit 70 in 1998 and 65 in 1999. The Baseball Writers Association of America named Sosa the National League's Most Valuable Player in 1998.

Samuel Sosa Peralta was born in the Dominican Republic and grew up in poverty. In 1985, Sosa, at the age of 16, came to the United States to play baseball after signing a contract with the Texas Rangers. He worked his way through the minor leagues, breaking into the majors with the Rangers in 1989. Sosa was traded from the Chicago White Sox to the Chicago Cubs in 1992.

Sosa founded the Sosa Foundation in October 1997 to help the people of the Dominican Republic. In September 1998, he contributed thousands of pounds of food and bottled water to the island nation when it was ravaged by Hurricane Georges.

See also **Baseball.**

Ventura, Jesse (1951–), a former profes-

sional wrestler nicknamed "The Body," became governor of Minnesota on Jan. 4, 1999. Ventura,

Sammy Sosa, Chicago Cubs outfielder

the Reform Party candidate, won 37 percent of the votes in the November 1998 election, defeating Democrat Hubert Humphrey III and Republican Norm Coleman. Ventura's election marked the first time a candidate of the Reform Party had won a major statewide office.

Most political observers regarded Ventura as a moderate on issues such as budget, taxes, and education. The governor took more liberal positions on social issues, such as abortion and gay rights. In July 1999, Ventura succeeded in having his own candidate for Reform Party chairman, John Gargan, elected over the candidate of Ross Perot, the party's founder. Ventura's influence in the party fueled speculation about the governor's future in presidential politics.

Jesse Ventura was born James George Janos —still his legal name—in Minneapolis, Minnesota. He served in Vietnam from 1970 to 1974 in the U.S. Navy SEALS, an elite naval unit. From 1975 to 1986, he played the professional wrestling circuit and adopted his stage name. Ventura also worked as a film actor and radio talk show host. In the early 1990's, he served as mayor of Brooklyn Park, a suburb of Minneapolis.

See also **State government.**

Wahid, Abdurrahman (1940–) of
the National Awakening Party (PKB) was elected president of Indonesia on Oct. 20, 1999, by an electoral assembly that voters had chosen in June. The election marked the end of political dominance by the Golkar Party, which supported the dictatorship of former President Suharto for 32 years. In May 1998, Suharto had resigned and installed B. J. Habibie as president.

Wahid offered the vice presidency to rival presidential candidate Megawati Sukarnoputri of the Indonesian Democracy Party-Struggle. Wahid's health appeared frail in 1999 after allegedly suffering two strokes, and many observers speculated that he might not complete his five-year term. Wahid's government faced formidable challenges, including a severe recession and conflicts between pro-independence groups and pro-Indonesia militias in the province of East Timor.

Indonesians call Wahid "Gus Dur," combining a Muslim title of respect with an abbreviation of his first name. Wahid was born in the Indonesian province of East Java. He studied at Al Azhar University in Cairo, Egypt, and earned a degree in 1970 from the University of Baghdad in Iraq. As the leader of Indonesia's largest Islamic organization, Nahdlatul Ulama Muslims, Wahid advocated an inclusive, tolerant form of Islam. International human rights advocates have called Wahid a defender of human rights.

See also **Indonesia.**

Peru. The Peruvian General Workers Confederation, the nation's largest union, led a general strike on April 28, 1999, to protest President Alberto K. Fujimori's plan to run for a third term in 2000 in violation of Peru's Constitution. The union also blamed Fujimori for the political and social unrest in the Peruvian countryside, which was forcing people to move to the crowded capital, Lima.

On July 7, 1999, Peru's congress, dominated by Fujimori supporters, rejected an appeal for a new trial for four Chileans sentenced to life in prison after being convicted of terrorist acts by a Peruvian military court. The Inter-American Human Rights Court, the Costa Rica-based legal branch of the 35-nation Organization of American States, had issued the appeal. The government action was widely condemned. Former Peruvian President Alan Garcia said that Fujimori's government was marked by "brutality" and that the president should be forcibly removed.

In July, Oscar Ramirez Durand, alleged commander of the Shining Path rebel group, was captured. He was tried for terrorist activity and sentenced to life in prison. Claiming responsibility for Ramirez's capture, Fujimori announced that the high command of the terrorist organization had been "decapitated."   □ Nathan A. Haverstock

See also **Latin America.**

Petroleum and gas. See Energy supply.

Philadelphia. Democrat John F. Street was
elected to a four-year term as mayor of Philadelphia in a close vote on Nov. 2, 1999. Street, 55, had been the president of the city council for seven of the eight years that outgoing Mayor Ed Rendell held office. Street won the election with just over 50 percent of the vote. Republican candidate Sam Katz, a private consultant who specialized in arranging business partnerships between government and corporations, received almost 49 percent of the vote.

Philadelphia has not had a Republican mayor since Barney Samuel was elected in 1947. The city's registered Democrats outnumbered Republicans about four to one in 1999. Nevertheless, Street and Katz both ran competitive, hard-fought campaigns that set a spending record before Labor Day (September 6).

Campaign controversies. Mayor Rendell, who was, according to the polls, the most popular leader in Philadelphia's modern history, generated campaign money for Street and defended him against advertisements that attacked Street's character and competence. These ads brought attention to Street's two personal bankruptcies and his unpaid water, gas, and tax bills in the 1980's. Street's personal finances were an embarrassing irony when compared with his political career, which included helping rescue Philadelphia from its impoverished financial condition when he was in the city council.

Street campaigned on his city council record and emphasized his positions in favor of expanding Philadelphia's day-care services, adding officers to the police force, and creating a program to demolish abandoned buildings. He and Katz, who had been a school board member, disagreed on the issue of *school vouchers* (legislation that would allow parents to use public funds for private schools). Although Katz maintained that vouchers would entice families to remain within the city, Street opposed the idea.

Republican convention. In January 1999, the Republican National Committee chose Philadelphia to host the party's presidential nominating convention in 2000. A group of Philadelphia political and business leaders offered the Republicans a $50-million package that would cover construction costs and other expenses. Local officials said the costly incentive package would be offset by an estimated $400 million in economic benefits that would be generated by the convention. They also suggested that the convention, expected to draw 40,000 people to the city, would promote Philadelphia as a tourist destination.

New baseball stadium. Philadelphia Phillies baseball team officials announced in May 1999 that they planned to build a new stadium in the heart of the city, but they later changed their minds about the location. Philadelphia and the state of Pennsylvania had previously agreed to provide about two-thirds of the cost of a $250-million stadium for the Phillies, as well as additional financing for a new stadium for the Eagles football team. However, the downtown location for the stadium would have cost $396 million and was heavily challenged by residents of the area.

In late 1999, Phillies officials looked for an alternate site for the stadium. Team owners maintained that the current home of the Phillies and Eagles—Veterans Stadium, which opened in 1971—was antiquated.

Crime statistics. While murders, robberies, and car thefts were down in Philadelphia in 1998, total crime was up by 11 percent, according to Federal Bureau of Investigation (FBI) statistics released in May 1999. United States cities are required to report their crime statistics to the FBI, which analyzes and distributes the information.

Philadelphia officials had expected the 1998 crime statistics to show an increase, because the city's police department had been forced to change a long-time practice of falsifying crime records. Auditors in 1998 discovered that many crimes committed in Philadelphia were not being reported to the FBI in order to make the city appear safer.   □ Howard S. Shapiro

See also **City.**

Philippines. In 1999, President Joseph Estrada's plans to amend the Constitution provoked the largest demonstrations in the Philippines since the 1986 overthrow of then-president Ferdinand E. Marcos.

Estrada appointed a preparatory commission to recommend changes to the Constitution, which had been hastily written by an unelected body in 1987. Estrada wanted to reduce the document's economic protectionism to encourage foreign investment, with political changes to be considered later.

Estrada's opponents, led by former President Corazon Aquino and Roman Catholic leader Jaime Cardinal Sin, staged protest rallies that attracted large numbers of Filipinos in August and September 1999. Opponents of constitutional revision said that any changes might invite removal of constitutional checks, such as congressional and presidential term limits.

Estrada vowed to continue his efforts to change the constitution. He argued that the proposed economic reforms would enable the Philippines to retain a strong economy and reduce poverty.

The Philippine economy grew at a rate of 3.6 percent in mid-1999, according to economists. It had staged a strong recovery from recession in 1998, when domestic output contracted by 0.5 percent. Inflation in mid-1999 ran at under 6 percent and showed no sign of heating up.

Estrada claimed credit for the improving economy. Some economists noted, however, that monsoon rains that broke a long drought were primarily responsible for the economy's strong showing. While agricultural output rose, industrial output remained low.

TIME CAPSULE   1942
PHILIPPINES

BATAAN. After a valiant four-months' stand, the 37,000 American-Filipino defenders of the Bataan Peninsula were forced to surrender to the Japanese on April 9. Although the enemy outnumbered them six to one, their defeat was finally caused by hunger and disease, due to the fact that reinforcements, equipment, supplies, and food could not be taken to them through the Japanese blockade. The heroic stand made by the troops wrote another glorious chapter in the annals of American military history.

Peace talks between the Philippine government and the Moro Islamic Liberation Front (MILF), long delayed, began in October 1999. A sticking point was the MILF's insistence on independence for MILF-dominated areas on the island of Mindanao. The government rejected any plan for independence. According to some estimates, the 30-year conflict between government forces and the MILF had cost up to 100,000 lives.

Relations with U.S. military. The Philippine Senate in May 1999 approved resumption of visits by U.S. naval ships and U.S.-Philippine joint military exercises, following clashes between Chinese and Philippine vessels in the South China Sea. In the early 1990's, the Philippine government had demanded the withdrawal of U.S. armed forces. U.S. Secretary of Defense William Cohen met in October 1999 with Orlando Mercado, the Philippine defense secretary, and signed an agreement for joint exercises. He also pledged U.S. aid to modernize the Philippine armed forces.

The first execution in the Philippines in 23 years took place on February 5. A man convicted of child rape was executed by lethal injection. By late October, five additional convicted criminals had been executed, despite protests from Roman Catholic church leaders.　　□ Henry S. Bradsher

See also **Asia**.

Physics.

Three teams of physicists in 1999 demonstrated how to reduce the speed of light to a virtual crawl. Light is normally the fastest-moving form of energy. In February, a group led by Lene Hau of Harvard University in Cambridge, Massachusetts, reported on a study in which light moved millions of times slower than normal as it passed through a gas of ultracold sodium atoms. In June, teams led by scientists at Texas A&M University at College Station and the University of California at Berkeley duplicated the feat using rubidium gas at more ordinary temperatures.

According to the theory of relativity, the speed of light in a vacuum—186,282 miles (299,792 kilometers) per second—cannot be altered. However, in a transparent medium, such as water or glass, light slows down somewhat due to its absorption in the medium—a process known as *refraction.* While the modest refractive properties of water and glass have long been known, the slowdowns achieved in 1999 were obtained using much more technical methods.

Hau's group worked with a Bose-Einstein condensate (BEC)—an unusual form of matter in which millions of atoms are confined in an extremely small cloud of gas cooled to billionths of a degree above absolute zero (−460 °F, or −273 °C). After cooling a cloud of sodium atoms, the researchers fired two *laser beams* (powerful, focused beams of light) into the gas. The laser beams were precisely tuned to slightly different frequencies. Although light would normally be absorbed by atoms of a BEC or other gas, the interaction of the two laser beams altered the subatomic states of the atoms, preventing them from absorbing the light. Therefore, the light continued to pass through the gas.

The interaction of the two laser beams greatly increased the refractive properties of the gas. This refraction caused a third beam of light, which was created by the combination of the original light beams, to move at a vastly reduced speed through the gas—38 miles (61 kilometers) per hour.

The physicists who used rubidium gas achieved similar results at temperatures that are much more convenient to work with. The Texas A&M group slowed the speed of laser beams to approximately 220 miles (354 kilometers) per hour at about 190 °F (87 °C), and the University of California team cut the speed of light to 18 miles (29 kilometers) per hour at room temperature.

The practical possibilities for these discoveries include rapid "light switches," in which a weak light beam either stops a stronger beam or allows it to pass through. This could be useful in a number of communications and computing devices, including computers based on light rather than electronics.

Three new elements? The periodic table of chemical elements, which ended with element 112 in 1998, may have been extended in 1999. Researchers from the Joint Institute for Nuclear Research in Dubna, Russia, and the Lawrence Livermore National Laboratory in Livermore, California, reported evidence of the existence of element 114 in January. In June, a team at the

TIME CAPSULE 1939

PHYSICS

OTTO HAHN and F. Strassmann of the Kaiser Wilhelm Research Institute, basing their investigations on the earlier work of Hahn with Lise Meitner and of Enrico Fermi of the University of Rome, succeeded in splitting the uranium atom by bombardment with neutrons. The neutron is a slow neutral particle of an energy of only 1/30 volt, which splits the uranium atom into two heavy elements, each constituting a gigantic radioactive atomic "cannon ball" of 100,000,000 volts, the greatest amount of atomic energy yet liberated.

Lawrence Berkeley National Laboratory in Berkeley, California, announced the discovery of what it believed to be elements 116 and 118.

An element's designated number refers to the number of *protons* (positively charged subatomic particles) that an atom of the element has in its *nucleus* (central region). The heaviest elements found in nature are uranium (number 92) and plutonium (number 94). Physicists create heavier elements in particle accelerators, devices in which speeding atoms or subatomic particles are bombarded together to fuse. These superheavy elements have short lifetimes, some lasting just thousandths of a second before their nuclei break apart. Nuclear theory suggests that between elements 114 and 120, an "island of stability" exists in which nuclei can survive for years or even centuries, enabling scientists to study chemical compounds formed by them.

The research reported by the Livermore and Russian scientists indicated that element 114 lies on the shore of this island of stability, because its nucleus lasted 30 seconds—more than a thousand times longer than previously known *isotopes* (forms) of element 112. Elements 116 and 118 lasted only fractions of a second, but still longer than would be expected for elements outside the island of stability.

☐ Robert H. March

Poetry. Mark Strand, former United States poet laureate (1990-1991), won the Pulitzer Prize in April 1999 for his collection *Blizzard of One,* his ninth volume of poetry. The Canadian-born author is one of the most distinguished of contemporary American poets. His poetry often confronts the experience of failure and seeks to find redemption in losing situations. In "Lines for Winter," which appears in his 1999 volume *Selected Poems,* he writes, "And if it happens that you cannot / go on or turn back / and you find yourself / where you will be at the end, / tell yourself / In that final flowing of cold through your limbs / that you love what you are."

Several distinguished poets published memorable translations of classic poetry, including 1995 Nobel Prize winner Seamus Heaney, who translated the narrative poem *Beowulf* into modern English verse. Heaney revives the story's emotional depth by concentrating on how the hero Beowulf must live long beyond the accomplishment of his greatest deed, slaying the monster Grendel. In 1999, Heaney also translated work by the Czech composer and librettist Leos Janacek for the English National Opera and a volume of poems by the Russian poet Alexander Pushkin.

The late Ted Hughes's (1930-1998) retelling of *Alcestis,* by the ancient Greek dramatist Euripides, was shortlisted for Great Britain's Whitbread Poetry Award. The story concerns a selfless woman, Queen Alcestis, who journeys to the underworld to protect her husband, King Admetos.

American poet David Ferry's work, collected in *Of No Country I Know,* included many of his translations of Latin poets Virgil and Horace and an extraordinary translation of the ancient *Epic of Gilgamesh.* While much of the work had been published before 1999, this collection shows the remarkable range of a poet who often captures an ordinary moment and makes it extraordinary with formal meter and language. In "Herbsttag," written as a kind of prayer, he writes, "Now is the right time, Lord. Summer is over. / Let the autumn shadows drift upon the sundials, / And let the wind stray loose over the fields."

Mysteries of Small Houses (1998) by Alice Notley received the Los Angeles Times Book Prize in poetry in April 1999. Notley, known for her use of experimental language, uses earthy language and long chatty lines to write poems that resemble memoir. By turns, the poems describe her in many female identities: child, poet, wife, friend, mother, youth, lover, and widow.

National Book Award Contenders. The poet Ai received the 1999 National Book Award in poetry for her collection *Vice: New and Selected Poems.* In a voice forceful and appropriate for dramatic monologues, Ai offers poems from the points of view of such cultural icons as movie star Marilyn Monroe and comedian Lenny Bruce, as well as priests, presidents, and urban strangers.

C. K. Williams published *Repair* in 1999, also shortlisted for the National Book Award. Williams is a passionate and careful observer, and his poetry uses a trademark long line that manages to be both musical, like lyric poetry, and narrative, like prose. Another NBA finalist, Louise Gluck, was shortlisted for the award with *Vita Nova: Poems.* Gluck has mastered lyric, short-lined poems, especially those that allude to mythological figures and themes. Poet Clarence Major was nominated for a National Book Award for *Configurations: New & Selected Poems.* In his direct style, he writes in "Un Poco Loco," "To keep going I watch / my grandmother hold / the chicken by its legs— / bauk bauk bauk!"

Short takes. Chicano poet Gary Soto wrote *A Natural Man,* a collection of verse championing society's outcasts. Rita Dove, a former poet laureate of the United States (1993-1995), also illuminates the lives of obscure people in her newly published *On the Bus With Rosa Parks.* William Stafford's *The Way It Is: New & Selected Poems* pulls together almost 40 years of poems about Native Americans, nature, war, and the extraordinary in the ordinary. ☐ Brian Bouldrey

See also **Literature, American; Literature, World.**

Poland joined the North Atlantic Treaty Organization (NATO) on March 12, 1999. European Union (EU) officials encouraged Poland to speed up economic reforms in 1999 to hasten its entry into the EU. In April, the World Bank agreed to a $30-million loan to help reform the Polish mining industry. The bank offered another $500 million in loans for agriculture. But the government struggled to implement reforms, especially making spending cuts to strengthen the economy.

In June 1999, Pope John Paul II visited Poland. Prior to the visit, tensions flared between Polish Jews and Christians when a Roman Catholic group erected 300 crosses on land adjacent to Auschwitz, the former Nazi death camp where more than 1 million Jews were killed between 1939 and 1945. Jewish groups asked Polish officials to remove a large cross from outside the camp because it could be seen from inside. The government removed the smaller crosses before the pope's arrival but left standing the large cross—erected in 1979 to commemorate Catholic victims of Auschwitz.

On Sept. 2, 1999, Janusz Tomaszewski, Poland's interior minister and deputy premier, resigned. Officials suspected that Tomaszewski had lied when he formally declared that he had not collaborated

---

TIME CAPSULE 1939

POLAND

THE MIGHTY GERMAN MILITARY machine struck the Poles so quickly and suddenly [on September 1] that the three Polish armies never had a chance to carry out fully their mobilization and concentration plans . . . The far larger and stronger German air forces swept over Poland, destroying Polish planes and air bases, bombing railroads and bridges, and cutting telephone and telegraph wires, so that the Polish armies lost the directing eye from the air, and invaluable means of communication. . . . Germany was thus able to drive swiftly eastward toward Warsaw and to seize the invaluable Polish iron, coal, and industrial districts in the south. . . .

The city of Warsaw made a most heroic and desperate resistance to overwhelming numbers of German bombers, tanks, and siege cannon. Its radio, though several times destroyed or jammed by the Germans, still announced to the world that Poland would fight to the last man. . . .

Warsaw finally gave up its heroic but hopeless struggle on September 27.

TIME CAPSULE 1989

POLAND

POLAND saw a transformation of its domestic political scene in 1989, ending four decades of totalitarian Communist rule with the emergence of the independent labor union Solidarity as a political powerhouse. The confirmation of Solidarity adviser Tadeusz Mazowiecki as Poland's first non-Communist prime minister since 1945 . . . challenged the entire Communist world. Almost as striking was . . . Mikhail S. Gorbachev's advice to Poland's Communist Party that the party should work with the Mazowiecki administration.

---

with Poland's Communist-era secret police.

The unemployment rate in Poland stood at about 12 percent in October. Economists expected inflation to reach 7.7 percent for the year and the *gross domestic product* (value of all goods and services produced in a country in a given year) to grow by about 4 percent. ☐ Sharon L. Wolchik

See also **Europe; Roman Catholic Church.**

Pollution. See Environmental pollution.

Popular music. Fans witnessed profound upheavals and significant transitions in popular music in 1999, ranging from new musical forms and artists to new technology. Younger fans in 1999, as in the past, demanded music that was all their own, rather than following trends and tastes that had been popular with older listeners.

Rock and rap. Rap music was once considered a rival to rock, threatening the popularity of the guitar-driven music. In 1999, a number of artists that combined both forms became more and more popular. Such acts as Limp Bizkit, Kid Rock, and Eminem featured rap-styled rhymes that were more spoken or chanted than sung and themes reminiscent of urban, street-tough rap, over a musical backing that had the dynamics of hard rock.

Such music generated a chart-topping popularity, especially among white listeners. This led to charges of musical thievery and even racism that were as old as rock and roll music itself. Critics accused Elvis Presley in the 1950's and the Rolling Stones in the 1960's—artists who had been deeply influenced by such musical styles as blues and jazz—of attracting a much larger audience than the black artists who inspired them. However, many critics questioned whether the artists who enjoyed such crossover breakthroughs in 1999 would have the same staying power.

Woodstock '99. Thirty years after the most famous outdoor rock music concert of the 1960's, the Woodstock festival returned in 1999 to upstate New York. The three-day festival, which began July 23, drew more than 200,000 fans, most of whom had not yet been born when the first festival took place in 1969. The festival focused primarily on rock and rap groups and technologically driven hybrids, with Limp Bizkit, Kid Rock, Rage Against the Machine, and the Red Hot Chili Peppers among the headliners. There were also all-night dance "raves" with Fatboy Slim and Moby, two artists whose dance-club music attracted many rock converts. Artists from the older generation of musicians, including James Brown and Willie Nelson, played well-received sets.

Woodstock '99 shared little of the spirit of the original festival or a 25th anniversary festival in 1994. Where the original Woodstock festival represented a communal sharing of "peace, love, and music" in a natural setting, Woodstock '99, staged at a U.S. Air Force base in Rome, New York, seemed militaristic to many fans.

The festival's finale was marred by incidents of rioting, vandalism, looting, and accusations of sexual assault. Some people reported that a small number of festgoers destroyed parked tractor-trailers, vendor tents, and concert light stands in rebellion against the high prices and commercialism of the weekend. Others blamed the aggressiveness of the music for inciting the violence. Concert officials and local officials downplayed the incident as "a serious problem" that lasted only a few hours.

Kiddie pop. Pre-teen and teen-aged audiences showed their buying power in 1999, as younger acts such as Christina Aguilera, Backstreet Boys, 'N Sync, and Britney Spears sold millions of albums each and dominated pop radio with chart-topping hits. Many of these performers were themselves only teen-agers, inspiring the sort of excitement and identification among younger fans that the Beatles had during the 1960's.

Although older listeners discounted their music as lightweight fluff, music industry executives could not ignore the profits of such an expanding market, with even rock publications like *Rolling Stone* magazine devoting considerable space to younger groups. With ballads such as the Backstreet Boys's "I Want It That Way," some of the acts began appealing to older listeners as well.

Hispanic crossover. Singers of Latin-American heritage made their presence felt at the top of the pop charts in 1999. Ricky Martin captivated audiences with his hit singles "Livin' la Vida Loca" and "La Copa de la Vida" ("The Cup of Life"). In addition to Martin, a former member of 1980's teen-aged group Menudo, such artists as Jennifer Lopez and Enrique Iglesias also enjoyed populari-

ELVIS ARON PRESLEY became one of the most controversial people in the United States in 1956. The former $25-a-week truckdriver rocked and rolled to fame and fortune with such songs as "Hound Dog," "Heartbreak Hotel," and "Love Me Tender." His records sold for about $6,000,000. Teen-agers mobbed him at every appearance, but thousands of other Americans criticized his performances as distasteful.

Elvis Presley

ty with audiences. Lopez had starred in *Selena* (1997), the film tribute to the slain Mexican Tejano-style singer Selena Quintanilla. Iglesias's father is Julio Iglesias, the internationally popular crooner.

Carlos Santana, a guitarist of Mexican descent, made a popular comeback with his *Supernatural* album, his most successful endeavor in decades. The album paired Santana with such younger artists as Rob Thomas of the band Matchbox 20 and singer Lauryn Hill, who appealed to a more youthful audience.

Some music industry leaders linked the surge of the popularity of Latin music to the growing numbers of Hispanics in the United States and the popularity of the style's dance-club rhythms.

Veterans on tour. One of the most highly anticipated international tours in 1999 featured the reunion of Bruce Springsteen with the E Street Band. The concert tour played to sellout stadium crowds and rave reviews across Europe and North America. Springsteen had performed through most of the 1990's as a solo acoustic artist, but his reunion with his old band proved to be a highly-charged celebration of rock and roll.

Another of the most popular tours of 1999 teamed Bob Dylan and Paul Simon, considered by many to be two of the finest U.S. songwriters to come to prominence during the 1960's. Dylan

Grammy Award winners in 1999

Record of the Year, "My Heart Will Go On," Celine Dion

Album of the Year, "The Miseducation of Lauryn Hill," Lauryn Hill

Song of the Year, "My Heart Will Go On," James Horner and Will Jennings

New Artist, Lauryn Hill

Pop Vocal Performance, Female, "My Heart Will Go On," Celine Dion

Pop Vocal Performance, Male, "My Father's Eyes," Eric Clapton

Pop Performance by a Duo or Group with Vocal, "Jump Jive an' Wail," The Brian Setzer Orchestra

Traditional Pop Vocal Performance, "Live At Carnegie Hall— The 50th Anniversary Concert," Patti Page

Pop Instrumental Performance, "Sleepwalk," The Brian Setzer Orchestra

Rock Vocal Performance, Female, "Uninvited," Alanis Morissette

Rock Vocal Performance, Male, "Fly Away," Lenny Kravitz

Rock Performance by a Duo or Group with Vocal, "Pink," Aerosmith

Hard Rock Performance, "Most High," Jimmy Page and Robert Plant

Metal Performance, "Better Than You," Metallica

Rock Instrumental Performance, "The Roots of Coincidence," Pat Metheny Group

Rock Song, "Uninvited," Alanis Morissette

Alternative Music Performance, "Hello Nasty," Beastie Boys

Rhythm-and-Blues Vocal Performance, Female, "Doo Wop (That Thing)," Lauryn Hill

Rhythm-and-Blues Vocal Performance, Male, "St. Louis Blues," Stevie Wonder

Rhythm-and-Blues Performance by a Duo or Group with Vocal, "The Boy Is Mine," Brandy and Monica

Rhythm-and-Blues Song, "Doo Wop (That Thing)," Lauryn Hill

Rap Solo Performance, "Gettin' Jiggy Wit It," Will Smith

Rap Performance by a Duo or Group, "Intergalactic," Beastie Boys

New-Age Album, "Landmarks," Clannad

Contemporary Jazz Performance, "Imaginary Day," Pat Metheny Group

Jazz Vocal Performance, "I Remember Miles," Shirley Horn

Jazz Instrumental, Solo, "Rhumbata," Chick Corea and Gary Burton

Jazz Instrumental Performance, Individual or Group, "Gershwin's World," Herbie Hancock

Large Jazz Ensemble Performance, "Count Plays Duke," Count Basie Orchestra; Grover Mitchell, Director

Latin Jazz Performance, "Hot House," Arturo Sandoval

Country Album, "Wide Open Spaces," Dixie Chicks

Country Vocal Performance, Female, "You're Still the One," Shania Twain

Country Vocal Performance, Male, "If You Ever Have Forever In Mind," Vince Gill

Country Performance by a Duo or Group with Vocal, "There's Your Trouble," Dixie Chicks

Country Vocal Collaboration, "Same Old Train," Clint Black, Joe Diffie, Merle Haggard, Emmylou Harris, Alison Krauss, Patty Loveless, Earl Scruggs, Ricky Skaggs, Marty Stuart, Pam Tillis, Randy Travis, Travis Tritt, and Dwight Yoakam

Country Instrumental Performance, "A Soldier's Joy," Randy Scruggs and Vince Gill

Bluegrass Album, "Bluegrass Rules!" Ricky Skaggs and Kentucky Thunder

Country Song, "You're Still the One," Robert John "Mutt" Lange and Shania Twain

Singer Lauryn Hill wins five Grammy awards, including Album of the Year for "The Miseducation of Lauryn Hill," at the annual Grammy Awards ceremony on Feb. 24, 1999.

and Simon alternated as headliners from concert to concert and sang duets of each other's material.

Computer download. The Internet in 1999 continued as a formidable medium for distributing music, a fact that caused anxiety in the music industry. Some industry leaders speculated that downloading from the Internet might replace shopping for compact discs (CD's) as the major means of obtaining music in the 2000's.

Much of the year's computer activity concerned music-download Internet sites such as MP3.com, where some recording artists experimented with making songs available for free. Such Web sites store songs in a highly compressed format called MP3. The downloaded files use the same digital technology and have the sound quality as CD's but without the cost of manufacturing or distribution. Competing formats for music coded as MP3 files included Liquid Music, RealPlayer, and MusicMatch, each of which allowed a personal computer to function as a file-based stereo system.

Questions that remained to be resolved at the end of 1999 included the future cost of music available through Internet services, the means of preventing illegal recordings, and the involvement of the corporate record labels that

THE YEAR 1964 was overwhelmingly the Year of the Beatles in popular music, a field that is not unknown for its cultivation of fads and fancies.

Who were the Beatles? They were a rock-and-roll quartet from Liverpool, England, who wore Edwardian-styled clothes and haircuts like helmets, and who, in addition to wallets bulging with royalties from record sales, carried with them, wherever they went a rambunctious and irreverent sense of fun.

Three of the young men thwacked away at electric guitars; the fourth pounded a set of drums. All of them sang, shook their mop tops, and clowned their way through their concerts, though their voices could be only rarely heard over the screams of thousands of teen-age girls in their bouncing and squirming audiences. And this latter, interesting phenomenon occurred wherever guitarists George Harrison, 22; Paul McCartney 23; John Lennon, 24; and drummer Ringo Starr, 24, appeared. . . .

At Carnegie Hall in February, 2,900 girls drowned out the quartet and pelted the stage with jelly beans, which became a trademark of Beatlemania. . . . It was the same everywhere in the 30 or so U.S. cities the Beatles invaded in 1964: waves of baying teens and long lines of police.

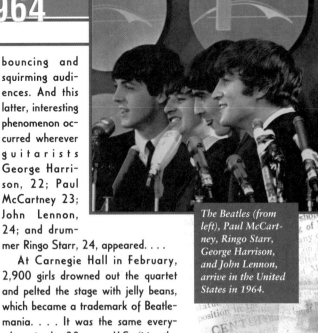

The Beatles (from left), Paul McCartney, Ringo Starr, George Harrison, and John Lennon, arrive in the United States in 1964.

have long dominated the music industry. Some observers speculated that the Internet might eventually make both record labels and record stores obsolete.

Country music gained new fans in 1999, in part due to the Dixie Chicks, a female trio from Texas. The Dixie Chicks sold more than 8 million copies of their 1998 debut album, *Wide Open Spaces,* which won both a 1999 Grammy Award and the Academy of Country Music Award for best country album.

Their 1999 follow-up album, *Fly,* released in August, quickly shot to the top of both the country and popular music album charts. Fans and critics alike applauded the fact that the Dixie Chicks played their own instruments on the album at a time when most country recordings were made using studio musicians.

A new album by Garth Brooks was less successful. In September, Brooks traded his cowboy hat for a black wig and the persona of fictional singer Chris Gaines and released *Garth Brooks in . . . the Life of Chris Gaines.* The album featured songs ranging from rock and folk to rhythm-and-blues. The effort received a lukewarm response from fans who viewed it as little more than a marketing tool.   □ Don McLeese

See also **Electronics; People in the news** (Martin, Ricky).

Population. The United Nations Population Fund (UNFPA) estimated that the world population reached 6 billion on Oct. 12, 1999. UNFPA is a United Nations (UN) agency that promotes greater access to reproductive information and services. This milestone was recorded at a time when population growth had actually slowed in most countries.

UN meeting. Delegates from 180 countries meeting at the UN headquarters in New York City in late June and early July reviewed the progress made in implementing a 20-year program adopted at the International Conference on Population and Development in Cairo, Egypt, in 1994. The program had called for nations to slow population growth through social programs, such as family planning, health care, and education, as well as by improving economic conditions.

The UN session revealed that an increasing number of countries were addressing population issues. Couples around the world had greater access to family planning methods, which enabled them to choose the number of children they had and to space births to enable them to take better care of their children.

The session reiterated that population issues also include social, health, education, and economic development factors. These factors can help limit population growth. The delegates urged governments to eliminate the gender gap in primary and secondary schools by 2005, increase primary school enrollment to 90 percent of children by 2010, and achieve universal access to primary education by 2015.

Unequal progress. Despite the positive results reported at the session, the delegates noted that progress to solve population problems had not been equal throughout the world. Some countries recorded setbacks in their population programs in 1999 because women and girls, according to the delegates, continued to suffer from discrimination. In addition, many individuals, including millions of Africans, did not have access to reproductive health care or basic health information. In some African countries, AIDS and other infectious diseases had caused drastic increases in death rates during the 1990's.

Need for more funds. To address the remaining problems, the delegates adopted a revised program of action. However, UN Secretary General Kofi Annan warned that the program's goals would not be met unless countries made more funds available to address the problems.

United States population. The U.S. Census Bureau projected in 1999 that the population of the United States would reach 274,634,000 in 2000.   □ J. Tuyet Nguyen

See also **AIDS; City.**

Portugal. The Socialist government of Prime Minister Antonio Guterres was reelected on Oct. 10, 1999. The Socialists won 112 seats in the 230-seat parliament, one seat short of an outright majority. The conservative Social Democratic Party, the main opposition group, won 80 seats. Guterres noted that the lack of a majority would hinder his party's ability to pass reforms that he had promised during the campaign.

The government benefited from a booming economy and Guterres's success in leading Portugal into the single European currency, the euro, launched in January 1999. Economists predicted that Portugal's *gross domestic product* (the value of all goods and services produced in a year) would grow by 3.2 percent in 1999 and that unemployment would drop to 4.7 percent, one of the lowest rates in the European Union (EU).

Bank battle. In June, the Portuguese government vetoed a takeover of the Portuguese banking group Champalimaud by Banco Santander Central Hispano SA of Spain. However, the European Commission, the agency that enforces competition rules in the EU, ruled that the merger could proceed. Santander agreed to a partial takeover of Champalimaud in November, buying two of the group's three banks for $1.5 billion.
                                                              □ Tom Buerkle

See also **Europe.**

Prison. The United States Department of Justice in March 1999 reported that the U.S. prison population was still increasing, though at the lowest rate since 1979. In December 1998, U.S. prisons held approximately 1,894,000 inmates. Two-thirds, or about 1,302,000 prisoners, were in state and federal prisons. The rest were in local jails, which hold offenders with terms of one year or less and people who are awaiting trial.

The number of prisoners, excluding inmates in jails, increased by 4.8 percent in 1998, below the average 6.7-percent annual increase since 1990. However, 59,866 more prisoners were in prison in 1998 than in 1997. One of every 149 U.S. residents was serving a sentence of one year or longer in 1998, compared to 1 of every 217 residents in 1990. The rate was higher than that of any other country except Russia.

The Department of Justice study cited three reasons for the increase. First, offenders were receiving longer sentences. In 1990, inmates entering state prison could expect to serve 38 months. By 1997, the length of an average sentence had increased to 43 months.

Second, fewer inmates were paroled, and the number of parole violators returned to prison increased by 39 percent.

Third, under harsher sentencing laws adopted in the 1990's, more prisoners served long sentences. Statistician Allen J. Beck, coauthor of the 1999 Department of Justice study, cited longer stays as "the biggest factor in pushing prison populations up," with the greatest increase in prisoners serving 3 to 5 years and a smaller increase in prisoners serving 20 years to life.

Gender trends. For the sixth time since 1990, the rate of increase in prisoners was greater for women (6.5 percent) than for men (4.7 percent). At a September 1999 conference in Chicago, criminal justice workers reported that the number of women in U.S. prisons had increased from 12,000 women in 1980 to 87,472 in 1998.

Racial disparities increased. In 1998, a black American was at least six times more likely than a white American to be in prison. Black Americans numbered only 13 percent of the total U.S. population in 1998 but constituted nearly half the prison population. Non-Hispanic white Americans numbered two-thirds of the total population but only 35 percent of prisoners.

Death row inmates. In mid-1999, death rows of U.S. prisons held more than 3,500 prisoners. By the end of September, 76 prisoners had been executed in 1999, the highest total since 1954. However, the number of people sentenced to death declined from an average of 300 per year between 1986 and 1996 to 265 in 1997.
                                                              □ Michael Tonry

Prizes. See **Nobel Prizes; Pulitzer Prizes.**

Protestantism. Representatives from the Roman Catholic Church and the Lutheran World Federation, an international communion representing some 57 million Lutherans, met on Oct. 31, 1999, in Augsburg, Germany, to sign a joint declaration that people are reconciled with God through "grace alone." The declaration took place on Reformation Day, when Lutherans celebrate the beginning of the Protestant faith in the 1500's under the leadership of Martin Luther. Many religious leaders heralded the agreement as a step in healing centuries-old divisions among Christians.

Other reconciliations. At a Churchwide Assembly in Denver, Colorado, in August 1999, representatives of the Evangelical Lutheran Church in America (ELCA) voted to enter into "full communion" with the Moravian Church in America and the Episcopal Church. The agreements allowed for the recognition of each church's sacraments, cooperation in various programs, and the exchange of clergy. The agreement with the Episcopal Church was controversial because Lutherans in the United States, unlike Episcopalians, do not recognize a *historic episcopate,* a continuous succession of ordained bishops that, according to tradition, originated in the early Christian church.

Mainline Protestant churches in the United States, churches generally considered to be moderate or liberal, experienced internal divisions in

1999 over issues involving homosexuality. Almost without exception, the mainline churches were torn over such questions as whether a minister could perform union ceremonies for gay couples and whether sexually active homosexuals could serve as ordained ministers.

On March 26, Gregory Dell, a Methodist minister in Chicago, was suspended for an indefinite length of time from service in the church for presiding at a same-sex union. In September, an appeals committee upheld the judgment against Dell but changed his suspension to one year. In March, 69 Methodist ministers of the California-Nevada Annual Conference protested church rules by presiding as a group over a ceremony for a lesbian couple. Bishop Melvin Talbert filed a complaint against the clergy but stated that he disagreed with the rule he was obligated to enforce.

The First United Methodist Church in Marietta, Georgia, voted to withhold $268,000 from denominational programs after Bishop G. Lindsey Davis barred Charles Sineath from continuing to serve as senior minister of the congregation. Sineath had been outspoken about the Methodist Church's refusal to condemn homosexual activity.

The Presbyterian Church (U.S.A.), at a General Assembly in June, gave a Women of Faith Award to lesbian minister Jane Spahr, after much debate. In August, delegates at the ELCA

Gregory Dell, a Methodist minister in Chicago, greets supporters in March 1999 during a church trial for conducting a blessing ceremony for two gay men. Found guilty, Dell was given an indefinite suspension from serving as a minister, which was later reduced to one year.

Churchwide Assembly voted to continue studying homosexual issues but voted against the ordination of practicing gays and lesbians.

Paul Weyrich, a political spokesperson for Evangelical Christians, posted a letter on the Internet in February that called for conservative Christians to back away from politics. Weyrich claimed that Evangelical Christians had lost the "culture war" in the United States. Rather than promoting political involvement, he suggested that Evangelicals should be "set apart" from U.S. culture by doing such things as shutting off their televisions and teaching their children at home.

The Christian Coalition, an organization that promotes conservative Protestant values, announced in June 1999 that it would restructure itself as two separate entities. During the 1990's, the U.S. Internal Revenue Service had denied the organization the tax-free status granted to religious groups because of the Christian Coalition's political activities. One of the new organizations, the Christian Coalition of America, conducted nonpartisan voter education programs, making it eligible for a tax-exempt status. The other group, the Christian Coalition International, engaged directly in political activities, barring it from tax exemption.   □ Martin E. Marty

See also **Roman Catholic Church.**

Psychology. See Mental health.

Public health and safety. Advances

in public health and in battling infectious diseases were the major factors that increased life expectancy in the United States between 1900 and 1999, the Atlanta, Georgia-based Centers for Disease Control and Prevention (CDC) reported in July. The increase, from 47.3 years in 1900 to 76.1 years in 1996, was largely due to public health measures, such as the chlorination of drinking water to kill disease-causing organisms and development of vaccines and antibiotics to treat infections. The advances were especially important for children. Infants and children under age 5 accounted for about 30 percent of all deaths in 1900, but just 1.4 percent of deaths in 1997.

The CDC noted, however, that infectious diseases remained a serious threat. New strains of antibiotic-resistant bacteria were making infections harder to treat, and new diseases, such as AIDS, continued to appear.

Reye's syndrome. In May 1999, the CDC reported that Reye's syndrome, a childhood disease much-feared in the 1980's, had almost disappeared. Reye's syndrome, a serious nerve disorder, usually develops in children who have been treated with aspirin for viral infections, such as chicken pox. After health agencies began warning parents in 1980 not to give aspirin to children with viral infections, the number of cas-

es dropped from 555 in 1980 to 2 in 1997.

Teen births. Births to teen-age mothers fell for the sixth straight year in 1997, the National Center for Health Statistics (NCHS) reported in April 1999. The rate dropped from 62.1 births per 1,000 girls aged 15 to 19 in 1991 to 52.3 births in 1997. NCHS officials attributed the decline to such factors as decreasing sexual activity and greater availability of contraceptives.

Centenarian boom. The number of *centenarians,* men and women who have reached age 100, almost doubled during the 1990's, reaching nearly 70,000 by 1999, the U.S. Census Bureau announced in April. Researchers at the bureau predicted that by 2050, the United States could have about 834,000 centenarians. The bureau said healthier lifestyles and better health care were among the reasons for the increases.

Disease outbreaks. A mysterious outbreak of viral disease began in Malaysia in March 1999, killing more than 50 people and forcing the slaughter of hundreds of thousands of pigs, which health officials feared could spread the disease to people. Neighboring countries banned imports of pork from Malaysia, the leading pork producer in Southeast Asia. Experts from the CDC who helped investigate said the disease might be a form of Japanese encephalitis, which is spread from pigs to humans by mosquito bite.

The government of Belgium in June ordered 14 million cases of Coca-Cola products recalled when about 100 consumers, including schoolchildren, became ill after drinking the soft drinks. Concern about Coke products spread to France, the Netherlands, and Luxembourg, which also banned the beverages. The bans were lifted in July, after Coke bottling factories took extra precautions to ensure the safety of their products.

Highway safety. The number of Americans killed in motor vehicle accidents decreased to 41,840 in 1998, the smallest number since 1994, the U.S. Department of Transportation (DOT) reported in May 1999. The 1998 death toll was 1.3 percent less than the 42,013 deaths recorded in 1997, and alcohol-related fatalities declined to a record low of 15,936, or 38.4 percent, of 1998 deaths. However, 62 percent of those killed were not wearing safety belts, which DOT officials said could have prevented thousands of deaths. Crash-related injuries declined by 4.4 percent, from 3.4 million in 1997 to 3.25 million in 1998.

U.S. President Bill Clinton announced in February 1999 new DOT regulations to help parents anchor child safety seats in cars. Rear seats of all cars beginning with 2000 models were to have standard anchoring points. All new child seats were to have attachments that easily fit the anchors.   □ Michael Woods

See also **Medicine.**

Puerto Rico. United States President Bill Clinton on Dec. 3, 1999, ordered a halt to live-fire U.S. military exercises on and near the Puerto Rican island of Vieques. His action followed months of protests, after a U.S. fighter jet dropped two bombs off-target on April 19, killing a civilian and injuring four other people. In July, a commission, appointed by Governor Pedro J. Rossello, concluded that U.S. Navy training operations in the region violated the constitutional and human rights of the island's 9,300 residents and caused severe environmental and economic damage.

The U.S. Navy reported in June that pilots also mistakenly fired 263 shells tipped with depleted uranium, a material with low radioactivity, at targets on Vieques. In response to this announcement and other recent reports, Puerto Rico's legislature allocated $100,000 for a study to determine why people of Vieques have a cancer rate 27 percent higher than the average rate in Puerto Rico.

U.S. President Bill Clinton on August 11 offered pardons to 16 convicted members of the Armed Forces of National Liberation (FALN), a Puerto Rican proindependence group that had been involved in more than 130 bombings in the United States from 1974 to 1983. None of the 16 people offered clemency were convicted of a crime that resulted in death or injury.

Twelve FALN members accepted the pardons and, as a condition of their release, renounced the use of terrorism. Two people, who had finished serving sentences but owed fines, did not respond to Clinton's offer. Two other prisoners refused to renounce terrorism and remained in prison. Federal and state law enforcement agencies and many U.S. congressional leaders criticized Clinton for pardoning the FALN members.

Telecommunications. The U.S. Federal Communications Commission on Feb. 12, 1999, approved the sale of shares in the commonwealth-owned Puerto Rico Telephone Company. GTE Corp. of Stamford, Connecticut, acquired a 51 percent share of the company for $2 billion. The Commonwealth government retained a 44 percent share. The remaining shares, 5 percent of the total, were offered for sale to local investors. Many Puerto Ricans bitterly opposed the sale.

On May 3, Telefonos de Mexico S.A. (Telmex), of Mexico City, and SBC Communications, of Houston, agreed to purchase Cellular Communications of Puerto Rico Inc., the largest wireless telephone company in Puerto Rico, for $814 million in cash and assumed debt.

Ricky Martin, a Puerto Rican singer, became a Latin music superstar throughout the United States in 1999 through his Spanish- and English-language recordings.   ☐ Nathan A. Haverstock

See also **Latin America; People in the news** (Martin, Ricky); **United States, President of the.**

Pulitzer Prizes in journalism, letters, and music were awarded on April 12, 1999, by Columbia University in New York City on the recommendation of the Pulitzer Prize Board.

Journalism. The Washington Post won the public service award for a series on reckless gunplay by city police officers. The Hartford (Connecticut) Courant took the breaking news award for its coverage of shootings by a state lottery worker. The Miami Herald staff received the investigative reporting award for revealing voter fraud in a city mayoral election. The explanatory reporting award went to Richard Read of The (Portland) Oregonian, for demonstrating the impact of the Asian economic crisis on a local industry. Chuck Philips and Michael A. Hiltzik of the Los Angeles Times won the beat reporting award for a series on entertainment industry corruption.

Maureen Dowd of The New York Times captured the commentary prize for her columns on the impact of U.S. President Bill Clinton's relationship with Monica Lewinsky. The Times staff—notably Jeff Gerth—won the national reporting prize for a series on the government-approved sale of U.S. technology to China. The Wall Street Journal staff won the international reporting prize for its stories on the Russian financial crisis. The Journal's Angelo B. Henderson took the feature writing award for his portrait of a druggist driven to violence by frequent armed robberies.

Blair Kamin of the Chicago Tribune received the criticism prize for his coverage of city architecture and his articles supporting lakefront development. The editorial writing award went to the New York Daily News editorial board for its campaign to rescue Harlem's Apollo Theatre from mismanagement. David Horsey of the Seattle Post-Intelligencer won the editorial cartooning prize. The Associated Press photo staff took the spot news photography award for photos of the embassy bombings in Kenya and Tanzania, as well as the feature photography prize for images of the key players and events surrounding President Clinton's relationship with Monica Lewinsky.

Letters and music. Michael Cunningham won the fiction prize for The Hours. The drama prize went to Margaret Edson for Wit. Edwin G. Burrows and Mike Wallace took the history prize for Gotham: A History of New York City to 1898. A. Scott Berg won the biography award for Lindbergh. Mark Strand earned the poetry prize for Blizzard of One. John McPhee's Annals of the Former World won the general nonfiction prize.

The prize in music went to Melinda Wagner for "Concerto for Flute, Strings and Percussion." A posthumous award was bestowed on Edward Kennedy "Duke" Ellington, commemorating the 100th year of his birth.   ☐ Brian Bouldrey

Quebec. See Canadian provinces.

Radio.

After three years of frenzied consolidation, the pace of mergers and acquisitions in the United States radio industry slowed during the first eight months of 1999. But two huge transactions in September and October established 1999 as a record-setting year, when measured by the dollar value of stations bought and sold. Radio industry deals totaled about $34.6 billion in 1999, far surpassing the 1997 record of $15.5 billion. That record followed the passage of the Telecommunications Reform Act of 1996, which eliminated most restrictions on radio ownership.

Big mergers. On Sept. 7, 1999, media giant Viacom, Inc. of New York City announced its proposed entry into the U.S. radio market with the acquisition of CBS Corp., also of New York City. In addition to owning a television network, CBS controlled the 163-station Infinity Broadcasting Corp. —valued at $15 billion—the largest U.S. radio network in terms of number of stations. Viacom's holdings included the world's largest cable-television network and film and television studios.

On October 4, Clear Channel Communications Inc. of San Antonio, Texas, the third-largest U.S. radio network in terms of revenue, announced plans to buy AMFM Inc., of Dallas, ranked second in number of stations and first in annual revenues. The $16.6-billion acquisition gave Clear Channel 955 stations and a presence in nearly every major U.S. market. Industry analysts expected both the Viacom and Clear Channel mergers to win approval from the Federal Communications Commission (FCC), an agency that regulates the radio and television industries, and the Department of Justice after some modifications.

Low-power FM debate. Many segments of the U.S. radio industry reacted angrily to an FCC proposal issued on January 28 to create a new class of radio stations, known as low-power FM stations. The FCC announced that it hoped that these inexpensive stations, which would be able to broadcast only within a radius of up to 9 miles (14 kilometers), would bring more diversity to the radio business. In 1998, more than 13,000 individuals and groups, including schools, churches, and local governments, had contacted the FCC expressing an interest in starting such a station.

Owners of commercial stations as well as other industry groups argued that low-power stations would cause "devastating" interference to the signals broadcast by larger existing stations. FCC Chairman William E. Kennard, however, cautioned the industry against using signal interference as a "smoke screen" for fears that low-power stations would siphon off listeners and advertising.

Pacifica battle. Charges of censorship and commercialism, staff firings, a three-week employee lockout, mass protests, and arrests for trespass-

TIME CAPSULE
RADIO
1922

This 14-year-old high school boy has one of the best-equipped radio outfits in a city of 3 million people, and he constructed it himself, even to the batteries. He also made a machine for charging the batteries. Johnnie Pringle may rightly be proud of his achievement, but he says he is not an exceptional boy, for thousands of others no older, possess expert knowledge of the mysteries of radio.

Texas Governor George W. Bush and his wife, Laura, pass beneath an honor guard outside the Texas statehouse in Austin following his inauguration on Jan. 19, 1999. Bush's landslide reelection catapulted him into the forefront as the Republican Party's leading candidate for the presidential nomination in 2000.

ing marked a battle over programming at KPFA-FM in Berkeley, California. KPFA, one of five stations owned by the nonprofit Pacifica Foundation, is known as a platform for free speech and unconventional programming.

The dispute arose in early 1999 when Pacifica's board of governors eliminated representatives from local-station advisory boards. The board of governors argued that the change was needed to satisfy requirements for the $2 million received annually from the Corporation for Public Broadcasting. The board also said it wanted to broaden KPFA's programming to attract more listeners.

Opponents of the changes charged the board with muzzling free speech in order to boost advertising revenues. After the board fired several staff members, including some who had criticized the board members on the air, it locked up the station for 23 days in July. The board reinstated the fired employees and reopened the station on July 30, though many issues remained unresolved.

Country and talk. Country music continued to be the most popular music format on U.S. radio in 1999, playing on about 2,500 of about 13,000 U.S. radio stations. For the fifth consecutive year, news/talk stations won the highest overall ratings, according to the Arbitron Company, a media ratings firm in New York City. □ Gregory Paeth

See also **Telecommunications; Television.**

Republican Party. Many Republican Party members rallied behind Texas Governor George W. Bush in 1999 as the party's prospective presidential candidate in 2000. The support followed his landslide reelection as governor. Bush, the son of former President George H. W. Bush, raised more than $50 million in 1999 to finance his campaign.

Republican fund-raising efforts for the next presidential contest began earlier than in past elections because of the increasing number of key primary elections in the first few months of the campaign. Political analysts predicted that the nominees for both the Republican and Democratic parties would be decided by early March 2000, when voters in California and New York were scheduled to cast ballots in primary elections.

Several Republican presidential hopefuls dropped out of the race in 1999, claiming they were unable to raise enough money to compete with Bush. They included Dan Quayle, who had served as vice president under President Bush; Elizabeth Dole, the former American Red Cross president and wife of former senator and Republican presidential candidate Bob Dole; U.S. Representative John Kasich (R., Ohio); and Lamar Alexander, the former governor of Tennessee.

Another Republican hopeful, conservative political commentator Patrick J. Buchanan, who announced his candidacy on March 2, later withdrew from the party to join the Reform Party. By late 1999, only two major candidates, Senator John McCain (R., Arizona) and Steve Forbes, a multimillionaire publisher, remained in the running with Bush.

The candidates. Bush announced his candidacy for president on June 12, advocating "compassionate conservatism." Although he quickly assumed front-runner status, Bush was pressed by reporters to discuss personal aspects of his life and whether he was qualified for the presidency, particularly in the area of international affairs.

McCain began his quest for the Republican nomination on September 27, in New Hampshire. McCain, who was first elected to the Senate in 1987, issued a "patriotic challenge" to voters to restore the integrity of the political system and campaigned as a strong advocate of campaign finance reform. He also emphasized his military record. As a Navy pilot during the Vietnam War (1957-1975), he was shot down and spent more than five years in a prisoner-of-war camp in Hanoi.

Shifting balance? The Republican Party in 1999 faced the possibility that it would lose its narrow control of the House of Representatives in the 2000 election. Many political experts in 1999 predicted that GOP candidates in the 2000 election might face an uphill battle in some races. They claimed that Bush's reluctance to embrace certain Republican issues, including various controversial parts of the 1999-2000 budget, could jeopardize the chances of some GOP candidates.

Republicans retained control of both the House and the Senate in the 106th Congress, which convened in January 1999. The Republicans had a 223-seat majority in the House, compared with the Democrats' 211 seats, and one independent who usually voted with the Democrats. In July 1999, however, U.S. Representative Michael Forbes (R., New York) announced that he was joining the Democratic Party. The Republicans maintained a 55 to 45 majority in the Senate.

Elections. Republicans won a historic victory in Virginia on Nov. 2, 1999, when the party gained control of both houses of the state legislature for the first time in state history. Following the elections, the Republican Party controlled 52 seats in the 100-member House and 21 seats in the 40-member Senate when the state legislature met in Richmond, the capital, in 2000.

In Louisiana, Governor Mike Foster, a Republican, defeated U.S. Representative William J. Jefferson, a Democrat, and 10 other challengers for the governorship in an open primary election on Oct. 23, 1999. Foster captured more than 60 percent of the vote, the first Louisiana governor since 1983 to avoid a runoff election.

In the governor's race in Mississippi, Lieutenant Governor Ronnie Musgrove, a Democrat,

edged Republican Mike Parker, a former congressman, by some 8,000 votes in the November 1999 election. Musgrove failed to take a majority of the popular vote, however, and for the first time in Mississippi history, an electoral vote by the state legislature was to determine which candidate would succeed the incumbent governor. The incumbent, Kirk Fordice, was prohibited under state term limits from seeking a third term.

Fund-raising report. The Federal Election Commission (FEC) in September reported that the Republican Party had raised $66.4 million for federal elections during the first six months of 1999, compared with $38.1 million raised by the Democratic Party. The Republicans raised $30.9 million in soft money, compared with $26.4 million for the Democrats. Soft money refers to individual contributions to political parties that are not subject to the same restrictions placed on contributions to candidates.

GOP national chairman. Members of the Republican National Committee on January 22 voted 127 to 36 to reelect Jim Nicholson as chairman. Nicholson defeated Florida Republican Chairman Tom Slade.   □ William J. Eaton

See also **Congress of the United States; Democratic Party; Elections; People in the news** (Bush, George W.); **State government,**

Rhode Island. See State government.

Roman Catholic Church.

Pope John Paul II made a pointed attack on "materialist consumerism" in his World Peace Day Message on Jan. 1, 1999. The pope, who had long criticized the economic and political hardships under Communist rule, sharply denounced what he called the inadequacies of free-market economies. He denounced consumerism as an ideology in which the "exaltation of the individual and the selfish satisfaction of personal aspirations become the ultimate goal of life." He said that a consumer culture is a threat to human dignity and denies the economic rights of many underprivileged individuals.

John Paul II, who turned 79 years old in May, appeared to be in poor health during his papal visits in 1999. Many people commended him, however, for maintaining a strong spirit. On January 22, the pope began a visit to Mexico, where he called on government leaders and Roman Catholics to work for justice for the poor and marginalized people of the nation.

On January 27, the pope traveled to St. Louis, Missouri. On his two-day visit, he urged Roman Catholics to denounce abortion and capital punishment with a renewed vigilance and to follow faithfully the teachings of the Roman Catholic Church. The pope also appealed to Missouri Governor Mel Carnahan to commute the death sentence of Darrell Mease, who was scheduled to be

Pope John Paul II greets crowds in Rome from a balcony at St. John Basilica draped with a tapestry depicting Italian monk Padre Pio, who died in 1968. The Vatican in May 1999 beatified Padre Pio, who is revered for his association with miracles. Beatification is the last step before sainthood.

executed on February 10. Mease had been convicted of murdering three people in 1988. Carnahan's political opponents severely criticized him for heeding the pope's appeal and commuting Mease's sentence to life in prison.

On a visit to India in November 1999, John Paul II met with leaders of the nation's Hindus, Sikhs, Muslims, Buddhists, and Jews. Many leaders praised the pope's efforts to promote cooperation among people of different faiths, but some leaders criticized him for asking Roman Catholics to seek religious converts. John Paul II responded that religious freedom included people's right "to change religion, if their conscience so demands."

Reconciliation. On October 31, representatives from the Vatican and the Lutheran World Federation, an international communion representing some 57 million Lutherans, signed a joint declaration that people are reconciled to God through "grace alone." The declaration ceremony took place in Augsburg, Germany, where in 1530, Roman Catholic bishops and early Protestant leaders had tried to reconcile disagreements.

Universities. Roman Catholic bishops in the United States voted in November 1999 to require theologians at Catholic universities to receive a mandate from a local bishop in order to teach. The bishop would certify that the professor was teaching "authentic Catholic doctrine." The ruling was part of a document called *Ex Corde Ecclesiae* (From the Heart of the Church), which called on Roman Catholic universities to work closely with bishops and to appoint devout Catholics to their boards of directors, administrations, and faculties. The document did not grant bishops direct authority over firing and hiring decisions.

Many Roman Catholic theologians believed that the requirement of a bishop's mandate restricted their academic freedom, affected their stature in the academic community as a whole, and compelled them to abandon more controversial scholarly pursuits.

Environmental issues. In May, Roman Catholic bishops in British Columbia, Idaho, Montana, Washington, and Oregon issued a pastoral "reflection" on the use and conservation of the Columbia River and its natural resources. The river basin is of concern to Native Americans, environmentalists, logging companies, farmers who use the water for irrigation, hydroelectric power suppliers, and people in other industries. The 66-page document, scheduled to be completed in 2000 as a pastoral letter to priests and parishes, was the first official document of the Roman Catholic Church regarding the environment. The bishops called for a "sacramental understanding" of the Columbia River and justice for all its inhabitants—persons, animals, and plants. ☐ Thomas C. Fox

See also **Protestantism.**

Romania. In February 1999, Romania's central bank took control of Bancorex, the country's largest state bank, following the resignation of Bancorex's top officials. The managers resigned over differences regarding the restructuring of the bank. The International Monetary Fund (IMF—a United Nations-affiliated organization that provides short-term credit to member nations) and the World Bank (a United Nations agency that provides long-term loans to countries for development) had made the restructuring of Bancorex a condition for approving important loans to Romania. The government took over Bancorex after withdrawals by nervous depositors threatened the bank's solvency.

Domestic affairs. Romania's parliament passed a bill in June 1999 giving ethnic minorities in Romania the right to use their own language for government business in areas in which they comprised 20 percent of the population. In July, the supreme court supported the government's 1998 decision to establish a multicultural university, overturning a lower court's ruling on appeal. Opposition parties had sued in December 1998 to reverse the government's decision.

Economy. In the first half of 1999, the national currency, the leu, depreciated by approximately 27 percent, and Romania's *gross domestic product* (the value of all goods and services produced in a country in a given year) fell by 3.9 percent. The IMF agreed in April to loan Romania $500 million to help ease the country out of a steep economic decline, after the government adopted a plan of reforms intended to stabilize the leu. The reforms included strengthening the banking system and simplifying regulations governing business.

Foreign relations. Romania leaders supported the North Atlantic Treaty Organization (NATO) in its actions to end hostilities in Kosovo and made Romanian airports and air space available to NATO planes. Romania also reaffirmed its desire to join NATO.

Government collapses. President Emil Constantinescu dismissed Prime Minister Radu Vasile on December 13, after seven cabinet ministers resigned to protest Vasile's failure to enact economic reforms. Constantinescu declared that the loss of support from his coalition partners had rendered Vasile unable to carry out his duties. Vasile initially refused to step down, arguing that Constantinescu had no constitutional authority to dismiss him. Vasile eventually relented, and Constantinescu chose Central Bank Governor Mugur Isarescu as prime minister-designate on December 17. The crisis occurred after the European Union (EU) had invited Romania to discuss future membership in the EU. ☐ Sharon L. Wolchik

See also **Europe; Hungary.**

Rowing. See Sports.

Rugby football. Australia triumphed in the 1999 Rugby Union World Cup, becoming the first nation to win the coveted William Webb Ellis Trophy twice, and Scotland became the European Five Nations champion in 1999. In Rugby League, Australia continued its domination of the world stage with a victory in the Tri-Nations Tournament in October 1999.

International Rugby Union (RU). Wales hosted the 1999 World Cup, a tournament staged every four years. The 1999 tournament was the first to permit professional players to participate. On October 30, in the first semifinal match, Australia narrowly scraped through in a tryless encounter against South Africa, 27-21, after extra time. France caused the biggest upset by defeating New Zealand, 43-31, in the semifinals at Twickenham, near London, on October 31. In a disappointing finale at the new Millennium Stadium in Cardiff, Wales, on November 6, Australia beat France to become the first two-time world champion. (Australia had also won in 1991.)

In April 1999, Scotland became the Lloyds TSB European Champion in the Five-Nations Tournament, but only on points difference. Wales, already defeated by Scotland, denied England the title with a surprising 32-31 victory, on a converted try in the final seconds of an extremely tense contest at London's Wembley Stadium.

New Zealand won the fourth annual Tri-Nations Series, a six-match tournament contested in July and August by Australia, New Zealand, and South Africa. The Australians retained the Bledisloe Cup, due largely to their two victories over New Zealand. On August 28, in the final match, which attracted a crowd of 107,000, the largest ever for an international rugby match, Australia defeated New Zealand, 28-7.

In the Super 12 Series, contested by 12 provincial teams from Australia, New Zealand, and South Africa, reigning champions Canterbury Crusaders defeated Otago Highlanders, 24-19, in the final at Dunedin, New Zealand, on May 29. In the Pacific Rim Championship, played by Japan, the United States, Hong Kong, Canada, Fiji, Tonga, and Samoa, Japan won the Epson Cup in July.

RU national competitions. In the European Cup final, Ulster defeated Colomiers, 21-6, in Dublin on January 30 to become the first Irish team to win rugby union's top European trophy. In the final of the European Shield, for teams not qualified to contest the European Cup, Montferrand overcame Bourgoin, 35-16, on February 27.

In England, London Wasps captured the Tetley's Bitter Cup by defeating Newcastle Falcons, 29-19, in the final at Twickenham on May 15. Leicester finished at the top of the Allied Dunbar Premier Division in May. Tetley's also sponsored the County Championship, which Cornwall won by defeating Gloucester, 24-15, in the final at Twickenham in May.

Heriot's FP won the Tennents Velvet First Division Championship in Scotland. Gala triumphed over Kelso, 8-3, in the SRU Tennents Velvet Cup final on April 24. Llanelli won the National League Premier Division title in Wales, but lost to Swansea, 37-10, in the final of the SWALEC Cup at Cardiff on May 15. Cork Constitution defeated Garryowen, 14-11, on May 1 to take the Allied Irish Bank League final in Ireland. Munster won Ireland's Guinness Interprovincial Championship title in November.

On September 11, the Golden Lions won South Africa's Bankfin Currie Cup by defeating Natal, 32-9, in the final at Kings Park Stadium. The Lions also won the Vodacom Cup on May 29, by beating Griqualand, 73-7. In New Zealand, Waikato retained the Ranfurly Shield with a 30-24 win over Wellington. In New Zealand's National Provincial Championship final on October 23, Auckland defeated Wellington, 24-18. In Australia, Eastern Districts defeated Western Districts, 16-15, in the Brisbane Premiership grand final.

International Rugby League (RL). Australia once again confirmed its status as the top Rugby League nation, overcoming New Zealand in a test match on April 23 in Sydney and then winning the Tri-Nations Tournament over New Zealand and Great Britain, in October. After being beaten by New Zealand in their preliminary round match, Australia overcame the same opponents, 22-20, in the final at Auckland on November 5.

In a separate test match played on October 22, the New Zealanders crushed Tonga, 74-0, in Auckland. In a World Cup qualifying competition in Orlando, Florida, in November, Lebanon trounced an inexperienced United States, 62-8, in the final.

RL national competitions. In England, Leeds Rhinos routed London Broncos, 52-0, in the Silk Cut Challenge Cup at Wembley Stadium in London on May 1. On September 25, in the Northern Ford Premiership Grand final, Hunslet Hawks narrowly defeated Dewsbury Rams, 12-11. In the Super League grand final at Old Trafford, Manchester, on October 9, St. Helens Saints defeated Bradford Bulls, 8-6.

In Australia, Melbourne Storm won the National Rugby League championship on September 26, with a victory over St. George-Illawarra, 20-18, before a league-record crowd of 107,558. In the annual State of the Origin Series, contested in May and June, between New South Wales and Queensland, the honors were even after one victory apiece. The final match was a draw, 10-10. The draw—the first in 57 Origin matches between the two states since the series began in 1980—meant that Queensland retained the Origin trophy as winners of the 1998 series.   □ David Duckham

Russia. On Dec. 31, 1999, Boris Yeltsin announced his immediate resignation as president of Russia and named Prime Minister Vladimir V. Putin as acting president. The resignation came six months before the scheduled end of Yeltsin's second term. Although Yeltsin had been hospitalized repeatedly since undergoing coronary bypass surgery in 1996, his resignation shocked the people of Russia and political leaders around the world.

Russia's political climate for much of 1999 was characterized by internal turmoil and international isolation stemming largely from Russia's war against the breakaway region of Chechnya. The Russian economy, however, began to recover in 1999 from the financial collapse of 1998.

Impeachment. In May 1999, Yeltsin faced impeachment by the State Duma, the lower house of the parliament. Communist deputies, who dominated the Duma, had agreed in December 1998 to present five articles of impeachment, charging Yeltsin with offenses ranging from waging the 1994-1996 war in Chechnya to implementing economic reforms that produced "genocide" in Russia by leading to a lower national birthrate and a drop in average life expectancy.

On May 12, 1999, the day before the Duma was to open the impeachment debate, Yeltsin dismissed Prime Minister Yevgeny Primakov, citing his lack of progress on economic improvements. In Primakov's place, Yeltsin appointed Sergei Stepashin, the Interior Minister and First Deputy Premier. Many political analysts viewed the ouster of Primakov—who had been appointed in a compromise between Yeltsin and his Communist Party opponents—and the choice of Stepashin—a Yeltsin loyalist—as a gesture of defiance toward the Duma on the eve of the impeachment vote. The Duma, apparently reluctant

to provoke yet another confrontation with Yeltsin, rejected all five impeachment counts. The strongest charge, relating to the war in Chechnya, fell 17 votes short of the required 300 votes. On May 19, the Duma approved Stepashin's nomination as prime minister on the first ballot.

Stepashin's government. The Russian economy began to rebound under Stepashin's leadership. On July 28, Russia won approval from the International Monetary Fund (IMF—a United Nations-affiliated organization, located in Washington, D.C., that provides short-term credit to member nations) for $4.5 billion in new loans. Russia's obligations to the IMF had gone unpaid since Russia defaulted on its debts in August 1998. The deal with the IMF cleared the way for negotiations to reschedule Russia's other outstanding debts. By July 1999, the government had also reduced the federal budget deficit, and the annual inflation rate had dropped to 50 percent (from 85 percent in 1998). The collapse of the ruble made imports more expensive, fueling an increased demand for Russian goods.

Financial scandals. In February 1999, the former head of the Russian Central Bank confirmed that from 1993 to 1998 the bank had hidden billions of dollars in hard currency from international lenders in an obscure offshore financial company in the Channel Islands off Great Britain. The revelation triggered a series of international probes into other financial dealings at the highest levels of the Russian government. In August 1999, investigators in Switzerland uncovered evidence that Mabatex, a Swiss construction company that had received lucrative contracts to restore the Kremlin and other government buildings, may have been paying kickbacks to members of Yeltsin's inner circle, including his daughter and close adviser, Tatyana Dyachenko.

In the United States, government officials began an investigation in August into whether the Bank of New York had served as a conduit for Russian funds in what appeared to be one of the biggest money-laundering schemes ever uncovered. U.S. bank officials were charged with helping Russian banks move billions of dollars—including funds from international lending agencies such as the IMF—out of Russia.

Stepashin dismissed. On August 9, Yeltsin abruptly fired Stepashin. Analysts speculated that Yeltsin was angry at Stepashin for failing to halt Yeltsin's opponents from forming an electorate bloc or resentful of the prime minister's growing popularity. In Stepashin's place, Yeltsin appointed Vladimir Putin, an obscure former intelligence agent and political operative who was head of the Federal Security Service. Yeltsin's nomination of Putin, who had spent his entire career working behind the scenes, stunned Russia's political elite.

TIME CAPSULE 1923

RUSSIA

A VAST NEW REPUBLIC, more than twice as large as the United States or Canada, was ushered into existence during August 1923. The organizing genius behind the movement was the leadership of the Russian Socialist Federated Soviet Republic, the legal designation of the communistic state established by [V. I.] Lenin and [Leon] Trotsky after the revolution of 1918. The original Russian Soviet government has welded together under the flag of communism six states, which now constitute the Union of Socialist Soviet Republics.

Parliamentary elections. Putin's appointment coincided with the start of campaigning for the December 1999 parliamentary elections. While the Communist Party repeated its 1995 showing and won about 24 percent of the vote, Unity, a centrist party organized by the new prime minister, took more than 23 percent, which observers suggested was an indication of greater public support for the government than analysts had suspected. The Fatherland-All Russia Party, organized around the alliance of Moscow Mayor Yuri Luzhkov and former Prime Minister Yevgeny Primakov, garnered 12 percent of the vote, far below expectations. The Union of Right Forces, a reform party led by Anatoly Chubais, architect of Russia's privatization program, took 8.7 percent.

Unlike Yeltsin's successful campaign against the Communists in the 1996 presidential campaign, the 1999 parliamentary election did not offer voters a stark choice between reform and a return to Communism. There were important issues at stake, however. Several parties pledged to introduce constitutional changes to strengthen the Duma, a relatively weak institution under the 1993 constitution. The most popular proposals included schemes to reduce the vast powers of the Russian president.

Yeltsin resigns. Many political experts characterized Boris Yeltsin's unexpected resignation on Dec. 31, 1999, as a brilliant stroke of political timing. After announcing the resignation during a televised address, Yeltsin named Prime Minister Putin as acting president and noted that presidential elections would be held in March 2000, three months ahead of schedule. Analysts theorized that Yeltsin's departure six months early was intended to capitalize on Putin's popularity to ensure his election as Russia's president. Popular support for the prime minister was at a high point in the wake of the parliamentary elections in December and the force with which Putin was waging the war in Chechnya. Putin, immediately after taking office as president, granted Yeltsin immunity from prosecution for any crimes committed during his nine years in office.

War with Chechnya flared again on Aug. 7, 1999, when a force of between 1,000 and 4,000 self-proclaimed Islamic militants from Chechnya invaded neighboring Dagestan, a republic in southern European Russia, and on August 10 declared Dagestan to be an independent Islamic state. In response, Russia reintroduced troops to Chechnya in an effort to wipe out the militants. Russia's military mission in Chechnya expanded dramatically in September, after three massive explosions destroyed apartment buildings in Moscow and the southern Russian city of Volgadonsk, killing more than 200 people. Russian investigators declared the explosions to be the

work of terrorists and blamed Chechens for the carnage. The military objectives in Chechnya quickly expanded to include the eradication of all terrorists based in the republic.

The renewed Russian military campaign in Chechnya was reminiscent of the unsuccessful campaign that had ended in 1996. While military officials in Moscow declared that their forces were attacking only military targets, reports from

---

TIME CAPSULE 1941
RUSSIA

By far the most important development in the war in 1941 was Hitler's sudden attack upon Soviet Russia on June 22. His reasons, as set forth in a long excited speech, were that he had never trusted Stalin, and only from necessity and with a heavy heart had entered into the pact with him a week before World War II began. . . .

Hitler, according to his own admission, had made a very serious miscalculation when he plunged into his Russian adventure. He had greatly underestimated the number and quality of the airplanes, tanks, and other equipment which Stalin had been secretly preparing for years. . . .

Moreover, Stalin adopted the "scorched-earth" policy. As Russian troops and peasants withdrew eastward, they destroyed everything in the path of the advancing Germans. Villages were burned. Factories, power plants, and bridges were blown up. Grain was set on fire. Cattle were driven deeper into Russia. As far as possible, nothing was left which the Germans could use.

TIME CAPSULE 1943
RUSSIA

The Russian People continued to make almost incredible sacrifices to drive the Nazi invader from their land. Food and clothing rations were cut to bare necessities in order to give the best of nourishment and protection to the Red Army. Laborers in Leningrad received only four slices of black bread and one glass of water a day. Regardless of the food scarcity, workers continued to labor at high speed in all Russian factories, often 11 hours a day and 6 days a week.

the region described relentless assaults generating many civilian casualties and even larger numbers of civilian refugees. On Oct. 21, 1999, as many as 150 people were killed when Russian rockets fell on a marketplace in the Chechen capital, Grozny. By mid-November, Russian troops had laid siege to Grozny, as floods of refugees headed for cover in the mountains, despite the coming of winter.

The Russian military issued an ultimatum to the people of Grozny on December 6, warning them to flee the besieged city by December 11 or face a massive assault. The ultimatum provoked outrage in the West, with some leaders considering imposing economic sanctions against Moscow unless it rescinded the threat. On December 10, Russia offered to negotiate with Chechen leaders to organize the safe exit of civilians from Grozny.

While the attack on Chechnya triggered an outpouring of international concern, the campaign had boosted the popularity of Putin, the new prime minister, at home. Public opinion polls showed that most Russians supported the new offensive. This was in contrast to the earlier war in Chechnya, which was highly unpopular with the Russian public. As a consequence, virtually all Russian political parties were united in their support of the war effort in 1999. Many Russians viewed the 1999 invasion as an opportunity to erase the memory of what they considered a humiliating defeat in Chechnya in 1996.

Tensions with the West over Chechnya capped a year of rising alienation and international isolation that began with the formal expansion of the North Atlantic Treaty Organization (NATO) on March 12, 1999. Poland, Hungary, and the Czech Republic, all former adversaries of NATO as members of the Communist Bloc, became NATO's newest members. Although NATO officials assured Russia that NATO remained a purely defensive alliance, Russian military and security officials remained wary. They were also uneasy about plans to consider NATO expansion into the former Soviet republics in the Baltics.

Yugoslavia. Russia's unease over NATO expansion turned into anger on March 24, when NATO began bombing Yugoslavia to force Serbian forces out of the province of Kosovo. Russia, a traditional ally of Serbia, continued to speak for the Serbian cause, with former Prime Minister Viktor Chernomyrdin shuttling between Belgrade, the Yugoslav capital, and NATO headquarters in Brussels, Belgium, seeking an end to the bombing.

Russia's frustration with its diminished authority in international affairs spilled over into action on June 11, when some 200 Russian troops stationed in Bosnia-Herzegovina raced across the border into Kosovo after the NATO bombings ended. The Russians arrived in Pristina ahead of NATO peacekeepers and set up a command post at the city's airport, where British forces were to have been based. Although the commanders avoided a confrontation, the move forced NATO to define a larger role for Russia in the Kosovo peacekeeping mission.   □ Steven L. Solnick

See also **Europe; Yugoslavia; Yugoslavia: A Special Report.**

San Francisco

San Francisco was ranked number one on *Money* magazine's 1999 list of the best places to live in the United States. The listing reflected the city's wealth, beauty, and cultural richness. These assets, however, continued to pose problems in the Bay Area—San Francisco and the suburbs and towns ringing San Francisco Bay.

Mayoral election. The downside of San Francisco's prosperity dogged the fall reelection campaign of Mayor Willie L. Brown, Jr., first elected in 1995. Brown boasted of the city's booming economy, budget surplus, low unemployment rate, and falling crime rate. But voters seemed more inclined to focus on such issues as congestion in both public and private transportation and the rise in homelessness and lack of affordable housing resulting from soaring housing costs. Brown also faced criticism for alleged corruption in the city's housing department.

Initially, Brown, Frank Jordan, a former mayor and police chief, and Clint Reilly, a millionaire former political consultant, were the front-runners in a field of 14 candidates. On Oct. 13, 1999, Tom Ammiano, president of the San Francisco Board of Supervisors and a leader in the city's gay and more liberal communities, mounted a write-in campaign. Ammiano said he was entering the race because so many people felt "despair" about the choice of candidates.

TIME CAPSULE **1991**

RUSSIA

The Soviet Union officially ceased to exist as a political entity on Dec. 25, 1991. That day, Soviet President Mikhail S. Gorbachev resigned, after six years in power. And the Soviet red flag, with its hammer standing for the workers and its sickle for the peasants, was lowered from the Kremlin in Moscow, which had been the center of the Soviet government. . . .

The collapse of the Soviet Union had occurred rapidly in the wake of a failed coup against Gorbachev in August.

On election day, November 2, Ammiano gathered 25.4 percent of the vote, surpassing Jordan and Reilly and forcing Brown into a runoff on December 14. In that election, Brown captured more than 126,000 votes—60 percent of the vote—to win a second term in office. Some political experts claimed that though Brown was a liberal, many voters considered Ammiano too liberal.

FBI probes. On November 15, a federal grand jury in San Francisco indicted four people, including three current or former employees of the San Francisco Housing Authority, on charges of bribery and conspiracy. Prosecutors accused the four of selling federal housing vouchers, documents that entitle low-income residents to federal rent subsidies. Federal law enforcement officials previously had filed charges against 25 people for their alleged roles in the scandal.

Federal investigators also launched a probe in 1999 of a San Francisco government agency that assists businesses owned by minorities and women to obtain city contracts. In September, the city filed a civil suit against a white-owned company that, the city charged, used a black-owned firm as a front to obtain city business.

One-newspaper town. The Hearst Corporation, owner of the *San Francisco Examiner*, the city's afternoon newspaper, announced on August 6 its purchase of the *San Francisco Chronicle*, its long-time morning rival. The announcement came two months after the Chronicle Publishing Company had put the largest-circulation paper in Northern California up for sale. Hearst announced it would try to sell the *Examiner*, but if no one bought the paper, Hearst would merge the *Examiner* into the *Chronicle*.

Many San Franciscans feared that without competition, the *Chronicle* would be less inclined to report on official corruption or inner-city issues. In October, officials from the U.S. Department of Justice announced an investigation of Hearst's merger plan to determine if it violated federal antimonopoly laws. State and city officials also launched investigations.

Pie brigade. Three members of San Francisco's Biotic Baking Brigade, a loosely organized group that throws pies to protest perceived social wrongs, received six-month jail sentences for battery on February 24 for hurling pastries at Mayor Brown. The three had pelted Brown with cherry, pumpkin, and tofu pies at the kickoff of the mayor's "San Francisco Cares" program for the homeless in November 1998. The pie-throwers contended they were trying to use humor to register their criticism of Brown's homeless policies. Brown testified that he feared a riot would break out after the attack. ☐ Brian Bouldrey

See also **City; Radio.**

Saudi Arabia played a key role in forging a March 1999 agreement by the Organization of Petroleum Exporting Countries (OPEC), an association of the world's major oil-producing nations, to cut OPEC's oil production. The move was made to raise oil prices, which in late 1998 had fallen to less than $10 a barrel—their lowest level in more than a decade. The production cutback helped oil prices surge to beyond $25 a barrel late in 1999.

Economy. Saudi Arabia acted in 1999 to increase its petroleum revenues, upon which its economy depends. In 1998, the kingdom's oil revenues fell to $30 billion—down from $50 billion in 1997. Saudi Arabia also suffered in 1998 from a budget deficit of $13 billion and a drop in *per capita gross domestic product* (the value of goods and services produced per person in a given period) from $7,000 in 1997 to $6,300 in 1998.

The Saudi government enacted austerity measures in 1999 to strengthen the economy. It cut state spending by 16 percent, suspended construction projects and military contracts, delayed contract payments, and continued a freeze in government hiring. The government also raised prices for some utilities.

Improved relations with Iran. Saudi officials in 1999 continued their efforts, begun in 1998, to improve relations with Iran. Saudi ties with Iran had been strained since the 1979 Islamic Revolution, in which a conservative Islamic regime assumed power in Iran. In mid-May 1999, Mohammed Khatami became the first Iranian president to visit Saudi Arabia since the revolution. Earlier that month, the two countries agreed to exchange defense *attaches* (persons on the staff of a minister to a foreign country).

Analysts believed the Saudis hoped to strengthen the hand of President Khatami, a moderate Islamic cleric, who was engaged in a political battle with conservative forces in Iran. However, Saudi Arabia's growing ties with Iran created friction with the United Arab Emirates (UAE), a traditional Saudi ally. The UAE and Iran have long disputed the sovereignty of three Persian Gulf islands.

Terrorism. In October 1999, the United States deported suspected terrorist Hani al-Sayegh to Saudi Arabia. Sayegh, a Saudi national, was to be tried in a Saudi court for his alleged role in a 1996 bombing that killed 19 U.S. troops at a military base near Dhahran, Saudi Arabia. Sayegh was deported after he backed out of a deal to provide U.S. agents with information on the bombing in exchange for not being returned to Saudi Arabia. ☐ Christine Helms

See also **Energy supply; Iran; Middle East; Middle East: A Special Report; Terrorism.**

School. See **Education.**

Senegal. See **Africa.**

Sierra Leone. On July 7, 1999, the government of Sierra Leone and the Revolutionary United Front (RUF), the nation's main rebel group, signed a peace accord to end an eight-year-long civil war. Under the accord, the government agreed to cancel the death sentence imposed on RUF leader Foday Sankoh for treason and mass murder and to name him vice president. The agreement also granted the rebels a general amnesty from prosecution for war crimes, gave the RUF seven additional ministerial posts, and provided for the transformation of the RUF into a political party.

In return, the RUF agreed to lay down its arms and drop demands for the expulsion from Sierra Leone of a Nigerian-led West African peacekeeping force, the Economic Community Monitoring Group (ECOMOG). However, by the end of 1999, the rebels, who controlled about half of Sierra Leone, showed little sign of demobilizing or handing in their weapons.

Freetown invaded. The civil war had escalated in January, when rebel forces nearly succeeded in capturing Freetown, the capital, after a three-month campaign. The antigovernment forces included both RUF fighters and the Armed Forces Revolutionary Council (AFRC), the ousted military regime headed by Major Johnny Paul Koromah. In 1997, military officers led by Koromah, in an alliance with the RUF, had overthrown President Ahmed Tejan Kabbah, whose 1996 election had been part of a previous peace settlement to end civil war. In early 1998, ECOMOG overthrew the AFRC and reinstated Kabbah. Since then, the RUF had continued its fight against the government, mainly with a campaign of mutilation, rape, and murder against civilians in rural areas.

During the attack on Freetown, RUF forces and their AFRC allies killed an estimated 3,000 civilians and burned large areas of the city. Thousands more—many hideously mutilated by rebel forces—fled the capital into the surrounding hills. ECOMOG forces ultimately stopped the offensive, but the insurgents left a trail of death and destruction in their wake.

Hostages. The fragile agreement nearly collapsed on Aug. 4, 1999, when renegade rebels seized several dozen hostages outside Freetown. The captives included United Nations military observers monitoring the cease-fire and aid workers sent to witness the release of some 200 abductees, mainly children, held by rebel forces. The kidnappers were former members of the AFRC regime, who felt that they had been left out of the July peace accord. The release of the hostages on August 10 followed an appeal by Koromah, who in 1999 ranked second in the RUF hierarchy.   □ Simon Baynham

See also **Africa.**

Sikhism. During the spring festival of Vaisakhi on April 14, 1999, Sikhs around the world celebrated the 300th anniversary of the founding of the Khalsa. The Khalsa (literally translated *pure*) is the community of Sikhs who follow a code of discipline established by the religion's 10th spiritual leader, Guru Gobind Singh. The festivities were highlighted by the completion of a four-year project to replace the gold-plated copper sheets covering the Golden Temple in Amritsar, India, and with an exhibition of Sikh treasures at the Victoria and Albert Museum in London.

On March 16, Bibi Jagir Kaur became the first woman president of Sikh's highest elected body, the Shiromani Gurdwara Parbandhak Committee, which was established in 1925. Months of conflict had led to the dismissal of Jagir Kaur's predecessor of 25 years, Gurcharan Singh Tohra, and of Bhai Ranjit Singh, manager of the Akal Takht, the shrine from which rulings are proclaimed.

Sikhs took steps in 1999 to introduce a solar calendar in place of a traditional lunar calendar from India. With the new system, festivals would occur on the same date every year.

In July 1999, Prince Charles of Great Britain unveiled in Thetford, England, a statue of Maharaja Duleep Singh, England's first Sikh resident and the last Sikh ruler in India. The British had deposed him in 1849.   □ Eleanor M. Nesbitt

Singapore. President Ong Teng Cheong announced in July 1999 that he could find "no compelling reason" to seek reelection as president. Ong expressed frustration about the largely ceremonial role of the office, saying that he had experienced difficulty obtaining cooperation from ministers and civil servants. In Singapore's parliamentary system, the prime minister, selected by parties in parliament, is the primary leader.

As the scheduled presidential election approached in August, the Elections Commission disqualified two of the three candidates, declared former intelligence chief S. R. Nathan the winner, and canceled the election. An opposition leader charged that the presidential selection was "stage-managed" by the People's Action Party, the ruling party in parliament. The new president began a six-year term on September 1.

An opposition politician, Chee Soon Juan, tested official limits on free speech in early 1999 by giving an impromptu speech in a Singapore park. He was arrested and convicted of violating the Public Entertainments Law, which requires public speakers to obtain a government permit. Government officials said that restricting public speaking was necessary to maintain order.   □ Henry S. Bradsher

See also **Asia.**

Skating. See Hockey; Ice skating.

Norwegian skier Lasse Kjus streaks toward the finish line in the final men's downhill race of the 1998-1999 World Cup season in Spain in March 1999. The victory earned Kjus the World Cup downhill championship.

Skiing. Lasse Kjus of Norway and Alexandra Meissnitzer of Austria were the preeminent skiers of 1999. Both excelled in the World Cup professional season and at the World Alpine Skiing Championships in Vail, Colorado, in February. Austria topped the overall count at Vail with 12 medals, 4 more than runner-up Norway. No other country won more than two medals, and the United States team was shut out.

Lasse Kjus topped the World Cup overall standings with 1,465 points—23 more than his chief challenger, fellow Norwegian Kjetil Aamodt. Kjus was also the season's downhill champion. Hermann Maier of Austria, the 1998 World Cup and Olympic champion, finished third in the final standings.

The high point of Kjus's season came on Feb. 14, 1999, the final day of the World Alpine Championships. By finishing second in the men's slalom, Kjus became the first skier ever to capture a medal in all five Alpine events. Kjus began his two-gold, three-silver performance by tying Maier for the Super-G gold medal on February 2. It was the first dead heat in a title race, and only 0.01 second separated Kjus and Maier from Hans Knauss of Austria, who finished third.

Kjus also struck gold in the giant slalom and silver in the downhill, the combined slalom, and the slalom. Palander beat Kjus by 0.11 second for the slalom title, becoming the first Finn to win a medal in a recognized Alpine race. Maier captured his second gold medal on February 6, when he held off Kjus in the downhill.

Meissnitzer, a 1998 Olympic medalist, topped the women's overall World Cup standings and also was the Super-G and giant slalom champion for the 1999 season. More impressively, she set the pace for the Austrian team at the World Alpine Championships. Meissnitzer's first gold in that competition led to an Austrian sweep of the Super-G on February 3. Meissnitzer won her second gold of the championships in the giant slalom. Austria also gained gold medals in the downhill and combined downhill from Renate Goetschl.

Sweden's Pernila Wiberg took the gold in the women's combined slalom at Vail, and Zali Skeggall of Australia won the women's slalom to become the first skier from the Southern Hemisphere to capture an Alpine Championships gold medal.

Nordic skiing. At the Nordic Skiing World Championships in February, at Ramsau, Austria, Mika Myllyla of Finland took the gold medals for the 10-, 30-, and 50-kilometer (6.2-, 18.6-, and 31.07-mile) races and barely missed winning the 15-kilometer (9.3-mile) pursuit race. Bjarte Engen Vik of Norway earned a pair of gold medals at Ramsau, in the men's combined and combined sprint competitions.   □ Ron Reid

Slovakia. The four-party coalition government of Prime Minister Mikulas Dzurinda spent 1999 attempting to put Slovakia back on track for membership in the European Union (EU) and the North Atlantic Treaty Organization (NATO). In February, Dzurinda formally apologized to the Hungarian government after Slovak intelligence officials admitted that, under the previous Slovak government, their agency had tried unsuccessfully to undermine Hungary's bid to join NATO. In July, the parliament passed legislation allowing ethnic minorities to use their own language in official business in areas in which they comprised more than 20 percent of the population.

New president. Rudolf Schuster, a member of the ruling coalition, was elected president of Slovakia in May. The largely ceremonial office had been vacant since March 1998, when the term of President Michal Kovac expired. Schuster was elected not by the parliament but by the public in a direct election. This change had been promised by the coalition in the 1998 elections.

Economy. Economists expected Slovakia's *gross domestic product* (the value of all goods and services produced in a country in a given year) to grow by 2 percent in 1999. Unemployment continued to rise, reaching 18.65 percent in October. Foreign investment in Slovakia rose as investors gained confidence in the government.

Foreign relations. In October, the EU gave encouraging signals that it might begin membership negotiations with Slovakia, as well as Lithuania, Latvia, Malta, Bulgaria, and Romania. In 1998, the EU had invited Hungary, Poland, the Czech Republic, Slovenia, Estonia, and Cyprus to the first round of EU expansion talks. EU officials recognized the progress Slovak leaders had made with regard to democratic and economic reforms. In September, the Slovak parliament had approved a law easing restrictions on the sale of large companies, including telecommunications and banking firms, to private owners. The measure repealed an exemption for such "strategically important" companies, which was a condition set by the EU for invitation to membership talks.

Slovakia continued its efforts in 1999 to join NATO. The Slovak government supported the NATO bombing of Yugoslavia even though opposition parties and most of the population disapproved of the campaign.

Czech and Slovak leaders resolved one of the last issues remaining from the negotiated break-up of Czechoslovakia in 1993, the division of national property.

In October 1999, Slovakia announced measures that allow Czech citizens to regain their Slovak citizenship or to keep dual Slovak-Czech citizenship.

☐ Sharon L. Wolchik

See also **Czech Republic; Europe.**

Soccer. Women's soccer took center stage in the summer of 1999, when the Federation Internationale de Football Association (FIFA) held its Women's World Cup tournament in the United States. The tournament ended in victory for the U.S. team, after a penalty shootout in the final against China. In men's soccer, Brazil won the Copa America, and Mexico was the surprise winner of the FIFA Confederations Cup.

International tournaments. The United States reestablished itself as the top women's soccer nation when the U.S. team won the third Women's World Cup, which was played from June 19 to July 10. The U.S. had won the first World Cup in 1991 and finished third in 1995.

The United States won all three of its group matches to reach the quarterfinals, where the team edged Germany 3-2. The United States then beat Brazil 2-0 in the semifinals. China defeated Russia in the quarterfinals and then beat reigning champion Norway 5-0 to reach the final.

The stage was set for a final between the two outstanding teams of the competition, and more than 90,000 people turned up at the Rose Bowl in Pasadena, California. The attendance set a record for a single women's sporting event.

The match was scoreless through 90 minutes of normal time and 30 minutes of "sudden death" extra time. The game, therefore, had to be decided by penalty kicks. Only one kick failed, when U.S. goalkeeper Brianna Scurry turned away the attempt of China's Liu Ying. Brandi Chastain scored the winning goal on the U.S. team's fifth and final penalty kick to claim the victory by 5-4 on penalties.

In June and July 1999, the South American Championship for the Copa America was staged in Paraguay for the first time. The tournament, held every two years, is contested by countries from South America plus two invited teams from other continents. In 1999, Mexico and Japan were the invitees, the latter being the first guest from outside the Americas to take part. Brazil, the reigning champion, retained the Copa America by beating Uruguay 3-0 in the final in Asuncion on July 18. Earlier, Brazil had beaten Venezuela 7-0 in their opening group match, a record score for the competition.

The first FIFA Confederations Cup began in Mexico on July 28, with eight teams playing in 2 groups of 4. Originally scheduled for January, the tournament received a setback in October 1998 when France, the World Cup champion, withdrew due to scheduling problems. The tournament was postponed for six months, but countries representing all of the continental federations eventually took part. The biggest shock of the competition was the U.S. team's 2-0 defeat of European champion Germany in Group B. This victory qualified the United States for the semifinals. Although the United States lost 1-0 to Mexico after extra time, it went on to beat Saudi Arabia 2-0 in the match for third place. Mexico won the Cup with a thrilling 4-3 victory over Brazil in the final, before a crowd of more than 100,000 at the Azteca Stadium in Mexico City on August 4.

International club competition. Manchester United of England won the European Champions Cup with a 2-1 final-match victory over Germany's Bayern Munich in Barcelona on May 26. The victory was the English club's first triumph in the competition since 1968. England trailed by a goal from the sixth minute, but scored twice in three minutes of stoppage time. This was the climax of a record season for Manchester, which had won the English Premier League title and the English Football Association (FA) Cup, to complete an unprecedented "treble" for an English team.

The two-match final of the Copa de los Libertadores, the major South American club competition, was decided on penalty kicks after a 2-2 draw. The Brazilian club Palmeiras won the shoot-out 4-3, defeating Deportivo Cali of Colombia. Deportivo had won the first leg 1-0 in Cali on June 2, but Palmeiras had forced the penalty decider with a 2-1 win in the second game in Sao Paulo on June 16.

Manchester United, the European club champion, and Palmeiras, the South American club champion, met in Tokyo on November 30 to contest the FIFA World Club Championship for the Toyota Cup. Manchester United claimed their fourth major title of the year by edging Palmeiras 1-0 to become the first English club to win the championship. The Italian club Lazio, of Rome, defeated the Spanish club Mallorca 2-1 in the final of the European Cup-Winners' Cup in Birmingham, England, on May 20. The match marked the end of this competition, held annually since 1961. It was discontinued because of the expansion of the Champions Cup. The Union of European Football Associations (UEFA) Cup was also won by an Italian club, Parma, which defeated the French club Marseille 3-0 in the final match in Moscow on May 12, 1999.

CONCACAF Champions Cup. The inaugural tournament for the CONCACAF (Confederation of North, Central America and Caribbean Associations of Football) championship was staged in Las Vegas, Nevada, from September 28 to October 3, with eight clubs from the region taking part. The two participating U.S. teams, DC United and the Chicago Fire, reached the semifinals. United fell 3-1 to Mexican winter champions Necaxa, and the Fire lost 5-4 on penalties (after a 1-1 draw) to the surprise team of the tournament, Alajuela

Goalkeeper Brianna Scurry of the United States blocks a penalty shot made by China's Liu Ying in the Women's World Cup soccer final at the Rose Bowl in Pasadena, California, in July 1999. The block set up the U.S. team for a 5-4 victory on penalty kicks to win the World Cup championship.

from Costa Rica. Necaxa defeated Alajuela in the final match 2-1.

Major League Soccer (MLS). On Nov. 21, 1999, DC United, the two-time MLS Cup champion, made it to the championship game for the fourth consecutive year. DC United won the MLS Cup in Foxboro, Massachusetts, for the third time by defeating the Los Angeles Galaxy 2-0.

To reach the final, the Galaxy beat the Colorado Rapids, 2 games to 0, then eliminated the Dallas Burn, 2 games to 1, for the Western Conference title. In the Eastern Conference, DC United beat the Miami Fusion, 2 games to 0, in the semifinals and the Columbus Crew, 2 games to 1, in the conference finals.

Los Angeles suffered a major setback in the final when team captain and central defender Robin Fraser suffered a broken collarbone just five minutes into the game. United scored both of its goals in the first half and then shut out the potent Galaxy offense.

Records, rankings, rules, and awards. Internazionale of Milan paid a new record price for the acquisition of a player in June. The team paid Lazio of Rome almost $50 million to acquire striker Christian Vieri.

The number of national soccer associations in the FIFA World Rankings rose above 200 for the first time in 1999. Brazil remained at the head of the list at the end of the year. France was in second place above the Czech Republic, which moved up five places during the year thanks to the team's exploits in the European Championships qualifying competition. The Czechs were the only team in the nine groups to finish with a perfect record. The United States moved up two places to end 1999 in 21st place.

An addition to the definitions of "unsporting behavior" proved to be a significant change to FIFA's *laws* (rules) of the game in 1999. The new law enabled referees to punish a player who pretends to have been fouled by an opponent, a practice known as "diving." FIFA sanctioned the use of two referees per match on a trial basis in some leagues for the 1999-2000 season. Each referee had jurisdiction over the entire field of play and had equal responsibilities, except that one was the timekeeper for the match.

In January 1999, Zinedine Zidane, the French midfielder and hero of France's 1998 World Cup championship, was named FIFA World Player of the Year. Zidane, who played professionally for the Italian club Juventus, received 518 points in the voting. Brazilian striker Ronaldo, the winner in the previous two years, was second with 164 points, followed by Davor Suker of Croatia with 108. The 1998 Fair Play award went jointly to the national associations of the United States, Iran, and Northern Ireland.   □ Norman Barrett

Social Security. While Democrats and Republicans both claimed to be the leading protectors of Social Security, the United States Congress did nothing in 1999 to deal with the system's long-term financial problems. Slightly rosier forecasts from the Trustees of the Social Security and Medicare trust funds in their March 30 report helped to reduce the sense of urgency. The Trustees projected that the Social Security fund would have adequate revenues until 2034, two years longer than the 1998 forecast. They said that the Hospital Insurance fund, once expected to run out of money in 2008, will be able to pay full benefits until 2015. The Trustees attributed the improved outlook to "the continued strong performance of the U.S. economy," which led to high employment and boosted payroll taxes that funded the program.

In October 1999, Social Security Commissioner Kenneth S. Apfel announced a 2.4-percent cost-of-living increase in benefits, starting in January 2000. The increase amounted to an average of $19 per month for individuals and $32 per month for couples. The maximum benefit increased by $60, to $1,433 in 2000. The maximum benefit under the Supplemental Security Income program rose from $500 to $512 a month for individuals and from $751 to $769 a month for couples. The Medicare Part B premium, which pays doctor bills and outpatient expenses, remained unchanged at $45.50 per month.

On Oct. 1, 1999, the Social Security Administration began a program to provide annual Social Security statements to all workers aged 25 and older. When the program was fully implemented, each worker would automatically receive a statement of benefit estimates three months before his or her birth month.   □ William J. Eaton

TIME CAPSULE   1935

SOCIAL SECURITY

THE SOCIAL SECURITY ACT was passed and approved on August 14. This measure, it was estimated, will affect in its various aspects more than 28,000,000 people. The act provides for temporary old-age assistance, a permanent old-age pension system, unemployment compensation, and for grants to states for the aid of dependent children, for maternal and child welfare, public health work, and assistance to the blind.

South Africa

Nelson R. Mandela, the first black president of South Africa, resigned in 1999, as he had planned, after the country held its second multiracial, nationwide election on June 2. Thabo Mbeki, deputy president since 1994 and leader of the ruling African National Congress (ANC) since 1997, succeeded Mandela as president. In the election, the ANC won an overwhelming majority in Parliament and majorities in all but two of South Africa's provincial legislatures.

Last address. Mandela gave his last state-of-the-nation address at the opening of South Africa's Parliament on Feb. 5, 1999. Mandela spoke of the ANC's achievements since entering office in 1994, especially in providing water, electricity, and housing to millions of deprived South Africans. He acknowledged that the government needed to do more to fight crime and corruption, which he described as signs of "a sick society." Mandela, who won the 1993 Nobel Peace Prize, also noted he was saddened by continuing tensions and mistrust between South Africa's blacks and whites.

Election campaign. Sixteen political parties, three fewer than in the country's first all-race election in 1994, fielded candidates for office in the June 1999 election. During the campaign, the ANC's political opponents attempted to capitalize on widespread voter anger and frustration over government attempts to tackle the high crime rate, the housing shortage, and unemployment. In 1999, South Africa's unemployment rate stood at about 35 percent. The ANC claimed it had built 500,000 new housing units, a figure hotly disputed by the party's political opponents, who claimed the total was half that number.

Former South African President Nelson Mandela congratulates his successor, Thabo Mbeki, after Mbeki's inauguration on June 16. Mbeki was Mandela's deputy president since 1994 and had headed the ruling African National Congress party since 1997.

In addition, opposition parties warned voters against giving the ANC a two-thirds majority in Parliament, which would allow the party to amend South Africa's Constitution unilaterally. Opponents raised fears that Mbeki and the ANC then would expand the power of the central government at the expense of provincial governments and independent agencies. In May, Mbeki promised that the ANC would not rewrite the Constitution if it won a two-thirds majority.

Several mainly white parties also complained that complicated reforms to voting registration rules introduced by the ANC would exclude many whites from the voting. In January, Johann

The Ministry of South Africa*

Thabo Mvuyelwa Mbeki—president
J. Zuma—executive deputy president
A. K. Asmal—minister of education
N. Balfour—minister of sport and recreation
M. G. Buthelezi—minister of home affairs
A. T. Didiza—minister of agriculture and land affairs
A. Erwin—minister of trade and industry
G. J. Fraser-Moleketi—minister for the public service and administration
R. Kasrils—minister of water affairs and forestry
P. Lekota—minister of defence
P. M. Maduna—minister of justice
T. A. Manuel—minister of finance
I. Matesepe-Casaburri—minister for posts, telecommunications, and broadcasting
M. M. S. Mdladlana—minister of labour
P. Mlambo-Neguka—minister of minerals and energy
M. V. Moosa—minister of environmental affairs and tourism
S. D. Mthembi-Mahanyele—minister of housing
F. S. Mufamadi—minister for provincial affairs and constitutional development
B. S. Ngubane—minister of arts, culture, science, and technology
J. M. Nhlanhla—minister of intelligence
D. Omar—minister of transport
E. G. Pahad—minister in the office of the president
J. T. Radebe—minister for public enterprises
S. N. Sigcau—minister of public works
B. Skosana—minister of correctional services
Z. S. T. Skweyiya—minister for welfare and population development
M. E. Tshabalala-Msimang—minister for health
S. V. Tshwete—minister for safety and security
N. C. Dlamini Zuma—minister of foreign affairs

*As of Dec. 31, 1999.

Kriegler, head of the Independent Electoral Commission (IEC), resigned, charging the government with meddling in IEC efforts to organize the election. Mandela denied the charges.

KwaZulu-Natal violence. Compared with South Africa's first all-race election in 1994, the 1999 campaign was relatively peaceful. Nevertheless, political tensions increased sharply around Richmond in KwaZulu-Natal province, the site of a bitter feud between the predominantly black ANC and the multiracial United Democratic Movement (UDM). On January 23, Sifiso Nkabinde, secretary-general of the UDM, died in a hail of gunfire near his home in Richmond. In 1997, Mandela had expelled Nkabinde from the ANC for allegedly spying on party leaders for South Africa's former white supremacist government. Within hours of Nkabinde's assassination, gunmen massacred 11 members of a Richmond family allied with the ANC.

Although the government put thousands of troops and police on alert in the province in the wake of the killings, violence continued. In March and April 1999, an estimated 120 people died in clashes between the ANC and the Inkatha Freedom Party (IFP), which had won control of KwaZulu-Natal in 1994. The politically motivated killings fueled fears of a resurgence in the virtual civil war that enveloped the province from the late 1980's to the mid-1990's. On May 11, 1999, government security forces uncovered an enormous cache of weapons, including rifles, grenades, explosives, and mines, in KwaZulu-Natal. Police linked the arsenal, the largest ever found in South Africa, to the IFP.

In early March, violence erupted in the Cape Town township of Nyanga, where five political activists were murdered in what appeared to be an escalation of the ANC-UDM feud. The killings followed the January 24 assassination of Vulindlela Matiyase, a high-ranking UDM official.

Peace pact. Despite the preelection political violence, the ANC and the IFP signed a peace pact in Durban in mid-May. The pact committed the two parties to peaceful political campaigning. They each agreed to allow the other party free access to voters in their respective political strongholds. As a result, on election day, there was little of the violence and intimidation that preceded the balloting, even in the most politically volatile regions.

Election results. The ANC won 266 of 400 seats (66.4 percent) in the National Assembly, one parliamentary seat short of a two-thirds majority. Tony Leon's mostly white liberal Democratic Party (DP) won 38 seats (9.6 percent) to establish itself as the new official opposition. The IFP came in third with 34 seats (8.6 percent), winning most of its support in the mainly Zulu province of KwaZulu-Natal. The New National Party (NNP, the former National Party), which had governed South Africa under apartheid, took 28 seats (7 percent), down from the 20 percent it held in 1994. Bantu Holomisa's UDM won 14 seats (3.4 percent).

Eight other political parties shared the remaining 20 National Assembly seats. Barely 2 percent of the vote went to parties of either political extreme. Most of South Africa's 18 million registered voters cast their ballots along racial lines in the election, exposing the deep divisions that remained after the official end of *apartheid* (strict racial segregation) in 1994.

As expected, the ANC won clear majorities in seven of nine provincial legislatures. In Western Cape, an NNP stronghold, the ANC won 18 of 42 seats. In KwaZulu-Natal, the ANC took 32 seats, compared with 34 for the IFP. Independent electoral monitors declared their satisfaction with the fairness of the poll.

The ANC finally achieved a two-thirds parliamentary majority on June 9, 1999, when it joined forces with the chiefly Indian Minority Front, which had won one seat.

New government. After being sworn in as president on June 16, Mbeki consolidated power by appointing his cabinet. Eight of his 27 cabinet members were women. To the surprise of many, Winnie Madikizela-Mandela, Nelson Mandela's ex-wife, failed to secure a cabinet post. Analysts concluded that Madikizela-Mandela's 1993 conviction on kidnapping and assault charges following the death of a youth activist had disqualified her for a position in the government.

Speculation that IFP leader Mangosthu Buthelezi would accept the deputy presidency in exchange for ANC control over KwaZulu-Natal province proved false. Buthelezi retained his cabinet position as the minister of home affairs, and Mbeki appointed Jacob Zuma, deputy president of the ANC, as executive deputy president.

Political developments. Opening the new parliament on June 25, 1999, Mbeki devoted most of his speech to domestic issues, particularly South Africa's high crime rate. He proposed initiatives to increase penalties for crimes committed with guns and to create special investigative units to tackle government corruption.

In July, a government proposal to curb firearms ownership by requiring all gun owners to reapply for a license and undergo a mental health examination triggered a fierce response from the gun lobby. The South African Gun Owners' Association claimed that the proposed legislation would leave law-abiding citizens defenseless against armed criminals, many of whom carry such powerful weapons as the AK-47 assault rifle. South Africa has the world's second-highest firearm murder rate after Colombia. Guns were

[SOUTH AFRICAN PRIME MINISTER Johannes G.] Strydom cracked down hard with his *apartheid* (strict racial segregation) policies. In February, the government began to force 60,000 nonwhite Africans to leave their homes in Johannesburg and move to a housing project in nearby Meadowlands. This marked the government's biggest effort so far to carry out the Group Areas Act of 1950. This law provides for separate residential areas for whites and nonwhites.

used in approximately half of the 25,000 murders that occurred in South Africa in 1998 and in at least 70 percent of robberies and car thefts.

Strike. Mbeki's government faced its first major challenge when it dealt with the largest labor strike since the ANC took office in 1994. The strike, which began on July 29, 1999, and continued into early August, involved more than 500,000 public service workers, including teachers, health care providers, and police officers. Strikers demanded a wage hike exceeding the inflation rate, which stood at about 7 percent. In September, the government offered a 6.3-percent wage hike, which was met with protests. The unions called off a nationwide strike scheduled for September 15 when the government announced its willingness to return to the bargaining table.

Bombings. On January 28, 11 people were injured when a bomb exploded outside Cape Town's main police station. The explosion followed a January 2 attack in which a bomb blew up cars outside a city theater and the January 14 assassination of a policeman investigating extremist Muslim groups. On November 28, a bomb exploded inside a pizzeria, injuring more than 40 people. No one claimed responsibility for these terrorist actions during 1999. Government forces suspected the violence was related to a three-way conflict among police, criminal gangs, and Islamic vigilantes, the most prominent of which was the People Against Gangsterism and Drugs.

Relations with the United States. South Africa and the United States laid the foundations for closer military cooperation when the U.S. Air Force provided transport planes for an African peacekeeping exercise, Operation Blue Crane, in April. In the largest such exercise ever held in Africa, U.S. aircraft helped ferry thousands of soldiers from 12 southern African nations to the South African Army Battle School at Lohathla.

Other foreign relations. On April 28, Mandela began an official visit to Russia. He said that he had a personal debt to pay for the assistance the former Soviet Union gave to South Africa in the fight against apartheid.

In his final act of foreign policy, Mandela invited Libyan leader Muammar Muhammad al-Qadhafi to visit South Africa in mid-June. The invitation aimed to hasten Libya's international rehabilitation after the United Nations suspended sanctions against Libya in April. The action followed an agreement, brokered partly by Mandela, involving two Libyans wanted in connection with the 1988 bombing of Pan American Flight 103 over Lockerbie, Scotland. Qadhafi, who donated millions of dollars to the ANC during the 1999 election campaign, was given a prominent place among the dozens of foreign dignitaries who attended Mbeki's inauguration on June 17.

Boesak conviction. In a major embarrassment for the ANC, Allan Boesak, one of South Africa's most prominent leaders in the struggle against apartheid, was found guilty in March of theft and fraud totaling several hundred thousand dollars. On March 24, a High Court sentenced him to six years in jail for stealing the money from his charity, The Foundation for Peace and Justice, which Boesak set up to help child victims of apartheid. ☐ Simon Baynham

See also **Africa; South Africa, President of.**

South Africa, President of. Thabo

Mbeki, deputy president of South Africa since 1994, assumed the presidency from Nelson R. Mandela on June 16, 1999. The National Assembly elected Mbeki president following the ruling African National Congress (ANC) party's overwhelming victory in national elections on June 2. Mbeki had served as president of the ANC since Mandela's retirement from the post in December 1997.

In his inaugural address, Mbeki paid tribute to Mandela but painted a bleak picture of a nation plagued by racial divisions, crime, and corruption. His 1999 speeches included references to his vision of an "African *renaissance*" (rebirth) and the need for "transformation"—altering South Africa's huge economic inequalities.

During Mbeki's first 100 days in office, the president played a key role in the July resolution by the Organization of African Unity, an association of 52 African nations, to exclude African leaders who seize power in future military *coups* (overthrows). Also in July, he helped broker a cease-fire pact to end the civil war in Congo (Kinshasa). In September, Mbeki addressed the United Nations General Assembly, urging world leaders not to ignore Africa. ☐ Simon Baynham

South America. See **Latin America.**
South Carolina. See **State government.**
South Dakota. See **State government.**

Space exploration. Two Mars probes were lost in 1999. On December 3, the Mars Polar Lander, a spacecraft that was due to make a soft landing about 620 miles (1,000 kilometers) from the planet's south pole, failed to radio back to Earth. The craft, which was launched by the National Aeronautics and Space Administration (NASA) on January 3, had been on a correct trajectory to Mars. Among the systems the vehicle was carrying were two "microprobes" to analyze the Martian soil and a microphone to detect sounds on the planet's surface. At year-end, NASA engineers were still trying to determine what had gone wrong.

Earlier in 1999, a probe called the Mars Climate Orbiter was lost due to a navigation error. The spacecraft had been launched in December 1998. As it was set to enter an orbit of Mars on Sept. 23, 1999, it came too close to the surface. Instead of being slowed by friction within the thin Martian atmosphere, the Mars Climate Orbiter either burned up or broke apart.

The failure of the Mars Climate Orbiter was caused by a mix-up among the project's engineers between metric and English units of measurement. For data used to operate the thrusters on the spacecraft, engineers at the Jet Propulsion Laboratory in Pasadena, California, who were operating the spacecraft, had used the metric system. The engineers at the Lockheed Martin Corporation who had built the craft had used the English system. The revelation that such an inconsistency would go undetected proved to be one of NASA's most embarrassing space-mission failures in years.

Another NASA spacecraft, the Mars Global Surveyor, experienced troubles on April 15 as it orbited Mars. The satellite went into an emergency mode, shutting down scientific instru-

TIME CAPSULE **1957**

SPACE EXPLORATION

SPACE TRAVEL became a reality late in 1957. The Soviet Union launched the first Earth satellite on October 4. . . . Sputnik I, a sphere, shot into space at about 8:00 a.m. It weighed 184.3 pounds (83 kilograms) and measured 22.8 inches (58 centimeters) in diameter. It traveled approximately 18,000 miles (28,800 kilometers) per hour, and circled the Earth every 96.2 minutes in a slightly elliptical orbit that carried it from about 143 to 583 miles (229 to 933 kilometers) above the Earth.

SPACE EXPLORATION

KENNEDY ACTS. On May 25, 1961, President John F. Kennedy served notice that the United States must catch up with Russia's space achievements. In August, he presented to Congress a program aimed at putting explorers on the moon before 1970. It was approved wholeheartedly, although the president estimated that the undertaking would ultimately cost billions. The vehicle scheduled to be used for the manned lunar landing is the three-man Apollo spacecraft now on the drawing boards.

ments, because the main antenna was not moving properly. Controllers deferred the spacecraft's mapping mission while they grappled with the problem. Eventually the mapping began, but the technical difficulty slowed the work.

Shuttle flights. The Discovery space shuttle took off for the International Space Station on May 27 with an international crew of seven, including five Americans, Canadian astronaut Julie Payette, and Russian cosmonaut Valery Tokarev.

During the five days that Discovery was docked to the space station, the crew transferred gear into its two sections—the Russian-built Zarya module and the U.S.-built Unity module.

The first U.S. space mission commanded by a woman—Air Force Colonel Eileen Collins—was launched on July 23. On a five-day flight aboard the shuttle Columbia, Collins and four colleagues deployed the Chandra X-ray Observatory, which was designed to make observations of the heavens in the relatively high-energy X-ray portion of the electromagnetic spectrum.

On December 19, following a two-month delay due to fuel-line and wiring repairs, Discovery, with a crew of seven, undertook a mission to service the nearly 10-year-old Hubble Space Telescope. NASA had originally scheduled the service mission for 2000, but the space agency decided to do part of the job early in an effort to get to the Hubble before the telescope developed problems that could halt its observations. However, because of the shuttle delay, the mission was still

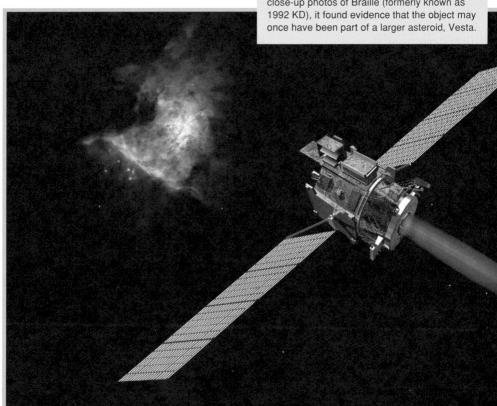

An advanced U.S. space probe, Deep Space 1 (shown in an illustration), passed within 10 miles (16 kilometers) of an asteroid named Braille in July 1999. Although the probe failed to obtain close-up photos of Braille (formerly known as 1992 KD), it found evidence that the object may once have been part of a larger asteroid, Vesta.

too late. The Hubble became inoperable on Nov. 13, 1999, when the fourth of its six gyroscopes failed. The telescope relies on the gyroscopes to point itself at astronomical objects. The telescope was expected to be fully operable by early 2000.

Space stations. Construction of the International Space Station was slowed in 1999 when a key component, the service module Zvezda, was not ready for launching on schedule.

Russia decided in 1999 to halt operations on its aging space station Mir. Russian cosmonauts departed the complex on August 28. One more crew was set to visit Mir early in 2000 but only to prepare the station for reentry into the atmosphere and disintegration over the Pacific Ocean.

China steps forward. China took a step in 1999 toward becoming the third nation capable of sending humans into space by orbiting a spacecraft similar to a Russian Soyuz manned spacecraft. China's Shenzhou vehicle was launched without a crew on November 20 from the Jiuquan launch site in the Gobi Desert. After a 21-hour test flight, controllers in Beijing ordered the descent module to separate. It landed on the plains of Inner Mongolia.

U.S. launcher troubles. In 1999, the United States suffered its worst spate of launch failures in more than a decade. In just eight days in April and May, three different kinds of rockets—the Athena II, the Titan IV-B, and the Delta III—failed to get their payloads into a proper orbit. The Titan mishap was the third failure in a row for the huge rocket. The string of problems sparked a series of investigations in which the government concluded that quality had slipped in the space industry.

A unique and successful system of launching rockets at sea was introduced in 1999. Two oceangoing vessels were used in the project—called Sea Launch—which was a partnership among the United States, Russia, and Norway. The launch platform, which was on one of the ships, was similar to an offshore oil-drilling platform. The other vessel served as a command ship.

Science missions. Several small science missions were sent into space in 1999. One, called Stardust, was launched on February 7 on a seven-year journey to intercept a comet, collect some of the material from the comet's tail, and return the samples to Earth. Stardust was expected to encounter the comet Wild-2 (pronounced *Vilt-2*) in January 2004 and capture matter spewing from it. Stardust was also expected to collect dust in "empty" space. Stardust was scheduled to return to Earth in January 2006.

Terra. On Dec. 18, 1999, NASA launched a large spacecraft called Terra on a Titan IV rocket from Vandenberg Air Force Base in California.

TIME CAPSULE 1969
SPACE EXPLORATION

MEN FLEW TO THE MOON, walked on its surface, and returned safely to Earth in 1969. The historic first journey marked the achievement of the U.S. space exploration goal of the decade and stimulated the projection of new goals for the 1970's and 1980's. . . .

The Apollo 11 mission of Neil A. Armstrong, Edwin E. Aldrin, Jr., and Michael Collins from July 16 to 24 demonstrated that men can land on the moon, collect soil samples and emplace instruments to operate from its surface, and return safely to Earth. Armstrong and Aldrin landed the lunar module Eagle in the southwestern part of the Sea of Tranquility, while Collins remained in orbit in the command module Columbia.

Astronaut Edwin E. "Buzz" Aldrin, the second man to walk on the moon

SPACE EXPLORATION

TWO UNITED STATES VIKING SPACECRAFT made the first landings on Mars in 1976 and sent back spectacular pictures of the Martian surface. Viking 1 touched down on July 20 and sent pictures back to Earth showing a reddish desert strewn with rocks of all sizes. The Viking 2 spacecraft landed on September 3 on a Martian plain called Utopia, 4,600 miles (7,400 kilometers) northeast of the Viking 1 site. Photographs again showed a reddish, sandy, rock-littered surface.

Terra, weighing 10.5 tons (9.5 metric tons), was one of the largest of a score of satellites planned in a 15-year program to study Earth from space. Terra's five science instruments were designed to provide data about how Earth's atmosphere, oceans, and land masses interact.

Private "spy" satellite. A small spacecraft called Ikonos was launched from Vandenberg Air Force Base on September 24. Ikonos was the world's first commercial imaging satellite able to take pictures with detail approaching that available to government intelligence agencies. Ikonos could make out details as small as 3 feet (1 meter) across. The satellite's owner, Space Imaging, Inc., a Denver, Colorado-based company that specializes in Earth-observation technologies, began selling the pictures in late 1999. The U.S. government, however, reserved the right to block some sales because of the level of detail.

☐ James R. Asker

See also **People in the news** (Collins, Eileen).

SPACE EXPLORATION

SALLY KRISTEN RIDE, a physicist and United States astronaut, in 1983 became the first American woman to travel in space. . . . As a mission specialist, Ride helped carry out many of the scientific experiments aboard the shuttle, including the launching of communication satellites for the Canadian and Indonesian governments. . . .

Ride was born on May 26, 1951, in Los Angeles. A gifted athlete, she was a nationally ranked junior tennis player.

Spain enjoyed one of Europe's strongest economies in 1999, which economists attributed to the country's participation in the single European currency, the euro. The government forecast that Spain's *gross domestic product* (GDP—the value of all goods and services produced in a country in a year) would increase by 3.6 percent in 1999, nearly double the average 2.1 percent rate for the 15-nation European Union. Spain experienced its fourth straight year of above-average growth, much of it fueled by lower interest rates set by the European Central Bank and increased investment generated by the country's successful effort to join the euro.

The strong growth helped to create new jobs in 1999 and reduced the country's unemployment rate to 15.7 percent from nearly 19 percent in 1998. The booming economy, however, boosted consumer prices and pushed the inflation rate above 2 percent, nearly double the average rate of the 11 countries participating in the euro. The inflation rate raised the risk that Spain could lose competitiveness against other euro countries.

The government of Prime Minister Jose Maria Aznar approved a 2000 budget in September 1999 that was intended to keep the economy and job market growing quickly while restraining inflation. The budget lowered the government's deficit target from 1.0 percent to 0.8 percent of GDP and aimed at achieving a balanced budget by 2002.

Takeovers. Spanish banks played an active role in the consolidation of Europe's banking industry, a trend that was encouraged by the launch of the euro in 1999. In January, the country's largest and third-largest banks, Banco Santander SA and Banco Central Hispano SA, respectively, agreed to merge in a deal worth $11.3 billion. The new Banco Santander Central Hispanoamericano ranked as one of Europe's largest banks and also controlled the largest foreign-owned banking business in Latin America. In October, Banco Bilbao Vizcaya SA (BBV) agreed to buy a smaller Spanish rival, Argentaria SA, for $11 billion to strengthen its position as Spain's second-largest bank. That same month, BBV began to negotiate an alliance with Unicredito Italiano, Italy's third-largest bank.

Basque separatism. The Spanish government in May 1999 held its first talks with the separatist group ETA, which seeks independence for the Basque region of northern Spain. ETA, whose initials stand for Basque Homeland and Freedom in the Basque language, declared a cease-fire in 1998 after a 30-year terrorist campaign that claimed some 800 lives. ETA declared an end to the cease-fire Dec. 3, 1999, when the talks failed to produce immediate results. ☐ Tom Buerkle

See also **Europe.**

Sports. In 1999, Wayne Gretzky, Michael Jordan, and John Elway, three of the greatest stars in professional team sports in the United States, retired. German tennis sensation Steffi Graf also decided that 1999 would be her final year on the international circuit, and Charles Barkley saw his final basketball season cut short in December by a career-ending knee injury. The year's most outstanding team accomplishment belonged to the United States women's soccer team, which raised women's soccer from obscurity to national prominence with a surprising performance in the World Cup tournament, culminating in a victory over China in the final match.

Sports fans in 1999 also mourned the passing of Joe DiMaggio, the legendary New York Yankees baseball star; James "Catfish" Hunter, who pitched in six World Series, three each for the Yankees and Oakland Athletics; Wilt Chamberlain, the dominating center who set the career record for rebounds during 14 seasons in the National Basketball Association (NBA); and former Chicago Bear great Walter Payton, the leading rusher in National Football League (NFL) history.

Legends retire. On March 29, Wayne Gretzky scored his 1,072nd career goal, surpassing Gordie Howe, Gretzky's boyhood hero, as the top goal scorer in professional hockey. Twenty days later, Gretzky retired from the National Hockey League (NHL) at the age of 38. In 20 seasons, Gretzky became the NHL's all-time scoring leader, with 2,857 points on 894 goals and 1,963 assists. He set 61 NHL records, won four Stanley Cups with the Edmonton Oilers in the 1980's, and was voted the NHL's Most Valuable Player nine times. As a result, the Hockey Hall of Fame Selection Committee voted to set aside the usual, three-year waiting period and inducted Gretzky on Nov. 22, 1999.

Michael Jordan announced his retirement from the Chicago Bulls, after 16 seasons in the NBA, on January 13. (Jordan had previously retired in October 1993, to play minor-league baseball, but returned to the Bulls in 1995.) Jordan was only the third player in NBA history to reach 29,000 career points. He led the league in scoring nine times and had the highest career scoring average in league history—31.5 points. Of the six NBA titles the Bulls won with Jordan, none ever required a seventh game.

Denver Broncos quarterback John Elway retired on May 2, 1999, after 16 seasons in the NFL. Elway went out after winning two straight Super Bowl championships, with the most victories (148) and with 47 game-winning or game-tying fourth-quarter comeback drives. He and Dan Marino of Miami, who also came into the NFL in 1983, are the only quarterbacks to pass for more than 50,000 career yards.

Other retirements. Steffi Graf, the dominant woman player in tennis in the late 1980's and early 1990's, announced on Aug. 13, 1999, that her career was over. She cited diminished motivation to excel. Graf was the only tennis player, male or female, to win all four Grand Slam events four times. She earned $21.8 million in prize money, more than any other woman athlete in history and was the top-ranked player for a longer period than any other player.

Charles Barkley, the Houston Rockets forward, announced on October 24 that the 1999-2000 NBA season would be his last. But he called it fate when a knee injury ended his career early, on Dec. 8, 1999, in Philadelphia, the city where his NBA career had begun 16 years before. Named one of the 50 Greatest Players in NBA History in 1996, Barkley was the NBA's Most Valuable Player in 1992-1993. He ranked 13th on the NBA's career scoring list but will be remembered best for his outspoken candor.

Transgressions. The biggest sports-related scandal reported in 1999 involved the bribing of members of the International Olympic Committee (IOC). The IOC expelled six of its members in January for accepting cash bribes and illegal gifts in exchange for awarding the 2002 Winter Olympics to Salt Lake City, Utah.

In the NFL, a feud erupted between Eddie DeBartolo Jr., co-owner of the San Francisco 49ers, and his sister, Denise DeBartolo York. The dispute began shortly after DeBartolo pleaded guilty in 1998 to a felony charge of failing to report a bribe when he paid $400,000 to acquire a riverboat gambling license in Louisiana. The NFL suspended DeBartolo for one year and turned control of the 49ers over to York. On April 8, 1999, the Edward J. DeBartolo Corporation, a holding company in Youngstown, Ohio, run by York, sued DeBartolo, accusing him of reneging on a $94-million debt to the corporation. DeBartolo countersued, and the situation effectively ended DeBartolo's association with the 49ers.

In early September, a videotape of a 1995 NFL Players Association (NFLPA) meeting revealed to the public that 16 NFL players had failed drug tests that year but avoided discipline by the league. The tape showed that the lack of punishment had been a concession by the NFL to the NFLPA in exchange for securing the NFLPA's support for a new, stronger drug-testing policy for the league.

In one of several collegiate sport scandals that surfaced in 1999, a $1.5-million investigation by the University of Minnesota revealed widespread cheating, grade manipulation, payoffs, and other infractions at the Big Ten school from 1993 through 1998. That charge, along with evidence of other illegal activity compelled University President Mark Yudof to suspend four players from the Minnesota basketball team on March 11, 1999, hours before Minnesota's first game in the National Collegiate Athletic Association (NCAA) tournament. Clem Haskins, the head basketball coach at Minnesota, later agreed to an early, $1.5-million buyout of his contract but accepted no blame for the scandal. Yudof also dismissed Mark Deinhart, the university's athletic director, and three other officials.

Dennis Lundy, a former Northwestern University football player, was sentenced to a month in prison and two years probation on May 5, for lying to a federal grand jury investigating gambling by Northwestern athletes. Lundy was among four football players charged in the scandal. Lundy admitted that he not only bet on games but also deliberately fumbled on the one-yard line in a 1994 game against Iowa to win a $400 bet.

For sale. In May 1999, Dan Snyder purchased the NFL's Washington Redskins and the team's Jack Kent Cooke Stadium, for $800 million, the highest price ever paid for a professional sports franchise. Richard Jacobs put the Cleveland Indians major league baseball team up for sale in May, less than one year after selling shares of the team to the public. *Forbes* magazine valued the Indians at $359 million, an evaluation for a baseball franchise second only to the New York Yankees, at $491 million. On May 12, Abe Pollin announced he had sold the Washington Capitals NHL team and a minority interest in his other holdings, which included the Washington Wizards NBA team, for about $200 million. Bill Laurie, the owner of the NHL St. Louis Blues, bought the NBA's Vancouver Grizzlies for $200 million on September 23. Observers expected that Laurie was planning to move the basketball team to St. Louis.

Defections. Rigoberto Herrerra Betancourt, the pitching coach of Cuba's national baseball team, defected to the United States after an exhibition baseball game in which Cuba beat the Baltimore Orioles, 12–6, on May 3, 1999, in Baltimore. Betancourt hid in bushes at a nearby park for seven hours before he walked into a downtown Baltimore police station and requested asylum. Cuba suffered the same political embarrassment in early August when 11 athletes, a softball coach, and a journalist defected at the end of the Pan American Games in Canada.

Awards and milestones. Track star Marion Jones in February received the 1999 Jesse Owens International Trophy Award, which is presented to the world's outstanding amateur athlete. University of Tennessee women's basketball star Chamique Holdsclaw won the 69th James E. Sullivan award in February as the nation's top amateur athlete. Holdsclaw was the second straight Tennessee athlete to be honored. Tennessee football player Peyton Manning won the Sullivan Award in 1998.

Among the winners in 1999 were—

Cycling. Lance Armstrong, the American cyclist who had conquered advanced testicular cancer, turned in cycling's greatest performance of 1999 when he won the Tour de France in July, after a two-year absence. On July 3, the first day of the three-week, 2,290-mile (3,690-kilometer) race, Armstrong won the time trial prologue and donned the yellow leader's jersey for the first stage. He also won two time trial stages and a formidable mountain stage in Sestriere, Italy, to become only the second U.S. champion of the race.

Armstrong, riding for the United States Postal Service, covered the race in 91 hours, 32 minutes, and 16 seconds to finish 7 minutes and 37 seconds ahead of runner-up Alex Zulle of Switzerland. Armstrong's performance was not only among the most inspiring in Tour de France history but also the fastest, at an average speed of 25 miles (40 kilometers) per hour.

Gymnastics. The 34th World Gymnastics Championships were held in Tianjin, China, October 9-16. Russia won four of the five individual gold medals. Vanessa Atler, considered America's best hope for a medal, was forced to withdraw after suffering an ankle injury on the final day of competition. The U.S. men's and women's teams both finished sixth overall.

Marathon. Joseph Chebet of Kenya took the lead with 4 miles (6.5 kilometers) to go to win the 103rd Boston Marathon on April 19, in 2 hours, 9 minutes, and 52 seconds. Chebet was the ninth Kenyan in a row to win the race. Fatuma Roba of Ethiopia topped the women's field for the third straight year, in 2 hours, 23 minutes, and 25 seconds.

Kenya's Tegla Loroupe broke her world record for the women's marathon on September 26, by winning the Berlin Marathon in 2 hours, 20 minutes, and 43 seconds. Loroupe, a two-time winner of the New York City Marathon, had set the former record of 2 hours, 20 minutes, and 47 seconds at Rotterdam, the Netherlands, in 1998.

Khalid Khannouci, a Moroccan living in the United States, shattered the world marathon record in Chicago on Oct. 24, 1999. Khannouci finished in 2 hours, 5 minutes, and 42 seconds. The previous mark, set by Brazilian Ronaldo Da Costa in 1998 in Berlin, was 2 hours, 6 minutes, and 5 seconds. The women's race ended with two Kenyans finishing one second apart. Joyce Chepchumba, the defending champion, finished in 2 hours, 25 minutes, and 59 seconds, and Margaret Okayo in 2 hours, 26 minutes.

Chebet and Adriana Fernandez of Mexico won the 30th New York City Marathon on Nov.

U.S. cyclist Lance Armstrong races past the Arc de Triomphe in Paris on his way to winning the 1999 Tour de France on July 25. Armstrong, only the second American to win the prestigious race, returned to cycling in 1998 after a long battle with cancer.

7, 1999. Chebet pulled away late to finish the race in 2 hours, 9 minutes, and 14 seconds—six seconds ahead of Domingos Castro of Portugal. Fernandez finished in 2 hours, 25 minutes, and 7 seconds.

Rowing. In the World Rowing Championships held at St. Catharine's, Canada, August 22-29, the U.S. team took the gold medal for the men's eights after covering the 2,000-meter course in 6 minutes, 1.58 seconds. The U.S. won a total of 10 medals (including 6 gold) in 24 events. Among the best marks set on the Martindale Pond course, Rob Waddell of New Zealand established a new world record of 6 minutes, 36.68 seconds for the single sculls.

In the 160th Henley Royal Regatta in June and July, the Cambridge and Queen's Tower team outrowed the University of California to win the Ladies' Challenge Plate by 2⅛ lengths. Marcel Hacker, of Germany, defeated defending champion Jamie Koven of Boston by 3 lengths to win the Diamond Challenge Sculls.

Cambridge University extended its winning streak over Oxford University to seven in the 145th rowing of The Boat Race in April. Cambridge covered the 4¼-mile (6.8-kilometer) course in 16 minutes, 41 seconds.

Other champions

Equestrian. World Cup Equestrian Final individual champions: show jumping, Rodrigo Pessoa, Brazil; driving, Vilnos Lazar, Hungary.
Lacrosse. U.S. college champions: men, University

of Virginia; women, University of Maryland.

Modern Pentathlon. World champions: men, Hungary; women, Russia.

Motorcycle racing. FIM Grand Prix 500-cc champion, Alex Criville, Spain.

Sled dog racing. On March 17, 1999, Doug Swingley of Lincoln, Montana, won the Iditarod Trail Sled Dog Race for the second time. He covered the 1,100-mile (1,770-kilometer) trek from Anchorage to Nome in 9½ days, finishing with almost a 9-hour margin of victory over runner-up Martin Buser. Swingley previously won the Iditarod in 1995, when he set the course record.

Soap Box Derby. Masters champion: Allan Endres, Barberton, Ohio.

Triathlon. World champions: men, Dimitry Gaag, Kazakhstan; women, Loretta Harrop, Australia.

Volleyball. World Cup champions: men, Russia; women, Cuba

Weightlifting. World champions, total weight: Men (over 105 kilograms [231 pounds]), Andrey Chermerkin, Russia, 457.7 kilograms (1,009 pounds). Women (over 75 kilograms [165 pounds]), Ding Meiyuan, China, 285 kilograms (629 pounds). □ Ron Reid

See also **Baseball: A Special Report; Basketball; Deaths; Football; Hockey; People in the news** (Armstrong, Lance); **Soccer.**

Sri Lanka. President Chandrika Kumaratunga of the People's Alliance (PA) party won a second term as president in an election on Dec. 21, 1999. Kumaratunga took 51.2 percent of the vote. Her main rival, Ranil Wickremesinghe of the United National Party (UNP), won 43 percent.

Kumaratunga, who was first elected to a six-year term as president in 1994, had promised to end a civil war. Government forces had fought the Liberation Tigers of Tamil Eelam (LTTE), a guerrilla group seeking a homeland in the north for Sri Lanka's Hindu Tamil minority, since 1983. By 1999, an estimated 60,000 people had died in the conflict.

President Kumaratunga had sponsored constitutional measures to grant semi-independence to the Tamil regions. The proposals, however, remained stalled in a parliamentary deadlock in 1999, and the LTTE refused to compromise its demand of total independence. Seeking a new mandate to negotiate an end to the war, the president called for elections in October, almost a year earlier than required by the Constitution.

Violence. The LTTE launched a major offensive after the election was scheduled. Sri Lanka's army, which had made small advances in savage jungle fighting in 1995 and 1996, lost most of these gains in late 1999. In its worst defeat of the war, the army was unable to maintain an over-land route to the northern city of Jaffna, which the government controlled.

The LTTE also continued to use suicide bombings in 1999 to intimidate opponents or those who sought a compromise to keep Tamil areas in Sri Lanka. At Kumaratunga's last election rally in Colombo, the capital, a woman detonated explosives strapped to her body. The blast killed at least 24 people and wounded Kumaratunga. Moments later, a suicide bomber at a UNP rally killed 12 people. Some political observers believed that sympathy votes after the bomb attacks allowed Kumaratunga to win the election.

Neelan Tiruchelvam, a Tamil member of parliament and a leading advocate of peace between Sri Lanka's Hindu Tamil minority and the Buddhist Sinhalese majority, died in a suicide bombing when a man detonated a bomb beside Tiruchelvam's car in a busy intersection. Six other people were injured in the attack.

Sri Lanka's economy did not share in the economic resurgence that took place in other Asian countries in 1999. Exports declined by 11 percent in the first eight months. Low world prices for tea hurt Sri Lanka's leading export. Economic growth slowed to only about 3 percent in 1999, down from 4.7 percent in 1998 and 6.3 percent in 1997. □ Henry S. Bradsher

See also **Asia.**

State government. State governments ended fiscal year 1999 on June 30 with their highest financial balances since 1980. Of 44 states responding to a National Conference of State Legislatures (NCSL) fiscal survey, 32 reported ending fiscal 1999 with a balance exceeding 5 percent. Seventeen of the 44 states put surplus money into reserve funds, according to the report, released on September 17. Twenty states also cut taxes to reduce excess revenues. Minnesota cut taxes 18 percent. Colorado, Connecticut, and Missouri cut taxes by at least 3 percent. Personal income tax reductions totaled $2.4 billion, and cuts in sales taxes totaled more than $1.6 billion. Twenty-four states lowered personal income taxes, and 21 reduced sales taxes. The 44 states responding to the survey lowered taxes by a net $5.5 billion for fiscal 2000.

Several states also put their surplus funds toward government programs. The Texas legislature spent the bulk of the state's surplus on a $3.8-billion school funding law that gave all public school teachers a $3,000 pay raise. Maryland increased state spending by nearly 6 percent and placed a record $255 million into school construction.

Employment. State and local governments employed 307,000 workers in 1998, an increase of 35,000 workers over 1997, according to a Nelson A. Rockefeller Institute of Government report issued in April 1999. The report noted that states hired an additional 86,000 workers in 1998. Most of the new employees were in the field of education.

School safety. A shooting at Columbine High School in Littleton, Colorado, in April 1999 forced many state legislators to take a new look at violence in schools. In July, California Governor Gray Davis signed legislation to enact stricter gun safety laws, including a new ban on assault weapons. The state also provided $100 million for school safety block grants for grades 8 through 12 for equipment, training counselors, and school safety needs.

School vouchers. School choice remained a hotly debated issue in several states in 1999. Florida schools began using the nation's first statewide voucher program at the beginning of the 1999-2000 school year. Voucher programs typically permit the use of state funds to send students to private schools. Florida students attending public schools that receive a failing grade from the state for two of four years can receive funds to pay tuition at a private school. State officials were to grade all Florida schools annually. The voucher program, proposed by Florida Governor Jeb Bush, provided up to $4,000 to children in failing schools who transfer to a *parochial* (religious) or other private school.

Wisconsin continued its voucher program for low-income families in Milwaukee in 1999. About 8,000 students were participating in the program at the beginning of the 1999-2000 school year.

The Ohio legislature in June revived a voucher plan for Cleveland schools after the Ohio Supreme Court voided a 1995 law permitting a voucher system. In August 1999, a federal judge ordered that the implementation of the voucher program be stopped. In November the U.S. Supreme Court ruled that the Cleveland voucher program could continue while a federal Circuit Court of Appeals pondered a ruling on the matter.

In June, the Illinois legislature enacted a state income tax credit of up to $500 per student for parents of private and parochial school students for the tuition and fees they pay.

Education. The California legislature in April passed Governor Davis's proposals to require a high school exit examination, establish a statewide ranking of school performance, establish a peer review for teachers, and create an elementary school reading program.

Iowa Governor Tom Vilsack in April signed a $150-million bill to hire additional teachers to reduce elementary school class sizes, improve reading skills, and upgrade technology in schools through 2003.

Maryland Governor Parris N. Glendening in May 1999 signed legislation to hire more teachers to reduce the size of first- and second-grade reading classes and to start a scholarship program for state high school graduates who maintained a B average or better in classes.

State legislatures in Alabama, Alaska, Louisiana, Maine, Michigan, and Nevada enacted similar scholarship programs during 1999. Voters in Alabama, however, rejected a proposal in October for a state lottery that would have funded the scholarship program.

Tobacco settlement. Forty-six states in 1999 began debate over how to spend a $206-billion tobacco settlement negotiated by state attorneys general in 1998. Various tobacco companies in the United States had agreed to pay the settlement to the states over a 25-year period beginning in 2000.

According to a report released in July 1999 by the NCSL, 21 states authorized spending $1.3 billion in settlement funds, with half the money going toward health care, 10 percent to antismoking campaigns, and 20 percent to education.

Minnesota officials planned to spend $17.7 million by 2001 to reduce smoking among teen-agers under an endowment fund created by the state legislature. The NCSL reported that officials in Kansas and Louisiana had also established endowment funds to create new antismoking initiatives.

North Carolina officials established a trust fund for health care issues and a second trust fund for tobacco farmers in the state. Florida planned to establish a trust fund for tobacco moneys for health programs benefitting children and the elderly.

Legislators in Maine, Montana, New Hampshire, New Jersey, and Wyoming budgeted their share of the tobacco money to address health care

TIME CAPSULE — 1959

STATE GOVERNMENT

PRESIDENT [DWIGHT D.] EISENHOWER issued a proclamation formally declaring Alaska a state on Jan. 3, 1959. Alaska's first congressional delegation was seated in the 86th Congress on Jan. 7, 1959, and July 4, 1959, was set as the date for adding a 49th star to the flag. . . .

Hawaii became the 50th state in the Union in 1959. President Eisenhower officially proclaimed statehood on August 21 . . . . Hawaiians voted for statehood on June 27 by a margin of 18 to 1.

Selected statistics on state governments

State	Resident population*	Governor†	Legislature† House (D)	(R)	Senate (D)	(R)	State tax revenue‡	Tax revenue per capita‡	Public school expenditure per pupil§
Alabama	4,351,999	Don Siegelman (D)	69	36	23	12	$ 14,008,000,000	$ 3,240	$ 4,580
Alaska	614,010	Tony Knowles (D)	16	24	5	15	9,439,000,000	15,500	8,840
Arizona	4,668,631	Jane Dee Hull (R)	20	40	14	16	13,692,000,000	3,010	4,600
Arkansas	2,538,303	Mike Huckabee (R)	77	23	29	6	8,844,000,000	3,510	5,320
California	32,666,550	Joseph Graham (Gray) Davis (D)	47	32	25	15	131,099,000,000	4,060	5,870
Colorado	3,970,971	Bill F. Owens (R)	25	40	15	20	12,780,000,000	3,280	5,280
Connecticut	3,274,069	John G. Rowland (R)	96	55	19	17	14,520,000,000	4,440	9,180
Delaware	743,603	Tom Carper (D)	15	26	13	8	4,211,000,000	5,750	8,060
Florida	14,915,980	Jeb Bush (R)	48	72	15	25	41,432,000,000	2,830	5,580
Georgia	7,642,207	Roy Barnes (D)	102	78	33	23	24,028,000,000	3,210	5,870
Hawaii	1,193,001	Benjamin J. Cayetano (D)	39	12	23	2	6,701,000,000	5,640	6,230
Idaho	1,228,684	Dirk Kempthorne (R)	12	58	4	31	4,289,000,000	3,540	5,050
Illinois	12,049,326	George H. Ryan (R)	62	56	27	32	39,038,000,000	3,280	5,840
Indiana	5,899,195	Frank L. O'Bannon (D)	53	47	19	31	17,537,000,000	2,990	6,640
Iowa	2,862,447	Tom Vilsack (D)	44	56	20	30	9,509,000,000	3,330	5,730
Kansas	2,629,067	Bill Graves (R)	48	77	13	27	7,950,000,000	3,060	5,890
Kentucky	3,936,499	Paul E. Patton (D)	66	34	18	20	15,033,000,000	3,850	5,930
Louisiana	4,368,967	Murphy J. (Mike) Foster (R)	76	29	28	11	15,929,000,000	3,660	5,300
Maine	1,244,250	Angus S. King, Jr. (I)	#79	71	#20	14	5,215,000,000	4,200	7,110
Maryland	5,134,808	Parris N. Glendening (D)	106	35	32	15	20,128,000,000	3,950	7,060
Massachusetts	6,147,132	Paul Cellucci (R)	#131	28	33	7	26,538,000,000	4,340	7,310
Michigan	9,817,242	John Engler (R)	52	58	15	23	45,509,000,000	4,660	7,490
Minnesota	4,725,419	Jesse Ventura (Reform)	63	71	#40	26	22,882,000,000	4,880	6,950
Mississippi	2,752,092	Ronnie Musgrove (D)	‡‡**86	33	34	18	9,400,000,000	3,440	4,380
Missouri	5,438,559	Mel Carnahan (D)	#86	76	18	16	16,601,000,000	3,070	5,210
Montana	880,453	Marc Racicot (R)	41	59	18	32	3,524,000,000	4,010	5,950
Nebraska	1,662,719	Mike Johanns (R)	unicameral (49 nonpartisan)				5,537,000,000	3,340	5,650
Nevada	1,746,898	Kenny Guinn (R)	28	14	9	12	6,494,000,000	3,870	5,440
New Hampshire	1,185,048	Jeanne Shaheen (D)	#153	246	13	11	3,561,000,000	3,040	6,300
New Jersey	8,115,011	Christine Todd Whitman (R)	35	45	16	24	36,087,000,000	4,480	9,700
New Mexico	1,736,931	Gary E. Johnson (R)	40	30	25	17	8,188,000,000	4,730	4,890
New York	18,175,301	George E. Pataki (R)	98	52	26	35	95,442,000,000	5,260	8,860
North Carolina	7,546,493	James B. Hunt, Jr. (D)	66	54	35	15	25,527,000,000	3,440	5,770
North Dakota	638,244	Edward T. Shafer (R)	34	64	18	31	2,818,000,000	4,400	4,600
Ohio	11,209,493	Robert Taft (R)	40	59	12	21	45,250,000,000	4,050	6,220
Oklahoma	3,346,713	Frank Keating (R)	61	40	33	15	11,328,000,000	3,420	5,330
Oregon	3,281,974	John Kitzhaber (D)	25	34	13	17	15,004,000,000	4,630	6,640
Pennsylvania	12,001,451	Tom J. Ridge (R)	100	103	20	30	49,318,000,000	4,100	7,150
Rhode Island	988,480	Lincoln C. Almond (R)	#86	13	42	8	4,229,000,000	4,290	7,610
South Carolina	3,835,962	Jim Hodges (D)	56	68	24	22	13,805,000,000	3,670	5,720
South Dakota	738,171	William J. Janklow (R)	18	51	13	22	2,316,000,000	3,140	5,070
Tennessee	5,430,621	Don Sundquist (R)	59	40	18	15	15,696,000,000	2,920	5,170
Texas	19,759,614	George W. Bush (R)	78	72	15	16	63,864,000,000	3,290	5,970
Utah	2,099,758	Michael O. Leavitt (R)	21	54	11	18	7,724,000,000	3,750	3,810
Vermont	590,883	Howard Dean (D)	††77	67	17	13	2,370,000,000	4,020	6,780
Virginia	6,791,345	James S. Gilmore III (R)	#47	52	19	21	24,322,000,000	3,610	6,040
Washington	5,689,263	Gary Locke (D)	49	49	27	22	26,841,000,000	4,780	6,210
West Virginia	1,811,156	Cecil H. Underwood (R)	75	25	29	5	7,467,000,000	4,110	6,890
Wisconsin	5,223,500	Tommy G. Thompson (R)	44	55	17	16	23,859,000,000	4,610	7,260
Wyoming	480,907	Jim Geringer (R)	17	43	10	20	2,559,000,000	5,330	6,810

*July 1, 1998, estimates. Source: U.S. Bureau of the Census.
†As of December 1998. Source: National Governors' Association; National Conference of State Legislatures; state government officials.
‡1997 figures. Source: U.S. Bureau of the Census.
§1998-1999 figures for elementary and secondary students in average daily attendance. Source: National Education Association.

#One independent.
**Three independents.
††Two independents; four progressives.
‡‡Projection. Mississippi House of Representatives to break electoral vote tie in January 2000 vote.

President Bill Clinton speaks with Minnesota Governor Jesse Ventura in August, following the president's speech before the National Governors' Association meeting in St. Louis, Missouri. Ventura, a former professional wrestler, rose to prominence in 1999 as the Reform Party's highest-ranking elected official.

issues and antismoking educational programs.

Officials in other states, including Arkansas, Illinois, Iowa, Missouri, New Mexico, Ohio, and Pennsylvania developed commissions seeking public input on how to use the additional funds. The states had until June 30, 2000, to create a plan to manage the funds.

The U.S. Centers for Disease Control and Prevention in Atlanta, Georgia, also announced in August 1999 that six states—Hawaii, Maryland, Minnesota, New Jersey, Vermont, and Washington—had set aside major amounts of their settlement for antitobacco measures. The CDC encouraged additional states to put the money toward antitobacco campaigns, claiming that research had shown such programs to be effective.

Health care issues. Texas Governor George W. Bush signed a bill on June 20 allowing physicians to collectively negotiate with managed care health plans, such as Health Maintenance Organizations (HMO's), over fees and other contract provisions. Managed care is a form of health insurance in which costs are controlled by offering incentives to providers to practice more conservative care.

The Texas law places physician negotiations under state supervision, which enables doctors to jointly request certain fees and other contract terms. Supporters of the legislation claimed it would provide a check and balance to ensure that HMO's do not unfairly use their power to control patient care.

CHIP. On September 8, U.S. Health and Human Services Secretary Donna Shalala announced that she had given approval to plans proposed by officials in Washington state and Wyoming to provide health coverage for uninsured children through the federal Children's Health Insurance Program (CHIP). With the approval, Shalala said that all 50 states and 6 U.S. territories had a plan approved by the federal government. Washington state could receive over $46 million and Wyoming could receive over $7 million in new funds under CHIP, which was created in 1997.

CHIP provides $24 billion through 2002 to help states and U.S. territories expand health insurance to children whose families earn too much to qualify for traditional Medicaid, yet not enough to afford private insurance. Officials anticipated that the program would provide health insurance to more than 2.6 million uninsured children by September 2000. ☐ Elaine Stuart

See also **Courts; Education; Health care issues; People in the news** (Ventura, Jesse).

Stocks and bonds. Computer-technology stocks dominated the stock market in 1999. While the U.S. Federal Reserve System (the Fed), the central bank of the United States, cast a pall over the economy when it made three increases in interest rates in June, August, and November, computer-technology stocks advanced sharply. Fears that the economy was growing too quickly to keep inflation in check pushed interest rates higher throughout much of the year. But higher rates did not dampen enthusiasm for even highly speculative computer-technology stocks that traded at lofty prices.

The Dow Jones Industrial Average—a composite of the stock prices of 30 major companies traded on the New York Stock Exchange and on the Nasdaq Composite Index, consisting of the more than 3,000 stocks traded electronically on the system operated by the National Association of Securities Dealers—broke the 10,000 mark on March 29, 1999, when it closed at a record high of 10,006.78. The Dow had hovered near the 10,000 mark for most of March. Economists claimed that the achievement was connected to the strong U.S. economy. On August 23, the Dow reached another record when it closed at 11,299.76, up 23 percent for the year. In October, the Dow went into a slide, breaking below the 10,000 mark during two successive trading days in mid-October. A rebound in computer-tech stocks helped boost the Dow in November.

On November 1, *The Wall Street Journal,* which picks the stocks to be in the various Dow Jones averages, added two popular computer-technology stocks to the Dow industrial index— software giant Microsoft Corporation of Redmond, Washington, and semiconductor leader Intel Corporation of Santa Clara, California. The newspaper also added retailer Home Depot of Atlanta, Georgia, and phone company SBC Communications of San Antonio.

The Wall Street Journal removed retailer Sears Roebuck of Chicago, oil producer Chevron of San Francisco, chemical manufacturer Union Carbide of Long Beach, California, and Goodyear Tire & Rubber of Akron, Ohio. The changes were intended to make the Dow more relevant to the current economy.

The Dow's new configuration reflected the growing influence of computer-technology companies in the U.S. economy and on the stock market. The Nasdaq is dominated by such giant computer-technology stocks as Microsoft and Intel. The Nasdaq posted repeated record highs in November 1999, and reached a record high of 3,520.63 points on December 3.

Individual investors, many trading through online services, helped propel computer technology stocks higher. New electronic services for trading stocks beyond the traditional hours of New York Stock Exchange and Nasdaq trading prompted the two exchanges to announce plans for extended trading hours.

In the bond market, the three Fed rate hikes of 1999, intended to slow economic growth and preempt inflation, eroded the value of fixed-income investments for most of the year. When interest rates rise, prices of existing fixed-income securities paying lower rates decline. The yield on 30-year Treasury bonds, which reflect changes in price to accommodate current market rates, climbed to 6.4 percent in late October 1999 from 5.09 percent in December 1998.

Glass-Steagall Act. Among other sectors of the stock market, financial service stocks rallied in 1999 after President Bill Clinton signed legislation on November 12 that rewrote U.S. banking laws and essentially repealed the 1933 Glass-Steagall Act. One provision of Glass-Steagall prohibited an institution that accepted deposits and made loans from doing investment banking. The repeal was expected to launch a number of multibillion-dollar mergers among financial service firms.

Winners and losers. Oil company stocks and stocks related to oil extraction and marketing advanced unexpectedly in 1999 after the Organization of Petroleum Exporting Countries (OPEC), an association of 11 oil-exporting nations, set and maintained strict production quotas that more than doubled the price of oil in 1999 to beyond $25 a barrel by mid-November.

The failure of small-company stocks, which constituted many actively managed mutual funds, to keep up with the gains in a fairly small number of large-company stocks, provided the biggest stock market disappointment in 1999.

TIME CAPSULE   1929

STOCKS AND BONDS

THE CLOSING DAYS of October, 1929, will be long remembered by thousands of American investors and speculators as the time of the greatest scaling down of values ever known on the New York Stock Exchange. A prolonged orgy of speculation was succeeded by a period of panicky selling, continued day after day until a climax was reached on Tuesday, October 29. On that day transactions on the Stock Exchange rose to the enormous figure of 16,410,030 shares.

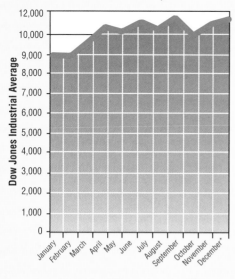

Stock market breaks 11,000

Closing monthly averages for 1999

*December figure is as of the 9th.

The Dow Jones Industrial Average broke 10,000 for the first time in March 1999. The Dow climbed to a new record high on August 23 when it broke 11,000.

Small stocks rallied from the end of March through mid-July, giving many fund managers encouraging second-quarter results. But they surrendered much of the gain from mid-July to mid-October, when higher interest rates took their toll on stock values in many sectors of the market.

The Russell 2000 index of small-company stocks rose 8 percent through mid-November 1999, but fell 7 percent below its all-time high, set in April 1998.

International stock markets. The rebound in the Japanese stock market was the biggest story for 1999 in international investing. Instability in the economies of Southeast Asia caused Asian stock markets to experience sharp swings in 1998. But the Nikkei 225 index of major stocks on the Tokyo Stock Exchange, boosted by government economic stimulus programs and a recovery in many Asian economies in 1999, climbed 33 percent through mid-November. On November 26, the Tokyo Stock Exchange closed at a record-high 18,914.50.

Major stocks in London were up 12 percent in 1999 through mid-November. German stocks rose 15 percent in the same period, and French stocks rose 33 percent.   □ Bill Barnhart

See also **Bank; Economics.**

Sudan. Controversy continued to grow in 1999 over the U.S. bombing on Aug. 20, 1998, of a factory in Sudan. In February 1999, the factory's owner, Saudi businessman Salih Idris, filed a lawsuit against the United States, demanding the release of some $24 million of his assets that the United States had frozen after destroying the factory in a missile attack. United States officials claimed that the factory had produced a chemical weapons agent called Empta and that the business was linked to the Islamic militant Osama bin Laden. The U.S. government accused bin Laden of plotting the bombings of U.S. embassies in Tanzania and Kenya in early August 1998.

Idris claimed his factory, in the Sudanese capital of Khartoum, had produced only pharmaceuticals. United States and British scientists hired by Idris's lawyers reported in February 1999 that they found no evidence of Empta in samples from the factory. In May, the U.S. government released the funds belonging to Idris, though it refused to retract its previous charge that his factory produced chemical weapons agents.

Parliament dissolved. Sudanese President Umar al-Bashir dissolved the parliament and declared a three-month state of emergency on December 12. Al-Bashir indicated that his action was prompted by friction with parliament Speaker Hassan Turabi, who had moved to reduce presidential powers.

Sudanese slavery. In February, the United Nations Childrens Fund (UNICEF), an agency concerned with protecting the rights of children around the world, strongly condemned the practice by some Western humanitarian groups of "redeeming" enslaved Sudanese people for cash. According to the United Nations (UN), enforced slavery of women and children had become widespread in Sudan since the resurgence of civil war in 1983. The war involved the mainly black Christians and *animists* (those believing that souls are present in all parts of nature) of southern Sudan fighting for autonomy from the Arab- and Muslim-dominated north.

UN officials charged that progovernment Arab militias often enslaved Christians and animists. Several Western humanitarian organizations had purchased the freedom of thousands of children from slave dealers in the 1990's. UNICEF concluded that profits from such purchases increased the incidents of enforced slavery.

U.S. aid to rebels. In November 1999, the Sudanese government condemned a new U.S. law that gave the U.S. president authority to send food aid to the Sudanese rebels. International aid groups also criticized the law for its use of food as a weapon of war.   □ Christine Helms

See also **Middle East; Middle East: A Special Report; United Nations.**

Supreme Court of the United States.

On June 22, 1999, the U.S. Supreme Court announced four decisions concerning the Americans with Disabilities Act (ADA). The ADA, passed by the U.S. Congress in 1990, was designed to prevent discrimination against disabled individuals in employment and in how the disabled are treated in public establishments.

In three cases involving employment issues, the justices established a more restrictive view of the definition of "disabled" that had been applied since the ADA became law in 1990. The court voted 7 to 2 in all three cases that people are not disabled under the provisions of the ADA if they have impairments that can be corrected with medication, glasses, or other devices. In the first case, the court ruled that two nearsighted sisters who had been denied airline pilot jobs because of vision problems were not disabled. In the second case, the court rejected a claim by a man who had sued a shipping company after he had been dismissed because high blood pressure prevented him from receiving federal certification to drive a truck. In the third case, the court rejected arguments that a man was discriminated against when he was dismissed as a supermarket truckdriver for being functionally blind in one eye.

The court decided in a fourth case involving the ADA that people who are mentally disabled may be able to use the law to force states to move them from public hospitals into smaller, homelike facilities. Voting 6 to 3, the court ruled that isolating disabled people unnecessarily in state institutions constituted discrimination. The court determined that the ADA requires states to move a patient into a group home, if one is available, when there is no medical reason to keep the individual in a large hospital.

State immunity. The court issued three 5-to-4 rulings on June 23, 1999, that made it more difficult for a person to sue states for violating federal laws. In a case involving the state of Maine, the justices ruled that state employees cannot sue their employers in state court for violating federal labor laws. Earlier in 1999, the Supreme Court had barred state employees from filing such labor suits in federal court.

In two cases involving Florida, the justices ruled that states cannot be sued in federal court by patent owners for infringement of their patents by state universities or for violation of patent and trademark laws by state agencies. The ruling struck down two 1992 federal laws that allowed such suits.

Equal welfare. In a 7-to-2 decision, the court determined on May 17, 1999, that states cannot limit new residents to the same welfare payments they had been receiving in their home states. The decision struck down a California law that capped the welfare benefits of new residents to the amount they had received in the states from which they had moved. The California law made new residents ineligible for full California-resident benefits until they had lived in the state for one year. The Supreme Court ruled that California's restrictions violated individuals' right to travel.

Sexual harassment. On May 24, the court determined that a school is obligated to pay monetary damages if the school fails to put an end to sexual harassment of one student by another. In a 5-to-4 vote, the court ruled that school districts can be held responsible if officials were "deliberately indifferent" to student-to-student sexual harassment. In the case involving a Georgia school, a student claimed that in 1992 and 1993, she and her mother had repeatedly told officials at the child's elementary school about offensive actions by a male classmate, who was never disciplined. The court determined that Title IX of the Education Amendment of 1972 requires school district officials to take action if they know about student-to-student sexual harassment.

Suspects' rights. In another decision handed down on May 24, 1999, the court unanimously ruled that police departments that allow journalists to observe or record a search or arrest on private property are violating the rights of criminal suspects. The court, ruling in separate cases from Maryland and Montana, decided that the protections against unreasonable searches and seizures guaranteed by the Fourth Amendment to the U.S. Constitution prevent police officers from inviting news media into a suspect's residence without the individual's consent. While the ruling makes police liable for monetary damages for bringing journalists onto private property, the court ruled, in a separate 8-to-1 vote, that the officers in the Maryland and Montana cases could not be sued. The law at the time of the raids in 1992 and 1993 was unclear regarding invasion of privacy by police.

Antiloitering law. The court ruled in a 6-to-3 decision on June 10, 1999, that a Chicago antiloitering law aimed at clearing gang members from street corners violated the U.S. Constitution. The justices decided that the law threatened the personal liberty of innocent people because it did not give police officers enough guidance about when to ask people to move along.

Death penalty upheld. On June 21, 1999, the court voted 5 to 4 to uphold a 1995 federal death sentence. The case was the first the court had reviewed under the 1994 Federal Death Penalty Act, which lists 40 federal crimes for which a defendant could receive a death sentence. The ruling involved Louis Jones, a former soldier in the U.S. Army, who was sentenced to

Police officers carry the remains of Harry Blackmun into the Supreme Court on March 8, 1999, where the former justice lay in state in the Great Hall. Blackmun, who died on March 4 at age 90, served on the court from 1970 to 1994.

death for kidnapping and killing a 19-year-old female private stationed at a U.S. Air Force base in Texas.

Jones claimed that jurors at his trial were unduly confused about their options and obligations in the case. He argued that the jury wrongly believed that he might eventually be released from prison if the jury did not hand down the death penalty. The Supreme Court ruled that while a judge in a federal capital case is required to hand down a sentence if a jury cannot decide on a verdict penalty, a judge need not explain that requirement to the jury.

Death row delays. The court on November 8 refused to hear appeals from two death row inmates—one in Nebraska and one in Florida—who claimed that keeping an inmate on death row awaiting execution constitutes cruel and unusual punishment. The cases failed to receive the four votes necessary for judicial review.

Statistical sampling. In a 5-to-4 vote, the court ruled on Jan. 25, 1999, that the U.S. Census Bureau may not use a technique called statistical sampling when counting the nation's population in the 2000 census. Results from the census, which is conducted every 10 years, are used to determine the number of members each state is entitled to in the U.S. House of Representatives.

The Census Bureau had claimed that such traditional counting methods as questionnaires, phone surveys, and door-to-door interviews miss many people, particularly racial and ethnic minorities in urban areas. The bureau had argued that sampling techniques would enable officials to estimate a region's total population based on a representative sample rather than a count of every person.

Blackmun dies. Former Supreme Court Justice Harry A. Blackmun died on March 4, 1999, at age 90. Blackmun was born in Nashville, Illinois, and was raised in St. Paul, Minnesota. Political experts considered Blackmun a conservative at the time of his appointment to the court in 1970 by President Richard M. Nixon. At the time of his retirement in 1994, many legal experts viewed Blackmun as one of the court's most liberal judges.

Blackmun wrote the Supreme Court's 1973 opinion that legalized abortion in the United States. In *Roe v. Wade,* the court ruled that states could not forbid a woman to have an abortion during the first *trimester* (three months) of pregnancy. The court further ruled that during the second trimester, states may regulate abortion only to protect a woman's health.

☐ Linda P. Campbell and Geoffrey A. Campbell
See also **Courts; Disabled; Welfare.**

Surgery. See Medicine.
Suriname. See Latin America.
Swaziland. See Africa.

SUPREME COURT

THE SUPREME COURT of the United States ruled unanimously on May 17 that segregation of the races in public schools is unconstitutional.

The decision overturned a ruling of the court in 1896 that blacks could be taught in "separate but equal" schools. The new decision held that "separate educational facilities are inherently unequal."

Opposition, amounting in many instances to refusal to abide by the decision, sprang up at once in [the] Southern States. Governors and legislators prepared methods which they hoped would enable them to get around the decision. Meanwhile, the court itself set no deadline for obeying the ruling. The decision does not apply to private schools.

The decision had the effect of wiping segregation laws from the books in 21 states, of which 17 had laws making segregation compulsory. . . . Sixteen other states had laws forbidding segregation, and 11 had no laws on the subject.

Sweden enjoyed one of the strongest economic growth rates of any European country in 1999, largely because of the rapid development of its high-technology and service industries. European economists expected Sweden's *gross domestic product* (the value of all goods and services produced in a year) to grow by 3.8 percent in 1999. The growth helped push Sweden's unemployment rate to less than 8 percent, compared with a high of nearly 10 percent in 1997.

Despite the strong growth, government officials grew concerned in 1999 that Sweden was losing control over its economic future in the face of the expanding global economy. In January, U.S.-based Ford Motor Company bought Volvo AB, the Swedish automobile manufacturer, for $6.5 billion. The acquisition followed a number of mergers that resulted in several companies moving their headquarters from Sweden to other countries. Industrial and business leaders claimed that Sweden's high tax rates were driving companies out of the country.

Government. Sweden's finance minister, Erik Asbrink, resigned in April after a policy disagreement with Prime Minister Goran Persson. Asbrink wanted to use a budget surplus to pay off part of Sweden's national debt, which had grown during the recession in the early 1990's. The prime minister, however, wanted to cut taxes to improve

Australian swimmer Ian Thorpe celebrates after breaking the men's 400-meter freestyle world record with a time of 3:41.83 at the Pan Pacific Swimming Championships in Australia in August 1999.

Sweden's competitiveness. Bosse Ringholm, an ally of Persson, replaced Asbrink as finance minister. In September 1999, Ringholm unveiled a budget for 2000 that contained Sweden's first significant income and business tax cuts in a decade.

Persson promised that his ruling Social Democratic Party would decide in the spring of 2000 whether to call a referendum on the question of Sweden's joining the single European currency, the euro. Most large companies wanted to join, to make it easier to compete in Europe. Opinion polls, however, showed slightly more than 50 percent of all Swedes opposed joining the euro.

Nuclear shutdown. A court in June 1999 ordered the closing of one of two reactors at a nuclear power plant in Barsebaeck, a city in southern Sweden. The shutdown was the first step of a program to phase out nuclear power. Swedes had voted to ban nuclear power in 1980, although the country's electric power industry contended that there were not enough alternative energy sources available.

Military cuts. Sweden's military chief of staff announced in March 1999 that the size of the armed forces would be cut in half because of budgetary pressures and the absence of the threat of invasion from the former Soviet Union.

☐ Tom Buerkle

See also **Denmark; Europe.**

Swimming. Jenny Thompson of the United States was arguably the top swimmer of 1999. But a number of others, including Lenny Krayzelburg, a Russian-born American, Pieter Van den Hoogenband of the Netherlands, and South Africa's Penny Heyns also turned in record performances.

Thompson set the world record for the 100-meter individual medley with a time of 1:00.41 in a World Cup short-course (25-meter pool) meet in Sydney, Australia, on January 16. She also won five gold medals at the meet, including the 50-meter butterfly, the 100-meter butterfly, and the 50-meter freestyle. In April, at the short-course world championships in Hong Kong, Thompson lowered the 100-meter individual medley record to 59.30 seconds in a preliminary heat. She also won six gold medals at the Pan Pacific Championships in Sydney, Australia, in August.

Other record breakers. Penny Heyns set breaststroke world records three times at the Pan Pacific Championships, breaking her own former standard in each race. She lowered her 100-meter world mark to 1:06.52 in a qualifying heat and set a 200-meter record of 2:23.64 four nights later, after breaking it earlier in the semifinals.

Lenny Krayzelburg broke the world records for the men's 50-, 100-, and 200-meter backstroke on his way to three gold medals at the Pan Pacific Championships. On August 24, he swam the 100 meters in 53.60 seconds, breaking the record of 53.86 set by American Jeff Rouse in 1992. On Aug. 27, 1999, Krayzelburg completed the 200-meter final in 1:55.87, 0.7 second faster than the former mark, set in 1991 by Martin Zubero of Spain. Krayzelburg broke his third record on Aug 29, 1999, swimming a 50-meter time trial in 24.99 seconds, beating the mark set by Rouse in 1993 by 0.14 second. Krayzelburg won his third gold medal as a member of the U.S. medley relay team.

Hoogenband's best showing came at the European Championships in Istanbul, Turkey, in July 1999, when he beat Russia's Aleksandr Popov, the world record holder, in the 100-meter freestyle. Hoogenband finished the meet with gold medals in the 50-, 100-, and 200-meter freestyle, the 50-meter butterfly, and in two relay events.

Older records also fall. Australia's Susie O'Neill broke one of swimming's oldest records on February 17, when she swam the 200-meter butterfly in 2:05.37 in a World Cup short-course meet at Malmo, Sweden. Her time was 0.28 second faster than the mark set by American Mary T. Meagher in 1981. Australia's Grant Hackett broke the oldest record in men's swimming on March 23, 1999, when he swam the first leg of the 4x200-meter relay in 1:46.67 at the Australian national championships. The former mark had been set in 1989 by Giorgio Lamberti of Italy. □ Ron Reid

Switzerland. The consensus that has long characterized politics in Switzerland was jolted in 1999 when the right-wing Swiss People's Party made dramatic gains in parliamentary elections in October. The People's Party waged a strongly nationalist campaign, calling for strict curbs on immigration and questioning attempts to strengthen links with the European Union (EU) and other international organizations. The party won 44 seats in the 200-member lower house of parliament, up from 29 seats in the previous election of 1995. The Social Democrats won 51 seats, compared with 54 seats in 1995. Switzerland's two centrist parties held steady. The Radical Democrats won 43 seats, down from 45 in the previous parliament, and the Christian Democrats took 35 seats, up from 34.

The People's Party demanded a greater voice in government, but in December 1999, all four parties agreed to continue the so-called magic formula that has kept them in coalition for 40 years. Under that formula, the Social Democrats, the Radical Democrats, and the Christian Democrats each held two ministerial posts in the government while the People's Party held one.

World War II investigations. Switzerland sought to settle controversy over its treatment of Jews and other refugees from Nazi Germany during World War II (1939-1945) with two reports in

Rescue workers search near Interlaken, Switzerland, in July 1999 for survivors of a flash flood down a mountain stream. Twenty-one people were killed in the flood while canyoning, an extreme sport involving sliding or jumping down mountain waterfalls and streams.

December 1999. A panel headed by Paul Volcker, a former U.S. Federal Reserve chairman, said it identified 54,000 unclaimed accounts in Swiss banks that may have belonged to victims of the *Holocaust* (the killing during World War II of Jews and other people by Germany's Nazi government). The panel recommended publishing the names of 25,000 account holders to enable survivors or heirs to claim funds. Claims would be paid from a $1.25-billion settlement that Switzerland's two largest banks, UBS AG and Credit Suisse Group, made in 1998. The panel said it found no evidence that banks conspired to steal funds in the accounts but criticized some banks for frustrating efforts by survivors to find old accounts.

A separate panel of historians criticized the country's treatment of refugees from Nazi Germany. Switzerland refused entry to more than 24,000 refugees during World War II.

Immigration. Swiss voters approved a referendum in June 1999 that tightened rules governing people seeking political asylum. The measure required refugees to request asylum individually rather than in groups and made it easier for the government to expel refugees who lacked identity papers. Switzerland had the highest number of refugees per inhabitant in Europe in 1999.

☐ Tom Buerkle

See also **Europe.**

Syria.

Syria. Syrian President Hafez al-Assad and Israeli Prime Minister Ehud Barak agreed to resume Syrian-Israeli peace talks in December 1999, following separate meetings with U.S. Secretary of State Madeleine Albright. In Washington, D.C., in mid-December, Barak and Syrian Foreign Minister Farouk Sharaa began the highest level talks ever held between the two countries.

Syrian-Israeli peace talks had been stalled since the 1996 election of a hard-line government in Israel. The election in May 1999 of Barak, a moderate, as prime minister of Israel had sparked hope in Syria for a Syrian-Israeli peace accord.

Problems remain. Despite the renewed hope, Syrian-Israeli differences remained wide. Assad continued to demand as a condition for peace that Israel return the Golan Heights, territory captured from Syria in the 1967 Arab-Israeli war. Assad claimed Israel had agreed to return this territory before previous peace talks broke down. Israel denied this. However, Barak indicated that, as a price for peace, Israel might have to give up at least some of the Golan.

Another difficulty concerned Lebanon, where Syria had 35,000 troops. Israel and Syria differed over how much influence Syria could bring to bear on Islamic guerrillas in southern Lebanon to end attacks on Israel. ☐ Christine Helms

See also **Israel; Lebanon; Middle East.**

Taiwan. A severe earthquake of magnitude 7.6 struck Taiwan in September. The quake left more than 2,300 people dead, 11,000 people injured, and caused more than $8 billion in property losses, according to government sources.

The earthquake damaged electric plants and power grids that supply electricity to Taiwan's booming export industries. Disruptions of factories that manufacture computer chips caused interruptions in production schedules of computer manufacturers worldwide.

Economy. Despite the huge cost of repairing earthquake-related damage, Taiwan's economy remained strong in 1999. Growth in domestic output continued in the range of 5.5 to 6.0 percent, according to government officials and independent economists. Inflation stayed low at about 1.5 percent.

President Lee Teng-hui announced on July 9 that Taiwan would henceforth negotiate with the People's Republic of China only on the basis of a "special state-to-state" relationship. China regards Taiwan as an estranged province and insists that China-Taiwan relations be based on the understanding that Taiwan is part of China.

Lee's new position prompted Chinese officials to repeat warnings that China would use force to block any move toward independence. Lee later explained that reunification could only be achieved democratically. Experts in China-Taiwan relations suggested that Lee's announcement signaled that he did not expect reunification as long as China was ruled by the Communist Party.

Chinese jet fighters began patrolling in 1999 the 100-mile (161-kilometer) strait separating Taiwan from the Chinese mainland. In response, Taiwan's government pushed ahead plans to develop an antimissile defense system that could destroy incoming Chinese missiles. Officials of Taiwan's military research institute announced in late 1999 a successful test of an antimissile missile.

Toward elections. At its August convention, Lee's Kuomintang (KMT) political party endorsed Vice President Lien Chan as its candidate for president in the March 2000 presidential election. The party chose Premier Vincent Siew as its candidate for vice president.

Lien faced a split in the long-dominant KMT. James Soong, a popular KMT leader who called for improved relations with China, announced his candidacy for president as an independent. The KMT expelled Soong from the party, but he ran ahead of Lien in most public opinion polls in late 1999. The opposition Democratic Progressive Party (DPP) backed former Taipei mayor Chen Shuibian for president. The DPP advocated independence for Taiwan. ☐ Henry S. Bradsher

See also **Asia; China.**

An earthquake with a magnitude of 7.6 topples a high-rise apartment building in Tungshih, Taiwan, in September. The quake, one of the strongest ever to strike Taiwan, left more than 2,300 people dead and caused billions of dollars in damages.

Taxation. United States President Bill Clinton and the Republican-led U.S. Congress clashed in 1999 over income tax reduction, setting the stage for a likely showdown over taxes in the 2000 election campaign. Voting mainly along party lines, Congress in August 1999 approved a Republican-designed bill to reduce federal taxes by $792 billion by 2010. The measure cleared the House on a vote of 221 to 206 but only narrowly won Senate approval by a vote of 50 to 49.

Republican legislators had hoped that the public would rally behind them and persuade President Clinton to lift a veto threat. However, the president received little criticism when he vetoed the bill on Sept. 23, 1999. The president said that the legislation would have used too great a percentage of a projected budget surplus and would have jeopardized future funding of such programs as Medicare and Social Security.

The bill was designed to lower the rates at which personal income and capital gains were taxed by one percentage point. Supporters claimed that 100 million taxpayers would have benefited from the proposed tax cut. It also would have repealed the federal inheritance tax.

President Clinton argued that he would have supported a smaller tax cut, targeting middle-income families. Democrats in Congress reported that the smaller reductions would not jeopardize efforts to bolster Social Security and Medicare trust funds by using the anticipated budget surplus. Speaker of the House Dennis Hastert (R., Illinois) said that tax relief would be a high-priority item on the agenda when the Congress reconvened in January 2000.

In November 1999, Congress approved a budget package that renewed a group of popular tax credits, including an $18.3-billion credit to companies that conduct research and development. A vote on a Republican proposal to reduce taxes on small business firms, which had been included as part of a bill to raise the minimum wage to $6.15 an hour, was postponed until the House of Representatives reconvened in January 2000 for the second session of the 106th Congress.

Anti-tax forces. Washington state voters approved a ballot measure on Nov. 2, 1999, that requires voter approval of future tax and fee increases at the state or local level. The restriction was adopted along with another referendum that eliminated an unpopular 2.2-percent tax on automobile registration. The fee was replaced with a flat $30 annual fee.

Voters in St. Paul, Minnesota, and Houston rejected separate proposals to use taxes to pay for new professional sports facilities.

☐ William J. Eaton

See also **People in the news** (Hastert, J. Dennis).

Telecommunications. The proposed merger of two giant telecommunications companies, MCI WorldCom and Sprint, epitomized the ambitious objectives of the telecommunications industry in 1999. For the fourth consecutive year, telecommunications companies aggressively pursued consolidation in hopes of gaining a competitive advantage. The volume and size of such mergers, however, prompted United States government regulators to question whether the consolidation of the communications giants was in the best interest of consumers.

The biggest merger in history. MCI WorldCom Incorporated, headquartered in Clinton, Mississippi, stunned the international telecommunications industry on October 5 when it announced that it planned to purchase Sprint Corporation of Westwood, Kansas, for $129 billion. MCI claimed that the merger would put the newly combined company in a better position to challenge the dominance of long-distance giant AT&T Corp.

The proposed marriage of the second- and third-largest long-distance carriers in the United States immediately provoked a sharp response from Federal Communications Corporation (FCC) Chairman William Kennard, who said he did not see how the merger would benefit consumers. The FCC is a federal agency that regulates radio, wire, and cable communications in the United States.

On October 6, one day after the MCI-WorldCom announcement, the FCC granted final approval to SBC Communications to purchase Chicago-based Ameritech for $72 billion. The merger made SBC Communications, of San Antonio, the largest local-telephone service provider in the United States.

Convergence. Years of talk about *technology convergence* (the melding of telephone, cable, television, and Internet-access services by one provider) began to become reality in 1999, as the

TIME CAPSULE **1958**

TELECOMMUNICATIONS

The United States climaxed a year of space-travel achievements by hurling the world's largest satellite into orbit on Dec. 18, 1958. The space vehicle, a monster "talking" Atlas missile weighing more than 4 tons, was the fifth satellite placed in orbit during the year by American scientists. An elaborate communications system enabled the rocket to broadcast a tape-recorded Christmas message from President Dwight D. Eisenhower back to Earth.

TELECOMMUNICATIONS

TIROS I, forerunner of a group of weather satellites, roared aloft April 1. The hatbox-shaped Tiros gave man his first global look at weather patterns by sending photographs back to receiving stations from an altitude of about 400 miles (640 kilometers). Using two television cameras, Tiros photographed cloud patterns, ice floes in a river, and later a hurricane that had not yet been reported . . . . Tiros gives great promise of allowing man to observe weather development over a vast track of Earth . . . .

distinctions between telephone and cable companies blurred. AT&T, which maintained its dominance in long-distance telephone services, led the transformation by becoming the largest cable television company in the United States in 1999.

On March 9, AT&T acquired Englewood, Colorado-based Tele-Communications Incorporated (TCI), the largest cable operator in the United States, for $55 billion. The merger provided AT&T with a way to avoid paying substantial access fees to local-service providers for millions of potential local and long-distance telephone customers. Local-service providers own the lines used by AT&T and other long-distance carriers. Telecommunication experts claimed that TCI's high-speed cable transmission lines also would provide AT&T with a way to enter the fast-growing Internet business as a major competitor.

Six weeks after the TCI acquisition, AT&T set off in pursuit of another big cable company, with the intent of expanding both its telephone and Internet-access business. The venture began on March 22, when Comcast Corporation of Philadelphia, the third-largest cable company, and MediaOne Group Incorporated of Englewood, Colorado, the fourth-largest cable provider, announced their plans to merge in a $49-billion deal. On April 22, AT&T surprised Comcast by making a $54-billion bid for MediaOne.

The three companies avoided an expensive bidding war by agreeing on May 4 to a compromise. AT&T won control of MediaOne for $58 billion and the ability to offer local-telephone service over Comcast's cable lines. Comcast was given the option to purchase 2 million new cable subscribers from AT&T for $9 billion in stock, boosting Comcast into third place among U.S. cable providers. AT&T's mergers with TCI and MediaOne gave AT&T cable access to more than 40 percent of U.S. households.

☐ Tim Jones

See also **Internet; Radio; Television.**

Television ratings compiled by Nielsen Media Research, a New York City-based agency that tracks television viewership, indicated that the combined share of the viewing audience of the six major networks—ABC, CBS, NBC, Fox, UPN, and WB—dropped to an all-time low of 55 percent during the 1998-1999 season. Some media experts explained that entertainment available via other sources, such as the Internet, played a role in the decline of television viewership. However, advanced sales of commercial advertising spots for the 1999-2000 season rose 13 percent to $7.25 billion. Advertising executives claimed that despite the overall decline in viewers, broadcast television programs still commanded the largest single audience per show.

Morning news. Some new faces appeared on the networks' early morning news shows during 1999. In January, the American Broadcasting Company (ABC) named Diane Sawyer and Charles Gibson as co-anchors of "Good Morning America" in an effort to reverse the morning news program's four-year ratings decline. CBS, Inc., perennially in last place in the morning show race, launched an entirely new early morning news show, "The Early Show" with Bryant Gumbel and Jane Clayson, which debuted in November.

Emmy Award winners in 1999

Comedy

Best Series: "Ally McBeal"
Lead Actress: Helen Hunt, "Mad About You"
Lead Actor: John Lithgow, "3rd Rock From the Sun"
Supporting Actress: Kristen Johnston, "3rd Rock From the Sun"
Supporting Actor: David Hyde Pierce, "Frasier"

Drama

Best Series: "The Practice"
Lead Actress: Edie Falco, "The Sopranos"
Lead Actor: Dennis Franz, "N.Y.P.D. Blue"
Supporting Actress: Holland Taylor, "The Practice"
Supporting Actor: Michael Badalucco, "The Practice"

Other awards

Drama or Comedy Miniseries or Special: *Horatio Hornblower*

Variety, Music, or Comedy Series: "Late Show with David Letterman"

Made for Television Movie: *A Lesson Before Dying*

Lead Actress in a Miniseries or Special: Helen Mirren, *The Passion of Ayn Rand*

Lead Actor in a Miniseries or Special: Stanley Tucci, *Winchell*

Supporting Actress in a Miniseries or Special: Anne Bancroft, *Deep in My Heart*

Supporting Actor in a Miniseries or Special: Peter O'Toole, *Joan of Arc*

Major acquisition. On September 7, Viacom Inc., a New York City-based broadcasting company, announced it would acquire the entire CBS Corporation, which included the broadcast network and 15 television stations, for $37.3 billion. The merger created the third-largest media company in the United States, after Time Warner, Inc., of New York City and Walt Disney Company of Burbank, California.

"Jenny Jones" penalized. In May, a jury ordered Warner Brothers, owner of "The Jenny Jones Show," to pay $25 million in damages to the family of a man who had been murdered after appearing on the talk show. The victim had revealed his infatuation for a male neighbor while both were appearing on the syndicated talk show in 1995. The neighbor later shot the man. Although the episode never aired, the jury ruled that the show was guilty of negligence.

Lawsuits. Producer Steven Bochco and actors David Duchovny and Alan Alda filed lawsuits in 1999 against the Fox network and its parent company, 20th Century Fox Film Corporation, of Beverly Hills, California. Although filed separately, the lawsuits involved a common issue—sales of series reruns—traditionally a rich source of income for networks. Bochco, Duchovny, and Alda charged that Fox sold the rights of the hit series "N.Y.P.D. Blue," "The X-Files," and "M*A*S*H" to its own FX cable channel at prices below fair market value. "The X-Files" aired on the Fox network while "M*A*S*H" and "N.Y.P.D. Blue" were produced by 20th Century Fox. Fox settled Alda's lawsuit in August. The other lawsuits remained unresolved in 1999.

Lack of integration? In July, Kweisi Mfume, president of the National Association for the Advancement of Colored People (NAACP), a civil

TIME CAPSULE 1939

TELEVISION

APRIL 30, 1939, marked the beginning of scheduled television service in the United States. Field tests of transmitters and receivers had resulted in technical improvements in equipment that enabled the National Broadcasting Company to offer entertaining programs on a reliable service basis. First schedules included 2 hours of broadcasting per week, but by the end of 1939 this had been increased to 15 hours, comprising two programs daily, five times per week.

TIME CAPSULE 1948

TELEVISION

A FOREST OF ODD-LOOKING ANTENNAS was sprouting on the rooftops of major United States cities. The word video, meaning "I see" in Latin, came to be a synonym for television. Baby sitters were easy to find if the family had a television set. All these were signs of the tremendous growth of television in 1948.

Television was America's fastest growing new business. Many authorities predicted that television will become one of the biggest industries in the country.

At the beginning of 1948 the United States had 19 television stations. In December it had 48 in 22 communities spread from coast to coast. Wayne Coy, chairman of the Federal Communications Commission . . . estimated that in a year all available channels in the nation's 140 metropolitan areas would be assigned, that 400 stations would be on the air within two years, and a thousand in seven or eight years.

rights organization headquartered in Baltimore publicly criticized executives at ABC, CBS, the National Broadcasting Company (NBC), and Fox for a lack of racially integrated casts on their shows, especially comedies. Mfume argued that none of the series scheduled for release for the 1999-2000 season had a minority star, and he threatened a network boycott during ratings sweeps week in November. His criticism resulted in apologies from TV executives and last-minute additions of black characters to new series. It was the first time that the NAACP had criticized television programming since 1951, when it challenged the stereotypes portrayed in the series "Amos and Andy."

Too much television can be bad for a child's health, according to a claim made by physicians in the August 1999 issue of the medical journal *Pediatrics*. The American Academy of Pediatrics declared that excessive television viewing poses a risk to children's social, mental, and physical health and may foster obesity and poor academic performance. The academy offered specific guidelines to parents, suggesting that children under the age of 2 should not be allowed to watch television at all and that older children should not be allowed to have television sets in their bedrooms.

School violence. A shooting rampage by two students at Columbine High School in Littleton, Colorado, on April 20 led network executives to change the air dates of some television programs. The WB network postponed the season finale of "Buffy the Vampire Slayer" from May 25 to July 13 out of respect for the incident. The episode featured threats of violence and an attempted mass poisoning of high school students.

Some people criticized ABC for their coverage of the Columbine shooting. ABC News paid a friend of one of the two alleged gunmen $16,000 for home videos of the youth and for an appearance on "Good Morning, America." Other television news executives criticized ABC for such a display of "checkbook journalism"—paying a source for an interview—especially since ABC did not disclose the arrangement when the show aired.

Public television was plagued by scandal in 1999 after a report issued by auditors of the Corporation for Public Broadcasting on September 9 revealed that 29 Public Broadcasting System (PBS) television stations had sold or exchanged donor lists with political organizations, most of them affiliated with the Democratic Party. The implication of political partisanship among PBS affiliates angered many members of the U.S. Congress, who threatened to cut federal contributions to public television's budget.

A network quiz show became a prime-time hit for the first time in decades in 1999. The ABC program "Who Wants To Be A Millionaire" gained 31 million viewers when it ran 13 episodes over two weeks in August. The program appealed to many viewers who were tired of summertime reruns. It returned for additional episodes in November. Morning show host Regis Philbin hosted the program, in which contestants answered multiple-choice questions with limited assistance from friends and the studio audience. The success of the quiz show prompted the other major networks to begin creating similar shows.

Nontraditional successes. The mid-August success of "Who Wants to be a Millionaire" indicated that hit shows can develop any time of the year, not just in the fall. The NBC series "Providence," about a doctor who returns to her native Rhode Island, became a surprise success following a debut in January 1999. "The Sopranos," a Home Box Office (HBO) cable series, proved to be another January success. The show, about the private and professional life of a mafia boss in therapy, drew an audience of 10 million viewers per week, the highest that any cable series had scored in years.

TELEVISION

TELEVISION DEBATES between Richard M. Nixon and John F. Kennedy in the autumn of 1960 made TV history, and they also may have helped to make national history. Never before were presidential candidates "seen" by so many voters during a campaign. An estimated 65,000,000 persons watched each of the four hour-long debates.

Top-rated U.S. television series

The following were among the most-watched television series for the 1998-1999 regular season, which ran from Sept. 23, 1998, to May 26, 1999.

1. "E.R." (NBC)
2. "Friends" (NBC)
3. "Frasier" (NBC)
4. "Jesse" (NBC)
5. "NFL Monday Night Football" (ABC)
6. "Touched by an Angel" (CBS)
7. "Veronica's Closet" (NBC)
8. "60 Minutes" (CBS)
9. "CBS Sunday Night Movie" (CBS)
10. "Home Improvement" (ABC)
11. "Everybody Loves Raymond" (CBS)
12. "20/20" (Wednesday) (ABC)
13. "The X-Files" (FOX)
14. "The Drew Carey Show" (ABC)
15. "N.Y.P.D. Blue" (ABC)
16. "Walker, Texas Ranger" (CBS)
17. "JAG" (CBS)
18. "Law & Order" (NBC)
19. "Providence" (NBC)
20. "Becker" (CBS)

CBS's long-anticipated news program "60 Minutes II" also debuted in mid-January. The news magazine show on March 31 aired an exclusive interview with President Bill Clinton, the first such interview since the U.S. Senate acquitted the president of impeachment charges.

The new fall season contained many shows that were spin-offs of more established series. "The Parkers" was derived from the United Paramount Network (UPN) sitcom "Moesha." Actress Jennifer Love Hewitt, one of the stars on Fox's drama "Party of Five," moved on to her own series, called "Time of Your Life." "Ally," another Fox show, was a unique repackaging of the already successful series "Ally McBeal." Episodes of the original one-hour series were cut into half-hour segments that emphasized the comic storylines.

End of the line. Several long-running shows departed the airwaves in 1999, including such still-popular *sitcoms* (situation comedies) as "Home Improvement," starring Tim Allen, and "Mad About You," starring Paul Reiser and Helen Hunt. The NBC police drama "Homicide" was canceled after a seven-year run, despite acclaim from the critics. NBC in April 1999 announced it had canceled "Another World." The soap opera debuted in 1964 and was NBC's longest-running daytime program. ☐ Troy Segal

Tennessee. See **State government.**

Tennis. Four women and three men won Grand Slam tennis titles in 1999, a year of continuing intense competition and rivalry on the women's professional tour. The public's interest in men's tennis was more erratic, thanks to a misleading ratings system and an early-season slump. Switzerland's Martina Hingis topped the women's rankings for the third straight year and led the money earnings list with $3.3 million. Andre Agassi of the United States, who won both the French and U.S. Open championships in 1999, ended Pete Sampras's six-year reign as the world's No. 1 player. Agassi also topped the men's earnings list with $4.3 million.

Women. On January 30, Hingis captured her third straight Australian Open title by beating unseeded Amelie Mauresmo of France. Mauresmo had upset American Lindsay Davenport, the 1998 U.S. Open champion, to reach the final. Hingis beat Mauresmo in the final, 6-2, 6-3, for her fifth Grand Slam singles title, but her victory brought an unforeseen consequence. After the match, Hingis called Mauresmo—a muscular woman who had announced earlier in the tournament that she was a lesbian—"half a man." A month later, in the quarterfinals of the Gaz de France Open in Paris, a rowdy crowd cheered Mauresmo and heartily booed Hingis during a match in which Mauresmo defeated Hingis in three sets.

Sisters Venus (right) and Serena Williams celebrate their victory in the women's doubles final at the French Open on June 6, 1999. The pair also won the doubles title at the U.S. Open in September.

The crowd's animosity resurfaced at the French Open in Paris on June 5, 1999, when Germany's Steffi Graf, backed by the highly partisan Parisian crowd, beat Hingis for her 22nd Grand Slam title. The match was humiliating for Hingis, who was booed so mercilessly that she broke down and had to be coaxed back onto the court for the awards ceremony. Graf's victory gave her a ninth French Open title, which she said would be her last.

On July 1, Graf advanced to the Wimbledon semifinals with a three-set victory over Venus Williams of the United States. Three days later, third-seeded Davenport beat Graf in straight sets, 6-4, 7-5, to claim the first Wimbledon championship of her career.

The highlight of the women's season came in New York City on September 11, when Serena Williams of the United States beat Hingis in an extraordinary match for her first Grand Slam singles title. Serena Williams, the younger and less-heralded sister of Venus Williams, was the first African American woman to win the U.S. Open since Althea Gibson in 1958.

Men. Pete Sampras began an erratic 1999 season by passing up the Australian Open in January and by playing badly—for the 10th straight year—at the French Open in May. Russian Yevgeny Kafelnikov, who credited his success to Sampras's absence, beat Sweden's Thomas Enqvist to win the Australian Open men's title on February 1. At the French Open, the only Grand Slam event Sampras has never won, he was knocked out in the second round by Andrei Medvedev of Ukraine.

The brightest moment of Sampras's inconsistent season came on July 4, when he completed a U.S. sweep at Wimbledon by beating Agassi in straight sets. Sampras played brilliantly to finish as the only man in the 1900's to conquer Wimbledon for the sixth time. It was Sampras's 12th Grand Slam title, matching the record of Australia's Roy Emerson.

Agassi bounced back heroically at the U.S. Open on Sept. 12, 1999, beating Todd Martin in a five-set final in which Agassi never lost his serve. Agassi previously won the U.S. Open in 1994. Sampras and Australian Patrick Rafter were forced to withdraw from the tournament due to injury.

Davis Cup. John McEnroe, inducted into the International Tennis Hall of Fame on July 10, 1999, was named captain of the U.S. Davis Cup team for 2000 by the U.S. Tennis Association on Sept. 8, 1999. McEnroe, one of the most successful American Davis Cup players, replaced Tom Gullikson. The fiery and competitive McEnroe said he hoped that he could persuade other top American players, including Sampras and Agassi, who had shown little enthusiasm for the competition in the past, to join him on the U.S. team. ☐ Ron Reid

Terrorism. Incidents of terrorism increased worldwide in 1999, after a decline in 1998. Many of the attacks were related to clashes between competing cultural, national, or religious groups.

Russia. A series of bombings, many connected with ethnic and nationalist conflicts in the Caucasus region, rocked Russia in 1999. On March 19, a bomb exploded in a market in Vladikavkaz, the capital of North Ossetia, where clashes between the Ossetian and Ingush ethnic groups had become frequent. At least 50 people were killed and more than 100 were wounded. The perpetrators remained unknown. Two days later, an attempt was made to assassinate Aslan Maskhadov, leader of Chechnya, a nearby region that had declared its independence from Russia in 1996.

In the summer of 1999, Islamic guerrillas supported by Chechnya conducted armed raids against Russian authorities in Dagestan, a region in southern Russia adjacent to Chechnya. After the Russians counterattacked, a series of bombs destroyed apartment buildings in several Russian cities, including Moscow, killing nearly 300 people and injuring more than 1,000.

Former Soviet republics. A series of car bombs exploded outside government headquarters in the central Asian country of Uzbekistan in February, killing 13 people and injuring more than 100. Authorities believed the bombings were attempts to assassinate the Uzbekistani President, Islam Karimov. In October, ultranationalist gunmen burst into the parliament building in Yerevan, the capital of Armenia, and assassinated Prime Minister Vazgen Sarkisian and seven members of parliament before surrendering. Political analysts speculated that progress in peace talks between Armenia and Azerbaijan after a 10-year war may have sparked the assault.

The Middle East and the Islamic world. On September 5 in Israel, two car-bombing attacks, one in Haifa and one in Tiberias, by Arab activists opposed to peace negotiations between the Israeli government and the Palestine authorities failed when the vehicles exploded prematurely, killing the activists. Two months later, pipe bombs packed with nails exploded in Netanya, Israel.

Struggles between militant Islamists and their opponents took hundreds of lives and destroyed property in Yemen, Algeria, Turkey, South Africa, and Pakistan throughout 1999. In August, a truck bomb exploded near the house of the leader of the *Taliban,* the Islamic militia that rules Afghanistan, killing seven people in the capital, Kabul. The United Nations invoked sanctions against Afghanistan in November when the Taliban regime refused to hand over fugitive Saudi businessman Osama bin Laden, who was wanted in the United States on charges of conspiring to blow up the

U.S. embassies in Kenya and Tanzania in 1998.

On Dec. 24, 1999, hijackers seized an Indian Airlines jet enroute to New Delhi, India's capital, after it took off from Kathmandu, Nepal. After stops in India, Pakistan, and the United Arab Emirates, the hijackers forced the crew to land in Afghanistan. The hijackers killed one passenger and held more than 150 passengers and crew members hostage, demanding that India give them $200 million and release imprisoned Kashmiri militants. The Indian government finally released three Kashmiri militants, and the hostages were released on December 31.

Western Europe. Three bombs exploded in various areas of London betwen April 17 and April 30, injuring more than 115 people and killing 3. Far-right extremist groups claimed responsibility, but the police attributed all three bombings to a single suspect with no ties to the groups.

In Spain in November, leaders of the Basque separatist group ETA (whose initials stand for Basque Homeland and Freedom in the Basque language) declared an end to a 14-month ceasefire with the Spanish government. ETA charged that the government failed to meet its demands for Basque autonomy.   ☐ Richard E. Rubenstein

See also **Afghanistan; Middle East; Russia.**

Texas. See Dallas; Houston; State government.

Thailand. The Thai economy began growing again in 1999 after a two-year period of decline. A collapse in the value of the Thai currency, the baht, in 1997 triggered a severe recession that spread to most of the nations of East and Southeast Asia. In 1998, Thailand's economy contracted by 8 percent.

In August 1999, the International Monetary Fund (IMF), a United Nations-affiliated organization that provides short-term credit to member nations, announced that Thailand's economy was growing at a rate of 3 to 4 percent and could reach 5-percent growth in 2000. An IMF line of credit of $17.2 billion had helped stabilize the Thai currency and enabled Thailand's government to deal with this bank's bad debts.

Bank losses. Thai banks reported huge losses in the first half of 1999. Finance Minister Tarrin Nimmanahaeminda in July revealed that the nation's banks would eventually have to write off a third of their total debt load of nearly $73 billion.

Unemployment. Despite economic gains in 1999, unemployment remained high. Some 2 million people who lost jobs in the Bangkok area in 1997 and 1998 returned to rural areas. However, drought and falling prices for rice made finding work on farms or in villages difficult. Many of these people drifted back to overcrowded Bangkok in 1999.

Economists credited Prime Minister Chuan Leekpai and Finance Minister Tarrin for making possible Thailand's economic recovery by maintaining a climate of political stability. Chuan, however, struggled to hold together his shaky parliamentary majority in 1999. Chuan's Democrat Party governed in coalition with the Chart Pattana Party and several other political groups. One partner in the coalition, the Social Action Party, withdrew in July after an internal battle between parties over who would control government leadership positions. Political observers expected party infighting to intensify as parliamentary elections approached in 2000.

Corruption and murder. The foreign business community in Thailand was shaken in 1999 by the murder of Michael Wansley, an Australian accountant. On March 10, Wansley was killed on a country road by a gunman on a motorcycle. An investigation led police to executives of a company Wansley was auditing. The executives had allegedly conspired in Wansley's murder to hide financial wrongdoing. The accused persons were arrested, tried, and found guilt of murder.

Army cuts. Commander-in-chief General Surayud Chulanont announced plans in 1999 to downsize the Thai army from 236,000 people to 190,000 by the year 2007.   ☐ Henry S. Bradsher

See also **Asia.**

Theater. The 1998-1999 theater season in New York City proved that legitimate plays still have a life on Broadway, even though Broadway's theaters had been almost exclusively the domain of musicals for several years. In striking contrast to the theatrical sensations of previous seasons, straight drama made the news and topped box-office records, while few musicals of note premiered.

Playwright David Hare. The first attention-grabbing play of the Broadway season was *The*

TIME CAPSULE 1943

THEATER

IN MARCH came one of the finest musical plays of many seasons, *Oklahoma*. The book was by Oscar Hammerstein II, based on the Lynn Riggs play, *Green Grow the Lilacs*; the music was by Richard Rodgers; and the dances were directed by Agnes de Mille. This will probably influence future musical comedies, making them more like folk operas instead of formless vaudeville. It was the theatrical high point of 1943.

Blue Room, an adaptation by British playwright David Hare of La Ronde, Arthur Schnitzler's 1900 play about love and infidelity. The Blue Room, which featured Hollywood star Nicole Kidman, transferred from London's Donmar Warehouse to Broadway for a limited run from December 1998 to February 1999. The show received nationwide publicity, with much of the hype focusing on the fact that Kidman briefly appeared nude on stage. Although the reviews in the United States were not as strong as those in Great Britain, the production sold out its limited run and made a significant profit.

Hare's London hit, Amy's View, a star vehicle for British actress Dame Judi Dench, also played on Broadway during the 1998-1999 season. In a performance that captured the 1999 Antoinette Perry (Tony) Award for best actress, Dench portrayed a veteran stage actress whose daughter is in love with a man embodying the worst qualities of the entertainment industry.

Hare appeared on Broadway himself in Via Dolorosa. In this solo show, Hare explored the conflicts of modern-day Israel through personal encounters with Arabs and Jews during his travels in Israel. (The title of the play refers to the name of a Jerusalem road, the "Way of Sorrows," the route that, according to tradition, Christ traveled on the way to Calvary.)

Best play. Three of the four Tony nominees for best play were productions imported from the United Kingdom or Ireland. The Tony voters, however, opted for the only new American play on the list, Warren Leight's Side Man, a poignant look back at the waning days of jazz. Most critics considered Side Man a long shot for Broadway success because it was an ensemble piece that initially featured unknown actors. It proved to be durable, however. The play's Tony Award success and casting changes with famous actors in the leading role—film actor Christian Slater and television star Scott Wolf of "Party of Five"—kept it afloat on Broadway through the end of 1999.

American classics. Perhaps the biggest surprise on Broadway in the 1998-1999 season was the commercial and critical success of plays by three of the greatest American playwrights, Arthur Miller, Tennessee Williams (1911-1983), and Eugene O'Neill (1888-1953). Chicago's Steppenwolf Theatre gave Miller's landmark American tragedy about the "common man," Death of a Salesman, a lauded 50th-anniversary Broadway revival. It won four Tony Awards, including best play revival and best actor in a play, for Brian Dennehy's portrayal of Willy Loman.

Williams' little-known play Not About Nightingales (1938), a harsh prison drama, transferred to Broadway from London's Royal National Theatre in a strikingly theatrical production directed

THEATER

[A] PLAY WHICH ATTRACTED most favorable attention [was] A Streetcar Named Desire by Tennessee Williams. . . . [The play] tells the tragic story of the disintegration of a young woman whose family had belonged to the older Southern aristocracy but had sunk into poverty. It is bold and brutal as a story, but Williams has the skill and human sympathy to make it pathetic and wring the hearts of audiences. He was hailed as the outstanding dramatist of 1947.

Tony Award winners in 1999

Best Play, Side Man by Warren Leight

Best Musical, Fosse

Best Play Revival, Death of a Salesman

Best Musical Revival, Annie Get Your Gun

Leading Actor in a Play, Brian Dennehy, Death of a Salesman

Leading Actress in a Play, Judi Dench, Amy's View

Leading Actor in a Musical, Martin Short, Little Me

Leading Actress in a Musical, Bernadette Peters, Annie Get Your Gun

Featured Actor in a Play, Frank Wood, Side Man

Featured Actress in a Play, Elizabeth Franz, Death of a Salesman

Featured Actor in a Musical, Roger Bart, You're a Good Man, Charlie Brown

Featured Actress in a Musical, Kristin Chenoweth, You're a Good Man, Charlie Brown

Direction of a Play, Robert Falls, Death of a Salesman

Direction of a Musical, Matthew Bourne, Swan Lake

Book of a Musical, Alfred Uhry, Parade

Original Musical Score, Jason Robert Brown, Parade

Orchestration, Ralph Burns and Douglas Besterman, Fosse

Scenic Design, Richard Hoover, Not About Nightingales

Costume Design, Lez Brotherston, Swan Lake

Lighting Design, Andrew Bridge, Fosse

Choreography, Matthew Bourne, Swan Lake

Regional Theater, Crossroads Theater Company, New Brunswick, New Jersey

Special Awards, Uta Hagen, Arthur Miller, Isabelle Stevenson, and the production of Fool Moon

Brian Dennehy portrays Willy Loman in the 50th-anniversary Broadway revival of Arthur Miller's *Death of a Salesman*. Dennehy's performance of the salesman who sacrifices his family and honor to the "American dream" won him the 1999 Tony Award for best actor in a play.

by Trevor Nunn. Film star Kevin Spacey gave what many critics and fans described as the performance of a lifetime as Hickey in O'Neill's grim barroom drama *The Iceman Cometh*. The Almeida Theatre Company of London transferred the show from London's West End to Broadway.

Musicals of the 1998-1999 season, new and revised, were wholly unspectacular. The Tony for best musical went to *Fosse*, a revue of dance numbers by the director and choreographer Bob Fosse (1927-1987). While critics and patrons lauded *Fosse* for its stylishness and the skill of its dancers, the show was not a traditional musical built around plot and character. The Tony Award for best direction of a musical also went to a dance production, a well-received version of *Swan Lake* in which men danced the roles of the swans. The critics drubbed *Footloose*, a musical version of the 1984 film that pits a young man's love of dancing against a conservative minister. The show managed, nonetheless, to play through 1999. *Parade*, an earnest story based on true accounts of the 1915 lynching of a Jewish man in Georgia, was nominated for nine Tony Awards and won two. It closed early in 1999, however, at a huge financial loss.

Problems with *Parade* were linked in part to the ongoing behind-the-scenes drama around Livent, Inc., a production company based in Toronto, Canada, which filed for bankruptcy protection in 1998 after serious accounting irregularities were discovered. The Livent saga drew to a close in July when SFX Entertainment, Inc., of New York City bought the remaining assets for $128 million.

TIME CAPSULE 1949
THEATER

THE OUTSTANDING NEW DRAMA was Arthur Miller's *Death of a Salesman*. In Willy Loman, the playwright has depicted many of the traits of much of current society. Through understatement, rather than heightened tragedy, great force is given to the story of Willy's collapse and the sorrows of Willy's family. This play was awarded both the Pulitzer Prize and the prize of the New York Drama Critics' Circle.

Walt Disney Theatrical Productions, a division of the Walt Disney Company of Burbank, California, had its ups and downs in the 1998-1999 season. In November 1998, the company fired the creative team of its new musical, *Elaborate Lives,* following a tryout production in Atlanta, Georgia. The pop musical, based on Guiseppe Verdi's opera *Aida* (1871), features music by Elton John and Tim Rice. The show opened for a second time in December 1999 under the title *Aida* at Chicago's newly renovated Cadillac Palace Theatre and was scheduled to move to Broadway in February 2000.

After the Walt Disney Company reported a 41-percent drop in net profits in April 1999, Disney Theatricals announced plans to scale back its Broadway production of *Beauty and the Beast,* by trimming the cast and moving to a smaller venue. The decision prompted a protest from Actors Equity, a union for professional actors.

In June, Disney Theatrical Productions experienced a comeback when a stage version of its animated film *The Hunchback of Notre Dame*—a light take on the 1831 Victor Hugo novel—opened in the German capital of Berlin. The production, the first Disney musical to premiere outside the United States, was well-received and was expected to transfer to Broadway in a couple of years. In October 1999, Disney's stage version of *The Lion King* opened at London's Lyceum Theatre and swept away both audiences and critics.

U.S. regional theater. The most important developments in U.S. regional theater in 1999 happened not in the usual hot spots—Chicago, Boston, and Los Angeles—but in Las Vegas, Nevada, where magic acts, variety shows, and popular musicians have been the mainstay of the city's resorts. *O,* a theatrical circus production created by Cirque du Soleil of Quebec, Canada, made show-business history by earning more on a weekly basis in 1999 than any previous theatrical offering. Tickets for *O* cost $100 each; the production played multiple performances each day; and the custom-built theater contained 1,800 seats. With all performances sold out, *O* earned up to $1.8 million a week.

The show is a montage of circus acts—including trapeze, high-wire, and clowning—played out around a 1.5 million-gallon (5.7 million-liter) onstage water tank. (The title *O* is a pun on *eau,* the French word for *water.*) Because the show, rather than the performers, was the attraction, its life span seemed virtually limitless.

Steve Wynn, the Las Vegas producer of *O* and owner of Mirage Resorts, announced in 1999 that he intended to build a theatrical empire in Las Vegas. He had already begun to import productions of such Broadway hits as the 1997 revival of the 1966 musical *Cabaret,* and he planned to de-

THEATER

THE AMERICAN THEATER will probably remember 1956 for the return of one of its greatest playwrights, Eugene O'Neill, to his place on the stage. . . . *Long Day's Journey Into Night,* a compassionate autobiographical drama forms a four-hour-long account of one critical day in the author's household. . . . The play was somewhat long and repetitive, but proved generally absorbing because of its truthfulness and pathos.

velop seven original musicals in the early 2000's. He offered artists excellent fees and custom-built theaters, which most regional theaters and Broadway producers cannot do. Many people in the theater industry expected Wynn's endeavors to be financially successful, but they watched with interest to see how theater in Las Vegas would integrate itself with and contribute to theater worldwide. □ Karen Fricker

See also **Literature, World: A Special Report; People in the news** (Dench, Dame Judi).

Togo. See Africa.

Toronto. The key to dealing with Toronto's problems with the homeless should be prevention, not crisis management, according to a Toronto city task force report released on Jan. 14, 1999. At least 26,000 people, including 5,300 children, use Toronto housing shelters annually. In addition, about 100,000 people, according to the report, are on a waiting list for subsidized housing.

The report, "Taking Responsibility for Homelessness," praised the Toronto government for increasing the capacity and number of city shelters. It linked the increase in homelessness to new federal restrictions on unemployment insurance and the Ontario government's decision to cut welfare benefits and shift responsibility for housing to municipalities. The federal and provincial governments also came under criticism for eliminating funding for affordable housing.

The report recommended increasing government housing benefits for welfare recipients and the working poor; creating additional housing units with support services for people with mental illness and addictions; and increasing the number of affordable rental units, partly through tax breaks and grants for private developers.

The report prompted Toronto Mayor Mel Lastman to organize Canada's first national conference on homelessness. Held on March 25 and

Hockey fans get their picture taken in front of Toronto's Maple Leaf Gardens before the final game was played in the arena on Feb. 13, 1999. The Maple Leafs played 2,329 games in the Gardens over a span of 67 seasons. The hockey team inaugurated its new home, the Air Canada Centre, on February 20.

26, the symposium attracted delegates from every major Canadian city as well as representatives of community and homelessness groups. At the conference, Lastman criticized the federal and Ontario governments for not providing adequate funding for Toronto's homelessness programs.

On March 23, Prime Minister Jean Chretien gave Labor Minister Claudette Bradshaw the additional title of minister for the homeless. That same week, the Ontario government promised $45 million for housing for people with mental illness over the next three years. In November, the federal government proposed spending $700 million over three years to fight homelessness in Toronto.

The Greater Toronto Services Board held its first meeting on January 22. The Ontario government created the 41-member board in 1998 to coordinate public services between the newly unified City of Toronto, including the surrounding regions of Peel, Halton, Durham, and York. Initially, the board was responsible only for regional commuter transportation. In August 1999, the board took control of the province-operated Government of Ontario Transit, which the board renamed the Greater Toronto Transit Authority.

Air Canada Centre. On February 13, the Toronto Maple Leafs of the National Hockey League played their final game in Maple Leaf Gardens, their home arena since 1931. On Feb.

20, 1999, the team played its first game in its new arena, the Air Canada Centre, beating the Montreal Canadiens 3-2. Over the years, Maple Leaf Gardens had become a Toronto landmark and cultural center, hosting concerts and political rallies as well as sporting events. On February 19, 20,000 fans cheered current and former Leafs as the team paraded to the new arena.

In April 1998, Steve Stavro, the Leafs' owner, acquired the Raptors of the National Basketball Association, along with the rights to the Raptors' arena, then under construction. On Feb. 21, 1999, the Raptors played their first game at the Centre, beating the Vancouver Grizzlies 102-87.

Waterfront rejuvenation. Mayor Lastman, joined by Prime Minister Chretien and Ontario Premier Mike Harris, on November 3 announced a grand, 10-year plan to renovate Toronto's aging waterfront. The plans for the 22-mile (46-kilometer) waterfront included constructing a network of parks and roads to replace a waterfront expressway and restoring the mouth of the Don River so that it flows directly into Toronto Harbour again. A citizens' task force was to report on the cost and funding of the project by early 2000. The project was expected to provide strong support for Toronto's bid to host the 2008 Summer Olympic Games. ☐ David Lewis Stein

See also **Canada; Canadian provinces; City.**

Toys and games. Retail toy sales in the United States rose 6 percent in 1999 over 1998 figures. Retailers reported strong sales in September 1999, the back-to-school shopping season and early benchmark for the holiday sales period, the last three months of the year.

Discount stores remained the top retailer for toys in the United States. According to 1998 sales (the latest available), Wal-Mart Stores, Incorporated, of Bentonville, Arkansas, surpassed Toys R Us, Incorporated, of Paramus, New Jersey, as the number one retailer of traditional (nonvideo) toys. Wal-Mart had a market share of 17.4 percent, versus TRU's 16.8 percent. Wal-Mart and other discounters accounted for nearly 42 percent of all traditional toy sales.

Online sales contributed significantly to toy industry sales. In 1999, toy purchases online mushroomed to nearly $200 million, compared with an estimated $80 million—or less than 1 percent of total toy industry sales of $21 billion—in 1998. All of the major toy and discount stores joined the rush to e-commerce, seeking to complement their store sales with online sales.

Toy retail chains Toys R Us, K-B Toys, of Pittsfield, Massachusetts, and FAO Schwarz, of New York City, as well as discounters Wal-Mart, Kmart Corporation of Troy, Michigan, and Target Stores of Minneapolis, Minnesota, sought to capture some of the market share held by the largest Internet toy retailer, eToys, Incorporated, of Santa Monica, California. Internet seller Amazon.com

Pokémon—Japanese "pocket monsters"—were the hottest toy craze of 1999. Nintendo introduced the characters in a video game, which was followed by a television cartoon, action figures, stuffed toys, and a movie. A series of collectible cards were by far the most popular form of the toy.

of Seattle, added toys to its online selection of books, music, and videos in July 1999.

The Force is out there. *Star Wars Episode 1—The Phantom Menace,* the first "prequel" to the popular science-fiction film series, was among the most anticipated movies of 1999. With the movie opening in mid-May, fans lined up outside theaters for weeks prior to the premiere to purchase tickets. Collectors of the film's licensed merchandise were equally excited when retail stores announced that Star Wars toys would go on sale at midnight of May 3, several weeks before the film's opening date. By late summer, more than $300 million worth of Star Wars toys had been sold, according to Hasbro, Incorporated, of Pawtucket, Rhode Island, the major toy licensee, with sales through the 1999 holiday season expected to surpass $500 million.

The Pokemon phenomenon. Sales of the Pokemon game and related toys and cards exploded in 1999. Originally appearing in Japan as an adventure game made by the Nintendo Company, Limited of Kyoto for the manufacturer's handheld video game player Game Boy, the Pokemon characters generated a tremendous response in that country. A television cartoon followed, along with a series of collector cards.

First introduced in the United States in late 1998, sales of the video game, cartoon series, and collectible cards took off in 1999, and the product line expanded to include action figures and stuffed toys, made by Hasbro. The card series, manufactured by Wizards of the Coast, Incorporated, of Renton, Washington, quickly became a staple of schoolyards and playgroups across the United States. The cards became hard to find, selling out as quickly as they appeared in stores. The Pokemon trainer (the person playing the game) attempts to capture all 151 Pokemon and train them for battle. Pokemon (short for pocket monsters) are fantastic, wild creatures with unique powers.

Welcoming the millennium. The toy industry in 1999 welcomed the new millennium with themed products. Millenniumopoly, made by Late for the Sky Production Company of Cincinnati, Ohio, took a light-hearted look at the people, places, and events of the last 1,000 years. The Millennium Time Capsule by Ludico Toys, Incorporated of Armonk, New York, was a craft kit that allowed children to collect things that are important in their lives and preserve them to be later "rediscovered" by their children or grandchildren. Mattel, Incorporated of El Segundo, California, created a tiny replica of the ball dropped in New York City's Times Square on New Year's Eve 1999 to place in the hand of the company's Millennium Barbie, one of the biggest sellers of the year. □ Diane P. Cardinale

Track and field. It is doubtful that any sport went through more ups and downs in 1999 than track and field. On the positive side, the Track & Field Association, a new professional league in the United States, was launched in June; television exposure of track and field events increased, thanks to a series of nationally televised indoor meets called the Golden Spike Tour; and thrilling performances highlighted the 1999 World Track and Field Championships. At the same time, track and field lost some of its best-known athletes through a series of highly publicized drug suspensions handed down by the International Amateur Athletic Federation (IAAF), the world governing body for track and field.

World championships. The 1999 World Track and Field Championships were held in Seville, Spain, over a nine-day period in August. The U.S. team led the competition with 11 gold medals and a total medal count of 17. The outstanding performer at the championships was Michael Johnson, the U.S. Olympic champion, who shattered the world record for the 400 meters at 43.18 seconds. Butch Reynolds of the U.S. set the previous record of 43.29 in 1988. Three nights after his world-record 400, Johnson anchored the U.S. 4x400-meter relay team to a victory that brought him his ninth gold medal in world-championship competition, a record total.

Maurice Greene, the powerful U.S. sprinter from Kansas City, Kansas, captured three gold medals at the world championships, taking his second straight 100-meter title along with gold medals for the 200 meters and the 4x100-meter relay. In June 1999 at a meet in Athens, Greece, Greene lowered the 100-meter world record to 9.79 seconds. Canada's Donovan Bailey set the former record of 9.84 seconds at the 1996 Atlanta Olympics.

American Stacy Dragila turned in the only other world-record performance at Seville by winning the women's pole vault with a jump of 15 feet 1 inch (4.60 meters). Dragila's effort equaled the world mark set by Australia's Emma George on Feb. 20, 1999. George set the former record, 15 feet ¾ inch (4.59 meters), in 1998.

Marion Jones of the United States had hoped to win four gold medals in Seville but was forced to withdraw on Aug. 26, 1999, after winning one gold in the 100-meter sprint and a bronze medal in the long jump. During the 200-meter semifinals, Jones suddenly stopped running and dropped to the track, obviously in pain. She was later diagnosed with back spasms, which ended her season and took her out of the running for the $1-million jackpot offered by the seven-meet European Golden League series.

Drug suspensions. Jamaican Merlene Ottey, Cuban Javier Sotomayor, and American Dennis

U.S. sprinter Maurice Greene (right) sets a new world record in the 100 meters—9.79 seconds—on June 16, 1999, at an invitational race for the world's top sprinters in Athens, Greece. Ato Boldon (left) of Trinidad finished in second place with a personal-best time of 9.86 seconds.

World outdoor track and field records established in 1999

Men

Event	Holder	Country	Where set	Date	Record
100 meters	Maurice Greene	USA	Athens, Greece	June 16	9.79
400 meters	Michael Johnson	USA	Seville, Spain	August 26	43.18
1,000 meters	Noah Ngeny	Kenya	Rieti, Italy	September 7	2:11.96
300-meter hurdles	Lewellyn Herbert	South Africa	Tampere, Finland	February 10	34.92
Decathlon	Tomas Dvorak	Czech Republic	Prague, Czech Republic	July 4	8994 pts
Mile	Hicham El Guerrouj	Morocco	Rieti, Italy	July 7	3:43.12

Women

Event*	Holder	Country	Where set	Date	Record
Pole Vault	Emma George	Australia	Sydney, Australia	February 20	15' 1" (4.6m)
	Stacy Dragila	USA	Seville, Spain	August 21	
Hammer throw	Michaela Melinte	Romania	Ruedlingen, Switzerland	August 29	249' 6½"(76.07m)

m = meters

* The International Amateur Athletic Foundation (IAAF), the world governing body for track and field, adopted a new women's javelin design effective April 1, 1999. The women's javelin world record (262 feet 5 inches, set on Sept. 9, 1988, by Petra Felke of East Germany) and the women's heptathlon world record (7,291 points, set by American Jackie Joyner-Kersee at the 1988 Olympics) were to be officially set aside and replaced with records set with the new javelin in 1999 on Jan. 1, 2000.

Source: International Amateur Athletic Federation (IAAF).

Mitchell were among the big-name athletes suspended for drug offenses by the IAAF in 1999. Ottey, who had won 14 medals for sprinting, more than any other athlete in world-championship history, tested positive for a performance-enhancing drug in July. In August, Pan American Games officials stripped Sotomayor, the world recordholder in the high jump, of his gold medal after he tested positive for cocaine. Also in August, the IAAF suspended Mitchell, the 1992 Olympic 100-meter sprint champion, for two years for failing a drug test taken 16 months earlier. Mitchell's suspension was retroactive to April 1, 1998, which meant that he could return to competition in April 2000 and would be eligible for the 2000 Olympics in Sydney, Australia.

Grand Prix. Gabriele Szabo of Romania and Wilson Kipketer of Denmark split $1 million as the winners of the Gold League series. Szabo earned an additional $250,000 by winning the women's 3,000 meters in the Grand Prix final at Munich on Sept. 11, 1999. Kenyan steeplechaser Bernard Barmasai took the men's Grand Prix title and won $250,000 but was disqualified from the Golden League jackpot after reports surfaced that he had asked fellow Kenyan Christopher Koskei to let him win during a Golden League meet in Zurich in August.   □ Ron Reid

Transit. See Transportation.

Transportation. Competition between railroads returned to the Northeastern United States in 1999 for the first time in more than 20 years. On June 1, Norfolk Southern Corporation of Norfolk, Virginia, and CSX Transportation Corporation of Jacksonville, Florida, completed the purchase of Philadelphia-based Conrail, Incorporated. Conrail's routes were divided between the two buyers. Despite assurances by Norfolk and CSX that services would not be disrupted, incompatibility between computer systems resulted in trains running late or to the wrong destinations and in shortages of crews and locomotives.

In a related move, CSX announced in July that it would sell Sea-Land, its international container shipping company, to rival A.P. Moller-Maersk of Denmark in order to concentrate on its railroad and domestic shipping operations. The deal involved 70 ships and over 200,000 containers.

On December 21, the Burlington Northern Santa Fe Corporation of Fort Worth, Texas, and the Canadian National Railway Company of Montreal announced that they would merge, creating the largest railroad in North America. The deal was subject to the approval of shareholders and the regulatory commissions of both countries.

High-speed rail. In March, Amtrak unveiled new, high-speed trains that were to begin operating on routes between Washington, D.C., New York City, and Boston in 2000. The "Acela" electric trains, manufactured by Bombardier of Canada and Alstom of France, travel at speeds of 93 to 103 miles (150 to 165 kilometers) per hour.

The first "Acela" train was to be in operation by September 1999, but problems with excessive wear on the wheels during test runs pushed the introduction of service back to the spring of 2000. Amtrak officials claimed the new train would cut the five-hour trip from New York City to Boston to three hours and the three-hour New York City to Washington, D.C., trip to two-and-a-half hours. Twenty of the new trains were expected to go into operation by the end of 2000.

Secretary of Transportation Rodney E. Slater announced in January 1999 that a system of high-speed rail lines would be constructed in Midwestern states surrounding Chicago. Florida governor Jeb Bush announced on taking office in January that he was scrapping a project that would have put trains similar to the French TGV (*train a grande vitesse*—very-high-speed train) into operation between Miami, Tampa, and Orlando.

Grade crossings. More than 400 people were killed at railroad crossings each year from 1983 to 1998. The danger of collisions between motor vehicles and trains was highlighted when Amtrak's "City of New Orleans" collided with a tractor-trailer truck near Bourbonnais, Illinois, on March 15, 1999, killing 11 passengers. The collision focused attention on whether the truck driver drove around the gates and whether his license should have been revoked because of traffic convictions in Illinois and other states. In July, the federal government introduced a "Federal Railroad Safety Enforcement Act," which would continue funding a successful campaign to install flashing lights and gates at the vast majority of crossings in the United States.

Mass transit. On June 12, Los Angeles opened a 4.6-mile (7.4-kilometer), five-station extension along Hollywood Boulevard of the city's multibillion-dollar subway system. The final phase of the project, a 6.3-mile (10-kilometer) segment to North Hollywood, was scheduled for completion in 2000. Critics of the line pointed to the very high cost and low ridership. In Miami, voters in July 1999 rejected a sales tax increase that would have paid for $16 billion in mass transportation projects over the next 20 years.

Penn Station. On May 19, President Bill Clinton promised federal funds to assist in the creation of a new Pennsylvania Station in New York City. The proposed structure was to be created from New York's former post office, built in 1913. The structure stands next to Madison Square Garden, which was constructed on the site of the old Pennsylvania Station. The razing of the much-loved station in the 1960's is widely credited with

In 1955, a 1,200-horsepower diesel engine, made by General Motors, pulls lightweight aluminum cars, capable of carrying 400 passengers, at speeds of more than 100 miles (160 kilometers) per hour.

sparking a movement to preserve heritage buildings in the nation's cities.

Hours of service. The U.S. Department of Transportation held hearings in 1999 to evaluate laws regulating how long truck drivers can work each day. Existing laws allow truckers to drive for 10 hours before taking a rest period and to drive for 70 hours in eight days. Concerns about accidents caused by fatigue prompted the review.

Oil spill. The "New Carissa," a 639-foot (195-meter) cargo vessel, ran aground off the coast of Coos Bay, Oregon, on Feb. 4, 1999. The U.S. Coast Guard, concerned that the ship was breaking up as fuel oil was leaking from its tanks, burned most of the ship's fuel in an attempt to save the area beaches from a dangerous spill. However, some oil still washed ashore. On March 11, the bow section was towed 300 miles (483 kilometers) into the Pacific Ocean and sunk.

Duty-free shopping between countries in the European Union was abolished on July 1. Previously, passengers on boats and aircraft could buy alcohol, tobacco, and luxury goods without paying taxes. Shipping companies and airports had derived considerable income from operating shops selling such goods.   □ Ian Savage

See also **Aviation; Environmental pollution.**

Trinidad and Tobago. See **West Indies.**
Tunisia. See **Middle East.**

Turkey. A devastating earthquake on Aug. 17, 1999, in northwestern Turkey killed more than 17,000 people. The quake, which registered 7.4 in magnitude, was Turkey's worst earthquake of the century. On November 12, a 7.2-magnitude earthquake hit the same region of Turkey, killing hundreds more. The quakes and their aftershocks destroyed or damaged tens of thousands of buildings and left hundreds of thousands of people homeless.

Most of the deaths in the August earthquake occurred in the collapse of poorly constructed apartment buildings. The government, which many Turks blamed for failing to properly regulate the building industry, arrested more than 30 engineers, contractors, and developers after the first disaster. In addition, government officials, fearing that aid from religious organizations would deepen public anger against the *secular* (nonreligious) government, sought to stop efforts by Islamic agencies to assist earthquake victims.

International relief organizations and the governments of more than 40 countries, including Turkey's long-time enemy Greece, provided aid to help Turkey recover from the earthquakes. In September, Turkey sent aid to Greece when that country suffered an earthquake.

Abdullah Ocalan. On June 29, a security court sentenced to death Kurdish leader Abdullah Ocalan for treason. Ocalan led the Marxist Kurdish Workers Party (PKK), which began waging a guerrilla war for Kurdish *autonomy* (self rule) against the Turkish government in 1984. The Kurds are an ethnic group who live in the mountainous region of southwestern Asia. By 1999, the guerrilla war had resulted in the deaths of 35,000 people, including many civilians. Ocalan's second-in-command at the PKK, Semdin Sakik, had been sentenced to death in May.

Turkish commandos captured Ocalan in February after he left the asylum of the Greek embassy in Nairobi, Kenya. Ocalan's capture led to triumphant celebrations by Turks and violent demonstrations by Kurds in Turkey and across Europe.

Western leaders hoped that Ocalan's capture might produce a Turkish-Kurdish peace. Although the PKK declared a unilateral cease-fire in August, the Turkish military launched a new offensive against the PKK and arrested PKK members who surrendered.

New government. In May, Bulent Ecevit, who had become prime minister in January, formed a new coalition government after his Democratic Left Party won 22 percent of the vote in an April parliamentary election. Ecevit accepted Devlet Bahceli's Nationalist Action Party in a coalition government after the nationalist party stunned analysts by winning a better-than-ex-pected 18 percent of the vote. Nationalist Action had been responsible for right-wing violence in Turkey in the 1970's, which ultimately resulted in a military coup in 1980. Bahceli announced in 1999 that his party had embraced democracy. The Motherland Party, the center-right party led by former Prime Minister Mesut Yilmaz, also joined the coalition government.

Many analysts believed that the nationalists' victory was prompted by Ocalan's capture, which stirred Turkish national sentiment. Support for the Islamic Virtue Party, a religious party that held the most parliamentary seats, fell from more than 20 percent in 1995 to 16 percent in 1999.

Islam and politics. Turkey's parliament erupted in tumult in May when Merve Kavakci, a newly elected female member of Virtue, arrived at the opening session of parliament wearing a traditional Muslim headscarf. Turkey's political establishment opposed the wearing of such headscarves in public buildings, fearing that the practice would undermine the secular nature of the state. Kavakci was later stripped of her parliamentary seat and Turkish citizenship and charged with subversion.   □ Christine Helms

See also **Disasters; Israel; Middle East; Middle East: A Special Report. People in the news** (Ecevit, Bulent).

Turkmenistan. See Asia.

Masked Turkish commandos restrain Kurdish rebel leader Abdullah Ocalan after his capture in Nairobi, Kenya, in February 1999. A Turkish court sentenced Ocalan to death in June for treason, but Ocalan appealed the sentence.

Uganda. President Yoweri Museveni announced a major reorganization of his Cabinet on April 6, 1999. The changes followed the censure of the junior minister for finance and the release of a parliamentary report charging corruption in the agriculture ministry. Museveni ousted the junior minister from the Cabinet and replaced the agriculture minister, while allowing her to remain as vice president. Museveni also named Apollo Nsibambi as the new prime minister, replacing Kintu Musoke, who, Museveni said, had retired.

Referendum Act dispute. Prodemocracy groups criticized a law, passed by Parliament in July, that called for a referendum in 2000 on Uganda's future political system. Voters would choose whether to allow the formation of political parties for future elections or to retain the current "movement" system that allows only Museveni's National Resistance Movement (NRM). Uganda's 1995 Constitution, which banned all political parties except the NRM, called for such a vote after five years. Museveni's opponents argued that Uganda was too poor to stage a national referendum and that the referendum was a ruse to entrench the NRM, which has ruled Uganda since seizing power in 1986.

Bombings. Four people died and at least 35 people were injured when two bombs exploded in Kampala, the capital, on Feb. 14, 1999. The attack followed a series of bomb explosions in 1998, which killed at least 24 people in Kampala. More bombs rocked the capital in April and May 1999, killing or wounding dozens of others. Independent observers blamed the violence on the rebel Allied Democratic Forces, which was operating in western Uganda, and on northern-based guerrillas from the Lord's Resistance Army.

Tourists massacred. Four Ugandan game wardens and eight Western tourists on safari to view rare mountain gorillas were hacked or shot to death by Hutu rebels from Rwanda in Uganda's Bwindi Impenetrable Forest National Park on March 1. The murders of four Britons, two Americans, and two New Zealanders apparently occurred in revenge for British and United States support for Rwanda's Tutsi-led government. The Hutu rebels also protested Uganda's involvement in the civil war in Congo (Kinshasa). On March 5, Museveni said that Ugandan soldiers had tracked down and killed 25 of the suspected attackers.

Royal wedding. The long-awaited marriage of Ronald Muwenda Mutebi II, the *kabaka* (king) of Buganda, the largest and most important of Uganda's ancient kingdoms, took place on August 27. The 43-year-old king, who is a highly respected symbol of Bagandan culture, married journalist Sylvia Nagginda Luswata in a glittering ceremony in Kampala.   □ Simon Baynham

See also **Africa; Congo (Kinshasa).**

Ukraine. President Leonid Kuchma won re-election on Nov. 14, 1999, in a runoff against Communist Party leader Petro Symonenko. Kuchma received 56 percent of the vote, warding off a challenge from left-wing forces that had forged an alliance after the first round of balloting on October 31.

Election. Symonenko, one of the most radical of Kuchma's 13 first-round opponents, advocated returning Ukraine to Communist rule and reunifying with Russia. When no candidate won a clear majority in the first round of balloting in October, Socialist Party head Oleksandr Moroz and radical Marxist candidate Natalia Vitrenko threw their support behind Symonenko. However, Symonenko's extreme views enabled Kuchma to portray himself as a defender of economic reform and political independence for Ukraine.

The presidential campaign dominated Ukrainian politics for most of 1999. For the most part, the country managed to avoid the displays of political violence that had characterized elections in Russia since the end of Communist rule. However on October 2, Vitrenko was wounded in a grenade attack during a campaign appearance.

Domestic affairs. Kuchma's first five-year term as president had been marked by extensive corruption and economic stagnation. His chief success was in maintaining peace among Ukrainians in the predominantly Russian and Orthodox Christian east, the largely Roman Catholic west, and the ethnically split Crimean peninsula in the south.

Ukraine made progress in 1999 in its recovery from a 1998 financial crisis. In September 1999, officials revised their forecast for inflation from 19.1 percent down to 16 percent for the year. In September, the International Monetary Fund (IMF—a United Nations-affiliated organization that provides short-term credit to member nations) released a $184-million loan installment after concluding that Ukraine was reducing its budget deficit and paying off its foreign debt.

Foreign affairs. In January, the Russian parliament refused to ratify the friendship treaty with Ukraine signed in 1997. In the treaty, Russian officials had agreed to grant sovereignty over the Crimean peninsula to Ukraine. Many influential Russian lawmakers, including Moscow Mayor Yuri Luzhkov, a leading contender in the Russian presidential election in 2000, maintained that the peninsula should belong to Russia. In April 1999, Ukraine joined Georgia, Uzbekistan, Azerbaijan, and Moldova in a joint security alignment that excluded Russia.   □ Steven L. Solnick

See also **Azerbaijan; Europe; Georgia; Russia.**

Unemployment. See Economics; Labor.

United Arab Emirates. See Middle East.

United Kingdom

Tony Blair's Labour government continued to enjoy the confidence of the British public in 1999. Before taking control of Parliament in the 1997 elections, Blair's party had promoted itself as "New Labour," taking a centrist political position by jettisoning much of its heritage as a trade union-backed party with a commitment to creating and maintaining a welfare state. In 1999, Labour continued to position itself in the center of the political spectrum. Midway through its term of office (governments in Britain are elected for up to five years), the Blair government displayed a confidence that opponents and some supporters claimed bordered on arrogance. Political debate in 1999 continued to center around whether Great Britain should participate in the euro, the European Union (EU) single currency.

In 1999, Labour pushed forward with its program to modernize the constitution, to grant a degree of self-government to Scotland and Wales, create a legislative body to govern London, and to reform the House of Lords.

TIME CAPSULE 1936
UNITED KINGDOM

ABDICATION OF EDWARD VIII. Some years ago the Prince of Wales had formed the acquaintance of Mrs. Wallis Simpson, an American woman who had grown up in Baltimore as Bessie Wallis Warfield. The acquaintance ripened into a strong attachment and Edward was determined to marry her. There was this embarrassing circumstance, however, that Mrs. Simpson had been twice married and once divorced. On October 27, she was granted a divorce from her second husband by a court sitting at Ipswich. Since the country seemed unwilling to accept a divorcee as queen and the government refused to introduce the special legislation necessary for a morganatic marriage, the King saw nothing to do but to surrender the throne.

The act of abdication was promptly approved by Parliament and by the proper authorities in the dominions; and the Duke of York was at once proclaimed king as George VI.

Relations with the European Union. Whether Great Britain would join the euro, launched by 11 EU nations on Jan. 1, 1999, remained the most divisive issue in British politics throughout 1999. Britain's Conservative Party, dominated by "Eurosceptics," argued that adopting the euro and abolishing the British currency, the pound, threatened the nation's sovereignty. Some Conservatives even urged that Britain withdraw from the EU. In elections in June, British Conservatives increased their representation in the European Parliament, an EU legislative body, which indicated an increase in popular resistance to joining the euro, according to political experts.

Blair's government announced in 1999 that whether Britain joined the euro would depend on the results of a referendum that would be held after the next general election, in 2001 or 2002. However, Blair instructed British civil servants in 1999 to prepare for a possible transfer to the euro, and he lent his support to an organization called Britain in Europe, established to campaign for Britain's entry into the single currency.

War in Kosovo. Great Britain played a key role in the North Atlantic Treaty Organization (NATO) campaign to end Serbia's ethnic cleansing of the Albanian majority in the Serb province of Kosovo. Yugoslav President Slobodan Milosevic began attacking ethnic Albanian civilians in Kosovo in the late 1990's in an attempt to stop an independence movement. On March 24, 1999, NATO began 78 days of bombing of Serb forces and installations to force Serbia to agree to a peace plan. British ships and submarines participated in the launching of cruise missiles at targets in Yugoslavia. After Milosevic agreed to sign a peace treaty on June 10, British Lieutenant General Sir Michael Jackson commanded the 50,000-troop NATO peacekeeping force sent to restore order to Kosovo.

New legislative bodies. The new Scottish Parliament and Welsh Assembly met for the first time in July. Before 1999, Scotland and Wales had been ruled directly by the British Parliament in London. British voters had approved the establishment of both legislatures in 1997. Elections for the legislatures took place in May 1999.

In Scotland, Donald Dewar of the Labour Party became first (prime) minister. Labour failed to win an overall majority and formed a coalition government with the Liberal Democrats. The Scottish National Party became the leading opposition party. Sir David Steel, former leader of the Liberal Democrats, was chosen speaker of the

Queen Elizabeth II rides in a procession up the Royal Mile in Edinburgh, Scotland, on July 1 to inaugurate the new Scottish Parliament, the first to meet in Scotland in almost 300 years.

AN EVENT OF ABSORBING INTEREST to the citizens of the United Kingdom and the British Commonwealth was the coronation of King George VI and his consort, Queen Elizabeth, in Westminster Abbey on May 12. The king was anointed and crowned by the Archbishop of Canterbury, who used an ancient ceremonial, parts of which are a thousand years old. [The archbishop] was assisted by several ecclesiastical dignitaries . . . and by a group of secular officials whose titles recall exalted authority in medieval times but whose functions at present are limited in most cases to assistance at a coronation service. Kings and princes, peers and government officials, ambassadors, members of Parliament, and highly favored commoners, all with their respective consorts, a concourse of about 7,000 in all, saw the ceremonial in the Abbey, while 1 million people lined the London streets to get a view of the procession as it moved in majesty to the Abbey, and back to Buckingham Palace when the services had been completed.

After the king had been consecrated, the queen was anointed and crowned by the archbishop of York. The new queen is the first of Scottish birth to have her throne in Westminster since the death of Edith Mathilda, who came to England in 1101.

King George VI (left), Princess Margaret, Princess Elizabeth, and Queen Elizabeth, on May 12, 1937, the day of his coronation.

new Parliament. The Scottish Parliament is responsible for local affairs and has limited powers to raise or reduce taxes. The new Welsh Assembly elected Labour's Alun Michael leader of a minority government.

Northern Ireland. The British Parliament transferred authority for local affairs in Northern Ireland to the new Northern Ireland Assembly on December 2, more than 19 months after the signing of the Good Friday agreement. The Good Friday agreement sought to end years of conflict between unionists, who favored the union of Northern Ireland with Great Britain, and nationalists, who favored the reunion of Northern Ireland with Ireland. The refusal by some unofficial military groups in Northern Ireland, particularly the Irish Republican Army, to surrender weapons had hindered the peace process.

House of Lords reform. The British government moved ahead in 1999 with legislation to abolish the right of *hereditary peers* (nobles who have inherited their title) to sit in the House of Lords, the upper house of Parliament. Historically, the House of Lords was made up of hereditary peers and *life peers* (persons of achievement given titles of nobility for their lifetime). In 1911, the House of Lords lost the power to block legislation, though it could still delay the passage of bills. During the 1999 debate on the bill to abol-

ish the parliamentary rights of hereditary peers, the Earl of Burford attacked the legislation as "treason." The House of Commons, the lower house of parliament, nevertheless passed the bill in November, ending an 800-year tradition. The legislation cut the membership of the Lords in half. As part of a compromise, 92 hereditary peers remained as part of an interim House of Lords until a Royal Commission could propose what form the new House of Lords would take.

Mayor of London. In 1998, the Labour government won voter approval to create both the new office of mayor of London and an elected assembly to oversee the affairs of the British capital. London had not had a ruling legislative body since 1986, when the Conservative government abolished the Greater London Council.

During 1999, the political process for selecting candidates for mayor fell into disarray. The Conservatives had chosen Jeffrey Archer, a novelist and former deputy-chairman of the party, as their candidate for mayor. In November, a friend of Archer's admitted giving false testimony on Archer's behalf during a 1987 libel suit that Archer had brought against a newspaper. The paper had alleged that the novelist had consorted with a prostitute. After the friend revealed that he had perjured himself in court, Archer withdrew as a candidate and was stripped of his right to represent the party in the House of Lords.

Members of the Labour Party accused Tony Blair of attempting to block Ken Livingstone, a left-wing Labour Member of Parliament (MP) and former leader of the Greater London Council, from gaining the party's nomination for mayor. Some Labour Party managers feared Livingstone would use the powerful position of mayor of London to attack the Labour government's centrist positions. In November, Labour was forced to place Livingstone onto the short list of candidates despite the fact that he opposed the party's policy to partially privatize the London Underground mass transportation system.

Oscar-winning actress Glenda Jackson, who had served as a junior government minister, and Frank Dobson, the former health secretary, were included on the short list for the nomination. The mayor and London council election was scheduled for May 2000.

Opposition politics. The Conservative Party, the main party on the right in British politics, made little progress in 1999 toward regaining control of the government. The party had governed Britain under Margaret Thatcher and then John Major from 1979 to 1997. In 1999, the Conservatives, under the leadership of William Hague, voiced frequent complaints that Prime Minister Blair had stolen their policies. The party remained divided in 1999 on the issue of British involvement in Europe, and several Conservatives who advocated joining in the euro were expelled from the party. Many party members looked forward to Michael Portillo's return to Parliament. Portillo, a leading right-wing party member, had lost his parliamentary seat in 1997 but was elected in November 1999 to replace Alan Clark, the Conservative MP for Kensington and Chelsea who had died earlier in 1999.

Paddy Ashdown, leader of the Liberal Democrats, a centrist party, announced in January that he would retire. Under Ashdown's leadership from 1988 to 1999, the party grew to become a considerable force, particularly in local government. In the 1997 election, the Liberal Democrats took 46 parliamentary seats, the party's best showing since the 1920's. In August 1999, the party selected the charismatic Charles Kennedy as leader.

Political scandals. In December 1998, Blair's close ally, Trade and Industry Minister Peter Mandleson, was forced to leave the cabinet because he had received a secret loan from the Paymaster General, Geoffrey Robinson, who was also forced to resign. Mandleson used the money to purchase a house in London's fashionable Notting Hill neighborhood. Losing Mandleson was a par-

TIME CAPSULE 1940
UNITED KINGDOM

THE IMMINENCE OF INVASION stirred the British at last to herculean efforts. They were no longer fighting an ideology or defending small distant nations whom they did not know, or the French, whom they did not really like. They were fighting for their very lives, their homes, and their independence, and doing it on their own soil. . . .

The strategy of that battle soon became clear. After knocking out France, Germany began an attempt to "soften" British resistance by increasingly severe air attacks on ships and on land. From bases held in France or the Low Countries, planes could be over British soil in six to ten minutes, and throughout July, August, and September, the number of German machines aimed at England mounted rapidly to at least 1,000 daily. The first targets were ships nearing port; the east and south coasts; and industrial, commercial, military, and naval centers in southern England; but in September the onslaught concentrated on London, both for day and night raids. . . .

The damage done to ships, wharves, and buildings was severe, but apparently the cost was too great, and gradually daylight raids gave place to heavier night attacks. Defense against these was much more difficult, for no country has yet found a way of seeing an enemy plane in the dark beyond the narrow range of searchlights. As the fall and winter nights grew longer, the nocturnal attacks grew in length and severity. . . .

These attacks put the civilian population "in the front line trenches," and made urban life more dangerous than that in the army. . . . But the new occupants of the front line were not defeated or driven to panic or surrender. They met danger with a poise and courage, an ability to "take it" and to "stand it" that won the unbounded admiration of the outside world.

Members of the British House of Commons

Queen Elizabeth II opened the 1999-2000 session of Parliament on Nov. 26, 1999. At that time, the House of Commons consisted of the following members: 416 Labour Party, 162 Conservative Party, 46 Liberal Democrats, 10 Ulster Unionists, 6 Scottish National Party, 4 Plaid Cymru, 3 Social Democratic and Labour Party, 2 Ulster Democratic Unionist Party, 2 Sinn Fein, 1 United Kingdom Unionist, 1 Independent, 1 Scottish Labour, and 1 Member of Parliament for Falkirk West. In addition, the unaffiliated speaker and 3 deputies attend sessions but do not vote. This table shows each legislator and party affiliation. An asterisk (*) denotes those who served in the Parliament at some time before the 1997 general election.

A
Diane Abbott, Lab.*
Gerry Adams, S.F.*
Irene Adams, Lab.*
Nick Ainger, Lab.*
Peter Ainsworth, Con.*
Robert Ainsworth, Lab.*
Douglas Alexander, Lab.
Richard Allan, L.Dem
Graham Allen, Lab.*
David Amess, Con.*
Michael Ancram, Con.*
Donald Anderson, Lab.*
Janet Anderson, Lab.*
James Arbuthnot, Con.*
Hilary Armstrong, Lab.*
Paddy Ashdown, L.Dem.*
Joe Ashton, Lab.*
Candy Atherton, Lab.
Charlotte Atkins, Lab.
David Atkinson, Con.*
Peter Atkinson, Con.*
John Austin, Lab.*
B
Norman Baker, L.Dem.
Tony Baldry, Con.*
Jackie Ballard, L.Dem.
Tony Banks, Lab.*
Harry Barnes, Lab.*
Kevin Barron, Lab.*
John Battle, Lab.*
Hugh Bayley, Lab.*
Nigel Beard, Lab.
Margaret Beckett, Lab.*
Anne Begg, Lab.
Roy Beggs, U.U.*
Alan Beith, L.Dem.*
Martin Bell, Ind.
Stuart Bell, Lab.*
Hilary Benn, Lab.*
Tony Benn, Lab.*
Andrew Bennett, Lab.*
Joe Benton, Lab.*
John Bercow, Con.
Sir Paul Beresford, Con.*
Gerald Bermingham, Lab.*
Roger Berry, Lab.*
Harold Best, Lab.
Clive Betts, Lab.*
Liz Blackman, Lab.
Tony Blair, Lab.*
Hazel Blears, Lab.
Bob Blizzard, Lab.
David Blunkett, Lab.*
Crispin Blunt, Con.
Paul Boateng, Lab.*
Sir Richard Body, Con.*
Betty Boothroyd, Speaker*
David Borrow, Lab.
Tim Boswell, Con.*
Peter Bottomley, Con.*
Virginia Bottomley, Con.*
Keith Bradley, Lab.*
Peter Bradley, Lab.
Ben Bradshaw, Lab.
Graham Brady, Con.
Tom Brake, L.Dem.
Peter Brand, L.Dem.
Julian Brazier, Con.*
Colin Breed, L.Dem.
Helen Brinton, Lab.
Peter Brooke, Con.*
Gordon Brown, Lab.*
Nick Brown, Lab.*
Russell Brown, Lab.
Desmond Browne, Lab.
Angela Browning, Con.*
Ian Bruce, Con.*
Malcolm Bruce, L.Dem.*
Karen Buck, Lab.
Richard Burden, Lab.*
Colin Burgon, Lab.

John Burnett, L.Dem.
Simon Burns, Con.*
Paul Burstow, L.Dem.
Christine Butler, Lab.
John Butterfill, Con.*
Stephen Byers, Lab.*
C
Vincent Cable, L.Dem.
Richard Caborn, Lab.*
Alan Campbell, Lab.
Anne Campbell, Lab.*
Menzies Campbell, L.Dem.*
Ronnie Campbell, Lab.*
Dale Campbell-Savours, Lab.*
Dennis Canavan, Lab.*
Jamie Cann, Lab.*
Ivor Caplin, Lab.
Roger Casale, Lab.
William Cash, Con.*
Martin Caton, Lab.
Ian Cawsey, Lab.
Ben Chapman, Lab.*
Sir Sydney Chapman, Con.*
David Chaytor, Lab.
David Chidgey, L.Dem.*
Malcolm Chisholm, Lab.*
Christopher Chope, Con.*
Judith Church, Lab.*
Michael Clapham, Lab.*
James Clappison, Con.*
David Clark, Lab.*
Lynda Clark, Lab.
Michael Clark, Con.*
Paul Clark, Lab.
Charles Clarke, Lab.
Eric Clarke, Lab.*
Kenneth Clarke, Con.*
Tom Clarke, Lab.*
Tony Clarke, Lab.
David Clelland, Lab.*
Geoffrey Clifton-Brown, Con.*
Ann Clwyd, Lab.*
Vernon Coaker, Lab.
Ann Coffey, Lab.*
Harry Cohen, Lab*
Iain Coleman, Lab.
Tim Collins, Con.
Tony Colman, Lab.
Michael Colvin, Con.*
Michael Connarty, Lab.*
Frank Cook, Lab.*
Robin Cook, Lab.*
Yvette Cooper, Lab.
Robin Corbett, Lab.*
Jeremy Corbyn, Lab.*
Sir Patrick Cormack, Con.*
Jean Corston, Lab.*
Brian Cotter, L.Dem.
Jim Cousins, Lab.*
Tom Cox, Lab.*
James Cran, Con.*
Ross Cranston, Lab.
David Crausby, Lab.
Ann Cryer, Lab.
John Cryer, Lab.
John Cummings, Lab.*
Lawrence Cunliffe, Lab.*
Jack Cunningham, Lab.*
Jim Cunningham, Lab.*
Roseanna Cunningham, S.N.P.
David Curry, Con.*
Clare Curtis-Thomas, Lab.
D
Cynog Dafis, P.C.*
Tam Dalyell, Lab.*
Alistair Darling, Lab.*
Keith Darvill, Lab.
Edward Davey, L. Dem.
Valerie Davey, Lab.
Ian Davidson, Lab.*
Denzil Davies, Lab.*
Geraint Davies, Lab.

Quentin Davies, Con.*
Ronald Davies, Lab.*
David Davis, Con.*
Terry Davis, Lab.*
Hilton Dawson, Lab.
Stephen Day, Con.*
Janet Dean, Lab.
John Denham, Lab.*
Donald Dewar, Lab.*
Andrew Dismore, Lab.
Jim Dobbin, Lab.
Frank Dobson, Lab.*
Jeffrey Donaldson, U.U.
Brian H. Donohoe, Lab.*
Frank Doran, Lab.
Stephen Dorrell, Con.*
Jim Dowd, Lab.*
David Drew, Lab.
Julia Drown, Lab.
Alan Duncan, Con.*
Iain Duncan Smith, Con.*
Gwyneth Dunwoody, Lab.*
E
Angela Eagle, Lab.*
Maria Eagle, Lab.*
Huw Edwards, Lab.*
Clive Efford, Lab.
Louise Ellman, Lab.
Sir Peter Emery, Con.*
Jeff Ennis, Lab.*
Bill Etherington, Lab.*
Nigel Evans, Con.*
Margaret Ewing, S.N.P.
F
David Faber, Con.*
Michael Fabricant, Con.*
Michael Fallon, Con.*
Ronnie Fearn, L.Dem.*
Frank Field, Lab.*
Mark Fisher, Lab.*
Jim Fitzpatrick, Lab.
Lorna Fitzsimons, Lab.
Howard Flight, Con.
Caroline Flint, Lab.
Paul Flynn, Lab.*
Barbara Follett, Lab.
Clifford Forsythe, U.U.*
Eric Forth, Con.*
Derek Foster, Lab.*
Don Foster, L.Dem.*
Michael J. Foster, Lab.
Michael Jabez Foster, Lab.
George Foulkes, Lab.*
Sir Norman Fowler, Con.*
Liam Fox, Con.*
Christopher Fraser, Con.
Maria Fyfe, Lab.*
G
Sam Galbraith, Lab.*
Roger Gale, Con.*
George Galloway, Lab.*
Mike Gapes, Lab.*
Barry Gardiner, Lab.
Edward Garnier, Con.*
Andrew George, L.Dem.
Bruce George, Lab.*
Neil Gerrard, Lab.*
Nick Gibb, Con.
Ian Gibson, Lab.
Christopher Gill, Con.*
Cheryl Gillan, Con.*
Linda Gilroy, Lab.
Norman A. Godman, Lab.
Roger Godsiff, Lab.*
Paul Goggins, Lab.
Llin Golding, Lab.*
Eileen Gordon, Lab.
Teresa Gorman, Con.*
Donald Gorrie, L.Dem.
Thomas Graham, S.Lab.*
Bernie Grant, Lab.*
James Gray, Con.

Damian Green, Con.
John Greenway, Con.*
Dominic Grieve, Con.
Jane Griffiths, Lab.
Nigel Griffiths, Lab.*
Win Griffiths, Lab.*
Bruce Grocott, Lab.*
John Grogan, Lab.
John Gummer, Con.*
John Gunnell, Lab.*
H
William Hague, Con.*
Peter Hain, Lab.*
Mike Hall, Lab.*
Patrick Hall, Lab.
Sir Archie Hamilton, Con.*
Fabian Hamilton, Lab.
Philip Hammond, Con.
Mike Hancock, L.Dem.*
David Hanson, Lab.*
Harriet Harman, Lab.*
Evan Harris, L.Dem.
Nick Harvey, L.Dem.*
Sir Alan Haselhurst, Deputy*
Nick Hawkins, Con.*
John Hayes, Con.
Sylvia Heal, Lab.*
Oliver Heald, Con.*
John Healey, Lab.
David Heath, L.Dem.
Sir Edward Heath, Con.*
David Heathcoat-Amory, Con.*
Doug Henderson, Lab.*
Ivan Henderson, Lab.
Stephen Hepburn, Lab.
John Heppell, Lab.*
Michael Heseltine, Con.*
Stephen Hesford, Lab.
Patricia Hewitt, Lab.
Keith Hill, Lab.*
David Hinchliffe, Lab.*
Margaret Hodge, Lab.*
Kate Hoey, Lab.*
Douglas Hogg, Con.*
John Home Robertson, Lab.*
Jimmy Hood, Lab.*
Geoffrey Hoon, Lab.*
Phil Hope, Lab.
Kelvin Hopkins, Lab.
John Horam, Con.*
Michael Howard, Con.*
Alan Howarth, Lab.*
George Howarth, Con.*
Gerald Howarth, Con.*
Kim Howells, Lab.*
Lindsay Hoyle, Lab.*
Beverley Hughes, Lab.
Kevin Hughes, Lab.*
Simon Hughes, L.Dem.*
Joan Humble, Lab.
John Hume, S.D.L.P.*
Andrew Hunter, Con.*
Alan Hurst, Lab.
John Hutton, Lab.*
I
Brian Iddon, Lab.
Eric Illsley, Lab.*
Adam Ingram, Lab.*
J
Michael Jack, Con.*
Glenda Jackson, Lab.*
Helen Jackson, Lab.*
Robert Jackson, Con.*
David Jamieson, Lab.*
Bernard Jenkin, Con.*
Brian Jenkins, Lab.*
Alan Johnson, Lab.
Melanie Johnson, Lab.
Sir Geoffrey Johnson Smith, Con.*
Barry Jones, Lab.*
Fiona Jones, Lab.*
Helen Jones, Lab.*

Ieuan Wyn Jones, P.C.*
Jenny Jones, Lab.
Jon Owen Jones, Lab.*
Lynne Jones, Lab.*
Martin Jones, Lab.*
Nigel Jones, L.Dem.*
Tessa Jowell, Lab.*
K
Gerald Kaufman, Lab.*
Sally Keeble, Lab.
Alan Keen, Lab.*
Ann Keen, Lab.
Paul Keetch, L.Dem.
Ruth Kelly, Lab.
Fraser Kemp, Lab.
Charles Kennedy, L.Dem.*
Jane Kennedy, Lab.*
Robert Key, Con.*
Piara S. Khabra, Lab.*
David Kidney, Lab.
Peter Kilfoyle, Lab.*
Andrew King, Lab.
Oona King, Lab.
Tom King, Con.*
Tess Kingham, Lab.*
Julie Kirkbride, Con.
Archy Kirkwood, L.Dem.
Ashok Kumar, Lab.*
L
Stephen Ladyman, Lab.
Eleanor Laing, Con.
Jacqui Lait, Con.*
Andrew Lansley, Con.
Jackie Lawrence, Lab.
Bob Laxton, Lab.
Edward Leigh, Con.*
David Lepper, Lab.
Christopher Leslie, Lab.
Oliver Letwin, Con.
Tom Levitt, Lab.
Ivan Lewis, Lab.
Julian Lewis, Con.
Terry Lewis, Lab.*
Helen Liddell, Lab.*
David Lidington, Con.*
Peter Lilley, Con.*
Martin Linton, Lab.
Ken Livingstone, Lab.*
Richard Livsey, L.Dem.*
Sir Peter Lloyd, Con.*
Tony Lloyd, Lab.*
Elfyn Llwyd, P.C.*
David Lock, Lab.
Michael Lord, Deputy*
Tim Loughton, Con.
Andrew Love, Lab.
Peter Luff, Con.*
Sir Nicholas Lyell, Con.*
M
John McAllion, Lab.*
Thomas McAvoy, Lab.*
Steve McCabe, Lab.
Chris McCafferty, Lab.
Ian McCartney, Lab.*
Robert McCartney, U.K.U.*
Siobhain McDonagh, Lab.
Calum McDonald, Lab.*
John McDonnell, Lab.
John McFall, Lab.*
Eddie McGrady, S.D.L.P.*
John MacGregor, Con.*
Martin McGuinness, S.F.
Anne McGuire, Lab.
Anne McIntosh, Con.
Shona McIsaac, Lab.
Andrew Mackay, Con.*
Rosemary McKenna, Lab.
Andrew Mackinlay, Lab.*
David MacLean, Con.*
Henry B. McLeish, Lab.*
Robert Maclennan, L.Dem.*
Patrick McLoughlin, Con.*
Kevin McNamara, Lab.*
Tony McNulty, Lab.
Denis MacShane, Lab.*
Fiona Mactaggart, Lab.
Tony McWalter, Lab.
John McWilliam, Lab.*
Sir David Madel, Con.*

Ken Maginnis, U.U.*
Alice Mahon, Lab.*
John Major, Con.*
Humfrey Malins, Con.*
Judy Mallaber, Lab.
Seamus Mallon, S.D.L.P.*
Peter Mandelson, Lab.*
John Maples, Con.*
John Marek, Lab.*
Gordon Marsden, Lab.
Paul Marsden, Lab.
David Marshall, Lab.*
Jim Marshall, Lab.*
Robert Marshall-Andrews, Lab.
Michael Martin, Deputy*
Eric Martlew, Lab.*
Michael Mates, Con.*
Francis Maude, Con.*
Sir Brian Mawhinney, Con.*
John Maxton, Lab.*
Theresa May, Con.
Michael Meacher, Lab.*
Alan Meale, Lab.*
Gillian Merron, Lab.
Alun Michael, Lab.*
Bill Michie, Lab.*
Ray Michie, L.Dem.*
Alan Milburn, Lab.*
Andrew Miller, Lab.*
Austin Mitchell, Lab.*
Laura Moffatt, Lab.
Lewis Moonie, Lab.*
Michael Moore, L.Dem.
Margaret Moran, Lab.
Alasdair Morgan, S.N.P.
Julie Morgan, Lab.
Rhodri Morgan, Lab.*
Elliot Morley, Lab.*
Estelle Morris, Lab.*
John Morris, Lab.*
Malcolm Moss, Con.*
Kali Mountford, Lab.
Marjorie Mowlam, Lab.*
George Mudie, Lab.*
Chris Mullin, Lab.*
Denis Murphy, Lab.
Jim Murphy, Lab.
Paul Murphy, Lab.*
N
Douglas Naysmith, Lab.
Patrick Nicholls, Con.*
Archie Norman, Con.
Dan Norris, Lab.
O
Mark Oaten, L.Dem.
Bill O'Brien, Lab.*
Mike O'Brien, Lab.*
Stephen O'Brien, Con.*
Eddie O'Hara, Lab.*
Bill Olner, Lab.*
Martin O'Neill, Lab.*
Lembit Opik, L.Dem.
Diana Organ, Lab.
Sandra Osborne, Lab.
Richard Ottaway, Con.*
P
Richard Page, Con.*
James Paice, Con.*
Ian Paisley, U.D.U.P.*
Nick Palmer, Lab.
Owen Paterson, Con.
Ian Pearson, Lab.
Tom Pendry, Lab.*
Linda Perham, Lab.
Eric Pickles, Con.*
Colin Pickthall, Lab.*
Peter Pike, Lab.*
James Plaskitt, Lab.
Kerry Pollard, Lab.
Chris Pond, Lab.
Greg Pope, Lab.*
Michael Portillo, Con.
Stephen Pound, Lab.
Sir Raymond Powell, Lab.*
Bridget Prentice, Lab.*
Gordon Prentice, Lab.*
John Prescott, Lab.*
Dawn Primarolo, Lab.*

David Prior, Con.
Gwyn Prosser, Lab.
Ken Purchase, Lab.*
Q
Joyce Quin, Lab.*
Lawrie Quinn, Lab.
R
Giles Radice, Lab.*
Bill Rammell, Lab.
John Randall, Con.
Syd Rapson, Lab.
Nick Raynsford, Lab.*
John Redwood, Con.*
Andrew Reed, Lab.
John Reid, Lab.*
David Rendel, L.Dem.*
Andrew Robathan, Con.*
Laurence Robertson, Con.
Geoffrey Robinson, Lab.*
Peter Robinson, U.D.U.P.*
Barbara Roche, Lab.*
Marion Roe, Con.*
Allan Rogers, Lab.*
Jeff Rooker, Lab.*
Terry Rooney, Lab.*
Ernie Ross, Lab.*
William Ross, U.U.*
Andrew Rowe, Con.*
Ted Rowlands, Lab.*
Frank Roy, Lab.
Chris Ruane, Lab.
Joan Ruddock, Lab.*
David Ruffley, Con.
Bob Russell, L.Dem.
Christine Russell, Lab.
Joan Ryan, Lab.
S
Nick St. Aubyn, Con.
Alex Salmond, S.N.P.*
Martin Salter, Lab.
Adrian Sanders, L.Dem.
Mohammad Sarwar, Lab.
Malcolm Savidge, Lab.
Phil Sawford, Lab.
Jonathan Sayeed, Con.*
Brian Sedgemore, Lab.*
Jonathon Shaw, Lab.
Barry Sheerman, Lab.*
Robert Sheldon, Lab.*
Gillian Shephard, Con.*
Richard Shepherd, Con.*
Debra Shipley, Lab.
Clare Short, Lab.*
Alan Simpson, Lab.*
Keith Simpson, Con.
Marsha Singh, Lab.*
Dennis Skinner, Lab.*
Andrew Smith, Lab*
Angela Smith, Lab.
Chris Smith, Lab.*
Geraldine Smith, Lab.
Jacqui Smith, Lab.
John Smith, Lab.*
Llew Smith, Lab.*
Sir Robert Smith, L.Dem.
W. Martin Smyth, U.U.*
Peter Snape, Lab.*
Nicholas Soames, Con.*
Clive Soley, Lab.*
Helen Southworth, Lab.
John Spellar, Lab.*
Caroline Spelman, Con.
Sir Michael Spicer, Con.*
Richard Spring, Con.*
Rachel Squire, Lab.*
Sir John Stanley, Con.*
Phyllis Starkey, Lab.
Anthony Steen, Con.*
Gerry Steinberg, Lab.*
George Stevenson, Lab.*
David Stewart, Lab.
Ian Stewart, Lab.
Paul Stinchcombe, Lab.
Howard Stoate, Lab.
Gavin Strang, Lab.*
Jack Straw, Lab.*
Gary Streeter, Con.*
Graham Stringer, Lab.

Gisela Stuart, Lab.
Andrew Stunell, L.Dem.
Gerry Sutcliffe, Lab.*
Desmond Swayne, Con.
John Swinney, S.N.P.
Robert Syms, Con.
T
Sir Peter Tapsell, Con.*
Ann Taylor, Lab.*
Dari Taylor, Lab.
David Taylor, Lab.
Ian Taylor, Con.*
John D. Taylor, U.U.*
John M. Taylor, Con.*
Matthew Taylor, L.Dem.*
Sir Teddy Taylor, Con.*
Peter Temple-Morris, Lab.*
Gareth Thomas, Lab.
Gareth R. Thomas, Lab.
William Thompson, U.U.
Stephen Timms, Lab.*
Paddy Tipping, Lab.*
Mark Todd, Lab.
Jenny Tonge, L.Dem.
Don Touhig, Lab.*
John Townend, Con.*
David Tredinnick, Con.*
Michael Trend, Con.*
Jon Trickett, Lab.*
David Trimble, U.U.*
Paul Truswell, Lab.
Dennis Turner, Lab.*
Desmond Turner, Lab.
George Turner, Lab.
Neil Turner, Lab.*
Derek Twigg, Lab.
Stephen Twigg, Lab.
Paul Tyler, L.Dem.*
Bill Tynan, Lab.*
Andrew Tyrie, Con.
V
Keith Vaz, Lab.*
Peter Viggers, Con.*
Rudi Vis, Lab.
W
Cecil Walker, U.U.*
Jim Wallace, L.Dem.*
Joan Walley, Lab.*
Robert Walter, Con.
Claire Ward, Lab.
Charles Wardle, Con.*
Robert Wareing, Lab.*
Nigel Waterson, Con.*
Dave Watts, Lab.
Steven Webb, L.Dem.
Bowen Wells, Con.*
Andrew Welsh, S.N.P.*
Brian White, Lab.*
Alan Whitehead, Lab.
Sir Raymond Whitney, Con.*
John Whittingdale, Con.*
Malcolm Wicks, Lab.*
Ann Widdecombe, Con.*
Dafydd Wigley, P.C.*
John Wilkinson, Con.*
David Willetts, Con.*
Alan Williams, Lab.*
Alan W. Williams, Lab.*
Betty Williams, Lab.
Phil Willis, L.Dem.
Michael Wills, Lab.
David Wilshire, Con.*
Brian Wilson, Lab.*
David Winnick, Lab.*
Ann Winterton, Con.*
Nicholas Winterton, Con.*
Rosie Winterton, Lab.
Audrey Wise, Lab.*
Mike Wood, Lab.
Shaun Woodward, Con.
Phil Woolas, Lab.
Tony Worthington, Lab.*
James Wray, Lab.*
Tony Wright, Lab.*
Tony Wright, Lab.*
Derek Wyatt, Lab
Y
Tim Yeo, Con.*
Sir George Young, Con.*

Prince Edward, the youngest son of Queen Elizabeth II, and his bride, Sophie Rhys-Jones, leave the chapel at Windsor Castle after their marriage ceremony on June 19. The new princess announced that she would continue in her job as a public relations executive.

ticular blow for Blair. Mandleson had been one of the key figures in "New Labour" and among Blair's most trusted advisers. In October 1999, Blair named Mandleson Secretary for Northern Ireland.

Former Conservative minister Jonathan Aitken pleaded guilty in January to charges of perjury and conspiracy to pervert the course of justice. In 1997, Aitken had sued the *Guardian* newspaper for claims that he had used his position as a government minister to promote arms sales in return for money. The suit collapsed, however, and Aitken was charged with perjury and conspiracy. On June 8, 1999, he was sentenced to prison.

Economy. Unemployment in the United Kingdom continued to decline in 1999. According to the European Commission, the executive arm of the European Union (EU), unemployment fell to 6.5 percent in 1999, compared with an unemployment rate of 9.5 percent in the mid-1990's. Inflation remained under control through 1999. However, officials at the Bank of England expressed concern at year-end that rising house prices would trigger higher inflation in 2000. Government analysts forecast that the United Kingdom's *gross domestic product* (the value of all goods and services produced in a country in a given year) would grow by only 1 to 1.5 percent in 1999, one of the lowest growth rates in Europe.

Chancellor of the Exchequer (treasury secretary) Gordon Brown continued to emphasize fiscal prudence in 1999. In his budget statement to Parliament on March 9, Brown reduced the basic rate of taxation from 23 to 22 percent, to go into effect in April 2000. The move helped distance Labour from its previous "tax and spend" image of the 1960's and 1970's. Conservatives, however, complained in November 1999 that the overall tax burden had increased since Labour came to power in 1997.

Trade dispute. Anglo-French relations deteriorated in late 1999 over the safety of British beef. In the late 1980's, British scientists noted a marked increase in the number of cattle diagnosed with a deadly brain disease called bovine spongiform encephaolopathy. or "mad cow disease." The scientists concluded that the disease was most likely contracted from contaminated feed. By the mid-1990's, scientists suspected that a link existed between mad cow disease and an increase in cases of Creutzfeldt-Jakob disease, a fatal, degenerative disease of the human brain. The EU banned imports of British beef in 1996.

After Great Britain introduced new safety proce-dures, the EU lifted its ban in August 1999. France, however, refused to lift its ban on British beef, raising the prospect that Great Britain might take France into the European Court to settle the trade dispute.

Bombings. On April 17, 1999, a nail bomb ex-ploded in the racially mixed Brixton area of Lon-don, injuring 39 people. One week later, another bomb exploded in Brick Lane, a section of Lon-don with a large Bangladeshi population, injur-ing seven people. A third bomb exploded on April 30 in a gay bar in Soho, killing 3 people and wounding more than 70. Far-right extremist groups claimed responsibility for the attacks, but on May 5, the police charged a man who had no apparent connections to political groups.

Rail crash. In October, 31 people died when a train went through a stop light and struck an-other train near Paddington Station in London. The collision resulted in a public outcry over rail safety. Britain's rail service, formerly a national-ized industry, had been privatized by the Conser-vatives. Members of the media criticized Rail-track, the private company that took over the railroads in 1996, for not putting money into safety measures despite making huge profits.

Royal wedding. In June 1999, Queen Eliza-beth's son, Prince Edward, married Sophie Rhys-

UNITED KINGDOM

QUEEN ELIZABETH II of Great Britain was crowned on June 2 in Westminster Abbey. . . . Millions of Britons and about 200,000 visi-tors from other countries jammed sidewalks through the damp night before Coronation Day. Privileged ones had seats in grandstands. Peers and members of Parliament rode to the Abbey in the subway, which changed its schedule and routes and used a special train called the "Silver Bullet" for that purpose.

Jones. The wedding took place at Windsor Castle. Princess Sophie indicated she would continue her job as a public relations executive.

The Millennium Dome. Britain's celebration of the new millennium centered around an enor-mous structure, named the Millennium Dome, built in Greenwich and opened on December 31. The dome contained a world's fair-like exhibition showcasing human creativity in the past, present, and future.   □ Rohan McWilliam

See also **Europe; Northern Ireland; Yu-goslavia: A Special Report.**

United Kingdom, Prime Minister of.

Prime Minister Tony Blair's (1953-) popularity in opinion polls dipped in 1999. However, he con-tinued to be remarkably popular for a prime min-ister who had held office for more than two years. In 1999, Blair struggled with a deadlock in the peace process in Northern Ireland and with a crisis in the Serbian province of Kosovo. Blair also pushed ahead with plans to modernize Britain, particularly its constitution and welfare system.

Elected as leader of the Labour Party in 1997, Blair continued to court the votes of so-called "Middle England," the mildly conservative mid-dle class. During 1999, he offended Labour's nat-ural constituency, public sector workers, by call-ing for higher standards and higher quality in the delivery of public services. In his speech at the an-nual Labour Party conference on September 28, Blair promised a war on the forces of conserv-atism—the Conservative party and anyone trying to slow the pace of modernization. Since his elec-tion in 1997, Blair has frequently been attacked as a conservative and for being too dependent on focus groups in forming his policies.

In November 1999, Blair and his wife, attorney Cherie Booth, 45, announced that they were ex-pecting their fourth child.   □ Rohan McWilliam

See also **Northern Ireland; Yugoslavia: A Special Report.**

The Cabinet of the United Kingdom*

Tony Blair—prime minister; first lord of the treasury; minister for the civil service

John Prescott—deputy prime minister; secretary of state for the environment, transport, and the regions

Gordon Brown—chancellor of the exchequer

Robin Cook—secretary of state for foreign and Common-wealth affairs

Lord Irvine of Lairg—lord chancellor

Jack Straw—secretary of state for the home department

David Blunkett—secretary of state for education and employment

Margaret Beckett—president of the Privy Council and leader of the House of Commons

Marjorie Mowlam—minister for the cabinet office; chancellor of the Duchy of Lancaster

John Reid—secretary of state for Scotland

Geoff Hoon—secretary of state for defence

Alan Milburn—secretary of state for health

Ann Taylor—chief whip

Chris Smith—secretary of state for culture, media, and sport

Peter Mandelson—secretary of state for Northern Ireland

Paul Murphy—secretary of state for Wales

Clare Short—secretary of state for international development

Alistair Darling—secretary of state for social security

Nick Brown—minister of agriculture, fisheries, and food

Baroness Jay of Paddington—lord privy seal; leader of the House of Lords; minister for women

Stephen Byers—secretary of state for trade and industry

Andrew Smith—chief secretary to the treasury

*As of Dec.2, 1999.

United Nations. In 1999, the United Nations (UN) faced the challenge of restoring peace in two areas of the world in "extreme crises." One was Kosovo, a Serbian province in Yugoslavia; and the other, East Timor, a former Portuguese colony occupied by Indonesia since 1975.

Kosovo. The crisis in Kosovo flared in early 1999, when Yugoslav President Slobodan Milosevic refused to honor promises he had made in 1998 to stop Serb violence against the ethnic-Albanian majority in the province. On March 24, 1999, the North Atlantic Treaty Organization (NATO) began bombing targets in Yugoslavia to force Milosevic to withdraw Serb forces from Kosovo. The bombing ended when Milosevic signed a peace agreement on June 10.

That same day, the UN Security Council authorized a UN civilian mission to administer the province of Kosovo and supervise the return of more than 800,000 refugees from foreign countries. The council also authorized the deployment of an international peacekeeping force under NATO command in Kosovo. The UN mission and the NATO force were to maintain order in Kosovo until a political settlement could be reached.

East Timor. On May 5, Indonesia and Portugal signed agreements negotiated by the UN to conduct a referendum on the future of East Timor. On August 30, more than 450,000 East Timorese voted on whether to adopt a UN plan to make East Timor an autonomous state within Indonesia. More than 78 percent of the voters rejected the plan, indicating that most East Timorese wanted complete independence.

Angered by the independence movement, militia forces dedicated to keeping East Timor a part of Indonesia unleashed a campaign of burning, looting, and killing of the East Timorese people. Indonesian troops failed to stop the violence. Faced with world outrage, the Indonesian government on September 12 accepted the temporary deployment in East Timor of a multinational force under Australian command. On October 25, the Security Council set up the UN Transitional Authority in East Timor, as well as a peacekeeping operation with more than 10,000 military troops and police, to govern the territory until it becomes an independent state.

Libya. On April 5, the Security Council suspended its seven-year-old trade sanctions against Libya after the Libyan government surrendered two Libyan nationals to stand trial under a Scottish court in the Netherlands. The United States and Great Britain had accused the two Libyans of planting bombs that blew up Pan American Flight 103 over Lockerbie, Scotland, on Dec. 21, 1988, killing 270 people. At Libya's request, the Scottish court delayed the trial of the two suspects until May 2000.

Iraq refused to allow UN arms inspectors into the country during 1999 to monitor its weapons programs, despite the UN Security Council order of 1991 and nearly continuous U.S. and British bombing raids on Iraqi sites since December 1998. Nevertheless, the UN allowed a humanitarian program known as "oil-for-food" to continue. Under the program, revenue from Iraqi oil sales can be used to buy food, medicine, and other daily essentials.

On Dec. 17, 1999, the Security Council voted to suspend economic sanctions imposed on Iraq after its 1990 invasion of Kuwait provided that Iraq fully cooperate with UN arms inspectors. Iraq countered that inspectors would not be allowed into the country unless sanctions were first lifted. The United Nations Children's Fund (UNICEF) said in August that the UN sanctions were partly responsible for an increase in deaths among Iraqi children under five years of age during the 1990's—from 56 deaths per 1,000 live births in 1984–1989 to 131 deaths in 1994–1999.

U.S. dues. The U.S. Congress passed legislation in November to pay the UN $926 million in unpaid membership dues—approximately two-thirds of the amount that the UN claimed the United States owed. Congress was faced with the choice of paying the dues or losing U.S. voting rights in the UN General Assembly after December 31. Congress attached conditions to the payment, including the requirement that the UN agree to certain reforms, such as a reduction in the U.S. share of the UN budget and in the U.S. contribution to UN peacekeeping missions.

The UN General Assembly began its 54th annual session on September 14 with the election of Namibia's Foreign Minister Theo-Ben Gurirab as president. The Assembly admitted Kiribati, Nauru, and the Kingdom of Tonga—three island republics in the South Pacific Ocean—as members, bringing the UN membership to 188 nations. From September 20 to October 2, the Assembly conducted a general debate. UN Secretary-General Kofi Annan criticized the slow rate at which the Security Council had responded to humanitarian disasters, such as the crisis in Kosovo. China, Algeria, and India protested that military intervention violated national sovereignty.

Security Council. On October 14, the General Assembly elected Bangladesh, Jamaica, Mali, Tunisia, and Ukraine to the 15-nation Security Council. The five countries began their two-year term on Jan. 1, 2000, joining Argentina, Canada, Malaysia, Namibia, and the Netherlands, as well as the permanent members of the council—China, France, Russia, the United Kingdom, and the United States.   □ J. Tuyet Nguyen

See also **Australia; Indonesia; Iraq; Yugoslavia; Yugoslavia: A Special Report.**

United States, Government of the.

The U.S. Justice Department on Sept. 22, 1999, filed a lawsuit against the leading cigarette makers in the United States, accusing the tobacco industry of violating federal racketeering laws by misleading the public about the dangers of smoking. The federal government sought payment for the more than $20 billion spent annually to treat elderly Medicare patients, military veterans, and federal employees for smoking-related illnesses. Such costs were not covered by the $206 billion the industry agreed to pay the states to settle similar lawsuits in 1998.

Independent counsel law. On June 30, 1999, the U.S. Congress allowed the Ethics in Government Act of 1978, also known as the independent counsel law, to expire after critics claimed that it gave special prosecutors too much power to run unnecessarily long and expensive investigations of government officials. Congress had originally passed the law to curb the power of presidents to block investigations, fearing that the executive branch could not be trusted to impartially investigate itself.

The independent counsel law became particularly unpopular with the public during the more than five years that special prosecutor Kenneth Starr spent investigating the personal, professional, and business affairs of President Bill Clinton and First Lady Hillary Rodham Clinton. Starr, whose inquiry cost more than $47 million, also investigated whether the president lied or obstructed justice in trying to conceal his relationship with Monica Lewinsky, a former White House intern. Starr's investigation led to the impeachment of President Clinton in 1998.

Budget surplus. The U.S. government ended fiscal year 1999 on September 30 with a higher-than-expected $115-billion budget surplus. The Clinton administration had announced plans on August 4 to use portions of any federal budget surplus to pay down the national debt by buying back high-rate bonds before they mature and replacing them with new securities that have lower interest rates. The federal government in 1999 owed investors $3.6 trillion in the form of bonds and other securities. The plan was scheduled to be put into action in 2000, if interest rates remained low enough to make the debt buybacks worthwhile.

Economy. The U.S. Federal Reserve System (the Fed), the central bank of the United States, increased short-term interest rates on June 30, 1999, from 4.75 percent to 5 percent. On August 24, the Fed increased the interest rate to 5.25 percent and also increased the federal funds rate, the interest commercial banks are charged when borrowing from the Federal Reserve, from 4.5

Federal spending
United States budget for fiscal 1999*

	Billions of dollars
National defense	276.8
International affairs	15.3
General science, space, technology	19.4
Energy	1.0
Natural resources and environment	22.3
Agriculture	24.4
Commerce and housing credit	3.0
Transportation	38.9
Community and regional development	12.8
Education, training, employment, and social services	57.4
Health	140.8
Social security	390.0
Medicare	190.4
Income security	237.2
Veterans' benefits and services	43.2
Administration of justice	25.8
General government	16.1
Interest	230.3
Undistributed offsetting receipts	–40.4
Total budget outlays	**1,704.7**

*Oct. 1, 1998, to Sept. 30, 1999.
Source: U.S. Department of the Treasury.

U.S. income and outlays

Revenue receipts
Total outlays

Billions of dollars

1995 1996 1997 1998 1999
Fiscal year
Source: U.S. Department of the Treasury.

Selected agencies and bureaus of the U.S. government*

Executive Office of the President

President, Bill Clinton
Vice President, Albert Gore, Jr.
White House Chief of Staff, John D. Podesta
Presidential Press Secretary, Joe Lockhart
Assistant to the President for Domestic Policy, Bruce N. Reed
Assistant to the President for National Security Affairs,
  Samuel R. Berger
Assistant to the President for Science and Technology,
  Neal F. Lane
Council of Economic Advisers—Martin Neil Baily, Chair
Office of Management and Budget—Jacob J. Lew, Director
Office of National Drug Control Policy—
  Barry R. McCaffrey, Director
U.S. Trade Representative, Charlene Barshefsky

Department of Agriculture

Secretary of Agriculture, Daniel R. Glickman

Department of Commerce

Secretary of Commerce, William M. Daley
Bureau of Economic Analysis—J. Steven Landefeld, Director
Bureau of the Census—Kenneth Prewitt, Director

Department of Defense

Secretary of Defense, William S. Cohen
Secretary of the Air Force, F. Whitten Peters
Secretary of the Army, Louis Caldera
Secretary of the Navy, Richard J. Danzig
Joint Chiefs of Staff—
  General Henry H. Shelton, Chairman
  General Michael E. Ryan, Chief of Staff, Air Force
  General Eric K. Shinseki, Chief of Staff, Army
  Admiral Jay L. Johnson, Chief of Naval Operations
  General James L. Jones, Jr., Commandant, Marine Corps

Department of Education

Secretary of Education, Richard W. Riley

Department of Energy

Secretary of Energy, Bill Richardson

Department of Health and Human Services

Secretary of Health and Human Services, Donna E. Shalala
Office of Public Health and Science—
  David Satcher, Assistant Secretary
Centers for Disease Control and Prevention—
  Jeffrey P. Koplan, Director
Food and Drug Administration—
  Jane E. Henney, Commissioner
National Institutes of Health—Harold Varmus, Director
Surgeon General of the United States, David Satcher

Department of Housing and Urban Development

Secretary of Housing and Urban Development,
  Andrew M. Cuomo

Department of the Interior

Secretary of the Interior, Bruce Babbitt

Department of Justice

Attorney General, Janet Reno
Bureau of Prisons—Kathleen Hawk Sawyer, Director
Drug Enforcement Administration—vacant
Federal Bureau of Investigation—Louis J. Freeh, Director
Immigration and Naturalization Service—
  Doris M. Meissner, Commissioner
Solicitor General, Seth P. Waxman

Department of Labor

Secretary of Labor, Alexis M. Herman

Department of State

Secretary of State, Madeleine K. Albright
U.S. Ambassador to the United Nations, Richard C. Holbrooke

Department of Transportation

Secretary of Transportation, Rodney E. Slater
Federal Aviation Administration—
  Jane F. Garvey, Administrator
U.S. Coast Guard—Admiral James M. Loy, Commandant

*As of Dec. 31, 1999.

Department of the Treasury

Secretary of the Treasury, Lawrence H. Summers
Internal Revenue Service—Charles O. Rossotti, Commissioner
Treasurer of the United States, Mary Ellen Withrow
U.S. Secret Service—Brian L. Stafford, Director
Office of Thrift Supervision—Ellen S. Seidman

Department of Veterans Affairs

Secretary of Veterans Affairs, Togo D. West, Jr.

Supreme Court of the United States

Chief Justice of the United States, William H. Rehnquist
  Associate Justices—
  John Paul Stevens   David H. Souter
  Sandra Day O'Connor   Clarence Thomas
  Antonin Scalia   Ruth Bader Ginsburg
  Anthony M. Kennedy   Stephen G. Breyer

Congressional officials

President of the Senate pro tempore, Strom Thurmond
  Senate Majority Leader, Trent Lott
  Senate Minority Leader, Thomas A. Daschle
  Speaker of the House, J. Dennis Hastert
  House Majority Leader, Richard K. Armey
  House Minority Leader, Richard A. Gephardt
  Congressional Budget Office—Dan L. Crippen, Director
  General Accounting Office—David M. Walker, Comptroller
    General of the United States
  Library of Congress—James H. Billington, Librarian of Congress

Independent agencies

Central Intelligence Agency—George J. Tenet, Director
Commission on Civil Rights—Mary Frances Berry, Chairperson
Commission of Fine Arts—J. Carter Brown, Chairman
Consumer Product Safety Commission—
  Ann Winkelman Brown, Chairman
Corporation for National Service—
  Harris Wofford, Chief Executive Officer
Environmental Protection Agency—
  Carol M. Browner, Administrator
Equal Employment Opportunity Commission—
  Ida L. Castro, Chairwoman
Federal Communications Commission—William E. Kennard, Chairman
Federal Deposit Insurance Corporation—
  Donna A. Tanoue, Chairman
Federal Election Commission—Darryl R. Wold, Chairman
Federal Emergency Management Agency—James Lee Witt, Director
Federal Reserve System Board of Governors—
  Alan Greenspan, Chairman
Federal Trade Commission—Robert Pitofsky, Chairman
General Services Administration—David J. Barram, Administrator
National Aeronautics and Space Administration—
  Daniel S. Goldin, Administrator
National Endowment for the Arts—William J. Ivey, Chairman
National Endowment for the Humanities—
  William R. Ferris, Chairman
National Labor Relations Board—John C. Truesdale, Chairman
National Railroad Passenger Corporation (Amtrak)—
  George D. Warrington, President & CEO
National Science Foundation—Rita R. Colwell, Director
National Transportation Safety Board—James E. Hall, Chairman
Nuclear Regulatory Commission—Greta Joy Dicus, Chairman
Peace Corps—Mark D. Gearan, Director
Securities and Exchange Commission—Arthur Levitt, Jr., Chairman
Selective Service System—Gil Coronado, Director
Small Business Administration—Aida Alvarez, Administrator
Smithsonian Institution—I. Michael Heyman, Secretary
Social Security Administration—Kenneth S. Apfel, Commissioner
U.S. Postal Service—William J. Henderson, Postmaster General

percent to 4.75 percent. The Fed explained that the rate increases were made to reduce inflationary pressures on the economy. On November 16, the Fed raised short-term interest rates another one-quarter of a percentage point to 5.5 percent.

Chinese espionage allegations. Department of Energy Secretary Bill Richardson on March 8 dismissed Wen Ho Lee, a scientist at the Los Alamos National Laboratory in New Mexico, after Lee allegedly compromised national security by placing top-secret nuclear weapons information on unsecured computers. Lee, a Taiwan-born U.S. citizen, was also suspected of spying for China. He had been under surveillance by the The Federal Bureau of Investigation (FBI) since 1996 in a probe of the theft of nuclear secrets during the 1980's. On Dec. 10, 1999, the federal government charged Lee with 59 counts of removing nuclear secrets from Los Alamos. On December 20, Lee sued the FBI and the Justice and Energy departments, claiming that they violated his privacy and leaked "misleading information" about him.

The Clinton administration moved to tighten security following Lee's dismissal, but the president's Foreign Intelligence Advisory Board in June issued a report claiming that the nation's nuclear secrets were not safe. The board charged that the Energy Department had mishandled security since the 1970's and called for a reorganization of the

agency to enhance the security of nuclear secrets. In October 1999, Congress approved a defense spending bill that included provisions to reorganize the agency and tighten nuclear security.

Waco investigation. The FBI on August 25 admitted that federal agents may have used explosive tear gas grenades in a confrontation with cult leader David Koresh and his followers, the Branch Davidians, near Waco, Texas, in 1993. The admission followed six years of denials that agents used pyrotechnic devices to bring about an end to a standoff with the Branch Davidians.

The Waco compound used by the cult burst into flames on April 19, 1993, killing Koresh and about 80 of his followers. The FBI claimed that tear gas canisters used during the 51-day standoff bounced off a concrete structure within the compound and did not cause the blaze. Following the FBI's admission, Attorney General Janet Reno appointed John Danforth, a former Republican senator from Missouri, as special counsel to investigate the incident.

Crime. President Clinton on Sept. 11, 1999, announced the government had earmarked $100 million in grants for programs designed to reduce youth violence. The action was spurred in part by several incidents of school violence in 1999. The grants were part of the Safe Schools/Healthy Schools Initiative sponsored by the departments

U.S. Embassy employees in Beijing, China, remove the damaged seal of the United States from an embassy gate following anti-American protests in May 1999. The protests erupted after NATO planes accidentally bombed the Chinese Embassy in Belgrade during NATO's bombing campaign of Yugoslavia.

PEARL HARBOR. At 7:55 a.m. on Sunday, December 7, squadrons of Japanese planes and bombers suddenly appeared over Pearl Harbor, the United States naval base in the Hawaiian Islands. They began to rain incendiary and explosive bombs on the American fleet and on the airplane hangars at Hickam Field. Midget submarines, 41-feet long, and carrying only two men, launched torpedoes. Billowing clouds of heavy smoke soon made evident to startled Hawaiians the magnitude of the treacherous attack. The battleship *Arizona* exploded and sank as the result of a bomb which passed down her smokestack. The older battleship Oklahoma capsized and several other ships were badly damaged.

On December 16, Secretary of the Navy Frank Knox reported 2,897 officers and men killed; 907 wounded or missing; [and] the 32,600-ton *Arizona* destroyed.

of Education, Justice, and Health and Human Services. The initiative was implemented to find ways to identify troubled youths and prevent violence.

The Federal Communications Commission, a government agency that regulates radio, wire, and cable communications in the United States, issued rules in August 1999 that would enable the FBI and other law enforcement agencies to use new electronic surveillance techniques to monitor cellular phones and conference calls. Under the rules, law enforcement authorities would be able to obtain a cell phone user's location at the beginning and end of calls, provided the police have court approval. The ruling also allows the FBI to listen to cell and telephone conversations of all people on a conference call. Law enforcement agencies believed that the rules will aid in combating terrorism, organized crime, and illegal drug activities.

In July, the FBI launched the National Crime Information Center 2000, an information system designed to serve more than 80,000 criminal justice agencies nationally. The system, which replaced the bureau's National Crime Information Center, provides police with material such as fingerprints and mugshots and includes 17 databases with information ranging from stolen property to people on probation or parole. With the proper computer hardware, police officers in the field can access the system via police car radios.

Hate crimes decreased in 1997, according to an FBI report released in January 1999. According to the report, there were 8,049 hate crimes committed during 1997. Of those, 4,710 were motivated by racial bias; 1,102 by sexual-orientation bia; 836 by ethnicity bias; 12 by disability bias; and 4 by multiple biases. The statistics were gathered from incidents reported to the FBI by 11,211 law enforcement agencies in 48 states and the District of Columbia.

Vitamin settlement. On May 20, 1999, the Justice Department announced that two European vitamin manufacturers had agreed to pay the U.S. government a combined $725 million to resolve charges that they conspired to inflate vitamin prices worldwide in the 1990's. The government reported that F. Hoffmann-LaRoche Ltd., a Swiss pharmaceutical company, agreed to pay a $500-million fine. BASF of Germany agreed to pay a $225-million fine. The government claimed that the companies inflated vitamin prices in a scheme that ran from January 1990 until February 1999.

On September 9, the Justice Department announced that three Japanese drug firms would pay more than $137 million for participating in the same conspiracy.

Food safety. On March 23, the federal government began requiring more complete information on the labels of dietary supplement products. The regulations require a new "supplement facts" information panel that includes the quantity of nutrients in vitamin and mineral products and the parts of plants used in herbal products.

On July 3, President Clinton directed the Department of Health and Human Services and the Department of the Treasury to take increased action to prevent unsafe foods from being imported into the United States. The Food and Drug Administration (FDA) reported that food imports had doubled since the early 1990's and were expected to increase an additional 30 percent by 2002. To discourage the distribution of foods before the FDA determines the food is safe, the president ordered the departments to destroy imported foods that could pose a serious health threat and to increase the bond importers post.

The FDA on Oct. 1, 1999, issued a public health warning about illnesses linked to contact with dog-chew products made from pork and beef. The FDA determined that the products pose a risk of bacterial infection that could cause flu-like symptoms in healthy people and life-threatening illness in people with weakened immune systems. The FDA reported that chew products made from pigs' ears were particularly suspect and should be handled carefully.

Health disparities. Surgeon General David Satcher announced on September 30 that the Atlanta-based U.S. Centers for Disease Control and Prevention would provide $9.4 million to community coalitions in 18 states in an effort to eliminate racial and ethnic health disparities. Satcher said that minorities generally have an unusually high level of infant mortality, deaths related to breast and cervical cancers, cardiovascular disease, and diabetes. Minorities also have lower rates of immunization. Satcher said that the money would be given to groups that are effective in reaching and serving these affected communities.

Energy efficiency. President Clinton on June 3 issued an executive order requiring the federal government to improve energy management to save money and reduce air pollution. Clinton ordered federal agencies to reduce greenhouse-gas emissions at their facilities to 35 percent of the levels that existed in 1985. This was to be done by 2010.

The order also pledged that the federal government would make greater use of renewable energy sources. The government planned to install 2,000 solar energy systems at federal facilities by 2001 and 20,000 solar systems by 2010.

☐ Geoffrey A. Campbell and Linda P. Campbell
See also **Congress of the United States; Crime; Food; State government.**

United States, President of the.

The U.S. Senate on Feb. 12, 1999, acquitted President Bill Clinton of impeachment charges passed by the U.S. House of Representatives in December 1998. The Senate voted 45 in favor of and 55 against on one charge of perjury and 50 to 50 on an obstruction of justice charge. The U.S. Constitution requires that a two-thirds majority of the Senate vote in favor of impeachment in order to convict a president.

The charges brought against Clinton stemmed from the president's denial, while giving sworn testimony, that he had had a sexual relationship with former White House intern Monica Lewinsky. Republican House members who supported the impeachment charges accused President Clinton of lying to a federal grand jury in 1998 and of trying to conceal his relationship with Lewinsky. During the Senate trial, which began Jan. 7, 1999, the president's lawyers argued that he did not give false testimony or obstruct justice and that the alleged offenses were not serious enough to justify removal from office.

President Clinton's relationship with Lewinsky came to light after he gave a deposition in January 1998 in a sexual harassment lawsuit filed by a former Arkansas state employee. In August 1998, the president admitted that he had misled the public about his relationship with Lewinsky.

TIME CAPSULE 1933
U.S. PRESIDENT

In 1932 the United States came to the point of economic explosion; the country reached the rock bottom of the Depression. On March 4, 1933, the nation welcomed Franklin D. Roosevelt as the 32nd President of the United States. . . . Hopefully America heard the President's program for the New Deal; gave him overwhelming faith and support; accepted his largely national concept of the future destiny of the United States; acquiesced in giving him virtually dictatorial powers, as of wartime; and felt toward the end of the year that the country actually was lifting itself by the boot straps.

Franklin Delano Roosevelt takes the presidential oath of office on March 4, 1933.

President Bill Clinton walks into the White House Rose Garden to meet reporters on Feb. 12, 1999, after the U.S. Senate acquitted him on charges of perjury and obstruction of justice. The voting—45 to 55 on a charge of perjury and 50 to 50 on a charge of obstruction of justice—was primarily along party lines.

Clemency for FALN. President Clinton on Aug. 11, 1999, offered to commute the sentences of 16 members of a Puerto Rican nationalist group. All had been members of the Armed Forces of National Liberation (FALN). a group dedicated to achieving independence for Puerto Rico. Although the FALN had been blamed for carrying out bombings of political and military installations in the United States in the 1970's and 1980's, none of the 16 FALN members who received the offer of clemency were directly involved in the bombings. Most had been convicted on charges of conspiracy to overthrow the government, possession of an unregistered firearm, or interstate transportation of a stolen vehicle. Some of the members had been sentenced to more than 50 years in jail. The president judged the sentences out of proportion to the nature of the crimes. He required each member to renounce the use of violence and comply with normal parole requirements. Eventually, 12 of the 16 accepted his offer.

Tax-cut veto. On Sept. 23, 1999, Clinton vetoed a $792-billion tax cut passed by Congress in August. The bill was designed to lower the rates at which personal income and capital gains are taxed and repeal the federal inheritance tax. The president said that the tax cut would have used too much of a projected budget surplus.

☐ Geoffrey A. Campbell and Linda P. Campbell

See also **Congress of the United States; Puerto Rico; Social Security; United States, Government of the.**

TIME CAPSULE 1974
U.S. PRESIDENT

A YEAR OF GRAVE CRISIS beset the United States presidency in 1974. . . . As the year began, President [Richard] Nixon struggled to retain the presidency and to conceal his knowledge of the Watergate scandal. In his State of the Union message on January 30, Nixon declared that he would not "walk away from the job the people elected me to do. . . ." On August 5, the president released [an] incriminating transcript of a June 23, 1972, conversation that revealed he knew about the cover-up almost from the beginning. . . .

In the next few days, the president's former supporters in Congress informed him that they would vote to remove him from office. Faced with certain impeachment by the House of Representatives and probable conviction by the Senate, he announced on August 8 that he would resign the next day. At noon on August 9, [Vice President Gerald] Ford was sworn in as the 38th president of the United States.

Uruguay. Uruguayans elected Jorge Batlle, of the ruling Colorado Party, president on Nov. 28, 1999. Batlle, 72, a former senator, won the office on his fifth presidential bid. He defeated Tabare Vazquez, 59, a former mayor of Montevideo, the capital, by taking 52 percent of the vote compared with Vazquez's 44 percent. Vazquez headed the Frente Amplio (Broad Front), a left-wing coalition that, in October, won the largest block of votes in the legislature. Batlle formed a coalition government with the center-right Blanco (National) Party. The new government was expected to continue promarket reforms.

Exports to Brazil, Uruguay's largest trading partner, dropped sharply in the first half of 1999 due to the weakness of Brazil's currency. In February, the Uruguayan government cut tariffs on farm exports by as much as 50 percent to boost their competitiveness.

Truckers strike. A 72-hour work stoppage by 25,000 truckdrivers paralyzed the transportation of goods in Uruguay in late July. The drivers claimed new vehicle taxes put them at a disadvantage with truckers from neighboring Brazil and Argentina.   □ Nathan A. Haverstock

See also **Latin America.**

Utah. See State government.

Uzbekistan. See Asia.

Vanuatu. See Pacific Islands.

Venezuela. Hugo Chavez Frias, of the Fifth Republic Movement, was sworn in on Feb. 2, 1999, for a five-year term as president of Venezuela. Chavez, a former lieutenant colonel, had attempted a military coup (takeover) in 1992 and was subsequently imprisoned until 1994. Shortly after his 1999 inauguration, the new president began initiatives to rewrite Venezuela's Constitution and to remove the "cancer" of corruption in the government. On April 22, the Venezuelan congress, although controlled by Chavez's opponents, enacted a law that allowed the president to bypass the authority of congress for six months and rule by decree on economic matters.

National Constituent Assembly. On April 25, Venezuelans passed a referendum mandating a popularly elected assembly to write a new constitution. Individuals campaigning for a seat in what came to be called the National Constituent Assembly were forced to run without endorsements by political parties. In July 25 elections, 120 of the 131 assembly seats were won by supporters of Chavez. Political opponents believed that Chavez was using the assembly to concentrate political power in his hands.

On August 19, the assembly declared a "judicial emergency" and assumed the power to suspend or dismiss judges accused of corruption. In 1999, roughly half of Venezuela's 4,700 judges were facing such allegations. On August 23, the supreme court ruled in a 9-to-6 vote that the assembly's action was constitutional. The following day, Cecilia Sosa Gomez, chief justice of the supreme court, resigned in protest.

On August 30, the National Constituent Assembly disbanded congress. Assembly President Luis Miquilena claimed, "We are assuming a duty they have irresponsibly abandoned." The assembly and congress reached an agreement that allowed congress to resume on October 2, providing that the assembly could determine the legislative agenda.

New Constitution. On December 15, Venezuelans voted to accept a new Constitution. It included several of Chavez's recommendations, such as extending the term of president to six years and allowing an incumbent president to run for a second consecutive term. Chavez also suggested an article renaming the country The Bolivarian Republic of Venezuela, in honor of Simon Bolivar (1783-1830), the nation's founding father.

Torrential rains in December 1999 caused flooding and landslides that, according to Venezuelan officials, may have killed 15,000 to 25,000 people. Observers noted Chavez's prompt response in mobilizing the military to conduct rescue and relief efforts.   □ Nathan A. Haverstock

See also **Latin America; People in the news** (Chavez, Hugo).

Vermont. See State government.

Vietnam. Reformers and conservatives fought in 1999 for influence in the ruling Communist Party of Vietnam. About 2.3 million of Vietnam's 78 million people are party members.

In early January, the party expelled Tran Do, a former member of the party's powerful central committee. He had angered party leaders by warning that the Communist Party no longer commanded the public's trust and confidence.

Following Tran Do's expulsion, conservatives pressed their attack with an unsigned letter in the Communist-controlled press, blaming reformers for many of Vietnam's problems. When the Communist Party central committee met in late January and announced no major leadership changes or reforms, political experts concluded that hard-liners had gained the upper hand.

Corruption. In May 1999, the top Communist official, General Secretary Le Kha Phieu, called for a struggle against corruption. Phieu decried "degeneration" among party members and alluded to high-ranking officials who had "violated party principles" as well as "the state law."

Two men were sentenced to death and 72 were imprisoned at the end of May in Vietnam's largest smuggling case to date. The 74 defendants were found guilty of participating in a smuggling ring that imported $70 million worth of consumer goods into Vietnam, evading custom duties by bribing officials.

Vietnam's economy remained lackluster in 1999, even as other Asian economies rebounded from recession. Domestic output and industrial production grew, though more slowly than in previous years. The World Bank, a United Nations agency, estimated that the average Vietnamese had an annual income of $310.

Economists said that Vietnam's economy was

TIME CAPSULE 1975
VIETNAM

THE LONG WAR IN VIETNAM ended on April 30, 1975, with a complete Communist victory. North Vietnam immediately began reorganizing South Vietnam in preparation for reunification of the two countries on April 30, 1976.

Phuoc Binh, capital of Phuoc Long province, fell to North Vietnamese Army troops on Jan. 7, 1975. Encouraged by this victory, North Vietnam sent more troops into South Vietnam. The fall of Ban Me Thuot on March 10 caused South Vietnam's President Nguyen Van Thieu to order the Central Highlands evacuated. This turned into a rout. Hue and Da Nang, the main cities in northern South Vietnam, fell on March 26 and 29.

The South Vietnamese Senate on April 2 overwhelmingly approved a resolution that a "government of national union" be formed to end the war. . . . The senators criticized both Thieu and the United States for the position in which South Vietnam found itself.

still backward and that Vietnam needed foreign investment to help modernize industry. But some international companies, discouraged by the difficulty of doing business in Vietnam, cut back or abandoned operations in the country in 1999.

In July, the United States and Vietnam announced an agreement on a trade pact. The Clinton administration had ended an *embargo* (ban on trade) on Vietnam in 1994, but the United States still imposed high tariffs. The new agreement, which was to reduce tariffs, required approval by the U.S. Congress and Vietnam's parliament. However, neither body had approved the pact by year's end.

Consulate. On Sept. 7, 1999, U.S. Secretary of State Madeleine Albright opened a U.S. consulate in Ho Chi Minh City, on the site where the U.S. embassy had once stood in what was then South Vietnam's capital, Saigon. The United States opened an embassy in Hanoi, Vietnam's capital, in 1995.

Heavy rains in November 1999 in central Vietnam caused floods that killed nearly 600 people. More rain in December caused further flooding in the region, killing more than 130 people. Foreign organizations helped with relief work.

□ Henry S. Bradsher

See also **Asia**.

Virginia. See State government.
Vital statistics. See Population.

TIME CAPSULE 1968
VIETNAM

For a month preceding the Tet [a Vietnamese holiday that marks the lunar new year], Viet Cong infiltrators disguised as civilians had been moving quietly into some 27 key cities of South Vietnam. Elsewhere in the south, the Viet Cong were gathering clandestinely in the thick jungles surrounding dozens of provincial capitals, villages, and hamlets. On January 31, the first day of the Tet, they struck in what was to prove the fiercest and most coordinated attack of the war.

Washington, D.C. The new mayor of Washington, D.C., Anthony A. Williams, took office on Jan. 2, 1999. Williams inherited a city government that had been stripped of most of its powers in 1995 by a control board appointed by the United States Congress. In a vote of confidence in the new mayor, Congress returned authority for the city's day-to-day operations to the city government in February 1999. Williams, who had been the city's chief financial officer since 1995, was largely responsible for the capital's financial turnaround. In 1999, the city ran a budget surplus of $445 million, compared with a deficit of approximately $330 million in 1995.

The surplus allowed the city to keep and restore its dilapidated City Hall, a six-story building on Pennsylvania Avenue built in the Beaux-Arts style. The city had agreed in 1995 to lease the building to the federal government because the capital lacked the funds for restoration.

Capital improvements. In April 1999, the city council passed a $418-million tax cut, reducing income, property, and business taxes. The council hoped the tax cut would lure businesses to Washington and stem the flight of the middle class to the suburbs. From 1960 to 1999, the city's population dropped by more than 30 percent.

Washington began to enforce its four-year-old curfew law in 1999. The law, which made it illegal for children under 17 to be out without adult supervision between 11 p.m. and 6 a.m. during the week and between midnight and 6 a.m. on weekends, had been passed in an effort to make neighborhoods safer and to reduce juvenile crime but had never been enforced.

Problems. In January, Charles H. Ramsey, the chief of police hired in 1998 after a series of police scandals, asked the U.S. Justice Department to review all fatal shootings by D.C. police officers over the previous 10 years. The request was made in reaction to the high level of distrust of police officers in the city and the number of police shootings throughout the 1990's. From 1990 to 1999, 87 people were shot and killed by Washington police, well above the national average.

On January 15, David Howard, a mayoral aide, inadvertently caused a crisis while discussing his agency's budget. Howard's statement, "I will have to be niggardly with this fund because it's not going to be a lot of money," was interpreted by one of his black colleagues as a racial slur. The word "niggardly," though similar to a racial epithet, is derived from an old Scandinavian word meaning "miserly" or "stingy." Nevertheless, Howard, who is white, resigned. The mayor was engulfed in protests and seen as indecisive. Hoping to put the incident behind him, the mayor rehired Howard on February 3.

The Lincoln Memorial in Washington, D.C.

TIME CAPSULE 1922
WASHINGTON, D.C.

IN MAY 1922 there was dedicated in the city of Washington the only memorial of its kind in the United States, a massive building of white marble, a fitting climax to the efforts of Americans to honor the life and service of Lincoln. This building, known as the Lincoln Memorial, stands on a site isolated, where nothing else intrudes. . . .

The memorial stands in a great open space on a mound built of a series of terraces, rising to a total height above grade of 122 feet. A colonnade of great Doric columns of white marble surrounds the walls, within which, in the center space, is a colossal statue of Lincoln. Each column, 36 in all, represents a state, one for each state of the Union at the time of Lincoln's death. On the walls above the colonnade, supported at intervals by eagles, are 48 memorial festoons, one for each state existing at the present time.

The setting of the Memorial is magnificent . . . . To the east, nearly a mile away, stands in its austere dignity Washington's monument, which is to be connected with the Lincoln Memorial by a great lagoon that will reflect both monuments. . . .

Within the building is the towering statue of Lincoln, in which is expressed . . . the gentleness, power, and intelligence of the man.

The Washington Monument shines spectacularly, encased in a specially designed brick-patterned aluminum scaffolding and translucent covering during the 1999 restoration of the 555-foot (169-meter) obelisk.

Museums. Ground was broken in September for the National Museum of the American Indian, scheduled to open in 2002. The museum will fill the last open space facing the National Mall. The $110-million museum was established to preserve the culture and history of the more than 1,000 Native American groups of the United States.

Washington's Phillips Collection, one of the first museums of modern art in the United States, was remodeled in 1999. To honor the founder, the 78-year-old institution organized the exhibit "Renoir to Rothko: The Eye of Duncan Phillips." The show included more than 350 works of modern art collected by Phillips.

Washington's beloved football team, the Redskins, was sold in 1999. A local communications magnate, Daniel Snyder, bought the team in May for $800 million, a record price for a U.S. sports team.

Watergate redux. In May, George Washington University purchased the Howard Johnson motel located near the Watergate Hotel, which was the site of the break-in at the Democratic Party's National Headquarters in 1972, an event that brought about President Richard Nixon's resignation. The university converted the motel into a dorm and Room 723—the headquarters for the burglars—into a museum.   ☐ Robert Messenger

See also **City.**

Weather. The year 1999 began with severe weather over most of the northern United States. A widespread storm brought blizzard conditions to the Midwest. Chicago received 18.6 inches (47.2 centimeters) of snow on January 2, the most on any single day since record-keeping began in 1886. The same storm glazed parts of the Northeast with ice.

Waves of severe winter weather spread over the Great Lakes region and Northeast during the first half of January 1999. Detroit, Michigan, received 27.4 inches (69.6 centimeters) of snow within the first two weeks, its second snowiest January on record. A state of emergency was declared in Buffalo, New York, after more than 60 inches (152 centimeters) of snow had accumulated within the first 15 days of January. Canadian soldiers were called to Toronto, Ontario, to help deal with the more than 40 inches (101.6 centimeters) of snow that fell in January, which was more than three times the city's average snowfall for the month. A warming trend in mid-January drove the temperature on January 16 above freezing in Chicago for the first time in 18 days.

Tornadoes in January. Disturbances in the *jet stream* (a high-altitude river of air that flows from west to east) accompanying the surge of milder air in mid-January produced tornadoes in many areas of the United States. In Arkansas,

Mississippi, and Tennessee, more than 80 twisters on January 17, 21, and 22 killed 19 people. Overall, 169 tornadoes were counted in the United States in January, breaking the previous record of 52 in January 1975.

Snowfall records. Late in January 1999, polar air invading the West Coast states brought rare low-elevation snows to California's Central Valley. Bakersfield was hit by more than 3 inches (8 centimeters) on Jan. 25, 1999, the city's first snow since 1974 and greatest snowfall on record.

Cold air withdrew from much of the nation in February 1999. However, storms across the Northwest led to record-setting rain and mountain snow. The storms contributed to a new national record for seasonal snowfall at Mount Baker, Washington. During the winter and spring of 1999, Mount Baker received 1,140 inches (2,896 centimeters)—95 feet (29 meters)—of snow, breaking the nation's previous record for snow—1,122 inches (2,850 centimeters) set in the winter of 1971-1972 at Mount Rainier, in Washington.

European winter. In 1999, Northern Europe experienced its hardest winter in 100 years. On January 28, temperatures in Finland, Norway, and Sweden plummeted to –60 °F (–50 °C). Central Europe received record-breaking snowfalls, leading to avalanches in the Alps. Near the Austrian villages of Galtuer and Valzur, 38 people were buried by snow slides on February 23 and 24.

Spring brought heavy rains, tornadoes, and the beginnings of drought to the United States. On April 26, 3.79 inches (9.62 centimeters) of rain fell on Oklahoma City in 24 hours—just 0.01 inches (0.03 centimeters) shy of its 24-hour record for April. On May 17, parts of Iowa got over 7 inches (18 centimeters) of rain, bringing some rivers to higher crests than were measured during the floods of 1993.

Violent tornadoes ripped through parts of Kansas and Oklahoma on May 3, 1999, destroying more than 9,000 residences and businesses and causing 49 deaths. Moore, Oklahoma, an Oklahoma City suburb, and Wichita, Kansas, were especially hard hit. Preliminary estimates from portable instruments indicated that winds had reached speeds of 318 miles (512 kilometers) per hour in one of the twisters near Oklahoma City.

The spring ended dry and warm across the Middle Atlantic States and Northeast, while numerous jet stream disturbances brought cool, inclement weather to the West. The latest measurable snow of record occurred at Mount Laguna near Los Angeles on June 4, when 3 inches (7.6 centimeters) fell. On the same day, Las Vegas registered its coolest June afternoon on record, with a high temperature of only 67 °F (19 °C).

Drought and heat. The weather pattern of late spring persisted into the beginning of the

A family takes refuge under a viaduct (left) near Newcastle, Oklahoma, on May 3, as a tornado tears through the area. The tornado was one of a number of twisters that hit parts of Kansas and Oklahoma with winds as high as 318 miles (512 kilometers) per hour.

A Daytona Beach, Florida, pier, pounded by the surf, collapses (right), as Hurricane Floyd approaches on September 15. The hurricane veered north, forcing the evacuation of more than 3 million people. With damages in excess of $7 billion, Floyd was the costliest hurricane to hit the United States since Andrew in 1992.

The year 1999 brought record-breaking cold and snows, as well as long-lasting drought and devastating windstorms.

A Chicagoan skis through a snow-packed street during the January 2 blizzard that struck much of the Midwest. Chicago received 18.6 inches (47.2 centimeters) of snow, the largest snowfall on any single day in the city's history since record-keeping began in 1886.

A pond in Orefield, Pennsylvania (right), lies parched and cracked in August in the wake of a months-long drought. Several Middle Atlantic and Northeastern states were declared disaster areas because of crop failure from drought. Agricultural losses in the region in 1999 were estimated to exceed $1 billion.

summer. Extreme heat aggravated the parched conditions in the Northeast and Middle Atlantic states. In New York City, a record was set when the temperature exceeded 95 °F (35 °C) on 11 days during July. The month was the warmest of any month in the city's history and the driest July on record.

In summer, drought conditions worsened and spread across the Northeast. The April through July period was the driest in 100 years in Delaware, Maryland, New Jersey, and Rhode Island. By early August, several Middle Atlantic and Northeastern states were declared disaster areas because of crop failure from drought. Agricultural losses in the region were estimated to exceed $1 billion. Drought emergencies were declared in Maryland, Pennsylvania, and New Jersey, where stream flows were near record low levels.

By contrast, the Southwest stayed unusually cool and moist through the summer of 1999. The worst flash flood in 15 years swept through Las Vegas, Nevada, on July 8, after a downpour dumped 3 inches (7.6 centimeters) of rain in just a few hours. In Salt Lake City, Utah, a rare tornado touched down in the downtown area, killing one person and injuring more than 100.

Hurricane season. The first Atlantic hurricane of the autumn season, Bret, made landfall in south Texas on August 22 with winds near 120 miles (193 kilometers) per hour. A week later, Hurricane Dennis passed within 60 miles (97 kilometers) of the North Carolina coast where it stalled, weakened, and eventually returned, making landfall in eastern North Carolina as a tropical storm in early September. A prolonged period of onshore gales from the lingering storm caused extensive damage along the Outer Banks.

Hurricane Floyd, born in the central Atlantic, was initially on a westbound track toward Florida but veered north and ravaged the central and northwest Bahamas on September 13 and 14 with winds near 150 miles (241 kilometers) per hour. With Floyd poised to strike the United States, more than 3 million people evacuated the East Coast from Florida to North Carolina, the largest evacuation in U.S. history. Floyd eventually made landfall on September 16 at Cape Fear, North Carolina, with peak winds near 110 miles (177 kilometers) per hour.

Floyd's most destructive element proved to be excessive rain after the storm weakened. Over 19 inches (48 centimeters) fell on Wilmington, North Carolina. Rainfall greater than 5 inches (13 centimeters) was widespread from eastern North Carolina to New England. Severe flooding occurred in eastern North Carolina, where more than 1,500 people had to be rescued after 30,000 residences were flooded. In North Carolina alone, 500,000 people lost electricity while virtually all roads east

of Interstate 95 were closed at some point. Total damage from Floyd exceeded $7 billion, making it the costliest hurricane to hit the United States since Andrew in 1992. The rains from Floyd officially ended the drought in the Middle Atlantic and Northeastern States.

Hurricane Irene struck Florida on Oct. 15, 1999, and reached South Carolina on October 17. Although Irene was not as powerful as Floyd, with winds of only 85 miles (137 kilometers) per hour, the National Weather Service estimated that the volume of rain that fell across southeastern Florida during Irene was the greatest of any hurricane of record there.

Cyclone in Asia. A cyclone that struck the Indian state of Orissa on October 29 caused the deaths of nearly 10,000 people. The storm packed winds of more than 160 miles (260 kilometers) per hour, destroying more than a million houses and killing hundreds of thousands of cattle.

November 1999 was the warmest and the sixth driest November across most of the United States since 1895, when record-keeping began, according to the National Climate Data Center. On Nov. 8, 1999, temperatures in Kennebec, South Dakota, hit 89 °F (31 °C), a state record for that date.　　□ Todd Miner and Fred Gadomski

See also **Disasters.**

Weightlifting. See Sports.

Welfare.

The number of people on welfare in the United States continued to decline, falling to 7.3 million in August 1999. The new figure reflected a drop from 14.1 million people in 1993, the largest caseload decline in history. According to government officials, the percentage of the U.S. population on welfare in 1999 was the lowest since 1967.

Analysts attributed most of the decline to the welfare reform bill passed by the U.S. Congress in 1996. However, government officials attributed at least 10 percent of the drop to the country's strong economic growth, which cut the unemployment rate to 4.3 percent in 1999. In Wisconsin, the state that pioneered welfare-to-work legislation, almost 90 percent of people who had been on welfare in 1996 no longer received benefits in 1999.

The 1996 welfare reform bill did not affect the food stamp program. However, the number of people receiving food stamps fell to 18.5 million in mid-1999, compared with 27.5 million in 1994. A steady increase in jobs accounted for part of the decline. Analysts noted that some people who were eligible for food stamps failed to apply for them, mistakenly believing that they no longer qualified under the 1996 welfare law.

Two-tiered payments. The U.S. Supreme Court ruled on May 17, 1999, that states could not pay lower welfare benefits to newly arrived residents than they paid to longtime residents. The court's 7-2 ruling struck down California's two-tier system of welfare benefits, which gave lower benefits to people who moved to California from states that provided lesser benefits than California's. (California's welfare payments are among the highest in the nation.)

Justice John Paul Stevens, writing for the majority, stated that the California law limited individuals' freedom to travel across state lines in violation of the 14th Amendment. The ruling—the high court's first decision involving the 1996 welfare law overhaul—also affected 14 other states with similar laws.

New Markets. President Clinton toured poverty-stricken areas of the United States—eastern Kentucky; East St. Louis, Illinois; Clarksdale, Mississippi; the Watts neighborhood of Los Angeles; and the Pine Ridge Indian Reservation in South Dakota—in July 1999 to promote private investment as a way to help the poor. The president's approach, which he called "New Markets," advocated the use of government incentives to encourage businesses to locate in depressed rural and urban areas. He proposed a 25-percent tax credit for investment in community banks and similar facilities.   □ William J. Eaton

See also **Supreme Court of the United States.**

West Indies. At an April 1999 summit meeting of the Association of Caribbean States, held in Santo Domingo, the capital of the Dominican Republic, leaders from 25 Caribbean nations pledged to work toward the creation of a regional trading bloc. The summit participants also agreed that increased tourism represented the best hope for boosting their region's earnings and employment.

Death penalty. To discourage mounting crime, which posed a threat to the tourist industry, several Caribbean governments revived the death penalty in 1999. In early June, Trinidad and Tobago executed criminals for the first time in 20 years, hanging nine men convicted of murder. Several other nations, including Barbados, St. Lucia, and Jamaica, announced their intention to reinstate capital punishment.

Jamaican violence. Nine people in Jamaica were killed during a week of widespread rioting in late April. Rioters looted stores and blocked roads with burning tires in anger over a government-announced 30-percent hike in the price of gasoline. The protest subsided only after Jamaica's prime minister, P. J. Patterson, cut the new tax by half.

Other violence persisted. In July, Patterson gave Jamaica's soldiers wide authority to crack down on what he called "a spate of criminal

madness." The violence, which had left some 500 Jamaicans dead by mid-1999, included gang-style killings in poor areas of Kingston, the capital.

Money-laundering Caribbean banks. U.S. government prosecutors announced in August that financial records they had obtained from a defunct bank in the Cayman Islands would net the treasury an estimated $300 million in unpaid taxes and penalties from about 1,500 U.S. citizens. The investigation exposed widespread money laundering in the Caymans.

Elections. On January 18, Grenada's Prime Minister Keith Mitchell won another term in office, his New National Party taking all 15 seats in Parliament. On January 20, Prime Minister Owen Arthur of Barbados was also reelected when his Barbados Labour Party won in a landslide, taking 26 of 28 seats in parliament.

On March 9, Antigua and Barbuda's Prime Minister Lester Bird was returned to office, his Antigua Labour Party winning 12 of 17 seats in Parliament. On June 28, the people of Antigua and Barbuda mourned the loss of the prime minister's father, Vere C. Bird, 89, who led the nation from 1981 to 1994.   □ Nathan A. Haverstock

See also **Latin America.**

West Virginia. See **State government.**
Wisconsin. See **State government.**
Wyoming. See **State government.**

Yemen. Islamic militants belonging to the Aden-Abyan Islamic Army continued a bombing campaign in Yemen in 1999 aimed at destabilizing the government. The attacks came despite a security crackdown on the rebels, who had been increasingly active since 1998.

A Yemeni court in May 1999 sentenced to death three members of the group, including its commander Zein al-Abideen al-Mehdar, for acts of *sedition* (inciting rebellion against the state). The men had also been charged with kidnapping 16 Western tourists in December 1998. Four of the tourists were killed during a rescue attempt by Yemeni troops. Al-Mehdar was executed by firing squad in October 1999. Also in October, the government said that police had arrested Abul-Muhsin, al-Mehdar's successor as leader of the Aden-Abyan group.

Other terrorist cases. In August, a Yemeni court sentenced 10 foreigners, including 8 British Muslims and 2 Algerians, to jail terms of up to seven years for plotting various terrorist acts. Four of the men were convicted of planning to bomb the British consulate, a church, and a Western-owned hotel. One of the Britons was the son of an Islamic cleric in London, who Yemeni officials accused of links with al-Mehdar.

□ Christine Helms

See also **Middle East.**

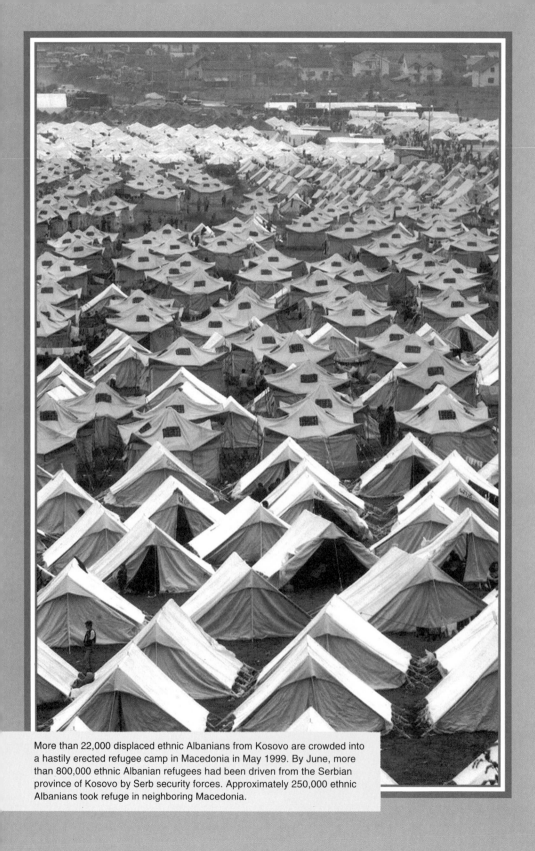

More than 22,000 displaced ethnic Albanians from Kosovo are crowded into
a hastily erected refugee camp in Macedonia in May 1999. By June, more
than 800,000 ethnic Albanian refugees had been driven from the Serbian
province of Kosovo by Serb security forces. Approximately 250,000 ethnic
Albanians took refuge in neighboring Macedonia.

Yugoslavia. The conflict between the government of Yugoslavia (which consisted of the republics of Serbia and Montenegro) and ethnic Albanians in the province of Kosovo escalated into open warfare in 1999. Serb police and Yugoslav Army units entered Kosovo with a mission to eliminate the Kosovo Liberation Army (KLA), an ethnic Albanian separatist group seeking independence from Serbia. International efforts to mediate the conflict, including face-to-face talks in France in early 1999, failed. On March 24, the North Atlantic Treaty Organization (NATO), after repeatedly warning Yugoslavia to cease its attacks on ethnic Albanians, began bombing Yugoslavia and Yugoslav forces in Kosovo.

NATO's offensive. NATO commanders implemented a strategy designed to cripple Yugoslavia's ability to wage war. During the 78-day campaign, NATO used more than 23,000 bombs and missiles to destroy military targets and infrastructure in Serbia and Kosovo. Inevitably, the air strikes also caused unintended damage. On April 12, NATO missiles aimed at a bridge near the Serbian town of Grdelica accidentally struck a passenger train, killing 17 people. A U.S. warplane mistakenly bombed the Chinese Embassy in Belgrade, Yugoslavia's capital, on May 7, killing three Chinese nationals. U.S. officials blamed the error on outdated intelligence. On April 14, NATO jets mistook a refugee convoy near Djakovica, Serbia, for Serbian troops and accidentally killed 75 civilians.

The fighting ends. The bombing campaign ended on June 10, after Serbia agreed to withdraw its forces from Kosovo and accept the presence of NATO peacekeeping troops in Kosovo under NATO control. The KLA, in turn, agreed to disarm. By the end of the conflict, thousands of people had been killed, and *ethnic cleansing* (the systematic removal of a particular ethnic group from an area) by Serbs had driven more than 800,000 ethnic Albanians out of Kosovo. Most of the refugees fled to neighboring Macedonia and Albania. The financial strain of feeding and housing so many refugees threatened to overwhelm the governments of those countries. Humanitarian organizations and Western governments provided funds and supplies to help ease the crisis, and Germany, the United States, and other NATO countries took in small numbers of refugees.

Tensions persist. On June 12, the first wave of 50,000 NATO troops began entering Kosovo. Some 3,600 troops from Russia, which had supported Serbia in the conflict, also served as peacekeepers. Many ethnic Albanians began returning soon after NATO forces moved in. Despite international efforts to deliver aid, many returning refugees faced extreme hardship. An estimated 27,000 dwellings in Kosovo had been destroyed in Serbia's ethnic cleansing campaign, and aid agencies warned that thousands of people would face the winter in Kosovo without adequate shelter.

In September, the KLA officially disarmed and its members organized as a civilian service corps of 5,000 former soldiers. However, few observers believed that the disarmament was genuine. In the months after the fighting ceased, international observers reported many instances of violence against Serbs. Nearly 200,000 Serbs fled Kosovo after the June peace agreement. The Serbs who remained continued to feel threatened despite NATO's promises of protection. In October, Serb leaders decided to organize their own defense force and to establish self-rule in areas where they remained the majority population.

International efforts. The International Criminal Tribunal for Yugoslavia in The Hague, the Netherlands, on May 27, indicted Yugoslav President Slobodan Milosevic and four other top officials as war criminals for their roles in the war in Kosovo. The United States and several European countries lifted economic sanctions against Kosovo and Montenegro in September. However, they left in place sanctions against Serbia. Foreign governments and international agencies also agreed to withhold reconstruction aid from Serbia as long as Milosevic was in power. In November, the United States announced that it would lift its sanctions when Yugoslavia held free national elections.

Economy. A group of Serb economists reported in July that the war in Kosovo had caused $29.6 billion in damage to the Yugoslav economy. The economists forecast that Yugoslavia's *gross domestic product* (the value of all goods and services produced in a country in a given year) would fall by 44.4 percent for 1999. The inflation rate rose sharply in October, as businesses regularly raised prices to keep pace with the rapidly declining value of the national currency, the dinar.

Opposition to Milosevic surged in Serbia after the end of the bombing. Opposition groups organized major protests in several Yugoslav cities in July and August, but turnout at the demonstrations slowly declined. Police in Belgrade forcibly dispersed a demonstration on September 29.

The government of Montenegro continued to distance itself from Serbia in 1999. In November, Montenegro introduced the German mark as its second legal currency alongside the dinar. Analysts saw the move as a step toward Montenegro's independence from Serbia. Later in November, Montenegrin premier Miodrag Vukovic said that a referendum on independence could take place in the first half of 2000.   □ Sharon L. Wolchik

See also **Albania; Armed forces; Europe; Macedonia; Russia; United Kingdom; United Nations; Yugoslavia: A Special Report.**

Yukon Territory. See **Canadian territories.**

Yugoslavia:
"A Decade of Ruin"

A series of civil wars in the 1990's
brought death and devastation to the
former Socialist Federal Republic of
Yugoslavia.

By Sharon L. Wolchik

The government of Yugoslavia, leaders of the Kosovo Liberation Army (KLA), and representatives of the North Atlantic Treaty Organization (NATO) signed an agreement on June 10, 1999, ending more than a year of armed conflict in Kosovo. Under the terms of this agreement, Yugoslavia, which consists of Serbia and Montenegro, was to withdraw its military and security forces from Kosovo, a province in southern Serbia where the majority of the people are ethnic Albanian Muslims. In return, NATO agreed to end its 11-week-old campaign of air strikes against Yugoslavia, and the KLA (a group seeking independence from Serbia) agreed to end hostilities and disarm their forces. On June 12, an international peacekeeping force under NATO command entered Kosovo to enforce the agreement and ensure the safe return of refugees. Meanwhile, thousands of Kosovar Serbs fled the province, fearing reprisals from returning refugees.

The conflict in Kosovo was the latest in a series of violent conflicts that occurred as the former Yugoslav state disintegrated during the 1990's. Brutal civil warfare killed, maimed, and displaced hundreds of thousands of people in the former federation. Physical destruction and international economic sanctions combined to disrupt the economy and greatly delay the creation of democratic political institutions to replace the Communist system that had been in place in Yugoslavia.

Forging a multiethnic nation

Yugoslavia, which means *Land of the South Slavs,* came into being at the end of World War I (1914-1918) as the Kingdom of Serbs, Croats, and Slovenes, with King Peter I of Serbia as head of state. The new kingdom consisted of Serbia, an independent nation that had broken free of the Ottoman Turks in 1878, and Croatia, Slovenia, Bosnia-Herzegovina, Montenegro, and Macedonia, territories that had been controlled by either Austria-Hungary or the Ottoman Empire. Both of these empires, weakened by the war, eventually collapsed.

In 1918, the Kingdom of Serbs, Croats, and Slovenes (renamed Yugoslavia in 1929) covered approximately 99,000 square miles (256,000 square kilometers) along the Adriatic Sea. It shared borders with Austria, Italy, Hungary, Romania, Albania, Bulgaria, and Greece. The six territories making up the new kingdom roughly followed the traditional boundaries of Yugoslavia's six largest Slavic nationality groups: Serbs, Croats, Bosnian Muslims, Slovenes, Macedonians, and Montenegrins. But, none of these states was peopled by a single ethnic group. There were pockets of Serbs in Croatia and Bosnia and Muslims living in Serbia and Montenegro. There were sizable non-Slavic minorities as well, including Albanians, Hungarians, Germans, and Romanians and smaller groups of Czechs, Slovaks, Italians, Ruthenians, Ukrainians, Turks, Romanies, and Jews.

From the beginning, Yugoslavia faced problems related to its diverse national composition. Each of the nationalities making up the new country retained its own sense of cultural identity. The Croats and Slovenes, who had been ruled by the Habsburg monarchy of Austria-Hungary, were more Western than the peoples to the east and south, who lived in regions formerly under Ottoman Turkish control. Most Croats and Slovenes were Roman Catholic; most Serbs, Macedonians, and Montenegrins were Eastern Orthodox Christians; the majority of people in Bosnia-Herzegovina were Muslim. There were also linguistic differences among the nationalities.

Significant economic differences also existed between the various republics. Slovenia and Croatia were more industrialized than Serbia, Macedonia, Montenegro, and Bosnia-Herzegovina. Like other new postwar European nations, Yugoslavia attempted to shift from a largely agricultural economy to an industrial economy. While the country achieved some success at reforms in the 1920's, the Great Depression of the 1930's hindered further efforts and led to widespread unemployment.

Conflicting views of government

Members of different national groups in Yugoslavia held conflicting views concerning the structure of the government. Officially, the government of the Kingdom of Serbs, Croats, and Slovenes was a democracy, with the powers of the monarchy balanced by an elected parliament. However, the fledgling government soon proved unable to deal effectively with the many challenges it faced and was replaced by authoritarian rule. In January 1921, the parliament approved a new constitution that created a strong, centralized state, a system favored by Serbs. Croatian political leaders opposed the new constitution and refused to cooperate with the Serbs. The Croats favored a decentralized system of government with significant autonomy for each of the political divisions within the kingdom.

The author:

Sharon L. Wolchik is a professor of political science and international affairs at George Washington University in Washington, D.C.

Violence soon erupted. A Montenegrin deputy shot five Croatian leaders on the floor of parliament in 1928, and King Alexander, who had succeeded King Peter I in 1921, abolished the constitution and established a dictatorship. Alexander was, in turn, assassinated by a Macedonian separatist in 1934. Alexander's son and heir, Peter, was too young to ascend the throne so the late king's brother, Paul, acted as regent for Prince Peter and carried on Alexander's highly unpopular policies.

The gathering shadows of World War II (1939–1945) brought further trouble to Yugoslavia. Paul attempted to shield the country from the threat of war by drawing closer to the fascist regimes of Italy and Nazi Germany. On March 25, 1941,

Yugoslavia officially became a German ally. Two days later, Paul was ousted by a military *coup* (overthrow), and his 17-year-old nephew, Prince Peter, was proclaimed king.

World War II

On April 6, 1941, Germany invaded Yugoslavia, and the new king and his supporters fled the country. The Yugoslav army offered the Germans little resistance, and the country was quickly carved up. The Germans set up puppet states in Croatia and Serbia. In Croatia and part of Bosnia-Herzegovina, power was handed to the Ustase, a right-wing nationalist group that collaborated with the Nazis to exterminate Jews and other minorities. This regime also persecuted non-Croats and fought with the Germans against the resistance forces that developed within Yugoslavia. Serb royalist forces, known as the Cetniks, also collaborated with the Germans.

The strongest resistance to German occupation came from Yugoslav guerrillas, called Partisans, who struggled to drive out occupation troops and bring down the Ustase. The Partisans were led by Josip Broz, then secretary-general of Yugoslavia's Communist Party. Josip Broz eventually became known as "Tito." Supplied by the Western allies, the Partisans, which included members of all national groups, were able to liberate parts of Yugoslavia from German control.

More than 1 million people died in Yugoslavia during World War II. (By comparison, approximately 400,000 U.S. and 350,000 British military personnel died in the war.) The large number of casualties was partially the result of the armed resistance to German occupiers. However, conflicts among Yugoslavia's various nationalities, particularly between Serbs and Croats, resulted in the death of many thousands of people. Each group committed atrocities against the other, and the memory of these atrocities help fuel the conflicts that tore Yugoslavia apart in the 1990's.

Communist rule

By the end of the war in 1945, Tito and the Communists controlled Yugoslavia and were ruling from the capital, Belgrade. Yugoslavia, under Tito, became a federation of six republics: Slovenia, Croatia, Serbia, Bosnia-Herzegovina, Montenegro, and Macedonia. Kosovo, in southern Yugoslavia between Bosnia and Macedonia, became an *autonomous* (self-governing) province within Serbia, as did Vojvodina, an area adjacent to Croatia in the north. The boundaries of the new political units left large numbers of ethnic minorities in each area.

The Communist government in Yugoslavia initially followed

Yugoslavia (top), lies in the Balkan Peninsula in southeastern Europe. When it was founded in 1918, it was approximately the size of the state of Oregon (bottom).

Yugoslavs honor Josip Broz (known as "Tito"), with flowers on his birthday, May 25 (far right). Tito, a Communist, led Yugoslavia from 1945 until his death in 1980. Under Tito, Yugoslavia consisted of six republics (right): Bosnia-Herzegovina, Croatia, Macedonia, Montenegro, Serbia, and Slovenia.

the model of government established by the Soviet Union. Although Yugoslavia was a federation of republics, actual power was exercised by the central Communist Party. The Communist government *nationalized* (assumed ownership of) industry, beginning with the confiscation of the property of Nazi collaborators in November 1944. The Communist leadership also transferred control of farms, farm equipment, and livestock to the government. Central planning was introduced, as were ambitious goals for rapid industrialization.

Tito's brand of communism

In 1948, Tito broke with Soviet dictator Joseph Stalin over Communist ideology and managed to hold the Soviet Union at arm's length until the Yugoslav leader died in 1980. Freed of Russian influence, Tito developed a new model of socialism that gave the diverse people of Yugoslavia some sense of shared statehood. Yugoslavs were allowed greater freedom to debate and discuss unorthodox ideas than people in most other Communist countries. The Yugoslav government also made innovations in the economic realm, including worker self-management and the introduction of certain elements of the free-market economy. In the area of foreign policy, Yugoslavia positioned itself between the two Cold War superpowers, the Soviet Union and the United States.

Decentralization was a key element of the Tito's new model of the Communist state. Beginning in the 1960's, the Yugoslav central Communist Party began sharing power with party leaders at the level of the six republics by delegating certain decisions regarding the economy. In late 1960's and early 1970's, Tito attempted to rein in growing *nationalism* (a people's sense of belonging together as a nation) within the six republics by reasserting central control at the federal level, but it was too late. Amendments to the constitution made in 1971 and a new consti-

Serbian President Slobodan Milosevic (far left), addresses the Communist Party of Serbia in 1992. Milosevic had the support of most Serbs in Serbia as well as in Croatia and Bosnia during the civil wars. Milosevic was elected president of Yugoslavia in 1997, which by then consisted only of Serbia and Montenegro (left). Vojvodina in the north and Kosovo in the south were provinces of Serbia.

The People of Yugoslavia in 1991*

Republic			Republic		
Bosnia-Herzegovina		**4,365,639**	**Serbia**		**9,721,177**
Muslim	44%		*Serbia proper*		*5,753,825*
Serb	33%		Serb	96%	
Croat	17%		Muslim	2%	
Other	6%		Other	1%	
Croatia		**4,703,941**	*Kosovo province*		*1,954,747*
Croat	75%		Albanian	83%	
Serb	15%		Serb	13%	
Other	10%		Other	4%	
Macedonia		**2,033,964**	*Vojvodina province*		*2,012,605*
Macedonian	64%		Serb	70%	
Albanian	21%		Hungarian	22%	
Serb	5%		Croat	5%	
Turk	5%		Romanian	3%	
Other	5%		**Slovenia**		**1,974,839**
			Slovene	91%	
Montenegro		**616,327**	Croat	3%	
Serb	90%		Serb	3%	
Albanian	4%		Other	3%	
Other	6%				

* From *Yugoslav Survey*, XXXII (March 1990-91),

tution adopted in 1974 increased the power of the republics at the expense of the federation.

The rise of Milosevic

The federation began to unravel after Tito's death. A global economic recession in the 1980's intensified Yugoslavia's economic problems, which included severe inflation, and contributed to growing dissatisfaction in many parts of the country. The economic gap that had long existed between the developed republics, such as Croatia and Slovenia, and the less developed republics, such as Macedonia and Montenegro, grew wider, and more economic resources were diverted from the developed to the undeveloped republics. This fueled resentment, particularly in Croatia and Slovenia. The government attempted to introduce

The wars in Yugoslavia

Where fighting occurred	When fighting began	Who fought whom	When fighting ended
Slovenia (1991)	Slovenia declares independence from Yugoslavia on June 25, 1991.	Serb-led Yugoslav National Army versus Slovenians.	The Yugoslav National Army retreats in late June after failing to crush Slovenia's independence movement.
Croatia (1991-1995)	Croatia declares independence from Yugoslavia on June 25, 1991.	Serb-led Yugoslav National Army and Croatian Serbs versus Croatians.	UN Protection Force places 14,000 peacekeeping troops in Croatia in early 1992. Croat offensives in 1995 recapture most Serb-held Croatian territory.
Bosnia-Herzegovina (1992-1995)	Serbian forces begin siege of Sarajevo in March 1992, after Bosnia's Muslims and Croats vote for independence in a referendum boycotted by the Serbs.	Serb-led Yugoslav National Army and Bosnian Serbs versus Bosnian Croats and Muslims; fighting occurs between Muslims and Croats between January 1993 and March 1994.	A cease-fire goes into effect in October 1995. Peace talks in Dayton, Ohio, in November produce the Dayton Peace Agreement. NATO peacekeeping forces arrive in Bosnia in December 1995.
Kosovo province of Serbia (1998-1999); Serbia proper (1999)	Serbia launches a crackdown against ethnic Albanian protesters in March 1998. NATO begins air strikes in Serbia in March 1999, after Yugoslavia ignores repeated international warnings to end ethnic cleansing operations in Kosovo.	Serb paramilitary forces and Serb-led Yugoslav National Army versus ethnic Albanians; NATO versus government of Yugoslav President Slobodan Milosevic.	NATO suspends bombing campaign on June 10, 1999, after Milosevic agrees to pull Serb troops out of Kosovo. NATO peacekeeping force enters Kosovo as Yugoslav National Army withdraws.

free-market reforms in order to relieve the faltering economy.

In Serbia, in 1987, a young politician named Slobodan Milosevic took control of the Communist Party by ousting a former political mentor. Milosevic had entered politics in 1984 and had swiftly risen through party ranks. Rather than developing relationships within the party, the usual route for advancement, Milosevic had preached ultranationalism to build a following among the Serb people. As head of the party, Milosevic strongly opposed any effort to strengthen Yugoslavia's ailing economy through reforms that undermined traditional Communism principles, particularly state control of the economy. In 1989, the Serbian assembly handed the presidency of Serbia to Milosevic after removing the sitting president from office.

Communism collapses

The Communist government in Yugoslavia, which had managed to keep rivalries among nationality groups largely under control, collapsed in 1990, in the wake of the democratic movement then sweeping across eastern Europe. At a party congress in January 1990, the Slovene delegates, frustrated by Serb opposition to their attempts to reform the Communist Party, walked out. When the Croatian delegates refused to continue without the participation of the Slovenes, the party's control over the national government of Yugoslavia was effectively over. Nationwide elections in April 1990 resulted in non-Communist government in 4 of the 6 republics. Only the voters of Montenegro and Serbia reelected the Communists, now renamed Socialists. Slobodan Milosevic was reelected president of Serbia.

Conflict between Serb, Slovene, and Croatian leaders increased. Serb President Milosevic insisted on a strong, centralized federal government, which the newly elected leaders of Slovenia and Croatia rejected. Leaders in both republics threatened to declare independence. The Yugoslav National Army, which was dominated by Serbs, supported Milosevic, and federal army commanders warned Slovenia and Croatia that they were prepared to use military force to preserve the federation.

On June 25, 1991, Slovenia and Croatia declared their independence from the federation. Leaders of the breakaway republics demanded a looser confederation consisting of essentially independent states. Milosevic responded by declaring that he would accept the breakup of the Yugoslav federation only if all Serb-inhabited areas, especially those in Croatia, were incorporated into Serbia. Slovenia, which did not have a sizable Serb population, was able to assert its independence relatively painlessly. But Milosevic was less inclined to allow Croatia to leave the Yugoslav federation, and the restrictive policies of the Croatian government against Serbs in Croatia provided a convenient pretext for intervention.

War in Croatia
In the summer of 1991, sporadic violence between Serbs and Croats in Croatia escalated to full-scale civil war. As the conflict deepened, most of the Yugoslav army sided with the Serbs, who instituted a policy of "ethnic cleansing," or the forced eviction of people from their houses and, in some cases, murder of civilians. The policy resulted in massive numbers of refugees and atrocities on both sides of the conflict. By the end of 1991, Croatian Serbs and Yugoslav National Army troops controlled about a third of Croatian territory.

In January 1992, a cease-fire agreement proposed by U.S. envoy Cyrus Vance went into effect, and the United Nations (UN) sent troops into Croatia to keep the peace. Hostilities between Croats and Serbs in Croatia, however, continued to flare sporadi-

Hundreds of victims of the Bosnian Serbs's 1992-1995 seige of Sarajevo, the Bosnian capital, are buried in a makeshift graveyard outside the walls of the city's Olympic Stadium, site of the 1984 Winter Olympics.

cally over the next two years, and Croatia steadfastly resisted any permanent peace plans that required it to surrender territory or join a reconstituted Yugoslav federation. In May and August 1995, the Croatian army launched major offensives and recaptured most of the areas that had been held by Serbia. In January 1998, Croatia regained eastern Slavonia, an area that borders Serbia.

War in Bosnia-Herzegovina

As armed conflict raged in Croatia in 1991, the fragile political agreement among Muslims, Serbs, and Croats in Bosnia-Herzegovina began to unravel. Bosnian Muslim and Croatian leaders favored independence. Bosnian Serb leaders wanted to remain within the Yugoslav federation. In September 1991, the Yugoslav National Army occupied key positions in Bosnia on the pretext of protecting the Bosnian Serb population.

In March 1992, a large majority of Bosnians voted for independence in a referendum boycotted by Bosnian Serbs. In response to the vote, the Bosnian Serbs declared independence and set up their own legislature. They then laid siege to the Bosnian capital, Sarajevo, shelling the city with heavy artillery placed in the surrounding mountains. Well-armed Serb paramilitary units and the Yugoslav National Army went on the offensive, and by the end of spring 1992, Serb forces controlled more than 60 percent of Bosnia-Herzegovina.

A Serb security officer patrols a burning village in Kosovo in March 1999. Serbia sent police and army reinforcements into Kosovo to eliminate the Kosovo Liberation Army (KLA), which had stepped up its guerrilla attacks against Serb forces in 1997 and 1998.

Attempts by various international agencies to achieve a political settlement in Bosnia failed, but the threat of international military intervention pushed President Milosevic of Serbia into withdrawing Yugoslav National Army troops from Bosnia. The army, however, left weapons and supplies in the hands of the Bosnian Serbs. As 1992 progressed, violence between Muslim and Bosnian Croatian forces on the one hand, and Bosnian Serbs on the other, escalated. Ethnic cleansing by Bosnian Serbs forced many Muslim and Croatian citizens out of their houses. Many educated Muslims in Bosnia were massacred in the streets or shipped to detention camps where they were killed. Bosnian Muslim and Croatian forces in Bosnia retaliated by committing atrocities against Serb civilians.

To complicate matters, the Bosnian Muslims and Croats began fighting among themselves in October. This conflict, which continued through 1993, ended in a cease-fire agreement in February 1994. In March, Bosnian Muslim and Croatian leaders met in Washington, D.C., where they formed a Muslim-Croat Federation within Bosnia-Herzegovina.

The Bosnian Serbs, however, refused to consider an international peace plan proposed in mid-1994 and continued to fight. In May and August 1995, NATO bombed Serb targets in Bosnia in retaliation for the repeated Serb shelling of Sarajevo. The NATO strikes combined with the loss in August of territory to the Muslim-Croat alliance finally forced the Bosnian Serbs to the bargaining table in late 1995.

Bosnian, Croat, and Serb representatives met in Dayton, Ohio, to negotiate a peace plan, which was signed in December. The Dayton Accords divided Bosnia into two parts—the Muslim-Croat federation consisting of 51 percent of the country; and a new Bosnian Serb republic with 49 percent. All war refugees were to be allowed to return to their homes, and 60,000 international troops under NATO command were to enter Bosnia to serve as peacekeepers. At the end of 1999, NATO troops remained in Bosnia keeping the peace.

Unrest in Kosovo

While centuries of strained relations have often sparked violence between Serbs and ethnic Albanians in Kosovo, the latest conflict in Kosovo can be traced to Slobodan Milosevic's rise in Serbian politics and to the repressive policies his government adopted regarding Kosovo and its ethnic Albanian majority. Upon becoming president of the Serbian Communist Party in 1987, Milosevic demanded that full control of the autonomous province be restored to Serbia. In 1988, as his policies gained increasing support, Milosevic replaced Communist Party leaders in Kosovo with his own supporters, and in 1990, he pushed the Serbian legislature into amending the constitution to strip Kosovo of its autonomy.

Milosevic's policies toward Kosovo grew out of the significance the province holds in Serb history and folklore. The Ottoman Empire conquered Serbia at the Battle of Kosovo Polje in 1389. Although a defeat, the battle became important in Serbian folklore as a place where Orthodox Christians took a stand against Muslim invaders. Over time, Serbs came to regard Kosovo as their heartland.

Many Serbs fled Kosovo during the period of Ottoman rule, and by the 1700's, the ethnic Albanians had become the majority and, according to legend, the oppressors of the Serbs who remained. Between 1912 and 1913, Serbia captured Kosovo with

Ethnic Albanians flee Kosovo for Macedonia in March 1999, after being driven from their homes by Serb forces. "Ethnic cleansing" in Kosovo made refugees of more than 890,000 ethnic Albanians by mid-1999.

other regions with Serb populations and, eventually, launched a campaign to resettle Serbs in the region. Ethnic Albanians in Kosovo responded by attacking the Serb settlements. Serb police retaliated by imprisoning whole families and seizing and destroying ethnic Albanian property.

When the Serbian legislature in 1989 stripped Kosovo of the autonomy that Tito had granted the province, Kosovo's ethnic Albanian population rioted for six days. Serb police attempting to quell the civil unrest shot and killed numerous civilians.

As war engulfed much of the former Yugoslav federation in the 1990's, Serb rule in Kosovo became more repressive. Milosevic's government placed restrictions on the use of the Albanian language, ordered many ethnic Albanian professionals removed from their jobs, and stepped up police attacks on civilians. Ethnic Albanian Kosovars responded with more demonstrations. When the Serbs used force to break up demonstrations in 1997, the Kosovo Liberation Army (KLA) retaliated by attacking Serb security forces.

Serbia attacks Kosovo

In March 1998, heavily armed Serb police and Yugoslav National Army troops swept into Kosovo on a mission to find and destroy KLA camps. Observers believed that the mission provided the Serbs with a convenient pretext for launching the same ethnic cleansing tactics on the ethnic Albanians that had been employed in Croatia and Bosnia. An international group led by U.S. envoy Richard Holbrooke forged a cease-fire agreement between Serbia and the KLA in October 1998, but the Serbs soon ignored its provisions and continued their ethnic cleansing operations. Between March 1998 and March 1999, an estimated 2,000 ethnic Albanians were killed in Kosovo. Peace talks, held in France in February 1999, broke down when Serb negotiators refused to discuss autonomy for Kosovo or allow NATO-led peacekeeping forces into the province.

Milosevic ignored repeated warnings to end the violence in Kosovo, and NATO on March 24 began bombing Serb military targets in Kosovo. The devastation of war touched Serbia for the first time since the 1991 breakup of the Yugoslav federation.

Serb troops, massed on the borders of Kosovo during the negotiations, responded to the bombings by stepping up attacks on Albanian villages and forcibly expelling ethnic Albanians from the province. Observers reported that the Serbs carried out ethnic cleansing on a scale not seen in Europe since the *Holocaust* (the systematic killing during World War II of 6 million Jews and other people considered undesirable by Germany's Nazi government). An estimated 860,000 ethnic Albanians were driven from Kosovo. Refugees poured into hastily assembled camps in neighboring Albania and Macedonia. Small groups were flown to temporary quarters in Germany, the United States, and other NATO member nations. United Nations officials labeled the situation a humanitarian crisis.

NATO bombings continued until Serb leaders finally agreed

in June to withdraw troops and allow international peacekeeping forces into Kosovo. The peace agreement required the KLA to disarm its troops in several stages by September. NATO became responsible for the security of Kosovo, and the first of approximately 50,000 peacekeeping troops arriving in Kosovo as Serb forces withdrew. Some 3,600 Russian troops also participated as peacekeepers.

The UN and other international organizations provided humanitarian aid, while NATO forces oversaw the return of approximately 720,000 ethnic Albanian refugees. Many returned to houses, or even whole towns, that had been destroyed.

As the ethnic Albanians returned, the Serbs fled. UN officials estimated that some 180,000 Serbs left Kosovo after the NATO bombing ended. Leaders of the approximately 50,000 Serbs who remained demanded an autonomous Serb enclave as protection against ethnic Albanians bent on revenge. Both the Serbs and ethnic Albanians in Kosovo occasionally threatened the fragile peace with sporadic acts of violence against each other and against NATO peacekeeping troops. In September 1999, the KLA officially disbanded. However, many international affairs experts believed that the breakup was more symbolic than real.

International peace-keeping forces under NATO command enter Kosovo in June 1999, after Serbia agreed to withdraw its forces from Kosovo. At year end, NATO troops remained in Kosovo to keep the peace, and Slobodan Milosevic remained president of Yugoslavia.

The aftermath

The war in Kosovo, beyond the loss of life and price in human misery, cost Yugoslavia approximately $64 billion in damages to the country's infrastructure. Yugoslavia's *gross domestic product* (the value of all goods and services produced in a country in a given year) declined by nearly half in 1999, and the country could not count on international aid in order to rebuild. The United Nations, most international organizations, and most Western governments refused to provide aid to Yugoslavia as long as Milosevic—deemed a war criminal by Western leaders and the international war crimes tribunal in The Hague, the Netherlands—remained in power. Serb opposition to Milosevic grew once the bombing stopped and Serb forces had left Kosovo, but Milosevic remained in power at the close of 1999.

The violent breakup of Yugoslavia has been attributed to ancient, deep-seated animosities between ethnic groups. Previous histories of conflict provided a convenient explanation for the hostilities and may have accounted for some of the savagery of the fighting. But in the opinion of some international experts, the disintegration of the Yugoslav nation also reflected an inability or unwillingness among leaders in the post-Tito era to reconcile the priorities and views of the individual republics. As the federal government's power diminished, the power of the leaders within the republics grew and different forces came to the fore. The wave of Serb nationalism that Milosevic manipulated to consolidate his power in Serbia in the mid-1980's stimulated the growth of nationalist sentiments among Serb populations in Croatia, Bosnia-Herzegovina, and Kosovo. Serb disregard for the rights of non-Serbs, in turn, stimulated nationalist responses and insensitivity among members of other ethnic groups. In the end, Serbia's use of violence to gain power forced its neighbors and the international community, through NATO, to respond in kind. For the third time in a century, the people of the former Yugoslav federation knew the horrors of full-scale war—the trauma of dislocation, loss of family members, and disruption of ordinary life. ■ ■ ■

For further reading:

Cohen, Lenard J. *Broken Bonds: The Disintegration of Yugoslavia.* Westview Press, 1993.

Ramet, Sabrina P. *Balkan Babel: Politics, Culture, and Religion in Yugoslavia.* Westview Press, 1992.

Woodward, Susan L. *Balkan Tragedy: Chaos and Dissolution After the Cold War.* Brookings Institute, 1995.

Zimbabwe. President Robert Mugabe faced widespread political unrest in 1999, the result of government corruption, controversy over Zimbabwe's involvement in the civil war in Congo (Kinshasa), and a government crackdown on journalists critical of his government. Zimbabweans also struggled with a record 70-percent inflation rate and a 50-percent unemployment rate.

Journalists tortured. Riot police in the capital, Harare, used tear gas on January 26 to break up a protest by lawyers and journalists against the arrest and torture of Zimbabwean reporters Ray Choto and Mark Chavunduka. Military police had detained the two in mid-January after they reported that 23 army officers had been arrested in December 1998 for plotting to overthrow Mugabe. While in confinement, the men had suffered "sustained, severe torture," according to independent medical reports. On Feb. 6, 1999, Mugabe, who denied the report, called for the resignation of three Supreme Court justices who had opposed the army's actions in the case. Human rights groups widely condemned the Zimbabwean army for the treatment received by the journalists.

Growing opposition. More than 120,000 civil servants, teachers, and physicians joined a nationwide pay strike on June 16, one day after the government imposed a 5-percent wage increase. The workers, who had been negotiating with the government since February 1998, had demanded 25 percent. On June 16, 1999, the strikers returned to work after the Cabinet agreed to continue negotiations. In early November, state-paid physicians and nurses ended a six-week strike after the government promised higher salaries in 2000.

About 20,000 people attended a rally on Sept. 11, 1999, to launch a new opposition party, the Movement for Democratic Change (MDC). Backed by the powerful Zimbabwe Congress of Trade Unions, the MDC announced that it would field candidates in parliamentary elections scheduled for 2000. In 1999, Mugabe's ruling Zimbabwe African National Union-Patriotic Front held 117 of the parliament's 120 elective seats.

Foreign affairs. During 1999, the government deployed some 10,000 Zimbabwean troops in Congo (Kinshasa) to help fight rebels backed by Rwanda and Uganda. Reports of hundreds of Zimbabwean casualties—together with the huge economic burden of the military operation—fueled more popular opposition to Mugabe. Mugabe had sent the soldiers to Congo in mid-1998 without consulting the Zimbabwean parliament.

Nkomo's death. On July 1, 1999, Vice President Joshua Nkomo died of cancer at age 83. Nkomo was known as the "Father of Zimbabwe" for his leadership role in the struggle for independence in 1980. □ Simon Baynham

See also **Africa; Congo (Kinshasa).**

Zoos. New York City's Bronx Zoo celebrated its 100th anniversary in June 1999 with the opening of Congo Gorilla Forest. The 6.5-acre (3-hectare) exhibit, which recreates a Central African rain forest, cost $43 million and includes 300 animals representing 75 species.

Visitors enter the Congo Gorilla Forest through a tunnel built to look like a fallen tree trunk. They pass black-and-white colobus monkeys foraging in trees and rare okapi, the only living relatives of the giraffe. In another panorama, mandrills—baboons with blue, grooved muzzles—scamper in trees and on the ground while De-Brazza's monkeys inhabit the treetops and Red River hogs root about the forest floor. The main attraction of the exhibit are two separate families of western lowland gorillas.

Most of the exhibit's vegetation—15,000 plants of 400 species—is real. In addition, artificial materials were used to create vines, rock outcrops, mudbanks, waterfalls, ponds, and streams. Within the mudbanks, a misting system generates ground fog. Hidden in the gorilla exhibit, an electronically timed feeder stimulates the animals to forage, just as they would in the wild.

The depths of California. The Monterey Bay Aquarium in Monterey, California, premiered the world's first major exhibit of deep-sea creatures—"Mysteries of the Deep"—in March. Most of the 300 animals of more than 40 species have never been exhibited before. All of the animals were taken from the Monterey submarine canyon just off the California coast, many collected from a depth of 3,300 feet (1,006 meters).

The exhibit focuses on three deep-water habitats: steep canyon walls, the mid-water zone, and the canyon floor. Most of the animals are *invertebrates* (animals without backbones), such as king crabs; mushroom corals that trap tiny animals in their feathery tentacles; pompom anemones; feather stars; sea whips; and predatory tunicates with hooded stalks that snap shut to capture prey. Fish on display include ratfish, filetail cat sharks, pallid eelpouts, and Pacific hagfish.

Tunnelvision. The Oceanic Adventures Newport (Kentucky) Aquarium opened in May across the Ohio River from Cincinnati, Ohio. More than 60 salt and freshwater exhibits introduce visitors to 11,000 aquatic animals of 600 species. Several galleries featuring acrylic underwater tunnels allow visitors to get unusually close to the wildlife.

One of the five underwater tunnels runs through a habitat that resembles the Amazon River. Visitors in the tunnel are surrounded by 1,100 fish. Another passage runs through a coral reef inhabited by such exotic creatures as emperor angelfish. At the "Surrounded by Sharks" exhibit, the longest tunnel—84 feet (26 meters) in length—winds through a 380,000-gallon (1.4-million-liter) tank. More than 25 sharks, including nurse, sand-tiger, and sandbar sharks—some 9 feet (3 meters) long—swim amid 2,200 tropical fish, including barracudas, above, below, and around visitors.

One of the most popular exhibits is a gallery where visitors can watch king penguins. The penguin habitat includes icy white mountains, frigid water, and twice-a-day snowstorms.

Tale of two rivers. Another new aquarium, Ocean Journey, opened in Denver, Colorado, in June with more than 15,000 animals representing 300 species. Ocean Journey simulates treks along two rivers that empty into the Pacific Ocean—the Colorado River in North America and the Kampar River on the Indonesian island of Sumatra.

The Colorado River trail begins with the Colorado's birth in the Rocky Mountains, then travels through wetlands, deep sandstone canyons, and hot, arid desert until it reaches the Gulf of California, an arm of the Pacific Ocean. Visitors encounter wildlife adapted to various freshwater environments—fish, river otters, waterfowl, and amphibians—and ocean creatures, such as sea horses and moray eels. The final stop is a California cove sheltering endangered southern sea otters.

Along the Indonesian trail, the Kampar River plunges down steep mountainsides to misty rain forests. As visitors walk through the warm, humid air, they see mountain caves inhabited by bats, ponds filled with freshwater tropical fish, and a lush forest, the domain of Sumatran tigers. The trail continues through a mangrove forest and a coral lagoon and ends in a South China Sea coral reef populated by sharks and colorful fish.

The seas of Texas. In June, a new aquarium containing more than 10,000 animals opened at Moody Gardens in Galveston, Texas. Housed in a 10-story, blue-glass pyramid, the facility highlights four major oceanic regions. The North Pacific gallery features fur seals, sea urchins, sea anemones, and a kelp forest. The Tropical Pacific exhibit simulates Australia's Great Barrier Reef and the Coral Sea and houses 200 tropical fish species. In the Edge of the Antarctic gallery, a replica of the rocky beaches of South Georgia Island is home to some 40 king penguins, raised from eggs by the aquarium staff. In the largest exhibit, visitors walk through an acrylic tunnel that provides panoramic views of such Caribbean Sea species as angelfish, damselfish, moray eels, puffers, sharks, and stingrays.

Goodwill ambassador dies. Hsing Hsing, a giant panda, died at Washington, D.C.'s Smithsonian National Zoo on Nov. 28, 1999, at the age of 28. The panda was one of a pair presented to U.S. President Richard Nixon during his trip to China in 1972. ☐ Eugene J. Walter, Jr.

A western lowland gorilla surveys its new home, the Congo Gorilla Forest, at New York City's Bronx Zoo. The exhibit, which opened in June 1999, recreates a Central African rain forest and features 300 animals and 15,000 plants native to equatorial Africa.

Index

How to use the index

This index covers the contents of the 1999 and 2000 editions.

R

Red Brigades (group), **00:** 396
Redington, Joe, **00:** 164
Reed, Oliver, **00:** 164
Reese, Pee Wee, **00:** 163 (il.), 164
Reform Party: Canada, **00:** 116; U.S., **00:** 340, 354
Refugees: African, **00:** 38, 362; Asian, **00:** 65–66; Cuban, **00:** 156; Kosovar, **00:** 48, 83–84, 107, 198, 254–255, 283, 416, 433, 435, 441–445; Switzerland referendum, **00:** 388; U.S. rules, **00:** 235; World War II, **00:** 387–388
Reich, Steve, **00:** 139
Reichstag (Berlin), **00:** 54, 113, 215 (il.)
Richard III (film), **00:** 278
Rock music. See **Popular music**
RUGBY FOOTBALL, **00:** 357, **99:** 357; Australia, **00:** 83
Ruiz Massieu, Jose Francisco, **00:** 291
Rushdie, Salman, **00:** 268
Russell, David O., **00:** 311
Russell 2000 index, **00:** 382
RUSSIA, **00:** 358–360, **99:** 358–361; archaeology, **00:** 51; ballet, **00:** 159; chess, **00:** 129; Eastern Orthodox Church, **00:** 172–173; facts in brief, **00:** 65; ice skating, **00:** 234, 235; Kosovo conflict, **00:** 198, 433; Mandela visit, **00:** 370; space program, **00:** 371, 372; other references, **00:** 46, 92, 102, 205, 213, 407. See also **Chechnya; Terrorism; Union of Soviet Socialist Republics**
Ruth, Babe, **00:** 95
RWANDA, **99:** 361; facts in brief, **00:** 41; other references, **00:** 42, 141, 147, 407
Ryan, Nolan, **00:** 97
Ryder Cup, **00:** 217

S

Safeco Field (Seattle), **00:** 111, 112 (il.)
Safety. See **Public health and safety**
Salt Lake City (Utah), **00:** 178, 430
Samoa, **00:** 328; facts in brief, **00:** 327
Sampras, Pete, **00:** 395
San Andreas Fault, **00:** 213
San Antonio Spurs, **00:** 100
SAN FRANCISCO, **00:** 360–361, **99:** 361–362; elections, **00:** 178
Sara Lee Corp., **00:** 205
Sarajevo (Yugoslavia), **00:** 441 (il.), 442, 443
Sarazen, Gene, **00:** 164
Sargent, John Singer, **00:** 60 (il.)
Sarkisian, Vazgen, **00:** 395
Saskatchewan, **00:** 126
Sassou-Nguesso, Denis, **00:** 42
Satcher, David, **00:** 290, 420–421, **99:** 331
Satellites, Artificial, **00:** 370, 373, 390, 391
Satellites, Planetary, **00:** 67
Saturn (car), **00:** 86

Each index entry gives the edition year and the page number or numbers—for example, **Reed, Oliver, 00: 164.** This means that information on this person may be found on page 164 of the 2000 edition.

When there are many references to a topic, they are grouped alphabetically by clue words under the main topic. For example, the clue words under **Refugees** group the references to that topic under several subtopics.

The "see" and "see also" cross-references—for example, **Rock music**—refer the reader to other entries in the index or to Update articles in the volumes covered by the index.

When a topic such as **Russia** appears in all capital letters, this means that there is an Update article entitled Russia in at least one of the two volumes covered by this index. References to the topic in other articles may also appear after the topic name.

When only the first letter of a topic, such as **Ryder Cup,** is capitalized, this means that there is no article entitled Ryder Cup but that information on this topic may be found in the edition and on the pages listed.

The indication (il.) means that the reference on this page is to an illustration only, as in the picture of **Sarajevo** on page 441 of the 2000 edition.

A

ABC. See American Broadcasting Cos.
Abdullah II, 00: 253–254, 332
Abernathy, Ralph, 00: 225 (il.)
Abkhazia (region), 00: 213
Aborigines, 00: 80–81
Abortion, 00: 178, 385
Abubakar, Abdulsalam, 00: 38, 322
Abul-Muhsin, 00: 431
Academy Awards, 00: 313, 333, 335, 339
Accidents. See Disasters; Public health and safety
Aceh province (Indonesia), 00: 241
Acela (train), 00: 404
Acquired immunodeficiency syndrome. See AIDS
Adamkus, Valdas, 00: 282, 99: 324
Adams, Alice, 00: 160
Adams, Joey, 00: 160
Adams, John (composer), 00: 138
Addiction. See Drug abuse
Aden-Abyan Islamic Army, 00: 431
Adler, Kim, 00: 107
Admiral's Cup (boating), 00: 106
Advertising, 00: 123, 284
Aerospatiale Matra S.A. (company), 00: 211, 217
Aerotrain, 00: 405 (il.)
AFGHANISTAN, 00: 38, 99: 38; facts in brief, 00: 64; other references, 00: 62, 293, 395–396
AFRICA, 00: 38–44, 99: 39–43; AIDS, 00: 44, 47; cities, 00: 134; conservation, 00: 147–149
African Americans: civil rights, 00: 224–225, 228–231; hate crimes, 00: 154–155; prison, 00: 348; television, 00: 392
African National Congress, 00: 38, 367–370
Agassi, Andre, 00: 394, 395
AGRICULTURE, 00: 45–47, 99: 44–45. See also Food
Agriculture, U.S. Department of, 00: 45
Aguire-Aguire, Juan Annibal, 00: 235
Ahern, Bertie, 00: 247
Ahtisaari, Martti, 00: 198, 205
Ai, 00: 343
Aida (musical), 00: 399
AIDS, 00: 47, 99: 45–46; Africa, 00: 44, 47; France, 00: 210
Ainsworth, Mary D., 00: 160
Air Canada Centre (Toronto), 00: 400
Air pollution. See Environmental pollution
Airbags, 00: 89
Airports: Athens, 00: 111; Dallas, 00: 157; Miami, 00: 292
Aitken, Jonathan, 00: 414
Al-Bashir, Umar, 00: 382
Al-Mehdar, Zein al-Abideen, 00: 431
Alabama, statistics, 00: 379
Alarcon Rivera, Fabian, 00: 263
Alaska, 00: 122, 220, 378; statistics, 00: 379
Alawi dynasty, 00: 296
ALBANIA, 00: 48, 99: 46–47; facts in brief, 00: 200; refugees, 00: 433
Albanians, Kosovar, 00: 48, 198, 255, 283, 433, 435, 443–445
Alberta, 00: 123–124
Albright, Madeleine Korbel, 00: 114, 388, 424
Albuquerque (New Mexico), 00: 137
Alcestis (Euripides), 00: 343
Alcohol abuse, 00: 171
Alda, Alan, 00: 392
Aldrin, Edwin E., Jr., 00: 372
Alexander, Lamar, 00: 353
Alexei II, Patriarch, 00: 172–173
ALGERIA, 00: 49, 99: 47–48; facts in brief, 00: 40; Middle East history, 00: 298, 302, 308; population growth, 00: 306; terrorism, 00: 395; unemployment, 00: 307
All-Africa Games, 00: 44
Alliance of Small Island States, 00: 195
Allied Pilots Association, 00: 258–259
Almutawakel (horse), 00: 223
Alphabet, Ancient, 00: 51
Alpher, Ralph, 00: 75
Alps, 00: 86, 171, 251, 427
Altruism, in animals, 00: 104
Amarjargal, Rinchinnyamin, 00: 66
Amazon: languages, 00: 264; rain forest, 00: 149
Amazon.com (company), 00: 401–402
Ambon Island (Indonesia), 00: 241
America West Airlines, 00: 259
American Airlines, 00: 90–92, 157, 258–259, 263
American Airlines Center (Dallas), 00: 157
American Beauty (film), 00: 311
American Broadcasting Cos., 00: 391–393
American Football Conference, 00: 209
American Health (magazine), 00: 284

American Indian Religious Freedom Act (U.S., 1978), 00: 232
American Institute of Architects, 00: 54
American Library Association, 00: 265, 266, 281
American Postal Workers Union, 00: 258
American Society for Landscape Architects, 00: 212
Americans with Disabilities Act (U.S., 1990), 00: 167, 383
Ameritech, 00: 390
AMFM Inc., 00: 352
Amman (Jordan), 00: 253
Ammiano, Tom, 00: 360–361
Amnesty International, 00: 134, 314
Amparano, Julie, 00: 321
Amtrak, 00: 404
Amy's View (Hare), 00: 397
Anderson, Ross "Rocky," 00: 178
Andorra, facts in brief, 00: 200
Andreotti, Giulio, 00: 251
Angola, 00: 42, 141; facts in brief, 00: 40
Anheuser Busch Companies, Inc., 00: 264
Animals: abuse, 00: 310; altruism, 00: 104; endangered, 00: 147–150; research, 00: 289, 290.
  See also Biology; Fossils
Animation (film), 00: 312
Annan, Kofi A., 00: 42, 246, 295, 348, 416
"Another World" (TV show), 00: 394
Antarctica, 00: 212, 319–320
ANTHROPOLOGY, 00: 49–50, 99: 48–49
Anti-Semitism, 00: 214
Antiballistic Missile Treaty (1972), 00: 360
Antibiotics, 00: 171
Antigua and Barbuda, 00: 431; facts in brief, 00: 262
Antley, Chris, 00: 222
Antoinette Perry Awards. See Tony Awards
Antona, Massimo d', 00: 396
Anwar Ibrahim, 00: 284
Apartheid, 00: 369
Apfel, Kenneth S., 00: 366
Apollo program, 00: 371, 372
Apple Computer, Inc., 00: 140
Aquariums. See Zoos
Aquino, Corazon, 00: 341
Arab League, 00: 301, 308
Arabs, 00: 296–309. See also Islam; Middle East; Palestinians
Arafat, Yasir, 00: 114, 248, 304, 305
ARCHAEOLOGY, 00: 51–53, 99: 49–50
Archaeoraptor liaoningensis (dinosaur), 00: 330
Archean Eon, 00: 213
Archer, Jeffrey, 00: 410–411
ARCHITECTURE, 00: 53–54, 99: 50–52; landscape design, 00: 212. See also Building and construction
Argana, Luis Maria, 00: 332
ARGENTINA, 00: 55–56, 99: 52–53; agriculture, 00: 45; air crash, 00: 168; facts in brief, 00: 262; other references, 00: 56, 263, 264
Argument, The (dance), 00: 158
Arias Cruz, Jacinto, 00: 292
Aris, Michael, 00: 314
Aristotle, 00: 70–73
Arizona, statistics, 00: 379
Arizona, University of, 00: 206
Arizona Republic, 00: 321
Arkansas, 00: 380, 427; statistics, 00: 379
ARMED FORCES, 00: 56–59, 99: 53–63; other references, 00: 351, 386. See also Defense, U.S. Department of
Armed Forces of National Liberation (group), 00: 351, 422
Armed Forces Revolutionary Council (Sierra Leone), 00: 362
Armed Islamic Group, 00: 49
ARMENIA, 99: 64; facts in brief, 00: 64; terrorism, 00: 395
Armstrong, Lance, 00: 332, 375, 376 (il.)
Armstrong, Neil A., 00: 372
Army, U.S., 00: 283. See also Armed forces
Army Corps of Engineers (U.S.), 00: 196
Arnault, Bernard, 00: 204
Arnett, James, 00: 310
Arnulfista Party (Panama), 00: 337–338
Around Alone race, 00: 106
ART, 00: 59–61, 99: 64–66
Art of Happiness, The (book), 00: 109–111
"Arthur" (TV program), 00: 266
Arthur, Owen, 00: 431
Asbrink, Erik, 00: 385–386
Ashbrook, Larry, 00: 155

Ashby, Richard, 00: 58
Ashdown, Paddy, 00: 411
Ashley, Maurice, 00: 129
ASIA, 00: 62–66, 99: 66–70; cities, 00: 134; cyclone, 00: 430; financial crisis, 00: 62, 173, 242, 99: 170–179
Asia-Pacific Economic Co-operation, 00: 317
Asian Americans, 00: 155
Asian Development Bank, 00: 62
Assad, Hafez al-, 00: 248, 304, 388
Association of Caribbean States, 00: 431
Association of Professional Flight Attendants, 00: 259
Association of Southeast Asian Nations, 00: 62–64, 115
Assoumani, Azaly, 00: 44
Astrodome (Houston), 00: 223
Astronauts. See Space exploration
ASTRONOMY, 00: 66–79, 99: 71–72
Astros, Houston, 00: 223
AT&T Corp., 00: 391
Athens (Greece), 00: 168, 218
Athens International Airport, 00: 111
Atlanta (Georgia), 00: 155
Atlanta Braves, 00: 95–97
Atlanta Falcons, 00: 209
Atlanta Journal-Constitution, 00: 321
Atlantic Ocean, 00: 321
Atler, Vanessa, 00: 375
Atom, Splitting of, 00: 342
Atomic bomb, 00: 252
Atomic energy. See Nuclear energy
Auctions: Marilyn Monroe, 00: 320; online, 00: 243
Aung San Suu Kyi, Daw, 00: 314
Auschwitz (Poland), 00: 344
AUSTRALIA, 00: 80–85, 99: 72–77; agriculture, 00: 45, 46; Asian refugees, 00: 66; cricket, 00: 152, 153; facts in brief, 00: 64, 327; population growth, 00: 306; rugby, 00: 357; unemployment, 00: 307
AUSTRALIA, PRIME MINISTER OF, 00: 85, 99: 77. See also Howard, John
AUSTRALIAN RULES FOOTBALL, 00: 85, 99: 78
Australopithecus (hominid), garhi, 00: 50
AUSTRIA, 00: 86, 99: 78; facts in brief, 00: 200; Nazi art looting, 00: 60, 61; other references, 00: 157, 205, 363
Austria-Hungary, 00: 435
Author's Club, 00: 268
Autissier, Isabelle, 00: 106
Autobiography of Alice B. Toklas, The (Stein), 00: 269
Automated teller machines, 00: 178
AUTOMOBILE, 00: 86–89, 99: 78–80; environmental pollution, 00: 196; labor, 00: 259–260; safety, 00: 89, 350
AUTOMOBILE RACING, 00: 89–90, 99: 81
Avalanches, 00: 86, 126, 169, 211, 310, 427
AVIATION, 00: 90–92, 99: 82; labor, 00: 258–259.
  See also Airports; Armed forces; Aviation disasters
Aviation disasters, 00: 91–92; Argentina, 00: 56; EgyptAir, 00: 177, 295; Lockerbie, Scotland, 00: 370, 416; Netherlands, 00: 314
Ayadi, Mohammed, 00: 51 (il.)
Azarian, Mary, 00: 281
AZERBAIJAN, 00: 92, 99: 83; facts in brief, 00: 64; other references, 00: 213, 395
Aznar, Jose Maria, 00: 373
Azores Islands, 00: 168
Aztecs, 00: 187

B

Babbitt, Bruce, 00: 149, 239
Bacteria, 00: 104, 171, 205–206, 350
Baha'i Faith, 00: 299
Bahamas, 00: 430; facts in brief, 00: 262
Bahceli, Devlet, 00: 406
BAHRAIN: facts in brief, 00: 294; population growth, 00: 306; unemployment, 00: 307
Baker, Mount (Washington), 00: 427
Bakersfield (California), 00: 427
Balanchine, George, 00: 158, 159
Balfour Declaration (1917), 00: 299
Balloons, Hot-air, 00: 318
Baltimore (Maryland), 00: 178
Baltimore Orioles, 00: 97, 155, 156 (il.), 375
Banco Bilbao Vizcaya (bank), 00: 373
Banco Santander Central Hispano SA (bank), 00: 348, 373
Bancorex (bank), 00: 356

Bangkok, **00:** 111, 396
BANGLADESH, **00:** 92–93, **99:** 83–84; facts in brief, **00:** 64; other references, **00:** 152, 169, 416
Bangladesh National Party, **00:** 92
BANK, **00:** 94–95, **99:** 84–85; Ecuador, **00:** 175; France, **00:** 210; Japan, **00:** 253; Mexico, **00:** 292; Portugal, **00:** 348; Romania, **00:** 356; Russia, **00:** 358; Spain, **00:** 373; Thailand, **00:** 396; West Indies, **00:** 431
Bank of New York, **00:** 358, 360
Bank Savings Protection Institute, **00:** 292
Banque Nationale de Paris S.A. (bank), **00:** 203, 210
Banzer Suarez, Hugo, **00:** 263
Barak, Ehud, **00:** 114, 248, 249, 254, 265, 305, 333, 388
Barbados, **00:** 431; facts in brief, **00:** 262
Barkley, Charles, **00:** 374
Barmasai, Bernard, **00:** 404
Barnum's Kaleidoscape (show), **00:** 320–321
Bart, Lionel, **00:** 160
Barton, Mark, **00:** 155
Baryshnikov, Mikhail, **00:** 158
BASEBALL, **00:** 95–99, **99:** 86–88; Houston, **00:** 223; other references, **00:** 374, 375. See also **Cuba**
Baseball Hall of Fame, **00:** 97
BASF (company), **00:** 420
BASKETBALL, **00:** 100–102, **99:** 89–91; other references, **00:** 223–224, 374–375
Basketball Hall of Fame, **00:** 101
Basque Homeland and Freedom (group), **00:** 373, 396
Basques, **00:** 373, 396
Basri, Driss, **00:** 295
Bataan Death March (1942), **00:** 341
Bates, Daisy, **00:** 160
Batlle, Jorge, **00:** 423
Baumann, Michael, **00:** 292
Bayne, Beverly, **00:** 276 (il.)
Beaches Environmental Awareness, Cleanup and Health Act (U.S., 1999), **00:** 146, 147
Beatles, **00:** 347
Beauty and the Beast (musical), **00:** 399
Beck, Allen J., **00:** 348
Beef, **00:** 47, 414–415
Beethoven, Ludwig van, **00:** 158–159
Beetles, Asian long-horned, **00:** 212
Begin, Menachim, **00:** 305
Begum Zia. See **Khaleda Ziaur Rahman**
Beijing, **00:** 131, 419 (il.)
Being John Malkovich (film), **00:** 311
Beipiaosaurus inexpectus (dinosaur), **00:** 330
Beirut (Lebanon), **00:** 247
BELARUS, **00:** 102–103, **99:** 92; facts in brief, **00:** 200; stampede, **00:** 171
Belfast (Northern Ireland), **00:** 324
BELGIUM, **00:** 103–104, **99:** 92–93; Coca-Cola recall, **00:** 350; facts in brief, **00:** 200
Belgrade (Yugoslavia), **00:** 133, 360, 437
Belize, facts in brief, **00:** 262
Belladonna (Rands), **00:** 138
Bellow, Saul, **00:** 266
Benavides, Ted, **00:** 157
Benigni, Roberto, **00:** 313 (il.), 314, 333
Benin, facts in brief, **00:** 40
Benzinger, Theodor H., **00:** 160
Beowulf, **00:** 343
Berbers, **00:** 298
Berenger, Paul, **00:** 288
Berezhnaya, Yelena, **00:** 235
Berger, Oscar, **00:** 219
Berio, Luciano, **00:** 138
Berlin, **00:** 111–113, 216
Berlin Philharmonic Orchestra, **00:** 138
Berlin Wall, **00:** 216, 217
Berry, Shawn, **00:** 225
Bertelli, Angelo, **00:** 160
Betancourt, Rigoberto Herrerra, **00:** 375
Bezos, Jeff, **99:** 324–325
Bharatiya Janata Party (India), **00:** 220, 235, 236, 238
Bhattarai, Krishna Prasad, **00:** 66
BHP (company), **00:** 83
Bhutan, **00:** 238; facts in brief, **00:** 64
Bhutto, Benazir, **00:** 329
Big bang, **00:** 75–79
"Bill of rights" (health care), **00:** 146, 219
Bin Laden, Osama, **00:** 38, 293, 382, 396
Biographies. See **Deaths; People in the news**
Biological weapons. See **Chemical and biological weapons**

BIOLOGY, **00:** 104–106, **99:** 93–94
Biotic Baking Brigade (group), **00:** 361
Biped (dance), **00:** 158
Birch, Ric, **00:** 83
Bird, Lester, **00:** 431
Bird, Vere C., **00:** 431
Birth rate. See **Census; Population**
Birthday Letters (Hughes), **00:** 268
Bison, **00:** 150, 240
Black Americans. See **African Americans**
Black Pearls of Micronesia (company), **00:** 328
Blackmun, Harry A., **00:** 160, 385
Blair, Tony, **00:** 324, 408, 411–415, **99:** 428
Blair Witch Project, The (film), **00:** 313–314
Blissful Hall (horse), **00:** 222–223
Blizzard of One (Strand), **00:** 343
Blizzards, **00:** 169, 427, 428 (il.)
Blobel, Gunter, **00:** 323
Bloc Quebecois (party, Canada), **00:** 116
Blue Room, The (Hare), **00:** 396–397
Blues, Carlton (team), **00:** 85
Boat people, **00:** 65–66
BOATING, **00:** 106, **99:** 95
Bobbyjo (horse), **00:** 223
Bochco, Steven, **00:** 392
Boeing, Inc., **00:** 259
Boesak, Allan, **00:** 370
Bogarde, Dirk, **00:** 160, 164 (il.)
Bogota (Colombia), **00:** 139, 140
Bohn, Parker, III, **00:** 107
Boivin, Pierre, **00:** 310
Bolcom, William, **00:** 138
Boldon, Ato, **00:** 403 (il.)
BOLIVIA: facts in brief, **00:** 262; human rights, **00:** 263
Bologna (Italy), **00:** 250
Bolton, Terrell, **00:** 157
Bombings. See **Terrorism**
Bonds. See **Stocks and bonds**
Bonn (Germany), **00:** 216
Booker Prize, **00:** 268
Books. See **Literature, American; Literature, World; Literature for children; Poetry**
Booth, Cherie, **00:** 415
Borges, Jorge Luis, **00:** 269
Bose-Einstein condensate, **00:** 342
BOSNIA-HERZEGOVINA, **00:** 106–107, **99:** 96; facts in brief, **00:** 200; Yugoslavia history, **00:** 435–443, 446; other references, **00:** 56, 119, 360
Boston Symphony Orchestra, **00:** 338–339
BOTSWANA, **99:** 96; facts in brief, **00:** 40
Bouchard, Lucien, **00:** 116, 118
Boulemia, Fouad, **00:** 49
Boutefitka, Abdelaziz, **00:** 49
Bouterse, Desi, **00:** 263
Bovine spongiform encephalopathy, **00:** 414–415
Bowdler, Thomas, **00:** 273
Bowl Championship Series, **00:** 206
Bowles, Paul, **00:** 160
BOWLING, **00:** 107, **99:** 97
BoxCar Willie, **00:** 160
BOXING, **00:** 107–108, **99:** 97–98
Brack, Kenny, **00:** 89
Bracks, Steve, **00:** 83, 84
Bradley, A. C., **00:** 274–275
Bradley, Bill, **00:** 166–167, 333–334
Bradley, Marion Zimmer, **00:** 160
Bradshaw, Claudette, **00:** 400
Braille (asteroid), **00:** 371 (il.)
Branch Davidians (group), **00:** 419
BRAZIL, **00:** 109, **99:** 98; Amazon destruction, **00:** 149; economy, **00:** 174; facts in brief, **00:** 262; soccer, **00:** 364, 366; other references, **00:** 263, 264, 423
Brcko (Bosnia-Herzegovina), **00:** 106–107
Breast cancer, **00:** 319–320
Bregenz music festival, **00:** 137 (il.)
Breitling Orbiter 3 (balloon), **00:** 318
Brett, George, **00:** 97
Brewer, Lawrence Russell, **00:** 225
British Airways, **00:** 90
British Columbia, **00:** 122, 123, 124, 356
British Library (London), **00:** 265
Broncos, Denver, **00:** 207–209
Bronx Zoo, **00:** 447
Brooklyn Museum of Art (New York City), **00:** 61, 315
Brooks, Garth, **00:** 347
Brown, Gordon, **00:** 414
Brown, Lee, **00:** 223
Brown, Tina, **00:** 284
Brown, Willie L., Jr., **00:** 178, 360–361

Brown v. Board of Education of Topeka, **00:** 228
Browner, Carol, **00:** 196, 197
Browns, Cleveland, **00:** 209
Brundtland, Gro Harlem, **99:** 325
Brunei, **00:** 64, 66; facts in brief, **00:** 64
Bruner/Cott & Associates, **00:** 54
Buchanan, Patrick J., **00:** 353–354
Bucharest (Romania), **00:** 356
Buchenwald (concentration camp), **00:** 216
BUDDHISM, **00:** 109–111, **99:** 99
Budget, Federal. See **Federal budget**
Buenos Aires (Argentina), **00:** 55, 56
Buffalo (New York), **00:** 427
Buffalo Sabres, **00:** 220–221
"Buffy the Vampire Slayer" (TV program), **00:** 393
BUILDING AND CONSTRUCTION, **00:** 111–113, **99:** 99–101; Chicago, **00:** 130. See also **Architecture** and specific country and city articles
BULGARIA, **00:** 113, **99:** 101; EU membership, **00:** 202; facts in brief, **00:** 200
Bulge, Battle of the (1944), **00:** 202
Bullfights, **00:** 310
Bulls, Chicago, **00:** 100–101, 374
Burckhardt, Rudy, **00:** 160
Bureau of Indian Affairs (U.S.), **00:** 239
Bureau of Labor Statistics (U.S.), **00:** 258
Burglary, **00:** 153
Burj Al Arab (building), **00:** 111
Burkina Faso, **00:** 44; facts in brief, **00:** 40
Burlington Northern Santa Fe Corp., **00:** 404
Burma. See **Myanmar**
Burton, Tim, **00:** 311
BURUNDI: facts in brief, **00:** 40; life expectancy, **00:** 44
Bush, George Walker, **00:** 166, 167, 178, 334, 353–354, 380
Bush, Jeb, **00:** 175, 378, 404
Bush, Laura, **00:** 353 (il.)
Bushman, Francis X., **00:** 276 (il.)
Buthelezi, Mangosthu, **00:** 369
Butterflies, Monarch, **00:** 46, 106
Butyrskaya, Mariya, **00:** 234, 235
Bwindi Impenetrable Forest (Uganda), **00:** 147
Byrd, James, Jr., **00:** 225
Byrd, Joe, **00:** 240
Byrdsong, Ricky, **00:** 154–155
Byzantine Empire, **00:** 182–183

C

CABINET, U.S., **00:** 114, **99:** 102
Cabinet (UK), **00:** 415
Cable-car disaster, **00:** 58, 251
Cairo (Egypt), **00:** 308 (il.), 347
Caldecott Medal, **00:** 281
Calgary Stampeders, **00:** 209
Calhoun, Rory, **00:** 160
California, **00:** 150, 212, 378, 383, 431, 447; statistics, **00:** 379. See also **Los Angeles; San Francisco**
Callahan, Harry, **00:** 160
Callaway Gardens (Georgia), **00:** 212
Calvin, Marie-Claude, **00:** 219
Calvino, Italo, **00:** 269
Camara, Helder Pessoa, **00:** 109
Cambridge University, **00:** 376
Cameron, James, **99:** 325
Cameroon, facts in brief, **00:** 40
Camp David Accords (1979), **00:** 305
Campbell, Naomi, **00:** 205
CANADA, **00:** 116–123, **99:** 104–110; agriculture, **00:** 45, 47; cities, **00:** 134; hockey, **00:** 221; population growth, **00:** 306; unemployment, **00:** 260, 307. See also **Montreal; Toronto**
CANADA, PRIME MINISTER OF, **00:** 123, **99:** 111. See also **Chretien, Jean**
Canadian Football League, **00:** 209
Canadian National Railway Co., **00:** 404
CANADIAN PROVINCES, **00:** 123–126, **99:** 111–114
CANADIAN TERRITORIES, **00:** 126–127, **99:** 114
Canadiens, Montreal, **00:** 310
Cancer, **00:** 289, 319–320, 332
Cannibalism, **00:** 50
Cape Verde, facts in brief, **00:** 40
Capital punishment, **00:** 224, 342, 348, 383–385, 431, **99:** 138–145
Carbon dioxide, **00:** 128, 195, 212
Cardenas Solorzano, Cuauhtemoc, **00:** 263
Cardoso, Fernando Henrique, **00:** 109, 264

Care Australia (charity), **00:** 83
Cargill, Inc., **00:** 46
Carl Fischer Music, **00:** 131
Carlton Blues (team), **00:** 85
Carnahan, Mel, **00:** 354–356
Carnegie Corp. of New York, **00:** 265
Carpal-tunnel syndrome, **00:** 260
Carr, Allan, **00:** 160
Carr, Bob, **00:** 83
Carrefour S.A. (company), **00:** 211
Carson, Rachel, **00:** 196
Carter, Anita, **00:** 160
Carter, Jimmy, **00:** 322
Cartoons. See **Animation**
Cartwright, Justin, **00:** 268
Case Corp., **00:** 46
Caspian Sea oil, **00:** 92
Cass, Peggy, **00:** 160, 164 (il.)
Castillo, John, **00:** 224
Castle, The (Kafka), **00:** 269
Castro, Fidel, **00:** 155, 156 (il.)
Caterpillars, **00:** 105–106
Catholic Church. See **Roman Catholic Church**
"Cavallo, II" (sculpture), **00:** 320 (il.)
Cayman Islands, **00:** 431
CBS Corp., **00:** 352, 391–394
Cell (biology), **00:** 323
Cellular Communications of Puerto Rico, Inc.,
  00: 351
CENSUS: Cambodia, **00:** 115. See also **Population**
Census Bureau (U.S.), **00:** 385
Centenarians, **00:** 350
Center of Science and Industry (Columbus, Ohio),
  00: 113
Centers for Disease Control and Prevention
  (U.S.), **00:** 154, 172, 205, 350, 380, 420–421
Central African Republic, **00:** 39; facts in brief, **00:**
  · 40
Central America. See **Latin America**
Central Park (operas), **00:** 138
CEO America (group), **00:** 176
Cervical cancer, **00:** 289
Chad, **00:** 141; facts in brief, **00:** 40
Chaebols (companies), **00:** 257–258
Challenger (eagle), **00:** 148 (il.)
Chamberlain, Wilt, **00:** 160, 162 (il.), 374
Champalimaud (company), **00:** 348
Championship Auto Racing Teams, **00:** 89
Chandrabadu Naidu (party, India), **00:** 236
Charismatic (horse), **00:** 222
Charlemagne, **00:** 183
Charles, Prince, **00:** 362
Charter schools, **00:** 176
Chattanooga Times, **00:** 321
Chaudhry, Mahendra, **00:** 220, 327
Chaudhuri, Amit, **00:** 268
Chaudhuri, Nirad C., **00:** 160
Chavez, Hugo, **00:** 263, 334, 423
Chavunduka, Mark, **00:** 447
Chebet, Joseph, **00:** 375–376
Chechnya (Russia), **00:** 358–360, 395
Chee Soon Juan, **00:** 362
Chemical and biological weapons, **00:** 382, **99:**
  56–63
Chemical reactions, **00:** 128
CHEMISTRY, **00:** 128–129, **99:** 115; Nobel Prizes,
  00: 323
Chemotherapy, **00:** 289
Chen Shuibian, **00:** 388
Chernomyrdin, Viktor, **00:** 198, 360
Cherokee Nation, **00:** 240
CHESS, **00:** 129, **99:** 116
Chiang Kai-shek, **00:** 132
Chiapas (Mexico), **00:** 292
CHICAGO, **00:** 129–131, **99:** 116–117; classical
  music, **00:** 138; elections, **00:** 178; schools, **00:**
  136; theater, **00:** 397; weather, **00:** 427, 428
  (il.); other references, **00:** 212, 383
Chicago Bulls, **00:** 100–101, 374
Chicago Cubs, **00:** 339
Chicago Fire (team), **00:** 365
Chicago Housing Authority, **00:** 129
Chick's Beach (boat), **00:** 106
Children: Africa, **00:** 44; diseases, **00:** 350; drug
  abuse, **00:** 171; Iraq, **00:** 246, 416; TV viewing,
  00: 392. See also **Adolescent; Conflicts and vi-
  olence; Education; Literature for children;
  Teen-agers; Welfare**
Children's Health Insurance Program, **00:** 380
Children's Scholarship Fund, **00:** 176
Childs, David, **00:** 53
CHILE, **00:** 131, **99:** 118; facts in brief, **00:** 262;

other references, **00:** 263, 264
Chimpanzees, **00:** 47, 50 (il.)
CHINA, **00:** 131–134, **99:** 118–120; Australia immigration, **00:** 84; Buddhism, **00:** 109, 111; disasters, **00:** 168; espionage case, **00:** 419; facts in
  brief, **00:** 64; paleontology, **00:** 329–330; Panama visa scheme, **00:** 332; soccer, **00:** 364;
  space program, **00:** 372; trade, **00:** 47, 242; Yu-
  goslav embassy bombing, **00:** 133, 419 (il.),
  433; other references, **00:** 62–66, 224, 253,
  283, 388. See also **Hong Kong; Taiwan**
Chiquita Brands International, **00:** 321
Chirac, Jacques, **00:** 126, 210
Chongqing, **00:** 132
Choto, Ray, **00:** 447
Chretien, Jean, **00:** 116, 119, 122–124, 126, 400,
  99: 111
Christian Coalition, **00:** 350
Christian Democratic Party: Germany, **00:** 214;
  Switzerland, **00:** 387
Christian fundamentalism, **00:** 150
Christiana Bank, **00:** 325
Christianity: India, **00:** 220, 236, 237; Indonesia,
  00: 241; Israel, **00:** 249; Middle East, **00:** 299.
  See also **Eastern Orthodox Churches; Protes-
  tantism; Roman Catholic Church**
Chrysler Corp. See **DaimlerChrysler AG**
Chuan Leekpai, **00:** 396
Churchill, Winston, **00:** 193
Ciampi, Carlo, **00:** 251
Cigarettes. See **Tobacco industry**
Cine Cite Montreal (studio), **00:** 310
Circuit Court of Appeals (U.S.), **00:** 196–197
Circus, **00:** 320–321, 399
Citizen Kane (film), **00:** 312
Citizens' Union (Georgia), **00:** 213
CITY, **00:** 134–137, **99:** 120–123; crime, **00:** 153
City of New Orleans (train), **00:** 404
CIVIL RIGHTS: U.S. history, **00:** 226–233. See also
  Human rights
Civil Rights Act (U.S., 1964), **00:** 229, 233
Clark, Glen, **00:** 124
Clark, Joe, **00:** 116
Clark, Wesley, **00:** 59
Clarkson, Adrienne, **00:** 118–119
CLASSICAL MUSIC, **00:** 137–139, **99:** 123–125;
  Pulitzer Prizes, **00:** 351
Clean Air Act (U.S., 1970), **00:** 197
Clear Channel Communications, Inc., **00:** 352
Cleveland (Ohio), **00:** 175
Cleveland Browns, **00:** 209
Cleveland Indians, **00:** 375
Cleveland Orchestra, **00:** 138
Climate, **00:** 330. See also **Global warming;
  Weather**
Climate Modeling Consortium, **00:** 128–129
Clinton, Bill, **00:** 421–423, **99:** 434–435; agricul-
  ture policy, **00:** 45, 47; banking laws, **00:** 94;
  budget surplus, **00:** 417; cabinet, **00:** 114; Canada trade, **00:** 122–123; China trade, **00:** 133;
  crime policy, **00:** 419; Cuba restrictions, **00:**
  155–156; energy policy, **00:** 421; environmental
  issues, **00:** 149, 150, 195, 196; espionage case,
  00: 419; FALN pardons, **00:** 314; film violence
  agreement, **00:** 314; food safety, **00:** 420; governors' meeting, **00:** 380 (il.); Guatemala visit, **00:**
  219; health care policy, **00:** 219, 220; highway
  safety, **00:** 350; impeachment, **00:** 142, 167,
  417; Indian affairs, **00:** 240; mental health policy, **00:** 290; New Zealand visit, **00:** 317; Panama
  Canal transfer, **00:** 331; presidential race, **00:**
  166; smallpox virus preservation, **00:** 288; tax
  policy, **00:** 146, 390, 422; test ban treaty defeat,
  00: 142; urban sprawl remedy, **00:** 136–137;
  welfare policy, **00:** 431; other references, **00:** 53,
  57, 147, 238, 245, 335, 394, 404
Clinton, Hillary Rodham, **00:** 58–59, 167, 317, 417
Clothing. See **Fashion**
Coal, **00:** 125, 195, 197
Coburn, James, **00:** 313 (il.)
Coca-Cola Co., **00:** 104, 193 (il.), 287, 350
Cocaine, **00:** 171
Cockerell, Sir Christopher, **00:** 160
Coetzee, J. M., **00:** 268
Cohen, William S., **00:** 245, 342
Cold War, **00:** 192–193
Coleman, Michael, **00:** 178
Coles, Phil, **00:** 83
Colleges. See **Education**
Collins, Eileen, **00:** 334–335, 371
Collins, Michael, **00:** 372
Colom, Alvaro, **00:** 219

COLOMBIA, **00:** 139–140, **99:** 126; earthquake,
  00: 140, 168; facts in brief, **00:** 262; other ref-
  erences, **00:** 261, 263, 264
Colonialism, Middle East, **00:** 298–304
Colony of Unrequited Dreams, The (Johnston),
  00: 268
Colorado, **00:** 377, 448; Littleton school shoot-
  ings, **00:** 153–154, 176, 378, 392–393; statis-
  tics, **00:** 379
Colorado Party (Uruguay), **00:** 92, 423
Colorado River, **00:** 448
Columbia River, **00:** 356
Columbia University, **00:** 53–54
Columbine High School (Colorado), **00:** 153–154,
  176, 378, 392–393
Columbus, Christopher, **00:** 186
Columbus (Ohio), **00:** 113, 178
Comcast Corp., **00:** 391
Comets, **00:** 372
Comets, Houston, **00:** 101, 223–224
Commerce, U.S. Department of, **00:** 242
Common Market. See **European Union**
Commonwealth of Independent States, **00:** 92,
  213
Commonwealth of Nations, **00:** 38, 322, 328
Communism: China, **00:** 132; containment policy,
  00: 192–193; Cuba, **00:** 155; Vietnam, **00:** 424;
  Yugoslavia, **00:** 437–441
Communist Party: China, **00:** 131, 388; Germany,
  00: 214; Russia, **00:** 358, 359; Ukraine, **00:**
  407; Vietnam, **00:** 424; Yugoslavia, **00:**
  438–441, 443
Community Reinvestment Act (U.S., 1977), **00:**
  94
Commuting time, **00:** 137
Comoros, **00:** 44; facts in brief, **00:** 40
Compact discs, **00:** 179, 346
Compaq Center (Houston), **00:** 223
Comprehensive Test Ban Treaty (1996), **00:** 142
Computer chips, **00:** 140–141
COMPUTERS, **00:** 140–141, **99:** 126–127; books,
  future of, **00:** 266; football championship, **00:**
  206; injuries, **00:** 260; molecular, **00:** 179;
  Shakespeare, **00:** 276; technology stocks, **00:**
  381; Y2K problem, **00:** 173, 287. See also **In-
  ternet**
CONCACAF Champions Cup (soccer), **00:**
  365–366
Cone, David, **00:** 97
Confederate flag, **00:** 224
Confederations Cup (soccer), **00:** 364–365
Configurations: New & Selected Poems (Major),
  00: 343
Conflicts and violence: Afghanistan, **00:** 38; Africa,
  00: 38, 42, 44; Albania, **00:** 49; Algeria, **00:** 49;
  Asia, **00:** 62, 65; Bangladesh, **00:** 92; China, **00:**
  133; Colombia, **00:** 139, 140; Congo (Kinshasa), **00:** 42, 141; Ecuador, **00:** 175; Haiti, **00:**
  219; India, **00:** 220, 237–238; Indonesia, **00:**
  84, 85, 240–241, 416; Iran, **00:** 244; Islamic
  fundamentalism, **00:** 306; Kenya, **00:** 256; Mauritius, **00:** 288; Mexico, **00:** 292; motion pictures, **00:** 314; Northern Ireland, **00:** 324; Pacific Islands, **00:** 327, 328; Paraguay, **00:** 332;
  Romania, **00:** 356; Sierra Leone, **00:** 42, 362;
  South Africa, **00:** 38–42, 368, 369; Spain, **00:**
  373; Sri Lanka, **00:** 377; Turkey, **00:** 406; U.S.
  schools, **00:** 153–154, 176, 378, 392–393, 419;
  Woodstock '99, **00:** 345; World Trade Organization, **00:** 243; Yugoslavia, **00:** 433; Zimbabwe,
  00: 447. See also **Crime; Terrorism**
CONGO (BRAZZAVILLE): conflict, **00:** 42; facts in
  brief, **00:** 40
CONGO (KINSHASA), **00:** 141, **99:** 127–128; conservation threats, **00:** 147, 149; facts in brief,
  00: 40; other references, **00:** 42, 447
Congo Gorilla Forest (exhibit), **00:** 447, 448 (il.)
CONGRESS OF THE UNITED STATES, **00:**
  142–147, **99:** 128–134; armed forces, **00:** 56,
  58; banking, **00:** 94; Cabinet confirmations, **00:**
  114; Canada trade, **00:** 122–123; Clinton impeachment, **00:** 417; environmental pollution,
  00: 195–197; farm aid, **00:** 45; health care, **00:**
  219–220; independent counsel law, **00:** 417;
  Social Security, **00:** 366; sweepstakes promotions, **00:** 284; taxes, **00:** 390, 422; UN dues,
  00: 336–337; other references, **00:** 176, 336
Congress Party (India), **00:** 236
Connecticut, **00:** 377; statistics, **00:** 379
Connecticut, University of, **00:** 101–102
Conrad, Charles "Pete", **00:** 161
Conrail, Inc., **00:** 404

CONSERVATION, 00: 147–150, 99: 134–135; Roman Catholic pastoral, 00: 356
Conservative Party (United Kingdom), 00: 408, 410 411, 415
Constantine I, 00: 182
Constantine IX (il.), 00: 182
Constitution: Australia, 00: 80, 85; China, 00: 132; Kenya, 00: 256; Korea, 00: 258; Philippines, 00: 341; South Africa, 00: 368; Uganda, 00: 407; Venezuela, 00: 423; Yugoslavia, 00: 436, 438–439
Constitution, U.S.: 4th Amendment, 00: 383; 19th Amendment, 00: 227; 24th Amendment, 230. See also Supreme Court of the United States
Construcciones Aeronauticas SA (company), 00: 217
Construction. See Building and construction
Consumer Price Index, 00: 195, 258
Continental Grain, 00: 46
Contraceptives, 00: 261–263
Copa America Championship (soccer), 00: 364
Copa de los Libertadores (soccer), 00: 365
Copernicus, Nicolaus, 00: 71, 72
Coral reefs, 00: 325–326
Corby, Ellen, 00: 161
Corn, 00: 46, 106
Corporate Resources Group, 00: 134
Corrositex (test), 00: 289
Corruption: European Commission, 00: 199; Ireland, 00: 247; Latin America, 00: 263; Mexico, 00: 291; Russia, 00: 358; San Francisco, 00: 361; sports, 00: 374; Thailand, 00: 396; Uganda, 00: 407; Venezuela, 00: 423; Vietnam, 00: 424
Cortes, Hernando, 00: 187
Cosmic Background Explorer (satellite), 00: 79
Cosmic microwave background radiation, 00: 76
Cosmology, 00: 75–79
COSTA RICA, 99: 136; facts in brief, 00: 262
Costello, Peter, 00: 80, 81
Cote d'Ivoire. See Ivory Coast
Couch, Jason, 00: 107
Country music, 00: 347, 353
COURTS, 00: 150–151, 99: 136–145. See also Supreme Court of the United States
Cows on Parade (exhibit), 00: 130
Cozma, Miron, 00: 356
Crawford, Shane, 00: 85
Credit Suisse Group (bank), 00: 388
Creutzfeldt-Jakob disease, 00: 414–415
Crew, Rudy, 00: 317
Crichton, Charles, 00: 161
CRICKET, 00: 152–153
CRIME, 00: 153–155, 99: 147–148; Chicago, 00: 130–131; cities, 00: 134; immigrants, 00: 235; Philadelphia, 00: 341; South Africa, 00: 369; Supreme Court rulings, 00: 383; U.S. government actions, 00: 419–420; West Indies, 00: 431. See also Conflicts and violence; Courts; Drug abuse; Drug trafficking; Hate crimes; People in the news; Prison; Terrorism
Crisp, Quentin, 00: 161
CROATIA, 00: 155, 99: 148; facts in brief, 00: 200; Yugoslavia history, 00: 435–444, 446
Croatian Democratic Union, 00: 155
Cronaca de Luogo (Berio), 00: 138
Crusades, 00: 183
Cruz Leon, Raul Ernesto, 00: 179
CSX Transportation Corp., 00: 404
CUBA, 00: 155–156, 99: 149; baseball, 00: 97, 155, 375; facts in brief, 00: 262; Pan American Games, 00: 330; terrorism, 00: 179; U.S. immigration, 00: 235, 292
Cubas Grau, Raul, 00: 332
Cubs, Chicago, 00: 339
Culinar Inc., 00: 310
Cunningham, Merce, 00: 158
Cyanobacteria, 00: 104, 213
Cycling, 00: 332, 375, 376 (il.)
Cyclones, 00: 169, 170, 430
Cyprus, 00: 201, 218, 295, 99: 150; facts in brief, 00: 294; population growth, 00: 306; unemployment, 00: 307
CZECH REPUBLIC, 00: 156–157, 99: 150; facts in brief, 00: 200; other references, 00: 198–199, 201, 221, 360, 366

D

D-Day, 00: 57
Daewoo (company), 00: 258
Dagestan (Russia), 00: 359, 395
DaimlerChrysler AG (company), 00: 87, 89, 217, 259–260

Dalai Lama, 00: 109–111
D'Alema, Massimo, 00: 250
Daley, Richard M., 00: 129, 136, 178
DALLAS, 00: 157, 99: 152
Dallas Area Rapid Transit, 00: 157
Dallas/Fort Worth International Airport, 00: 157
Dallas Stars, 00: 157, 220
DANCE, 00: 158–159, 99: 152–154
Danes, Claire, 00: 276 (il.)
Danforth, John, 00: 419
Danko, Rick, 00: 161
Darabont, Frank, 00: 311
Dark matter (space), 00: 79
Darrow, Whitney, Jr., 00: 161
Davis, G. Lindsey, 00: 349
Davis, Gray, 00: 378
Davis Cup (tennis), 00: 395
Day, Stockwell, 00: 123–124
Dayne, Ron, 00: 207
Dayton Accords (1995), 00: 443
DC United (team), 00: 365, 366
DDT (pesticide), 00: 149
Death of a Salesman (Miller), 00: 397, 398
Death penalty. See Capital punishment
Death rates. See Population
Deaths: AIDS, 00: 47; highway, 00: 350; rail crossing, 00: 404. See also Disasters
DEATHS (obituaries), 00: 160–165, 99: 154–160
DeBartolo, Eddie, Jr., 00: 374
Decibe, Susana, 00: 55
Decommissioning, 00: 324
Deep Space 1 (space probe), 00: 371 (il.)
Defense, U.S. Department of, 00: 57–59
Deformities, in frogs, 00: 105
Dehaene, Jean-Luc, 00: 103
De La Hoya, Oscar, 00: 108
De la Rua, Fernando, 00: 55, 263
Delaware, 00: 430; statistics, 00: 379
DeLay, Tom, 00: 335
Dell, Gregory, 00: 349
Delphi Automotive Systems, 00: 260
Delta Air Lines, 00: 91
Del Tredici, David, 00: 138
Democratic Left Party (Turkey), 00: 406
Democratic Party: Australia, 00: 83; South Africa, 00: 368
DEMOCRATIC PARTY (U.S.), 00: 166–167, 99: 160–161; elections, 00: 177–178; health care, 00: 219; public TV scandal, 00: 393; taxes, 00: 390; other references, 00: 146, 353, 354
Democratic Progressive Party (Taiwan), 00: 388
Dench, Dame Judi, 00: 313 (il.), 335–336, 397
DENMARK, 00: 167, 99: 162; agriculture, 00: 46; facts in brief, 00: 200
Dennehy, Brian, 00: 397, 398 (il.)
Denver (Colorado), 00: 448
Denver Broncos, 00: 207–209
Depression (disorder), 00: 290
Depression, Great, 00: 94, 173, 382, 421
Destination: Technodrome (park, Montreal), 00: 310
Detroit (Michigan), 00: 427
De Valera, Eamon, 00: 247
DeVol, Frank, 00: 161
Dewar, Donald, 00: 408
Dhaka, 00: 92
Dhammachayo, Phra, 00: 111
Di-Ichi Kangyo Bank, Ltd., 00: 95
Diabelli (dance), 00: 158–159
Diallo, Amadou, 00: 317
Diamond mining, 00: 126–127
Diamond Multimedia Systems, Inc., 00: 179
Diana, Princess of Wales, 99: 424–425
Diavik Mine (Northwest Territories), 00: 126–127
DiCaprio, Leonardo, 00: 276 (il.), 279
Digital subscriber lines, 00: 244
DiMaggio, Joe, 00: 98–99, 374
Dingell, John, 00: 219
Dinosaurs, 00: 329 (il.), 330
Dioxin, 00: 103
DISABLED, 00: 167, 99: 163; Supreme Court rulings, 00: 383
DISASTERS, 00: 168–171, 99: 163–166; auto racing, 00: 89; Bangladesh ferry, 00: 92; Doctors Without Borders, work of, 00: 323; Indian pilgrim stampede, 00: 220; Italian cable car, 00: 58, 251; Japan uranium plant, 00: 251; Texas bonfire collapse, 00: 206–207. See also Avalanches; Aviation disasters; Earthquakes; Fires; Flooding; Railroads; Terrorism; Weather
Discovery (space shuttle), 00: 371–372

Discrimination. See Civil rights
Disease. See Medicine; Public health and safety; and specific diseases
Disgrace (Coetzee), 00: 268
Dixie Chicks (pop group), 00: 347
Dixit Dominus (dance), 00: 158
Djibouti, facts in brief, 00: 40
Dmytryk, Edward, 00: 161
DNA, 00: 128
Dobson, Frank, 00: 411
Doctors Without Borders, 00: 323
Dodik, Milorad, 00: 107
Doer, Gary, 00: 124
Dog chew products, 00: 420
Dogs, Sled. See Sled dog racing
Dole, Elizabeth, 00: 353
Dole Food Co., 00: 264
Dome of the Rock, 00: 300 (il.)
Dominica, facts in brief, 00: 262
Dominican Republic, 00: 431; facts in brief, 00: 262
DOPA (chemical), 00: 128
Douglas, Katie, 00: 101 (il.)
Dow Jones Industrial Average, 00: 381
Doyle, Roddy, 00: 268
Dracula (music), 00: 138
Dragila, Stacy, 00: 402
Drapeau, Jean, 00: 310
Drought, 00: 45 (il.), 427–430
DRUG ABUSE, 00: 171, 99: 166; athletes, 00: 330, 374, 402–404; Australia, 00: 84
Drug trafficking: Afghanistan, 00: 38; Colombia, 00: 140; Latin America, 00: 263–264; Mexico, 00: 291; Miami, 00: 292
DRUGS, 00: 171–172, 99: 166–167; mental health, 00: 290
Druse religion, 00: 299
Dubai World Cup, 00: 223
Du Bois, W. E. B., 00: 226
Duch, 00: 115
Duchovny, David, 00: 392
Duhalde, Eduardo, 00: 263
Duisenberg, Wim, 99: 325–326
Duke! (dance), 00: 158
Duke Energy Corp., 00: 179
Duke University, 00: 101–102
Dylan, Bob, 00: 345–346
Duma (Russia), 00: 358, 360
Dunquerque (France), 00: 210
Dusenbury, Harold, 00: 225
Dutch (Morris), 00: 268
DVD-Audio, 00: 179
Dyson, Rob, 00: 90
Dzurinda, Mikulas, 00: 364

E

E-commerce, 00: 243
E Street Band, 00: 345
E-trading, 00: 243–244
Eagle, Bald, 00: 149
Eagle, Dale, 00: 107
Earthquakes, 00: 168; Colombia, 00: 140, 00: 168; Greece, 00: 218, 295; Los Angeles area, 00: 213; Taiwan, 00: 388; Turkey, 00: 168, 218, 295, 405
East India Co., 00: 190
East Timor, 00: 62, 240–241; Australia's role, 00: 81 (il.), 84, 85; Canada's role, 00: 119; New Zealand's role, 00: 317; UN actions, 00: 416
EASTERN ORTHODOX CHURCHES, 00: 172–173, 99: 167–168
eBay (company), 00: 243
Ecevit, Bulent, 00: 336, 406
Eclipse, Solar, 00: 320 (il.)
Economic Community Monitoring Group, 00: 362
ECONOMICS, 00: 173–175, 99: 168–169; Nobel Prizes, 00: 323. See also specific country articles
ECUADOR, 00: 175, 99: 180; facts in brief, 00: 262; other references, 00: 263, 264
Edah (organization), 00: 255
Edison Schools, Inc., 00: 176
EDUCATION, 00: 175–176, 99: 180–181; Chicago, 00: 129, 136; civil rights, 00: 233; congressional action, 00: 146; Dallas, 00: 157; New York City, 00: 317; Roman Catholic mandates, 00: 356; school violence, 00: 153–154, 176, 378, 392–393; segregation, 00: 385; sexual harassment, 00: 383
Education, U.S. Department of, 00: 175, 419
Education Amendments (U.S., 1972), 00: 233
Education Flexibility Partnership Act (U.S., 1999), 00: 146

Education management organizations, 00: 176
Edward VIII, 00: 408
Edward, Prince, 00: 415
Eggs, 00: 206
EGYPT, 00: 176–177, 99: 181; facts in brief, 00: 294; Middle East history, 00: 301, 302, 304, 305, 307, 308; population growth, 00: 306; unemployment, 00: 307
Egypt, Ancient, 00: 51, 52, 61
EgyptAir (airline), 00: 92, 177, 295
Ehrlichman, John, 00: 161
Eichel, Hans, 00: 214
Eilber, Janet, 00: 159
Elaborate Lives (musical), 00: 399
ELECTIONS, 00: 177–178, 99: 182–183; campaign finance reform, 00: 142; presidential race, 00: 353–354; voting rights, 00: 227, 230. See also specific country, province, and city articles
ELECTRONICS, 00: 179, 99: 183–184. See also Computers; Telecommunications
Elementary and Secondary Education Act (U.S., 1965), 00: 176
Elements, Chemical, 00: 342–343
Elf Aquitaine S.A. (company), 00: 203, 210–211, 325
Elion, Gertrude Belle, 00: 161, 162 (il.)
Elizabeth (wife of George VI), 00: 410
Elizabeth II, 00: 85, 119, 319, 409 (il.), 415
Ellison, Ralph, 00: 267
El Niño, 00: 325
EL SALVADOR, 00: 179, 99: 182; election, 00: 263; facts in brief, 00: 262
Elway, John, 00: 207, 374
Emmy Awards, 00: 391
Emotional disorders. See Mental health
Empire State Building, 00: 315 (il.)
Empires, 00: 180–193
Employment. See Labor and employment
Empta (chemical weapon), 00: 382
Encephalitis, 00: 284
Encyclopaedia Britannica, 00: 244
Energy, U.S. Department of, 00: 195
Energy Information Agency, 00: 195
ENERGY SUPPLY, 00: 194–195, 99: 184–186; U.S. government action, 00: 421. See also Natural gas; Nuclear energy; Petroleum
Engineering. See Building and construction
England. See United Kingdom
ENVIRONMENTAL POLLUTION, 00: 195–197, 99: 186–188; Brazil, 00: 109; congressional action, 00: 146
Environmental Protection Agency (U.S.), 00: 146, 196–197
Episcopal Church, 00: 349
Equal Credit Opportunity Act (U.S., 1975), 00: 233
Equal Music, An (Seth), 00: 268
Equal Pay Act (U.S., 1963), 00: 233
Equatorial Guinea, facts in brief, 00: 40
Equestrian events, 00: 376
Eran, Oded, 00: 294
Ergonomics, 00: 260
Eritrea, 00: 42
Espionage, 00: 245, 419
ESTONIA, 00: 197, 99: 188; facts in brief, 00: 200; other references, 00: 201, 282
Estrada, Joseph, 00: 341, 99: 326
ETA (group). See Basque Homeland and Freedom
Ethics in Government Act (U.S., 1978), 00: 417
Ethiopia, 00: 42, 44, 254; facts in brief, 00: 40
Ethnic cleansing, 00: 433, 441, 442, 444
eToys, Inc., 00: 401
EU. See European Union
Eukaryotes (organisms), 00: 104
Eurasian steppe, 00: 51
Euro (currency), 00: 174, 202, 242, 99: 194–199; Denmark, 00: 167; Greece, 00: 218; Portugal, 00: 348; Sweden, 00: 386; United Kingdom, 00: 408, 411
Europa (moon), 00: 67
EUROPE, 00: 199–203, 99: 188–199; economy, 00: 174; football, 00: 209; weather, 00: 427
European Aeronautic, Defense and Space Co., 00: 211, 217
European Central Bank, 00: 202
European Champions Cup (soccer), 00: 365
European Commission, 00: 199, 202. See also European Union
European Community. See European Union
European Cup (rugby), 00: 357

European Parliament, 00: 408
European People's Party, 00: 201
European Union, 00: 64–66, 200–203, 242, 264, 295, 99: 194–199; agriculture, 00: 46; Belgium, 00: 103; Croatia, 00: 155; Denmark, 00: 167; Estonia, 00: 197; Finland, 00: 205; France, 00: 210; Germany, 00: 214; Greece, 00: 218; Ireland, 00: 247; Italy, 00: 250; Latvia, 00: 265; Lithuania, 00: 282; Poland, 00: 344; Portugal, 00: 348; Slovakia, 00: 364; Switzerland, 00: 387; transportation, 00: 405; United Kingdom, 00: 408, 414–415. See also Euro
Euthanasia, 00: 315
Evangelical Christians, 00: 350
Evangelical Lutheran Church in America, 00: 349
Everest, Mount, 00: 319
Everglades, 00: 196
Evolution, 00: 150
Ewing, Patrick, 00: 100
Ex Corde Ecclesiae (document), 00: 356
Exercise therapy, 00: 290
Explosions, 00: 168. See also Terrorism
Exports. See Agriculture; International trade; Manufacturing

F

F. Hoffmann-LaRoche Lt., 00: 420
Fabius, Laurent, 00: 210
Fadiman, Clifton, 00: 161
Fair Housing Act (U.S., 1968), 00: 231
Falcons, Atlanta, 00: 209
Falcons, Peregrine, 00: 149
Falkland Islands, 00: 56
FALN (group). See Armed Forces of National Liberation
Falun Gong (group), 00: 111, 131, 133 (il.), 224
Families, in Latin America, 00: 261–263
Famine, 00: 44, 256
FARC. See Revolutionary Armed Forces of Colombia
Farm and farming. See Agriculture
Farmer, James, 00: 161, 165 (il.)
Farrell, Suzanne, 00: 159
Fascists, 00: 250
FASHION, 00: 204–205, 99: 200–201
Fatherland-All Russia Party, 00: 359
FBI. See Federal Bureau of Investigation
FCC. See Federal Communications Commission
Feathers, on dinosaurs, 00: 330
Federal Agricultural Improvement and Reform Act (U.S., 1996), 00: 45
Federal Aviation Administration (U.S.), 00: 90
Federal budget, 00: 417
Federal Bureau of Investigation (U.S.), 00: 92, 224, 341, 361; crime statistics, 00: 153; Waco case, 00: 419
Federal Communications Commission (U.S.), 00: 351, 352, 390, 420
Federal Death Penalty Act (U.S., 1994), 00: 383–383
Federal Election Campaign Act (U.S., 1971), 00: 142
Federal Express, 00: 258
Federal funds rate, 00: 175, 417–419
Federal Reserve System (U.S.), 00: 94, 95, 174–175, 286–287, 417–419
Federation Internationale de Football Association, 00: 364, 366
Feininger, Andreas, 00: 161
Feinstein, Dianne, 00: 147 (il.)
Femtosecond spectroscopy, 00: 323
Fernandez, Adriana, 00: 375–376
Ferry, David, 00: 343
Fianna Fail Party (Ireland), 00: 247
Fiennes, Joseph, 00: 270 (il.)
Fight Club (film), 00: 311
Fiji, 00: 220, 327, 328; facts in brief, 00: 327
Fila (boat), 00: 106
Filmon, Gary, 00: 124
Films. See Motion pictures
Filo, David, 99: 326–327
Financial Services Modernization Act (U.S., 1999), 00: 94
Fincher, David, 00: 311
FINLAND, 00: 205, 99: 201; facts in brief, 00: 200; skating, 00: 235
Fire, Chicago (team), 00: 365
Firearms, 00: 146, 150, 292, 369
Fires, 00: 168; Amazon rain forest, 00: 149; Asian rain forest, 00: 66; France, 00: 211
First International Conference on the Ocean Observing System for Climate, 00: 326
FIS. See Islamic Salvation Front

Fish, Hugh, 00: 161
Fish and Wildlife Service, U.S., 00: 149–150
Fishburne, Laurence, 00: 278 (il.), 279
Fishing industry, 00: 119–122
Flatworms, 00: 105
Fleischer, Bruce, 00: 217
Flockhart, Calista, 00: 278, 279
Flooding, 00: 169–170; Asia, 00: 66, 92, 132, 169–170, 256, 424; Europe, 00: 234, 387 (il.); Latin America, 00: 170, 261 (il.), 291 (il.); U.S., 00: 169–170, 430
Flores Perez, Francisco Guillermo, 00: 179
Florida, 00: 151, 175, 378, 383, 428 (il.), 430; statistics, 00: 379. See also Miami
Florida State University, 00: 206
Fly (recording), 00: 347
Flynn, Padraig, 00: 247
FM radio, Low-power, 00: 352
Foden, Giles, 00: 268
FOOD, 00: 205–206, 99: 202; Africa shortages, 00: 44; North Korea shortages, 00: 256; safety, 00: 103, 104, 205–206, 284, 350, 414–415, 420. See also Agriculture; Famine; Pesticides
Food and Agriculture Organization (UN), 00: 44
Food and Drug Administration (U.S.), 00: 171, 172, 205, 420
Food Quality Protection Act (U.S., 1996), 00: 196
Food Safety and Inspection Service (U.S.), 00: 206
Food stamps, 00: 430
FOOTBALL, 00: 206–209, 99: 202–205; other references, 00: 223, 374, 375. See also Australian rules football; Rugby football; Soccer
Footloose (musical), 00: 398
Forbes (magazine), 00: 375
Forbes, Steve, 00: 354
Forbes-Robinson, Elliott, 00: 90
Ford Motor Co., 00: 86–89, 260, 286 (il.), 385
Formula One racing, 00: 89–90
Forrest, Helen, 00: 161
Fort Worth (Texas), 00: 155
Fosse (musical), 00: 398
Fossil fuels, 00: 212. See also Coal; Global warming; Natural gas; Petroleum
Fossils, 00: 49–50, 213, 329–330
Foster, Mike, 00: 178, 354
Foster, Sir Norman, 00: 54, 113
Fountain of Bakhchisaria, The (ballet), 00: 159
Four Seasons (Torke), 00: 138
Fox Broadcasting Co., 00: 391, 392, 394
FRANCE, 00: 210–211, 99: 206–207; agriculture, 00: 46; empire, 00: 187–189; facts in brief, 00: 200; literature, 00: 269; Middle East history, 00: 296–298, 302–304; Mont Blanc tunnel fire, 00: 171, 211; soccer, 00: 364, 366; UK beef ban, 00: 415; other references, 00: 266, 350
Frankfurt Galaxy (team), 00: 209
Fraser, Malcolm, 00: 83
Freedom Party (Austria), 00: 86
Freedom's Song (Chaudhri), 00: 268
Freetown (Sierra Leone), 00: 42, 362
Friedan, Betty, 00: 233
Frog deformities, 00: 105
Fuchs, Sir Vivian, 00: 161
Fuel. See Energy supply
Fuji Bank, Ltd., 00: 95
Fujimori, Alberto K., 00: 340
Fundamentalism. See Christian fundamentalism; Islamic fundamentalism
Funt, Allen, 00: 161
Furrow, Buford O'Neal, 00: 225

G

Gabon, facts in brief, 00: 40
Gadhafi, Muammar Muhammad al-. See Qadhafi, Muammar Muhammad al-
Galaxies, 00: 74–75, 78–79
Galaxy, Frankfurt (team), 00: 209
Galaxy, Los Angeles (team), 00: 366
Galileo (space probe), 00: 67
Galileo Galilei, 00: 72, 73
Gallagher, Mike, 00: 321
Gambia, facts in brief, 00: 40
Gamboa Tropical Rainforest Resort (Panama), 00: 332
Games. See Chess; Sports; Toys and games
Gamow, George, 00: 75
Gandhi, Mohandas K., 00: 238
Gandhi, Sonia, 00: 236
Garcia, Alan, 00: 340
Garcia, Sergio, 00: 217
Garden of Light (Kernis), 00: 138

GARDENING, 00: 212
Garth Brooks in...the Life of Chris Gaines (recording), 00: 347
Garzon, Baltazar, 00: 263
Gasoline, 00: 195, 196
Gass, William, 00: 266
Gates, Bill, 00: 265
Gates (Bill and Melinda) Foundation, 00: 265
Gay rights. See Homosexuality
Gaza Strip, 00: 248, 304, 305
Gedhun Choekyi Nyima, 00: 109
Gehry, Frank, 00: 54
General Accounting Office (U.S.), 00: 290
General Motors Corp., 00: 87, 89, 259–260
Genes, 00: 288
Genetic engineering, 00: 46, 105 (il.), 106, 287
Genetically modified foods, 00: 46
Genghis Khan, 00: 184, 185
Genome, 00: 288
GEOLOGY, 00: 212–213, 99: 208–210. See also Ocean
George (magazine), 00: 284
George V, 00: 189 (il.)
George VI, 00: 408, 410
George Washington University, 00: 427
GEORGIA (country), 00: 213, 99: 210; facts in brief, 00: 64
Georgia (state), 00: 383; statistics, 00: 379
GERMANY, 00: 214–217, 99: 210–212; agriculture, 00: 46; art looting, 00: 59–61; buildings, 00: 111–113; economy, 00: 174; facts in brief, 00: 200; Nazi Empire, 00: 190–191; stocks, 00: 382; other references, 00: 202–203, 205, 260. See also Nazis; World War II
Gershon, Nina, 00: 315
Gerstein, Erez, 00: 249
Ghana, facts in brief, 00: 40
Giant Mine (Northwest Territories), 00: 126
Gilchrist, Adam, 00: 152 (il.)
Gilmartin, Tom, 00: 247
Gingrich, Newt, 00: 178
Ginsberg, Ruth Bader, 00: 317
Giuliani, Rudolph, 00: 61, 136, 315, 317
Glass, Philip, 00: 138
Glass-Steagall Act (U.S., 1933), 00: 94, 381
Glendening, Parris N., 00: 378
Global warming, 00: 128, 149, 195, 325
Globe Theatre: new, 00: 271; old, 00: 272
Gluck, Louise, 00: 343
Glue, Waterproof, 00: 128
Golan Heights, 00: 249, 388
Gold Cup (boating), 00: 106
GOLF, 00: 217, 99: 212–213
Gonchar, Viktor, 00: 102–103
Goncz, Arpad, 00: 234
Gonzalez Macchi, Luis, 00: 332
Good Friday peace agreement (1998), 00: 324, 410
Goodman, Oscar, 00: 178
Goods and services tax (Australia), 00: 81–83, 85
Gorbachev, Mikhail S., 00: 360
Gorbachev, Raisa, 00: 162
Gordon, Jeff, 00: 89
Gore, Albert, Jr., 00: 166–167
Gorillas, 00: 147, 149, 447, 448 (il.)
Gould, Sandra, 00: 162
Gover, Kevin, 00: 239
Government. See City; State government; United States, Government of the; and specific countries
Governor-General of Canada, 00: 118–119
Graf, Steffi, 00: 374, 395
Graham, Martha, 00: 159
Grammy Awards, 00: 138, 337, 346
Grand Prix (track), 00: 404
Grand Slam (tennis), 00: 394–395
Grange, Harold (Red), 00: 209
Grant, Shannon, 00: 85
Grass, Gunter, 00: 268, 323
Graves, Michael, 00: 53
Gravitation, 00: 73
Great Gatsby, The (Harbison), 00: 138
GREECE, 00: 218, 99: 213–214; earthquake, 00: 168; facts in brief, 00: 200; Serbia conflict, 00: 198; other references, 00: 111, 295, 405
Greek Orthodox Church, 00: 173
Green, Mark, 00: 317
Green Mile, The (film), 00: 311
Green Party (Germany), 00: 216
Greene, Maurice, 00: 402
Greenfield, Meg, 00: 162
Greenhouse effect, 00: 195, 212, 325, 421
Greenpeace, 00: 46
Greenwich (England), 00: 318–319

Grenada, 00: 431; facts in brief, 00: 262
Gretzky, Wayne, 00: 221, 374
Grey Cup (football), 00: 209
Gross domestic product, U.S., 00: 136, 287. See also specific country articles
Grosse Sonate (dance), 00: 158
Ground Beneath Her Feet, The (Rushdie), 00: 268
Grozny (Chechnya), 00: 359
GTE Corp., 00: 351
Guadalcanal Island (Pacific), 00: 327
Guadalcanal Revolutionary Army, 00: 327
GUATEMALA, 00: 219, 99: 214; election, 00: 263; facts in brief, 00: 262
Gucci Group NV (company), 00: 204, 249
Guernica (Picasso), 00: 59
Guinea, facts in brief, 00: 40
Guinea-Bissau, 00: 44; facts in brief, 00: 40
Gulf War syndrome, 00: 57
Guns. See Firearms
Gurirab, Theo-Ben, 00: 416
Gusmao, Jose "Xanana," 00: 241
Guterres, Antonio, 00: 348
Guth, Alan, 00: 78–79
GUYANA: election, 00: 263; facts in brief, 00: 262
Gwynn, Tony, 00: 97
Gyancain Norbu, 00: 109
Gymnastics, 00: 375
Gypsies, 00: 156

H

Ha Jin, 00: 266
Habibie, Bacharuddin Jusuf, 00: 84, 85, 240, 241, 99: 327
Hachani, Abdelkader, 00: 49
Hacker, Marcel, 00: 376
Hackett, Grant, 00: 387
Hague, William, 00: 411
Haider, Joerg, 00: 86
HAITI, 00: 219, 99: 215; facts in brief, 00: 262
Hale, George Ellery, 00: 74
Hall, Huntz, 00: 162
Hall, Steve, 00: 321
Hamas, 00: 254, 307
Hamilton Tiger-Cats, 00: 209
Hamm, John, 00: 125
Hammerstein, Oscar, II, 00: 397
Hanauer, Chip, 00: 106
Handguns. See Firearms
Handicapped. See Disabled
Haqani, Sheik Nazem Rabbani, 00: 247
Harare (Zimbabwe), 00: 134
Harbison, John, 00: 138
Hardy Holzman Pfeiffer Associates, 00: 53
Hare, David, 00: 396–397
Harradine, Brian, 00: 83
Harris, Eric, 00: 153–154
Harris, Mike, 00: 125, 400
Hashemite dynasty, 00: 296, 298, 304
Hasina Wajed, 00: 92
Haskins, Clem, 00: 375
Hassan II, 00: 162, 293 (il.), 295, 296
Hassan, Prince, 00: 254
Hastert, J. Dennis, 00: 142, 336, 390
Hate crimes, 00: 154–155, 225, 255, 420
Haughey, Charles, 00: 247
Havel, Vaclav, 00: 156
Hawaii, 00: 151, 378, 380; statistics, 00: 379
Hazard Analysis and Critical Control Point system, 00: 206
HBO. See Home Box Office
Health. See Health-care issues; Medicine; Mental health; Public health and safety
Health (magazine), 00: 284
Health and Human Services, U.S. Department of, 00: 171, 380, 419, 420
HEALTH-CARE ISSUES, 00: 219–220, 99: 215; other references, 00: 146, 380, 421
Health insurance, 00: 219–220
Health maintenance organizations, 00: 219, 380
Heaney, Seamus, 00: 343
Hearst Corp., 00: 361
Heisman Trophy, 00: 207
Heliocentric theory, 00: 71–72
Heller, Joseph, 00: 162
"Hello, President" (radio program), 00: 423
Hemingway, Ernest, 00: 267, 268
Henderson, Russell, 00: 150, 225
Herbert, Zbigniew, 00: 269
Herlihy, Ed, 00: 162
Herman, Robert, 00: 75
Heroin, 00: 171
Herschel, William, 00: 74
Herzberg, Gerhard, 00: 162

Heyns, Penny, 00: 386
Hezbollah (group), 00: 249, 265
Hieroglyphics, 00: 51
Hill, Lauryn, 00: 345, 346 (il.)
Hindenburg (airship), 00: 170
HINDUISM, 00: 220, 99: 216–217; India, 00: 220, 236–238; Mauritius, 00: 288
Hingis, Martina, 00: 394–395
Hinomaru (flag), 00: 253
Hiroshima (Japan), 00: 252
Hirt, Al, 00: 162
"His Majesty's Reign" (anthem), 00: 253
Hispanic Americans, 00: 345
Hitler, Adolf, 00: 190–191, 214, 359
HIV. See AIDS
Ho, Edmund, 00: 134
Ho Chi Minh City (Vietnam), 00: 424
HOCKEY, 00: 220–221, 99: 217–218; other references, 00: 374, 375
Hoffa, James P., 00: 259
Hogs, 00: 47
Holbrooke, Richard, 00: 114, 336–337, 444
Holdsclaw, Chamique, 00: 375
Holes (Sachar), 00: 281
Holland. See Netherlands
Holocaust, 00: 59, 156, 216, 224, 255, 388
Holy Roman Empire, 00: 183–184
Holyfield, Evander, 00: 107–108
Homan, Paul, 00: 239
Home Box Office, 00: 393
Homelessness, 00: 399–400
Hominids. See Prehistoric people
Homo erectus (hominid), 00: 50
Homo habilis (hominid), 00: 49
Homosexuality, 00: 58, 151, 225, 349–350
Honda Motor Co., 00: 89
Hong Kong, 00: 66, 110 (il.), 133–134
Honolulu Star-Bulletin, 00: 321
Hoogenband, Pieter van den, 00: 386, 387
Hoover Dam, 00: 113 (il.)
HORSE RACING, 00: 222–223, 99: 219–220
Horst, Horst P., 00: 162
Houghton, Richard A., 00: 128
House of Commons: Canada, 00: 120; UK, 00: 410, 412–413
House of Lords (UK), 00: 410
House of Representatives (Australia), 00: 82
House of Representatives (U.S.). See Congress of the United States
Housing discrimination, 00: 231
HOUSTON, 00: 223–224, 99: 220
Houston Astros, 00: 223
Houston Comets, 00: 101, 223–224
Houston Rockets, 00: 223
Howard, David, 00: 425
Howard, John, 00: 80–81, 84, 85
Hsing Hsing (panda), 00: 448
Hu Jintao, 00: 131
Hubble, Edwin, 00: 74–75, 76 (il.)
Hubble Space Telescope, 00: 77, 371–372
Hughes, Ted, 00: 268, 343
Hull, Brett, 00: 220
Human Genome Project, 00: 288
HUMAN RIGHTS, 00: 224–233, 99: 221–227; Bolivia, 00: 263; China, 00: 131, 134; Cuba, 00: 156; Egypt, 00: 176; Guatemala, 00: 219; Myanmar, 00: 314; Nigeria, 00: 322; Peru, 00: 340; Sierra Leone, 00: 42; Zimbabwe, 00: 447. See also Civil rights
Hume, Basil Cardinal, 00: 162
Hun Sen, 00: 115
Hunchback of Notre Dame, The (musical), 00: 399
HUNGARY, 00: 234, 99: 228; facts in brief, 00: 200; other references, 00: 198–199, 201, 360, 364
Hunt, Helen, 99: 327
Hunter, James "Catfish," 00: 162, 374
Hurricanes: Brett, 00: 430; Floyd, 00: 169–170, 430; Irene, 00: 430
Hurtado, Jaime, 00: 140
Huss, Salim al-, 00: 265
Hussein I, 00: 253–254, 296, 297, 304, 305, 332
Hussein, Saddam, 00: 246, 308–309
Hustead, Ted, 00: 162
Hutu, 00: 147, 149, 407

I

i-drive (business), 00: 244
iBook (computer), 00: 141 (il.)
ICE SKATING, 00: 234–235, 99: 228–229
Icebergs, 00: 325

Iceland, facts in brief, **00:** 200
Iceman Cometh, The (O'Neill), **00:** 398
Idaho, **00:** 356; statistics, **00:** 379
Iditarod Trail Sled Dog Race, **00:** 377
Idris, Salih, **00:** 382
Iglesias, Enrique, **00:** 345
Ikonos (satellite), **00:** 373
Illinois, **00:** 378, 380; statistics, **00:** 379. See also **Chicago**
Illiteracy, **00:** 266
iMac (computer), **00:** 140
IMMIGRATION, **00:** 235, **99:** 229; Australia, **00:** 84; Miami, **00:** 292; Switzerland, **00:** 388. See also **Refugees**
Immigration Act (U.S., 1996), **00:** 235
Immigration and Naturalization Service (U.S.), **00:** 156, 235, 292
Impeachment: Clinton, **00:** 142, 167, 417; Yeltsin, **00:** 358
Imports. See **International trade; Manufacturing**
Inca, **00:** 187
Independent counsel law. See **Ethics in Government Act**
INDIA, **00:** 235–238, **99:** 230–232; British Empire, **00:** 189–190; cricket, **00:** 152, 153; disasters, **00:** 169–171, 430; facts in brief, **00:** 64; literature, **00:** 268; other references, **00:** 92, 329. See also **Hinduism**
INDIAN, AMERICAN, **00:** 239–240, **99:** 233; Canada, **00:** 119–122, 124; civil rights, **00:** 232; Kennewick Man, **00:** 53; Mexico, **00:** 292; Miami Circle, **00:** 292; museum, **00:** 427
Indian Self-Determination and Education Assistance Act (U.S., 1975), **00:** 232
Indiana, **00:** 197; statistics, **00:** 379
Indianapolis (Indiana), **00:** 178
Indianapolis 500, **00:** 89
Indianapolis News, **00:** 321
Indianapolis Star, **00:** 321
Indians, Cleveland, **00:** 375
INDONESIA, **00:** 240–241, **99:** 233–234; facts in brief, **00:** 64; shipwreck, **00:** 168; other references, **00:** 62, 65, 84, 340, 416. See also **East Timor**
Industrial Bank of Japan Ltd., **00:** 95
Indy Racing League, **00:** 89
Infectious disease, **00:** 350
Infinity Broadcasting Corp., **00:** 352
Inflation, **00:** 173, 195, 242
Influenza, **00:** 172
Inkatha Freedom Party (South Africa), **00:** 368–369
Inkster, Juli, **00:** 217
Insects, **00:** 330
Instant replay, **00:** 209
Institute for Creative Technologies, **00:** 283
Institute of Medicine (U.S.), **00:** 288
Institutional Revolutionary Party (Mexico), **00:** 291
Intel Corp., **00:** 140–141, 381
Interagency Coordinating Committee on the Validation of Alternative Methods, **00:** 289
Interest rates, **00:** 417–419; Europe, **00:** 202; U.S., **00:** 95, 174–175, 195, 286–287
Interior, U.S. Department of the, **00:** 146, 147, 239
International Association of Machinists, **00:** 259
International Brotherhood of Teamsters. See **Teamsters Union**
International Criminal Tribunal, **00:** 224, 433
International Energy Agency, **00:** 194
International Ice Patrol, **00:** 325
International Monetary Fund, **00:** 175; Albania, **00:** 48; Brazil, **00:** 109; Ecuador, **00:** 175; Romania, **00:** 356; Russia, **00:** 358; Thailand, **00:** 396; Ukraine, **00:** 407
International Olympic Committee, **00:** 326, 374
International Rugby League, **00:** 357
International Rugby Union, **00:** 357
International Space Station, **00:** 371, 372
INTERNATIONAL TRADE, **00:** 242–243, **99:** 235–236
Internazionale (team), **00:** 366
INTERNET, **00:** 243–244, **99:** 236–237; *Blair Witch Project*, **00:** 314; drug sales, **00:** 172; magazines, **00:** 284; music copying, **00:** 179, 346–347; Saudi Arabian women, **00:** 248; toy sales, **00:** 401–402
Intifada, **00:** 305–307
Inuit, **00:** 120
Ionatana, Ionatana, **00:** 328
Iowa, **00:** 378, 380; statistics, **00:** 379
IRAN, **00:** 244–245, **99:** 237–238; facts in brief, **00:** 294; Middle East history, **00:** 299, 306–308;

population growth, **00:** 306; Saudi Arabia, **00:** 361; unemployment, **00:** 307
IRAQ, **00:** 246, **99:** 239; facts in brief, **00:** 294; Middle East history, **00:** 298, 304, 308–309; oil production, **00:** 194; population growth, **00:** 306; UN actions, **00:** 416; U.S. military actions, **00:** 56–57
Iraqi National Council, **00:** 246
IRELAND, **00:** 247, **99:** 239–240; facts in brief, **00:** 200. See also **Northern Ireland**
Irish Republican Army, **00:** 324, 410
Iron smelting, **00:** 53
Irvine, Andrew, **00:** 319
Irwin, Hale, **00:** 217
Isakson, Johnny, **00:** 178
Ishihara, Shintaro, **00:** 252
ISLAM, **00:** 247–248, **99:** 240. See also **Muslims**
Islamic fundamentalism, **00:** 176, 177, 247–248, 306–309, 395
Islamic Salvation Army, **00:** 49
Islamic Salvation Front, **00:** 49, 308
Islamic Virtue Party (Turkey), **00:** 406
ISRAEL, **00:** 248–249, **99:** 240–241; facts in brief, **00:** 294; Judaism, **00:** 254; Middle East history, **00:** 302–306; population growth, **00:** 306; terrorism, **00:** 395; unemployment, **00:** 307; other references, **00:** 245, 265, 293–295, 333, 388. See also **Gaza Strip; Judaism; West Bank**
Istanbul, **00:** 320 (il.)
ITALY, **99:** 248; archaeology, **00:** 53; art restoration, **00:** 61; facts in brief, **00:** 200; ski tragedy, **00:** 58, 251; terrorism, **00:** 396; other references, **00:** 46, 202
Ivory Coast, facts in brief, **00:** 40
Iwo Jima, Battle of (1945), **00:** 328 (il.)

J

Jackson, Glenda, **00:** 411
Jackson, Jesse Louis, **00:** 225 (il.)
Jackson, Sir Michael, **00:** 408
Jackson, Milt, **00:** 162
Jackson, Thomas Penfield, **00:** 151, 287
Jacob, Irene, **00:** 278 (il.)
Jacobs, Richard, **00:** 375
Jagan, Janet, **00:** 263
Jagdeo, Bharrat, **00:** 263
Jagir Kaur, Bibi, **00:** 362
Jaguar (car), **00:** 87 (il.)
Jahn, Helmut, **00:** 111
Jamaica, **00:** 416, 431; facts in brief, **00:** 262
Jansky, Karl, **00:** 76
JAPAN, **00:** 251–253, **99:** 250–251; banks, **00:** 95; economy, **00:** 174; empire, **00:** 190–191; facts in brief, **00:** 64; literature, **00:** 269; stocks, **00:** 382; trade, **00:** 242; typhoon, **00:** 170; unemployment, **00:** 260; other references, **00:** 46, 62, 264
Jarrett, Dale, **00:** 89, 90 (il.)
Jazz, **00:** 158
Jefferson, William J., **00:** 178, 354
Jeholodens jenkinsi (animal), **00:** 330
"Jenny Jones" (TV show), **00:** 178
Jerusalem, **00:** 248, 255 (il.), 293–294, 300 (il.)
Jews: art looting, **00:** 59–61; Auschwitz crosses, **00:** 344; hate crimes, **00:** 154–155, 225; Middle East history, **00:** 296–309; Swiss bank accounts, **00:** 387–388. See also **Israel; Judaism**
Jezzin (Lebanon), **00:** 265
Jiang Zemin, **00:** 131, 133, 251 (il.), 317
Jobaria tiguidensis (dinosaur), **00:** 329 (il.)
John Paul II, **00:** 173, 344, 354–356
Johnson, Michael, **00:** 402
Johnson, Reggie, **00:** 108
Johnston, Wayne, **00:** 268
Jones, Brian, **00:** 318
Jones, James L., Jr., **00:** 59
Jones, Jenny, **00:** 392
Jones, Louis, **00:** 383–385
Jones, Marion, **00:** 375, 402
Jones, Roy, Jr., **00:** 108
Jonson, Ben, **00:** 272
Jonze, Spike, **00:** 311
JORDAN, **00:** 253–254, **99:** 251; facts in brief, **00:** 294; Middle East history, **00:** 296–298, 304, 305, 308, 309; population growth, **00:** 306; unemployment, **00:** 307; water supply, **00:** 294–295; other references, **00:** 53, 332
Jordan, Frank, **00:** 360–361
Jordan, Michael, **00:** 101, 131, 374
Jospin, Lionel R., **00:** 219
Journalism. See **Magazine; Newspaper; Pulitzer Prizes**

JUDAISM, **00:** 254–255, **99:** 252–253. See also **Jews**
Jugnauth, Sir Aneerood, **00:** 288
Juneteenth (Ellison), **00:** 267
Jupiter, **00:** 67, 72
Justice, U.S. Department of, **00:** 197, 361, 419, 425; airlines, **00:** 91; drug trafficking, **00:** 263; mental illness study, **00:** 290; Microsoft lawsuit, **00:** 151, 287; prison report, **00:** 348; tobacco lawsuit, **00:** 151, 417; vitamin settlement, **00:** 420
Juvenile Offenders Act (U.S.), **00:** 146

K

Kabbah, Ahmed Tejan, **00:** 42
Kabbani, Sheik Hisham, **00:** 247–248
Kabila, Laurent, **00:** 42, 141
Kabul (Afghanistan), **00:** 38
Kafka, Franz, **00:** 269
Kahn, Madeline, **00:** 162
Kamu, Luagalau Levaula, **00:** 328
Kanin, Garson, **00:** 162
Kansas, **00:** 427; statistics, **00:** 379
Karimov, Islam, **00:** 395
Karpov, Anatoly, **00:** 129
Kashmir (region), **00:** 62, 237, 329
Kasich, John, **00:** 353
Kasparov, Garry, **00:** 129
Kassem, Abdul Karim, **00:** 304
Katz, Sam, **00:** 340–341
Kavakci, Merve, **00:** 406
Kawabata, Yasunari, **00:** 269
Kay, Jackie, **00:** 268
Kaya, **00:** 288
KAZAKHSTAN, **00:** 256, **99:** 253; agriculture, **00:** 45, 46; archaeology, **00:** 53; facts in brief, **00:** 64
Kazhgeldin, Alezhan, **00:** 256
Keats, John, **00:** 279
Kelley, DeForest, **00:** 162
Kendall, Henry W., **00:** 162
Kendall, Joe, **00:** 259
Kennard, William, **00:** 390
Kennedy, Carolyn Bessette, **00:** 161 (il.)
Kennedy, John F., **00:** 320, 371, 393
Kennedy, John F., Jr., **00:** 161 (il.), 162, 284
Kennedy, Robert F., **00:** 225
Kennett, Jeff, **00:** 83
Kennewick Man (fossil), **00:** 53
KENTUCKY, **00:** 177–178, 197; statistics, **00:** 379
Kentucky Derby, **00:** 222
KENYA, **00:** 256, **99:** 253; facts in brief, **00:** 40; other references, **00:** 152, 170, 375
Kepler, Johannes, **00:** 72–73
Kernis, Aaron Jay, **00:** 138
Kevorkian, Jack, **00:** 150, 220
KGB (secret police), **00:** 282
Khaleda Ziaur Rahman, **00:** 92
Khalifman, Alexander, **00:** 129
Khalsa (community), **00:** 362
Khamenei, Ali, **00:** 244
Khannouci, Khalid, **00:** 375
Khatami, Mohammed, **00:** 244, 361
Khmer Rouge, **00:** 115
Khomeini, Ruhollah, **00:** 245, 307
Kidman, Nicole, **00:** 205, 397
Kiley, Richard, **00:** 162
Killanin, Lord, **00:** 162
Kim Chong-il, **00:** 257
Kim Dae-Jung, **00:** 257–258, 317, **99:** 327–328
Kim Jong Pil, **00:** 258
King, John William, **00:** 225
King, Martin Luther, Jr., **00:** 225, 229, 231
King of the Ants (Herbert), **00:** 269
Kingston (Jamaica), **00:** 431
Kipketer, Wilson, **00:** 404
Kiribati, **00:** 327, 416; facts in brief, **00:** 327
Kirkland, Lane, **00:** 163
Kirov Ballet, **00:** 159
Kiwi International (airline), **00:** 91
Kjus, Lasse, **00:** 363
Klebold, Dylan, **00:** 153–154
Kleitman, Nathaniel, **00:** 163
Klima, Viktor, **00:** 86
Kline, Kevin, **00:** 273 (il.), 278
KMT. See **Kuomintang party**
Knickerbockers, New York, **00:** 100
Kohl, Helmut, **00:** 214
Kok, Wim, **00:** 314–315
Komorah, Johnny Paul, **00:** 362
KOREA, NORTH, **00:** 256–257, **99:** 254; facts in

brief, **00:** 64; other references, **00:** 62, 66, 192, 253
KOREA, SOUTH, 00: 257–258, **99:** 255; facts in brief, **00:** 64; floods, **00:** 169; other references, **00:** 62, 66, 192, 257
Korean War (1950-1953), **00:** 192
Koresh, David, 00: 419
Kosovo (province), **00:** 172, 198–199, 433; Albania, **00:** 48; Canada, **00:** 119; Finland, **00:** 205; Germany, **00:** 216; Jewish aid, **00:** 255; refugees, **00:** 83–84, 107, 283; Romania, **00:** 356; Russia, **00:** 360; UN actions, **00:** 416; United Kingdom, **00:** 408; U.S. military actions, **00:** 56; war crimes tribunal, **00:** 224; Yugoslavia history, **00:** 435, 437, 439, 440, 443–446
Kosovo Liberation Army, 00: 198, 433, 435, 444–445
Kosovo Polje, Battle of (1389), **00:** 443
KPFA-FM (station), **00:** 353
Kraus, Alfredo, 00: 163
Krayzelburg, Lenny, 00: 386–387
Kriegler, Johann, 00: 368
Kristopans, Vilis, 00: 265
Ku Klux Klan, 00: 317
Kubilius, Andrius, 00: 282
Kublai Khan, 00: 185
Kubrick, Stanley, 00: 161 (il.), 163
Kuchma, Leonid, 00: 407
Kumaratunga, Chandrika, 00: 377
Kumble, Anil, 00: 153
Kuomintang party (Taiwan), **00:** 388
Kurdish Workers Party, 00: 406
Kurds, 00: 218, 295, 298, 314 (il.), 405–406
KUWAIT: facts in brief, **00:** 294; population growth, **00:** 306; unemployment, **00:** 307; other references, **00:** 194, 254, 308
Kvaerner ASA (company), **00:** 325
Kwan, Michelle, 00: 234, 235
KwaZulu-Natal province (South Africa), **00:** 368–369
Kyoto Protocol on Climate Change (1997), **00:** 129, 195
Kyrgyzstan, facts in brief, **00:** 64

L
Laar, Mart, 00: 197
Labastida Ochoa, Francisco, 00: 291
Labels, Drug, 00: 172
Labor, U.S. Department of, 00: 258, 260
LABOR AND EMPLOYMENT, 00: 258–260, **99:** 255–259; airlines, **00:** 92; automobiles, **00:** 89; basketball, **00:** 100; states, **00:** 377–378. See also **Strikes**; **Unemployment**
Labor Party (Mauritius), **00:** 288
Labour Party (UK), **00:** 408, 410, 411, 414, 415
Lacrosse, 00: 376–377
Ladies Professional Golf Association, 00: 217
Lafontaine, Oskar, 00: 214
Lagos, Ricardo, 00: 131
Laguna, Mount (California), **00:** 427
Lalli, Frank, 00: 284
Lamberth, Royce, 00: 239–240
Landry, Bernard, 00: 125
Language extinction, 00: 264
La Niña, 00: 325
Laos, facts in brief, **00:** 64
Las Vegas (Nevada), **00:** 178, 399, 427, 430
Lasers, 00: 342
Last King of Scotland, The (Foden), **00:** 268
Last Life, The (Messud), **00:** 267
Last Supper, The (Leonardo da Vinci), **00:** 61
Lastman, Mel, 00: 399–400
LATIN AMERICA, 00: 261–264, **99:** 258–262; cities, **00:** 134
LATVIA, 00: 265, **99:** 263; EU membership, **00:** 202; facts in brief, **00:** 200
Laurie, Bill, 00: 375
Lava lamps, 00: 213
Lavin, Joaquin, 00: 131
Law of Return (Judaism), **00:** 254
Lawrie, Paul, 00: 217
Leading the Cheers (Cartwright), **00:** 268
Leakey, Louis S. B., 00: 49
Leakey, Richard, 00: 256
Learn, Bob, Jr., 00: 107
LEBANON, 00: 265, **99:** 263; facts in brief, **00:** 294; Middle East history, **00:** 298, 305, 306; population growth, **00:** 306; unemployment, **00:** 307; other references, **00:** 249, 388
Lee, Wen Ho, 00: 419
Lee Teng-hui, 00: 133, 388

Lees, Meg, 00: 83
Legionnaire's disease, 00: 314
Legorreta, Ricardo, 00: 54
Leight, Warren, 00: 397
Leitzinger, Butch, 00: 90
Lemon Drop Kid (horse), **00:** 222
Leonard, Justin, 00: 217
Leonardo da Vinci, 00: 61
Le Pen, Jean-Marie, 00: 210
Lerner (Alfred) Hall, 00: 53–54
Lesbianism. See **Homosexuality**
Lesotho, facts in brief, **00:** 40
Lewin, Lord, 00: 163
Lewinsky, Monica, 00: 142, 167, 417, 421
Lewis, Lennox, 00: 107–108
Li Hongzhi, 00: 131, 224
Liberal Democratic Party: Japan, **00:** 252; United Kingdom, **00:** 408–411
Liberal Party: Australia, **00:** 83; Belgium, **00:** 103–104; Canada, **00:** 116, 123–126; Japan, **00:** 252
Liberation Tigers of Tamil Eelam (group), **00:** 377
LIBERIA: facts in brief, **00:** 40
LIBRARY, 00: 265–266, **99:** 263–265
LIBYA, 00: 266, **99:** 265; facts in brief, **00:** 40; population growth, **00:** 306; unemployment, **00:** 307; other references, **00:** 370, 416
Liechtenstein, facts in brief, **00:** 200
Lien Chan, 00: 388
Life, Primitive, 00: 104
Life expectancy, 00: 350
Life is Beautiful (film), **00:** 314, 333
Light, Speed of, 00: 342
Lincoln Memorial, 00: 425
Lindbergh, Charles, 00: 91
Lipscomb, Albert, 00: 157
Lissouba, Pascal, 00: 42
Listeriosis, 00: 205
LITERATURE, AMERICAN, 00: 266–268, **99:** 267–269; Pulitzer Prizes, **00:** 351
LITERATURE, WORLD, 00: 268–279, **99:** 269–271; Nobel Prizes, **00:** 323
LITERATURE FOR CHILDREN, 00: 280–281, **99:** 266–267
LITHUANIA, 00: 282, **99:** 271; EU membership, **00:** 202; facts in brief, **00:** 201
Littleton (Colorado), **00:** 153–154, 176, 378, 392–393
Livent Inc., 00: 398
Livingston, Robert L., 00: 142, 178
Livingstone, Ken, 00: 411
Llewelyn, Desmond, 00: 163
Lobster fishing, 00: 119–122
Lockerbie, Scotland, explosion, 00: 370, 416
Lockett, Tony, 00: 85
Lockheed Martin Corp., 00: 259
Loitering, 00: 383
Lok Sabha (India), **00:** 235, 236
London, 00: 318–319, 382, 408; mayor, **00:** 410–411; terrorism, **00:** 396; theater, **00:** 397–398; train crash, **00:** 170–171
Long Day's Journey into Night (O'Neill), **00:** 399
Lopez, Jennifer, 00: 345
Lord, Bernard, 00: 124
Loroupe, Tegla, 00: 375
Lortel, Lucille, 00: 163
Los Alamos National Laboratory, 00: 419
LOS ANGELES, 00: 282–283, **99:** 271–272; commuting time, **00:** 137; geology, **00:** 213; railroad, **00:** 404
Los Angeles Galaxy (team), **00:** 366
Louima, Abner, 00: 225, 317
Louisiana, 00: 178, 354, 378; statistics, **00:** 379
Lucas, George, 00: 312
Lukas, D. Wayne, 00: 222
Lukashenko, Aleksandr, 00: 102–103
Lumber, 00: 123
Lundy, Dennis, 00: 375
Lusaka (Zambia), **00:** 42, 141
Luswata, Sylvia Nagginda, 00: 407
Lutheran World Federation, 00: 349, 356
Luxembourg, 00: 350; facts in brief, **00:** 201
Luyendyk, Arie, 00: 89
Luzhkov, Yuri, 00: 407
LVMH Moet Moet Hennessey-Louis Vuitton SA (company), **00:** 204, 249

M
Ma, Yo-Yo, 00: 212
Mabatex (company), **00:** 358
Macao, 00: 134
MACEDONIA, 00: 283; facts in brief, **00:** 201; Yu-

goslavia history, **00:** 435–439, 444; other references, **00:** 113, 433
Machover, Tod, 00: 138
Macintosh computer. See **Apple Computer, Inc.**
MacLellan, Russell, 00: 125
Mad cow disease, 00: 414–415
Madagascar, facts in brief, **00:** 41
Madame X (Sargent), **00:** 60 (il.)
Madikizela-Mandela, Winnie, 00: 369
Madura (Indonesia), **00:** 241
Mafia, 00: 251
MAGAZINE, 00: 284, **99:** 272; Canada, **00:** 123
Magazine Publishers of America, 00: 284
Mahathir bin Mohammad, 00: 284
Mahindra, Ibrahim Bare, 00: 44
Maine, 00: 178, 378–380, 383; statistics, **00:** 379
Majko, Pandeli, 00: 48
Major, Clarence, 00: 343
Major League Baseball. See **Baseball**
Major League Soccer, 00: 366
Malaita (Pacific Islands), **00:** 327
Malawi, facts in brief, **00:** 41
MALAYSIA, 00: 284–285, **99:** 272–273; disease, **00:** 350; facts in brief, **00:** 64; other references, **00:** 62, 64–66
Maldives, facts in brief, **00:** 65
Maldonado, Betti, 00: 224
Malevich, Kasimir, 00: 60–61
Mali, 00: 416; facts in brief, **00:** 41
Malielegaoi, Tuila'epa Sailele, 00: 328
Mallory, George, 00: 319
Malone, Karl, 00: 101
Malta, 00: 202; facts in brief, **00:** 201
Mammals, 00: 329–330
Managed care, 00: 219–220, 380
Manchester United (team), **00:** 365
Mandela, Nelson R., 00: 38–42, 367–370
Mandela, Winnie. See **Madikizela-Mandela, Winnie**
Mandleson, Peter, 00: 324, 411–414
Mane, Ansumane, 00: 44
Manitoba, 00: 124
Mannesmann AG (company), **00:** 202–203
Manning, Peyton, 00: 375
Manning, Preston, 00: 116
Mantle, of Earth, 00: 213
MANUFACTURING, 00: 286–287, **99:** 273–274; Japan, **00:** 400
Maple Leaf Gardens (Toronto), **00:** 400
Maple Leafs, Toronto, 00: 400
Marathon, 00: 375
Marijuana, 00: 171, 178
Marine Corps, U.S., 00: 58, 251
Maris, Roger, 99: 87
Marriage, Same-sex, 00: 151
Mars, 00: 66–67, 370–371, 373
Mars, Forrest, 00: 163
Mars Climate Orbiter (spacecraft), **00:** 66–67, 370
Mars Global Surveyor (spacecraft), **00:** 67, 370–371
Mars Polar Lander (spacecraft), **00:** 67, 370
Marshall Islands, 00: 328; facts in brief, **00:** 327
Martha Graham Dance Co., 00: 159
Martin, Paul, 00: 118
Martin, Ricky, 00: 337, 345, 351
Martins, Peter, 00: 158
Martz, Ron, 00: 321
Mary of Teck, 00: 189 (il.)
Maryland, 00: 377, 378, 380, 383, 430; statistics, **00:** 379
Maskhadov, Aslan, 00: 395
Massachusetts, statistics, **00:** 379
Massachusetts Museum of Contemporary Art, 00: 54, 61
Matisse, Henri, 00: 59
Matiyase, Vulindlela, 00: 368
Mature, Victor, 00: 163
Mauresmo, Amelie, 00: 394
Mauritania, facts in brief, **00:** 41
MAURITIUS, 00: 288, **99:** 275; facts in brief, **00:** 41
Maya, 00: 51
Mayi Mayi guerrillas, 00: 149
Mazda (car), **00:** 89
Mazowiecki, Tadeusz, 00: 344
Mbeki, Thabo, 00: 38–42, 367–370
McCain, John, 00: 354
McCann, Donal, 00: 163
McCourt, Frank, 00: 268
McDonald, Piers, 00: 127
McEnroe, John, 00: 395
McGwire, Mark, 00: 95, 97, **99:** 87, 328
MCI WorldCom (company), **00:** 390
McKellen, Ian, 00: 279 (il.)

McKenna, Frank, 00: 124
McKinney, Aaron, 00: 150–151, 225
McManus, Danny, 00: 209
McNair, Bob, 00: 223
McPherson, Wendy, 00: 107
Mease, Darrell, 00: 354–356
Meat, 00: 205–206, 414–415
MediaOne Group (company), 00: 391
Medicaid, 00: 167, 380
Medicare, 00: 146, 167, 219, 366, 390
MEDICINE, 00: 288–289, 99: 275–276; Nobel Prizes, 00: 323. See also AIDS; Drugs; Health-care issues; Mental health
Medinah Temple (Chicago), 00: 130
Meditation (dance), 00: 159
Meerkats, 00: 104
Megret, Bruno, 00: 210
Meijer, Inc., 00: 260
Meissnitzer, Alexandra, 00: 363
Melbourne Kangaroos (team), 00: 85
Mella, Patricia, 00: 125
Mellon, Paul, 00: 163
Mendes, Sam, 00: 311
Menem, Carlos Saul, 00: 55
MENTAL HEALTH, 00: 290, 99: 276–277
Menuhin, Yehudi, 00: 163, 165 (il.)
Mercado, Orlando, 00: 342
Mercosur (organization), 00: 264
Mergers: agriculture, 00: 46; Argentine oil companies, 00: 55–56; Europe, 00: 202–203; fashion, 00: 204; food company, 00: 206; France, 00: 203, 210–211; German aerospace industry, 00: 216–217; Italy, 00: 249–250; Japanese banks, 00: 95; Montreal, 00: 310; Norway, 00: 325; Portuguese banks, 00: 348; radio industry, 00: 352; railroad, 00: 404; Spanish banks, 00: 373; telecommunications, 00: 390–391
MeritaNordbanken Oyj (bank), 00: 325
Messud, Claire, 00: 267
Meta, Ilir, 00: 48
Methodist Church, 00: 349
Methyl parathion (pesticide), 00: 196
Methyl tertiary butyl ether (chemical), 00: 196
Metropolitan Museum of Art (New York City), 00: 61, 316 (il.)
MetroRail (Los Angeles), 00: 283
MEXICO, 00: 291–292, 99: 277–279; archaeology, 00: 51; disasters, 00: 168, 170; facts in brief, 00: 262; soccer, 00: 365; unemployment, 00: 260; other references, 00: 46, 194, 261, 263, 264
Mexico City, 00: 263, 264, 292
Mfume, Kweisi, 00: 392
MIAMI, 00: 292, 99: 279–280
Miami Circle (artifact), 00: 292
Miami International Airport, 00: 292
Michael, Alun, 00: 410
Michigan, 00: 378; statistics, 00: 379
Micronesia, Federated States of, facts in brief, 00: 327
Microsoft Corp., 00: 140, 141, 151, 284, 287, 381
MIDDLE EAST, 00: 293–309, 99: 280–283; cities, 00: 134
Midsummer Night's Dream, A (film), 00: 273 (il.), 278, 279
Mihajlovic, Svetozar, 00: 106
Mi'kmaq Indians, 00: 119
Milan (Italy), 00: 320 (il.)
Military. See Armed forces
Milky Way Galaxy, 00: 74
Millennium, 00: 247, 249, 318–319; astronomy, 00: 79; toys, 00: 402; year 2000 problem, 00: 173, 287
Millennium Dome (England), 00: 318–319, 415
Millennium Wheel (London), 00: 319
Miller, Arthur, 00: 397, 398
Miller, Dan, 00: 124
Mills, Donald, 00: 163
Milosevic, Slobodan, 00: 56, 103, 172, 198, 205, 224, 408, 416, 433, 439–446
Minas Gerais (Brazil), 00: 109
Mindanao (Philippines), 00: 342
Mining, 00: 125–127, 356
Minnesota, 00: 339–340, 378, 380; statistics, 00: 379
Minnesota, University of, 00: 374–375
Miquelena, Luis, 00: 423
Mir (space station), 00: 372
Miramar Mining Corp., 00: 126
Miranda, Altina Schinasi, 00: 163
Miss PICO (boat), 00: 106
Mississippi, 00: 177, 354, 427; statistics, 00: 379

Missouri, 00: 377, 380; statistics, 00: 379
Missouri, U.S.S. (ship), 00: 320 (il.)
Mitchell, Dennis, 00: 402–404
Mitchell, George, 00: 324
Mitchell, Keith, 00: 431
Models, Fashion, 00: 205
Modems, 00: 244
Modern pentathlon, 00: 377
Mohammed VI, 00: 295
Moi, Daniel arap, 00: 256
Moldova, 00: 213
Molecular computer, 00: 179
Molson Centre (Montreal), 00: 310
Monaco, facts in brief, 00: 201
Money. See Bank; Economics; International trade
Money (magazine), 00: 360
Mongol Empire, 00: 184–185
Mongolia, 00: 66; facts in brief, 00: 65
Monroe, Marilyn, 00: 98, 99, 320
Monsanto Co., 00: 46
Monsoons, 00: 66, 169
Mont Blanc Tunnel (France), 00: 171, 211
Montagu, Ashley, 00: 163
Montana, 00: 356, 378–380, 383; statistics, 00: 379
Montenegro, 00: 198, 433, 435–439, 441
Monterey Bay Aquarium (California), 00: 447
Montoya, Carlos, 00: 89
MONTREAL, 00: 310–311, 99: 283–284
Montreal Canadiens, 00: 310
Moody Gardens (Texas), 00: 448
Moon, 00: 371, 372
Moons. See Satellites, Planetary
Moore, Brian, 00: 163
Moore, Greg, 00: 89
Morauta, Sir Mekere, 00: 328
Moravian Church in America, 00: 349
Morgan Stanley Dean Witter & Co., 00: 264
Morgenthau, Robert M., 00: 60
Morita, Akio, 00: 163
Moro Islamic Liberation Front (group), 00: 342
Morocco, 00: 295; facts in brief, 00: 41; Middle East history, 00: 296, 298, 302, 309; population growth, 00: 306; unemployment, 00: 307
Morris, Edmund, 00: 268
Morris, Mark, 00: 158
Morris, Willie, 00: 163
Moscoso, Mireya, 00: 263, 331, 337–338
Moscow, 00: 359, 395
Moss, Kate, 00: 205
Moths, Rattlebox, 00: 105–106
MOTION PICTURES, 00: 311–314, 99: 284–287; books, future of, 00: 266; Montreal, 00: 310; Shakespeare, 00: 271, 272, 275–279
Motley, Marion, 00: 163
Motorcycle racing, 00: 377
Mount Baker (Washington), 00: 427
Mount Everest, 00: 319
Mount Laguna (California), 00: 427
Mount Union College, 00: 207
Movement for Democratic Change (party, Zimbabwe), 00: 447
Movement for the Liberation of Congo (group), 00: 141
Mowlam, Mo, 00: 324
Moynihan, Daniel Patrick, 00: 166, 167
Mozambique, 00: 38; facts in brief, 00: 41
MP3 format, 00: 179, 346
Mubarak, Hosni, 00: 176, 177
Mugabe, Robert, 00: 447
Mundell, Robert A., 00: 323
Murakami, Haruki, 00: 269
Murden, Tori, 00: 321
Murder rate, 00: 153
Murdoch, Iris, 00: 163
Murphy Family Farms, 00: 46
Murray, Kathryn, 00: 163
Murray, Les, 00: 80
Musaveni, Yoweri, 00: 407
Muscular-skeletal injuries, 00: 260
Museum of Modern Art (New York City), 00: 59–61
Musgrove, Ronnie, 00: 177, 354
Musharraf, Pervez, 00: 328–329
Music Alive (program), 00: 139
Music copying, 00: 179, 346. See also Classical music; Popular music
Musicals, 00: 398, 399
Muslims: India, 00: 236, 237; Indonesia, 00: 241; Mauritius, 00: 288; South Africa, 00: 369; Turkey, 00: 406; Yemen, 00: 431; Yugoslavia, 00: 435, 436, 439, 442, 443. See also Islam;

Islamic fundamentalism
Mussels, 00: 128
Mussolini, Benito, 00: 250
Mutebi, Ronald Muwenda, II, 00: 407
MYANMAR, 00: 314, 99: 287; facts in brief, 00: 65; other references, 00: 62–64
Mysteries of Small Houses (Notley), 00: 343
"Mysteries of the Deep" (exhibit), 00: 447

N

NAACP. See National Association for the Advancement of Colored People
Nairobi (Kenya), 00: 256
Namibia, 00: 42, 141; facts in brief, 00: 41
Nano, Fatos, 00: 48
Napoleon I, 00: 189
NASA. See National Aeronautics and Space Administration
NASCAR racing, 00: 89
Nasdaq Composite Index, 00: 381
Nasdaq exchange, 00: 203
Nasser, Gamel Abdel, 00: 302
National Academy of Recording Arts and Sciences. See Grammy Awards
National Academy of Television Arts and Sciences. See Emmy Awards
National Action Party (Mexico), 00: 291
National Aeronautics and Space Administration, 00: 334–335, 370–373
National Association for the Advancement of Colored People, 00: 150, 224, 392
National Association of Letter Carriers, 00: 258
National Association of Purchasing Management, 00: 287
National Basketball Association, 00: 100–101, 223
National Bipartisan Commission on the Future of Medicare, 00: 219
National Book Awards, 00: 266–268, 343
National Broadcasting Co., 00: 391–394
National Collegiate Athletic Association, 00: 100–102, 206
National Conference of State Legislatures, 00: 377, 378
National Constituent Assembly (Venezuela), 00: 423
National Crime Information Center 2000, 00: 420
National Democratic Alliance (India), 00: 235, 236
National Football Conference, 00: 209
National Football League, 00: 207–209, 223, 374, 375
National Front Party (France), 00: 210
National Gallery of Art (Washington, D.C.), 00: 61
National Highway Traffic Safety Administration, 00: 89
National Hockey League, 00: 374, 375
National Hot Rod Association, 00: 90
National Institutes of Health, 00: 288, 289
National League of Cities, 00: 134
National Liberation Army, 00: 139
National Museum of Anthropology (Mexico City), 00: 292
National Museum of the American Indian (Washington, D.C.), 00: 240, 427
National Park Service (U.S.), 00: 53
National Party (New Zealand), 00: 317
National People's Congress (China), 00: 132–134
National Postal Mail Handlers Union, 00: 258
National Resistance Movement (Uganda), 00: 407
National Transportation Safety Board (U.S.), 00: 91, 92
National Urban League, 00: 224
Nationalism, Middle East, 00: 299–309
Nationalist Action Party (Turkey), 00: 406
NATO. See North Atlantic Treaty Organization
Natural gas, 00: 92, 195
Nauru, 00: 327, 416; facts in brief, 00: 327
Navy, U.S., 00: 351
Nawaz Sharif, 00: 328–329
Nazarbayev, Nursultan, 00: 256
Nazis, 00: 214, 216, 325; art looting, 00: 59–61; empire, 00: 190–191; Yugoslavia invasion, 00: 437, 438
NBC. See National Broadcasting Co.
Neanderthals, 00: 49–50
Nebraska, 00: 224; statistics, 00: 379
Necaxa (team), 00: 365–366

Nepal, 00: 66; facts in brief, 00: 65
Netanyahu, Benjamin, 00: 248
NETHERLANDS, 00: 314–315, 99: 288; facts in brief, 00: 201; other references, 00: 202, 350
Nevada, 00: 378; statistics, 00: 379
Nevirapine (drug), 00: 47
Nevis. See St. Kitts and Nevis
New Brunswick, 00: 116, 119, 124
New Caledonia (Pacific Islands), 00: 327
New Carissa (ship), 00: 405
New Dehli, 00: 237
New Democratic Party (Canada), 00: 116, 124–126
New Hampshire, 00: 258, 378–380; statistics, 00: 379
New Holland N.V. (company), 00: 46
New Jersey, 00: 224, 378–380, 430; statistics, 00: 379
New Jersey Coastal Heritage Trail Route, 00: 147
New Markets (program), 00: 431
New Mexico, 00: 240, 258, 380; statistics, 00: 379
New Orleans (Louisiana), 00: 150, 212
New South Wales, 00: 83, 84
New York (state), 00: 167, 197, 345; statistics, 00: 379. See also New York City
NEW YORK CITY, 00: 315–317, 99: 289–290; architecture, 00: 53–54; art, 00: 59–61; civil rights, 00: 212, 225; classical music, 00: 137, 138; dance, 00: 158, 159; economics, 00: 134, 136; railroad, 00: 404–405; theater, 00: 396–398; weather, 00: 430; welfare, 00: 136; zoo, 00: 447
New York City Ballet, 00: 158
New York Knickerbockers, 00: 100
New York State Theater, 00: 137
New York Stock Exchange, 00: 264, 382
New York Yankees, 00: 95–97
New Yorker (magazine), 00: 267
NEW ZEALAND, 00: 317, 99: 290; cricket, 00: 152, 153; facts in brief, 00: 327; rugby, 00: 357; other references, 00: 46, 83
Newfoundland, 00: 116, 124–125
Newley, Anthony, 00: 163
NEWS BYTES, 00: 318–321, 99: 291–295
NEWSPAPER, 00: 321, 99: 295–305
Newton, Isaac, 00: 73
NICARAGUA, 99: 306; facts in brief, 00: 262
Nicholson, Jim, 00: 354
Nielsen Media Research, 00: 391
Nielson, Jerri, 00: 319–320
Niemann-Stirnemann, Gunda, 00: 235
Niger, 00: 44; facts in brief, 00: 41
NIGERIA, 00: 322, 99: 306; disasters, 00: 168–169, 170; facts in brief, 00: 41; other references, 00: 38, 42, 338
Nikkei 225 index, 00: 382
Nikon, Bishop, 00: 172
Nintendo Co., Ltd., 00: 402
Nisga'a (people), 00: 124
Nissan Motor Co., 00: 211
Nixon, Richard M., 00: 393, 423, 448
Nkabinde, Sifiso, 00: 368
Nkomo, Joshua, 00: 447
NMDA (substance), 00: 290
NOBEL PRIZES, 00: 323, 99: 307
Nordic skiing, 00: 363
Norfolk Southern Corp., 00: 404
Norris, Orlin, 00: 108
Norsk Hydro ASA (company), 00: 325
North Atlantic Treaty Organization: Azerbaijan, 00: 92; Canada, 00: 119; Czech Republic, 00: 157; expansion, 00: 198–199, 201–202; Hungary, 00: 234; Poland, 00: 344; Romania, 00: 356; Russia, 00: 360; Serbia bombing, 00: 48, 56, 103, 113, 198, 216, 408, 416, 433; Slovakia, 00: 364; Yugoslavia history, 00: 435, 443–446
North Carolina, 00: 169–170, 378, 430; statistics, 00: 379
North Dakota, statistics, 00: 379
North Korea. See Korea, North
Northern Alliance (Afghanistan), 00: 38
NORTHERN IRELAND, 00: 324, 99: 308; other references, 00: 410, 415
Northwest Territories, 00: 126–127
Norvo, Red (Kenneth), 00: 163, 164 (il.)
NORWAY, 00: 325, 99: 309; facts in brief, 00: 201
Norwood, Charles, 00: 219
Not About Nightingales (Williams), 00: 397–398
Notley, Alice, 00: 343
Notre Dame University, 00: 206
Nouri, Abdollah, 00: 244
Nova Scotia, 00: 119, 125

Nsibambi, Apollo, 00: 407
Nubians, 00: 298
Nuclear energy, 00: 194 (il.), 214–216, 251–252, 386
Nuclear weapons: China-U.S. spy case, 00: 419; India, 00: 237 (il.), 238; Japan, 00: 252; North Korea, 00: 257; Russia-U.S. conflict, 00: 360
Nunavut, 00: 116, 126, 127
Nurses, 00: 125–126
Nyachae, Simeon, 00: 256
Nyanga (South Africa), 00: 368
Nyerere, Julius Kambarage, 00: 164

O

O (show), 00: 399
Obasanjo, Olusegun, 00: 38, 322, 338
Obituaries. See Deaths
Obuchi, Keizo, 00: 242, 252, 253, 99: 329
Ocalan, Abdullah, 00: 218, 295, 314 (il.), 405–406
OCEAN, 00: 325–326, 99: 309. See also Atlantic Ocean; Pacific Ocean
Ocean Journey (Denver), 00: 448
Oceanic Adventures Newport Aquarium (Ohio), 00: 447
Odalisque (Matisse), 00: 59
Of No Country I Know (Ferry), 00: 343
Offili, Chris, 00: 61
Oglala Lakota Sioux, 00: 239 (il.), 240
Ohio, 00: 197, 378, 380, 447; statistics, 00: 379
Ohio State University, 00: 206
Oil, Chemical, and Atomic Workers International Union, 00: 260
Oil spill, 00: 405. See also Petroleum
Okalik, Paul, 00: 126
Oklahoma, 00: 240, 427, 428 (il.); statistics, 00: 379
Oklahoma! (musical), 00: 397
Olazabal, Jose Maria, 00: 217
Old Man and the Sea, The (Hemingway), 00: 267
Oldfield, David, 00: 83
Oliver, Solomon, 00: 175
Olivetti SpA (company), 00: 203, 249
Olmsted, Frederick Law, 00: 212
OLYMPIC GAMES, 00: 326; Australia, 00: 83
Olympic Stadium (Montreal), 00: 310
O'Malley, Martin, 00: 178
Oman, 00: 306; facts in brief, 00: 294
Omar, Mullah Mohammad, 00: 38
O'Meara, Mark, 99: 328–329
One Israel (party), 00: 248
O'Neill, Eugene, 00: 397–399
O'Neill, Susie, 00: 387
Ong Teng Cheong, 00: 362
Ontario, 00: 125. See also Toronto
OPEC, 00: 194, 361, 381
Open, U.S. (tennis), 00: 394, 395
Operation Blue Crane, 00: 369
Operation Condor, 00: 263
Orange Order (group), 00: 324
Oregon, 00: 122, 356; statistics, 00: 379
Oresund Fixed Link (bridge), 00: 167
Organization for Economic Cooperation and Development, 00: 260
Organization of African Unity, 00: 42, 288, 370
Organization of Petroleum Exporting Countries, 00: 194, 361, 381
Orioles, Baltimore. See Baltimore Orioles
"Oscars." See Academy Awards
Oslo Accords (1993), 00: 305
Ossetia, North (Russia), 00: 395
Othello (film), 00: 278 (il.), 279
Ottawa, 00: 117 (il.)
Ottey, Merlene, 00: 402–404
Otto I (Holy Roman emperor), 00: 183–184
Ottoman Empire, 00: 185–186, 296–298, 435, 443; map, 00: 302
Ovary transplant, 00: 288–289
Oviedo, Lino Cesar, 00: 332
Owens, Jesse, 00: 326 (il.)
Owensboro Messenger-Inquirer, 00: 321
Oxygen, 00: 213
Oz, Amos, 00: 269
Ozawa, Isihiro, 00: 252
Ozawa, Seiji, 00: 138, 338–339

P

PACE International Union, 00: 260
PACIFIC ISLANDS, 00: 327–328, 99: 318–319
Pacific Ocean, 00: 325
Pacifica Foundation, 00: 352–353
Paeniu, Bikenebeu, 00: 328
Pak, Se Ri, 99: 329

PAKISTAN, 00: 328–329, 99: 320; cricket, 00: 152, 153; cyclone, 00: 169; facts in brief, 00: 65; other references, 00: 237–238, 395
Paksas, Rolandus, 00: 282
Palau, facts in brief, 00: 327
PALEONTOLOGY, 00: 329–330, 99: 321–323
Palestine, 00: 248, 298–302
Palestine Liberation Organization, 00: 114, 304, 305, 307, 395
Palestinians, 00: 177, 248, 293–295, 298–304, 308
Palmeiras (team), 00: 365
Paltrow, Gwyneth, 00: 205, 313 (il.), 339
PAN AMERICAN GAMES, 00: 330
PANAMA, 00: 331–332, 99: 323; facts in brief, 00: 262; other references, 00: 263, 264, 337–338
Panama Canal, 00: 331–332
Panchen Lama, 00: 109
Panda, 00: 448
Papua New Guinea, 00: 328; facts in brief, 00: 327
Parade (musical), 00: 398
PARAGUAY, 00: 332, 99: 323; facts in brief, 00: 262; other references, 00: 263, 264
Paribas S.A. (bank), 00: 210
Paris, 00: 376 (il.)
Parker, Mike, 00: 177, 354
Parks, Rosa, 00: 224, 229
Parliament (UK), 00: 408, 410–411
Parti Quebecois, 00: 125–126
Particulates (pollution), 00: 196–197
Partisans (Yugoslavia), 00: 437
Party of God. See Hezbollah
Pascua, Charles, 00: 210
Pastrana Arango, Andres, 00: 139, 140, 99: 329–330
Pataki, George, 00: 53
Patents, 00: 383
Paterson, Jennifer, 00: 164
Paterson, Louise, 00: 164
Patterson, P. J., 00: 431
Patton, Paul, 00: 177–178
Pavle, Patriarch, 00: 172
Pawar, Sharad, 00: 236
Paxil (drug), 00: 290
Payton, Walter, 00: 131, 160 (il.), 164, 374
Peace Prize, Nobel, 00: 323
Pearl Harbor attack, 00: 420
Pearl industry, 00: 328
Peavy, John, Jr., 00: 224
Peck, Bob, 00: 164
Pennsylvania, 00: 380, 429 (il.), 430; statistics, 00: 379. See also Philadelphia
Pennsylvania State University, 00: 206
Pennsylvania Station (New York City), 00: 53, 404–405
Penzias, Arno, 00: 76, 78 (il.)
PEOPLE IN THE NEWS, 00: 332–340, 99: 324–334. See also Deaths; News bytes
People's Action Party (Singapore), 00: 362
People's Alliance (Sri Lanka), 00: 377
People's Consultative Assembly (Indonesia), 00: 240
People's Democratic Party (Nigeria), 00: 322
People's Liberation Front (Sri Lanka), 00: 377
People's Party: Austria, 00: 86; Switzerland, 00: 387
People's Republic of China. See China
Perez Balladares, Ernesto, 00: 332
Peron, Eva, 00: 55
Persian Gulf War (1991), 00: 57, 308–309
Persians, 00: 298. See also Iran
Persson, Goran, 00: 385, 386
PERU, 00: 340, 99: 334; facts in brief, 00: 262; other references, 00: 261 (il.), 264
Pesticides, 00: 149, 196
Petain, Henri Philippe, 00: 211
Peters, F. Whitten, 00: 59
Peterson, Bart, 00: 178
Petkovski, Tito, 00: 283
Petritsch, Wolfgang, 00: 107
Petrobangla (company), 00: 92
PETROBRAS (company), 00: 109
Petroleum, 00: 194–195; Argentina, 00: 55; Azerbaijan, 00: 92; Brazil, 00: 109, 264; France, 00: 210–211; Saudi Arabia, 00: 361; stocks, 00: 381; trade, 00: 242–243, 448. See also Oil spill
Petronas Twin Towers (Malaysia), 00: 285 (il.)
Pfeiffer, Michelle, 00: 273 (il.)
Phieu, Le Kha, 00: 424
PHILADELPHIA, 00: 340–341, 99: 334–335; elections, 00: 178
Philadelphia Phillies, 00: 341
Philbin, Regis, 00: 393

PHILIPPINES, **00:** 341–342, **99:** 335–336; facts in brief, **00:** 65; floods, **00:** 169; other references, **00:** 62, 64–66
Philips Electronics North America, **00:** 179
Phillips, Duncan, **00:** 427
Phillips Collection (Washington, D.C.), **00:** 427
Phnom Penh, Cambodia, **00:** 115 (il.)
Photosynthesis, **00:** 104
PHYSICS, **00:** 342–343, **99:** 336–337; Nobel Prizes, **00:** 323
Physiology Prize, Nobel, **00:** 323
Picasso, Pablo, **00:** 59
Piccard, Bertrand, **00:** 318
Pickering, Thomas, **00:** 246
Pine Ridge Indian Reservation, **00:** 240
Pinochet Ugarte, Augusto, **00:** 131, 263
Pio, Padre, **00:** 355 (il.)
Piracy, **00:** 65
Planets, **00:** 68–74; extrasolar, **00:** 66
Plath, Sylvia, **00:** 268
Plato, Dana, **00:** 164
PLO. See **Palestine Liberation Organization**
Plushenko, Yevgeny, **00:** 234, 235
Pluto (planet), **00:** 66, 67
Poaching, **00:** 149
POETRY, **00:** 343, **99:** 337–338; children's literature, **00:** 280. See also **Canadian literature; Literature for children**
Pokemon (toys), **00:** 401 (il.), 402
POLAND, **00:** 344, **99:** 338–339; facts in brief, **00:** 201; other references, **00:** 198–199, 201, 360
Police, **00:** 157, 225, 317, 383, 425
Polio, **00:** 172, 289
Political Islam, **00:** 305–309
Pollin, Abe, **00:** 375
Pollution credits, **00:** 195
Pope. See **John Paul II**
Poplasen, Nikola, **00:** 106–107
POPULAR MUSIC, **00:** 344–347, **99:** 339–347
POPULATION, **00:** 347–348, **99:** 348; China, **00:** 133; cities, **00:** 135–136; India, **00:** 238; Middle East, **00:** 306, 309. See also **Census** and specific continent and country articles
Pork, **00:** 350
Portillo, Alfonso, **00:** 219
Portillo, Michael, **00:** 411
PORTUGAL, **00:** 348, **99:** 348–349; facts in brief, **00:** 201; other references, **00:** 134, 416
Postal Service (U.S.), **00:** 212, 243 (il.), 258
Potter, Harry (character), **00:** 281
Poultry, **00:** 205–206
Pratt, Steve, **00:** 83
Preakness Stakes, **00:** 222
Pregnancy, **00:** 47
Prehistoric people, **00:** 49–50
Presbyterian Church (U.S.A.), **00:** 349–350
President of the United States. See **United States, President of the**
President's Council on Invasive Species, **00:** 212
Presley, Elvis, **00:** 345
Press. See **Magazine; Newspaper**
Preval, Rene, **00:** 219
Priceline.com (business), **00:** 243
Prices. See **Economics; Inflation; Labor and employment**
Primakov, Yevgeny, **00:** 358, **99:** 330
Prime Minister. See **Australia, Prime Minister of; Canada, Prime Minister of; United Kingdom, Prime Minister of**
Prince Edward Island, **00:** 125
Princess Mononoke (film), **00:** 312
Princeton University, **00:** 128–129
Pringle, Johnnie, **00:** 352 (il.)
PRISON, **00:** 348, **99:** 349; mentally ill, **00:** 290
Pristina (Kosovo), **00:** 360
Pritzker, Jay, **00:** 164
Pritzker Prize, **00:** 54
Privacy, and computers, **00:** 140–141
Prodi, Romano, **00:** 200
Profamilia (program), **00:** 261–263
Professional Bowlers Association, **00:** 107
Professional Golfers Association, **00:** 217
Professional Women's Bowling Association, **00:** 107
Progressive Conservative Party (Canada), **00:** 116, 124–126
Promodes S.A. (company), **00:** 211
Protas, Ron, **00:** 159
Proteins, **00:** 323
PROTESTANTISM, **00:** 349–350, **99:** 350–351
"Providence" (TV show), **00:** 393
Psychiatry. See **Mental health**

Psychologists, **00:** 290
Ptolemy, **00:** 70–71
Public Broadcasting System, **00:** 393
PUBLIC HEALTH AND SAFETY, **00:** 350, **99:** 351; airlines, **00:** 91–92; automobiles, **00:** 89, 350. See also **AIDS; Food; Medicine**
Pueblo Indians, **00:** 240
PUERTO RICO, **00:** 351, **99:** 352; facts in brief, **00:** 262; presidential clemency, **00:** 422
Puerto Rico Telephone Co., **00:** 351
PULITZER PRIZES, **00:** 351, **99:** 352; poetry, **00:** 343
Purdue University, **00:** 102
Putin, Vladimir, **00:** 102, 358–360
Putrajaya (Malaysia), **00:** 284
Puzo, Mario, **00:** 164
Pyewacket (boat), **00:** 106
Pyramids, Great (Egypt), **00:** 177

Q

Qadhafi, Muammar Muhammad al-, **00:** 266, 370
Qatar, **00:** 306; facts in brief, **00:** 294
Quayle, Dan, **00:** 353
Quebec, **00:** 116, 118, 125–126. See also **Montreal**
Quebecor Printing, Inc., **00:** 310
Queensland, **00:** 84
Quisling, Vidkun, **00:** 325

R

Rabbo, Yasir Abed, **00:** 293–294
Rabin, Yitzak, **00:** 305
Rabuka, Sitiveni, **00:** 328
Racing. See **Automobile racing; Horse racing; Motorcycle racing; Sled dog racing**
Radical Democrats (Switzerland), **00:** 387
RADIO, **00:** 352–353, **99:** 353
Radio City Music Hall (New York City), **00:** 53
Radisic, Zivko, **00:** 107
Railroads, **00:** 157, 283, 317, 404, 405 (il.); crashes, **00:** 170–171, 236 (il.), 238, 415
Rain forests, **00:** 66, 149, 447
Rally for Congolese Democracy (group), **00:** 141
Rally for France (party), **00:** 210
Rally for the Republic Party (France), **00:** 210
Ralston, Joseph, **00:** 59
Ramgoolam, Navinchandra, **00:** 288
Ramirez Durand, Oscar, **00:** 340
Ramsey, Sir Alf, **00:** 164
Ramsey, Charles H., **00:** 425
Rands, Bernard, **00:** 138
Rap music, **00:** 344
Rape, **00:** 153
Rape of Nanjing, The (book), **00:** 253
Raptors (team), **00:** 400
Rasmussen, Poul Nyrup, **00:** 167
Rattle, Sir Simon, **00:** 138
Raymond, Arthur, **00:** 164
Reagan, Ronald, **00:** 268
Real (currency), **00:** 174
Recession: Asia, **00:** 62, 173, 242, 284, **99:** 170–179; Latin America, **00:** 174, 264
Red Brigades (group), **00:** 396
Redington, Joe, **00:** 164
Reed, Oliver, **00:** 164
Reese, Pee Wee, **00:** 163 (il.), 164
Reform Party: Canada, **00:** 116; U.S., **00:** 340, 354
Refugees: African, **00:** 38, 362; Asian, **00:** 65–66; Cuban, **00:** 156; Kosovar, **00:** 48, 83–84, 107, 198, 254–255, 283, 416, 433, 435, 441–445; Switzerland referendum, **00:** 388; U.S. rules, **00:** 235; World War II, **00:** 387–388
Reich, Steve, **00:** 139
Reichstag (Berlin), **00:** 54, 113, 215 (il.)
Reilly, Clint, **00:** 360–361
Relenza (drug), **00:** 172
RELIGION. See also specific religions
Renault S.A. (company), **00:** 211
Rendell, Ed, **00:** 340
Reno, Janet, **00:** 419
Reno Air (airline), **00:** 259
Repair (Williams), **00:** 343
Repsol SA (company), **00:** 55–56
REPUBLICAN PARTY, **00:** 353–354, **99:** 353–355; Clinton impeachment, **00:** 421; elections, **00:** 177–178; fund-raising, **00:** 142; health care, **00:** 219; Philadelphia, **00:** 340, 341; taxes, **00:** 390; other references, **00:** 142, 146, 335
Resurrection (opera), **00:** 138
Revolutionary Armed Forces of Colombia, **00:** 139, 140
Revolutionary Democratic Party (Mexico), **00:** 291
Revolutionary United Front (Sierra Leone), **00:** 362
Reyes, Ben, **00:** 224
Reye's syndrome, **00:** 350

Rhode Island, **00:** 430; statistics, **00:** 379
Rhys-Jones, Sophie, **00:** 415
Ribeiroia (flatworm), **00:** 105
Richard III (film), **00:** 278
Richardson, Bill, **00:** 419, **99:** 330–331
Ride, Sally Kristen, **00:** 373
Ridgeway, Aden, **00:** 80
Ringholm, Bosse, **00:** 386
Ringling Brothers Barnum & Bailey Circus, **00:** 320–321
Rio (recorder), **00:** 179
Rio de Janeiro, **00:** 109
Ripken, Cal, Sr., **00:** 164
Rite Aid Corp., **00:** 260
Rivera, Mariano, **00:** 97
Robbery, **00:** 153
Robertson, Betty, **00:** 164
Robinson, Geoffrey, **00:** 411
Robles Berlanga, Rosario, **00:** 263
Rock music. See **Popular music**
Rocket launches, **00:** 372
Rockets, Houston, **00:** 223
Rodgers, Richard, **00:** 397
Roe v. Wade, **00:** 385
Rogers, Buddy, **00:** 164
Rojas, Waldemar, **00:** 157
Roma (people), **00:** 156
Roman, Ruth, **00:** 164
ROMAN CATHOLIC CHURCH, **00:** 354–356, **99:** 355–356; empires, **00:** 182, 184; Protestant communion, **00:** 349
Roman Empire, **00:** 180–181, 183
ROMANIA, **00:** 356, **99:** 356; facts in brief, **00:** 201; other references, **00:** 173, 202
Romanow, Roy, **00:** 126
Rome, Ancient, **00:** 53
Romeo and Juliet (film), **00:** 276–277, 279
Ronaldo, **00:** 366
Roosevelt, Franklin D., **00:** 421
Rose, Pete, **00:** 95
Rosello, Pedro J., **00:** 351
Rosenberg, Paul, **00:** 59
Rossington, Norman, **00:** 164
Rothschild family, **00:** 61
Rouse, Christopher, **00:** 138
Route 66, **00:** 147
Rowing, **00:** 321, 376
Rowling, J. K., **00:** 281
Royal Canadian Mounted Police, **00:** 124
Royal Library (Copenhagen), **00:** 265
Royal Teton Ranch, **00:** 150
Rubin, Robert E., **00:** 114, 239
RUGBY FOOTBALL, **00:** 357, **99:** 357; Australia, **00:** 83
Ruiz Massieu, Jose Francisco, **00:** 291
Rushdie, Salman, **00:** 268
Russell, David O., **00:** 311
Russell 2000 index, **00:** 382
RUSSIA, **00:** 358–360, **99:** 358–361; archaeology, **00:** 51; ballet, **00:** 159; chess, **00:** 129; Eastern Orthodox Church, **00:** 172–173; facts in brief, **00:** 65; ice skating, **00:** 234, 235; Kosovo conflict, **00:** 198, 433; Mandela visit, **00:** 370; space program, **00:** 371, 372; terrorism, **00:** 359, 395; other references, **00:** 46, 92, 102, 205, 213, 407. See also **Chechnya; Union of Soviet Socialist Republics**
Ruth, Babe, **00:** 95
RWANDA, **99:** 361; facts in brief, **00:** 41; other references, **00:** 42, 141, 147, 407
Ryan, Nolan, **00:** 97
Ryder Cup, **00:** 217

S

Sabarimala (shrine), **00:** 220
Sabres, Buffalo, **00:** 220–221
Sabunji, Taha, **00:** 247
Sachar, Louis, **00:** 281
Sadat, Anwar el-, **00:** 176, 304–305
Safeco Field (Seattle), **00:** 111, 112 (il.)
Safety. See **Public health and safety**
Saga Petroleum ASA (company), **00:** 325
St. Kitts and Nevis, facts in brief, **00:** 262
St. Lucia, **00:** 431; facts in brief, **00:** 262
St. Vincent and the Grenadines, facts in brief, **00:** 262
Saint Lawrence Seaway, **00:** 119
Saitoti, George, **00:** 256
Salaries, **00:** 258
Salinas de Gortari, Raul, **00:** 263, 291–292
Salk vaccine, **00:** 289
Salmon fishing, **00:** 122

Salmonella poisoning, **00:** 206
Salt Lake City (Utah), **00:** 178, 430
Samoa, **00:** 328; facts in brief, **00:** 327
Sampras, Pete, **00:** 395
San Andreas Fault, **00:** 213
San Antonio Spurs, **00:** 100
SAN FRANCISCO, **00:** 360–361, **99:** 361–362;
    elections, **00:** 178
San Francisco Chronicle, **00:** 361
San Francisco Examiner, **00:** 361
San Marino, facts in brief, **00:** 201
Sanders, Barry, **00:** 209
Sandpaper Ballet (dance), **00:** 158
Sankoh, Foday, **00:** 362
Santa Fe (New Mexico), **00:** 54
Santana, Carlos, **00:** 345
Santer, Jacques, **00:** 200
Santo Domingo (Dominican Republic), **00:** 431
Santos, Eduardo dos, **00:** 42
São Tome and Principe, facts in brief, **00:** 41
Saputo Group, Inc., **00:** 310
Sara Lee Corp., **00:** 205
Sarajevo (Yugoslavia), **00:** 441 (il.), 442, 443
Sarazen, Gene, **00:** 164
Sargent, John Singer, **00:** 60 (il.)
Sarkisian, Vazgen, **00:** 395
Saskatchewan, **00:** 126
Sassou-Nguesso, Denis, **00:** 42
Satcher, David, **00:** 290, 420–421, **99:** 331
Satellites, Artificial, **00:** 370, 373, 390, 391
Satellites, Planetary, **00:** 67
Saturn (car), **00:** 86
SAUDI ARABIA, **00:** 361, **99:** 362–363; facts in
    brief, **00:** 294; Internet, **00:** 248; Middle East
    history, **00:** 306, 308; population growth, **00:**
    306; other references, **00:** 194, 195, 214
Sautter, Christian, **00:** 210
Savimbi, Jonas, **00:** 42
Sayão, Bidu, **00:** 164
Sayegh, Hani al-, **00:** 361
SBC Communications, **00:** 351, 390
Schawlow, Arthur, **00:** 164
Schiele, Egon, **00:** 59–61
Schizophrenia, **00:** 290
Schools. See Education
Schroeder, Gerhard, **00:** 203, 214, 216, **99:**
    331–332
Schuster, Rudolf, **00:** 364
Schwartz, Charles, **00:** 225
Schweitzer, Joseph, **00:** 58
Scipionyx samniticus (dinosaur), **00:** 330
Scopes trial, **00:** 150
Scotland, **00:** 152, 357, 408–410; Lockerbie ex-
    plosion, **00:** 370, 416
Scott, George C., **00:** 163 (il.), 164
Scruggs, Kathy, **00:** 321
Scurry, Brianna, **00:** 364
Scythians, **00:** 53
Sea-Land (company), **00:** 404
Sea Launch (mission), **00:** 372
Seaborg, Glenn, **00:** 164
Seattle (Washington), **00:** 46, 112 (il.), 203, 243
Seattle Art Museum, **00:** 59
Second Avenue Subway (New York City), **00:** 317
Secure Digital Music Initiative, **00:** 179
Securities and Exchange Commission (U.S.), **00:**
    292
Seeing (music), **00:** 138
Segregation, **00:** 228, 229, 385
Seinfeld, Jerry, **99:** 332
Self Possessed (horse), **00:** 222
Semiautomatic assault weapons, **00:** 146
Semon, Waldo, **00:** 164
Senate. See Congress of the United States
Senegal, facts in brief, **00:** 41
Senor Wences, **00:** 164
"Sensations" (exhibit), **00:** 61, 315
Sepkoski, John, Jr., **00:** 165
Serbia, **00:** 433; Australia, **00:** 83; bombing, **00:**
    49, 56, 58 (il.), 113, 198, 360, 408, 414, 433,
    444–445; Eastern Orthodox Church, **00:** 172;
    Finland, **00:** 205; Yugoslavia history, **00:**
    436–446. See also Kosovo; Yugoslavia
Serbs, Croats, and Slovenes, Kingdom of, **00:**
    435–437
Sereno, Paul, **00:** 329 (il.)
Seth, Vikram, **00:** 268
Sexual harassment, **00:** 383
Seychelles, facts in brief, **00:** 41
Shakespeare, William, **00:** 271–279
Shakespeare in Love (film), **00:** 271, 272, 335,
    339

Shalala, Donna, **00:** 380
Sharif, Mohammad Nawaz, **00:** 237–238
Shas (party, Israel), **00:** 248
Shaw, Robert, **00:** 165
Shenzhou (spacecraft), **00:** 372
Shepard, Matthew, **00:** 150–151, 225
Shevardnadze, Eduard, **00:** 213
Shiites, **00:** 307
Shining Path (group), **00:** 340
Shinseki, Eric K., **00:** 59
Shipley, Jenny, **00:** 317
Shipping, **00:** 65, 405
Ships, Ancient, **00:** 53
Shipwrecks, **00:** 168–169
Shiromani Gurwara Parbandhak Committee, **00:**
    362
Shyness, **00:** 290
Sicily, **00:** 198
Side Man (Leight), **00:** 397
Sidney, Sylvia, **00:** 165
SIERRA LEONE, **00:** 362, **99:** 363–364; facts in
    brief, **00:** 41; other references, **00:** 42, 44
Siew, Vincent, **00:** 388
Sikharulidze, Anton, **00:** 235
SIKHISM, **00:** 362, **99:** 364
Silajdzic, Haris, **00:** 106
Silent Spring (Carson), **00:** 196
Sill, Aleta, **00:** 107
Silva Henriquez, Raul, **00:** 131
Silverstein, Shel, **00:** 163, 165
Simitis, Costas, **00:** 218
Simon, Paul (senator), **00:** 266
Simon, Paul (singer), **00:** 345–346
Simpson, Wallis, **00:** 408
Sin, Jaime Cardinal, **00:** 341
Sinatra, Frank, **99:** 341–347
Sineath, Charles, **00:** 349
SINGAPORE, **00:** 362, **99:** 364; facts in brief, **00:**
    65; other references, **00:** 62, 66
Singh, Maharaja Duleep, **00:** 362
Sinn Fein (group), **00:** 324
Sinornithosaurus millenii (dinosaur), **00:** 330
Sirivudh, Prince, **00:** 115 (il.)
Siskel, Gene, **00:** 131, 160 (il.), 165
Six-Day War (1967), **00:** 304
Sixth Sense, The (film), **00:** 313
"60 Minutes II" (TV show), **00:** 394
Skele, Andris, **00:** 265
Skidmore, Owings & Merrill (company), **00:** 53
SKIING, **00:** 363, **99:** 365
Skopje (Macedonia), **00:** 283
Slate (magazine), **00:** 284
Slater, Rodney E., **00:** 404
Slavery, **00:** 216, 382
Sled dog racing, **00:** 377
Sleeping Beauty, The (ballet), **00:** 159
Sleepy Hollow (film), **00:** 311
SLOVAKIA, **00:** 364, **99:** 366; EU membership,
    00: 202
Slovenia, **00:** 201, 435–441; facts in brief, **00:**
    201
Smallpox, **00:** 288
Smith, Benjamin, **00:** 154–155, 225
Smith, Chad, **00:** 240
Smith, Samantha, **00:** 332
Smithfield Foods, Inc., **00:** 46
Smog, **00:** 66, 196
Smoking. See Tobacco industry
Snow. See Blizzards
Snow, Hank, **00:** 165
Snowflake Bentley (Azarian), **00:** 281
Snyder, Daniel, **00:** 375, 427
Soap box derby, **00:** 377
SOCCER, **00:** 364–366, **99:** 366–374; other refer-
    ences, **00:** 374
Social anxiety disorder, **00:** 290
Social Democratic Party: Austria, **00:** 86; Ger-
    many, **00:** 214, 216; Switzerland, **00:** 387
Social promotion (policy), **00:** 317
SOCIAL SECURITY, **00:** 366, **99:** 374; other refer-
    ences, **00:** 142, 146, 390
Social Security Act (1935), **00:** 366
Social Union (Canada), **00:** 116–118
Socialist Party: Albania, **00:** 48; France, **00:** 210;
    Portugal, **00:** 348; Yugoslavia, **00:** 441
Societe General S.A. (bank), **00:** 203, 210
Solana, Javier, **00:** 199
Solar system, New, **00:** 66
Soldini, Giovanni, **00:** 106
Solidarity (Poland), **00:** 344
Solomon Islands, **00:** 327–328; facts in brief, **00:**
    327

SOMALIA: facts in brief, **00:** 41
Somar, Michael, **00:** 328
Sony Center (Berlin), **00:** 111–113
Sony Electronics, **00:** 179
Soong, James, **00:** 388
"Sopranos, The" (TV show), **00:** 393
Sosa, Sammy, **00:** 95, 97, 131, 339, **99:** 87
Sosa Gomez, Cecilia, **00:** 423
Sotomayor, Javier, **00:** 330, 402–404
SOUTH AFRICA, **00:** 367–370, **99:** 374–378; All-
    Africa Games, **00:** 44; cricket, **00:** 152–153;
    facts in brief, **00:** 41; other references, **00:**
    38–42, 141, 395
SOUTH AFRICA, PRESIDENT OF, **00:** 370, **99:**
    378. See also Mandela, Nelson R.; Mbeki,
    Thabo
South America. See Latin America
South American Common Market. See Mercosur
South Carolina, **00:** 224, 430; statistics, **00:** 379
South Dakota, **00:** 430; statistics, **00:** 379
South Korea. See Korea, South
South Lebanon Army, **00:** 265
South Pacific Games, **00:** 327
Southern California, University of, **00:** 283
Southern Christian Leadership Conference, **00:**
    224
Southern Methodist University, **00:** 157
Soviet Union. See Union of Soviet Socialist Re-
    publics
Soybeans, **00:** 46
SPACE EXPLORATION, **00:** 370–373, **99:**
    379–381. See also Astronomy
Space Imaging, Inc., **00:** 373
Space shuttle, **00:** 371–372
Spacey, Kevin, **00:** 398
Spahr, Jane, **00:** 349
SPAIN, **00:** 373, **99:** 381; economy, **00:** 202; em-
    pire, **00:** 186–187; facts in brief, **00:** 201
Spectrum (program), **00:** 265
Spencer, Lady Diana. See Diana, Princess of
    Wales
Sperm, **00:** 105–106
Sport-utility vehicles, **00:** 196
SPORTS, **00:** 374–377, **99:** 382–384. See also
    Olympic Games and specific sports
Sports stadiums: Australia, **00:** 83; Dallas, **00:**
    157; Houston, **00:** 223; Los Angeles, **00:**
    282–283; Montreal, **00:** 310; Philadelphia, **00:**
    341; Seattle, **00:** 111
Sportswear, **00:** 204
Spratly Islands (Asia), **00:** 64–65
Springfield, Dusty, **00:** 165
Springsteen, Bruce, **00:** 345
Sprint Corp., **00:** 390
Spurs, San Antonio, **00:** 100
Sputnik 1 (satellite), **00:** 370
Spyridon, Archbishop, **00:** 173
Sri Ganesha Mandir (temple), **00:** 220
SRI LANKA, **00:** 377, **99:** 385–386; conflict, **00:**
    62; cricket, **00:** 152, 153; facts in brief, **00:** 65
Stacy, Kim, **00:** 321
Stader, Maria, **00:** 165
Stadium Australia, **00:** 83
Stadiums, Sports. See Sports stadiums
Stalin, Joseph, **00:** 192 (il.), 359, 438
Stampedes, Calgary, **00:** 209
Stamps.com (business), **00:** 243 (il.)
Stanley Cup, **00:** 157, 220–221
Staples Center (Los Angeles), **00:** 282–283
Star Called Henry, A (Doyle), **00:** 268
Star Wars: Episode 1–The Phantom Menace
    (film), **00:** 312, 314, 402
Stardust (spacecraft), **00:** 372
Starr, Kenneth, **00:** 417, **99:** 332
Stars, **00:** 66
STATE GOVERNMENT, **00:** 377–380, **99:**
    386–388; elections, **00:** 177–178, 354;
    Supreme Court rulings, **00:** 383
State Peace and Development Council (Myan-
    mar), **00:** 314
"Statement of Principles" (document), **00:** 255
Statistical sampling, **00:** 385
Statoil (company), **00:** 325
Stavro, Steve, **00:** 400
Stears, John, **00:** 165
Steel industry, **00:** 83, 287
Steele, Sir David, **00:** 408–410
Stein, Gertrude, **00:** 269
Steinberg, Saul, **00:** 165
Stepashin, Sergei, **00:** 358
Stevens, John Paul, **00:** 431
Stewart, Payne, **00:** 165, 217

STOCKS AND BONDS, 00: 381–382, 99: 388–389; bank sales, 00: 94; Internet, 00: 243–244; Latin America, 00: 264; Miami, 00: 292
Storms, 00: 84, 169–170, 427–430
Strand, Mark, 00: 343
Strasberg, Susan, 00: 165
Strauss-Kahn, Dominique, 00: 210
Street, John F., 00: 178, 340–341
Streetcar Named Desire, A (Williams), 00: 397
Strickland, David, 00: 165
Strikes: Argentina, 00: 55; Bangladesh, 00: 92; Brazil truckers, 00: 109; Canadian nurses, 00: 125–126; Peru, 00: 340; Romanian miners, 00: 356; South Africa, 00: 369; Uruguay truckers, 00: 92; Zimbabwe, 00: 447
Strydom, Johannes G., 00: 369
Subatomic particles, 00: 323
Substance abuse. See Drug abuse
Suburbs, 00: 137
SUDAN, 00: 382, 99: 390; Congo, 00: 141; facts in brief, 00: 41; population growth, 00: 306; unemployment, 00: 307
Sudbury, Assabet, and Concord Wild and Scenic River Act (U.S., 1999), 00: 146
Suez Canal, 00: 300 (il.), 302–304
Sufis (people), 00: 247
Suicide, 00: 290; assisted, 00: 150, 220, 315
Sukarnoputri, Megawati, 00: 240
Suker, Davor, 00: 366
Suleiman I, 00: 185 (il.), 186
Summers, Lawrence, 00: 114
Sunjet International (airline), 00: 91
Super Audio Compact Disc, 00: 179
Super Bowl, 00: 207, 209
Supermodels, 00: 205
Superpowers, 00: 191–193
Supreme Court of Canada, 00: 116, 119
SUPREME COURT OF THE UNITED STATES, 00: 383–385, 99: 391–393; other references, 00: 130, 167, 175, 235, 383, 430–431
Surayud Chulanont, 00: 396
Suriname, 00: 263; facts in brief, 00: 262
Swan Lake (ballet), 00: 158, 393
Swaziland, facts in brief, 00: 41
SWEDEN, 00: 385–386, 99: 393; facts in brief, 00: 201; other references, 00: 167, 260
Sweepstakes promotions, 00: 284
SWIMMING, 00: 386–387, 99: 393–394
Swingley, Doug, 00: 377
Swissair, 00: 91
SWITZERLAND, 00: 387–388, 99: 394; facts in brief, 00: 201; other references, 00: 169, 358
Sydney (Australia), 00: 83, 84
Symonenko, Petro, 00: 407
Symphony No. 5 (Glass), 00: 138
Synercid (drug), 00: 171
SYRIA, 00: 388, 99: 394–395; facts in brief, 00: 294; Middle East history, 00: 298, 304, 308; population growth, 00: 306; unemployment, 00: 307; other references, 00: 248, 249
Szabo, Gabriele, 00: 404

T

't Hooft, Gerardus, 00: 323
Ta Mok, 00: 115
Tabloid journalism, 99: 296–305
TAIWAN, 00: 388–389, 99: 395–396; earthquake, 00: 168; facts in brief, 00: 65; other references, 00: 62, 133
TAJIKISTAN, 99: 396; facts in brief, 00: 65
"Taking Responsibility for Homelessness" (report), 00: 399
Taliban (group), 00: 38, 62, 293, 395–396
Talk (magazine), 00: 284
Tamiflu (drug), 00: 172
Tamils (people), 00: 377
Tanzania, facts in brief, 00: 41
Tariffs, 00: 46–47, 203
Tarrin Nimmanahaeminda, 00: 396
Tarzan (film), 00: 312, 314
TAXATION, 00: 390, 99: 396; Argentina, 00: 55; Australia, 00: 81–83, 85; Canada, 00: 123–125; Clinton policy, 00: 146, 390, 422; congressional actions, 00: 146; Germany, 00: 214
Taylor, Mark, 00: 152
Taymor, Julie, 99: 333, 334 (il.)
Teachout, Terry, 00: 266
Teamsters Union, 00: 259
Teen-agers: births to, 00: 350; drug abuse, 00: 171
Teheran, 00: 244
Tele-Communications Inc., 00: 391
Telecom Italia, 00: 203, 249
TELECOMMUNICATIONS, 00: 390–391, 99: 397.

See also Computers; Internet
Telefonos de Mexico (company), 00: 351
Telenor (company), 00: 325
Telenovelas, 00: 263
Telephones, 00: 390–391; cellular, 00: 420
Telescope, 00: 72–77
TELEVISION, 00: 392–394, 99: 397–400; cable, 00: 390–391, 393
Telia (company), 00: 325
Tennessee, 00: 427; statistics, 00: 379
Tennessee, University of, 00: 102
TENNIS, 00: 394–395, 99: 400–401; Graf retirement, 00: 374
Terra (spacecraft), 00: 372–373
TERRORISM, 00: 395–396, 99: 402–403; Afghanistan, 00: 38; Cuba, 00: 179; FALN, 00: 351, 422; India, 00: 237; Iran, 00: 244–245; Libya, 00: 266; Middle East, 00: 293, 395–396; Peru, 00: 340; Russia, 00: 359, 395; Saudi Arabia, 00: 361; South Africa, 00: 369; Sri Lanka, 00: 377; Uganda, 00: 407; United Kingdom, 00: 415; Yemen, 00: 431. See also Conflicts and violence
Tet offensive (1968), 00: 424
Texas, 00: 334, 377, 380, 448; statistics, 00: 379.
See also Dallas; Houston
Texas, University of, 00: 206, 207
Texas A&M University, 00: 206–207
THAILAND, 00: 396, 99: 403; facts in brief, 00: 65; other references, 00: 62, 111
Tharp, Twyla, 00: 158–159
THEATER, 00: 396–399, 99: 403–415
Them Too (dance), 00: 158
Theriault, Camille, 00: 124
Thiomargarita namibiensis (bacteria), 00: 104
Thompson, Jenny, 00: 386
Thorpe, Ian, 00: 386 (il.)
Three Gorges Dam (China), 00: 132
Three Kings (film), 00: 311
Tiberi, Jean, 00: 210
Tibet, 00: 109
Tiger-Cats, Hamilton, 00: 209
Time Inc. Health, 00: 284
Timor, East. See East Timor
Tiros 1 (satellite), 00: 391
Tiruchelvam, Neelam, 00: 377
'*Tis* (McCourt), 00: 268
Titan (rocket), 00: 372
Tito, Josip Broz, 00: 437–438, 444
Tobacco industry, 00: 151, 378–380, 417
Tobago. See Trinidad and Tobago
Tobin, Brian, 00: 124
Togo, facts in brief, 00: 41
Tokaimura (Japan), 00: 251
Tomaszewski, Janusz, 00: 344
Tomb of the Unknowns (Virginia), 00: 58
Tombs, 00: 51
Tonga, 00: 327, 416; facts in brief, 00: 327
Tony Awards, 00: 335, 397, 398
Topize, Joseph Reginald, 00: 288
Torke, Michael, 00: 138
Torme, Mel, 00: 161 (il.), 165
Tornadoes, 00: 427
TORONTO, 00: 399–400, 99: 416; weather, 00: 427
Toronto Maple Leafs, 00: 400
Toronto Music Garden, 00: 212
Total Fina S.A. (company), 00: 210–211
Tour de France, 00: 332, 375, 376 (il.)
Tourism, 00: 147, 177, 407, 431
Toussaint, Jean-Yvon, 00: 219
Toyota Cup (soccer), 00: 365
Toyota Motor Corp., 00: 86, 89
TOYS AND GAMES, 00: 401–402, 99: 416–418
Toys R Us, Inc., 00: 401
TRACK AND FIELD, 00: 402–404, 99: 418–419
Trade. See Economics; International trade
Trade deficits, 00: 242
Trains. See Railroads
Trajkovski, Boris, 00: 283
Trakatellis, Demetrios, 00: 173
Tran Do, 00: 424
Transit. See Transportation
Transjordan, 00: 298
Transpacific Yacht Race, 00: 106
Transplants (surgery), 00: 288–289
TRANSPORTATION, 00: 404–405, 99: 419–420.
See also Automobile; Aviation; Railroads; Strikes
Transportation, U.S. Department of, 00: 91, 350, 405

Treasury, U.S. Department of the, 00: 94, 240, 420
Tree Studios (Chicago), 00: 130
Trial, The (Kafka), 00: 269
Triathlon, 00: 377
Trinidad, Felix, 00: 108
Trinidad and Tobago, 00: 431; facts in brief, 00: 262
Triple Crown (racing), 00: 222
Triple Quartet (Reich), 00: 139
Tripp, Linda, 00: 151 (il.)
Trojan Nuclear Power Plant, 00: 194 (il.)
Tropical rain forests. See Rain forests
Tropical Storm Olga, 00: 169
Trucking, 00: 405
Trucks, Light, 00: 86–89, 196
True at First Light (Hemingway), 00: 268
Truman, Harry S., 00: 178
Trump, Donald, 00: 317
Trumpet (Kay), 00: 268
Tschumi, Bernard, 00: 53–54
Tudjman, Franjo, 00: 155, 165
Tunisia, 00: 298, 302, 306, 416; facts in brief, 00: 41
Turabi, Hassan, 00: 382
TURKEY, 00: 405–406, 99: 421–422; facts in brief, 00: 201, 294; Middle East history, 00: 306; population growth, 00: 306; terrorism, 00: 395; unemployment, 00: 307; other references, 00: 202, 218, 295, 336. See also Earthquakes; Ottoman Empire
Turkmenistan, facts in brief, 00: 65
Turks, 00: 298. See also Ottoman Empire; Turkey
Tutankhamen, 00: 52
Tutsi, 00: 407
Tuvalu, 00: 328; facts in brief, 00: 327
Typhoons, 00: 170
Tyson, Mike, 00: 107, 108
Tzotzil Indians, 00: 292

U

UAW. See United Automobile Workers
UBS AG (bank), 00: 388
UGANDA, 00: 407; facts in brief, 00: 41; tourist murders, 00: 147; other references, 00: 42, 47, 141
Uighurs (people), 00: 134
UKRAINE, 00: 407, 99: 422; explosion, 00: 168; facts in brief, 00: 201; other references, 00: 213, 416
Ulster Unionist Party, 00: 324
Umpires, 00: 95
UN. See United Nations
Unemployment: Middle East, 00: 307; U.S., 00: 258; world, 00: 260. See also specific country articles
UNICEF, 00: 44, 246, 382
Union of Soviet Socialist Republics, 00: 192–193, 282, 358, 359, 360, 438; Middle East history, 00: 304. See also Russia
United Arab Emirates, 00: 111, 223, 306, 361; facts in brief, 00: 294
United Automobile Workers, 00: 89, 259–260
United Democratic Movement (South Africa), 00: 368, 369
United Food and Confectionary Workers Union, 00: 260
United Jewish Communities, 00: 255
UNITED NATIONS, 00: 408–415, 99: 423–428; agriculture, 00: 46; British Empire, 00: 181, 187–192; cricket, 00: 152, 153; facts in brief, 00: 201; Falkland Islands, 00: 56; Libya, 00: 266; Middle East history, 00: 296–304; Millennium, 00: 318–319; Pinochet case, 00: 263; population growth, 00: 306; rugby, 00: 357; soccer, 00: 365; unemployment, 00: 307. See also Northern Ireland; Scotland; Wales
UNITED KINGDOM, PRIME MINISTER OF, 00: 415, 99: 428. See also Blair, Tony
United Kingdom Coalition to Stop the Use of Child Soldiers, 00: 44
United Malays National Organization, 00: 284
UNITED NATIONS, 00: 416, 99: 428–429; Afghanistan, 00: 38; African development, 00: 44; Albania, 00: 48; Angola, 00: 42; environmental pollution, 00: 195; Haiti, 00: 219; human rights, 00: 224; Indonesia, 00: 240–241; Iraq, 00: 194, 246; Libya, 00: 266; Macedonia, 00: 283; Middle East history, 00: 301; Pacific Islands, 00: 327; population, 00: 347; U.S. dues, 00: 336–337, 416; Yugoslavia, 00: 441, 444–446. See also International Monetary Fund; UNICEF; World Bank

United Nations Childrens Fund. See UNICEF
United Paperworkers International Union, 00: 260
UNITED STATES, GOVERNMENT OF THE, 00:
417–421, 99: 429–434; bin Laden case, 00: 38,
293; Canada trade, 00: 122–123; China relations, 00: 133; environmental pollution, 00:
195; European trade, 00: 203; Indian affairs,
00: 239–240; international trade, 00: 242, 243;
Iran relations, 00: 244–245; Iraq policy, 00:
246; Middle East history, 00: 304, 306, 308,
309; North Korea relations, 00: 257; Panama
Canal transfer, 00: 331; Philippines relations,
00: 342; Russia relations, 00: 358, 360; South
Africa relations, 00: 369; Sudan bombing, 00:
382; superpowers, 00: 192–193; Vietnam
trade, 00: 424. See also Armed forces; Clin-
ton, Bill; Congress of the United States;
Courts; Democratic Party; Elections; Republi-
can Party; Social security; State government;
Supreme Court of the United States
UNITED STATES, PRESIDENT OF THE, 00:
421–423, 99: 434–435. See also Clinton, Bill
Unity (group), 00: 359
Univac (computer), 00: 140
Universities. See Basketball; Education; Football
University of... See under keyword, as in Texas,
University of
Upsilon Andromedae (star), 00: 66, 68
Uranium, 00: 251
Uranus (planet), 00: 67
URUGUAY, 00: 423; facts in brief, 00: 262; other
references, 00: 263, 264
USAir (airline), 00: 259
U.S.S.R. See Union of Soviet Socialist Republics
Utah, statistics, 00: 379
Uteem, Sir Cassam, 00: 288
UZBEKISTAN, 99: 435; facts in brief, 00: 65; other
references, 00: 213, 395

V
Vaccines, 00: 47, 172
Vagnorius, Gediminas, 00: 282
Vaisakhi (festival), 00: 362
Vajpayee, Atal Behari, 00: 92, 220, 235–237, 99:
333
Vancomycin (drug), 00: 171
Vancouver Grizzlies, 00: 375
Van Gogh, Vincent, 00: 61
VanGorp, Michele, 00: 101 (il.)
Vanuatu, facts in brief, 00: 327
Vasile, Radu, 00: 356
Veldkamp, Bart, 00: 235
Veltman, Martinus J. G., 00: 323
VENEZUELA, 00: 423, 99: 436; facts in brief, 00:
262; flood, 00: 170; other references, 00: 194,
263, 264, 334
Venice (Italy), 00: 251 (il.)
Ventura, George, 00: 321
Ventura, Jesse, 00: 339–340, 380 (il.)
Verhofstadt, Guy, 00: 104
Vermont, 00: 151, 380; statistics, 00: 379
Vesicles, 00: 128
Via Dolorosa (Hare), 00: 397
Viacom, Inc., 00: 352, 392
Vice: New and Selected Poems (Ai), 00: 343
Victoria (Australia), 00: 83
Video games, 00: 402
Vieira, Joao Bernardo, 00: 44
Vieques (Puerto Rico), 00: 351
Vieri, Christian, 00: 366
VIETNAM, 00: 424, 99: 436; facts in brief, 00: 65;
rains, 00: 170, 424; refugees, 00: 65–66
Vietnam War, 00: 58, 192–193, 424
View from the Bridge, A (opera), 00: 138
Vike-Freiberga, Vaira, 00: 265
Vikenty, Bishop, 00: 172
Viking spacecraft, 00: 373
Villanueva Madrid, Mario, 00: 291
Vilsack, Tom, 00: 378
Violence. See Conflicts and violence
Virginia, 00: 177, 197, 354; statistics, 00: 379
Virginia Tech University, 00: 206
Viruses, 00: 284, 315–317
Vita Nova: Poems (Gluck), 00: 343
Vitamins, 00: 420
Vitter, David, 00: 178
Vodafone AirTouch Plc (company), 00: 202–203
Voigt, Barton, 00: 150–151
Vojvodina (Serbia), 00: 437, 439
Volgadonsk (Russia), 00: 359
Volkswagen (car), 00: 89
Volleyball, 00: 377
Volpe, Justin, 00: 225, 317

Volvo AB (company), 00: 87, 385
Voting Rights Act (U.S., 1965), 00: 230
Vouchers, School, 00: 175–176, 378
Vukovic, Miodrag, 00: 433

W
Waco (Texas), 00: 419
Waddell, Rob, 00: 376
Wages, 00: 258
Wahid, Abdurrahman, 00: 240, 340
Waiting (Ha Jin), 00: 266
Wal-Mart Stores, Inc., 00: 206, 401
Wales, 00: 408, 410
Wall Street Journal, 00: 381
Wallace, Andy, 00: 90
Wallace, Peter, 00: 83
Walt Disney Theatrical Productions, 00: 399
Wan Azizah Wan Ismail, 00: 284
Wanke, Daouda Malam, 00: 44
Wansley, Michael, 00: 396
Warner Brothers, 00: 391–393
Wars. See Conflicts and violence
Warsaw, 00: 344
WASHINGTON, D.C., 00: 425–427, 99: 436–438
Washington, Grover, Jr., 00: 165
Washington (state), 00: 122, 356, 380, 390;
statistics, 00: 379
Washington Capitals, 00: 375
Washington Monument, 00: 53, 426 (il.)
Washington Redskins, 00: 375, 427
Washington Wizards, 00: 375
Water: extraterrestrial, 00: 67; Middle East, 00:
294–295. See also Drought; Environmental
pollution; Ocean
Watergate scandal, 00: 423, 427
Watson, Bobs, 00: 165
Weapons. See Armed forces; Chemical and bio-
logical weapons; Firearms; Nuclear weapons
WEATHER, 00: 427–430, 99: 438–442; Asia, 00:
66; gardening impact, 00: 212. See also Disas-
ters; Flooding; Global warming; Hurricanes;
Storms; Tornadoes
Weber, Pete, 00: 107
Weightlifting, 00: 377
Weiss, Michael, 00: 234–235
WELFARE, 00: 430–431, 99: 442–443; immi-
grants, 00: 235; New York City, 00: 136;
Supreme court rulings, 00: 383, 430–431;
Toronto, 00: 399–400
Welles, Orson, 00: 312
Welser-Most, Franz, 00: 138
Wences, Senor, 00: 164
West Bank, 00: 248, 294, 304, 305
WEST INDIES, 00: 431, 99: 443; cricket, 00:
152–153
West Kalimantan (Indonesia), 00: 241
West Nile virus, 00: 315–317
West Virginia, 00: 197; statistics, 00: 379
Westendorp, Carlos, 00: 106, 107
Western Sahara (region), 00: 295
Western Wall (Jerusalem), 00: 300 (il.)
Weyrich, Paul, 00: 350
Wheat, 00: 45
Whitbread Book of the Year Prize, 00: 268
White, Reggie, 00: 209
Whitelaw, Lord William, 00: 165
Whitney Museum of American Art (New York
City), 00: 61
"Who Wants to be a Millionaire" (TV show), 00:
393
Why Read the Classics? (Calvino), 00: 269
Whyte, William H., 00: 165
Wide Open Spaces (recording), 00: 347
Wild-2 (comet), 00: 372
Williams, Anthony A., 00: 425
Williams, C. K., 00: 343
Williams, Joe, 00: 165
Williams, Serena, 00: 395
Williams, Tennessee, 00: 397–398
Williams, Venus, 00: 395
Wilson, Robert, 00: 76, 78 (il.)
Winair (airline), 00: 91
Windows (software), 00: 140, 141, 151
Winfrey, Oprah, 00: 266
Winnipeg, 00: 330
Winston Cup, 00: 89
Winter's Tale, A (Shakespeare), 00: 275 (il.)
Wisconsin, 00: 378, 430; statistics, 00: 379
Witt, Jamil Mahuad, 00: 175
Wolves, Mexican, 00: 149–150
Women: fashion, 00: 204; prison, 00: 348; rights,
00: 227, 233, 248; soccer, 00: 364–365, 374.

See also Abortion; Pregnancy; and specific
sports
Women's National Basketball Association, 00:
101, 223–224
Woo Yong Gak, 00: 258
Woods, Tiger, 00: 217
Woods Hole Research Center, 00: 128–129
Woodstock '99 (concert), 00: 345
Woolf, Sir John, 00: 165
Work Incentives Improvement Act (U.S., 1990),
00: 167
Workday, Length of, 00: 260
World Bank, 00: 48, 55, 103, 175, 344, 356
World Book Encyclopedia, The, 00: 244
World Color Press, Inc., 00: 310
World Cup: cricket, 00: 152; rugby, 00: 357; ski-
ing, 00: 363; soccer, 00: 364
World Health Organization, 00: 47, 288
World Series, 00: 95, 97
World Track and Field Championships, 00: 402
World Trade Organization, 00: 46–47, 197, 203,
242, 243, 317
World War II, 00: 190–191; art looting, 00: 59–61;
atomic bomb, 00: 252; Bataan Death March,
00: 341; Britain, attack on, 00: 411; Buchen-
wald liberation, 00: 216; Bulge, Battle of the, 00:
202; D-Day, 00: 57; Dunquerque evacuation,
00: 210; France, occupation of, 00: 211; Iwo
Jima, 00: 328 (il.); Norway, 00: 325; Pearl Har-
bor attack, 00: 420; Poland defeat, 00: 344;
Sicily invasion, 00: 198; U.S.S.R., 00: 359; Yu-
goslavia, 00: 436–437
World Watch Institute, 00: 195
World Wide Web. See Internet
Worrell 1000 (race), 00: 106
Wye Two agreement (1999), 00: 114
Wynn, Early, 00: 165
Wynn, Steve, 00: 399
Wyoming, 00: 150–151, 240, 378–380; statistics,
00: 379

X
Xie Jun, 00: 129
Xinjiang (China), 00: 134

Y
Yacimientos Petroliferos Fiscales (company), 00:
55–56
Yagudin, Alexei, 00: 234, 235
Yahoo! Inc., 00: 244
Yamani, Ahmed Zaki, 00: 195
Yang, Jerry, 99: 326
Yankees, New York, 00: 95–97
Yarbrough, Michael, 00: 224
Yazidi religion, 00: 299
Yellowstone National Park, 00: 150, 240
Yeltsin, Boris, 00: 358, 359
YEMEN, 00: 431, 99: 443–444; facts in brief, 00:
294; Middle East history, 00: 308; population
growth, 00: 306; terrorism, 00: 395; unemploy-
ment, 00: 307
Yen (currency), 00: 174
Yerevan (Armenia), 00: 395
Yixian Formation, 00: 329–330
York, Denise DeBartolo, 00: 374
Yount, Robin, 00: 97
Y2K. See Millennium
Yuan (currency), 00: 242
Yudof, Mark, 00: 374–375
YUGOSLAVIA, 00: 433–446, 99: 444; Chinese em-
bassy bombing, 00: 133; facts in brief, 00: 201;
Jews, 00: 254–255; other references, 00: 103,
198–199, 205, 234, 283, 364. See also Bosnia-
Herzegovina; Croatia; Serbia; Slovenia
Yukon Territory, 00: 127

Z
Zaire. See Congo (Kinshasa)
ZAMBIA, 99: 446; facts in brief, 00: 41; other refer-
ences, 00: 42, 44, 141
Zare, Richard N., 00: 128
Zedillo Ponce de Leon, Ernesto, 00: 291
Zewail, Ahmed H., 00: 323
Zhu Rongji, 00: 132
Zidane, Zinedine, 00: 366
ZIMBABWE, 00: 447, 99: 446; cricket, 00: 152,
153; facts in brief, 00: 41; other references, 00:
42, 134, 141
Zionism, 00: 299–302
Zoe, Empress, 00: 182 (il.)
Zoll, Paul, 00: 165
ZOOS, 00: 447–448, 99: 447–448
Zuma, Jacob, 00: 369

Acknowledgments

The publishers acknowledge the following sources for illustrations. Credits read from top to bottom, left to right, on their respective pages. An asterisk (*) denotes illustrations and photographs created exclusively for this edition. All maps, charts, and diagrams were prepared by the staff unless otherwise noted.

6 AP/Wide World; Granger Collection
7 Reuters/Archive Photos; Agence France-Presse; NASA
8 AP/Wide World
9 © Flip Horvat, Saba; AP/Wide World; © David Hume Kennerly, Sygma
10 Agence France-Presse; Reuters/Archive Photos
11 Goddard Space Flight Center from NOAA Goes-8 DATA/Hal Pierce/Fritz Hasler/NASA
12 Reuters/Archive Photos
15-22 AP/Wide World
24 Agence France-Presse
27 AP/Wide World
28 Goddard Space Flight Center from NOAA Goes-8 DATA/Hal Pierce/Fritz Hasler/NASA
31 Agence France-Presse
32-34 AP/Wide World
36 © Rendering of planets by Sylvain Korzennik, Harvard University; photograph by Till Credner, Max Planck Institute fur Aeronomie
39 Agence France-Presse
45-48 AP/Wide World
50 © Dani/Jeske from Animals Animals
52 Underwood Photo Archives
54 AP/Wide World
55 Popperfoto/Archive Photos
57 U. S. Navy
58 © David Hume Kennerly, Sygma
59 Reina Sofia Museum, Madrid (AP/Wide World)
60 Metropolitan Museum of Art, New York City, Arthur Hoppock Hearn Fund
63 Agence France-Presse
67 NASA
68 © Image Select/ Art Resource; © Rendering of planets by Sylvain Korzennik, Harvard University, photograph by Till Credner, Max Planck Institute fur Aeronomie
70 Granger Collection
71 Erich Lessing/Art Resource; Giraudon/Art Resource
72-74 Granger Collection
75 From the Philosophical Transactions of the Royal Society, London; Archive Photos
76 Observatories of the Carnegie Institution of Washington, D.C.
77 NASA/Smithsonian Institution/Lockheed Corporation; NASA
78 © Roger Ressmeyer, Corbis; NASA; NASA
79 NASA
81 Reuters/Archive Photos
84-86 AP/Wide World
87 Jaguar Cars
90 AP/Wide World
91 Underwood Photo Archives
93 Reuters/Archive Photos
95-97 AP/Wide World
98 Sporting News/Archive Photos
99 Archive Photos
101 Reuters/Archive Photos
103 AP/Wide World
105 Reuters/Archive Photos
108-110 AP/Wide World
112 © Jeff Larsen, Seattle Post-Intelligencer
114 AP/Wide World
115 Agence France-Presse
117 Reuters/Archive Photos
119 AP/Wide World
127 AP/Wide World; Government of Nunavut

130 William McBride with Pat Moss and Michael Stack (photo © Cathy Melloan)
133 AP/Wide World
137 Agence France-Presse
139 AP/Wide World
141 Apple Computer, Inc.
147 AP/Wide World
148-151 Reuters/Archive Photos
152-154 AP/Wide World
156 Agence France-Presse
158 © Valentin Baranovsky
160 AP/Wide World
161 Warner Bros./Archive Photos; Reuters/Archive Photos; Archive Photos
162 AP/Wide World; AP Wide World; Archive Photos
163 20th Century Fox/Archive Photos; Archive Photos; AP/Wide World
164 AP/Wide World; Archive Photos; Pop-perfoto/Archive Photos
165 Archive Photos; Reuters/Archive Photos; Archive Photos
166 Reuters/Archive Photos
168 AP/Wide World
170 Baldwin H. Ward, Corbis
177-178 AP/Wide World
182 Erich Lessing/ Art Resource
183 SCALA/Art Resource
184 Werner Forman Archives/ Art Resource
185 Giraudon/Art Resource
186 Granger Collection
188 Detail of the Coronation of Emperor Napoleon I (1807) oil on canvas by Jacques Louis David; The Louvre, Paris (Erich Lessing/ Art Resource)
189 © Hulton Getty/ Liaison Agency
191 Corbis/Bettmann
192 Archive Photos
193 Coca Cola™Company
194-197 AP/Wide World
199 Reuters/Archive Photos
203 Agence France Presse
204 Cathy Melloan*
207-211 AP/Wide World
215 Reuters/Archive Photos
218 © Yannis Kontos, Sygma
221 AP/Wide World
222 Reuters/Archive Photos
225 AP/Wide World
226 National Archives
227 National Archives; Library of Congress; Library of Congress
228 AP/Wide World; Carl Iwasaki, Life Magazine © Time Inc.
229 Library of Congress; AP/Wide World; National Archives
230 AP/Wide World
231 © Superstock; © Hulton Getty/ Liaison Agency
232 AP/Wide World; © Craig J. Brown, Liaison Agency
233 © J.P. Laffont, Sygma; © Sotographs, Liaison Agency
234 © Phil Cole, Allsport
236 Reuters/Archive Photos
237 Agence France-Presse
238-239 AP/Wide World
241 Reuters/Archive Photos
243 Stamps.com Inc.
245 AP/Wide World
249 Agence France-Presse
250-251 AP/Wide World

252 Archive Photos
254 Reuters/Archive Photos
255-261 AP/Wide World
267 American Stock/Archive Photos
269 AP/Wide World
270 Liaison Agency; Granger Collection
273 Fox Searchlight/Shooting Star
275 Granger Collection
276 Corbis/John Springer; Photofest
278-279 Photofest
281 Scholastic, Inc.
282 Metropolitan Transportation Authority
285-286 AP/Wide World
289 Corbis/Bettmann
291 AP/Wide World
293 Reuters/Archive Photos
297 Hulton Getty/Liaison Agency
300 © Will Yurman, Liaison Agency; Hulton Getty, Liaison Agency
301 © Saba
308 Agence France-Presse; © Thomas Hartwell, Sygma
311 Corbis/Bettmann
313-314 Agence France-Presse
316 Metropolitan Museum of Art
318 AP/Wide World
319 Reuters/Archive Photos
320 © Dean Sensui, Honolulu Star-Bulletin; AP/Wide World
321-324 AP/Wide World
326-328 Corbis/UPI-Bettmann
329 Reuters/Archive Photos
331 AP/Wide World
333 Reuters/Archive Photos; AP/Wide World
334 NASA
335 AP/Wide World; Reuters/Archive Photos
336-337 AP/Wide World
338 Reuters/Archive Photos; AP/Wide World
339-345 AP/Wide World
346 Agence France-Presse
347-349 AP/Wide World
352 Underwood Photo Archives
353-355 AP/Wide World
363 Agence France-Presse
365-367 AP/Wide World
371-372 NASA
376-387 AP/Wide World
389 Agence France-Presse
393 AP/Wide World
394 Reuters/Archive Photos
398 © Joan Marcus
400 Reuters/Archive Photos
401 Nintendo of America; Wizards of the Coast; Wizards of the Coast; Wizards of the Coast; Wizards of the Coast; Hasbro
403 Reuters/Archive Photos
405 New York Central System
406-409 Reuters/Archive Photos
410-422 AP/Wide World
425 Underwood Photo Archives
426 © Paul Irmiter
428 AP/Wide World; Reuters/Archive Photos
429 AP/Wide World
432 Agence France-Presse
434-438 AP/Wide World
439 © Tom Haley, Sipa Press
441 © Viviane Riviere, Sipa Press; AP/Wide World; © Flip Horvat, Saba
442 © George Merillon, Liaison Agency
448 Wildlife Conservation Society
449 WORLD BOOK illustration by Tim Hayward, Bernard Thornton Artists